Organizational Integration of Enterprise Systems and Resources:

Advancements and Applications

João Varajão
University of Trás-os-Montes e Alto Douro, Portugal

Maria Manuela Cruz-Cunha
Polytechnic Institute of Cavado and Ave, Portugal

António Trigo
Polytechnic Institute of Coimbra, Portugal

Managing Director:	Lindsay Johnston
Senior Editorial Director:	Heather A. Probst
Book Production Manager:	Sean Woznicki
Development Manager:	Joel Gamon
Development Editor:	Michael Killian
Acquisitions Editor:	Erika Gallagher
Typesetter:	Lisandro Gonzalez
Cover Design:	Nick Newcomer

Published in the United States of America by
Business Science Reference (an imprint of IGI Global)
701 E. Chocolate Avenue
Hershey PA 17033
Tel: 717-533-8845
Fax: 717-533-8661
E-mail: cust@igi-global.com
Web site: http://www.igi-global.com

Library of Congress Cataloging-in-Publication Data

International Conference on Enterprise Information Systems (2010: Viana do Castelo, Portugal)
Organizational integration of enterprise systems and resources: advancements and applications / Joao Varajao, Maria Manuela Cruz-Cunha, and Antonio Trigo, editors.
        p. cm.
  Papers presented at the International Conference on Enterprise Information Systems held in Viana do Castelo, Portugal, in October 2010.
  Includes bibliographical references and index.
  ISBN 978-1-4666-1764-3 (hardcover) -- ISBN 978-1-4666-1765-0 (ebook) -- ISBN 978-1-4666-1766-7 (print & perpetual access) 1. Management information systems--Congresses. 2. Information technology--Management--Congresses. I. Varajao, Joao, 1972- II. Cruz-Cunha, Maria Manuela, 1964- III. Trigo, Antonio, 1974- IV. Title.
  HD30.213.I583 2010
  658.4'038011--dc23
                2011053451

British Cataloguing in Publication Data
A Cataloguing in Publication record for this book is available from the British Library.

All work contributed to this book is new, previously-unpublished material. The views expressed in this book are those of the authors, but not necessarily of the publisher.

Editorial Advisory Board

Table of Contents

Detailed Table of Contents

Chapter 1

An Enterprise Architecture Approach for Designing an Integrated Wood Supply
Management System 1

A. F. Marques, Centre for Forest Studies, Instituto Superior de Agronomia, Technical University of Lisbon, Portugal, & INESC TEC, Portugal

J. G. Borges, Centre for Forest Studies, Instituto Superior de Agronomia, Technical University of Lisbon, Portugal

P. M. Sousa, IST, Technical University of Lisbon, Portugal

M. Fonseca, Link Consulting, Portugal

J. Gonçalves, Europac Group, Viana do Castelo, Portugal

J. Oliveira, Floresta Atlântica – SGFII, S.A., Portugal

The wood supply chains encompass a multitude of agents with independent business processes and information systems. The network of interrelationships and information flows among the agents is often neglected when designing information systems. Common processes and automatic data exchanges can enhance collaboration as well as improve IT alignment with business needs across multiple organizations in the supply chain. This chapter proposes an Enterprise Architecture methodological approach for designing an integrated modular Wood Supply Management System. Both Process Architecture Framework and Information Architecture were developed and used to define individual systems and integration requirements, discussed on the Applications Architecture. The Technological Architecture was further addressed. Results of its application to the Portuguese pulpwood, biomass and lumber-based supply chains are presented. Results show that this approach can effectively specify individual systems requirements driven from the processes descriptions built in collaboration with the agents. It further shows that a Service-Oriented Architecture can be derived, ensuring systems integration and interoperability.

Chapter 2

Governance, Sociotechnical Systems and Knowledge Society: Challenges and Reflections 22

Antonio J. Balloni, Center for Information Technology Renato Archer, Brazil

Paulo Henrique de Souza Bermejo, Federal University of Lavras, Brazil

Jeanne Holm, NASA/Jet Propulsion Laboratory, California Institute of Technology, USA

Adriano O. Tonelli, Federal University of Lavras, Brazil

This chapter presents some challenges and reflections about governance, knowledge society and socio-technical systems. Based on the Action Network Theory, Theory of Constraints and others techniques, questions are discussed in a systematic and innovative way. Points like the synergism and collaborative ecosystem research efforts, organizations knowledgeable and organization as a living being, the involvement of people and others IT resources regarding the questions, as well as others are discussed, while considering questions, challenges and future perspectives. In conclusion, points are made to offer governance the normative goals of sustainability, existing socio-technical systems, and to imply connecting and synchronizing changes among the knowledge society actors.

Jonatan Jelen, Parsons The New School for Design, USA

Billy Brocato, Sam Houston State University, USA

Thomas Schmidt, University of Phoenix, USA

Stuart Gold, Walden University, USA

The authors' meta-analysis showed that leadership studies have ignored pioneering research into the heuristic tools people employ that affect decision-making and subsequently judgments regarding effective group performance in organizational settings. Authors suggest a postmodern model superseding the modernist perspectives The authors' meta-analysis identified salient characteristics found in the selected leadership research, allowing for a disambiguation of the transformational and charismatic leadership operational traits. The meta-analysis comprised selected research studies from 1999 to 2008, and revealed distinctive intrapersonal (5 organizational referents) and interpersonal (5 social identity/normative referents) icons that inform emergent leader and follower behaviors. Then authors propose a postmodern evaluation matrix to reveal the structural biases and modernist conceptual ambiguities tied to the leader-worker dyadic in varying organizational contexts. The findings suggest that leadership researchers should consider complex behavioral decision-making processes that result in emergent group performances instead of focusing on a leader's ephemeral behavioral traits. A postmodern approach also helps leadership researchers identify a group's performance on a continuum that would demonstrate their willingness to act in a way that tests individual limits, stretches group boundaries, and exceeds company goals, what the authors term a Star Trek Affective State.

Vasco Vasconcelos, EGP- University of Porto Business School, Portugal

Pedro Campos, LIAAD - INESC TEC,FEP and University of Porto Business School, Portugal

Web 2.0 and Enterprise 2.0 concepts offer a whole new set of collaborative tools that allow new approaches to market research, in order to explore continuously and ever fast-growing social and media environments. Simultaneously, the exponential growth of online Social Networks, along with a combination of computer-based tools, is contributing to the construction of new kinds of research communities, in which respondents interact with researchers as well as with each other. Furthermore, by studying the networks, researchers are able to manage multiple data sources - user-generated contents. The main purpose of this paper is to propose a new concept of Distributed Informal Information Systems for Innovation that arises from the interaction of the accumulated stock of knowledge emerging at the individual (micro) level. A descriptive study unveils and reports when and how market research professionals use Social Networks for their work and therefore create distributed information systems for Innovation.

Higher education institutes like universities cannot ignore the need to teach well known information systems, like ERP systems. Case studies are the most chosen way to introduce the handling of these systems to fulfill the needs of the international employment market and to provide a practical focus within the education. Effective teaching concepts have to improve this situation by considering the pedagogical aspects, which support the individual learning process of each student. This chapter discusses the changes and challenges of enterprise systems in higher education and provides an overview about the learning theory and the actual learning supporting technology as a basis for our concept. The approach considers actual needs of higher education, e.g. present learning in a lab as well as e-Learning courses supported by new methods in technology-enhanced learning by recording students' behavior to guide them through the system. Therefore the authors introduce an Adaptive Learning Cycle which considers tracking and analyzing results deduced with mining methods to improve the learning progress. The aim is to achieve positive influences on the progress of the learning process to build up professional competence.

Organizations not only play an increasingly active role in today's society but also address every day's necessities and concerns of individuals. To achieve a competitive advantage, it is becoming more and more necessary that organizations perform efficiently in order to survive. As organizations can be defined as a group of people who work together to obtain common results, it is imperative that all its constituents represent themselves as part of the whole. Essential issues belonging to self-identity such as: who is the organization, what it does, for whom it operates and what its core values are can be answered by building a Business Model. In this context, the Business Model and artifacts like the Business Motivation Model, which help to specify the enterprise business architecture, can be complementary. This chapter shows how the Portuguese Air Force developed its generic Business Model and describes two example of application in the strategic and operational levels.

This chapter is an effort towards illustrating the use of expert panels (EP) as a means of eliciting knowledge from a group of enterprise resource planning (ERP) experts in an exploratory research. The development of a cost estimation model for ERP adoptions is very crucial for research and practice, and that was the main reason behind the willingness of experts to participate in this research. The use of EP was very beneficial as it involved various data collection and visualization techniques, as well as data validation and confirmation. Arguments for using EP over other group techniques are presented in this chapter. Experts modified and enhanced the initial cost drivers list and their sub-factors significantly, as they added, modified, merged and split different costs. Moreover, they ranked the cost drivers according to their weight on total costs. All of this helped the authors to better understand relationships among various cost factors.

Chapter 8

Ricardo Almeida, Faculdade de Engenharia da Universidade do Porto, Portugal

Miguel Nuno de Oliveira Teixeira, Universidade Trás-os-Montes e Alto Douro, Portugal

Information management has assumed an increasing importance at business organizations, over the last decades. Such trends lead companies to promote enormous efforts on organizing and optimizing their business processes, acquiring expensive enterprise information systems, aiming to promote an accurate answer to market uncertainty. Unfortunately, traditional software implementations have revealed low levels of satisfaction by Enterprise Resource Planning (ERP) systems' customers. This study aims to evaluate the reasons for success and failure of ERP systems implemented in Portugal and the methodologies taken by consulting teams. To achieve such a goal, it has been submitted a web survey to Portuguese companies and consulting teams, in order to confirm major errors, ERP systems' coverage and quality's response for business processes, and assessment of engineering requirements as a major concern. This study is concluded with the presentation of the web survey results and some conclusions about ERP systems' implementation at Portugal.

Chapter 9

Rebecca Angeles, University of New Brunswick Fredericton, Canada

This chapter features the results of an empirical online survey focusing on radio frequency identification initiatives and the revalidation of these results using brief case studies on Charles Voegele and Vail Resorts. The empirical study investigates the ability of information technology (IT) infrastructure integration and supply chain process integration to moderate the relationships between the importance of the perceived seven adoption attributes and system deployment outcomes, operational efficiency and market knowledge creation in radio frequency identification (RFID)-enabled supply chains. Using the online survey method, data was collected from members of the Council of Supply Chain Management Professionals in North America. The three adoption attributes, relative advantage, results, and image turned out to be the most important attributes in these RFID systems. Indeed, both IT infrastructure integration and supply chain process integration moderate the relationships between these three adoption attributes and the RFID system outcomes.

Chapter 10

Carlos Páscoa, Air Force Academy, Portugal & Instituto Superior Técnico, Technical University of Lisbon, Portugal

António Alves, Air Force Academy, Portugal

José Tribolet, Instituto Superior Técnico, Technical University of Lisbon, Portugal & CODE - Center for Organizational Design & Engineering, INOV, Portugal

In order to be able to plan, execute, and control its activities to achieve the desired results, it is essential that organizations tie together the academic knowledge and the operational experience by utilizing proven scientific theories in the organization executables. There are several theories about how to frame the models of corporate governance according to different perspectives; there are advantages and disadvantages in the adoption of each of them. The more or less complete dimension when related to the scope of each model is also an important aspect in its use and disclosure. The EX-ANTE and EX-POST model proposes a set of concepts that allow for the co-existence of mechanisms of access control and registration and validation, being the governance of the system based on four architectures: strategic, business, applications and technology. The model that the Portuguese Air Force uses for the definition of its annual flying hours regime includes five well-defined phases that may improve the level of coverage if the listed security mechanisms, control and audit, recommended in the Model EX-ANTE and EX-POST, are considered.

Ben Clegg, Aston University, UK
Yi Wan, Aston University, UK

The enterprise management (EM) approach provides a holistic view of organizations and their related information systems. In order to align information technology (IT) innovation with global markets and volatile virtualization, traditional firms are seeking to reconstruct their enterprise structures alongside repositioning strategy and establish new information system (IS) architectures to transform from single autonomous entities into more open enterprises supported by new Enterprise Resource Planning (ERP) systems. In this chapter, the authors see how ERP engage-abilities cater for three distinctive EM patterns and resultant strategies. The purpose is to examine the presumptions and importance of combing ERP and inter-firm relations relying on the virtual value chain concept. From a review of the literature on ERP development and enterprise strategy, exploratory inductive research studies in Zoomlion and Lanye have been conducted. In addition, the authors propose a dynamic conceptual framework to demonstrate the adoption and governance of ERP in the three enterprise management forms and points to a new architectural type (ERPIII) for operating in the virtual enterprise paradigm.

Paulo Andrade, ISCTE – Instituto Universitário de Lisboa, Portugal
Bráulio Alturas, ISCTE – Instituto Universitário de Lisboa, Portugal
Tiago Oliveira, ISEGI, Universidade Nova de Lisboa, Portugal

E-procurement systems make purchasing activities more effective in terms of both time and cost. However, over the past years there is evidence that some of the expected benefits have not been achieved. Among several causes, supplier's low adherence to such platforms has been regarded as one. The focus of this work is in supplier adoption of e-Procurement. It will help to better address the issues actually faced by suppliers within e-Procurement. The authors have conducted a questionnaire-based survey to 721 Portuguese companies and performed an empirical analysis of the data. The findings from this work provide evidence that the supplier perceived indirect benefits and business partner pressures are most important to e-Procurement adoption while barriers have a negative impact on their adoption. The main critical success factors on e-Procurement adoption are also presented.

Tiago Almeida, University of Aveiro, Portugal
Leonor Teixeira, GOVCOPP - University of Aveiro, Portugal, & IEETA, Portugal
Carlos Ferreira, University of Aveiro, Portugal, & CIO - University of Lisbon, Portugal

This chapter analyzes the impact of the implementation of SAP R/3 in a Multinational Portuguese Organization (MPO), defining some Critical Success Factors (CSFs). In order to understand the motivations of end-users prior to implementation and to analyze the behavior after a change (post-implementation), a study based on a questionnaire was carried out. The sample included 67 users of SAP R/3 that were present throughout the process. Considering the results, we can conclude that the implementation of SAP R/3 in MPO was successful, and the respondents consider their work more productive and achieve easier access to information. The existence of a solid team to support the project was established as a major facilitator in the whole process, as opposed to the limited time and lack of training that emerged as barriers to the implementation. It was also found that the learning period assumes a high importance in the success of the implementation, since increasing the training time reduces the need for support to the end-users.

Chapter 14

Lerina Aversano, University of Sannio, Italy
Fiammetta Marulli, University of Sannio, Italy
Maria Tortorella, University of Sannio, Italy

The relationship existing between a business process and the supporting software system is a critical concern for organizations, as it directly affects their performance. The knowledge regarding this relationship plays an important role in the software evolution process, as it helps to identify the software components involved by a software change request. The research described in this chapter concerns the use of information retrieval techniques in the software maintenance activities. In particular, the chapter addresses the problem of recovering traceability links between the entities of the business process model and components of the supporting software system. Therefore, an information retrieval approach is proposed based on two processing phases including syntactic and semantic analysis. The usefulness of the approach is discussed through a case study.

Chapter 15

Jan van den Berg, Delft University of Technology, The Netherlands
Guido van Heck, Accenture Consulting, The Netherlands
Mohsen Davarynejad, Delft University of Technology, The Netherlands
Ron van Duin, Delft University of Technology, The Netherlands

Enterprise Resource Planning systems have been introduced to support the efficient and effective execution of business processes. In practice, this may not fully succeed. This also holds in particular for inventory management (IM), which forms a part of supply chain management. Within this research, by analyzing the IM business process theoretically, eleven potential benefits are indicated. Next, by using a Business Intelligence approach, key performance indicators (KPIs) are selected to measure the performance of IM sub-processes. Integration of these approaches yields an IM performance decision support framework that can be used to obtain a generic, coherent picture of the fundamental IM processes in an organization. In addition, by tracking and analyzing KPI measurements, adequate decisions can be prepared towards the improvement of the operational IM performance. The proposed framework is validated using experts' opinions and a comparative case study. The experts' comments yielded a list of top-10 KPIs, based on the measurements of which a set of quick wins can be determined. The case study results show that some of the identified potential benefits are also observed in practice. Future research may reveal that comparable performance improvements are possible in other IM environments (and even in other supply chain domains) based on similar decision support frameworks.

Chapter 16

Traceability systems, including the approval and control of documents, are increasingly assuming a pivotal role in the workflow of information across an organization and they can be classified as an element of any internal control system at the organizational context which contributes for a continuous auditing and helps to manage and minimize organizational risk. RFID (Radio Frequency Identification) is a technology that can enable the development of architectures which provide an adequate response to this requirement of internal control. Thus, this chapter, as main objective, raises awareness of the importance of these systems in an organizational environment. Moreover this chapter's objective is to propose a modular and flexible solution which simultaneously traces, monitors, and searches the flow and location of documents in an organization, using RFID technology.

Collaborative workgroups have to make decisions, so it is necessary to have a good mechanism in order to make better decisions. Consensus decision-making helps organizations to process that, based on a diagnosis- and discussion-based approach to current and idealized future scenarios regarding a set of topics of interest. The model incorporates a mechanism that allows the comparison of personal opinion with the average group's opinion. Besides, it allows users to prioritize the topics evaluated, or agree about the potential risks in a specific field, with the aim of facilitate to take decisions about how and where to start actions. The model is presented within the dynamic context of an innovation community. A prototype of such consensus support system in which members provide their opinion in relation to some drivers that support and encourage their organization has been implemented. In such a way, the chapter provides a new consensus framework which can be applied to support web-based consensus and decision processes in different environments. Two case studies are presented; the first one is focused on the prioritization of the drivers that motivates researcher in an innovative group, and the second is dedicated to the assessment of the drivers for future internet.

Public Administrations are seeking more efficient alternatives for the use of information and communication technologies in terms of a cost-benefit analysis. Open source standards can offer them rational alternatives. Up to this moment one can find some good experiences in the implementation of open source software in Public Administrations worldwide. This study offers the results of research where a group of eighteen Public Administration experiences of integral systems migration to open software standards have been analyzed. Public Administrations perceive improvements in the way they offer services, a reduction of the costs, and better secured information systems. The authors think this analysis can be of value for IT decision makers at Public Administrations.

Chapter 19

Andrea Herrera, University of Los Andes, Colombia
Olga Lucía Giraldo, University of Los Andes, Colombia

Colombian healthcare industry has been growing since the late 90's and the amount of spending allocated to this sector is the highest proportion of GDP in Latin American countries. Those facts have increased the importance of this sector for the economy and national development. The authors performed a research project to find out if there are similarities amongst Colombian Health Sector Enterprises that have obtained positive results. In this project, the authors studied IT governance, operational model, engagement model, and portfolio management of twelve companies, all of them large o medium-sized. The results show that IT governance behavior of Colombian healthcare industry is not homogeneous. Different subsectors have different behavior; some perform as large superior global enterprises and other are beginning their journey.

Chapter 20

Jan Aalmink, Carl von Ossietzky Universität Oldenburg, Germany
Jorge Marx Gómez, Carl von Ossietzky Universität Oldenburg, Germany

Cloud Computing is finding its way into the architecture of current IT landscapes. The present chapter depicts the challenges of the required changes and transitions of Enterprise Data Centers from non-integrated on-premise solutions towards fully integrated on-demand systems in silo-free clouds. Cloud standardization in the context of the Open Cloud Manifesto is discussed as well as a reference model based upon semantic composition and federation (Federated ERP Systems and Corporate Environmental Information Management Systems CEMIS 2.0). How Enterprise Tomography can support the governance process is described as the Root-Cause-Analysis procedure and Integration Lifecycle Management of an Enterprise Cloud and by comparing different system states. On the basis of an operator-based approach, Root-Cause-Analysis and data integrity can be ensured. Finally, an outlook on an approach involving environmental aspects (Green Clouds) is given.

Chapter 21

Alberto J. Arroyo, ALAMCIA S. L, Spain.

IT Corporate governance is the information technology-governing discipline of corporate governance.. Governing IT is not a simple discipline: researchers and practitioners have developed frameworks, best practices, etc. The standard ISO/IEC 38.500 sets the principles and activities to be carried in the organization to implement corporate governance of IT. Family-owned enterprises introduce a specific particularity regarding governance: the family. This paper presents an analysis of corporate governance of IT in family owned enterprises, considering this singularity, from the Spanish perspective. Also, it introduces two examples of implementation in family owned enterprises.

Luís Ferreira, Polytechnic Institute of Cávado and Ave, Portugal
Goran Putnik, University of Minho, Portugal
Maria Manuela Cruz-Cunha, Polytechnic Institute of Cávado and Ave, Portugal
Hélio Castro, University of Minho, Portugal

The new (e)commerce/(e)business paradigms forced enterprises to undertake important transformations and reorganizations. It happened with the web and will be repeated in the Cloud and social networks. The tourism is no more only a traditional commercial activity but ever more social and information-oriented. The tourism services need to be effective to be aligned with tourist requirements. The globalization and easy access allows tourists to change their plans constantly. Dynamic services reconfiguration and resulting impact on their information systems need to be supported. The chapter explores new tourism services requirements as the ubiquity and dynamic reconfiguration, new brokering mechanisms and reliable integration processes, and human-to-human synchronous collaboration allow the natural involvement of the tourist on the co-creation of his activity plan with other agents (humans).

Preface

ABOUT THE SUBJECT

For the last few decades, it is being recognized that enterprise computer-based solutions no longer consist of isolated or dispersedly developed and implemented MRP (Material Requirements Planning) and MRP II solutions, CRM (Customer Relationship Management) solutions, electronic commerce solutions, ERP (Enterprise Resources Planning) solutions, or others, transposing the functional/technological islands to the so-called 'islands of information'. Solutions must be integrated, built on a single system, and supported by a common information infrastructure central to the organization, ensuring that information can be shared across all functional levels and management, so that users can see data entered anywhere in the system in real-time and, simultaneously, seamlessly allow the integration and coordination of most (if not all) the enterprise business processes.

The topic of Enterprise Information Systems (EIS) is gaining an increasingly relevant strategic impact on global business and the world economy, and organizations are undergoing hard investments (in cost and effort) in search of the rewarding benefits of efficiency and effectiveness that this range of solutions promise. As we all know, this is not an easy task! It is not only a matter of financial investment! It is much more, as this book shows. EIS are at same time responsible for tremendous gains in some companies and tremendous losses in others. So, their adoption should be carefully planned and managed.

Responsiveness, flexibility, agility and business alignment are requirements of competitiveness that enterprises search for. And we hope that the models, solutions, tools and case studies presented and discussed in this book can contribute to highlight new ways to identify opportunities and overtake trends and challenges of EIS selection, adoption and exploitation.

ORGANIZATION OF THE BOOK

This book integrates the enhanced versions of 22 papers selected from the international conference CENTERIS – Conference on ENTERprise Information Systems held in Viana do Castelo, Portugal, in October 2010. These selected contributions discuss the main issues, challenges, opportunities and developments related with Enterprise Information Systems from the social, managerial and organizational perspectives, in a very comprehensive way, and contribute to the dissemination of current achievements and practical solutions and applications in the field.

These 22 chapters are written by a group of more than 60 authors that includes many internationally renowned and experienced authors in the EIS field and a set of younger authors, showing a promising potential for research and development. Contributions came from USA, Canada, Latin America, Africa and Europe. At the same time, the book integrates contributions from academe, research institutions and industry, representing a good and comprehensive representation of the state-of-the-art approaches and developments that address the several dimensions of this fast evolutionary thematic.

"Organizational Integration of Enterprise Systems and Resources: Advancements and Applications" integrates 22 chapters.

In chapter one, "An Enterprise Architecture Approach for Designing an Integrated Wood Supply Management System", the authors propose an Enterprise Architecture methodological approach for designing an integrated modular Wood Supply Management System. Both Process Architecture Framework and Information Architecture were developed and used to define individual systems and integration requirements, discussed on the Applications Architecture. The Technological Architecture was further addressed. Results of its application to the Portuguese pulpwood, biomass and lumber-based supply chains are presented. Results show that this approach can effectively specify individual systems requirements driven from the processes descriptions built in collaboration with the agents. It further shows that a Service-Oriented Architecture can be derived, ensuring systems integration and interoperability.

"Governance, Sociotechnical Systems and Knowledge Society: Challenges and Reflections" presents some challenges and reflections about governance, knowledge society and sociotechnical systems. Based on the Action Network Theory, Theory of Constraints and others techniques, questions are pointed and discussed in a systematic and innovative way. Points like the synergism and collaborative ecosystem research efforts, knowledgeable organizations, and organizations as living beings, the involvement of people and others IT resources on the questions, and others are discussed considering questions, challenges and future perspectives. In conclusion, points are made to offer governance the normative goals of sustainability, existing socio-technical systems, and to imply connecting and synchronizing changes among the knowledge society actors.

Then authors of "In Search of a Star Trek Affective State" propose a postmodern evaluation matrix to reveal the structural biases and modernist conceptual ambiguities tied to the leader-worker dyadic in varying organizational contexts. The findings suggest that leadership researchers should consider complex behavioral decision-making processes that result in emergent group performances instead of focusing on a leader's ephemeral behavioral traits. A postmodern approach also helps leadership researchers identify a group's performance on a continuum that would demonstrate their willingness to act in a way that tests individual limits, stretches group boundaries, and exceeds company goals, what the authors term a Star Trek Affective State.

Chapter 4

Web 2.0 and Enterprise 2.0 concepts offer a whole new set of collaborative tools that allow new approaches to market research, in order to explore continuously and ever fast-growing social and media environments. Simultaneously, the exponential growth of online Social Networks, along with a combination of computer-based tools, is contributing to the construction of new kinds of research communities, in which respondents interact with researchers as well as with each other. Furthermore, by studying the networks, researchers are able to manage multiple data sources - user-generated contents. The main purpose of this chapter "The Role of Social Networks in Distributed Informal Information Systems for Innovation" is to propose a new concept of Distributed Informal Information Systems for Innovation that arises from the interaction of the accumulated stock of knowledge emerging at the individual (micro) level. A descriptive study is to unveil and report when and how market research professionals use Social Networks for their work, creating, therefore, distributed information systems for Innovation.

The fifth chapter, "Adaptive Learning Cycle to improve the Competence-Building for Enterprise Systems in Higher Education" discusses the changes and challenges of enterprise systems in higher education and provide an overview about the learning theory and the actual learning supporting technology as a basis for the authors' concept. Their approach considers actual needs of higher education, e.g. present learning in a lab as well as e-Learning courses supported by new methods in technology enhanced learning by recording student's behavior to guide him through the system. Therefore the authors introduce an Adaptive Learning Cycle which considers tracking and analyzing results deduced with mining methods to improve the learning progress. The aim is to achieve positive influences on the progress of the learning process to build up professional competence.

Organizations not only play an increasingly active role in today's society but also address every day's necessities and concerns of individuals. To achieve competitive advantage, it is becoming more and more necessary that organizations perform efficiently in order to survive. As organizations can be defined as a group of people who work together to obtain common results, it is imperative that all its constituents represent themselves as part of the whole. Essential issues belonging to self-identity such as: who is the organization, what it does, for whom it operates and what its core values are can be answered by building a Business Model. In this context, the Business Model and artifacts like the Business Motivation Model, which help to specify the enterprise business architecture, can be complementary. Chapter six, "Organization Identity: the Business Model", shows how the Portuguese Air Force developed its generic Business Model and describes two example of application in the strategic and operational levels.

Chapter seven, "The Use of Experts Panels in ERP Cost Estimation Research", represents an effort towards illustrating the use of expert panels (EP) as a mean of eliciting knowledge from a group of enterprise resource planning (ERP) experts in an exploratory research. The development of a cost estimation model for ERP adoptions is very crucial for research and practice, and that was the main reason behind the willingness of experts to participate in this research. The use of EP was very beneficial as it involved various data collection and visualization techniques, as well as data validation and confirmation. Arguments for using EP over other group techniques are presented in this chapter. Experts modified and enhanced the initial cost drivers list and their sub-factors significantly, as they added, modified, merged and split different costs. Moreover, they ranked the cost drivers according to their weight on total costs. All of this helped the authors to better understand relationships among various cost factors.

Chapter 8

Information management has assumed an increasing importance at business organizations, over the last decades. Such trends lead companies to promote enormous efforts on organizing and optimizing their business processes, acquiring expensive enterprise information systems, aiming to promote an accurate answer to market uncertainty. Unfortunately, traditional software implementations have revealed low levels of satisfaction by Enterprise Resource Planning (ERP) systems' customers. The study presented in "Evaluating the Success of ERP Systems' Implementation: A Study about Portugal" aims to evaluate the reasons for success and failure of ERP systems implemented at Portugal and the methodologies taken by consulting teams. To achieve such goal, it has been submitted a web survey to Portuguese companies and consulting teams, in order to confirm major errors, ERP systems' coverage and quality's response for business processes, and assessment of engineering requirements as a major concern. This study is concluded with the presentation of the web survey results and some conclusions about ERP systems' implementation at Portugal.

Chapter nine, "Two Case Studies on RFID Initiatives: Testing the Impact of IT Infrastructure Integration and Supply Chain Process Integration", features the results of an empirical online survey focusing on radio frequency identification initiatives and the revalidation of these results using brief case studies on Charles Voegele and Vail Resorts. The empirical study investigates the ability of information technology (IT) infrastructure integration and supply chain process integration to moderate the relationships between the importance of the perceived seven adoption attributes and system deployment outcomes, operational efficiency and market knowledge creation in radio frequency identification (RFID)-enabled supply chains. Using the online survey method, data was collected from members of the Council of Supply Chain Management Professionals in North America. The three adoption attributes, relative advantage, results, and image turned out to be the most important attributes in these RFID systems. Indeed, both IT infrastructure integration and supply chain process integration moderate the relationships between these three adoption attributes and the RFID system outcomes.

Chapter 10

In order to be able to plan, execute, and control its activities to achieve the desired results, it is essential that organizations tie together the academic knowledge and the operational experience by utilizing proven scientific theories in the organization executables. There are several theories about how to frame the models of corporate governance according to different perspectives; there are advantages and disadvantages in the adoption of each of them. The more or less complete dimension when related to the scope of each model is also an important aspect in its use and disclosure. The EX-ANTE and EX-POST model proposes a set of concepts that allow for the co-existence of mechanisms of access control and registration and validation, being the governance of the system based on four architectures: strategic, business, applications and technology. The model that the Portuguese Air Force uses for the definition of its annual flying hours regime includes five well-defined phases that may improve the level of coverage if the listed security mechanisms, control and audit, recommended in the Model EX-ANTE and EX-POST, are considered in chapter tenth, "EX-ANTE and EX-POST Model applied to the Portuguese Air Force Flying Regime".

The enterprise management (EM) approach provides a holistic view of organizations and their related information systems. In order to align information technology (IT) innovation with global markets and volatile virtualization, traditional firms are seeking to reconstruct their enterprise structures alongside repositioning strategy and establish new information system (IS) architectures to transform from single autonomous entities into more open enterprises supported by new Enterprise Resource Planning (ERP) systems. In "A New Dynamic Framework for Managing ERP Development and Enterprise Strategy", authors see how ERP engage-abilities cater for three distinctive EM patterns and resultant strategies. The purpose is to examine the presumptions and importance of combing ERP and inter-firm relations relying on the virtual value chain concept. From a review of the literature on ERP development and enterprise strategy, exploratory inductive research studies in Zoomlion and Lanye have been conducted. In addition, the authors propose a dynamic conceptual framework to demonstrate the adoption and governance of ERP in the three enterprise management forms and points to a new architectural type (ERPIII) for operating in the virtual enterprise paradigm.

Chapter 12

E-procurement systems make purchasing activities more effective in terms of both time and cost. However, over the past years there is evidence that some of the expected benefits have not been achieved. Among several causes, supplier's low adherence to such platforms has been regarded as one. The focus of this work is in supplier adoption of e-Procurement. It will help to better address the issues actually faced by suppliers within e-Procurement. Authors have conducted a questionnaire-based survey to 721 Portuguese companies and performed an empirical analysis of the data. The findings from this work provide evidence that the supplier perceived indirect benefits and business partner pressures are most important to e-Procurement adoption while barriers have a negative impact on their adoption. The main critical success factors on e-Procurement adoption are also in the chapter "Electronic Procurement: The Supplier Perspective".

Chapter 13 "End-user Attitude in ERP Post-Implementation: A Study in a Multinational Enterprise" analyzes the impact of the implementation of SAP R/3 in a Multinational Portuguese Organization (MPO), defining some Critical Success Factors (CSFs). In order to understand the motivations of end-users prior to implementation and to analyze the behavior after a change (post-implementation), a study based on a questionnaire was carried out. The sample included 67 users of SAP R/3 that were present throughout the process. Considering the results, we can conclude that the implementation of SAP R/3 in MPO was successful, and the respondents consider their work more productive and achieve easier access to information. The existence of a solid team to support the project was established as a major facilitator in the whole process, as opposed to the limited time and lack of training that emerged as barriers to the implementation. It was also found that the learning period assumes a high importance in the success of the implementation, since increasing the training time reduces the need for support to the end-users.

The relationship existing between a business process and the supporting software system is a critical concern for the organizations, as it directly affects their performance. The knowledge regarding this relationship plays an important role in the software evolution process, as it help to identify the software components involved by a software change request. The research described in "An Approach for Recovering the Connections between Business Process and Software System" concerns the use of information retrieval techniques in the software maintenance activities. In particular, the chapter addresses the problem of recovering traceability links between the entities of the business process model and components of the supporting software system. Therefore, an information retrieval approach is proposed based on two processing phases including syntactic and semantic analysis. The usefulness of the approach is discussed through a case study.

ERP systems have been introduced to support the efficient and effective execution of business processes. In practice, this may not fully succeed. This also holds in particular for inventory management (IM), which forms a part of supply chain management. Within this research, by analyzing the IM business process theoretically, eleven potential benefits are indicated. Next, by using a Business Intelligence approach, key performance indicators (KPIs) are selected to measure the performance of IM sub-processes. Integration of these approaches yields an IM performance decision support framework that can be used to obtain a generic, coherent picture of the fundamental IM processes in an organization. In addition, by tracking and analyzing KPI measurements, adequate decisions can be prepared towards the improvement of the operational IM performance. The framework proposed in chapter 15, "Inventory Management, a Decision Support Framework to Improve Operational Performance", is validated using experts' opinions and a comparative case study. The experts' comments yielded a list of top-10 KPIs, based on the measurements of which a set of quick wins can be determined. The case study results show that some of the identified potential benefits are also observed in practice.

Traceability systems, including the approval and control of documents, are increasingly assuming a pivotal role in the workflow of information across an organization and they can be classified as an element of any internal control system at the organizational context which contributes for a continuous auditing and helps to manage and minimize organizational risk. RFID (Radio Frequency Identification) is a technology that can enable the development of architectures which provide an adequate response to this requirement of internal control. Thus, this chapter has as main objective to raise awareness of the importance of these systems in an organizational environment. Moreover this chapter "Automation of the Approval and Control Process of Documents" has the objective to propose a modular and flexible solution which simultaneously traces, monitors and searches the flow and location of documents in an organization, using RFID technology.

Collaborative workgroups have to make decisions, so it is necessary to have a good mechanism to obtain the better decisions, consensus decision-making helps organizations to that process based on a diagnosis and discussion approach of current, and idealized future scenario of a set of topics of interest. The model incorporates a mechanism that allows comparing the personal opinion to the average group's opinion. Besides, it allows users to prioritize the topics evaluated, or agree about the potential risks in a specific field, with the aim of facilitate to take decisions about how and where to start actions. The model is presented within the dynamic context of an innovation community. A prototype of such consensus support system in which members provide their opinion in relation to some drivers that support and encourage their organization has been implemented. In such a way, we provide a new consensus framework which can be applied to support web-based consensus and decision processes in different environments. The chapter "Vector Consensus Model" presents two case studies: the first one is focused on the prioritization of the drivers that motivates researcher in an innovative group, the second is dedicated to the assessment of the drivers for future internet.

Public Administrations are each time more seeking for efficient alternatives in the use of information and communication technologies in terms of a cost-benefit analysis. Open source standards can offer them rational alternatives. Up to this moment the authors found some good experiences in the implementation of open source software in Public Administrations worldwide. The study presented in "Efficient Alternatives in the Adoption of Software for Public Companies" offers the results of a research where a group of eighteen Public Administration experiences of integral systems migration to open software standards have been analyzed. Public Administrations perceive improvements in the way they offer services, a reduction of the costs and better secured information systems.

Colombian healthcare industry has been growing since the late 90's and the amount of spending allocated to this sector is the highest proportion of GDP in Latin American countries. Those facts have increased the importance of this sector for the economy and national development. Furthermore, enterprises with IT governance focus on organizational objectives have yielded superior results than their competitors. Authors of chapter 19, "IT Governance State of Art in the Colombian Health Sector Enterprises", performed a research project to find out if there are similarities amongst Colombian Health Sector Enterprises that have obtained positive results. In this project, we studied IT governance, operational model, engagement model, and portfolio management of twelve companies, all of them large o medium-sized. Eesults show that IT governance behavior of Colombian healthcare industry is not homogeneous. Different subsectors have different behavior; some perform as large superior global enterprises and other are beginning their journey.

Cloud Computing is finding its way into the architecture of current IT landscapes. The present chapter depicts the challenges of the required changes and transitions of Enterprise Data Centers from non-integrated on-premise solutions towards fully integrated on-demand systems in silo-free clouds. Cloud standardization in the context of the Open Cloud Manifesto is discussed as well as a reference model basing upon semantic composition and federation (Federated ERP Systems and Corporate Environmental Information Management Systems CEMIS 2.0). Chapter 20, "Enterprise Tomography Driven Root-Cause-Analysis and Integration Lifecycle Management of Federated ERP in Green Clouds", describes how Enterprise Tomography can support the governance process, the Root-Cause-Analysis procedure and Integration Lifecycle Management of an Enterprise Cloud by comparing different system states. On basis of an operator-based approach, Root-Cause-Analysis and data integrity can be ensured. Finally, an outlook on an approach involving environmental aspects (Green Clouds) is given.

IT Corporate governance is the information technology-governing discipline of corporate governance. Governing IT is not a simple discipline: researchers and practitioners have developed frameworks, best practices, etc. The standard ISO/IEC 38.500 sets the principles and activities to be carried in the organization to implement corporate governance of IT. Family owned enterprises introduces a specific particularity regarding governance: the family. Chapter 21, "Corporate Governance of IT in Spanish Family Owned Enterprises" presents an analysis of corporate governance of IT in family owned enterprises considering this singularity, from the Spanish perspective, and also it introduces two examples of implementation in family owned enterprises

The new (e)commerce/(e)business paradigms forced enterprises to undertake important transformations and reorganizations. It happened with the web and will be repeated in the Cloud and social networks. The tourism is no more only a traditional commercial activity but ever more social and information-oriented. The tourism services need to be effective to be aligned with tourist requirements. The globalization and easy access allows tourists to change constantly their plans. Dynamic services reconfiguration and resulting impact on their information systems need to be supported. Chapter 22 explores new tourism services requirements as the ubiquity and dynamic reconfiguration, new brokering mechanisms and reliable integration processes, human-to-human synchronous collaboration to allow the natural involvement of the tourist on the co-creation of his activity plan with other agents (humans).

EXPECTATIONS

The book provides researchers, scholars, professionals with some of the most advanced research, solutions and discussions of Enterprise Information Systems design, implementation and management and is targeted to be read by academics (teachers, researchers and students of several graduate and postgraduate courses) and by professionals of Information Technology, IT managers, Information Resources managers, Enterprise managers (including top level managers), and also technology solutions developers.

We strongly hope it meets your expectations!

João Varajão
University of Trás-os-Montes e Alto Douro, Portugal

Maria Manuela Cruz-Cunha
Polytechnic Institute of Cavado and Ave, Portugal

António Trigo
Polytechnic Institute of Coimbra, Portugal

Acknowledgment

Editing a book is a quite hard but involves a set of enriching activities of discussion and exchange of ideas and experiences, process management, organization and integration of contents, and many others, with the permanent objective of creating a book that meets the public expectations. And this task cannot be accomplished without a great help and support from many sources. As editors we would like to acknowledge the help, support and believe of all who made possible this creation.

First of all, the edition of this book would not have been possible without the ongoing professional support of the team of professionals of IGI-Global. Special thanks go also to all the staff at IGI-Global, whose contributions throughout the process of production and making this book available all over the world was invaluable.

We are grateful to all the authors, for their insights and excellent contributions, and to the members of the editorial advisory board, which made possible this book.

Thank you.

The Editors,

João Varajão
University of Trás-os-Montes e Alto Douro, Portugal

Maria Manuela Cruz-Cunha
Polytechnic Institute of Cavado and Ave, Portugal

António Trigo
Polytechnic Institute of Coimbra, Portugal

Chapter 1

An Enterprise Architecture Approach for Designing an Integrated Wood Supply Management System

A. F. Marques
Centre for Forest Studies, Instituto Superior de Agronomia, Technical University of Lisbon, Portugal, & INESC TEC, Portugal

J. G. Borges
Centre for Forest Studies, Instituto Superior de Agronomia, Technical University of Lisbon, Portugal

P. M. Sousa
IST, Technical University of Lisbon, Portugal

M. Fonseca
Link Consulting, Portugal

J. Gonçalves
Europac Group, Viana do Castelo, Portugal

J. Oliveira
Floresta Atlântica – SGFII, S.A., Portugal

ABSTRACT

The wood supply chains encompass a multitude of agents with independent business processes and information systems. The network of interrelationships and information flows among the agents is often neglected when designing information systems. Common processes and automatic data exchanges can enhance collaboration as well as improve IT alignment with business needs across multiple organizations in the supply chain. This article proposes an Enterprise Architecture methodological approach for designing an integrated modular Wood Supply Management System. Both Process Architecture Framework and Information Architecture were developed and used to define individual systems and integration requirements, discussed on the Applications Architecture. The Technological Architecture was further addressed. Results of its application to the Portuguese pulpwood, biomass and lumber-based supply chains are presented. Results show that this approach can effectively specify individual systems requirements driven from the processes descriptions built in collaboration with the agents. It further shows that a Service-Oriented Architecture can be derived, ensuring systems integration and interoperability.

DOI: 10.4018/978-1-4666-1764-3.ch001

INTRODUCTION

The wood supply chains are commonly presented as a pipeline of activities starting on the raw material acquisition and ending on its delivery on the transformation centers, where the finish goods are produced according to the final clients' specifications. They involve several companies, various business units inside the companies, many locations and consequently a paraphernalia of distinct information systems for planning and controlling the activities and information flows. Proprietary, client-tailored systems prevail, often without interfaces to other company's systems nor interoperability features with other agents systems. Redundancy and data inconsistency problems are frequent and some transversal processes, such as products traceability along the chain, are difficult or even impossible to implement.

This chapter advocates the advantages of developing integrated computer-based approaches to support the management of the wood supply chain activities as well as the interactions among its agents. It further proposes an Enterprise Architecture approach for designing the Integrated Wood Supply Management System (iWS) with the involvement of the end-users.

The chapter is organized as follows: The background section provides the description of the Wood Supply Chain using as an example the Portuguese context. The currently adopted information systems are reviewed. An overview of the Enterprise Architecture (EA) methodologies is also presented. The following sections detail the applied EA road-map and its main results, namely, the hierarchical top-down Process Architecture, encompassing the Process Architecture framework and its individual business processes. The information entities described under the Information Architecture. The description of the iWS main modular components, driven from the CRUD matrix analysis in the course of the Applications Architecture. Finally, existing technologies that can adequately support the iWS modules as well

as the technological requirements and developing guidelines, included on the Technological Architecture. The last sections are devoted to the discussion of future and emerging trends and presenting the concluding remarks.

BACKGROUND

The Portuguese Wood Supply Chain Management: Activities, Agents, Systems

The maritime pine (*Pinus pinaster*) and eucalypt (*Eucaliptus globulus*) plantations are the dominant forest occupation in Portugal (885 thousand ha, 740 thousand ha, respectively). Their production is almost entirely absorbed by the pulp & paper and lumber-based sub-sectors (annual sales of $1623 \times 10^3 €$ and $1131 \times 10^3 €$ respectively), which are key contributors to the forest cluster that represent 14% of the GNP, 12% of exports and 9% of the industrial employment (INE, 2007).

Both pine and eucalypt-based supply chains can be seen as large networks of activities and agents throughout which the tree products are explored, stored and transported until they reach the transformation centers (Figure 1). The efficiency of this procurement stage will dictate the raw material acquisition costs, thus conditioning the following wood transformation activities (e.g. bucking, sawing, pressing, and drying) as well as the wood distribution and sales channels and the finish product price paid by the costumers. At the beginning of the supply chain, the forest owners and forest practitioners perform long-term forest operations planning in order to grow mature trees suitable for different utilizations. At the end, the transformation centers acquire timber on the national and international markets through wood supply contracts (usually with wood-trade entrepreneurs) complementary to its eventual self-supply availability, in order to accomplish the target finishing products production levels. In the middle, there are multiple agents conducting middle-term/short-term forest operations, wood storing and transportation planning. The role of these agents on these operational plans varies greatly with the forestland ownership structure and the supply chain context. Pine plantations are majority owned by public, private small-scaled land owners or their collective management structures. They often do not participate on the operational planning as they sell the wood on the forest to local entrepreneurs specialized on harvesting and trade. These are crucial business intermediates, actually responsible for planning the harvest and transportation of the total wood volume obtained on their multiple contracts with the owners. There is little if any direct contact between the mills and the forest owners. The majority of the pine production targets the lumber transformation units. There are more than 250 small-scaled sawmills and 12 panels production units operating mainly in the Center and North of the Country, sustaining more than 4500 carpentry and furniture small-scaled units, responsible for secondary transformation and consumer products commercialization (AIMMP, 2008). Alternatively, the wood importations, especially from Spain, Brazil and USA, are often delivered by boat to the port nearest to the mills facilities and then are transported by truck under the direct industry supervision. Contrarily, most of the eucalypt plantations were installed by the pulp & paper companies as part of their self-supply strategy. Together, they are the major Portuguese private forestland owners. There are 7 operating units, from 2 economical groups, producing annually 1833,2 and 188,5 $\times 10^3 m^3$ of hardwood and softwood pulp, respectively (equivalent to the consumption of 5593 and 731$\times 10^3 m^3$ of eucalypt and pine woodpulp respectively) (CELPA, 2008). The production targets European market although 45% is internally transformed into paper. These integrated companies, holding forestland areas and transformation centers, establish an internal target on the yearly self-supply levels, based on its approved pulp production plan and woodpulp

growth estimates. The yearly foreseen forest operations are subjected to a detailed operational planning, at monthly basis, taking into account the available resources (equipment, teams and vehicles) and the expected wood productions at the self-owned and rented forestlands. Transportation is often outsourced although the company may suggest the transportation plan or even coordinate the transportation in case of small-scaled hauliers. The wood yards, usually owned by woodpulp companies, are gaining importance as part of the company supply strategy, compensating for the wood offer seasonal fluctuation. Moreover, they contribute to transportation costs reduction due to log drying under open air conditions and the possibility of transporting higher log quantities using the railway network from these yards to the mills (Marques, Borges et al. 2011). The recent increase of the biomass sub-sector economical importance justifies its inclusion in this study. In fact, there are currently 6 biomass centrals operating in Portugal, and 4 new units planned until the end of 2010. The majority is located at pulp & paper mills facilities. Together they produce 133,6MW from about 1,4$\times 10^6$ton of forestry residues with origin in self-owned forestlands or internal market, usually chipped at the harvesting sites (Celpa, 2008). Up to now, the forest residues were managed independently in small-scale and trail operations conducted mainly by the pulp and paper industries. Its increasing demand fosters the systematic forest residues collection and chipping, preferably integrated with the traditional logs harvesting operations. Nevertheless, the transportation of chipped forest residues must be managed separately as distinct closed-trailers are required.

The forest products flows along the procurement network are accompanied by information flows, usually on paper basis, enabling the load control and assuring high-level traceability, especially when forest certification and chain of custody certification schemas are implemented. The concurrent supply chain agents (involved in the same activities) usually do not interact, con-

Figure 1. The Forest products procurement network represented the supply, demand and temporary storing locations as well as the eucalypt and pine transportation flows under the Portuguese pulp & paper, lumber-based and biomass supply chains.

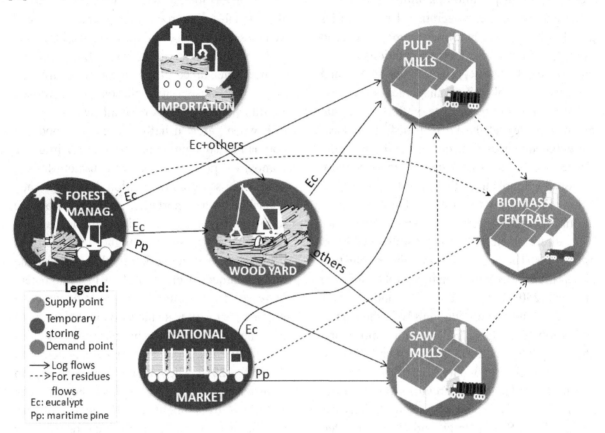

trary to the frequent data exchanges and process triggering among different-staged agents. Recent integrated supply chain approaches did model the pulpwood flows and the information exchange for pulp & paper companies (D'Amours, Ronnqvist et al., 2008). Yet fragmented activity modeling approaches and independent mono-activity information systems prevail among large-scaled forestland owners and industry (Ronnqvist, 2003). Often these systems were tailored to address single agents' planning requirements and built in the context of research projects that did not need to take into account robustness, scalability for continuous use nor the integration with other companies systems, such as the administrative Enterprise-Resource Planning Systems (e.g.

Falcão, Borges et al., 1999; Borges, Falcão et al., 2003; Falcão and Borges, 2005; Falcão, Próspero dos Santos et al., 2006). The activities performed by small-scaled forestland owners, entrepreneurs, hauliers and even small-scaled industries typically were not subjected to computer-based planning nor execution/performance indicators are properly recorded. Individually, they cannot lead the development of such tools and collective initiatives are uncommon. (Reynolds, Twery et al., 2007) presented an overview of Forest Management Decision Support Systems in use in North America, Europe, and Asia and underlined the importance of systems integration to achieve cooperation among the chain agents.

This research aims the design of an integrated wood supply management system (iWS). Emphasis is the support individual agents activities as well as automating data sharing and exchange, thus promoting cooperation and interoperability among the agents. The underling challenges are:

1. *Horizontal integration among the supply chain agents:* The definition of common processes and modular functional components – sub-systems - per supply chain activity/ agent profile, based on recognized best practices, can conduct to single-agent operations improvements and promote cooperativism, especially relevant for small-scaled agents. The modules should be easily adaptable/ parameterized to specific agents requirements in order to simplify the new systems development process. Its interfaces should be clearly defined, and efforts should be taken to enable easy integration with existing systems as well as assuring a scalable/ flexible systems architecture.

2. *Vertical integration among the supply chain agents:* The identification of the information shared and exchanged among agents can simplify the independent systems integration, thus enhancing interoperability and cooperation among the agents. It further can improve processes transversal to the entire wood supply chain, such as the wood traceability.

3. *Integration between the systems used for planning and activities execution control:* The control systems should relay on state-of-the-art mobile devices for real-time activities execution follow-up. It should also compile data from different sources, compute metrics and deviations in respect to the operational plans and trigger re-planning events when significant deviations are recorded.

Overview of Enterprise Architecture Approaches for Forest Information Systems Design

Enterprise Architecture (EA) methodology approaches have been successfully applied to design scalable information systems. It is based on processes' modeling and information characterization (Schekkerman, 2009) conducted in Process Architecture workshops with end-users (or supply chain agents). These workshops are instrumental for identifying system requirements to support business processes, ensuring the alignment between business requirements and the Information Technology (IT) function (Sousa and Pereira, 2005). (Ribeiro, Borges et al., 2005) demonstrated the EA potential for specifying the Integrated Forest Management System strategic module for a major pulp and paper industry in Portugal (Grupo Portucel Soporcel). (Marques, Borges et al., 2010) extended this approach to develop an information system for the entire pulpwood supply chain, also in the context of an integrated Portuguese pulp and paper company. The same authors also applied this methodology into the design of a regional forest management toolbox with the active collaboration of 32 representatives of 21 stakeholders groups with interests on the forest resources of the Chamusca county (Marques, Borges et al., 2011).

In this research we proposed and tested an extension of the EA methodology (Spewak & Hill, 1992) to involve several agents on the design of an Integrated Wood Supply Management System. The reasoning behind the selection of this methodological approach was:

• Disaggregates the business complexity throughout top-down business process representations

• Foresees the involvement of the agents in interactive process architecture workshops. The process representations are based on what they do and what they intent to do. No a priori assumptions are made. These workshops further address the information shared and exchanged among agents, which is the basis for establishing the interoperability and integration requirements.

- Identifies core information entities (manipulated within the processes). Any unjustified data is included.
- Identify the system modules using a well established approach based on the CRUD matrix manipulation and IT alignment rules, therefore assuring the alignment between the business and the IT function.
- Analyses existing technologies and specifies the most adequate to support the business and communication requirements.
- Creates dynamic and exportable knowledge repositories with all EA artifacts, whose HTML version is easy to use and can be embedded on the agents internal web sites.

APPLYING ENTERPRISE ARCHITECTURE TO THE DESIGN OF THE INTEGRATED WOOD SUPPLY CHAIN MANAGEMENT SYSTEM

Enterprise Architecture Methodology

The expertise and representativeness of the EA team was a key success factor. The team leader was a well experienced EA architect who coordinated the work of the IT technicians, forest practitioners and logistic experts. They worked in straight collaboration with a consultants committee, consisting of forest production experts, entrepreneurs, representatives of the pulp & paper and lumber-based industries. They were actively involved during the Process Architecture stage

and validated the outcomes of the other three methodological stages (Figure 2).

The Process Architecture (PA) focused on forest production, logistics, and plant supply processes as well as on the business information of the Portuguese pulpwood, biomass and lumber-based supply chains. An average of 8 experts met in three half-day interactive process architecture workshops. The Post-It method was applied for hierarchical top-down decision process interactive design. During the first session, the eucalypt and pine supply and demand points were represented on the wood procurement network and further described (in line with the overview presented on section 2.1). This representation motivated the discussion among agents about the current characteristics, problems and future trends of the Portuguese wood supply chain. Additionally, it contributed for the cohesion among the consultants committee and their acquaintance with the concepts and the drawing approach. The following sessions were used to build and detail the hierarchical Process Architecture Framework. This framework extended the referential presented on (Marques, Borges et al,. 2010) to include the lumber-based and biomass supply chains. The process element was the elementary object. Similar to SCOR Supply Chain Operations Reference Model (Supply Chain Council, 2008), the first and second levels grouped the process elements into process types and categories, respectively. These were the levels represented on the Wood Supply Chain Process Framework. Afterwards, individual meetings were conducted with the interested agents in order to complete the process elements description, its tasks (fourth level), and their input/output information. This description is often complemented with process flowcharts or other representations where standard notations are often used (e.g. Business Process Modeling Notation). In this case, common representations could not be produced, as the tasks sequencing was highly agent-dependent. Still, the tasks and information flows were displayed on

Figure 2. Enterprise Architecture four-stage methodology, including the activities and the outcome of each stage

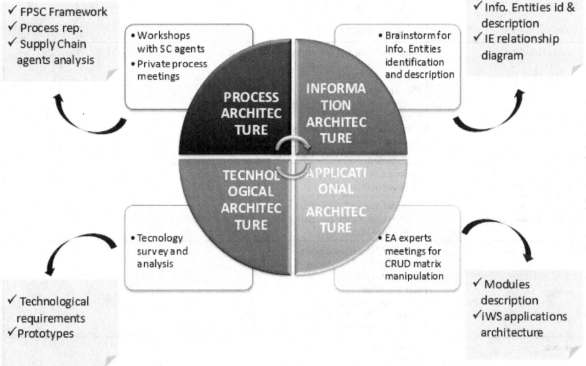

proper tables and complemented with tasks and information dictionaries compiled at the end of the process architecture. Both process elements and tasks are generic and propose operating standards based on recognized best practices (e.g. CAP, 2004), upon which recommendations, guidelines and system requirements were driven. These tasks should be adapted according to individual entities context and sub-tasks (fifth level) can be dawned. Additionally, the agents involved on the Portuguese wood supply chain were identified and their role on the tasks was acknowledged. As so, the identified agents and processes were displayed across the columns and lines of a RACI responsibility assignment matrix. The RACI is an acronym derived from the four key responsibilities most typically used: Responsible, Accountable, Consulted and Informed (IIBA, 2009).

The second stage - Information Architecture – encompassed brainstorm meetings with the forest experts and IT managers for core information entities identification, based on the information flows handled by the process elements. These information entities were further characterized in respect to their business responsible, single identifier defined from a business perspective, a brief description and a set of attributes (Marques, Borges et al. 2010) (Table 1). The high level entity-relationship model was also produced. The information entities were represented on boxes with their main attributes and the connectors among entities expressed logical relationships. This model was the precursor of the future Data Base structure. These meetings were also instrumental for creating awareness on the agents about the importance of their business information. It should be considered an asset of the organiza-

Table 1. Characterization of the EA artifacts, based on (Marques, Borges et al. 2010)

EA artifact	Properties
Agent/Role	Identifier, Name and Description Organization Physical location
Process element	Identifier, Name and Description Category (business or support) Objectives Physical location Frequency (daily, monthly, triggered by client, other) [Tasks] [Responsible Role and Participant Roles] [Input and output information] [Relationship with other processes]
Task (and Tasks Dictionary)	Identifier, Name, Description [Associated Processes]
Information flow (and Information Dictionary)	Identifier, Name, Description Support type (paper, electronic flow, oral communication…) [Associated Processes]
Information entity	Identifier, Name, Description Objective [Associated Information flows] Key-Identifier [Associated Attributes] [Relationship with other information entities] [Relationship with the processes, based on CRUD matrix]
Attribute	Abbreviator, Name Units Source Optional (yes/no) Data type: Check box, value list, text (char number), date, integer, decimal, logic (V, F) Table name and field name on the data model
Information system (IS)	Identifier, Name, Description Objective [Supported processes, based on CRUD matrix] [Supported information entities, based on CRUD matrix] [Supported activities] Interfaces (GUI, with external IS, with other internal IS) Migration and integration requirements Technological requirements
Module (or sub-system)	Identifier, Name, Description Interfaces (GUI, with external IS, with other internal IS) Functional requirements

tion therefore subjected to proper management. Lastly, the information entities were mapped into the processes, in the course of the CRUD matrix elaboration. Accordingly, the processes and information entities were positioned as rows and columns of a CRUD matrix, respectively. Then, the processes flowcharts were revisited in order to identify the behavior (Create, Read, Update, Delete) of the process concerning each information entity. For example, if a given information flow is created and can be deleted in the course of a process execution then the process has a CRUD behavior over its correspondent information entity.

The third stage - Application Architecture - started with the CRUD matrix reorganization. Clusters of functionally-related processes were built and the information entities were also grouped until all the Create, Update, Delete behaviors were displayed diagonally. Proper system consistency and business-IT alignment rules were applied to identify the future system functional modular components (Sousa and Pereira, 2005) (Table 1). Accordingly, each process should only be supported in one module and each information entity should only be CRUD in one module. The overall iWS application architecture diagram was drawn following the traditional three layer representations (Interfaces, applications, information). It displayed the modules (or sub-systems) general architecture schema, its main end-users agents profiles and the handled information entities. The information entities entirely managed by the sub-system - had a "Create", "Update" and "Delete" behavior on the CRUD matrix - are those relying solely on its data repository and available for query by the other systems, while those simply accessed – had a "Read" behavior on the matrix - correspond to interfaces with other modules or systems. The modules were further described regarding its data repositories, graphical user interfaces, interfaces with other existing or foreseen systems and a set of functional requirements to manage its information entities life cycle and to automate the activities of its specific business processes. Additional solution components were added to address interoperability among the sub-systems to be used by the supply chain agents. Interoperability was generally defined as the capability to communicate, execute programs, or transfer data among various functional units in a manner that requires the user to have little or no knowledge of the unique characteristics of those units (ISO/IEC 2382-1, 1993).

The fourth last stage - Technological Architecture - proposed the most adequate technologies to support the iWS sub-systems and implement the interoperability requirements. This stage encompassed a detailed analysis of existing Information & Communication technologies. When adequate technologies were found, the analysis further specified the adaptations needed to fully address the requirements previously established and achieve it integration on the overall iWS solution. Complementary, when such technologies were not available, it further detailed the guidelines for its deployment and evaluated the effort involved on its development on the course of a forthcoming prototype phase.

Process Architecture

The process architecture started by identifying the wood supply agents, namely: Public forestland owners, private small-scaled forestland owners, industrial forestland owners, entrepreneurs/wood suppliers, hauliers/other service providers, wood yard technicians (manager, receptionist) and mill supply technicians (manager, receptionist). The Wood Supply Chain Process Architecture Framework foreseen standard processes performed by these agents for producing tree products at the supply points – 1. Forest production –, fulfill the wood demands at the consumption points – 3. Plant supply – and manage wood storing and transportation between the wood procurement network locations – 2. Wood logistics (Figure 3). The first type grouped the common high-level processes conducted by forest practitioners and landowners (public, industrial, private small-scaled and collective) into 4 categories: The forestland management (1.1.) assured an updated knowledge of the forest status; including the forest properties registration (1.1.1) (i.e. spatial representation, biophysical characterization, ownership structure, forest and forest products characteristics), the biotic and abiotic hazards monitoring (1.1.2.) and the stands biometric indicators collected at the forest inventories (1.1.3.). It further included the negotiation procedures related with new forestland properties acquisition or rental (1.1.4), especially for industrial forestland owners. The forest operations planning (1.2.) was divided according to its main spatial-temporal scales, although its processes and management objectives

Figure 3. The Wood Supply Chain Process Architecture Framework grouped the process elements into process categories, displayed into 3 main process types: 1. Forest production, 2. Wood logistics and 3. Plant Supply.

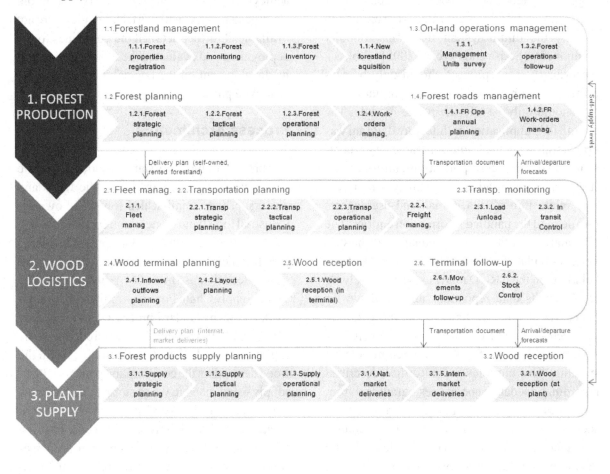

were highly agent-dependent. In general terms, the long-term strategic plan (1.2.1) for the entire owners patrimony, presented the operations scheduled to occur over the next decades. The industrial forestland owners typically had optimal management models to assure the mills self-supply levels while addressing other ecological, economical and social objectives. On the opposite, the remaining landowners typologies adopted descriptive plans with few econometrics, following the pre-establish plan template imposed by the national forestry regulation. The tactical and operational planning levels often conducted by the industrial forestland owners at local/short-term scales (1.2.2., 1.2.3.)

enabled optimal use of the available resources and provided input for establishing the work-orders which were then allocated to internal crews or outsourced to service providers (1.2.4). Lastly, the internal forest roads management (1.4.) scheduled the roads maintenance operations in order to assure forest sites access during the harvest operations. The next process type related to wood intermediate storing and transportation, mainly performed by the yard managers, entrepreneurs and hauliers. Specifically, the fleet management (2.1.), transportation planning (2.2.) and transportation monitoring (2.3.) aimed overall transportation management, while wood terminal planning (2.4.), wood reception (2.5.) and terminal follow-up (2.6.) assured complete wood yard management. The third process type focused on wood and forest residues deployment to the transformation units and biomass centrals. Thus, the Forest products supply planning (3.1.) included the wood supply hierarchical planning, considering the self-supply levels as well as the acquisitions at the national (wood suppliers) and international markets. The plant wood reception (3.2.1.) presented similarities with the process 2.5.1 (Table 2). The correspondent tasks regulated the wood trucks unload and assured the load evaluation. It further managed the truck queuing at the mill/yard entrance based on the anticipation of the next incoming truck, obtained from the arrivals/departures forecasts produced by the In-transit control (2.3.2.) process. The RACI matrix was further drawn synthesizing the role of the agents over the described processes. This matrix was instrumental for identifying the end-users of the sub-systems as well as the users-access control features for the entire iWS solution. All the dictionaries (tasks, agents, information) and the process descriptions were placed on a VISIO-based knowledge repository, whose HMTL export files were deployed to the agents and used for their content validation.

Information Architecture

The definition of the nuclear information handled by the supply chain agents was instrumental to avoid data inconsistency and establishing the data exchanges among agents/systems. In fact, it was recognized by the agents that the integration and interoperability relied both on proper technologies and the adoption of a common ontology, which could be based on this information entities definitions.

More than 100 information types were identified on the brainstorm meetings, grouped afterwards into 22 independent Information Entities, namely: E1. Management Unit, E2. Forest property, E3. Harvesting Unit, E4. Forest Operation, E5. Transformation Center, E6. Wood Yard, E7. Forest Product, E8. Supply plan, E9. Freight, E10. Transportation Vehicle, E11. Wood supplier/entrepreneur, E12. Work order, E13. Service provider, E14. Equipment, E15. Forest road, E16. Crew, E17. Wood pile, E18. Wood load, E19. Forest hazard, E20. Forest inventory, E21. Forest plan, E22. Logistic plan. The information entity represented a set on functionally interrelated information, which in term could be related with several other entities, creating the basis for a data base relational model. As an example, the E1.

Table 2. Description of the Plant wood reception (3.2.1.) process element

Input information	Task	Output information
• *Arrival/departure estimates* • *Transportation document*	3.2.1.1. Anticipate next incoming truck • Estimate arrival date • Provide destination • Notify unloading team and equipment (if needed) • If there is a delay,	• *Unloading notification*
	3.2.1.2. Verify truck load • Load quality evaluation • Wood weight	• *Load entrance registration*
	3.2.1.3. Truck unload	
• *Truck daily schedule*	3.2.1.4. Record truck exiting • Truck exiting date • Update next trip origin (if needed)	• *Load entrance registration update*
• *Trucks queue at plant entrance*	3.2.1.5. Manage truck queuing • Prioritize and display truck entrance sequence	• *Next entering truck*

Management unit information entity included the biophysical characteristics (e.g. slope, soil, climate), forest occupation (forest species), biometric indicators, type of ownership and other management information. Included historic information on the annual surveys conducted prior to forest operational planning. It was related with several other entities, such as the forest inventory, since each forest inventory addressed several management units and each unit had at least one forest inventory. Similarly, each unit produced at least two products (biomass, logs) while each product was obtained in one or several units. Lastly, the entities were mapped on the described processes as part of the CRUD matrix preparation (Figure 4). Accordingly, the Forest Production process elements handled (Create, Read, Update, Delete) 15 main information entities (IEs), namely: E1. Management Unit, E2. Forest Property, E3. Harvesting Unit, E4. Forest Operation, E17. Forest Product, E12. Work order, E13. Service Provider, E14. Equipment, E15. Forest road, E16. Crew, E17. Wood pile, E19. Forest hazard, E20. Forest inventory and E21. Forest Plan. The Management Unit and Forest Operation were accessed ("Read") by all of these processes. The first was managed ("Create", "Read", "Update", "Delete") by the Forest properties Registration process (1.1.1.)

Figure 4. CRUD matrix produced at the Applications Architecture stage. It established the behavior ("Create", "Read", "Update", "Delete") of the business processes over the information entities, displayed in the rows and columns respectively. Its reorganization and the appliance of business-IT alignment rules allowed the identification of the 12 sub-systems.

CRUD MATRIX	Management Unit E1	Forest property E2	Forest hazard E19	Forest inventory E20	Forest plan E21	Harvesting Unit E3	Forest Road E15	Forest Operation E4	Work order E12	Haulier/Service provider E13	Equipment E14	Crew E16	Wood pile E17	Forest Product E7	Transport Vehicle E10	logistic plan E22	Freight E9	Wood Yard E6	Wood load E18	Transf. Center E5	Supply plan E8	Wood supplier/entrepreneur E11
1.1.1 Forest properties registration	CRUD	CRUD																				
1.1.4 New forestland aquisition		CRUD												RU								
1.1.2 Forest monitoring	RU	R	CRUD																			
1.1.3 Forest inventory	RU	R		CRUD									RU	RU								
1.2.1 Forest strategic planning	RU		R		CRUD															R	RU	R
1.2.2 Forest tactical planning	RU		R		CRUD	CRUD		RU						R				R		R	R	R
1.4.1 FR Ops annual planning					RU	CRUD		R														
1.2.3 Forest operational planning	RU	R		R	CRUD	RU	R	RU	RU	RU	RU			R				R	R	R	R	R
1.3.1 ManagementUnits survey	R	R			RU			CRUD		R		R										
1.3.2 Forest operations follow-up	RU				R			CRUD	RU	CRUD	CRUD	CRUD	CRUD	CRUD								
1.2.4 Work-orders manag.								CRUD	RU	RU	RU											
1.4.2 FR Work-orders manag							RU	CRUD	CRUD	RU	RU											
2.1.1 Fleet manag								R		R					CRUD							
2.2.1 Transp strategic planning	R				R	R	R	R						R	R	CRUD			R			
2.2.2 Transp tactical planning	R				R	R		R							RU	CRUD		R		R		
2.2.3 Transp operational planning	R				R	R		R							RU	CRUD		R		R		
2.4.1 Inflows/outflows planning														R	R	CRUD						
2.2.4 Freight manag.	R				R	R		R			R	R	R	R		CRUD	R	R				
2.3.2 In transit Control														R		CRUD						
2.4.2 Layout planning														RU			CRUD					
2.3.1 Load/unload					R			R		R	RU		R				CRUD	RU				
2.6.1 Movements follow-up									R	R	R	R					CRUD	RU	R			
2.6.2 Stock Control														R			CRUD					
3.2.1 Wood reception (at plant)								RU						R				R		R		RU
2.5.1 Wood reception (in terminal)								RU						R			R	R	RU			
3.1.1 Supply strategic planning					RU									R						RU	CRUD	R
3.1.2 Supply tactical planning														R						RU	CRUD	R
3.1.3 Supply operational planning								R						R						RU	CRUD	R
3.1.4 Nat. market deliveries														R						R		CRUD
3.1.5 Interm. market deliveries														R						R		CRUD

whenever a new property was acquired or a forest hazard, like a forest fire, obliged to new forestland segmentation. Each management unit, usually with a geographical representation, was considered homogeneous in terms of its characterization, foreseen and executed forest operations, although it could include several non-contiguous forest properties. The forest operations were planned at the management unit level. The on-land operations management processes (1.3.) handled the executed Forest Operations, and associate it to a Management Unit. The Wood Logistics processes managed the E6. Yard, E9. Freight, E10. Transportation Vehicle, E18. Wood load and E22. Logistic Plan. The freight was the main information entity of the transportation monitoring process (2.3.). It was "Created" at the origin (harvest unit or yard), when a new transportation document was issued and "Deleted" (or sent to historic records) when the truck was unloaded. It included the arrival time estimates at the origins and destinations, which should be periodically updated based on the vehicle real-time positioning. Finally, the Plant Supply processes were responsible for the E8. Supply Plan and E11. Wood Supplier. The E5. Industrial Unit was accessed (Read) by these processes but its information was managed by external systems.

Applications Architecture

The 12 sub-systems suggested by the CRUD matrix manipulation assured univocal relationships between processes and information entities, thus, avoiding functional redundancy. They were the main elements of the iWS architecture diagram (Figure 5), which also emphasized the interoperability and integration mechanisms. The diagram initial analysis revealed a clear separation between the planning and operations control sub-systems. In fact, the forestry, wood logistics and mills supply plans could be produced centrally by the agents with management responsibilities, while the control sub-systems encompassed several mobile devices used by the on-land agents' profiles to col-

lect real-time execution metrics, which should be centrally consolidated for operations monitoring (backoffice) and then shared among the agents. Accordingly, the Forest production processes were addressed by 1 planning sub-system and 4 control sub-systems. The S1. Forest Operations Planning produced all the forest plans (E21), including the strategic, tactic and operational plans used by the industrial forestland owners, the PGF template adopted by public and small-scaled managers and other collective forest management plans. It also established the harvest units (E5) and the forest roads interventions schedules (E15). The S2. Properties Management relied on mobile GPS devices for property delimitation (included on E2) and on-land data collection (e.g. biophysical characteristics of the forest properties, forest operations performed (E1)). Similar devices were specified for supporting the forest inventory activities (S4) and on-land Operations Management (S5). In the first case, they provided the location of the pre-defined forest inventory plots (E20) and recorded its biometrical data, according to the inventory protocol previously established. Their main users were forest practitioners prior to forest planning processes, although they were also adequate for outsourced inventory teams conducting national forest inventory or for entrepreneurs requiring precise wood estimates during the negotiations with the landowners. In the second case, they located the ongoing forest and road management operations (E1) and collected its execution metrics, thus improving the work conducted by the forestland owners and entrepreneurs. The information collected was synchronized to central data repositories, subjected to validation schemas and then available to other sub-systems. The S1. Forest monitoring, encompassed surveillance cameras and other fixed equipment for early forest hazards detection (E19), as well as a central backoffice for alarms management and recording the following monitoring events. The Wood Logistic processes were addressed by 2 planning sub-systems and 3 operations control sub-systems. The S6. Trans-

Figure 5. iWS application architecture diagram, representing the 12 modular components (sub-systems) identified from the CRUD matrix analysis, namely: S1.Forest Operations Planning, S2. Properties Management, S3. Forest Monitoring, S4. Forest Inventory, S5. Operations Management, S6. Transportation Planning, S7. Fleet Management, S8. Wood Stock Control, S9. Transportation Follow-up, S10. Yard Planning, S11. Wood Purchase, S12. Supply Planning. It includes the information entities managed by the sub-systems and exchanged among them trough the Interoperability module, namely: E1. Management Unit, E2. Forest property, E3. Harvesting Unit, E4. Forest Operation, E5. Transformation Center, E6. Wood Yard, E7. Forest Product, E8. Supply plan, E9. Freight, E10. Transportation Vehicle, E11. Wood supplier/entrepreneur, E12. Work order, E13. Service provider, E14. Equipment, E15. Forest road, E16. Crew, E17. Wood pile, E18. Wood load, E19. Forest hazard, E20. Forest inventory, E21. Forest plan, E22. Logistic plan. If further displays the sub-systems end-users according to the agents profiles.

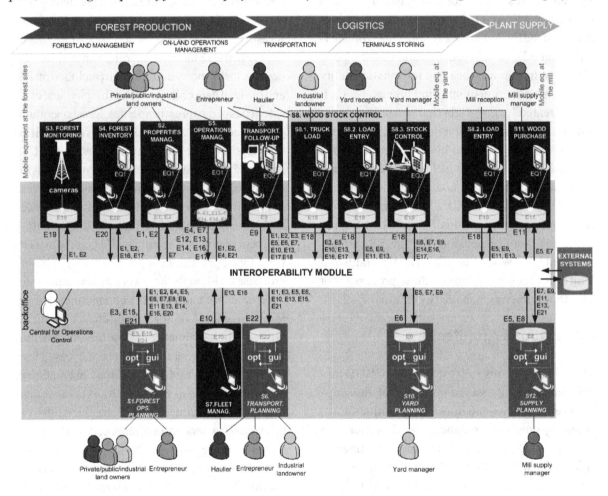

portation planning provided the wood distribution plans, the daily trucks and crews schedules and budgeting estimates (E22), according to the specificities of the transportation planner (e.g. haulier, entrepreneur, industrial landowner). The

wood transportation fleet was managed by the haulier on the S7 central sub-system. The daily transportation monitoring (S9) was performed by embedded devices responsible for displaying the trucks location (and other information recorded by the driver) on a Central backoffice managed by the haulier. This information was instrumental for managing the wood reception on the yards and mills, under a just-in-time delivery schema. The internal configuration of the wood yards, the daily schedules for the loading/unloading equipment and crew as well as the qualified daily stock management was addressed by the S10. Yard Planning sub-system. The wood stock control sub-system (S8), encompassed a series of mobile devices grouped into sub-modules aiming Truck load (S8.1), Load reception at the yards and mills (S8.2.) and wood stock control at the yards (S8.3). This was a transversal system thus assuring the wood flows quantitative control across the entire wood procurement network, according to industrial owners requirements. Finally, the supply of sawmills, pulp mills and biomass centers relied on 1 planning sub-system and 2 wood deliveries control sub-systems. The S12. Supply Planning sub-system defined the strategic target levels for self-supply and national/international market acquisitions, based on the approved production plans, which were mandatory for the transportation and supply contracts/agreements. Moreover, it produced the daily delivery plans at the yards and mills based on the actual agreements and the transportation/crews/equipment daily availabilities. The entrepreneurs are other wood suppliers prior qualification process and negotiation terms were supported on the S11. Wood Purchase sub-system.

The sub-systems general functional requirements and the interfaces with other internal and external systems were properly characterized. As an example, the requirements for the S8.2. Load Entry sub-module, used on the yard and mill reception were:

- Receive the real-time estimates for truck arrivals and update the daily delivery plans.
- Display an alarm for truck delays and trigger new daily delivery plans.

- Consolidate and display information on the next arriving truck (e.g. truck and driver identification, load characteristics, origin).
- Consolidate and display information on the truck unload operations (e.g., destination, unload equipment, crew).
- Query/edition/exportation/report of truck entry records.
- Automatic integration with the weighing-machine records.
- Record the truck exiting hour.

Like the remaining S8. Wood stock control sub-modules, all the information managed (Create, Update, Delete) was included on the E18. Wood load information entity, thus suggesting a shared data-base infra-structure. This sub-module further accessed (Read) information managed by other iWS modules or external systems, such as:

- Description of the transportation service provider (haulier) or entrepreneur/wood supplier contract, supported on S5 and S11, respectively.
- Information on the freight for the next arriving truck, managed by S9.
- Mills/yards loading/unloading equipment and crews, real-time time information on the mills/yards status available at S8.3. module or other mills' systems.

The applications architecture further suggested an interoperability module and a Central for Operations Control. This module was a key component of the distributed iWS applications architecture. It was responsible for automating information exchange among sub-system and with external systems. It also recognized and handled triggering events among systems. Specifically, when certain events were recorded on a given sub-system, a specific message was delivered to other related sub-systems in order to trigger the execution of consecutive events. As an example, when a truck damage record was created on the S7. Fleet management sub-system, a replan event should be received at the S6. Transportation Planning sub-system for updating the daily truck schedules. This module did not implement specific business processes and so it was considered invisible for the supply chain agents. Yet, the data exchanges required proper monitoring performed at Central for Operations Control, operated by an independent IT team. This central further undertake the necessary actions for solving trouble-shooting situations and assured the integration of legacy systems into the overall iWS solution. It could also aggregate the BackOffice Operations consolidation modules, foreseen for sub-systems S2., S3., S4., S5., S8., S9., especially useful for integrated industries.

Technological Architecture

The Information and Communication Technologies analysis focused on existing state-of-the-art solutions with similarities with the planning and operations control sub-systems described previously. Forest planning was been recently addressed by state-of-the-art Decision Support Systems (e.g. Borges, Falcao et al,. 2003, Reynolds, Twery et al., 2007, Hetemaki and Nilsson 2005). An ongoing survey on forest management decision support systems in Portugal revealed two systems that seemed to meet the majority of the S1 functional requirements. Specifically, the SAGFLOR (fp0804.emu.ee/wiki/index.php/SADfLOR/SAGfLOR) was a research prototype developed by the Technical University of Lisbon to address forest long-term optimal planning, taking into account the ecological and economical objectives and constraints that characterize the planning problem under the public or industrial forestland owner perspectives. Complementary, the SADPOF (http://fp0804.emu.ee/wiki/index.php/SADPOF) was a web based application for optimized forest tactical/operational forest planning. Currently solved harvest scheduling integrated with eucalypt wood logs and biomass assortment

and assignment, under the scope of an integrated pulp and paper company. No solutions were found in Portugal that could comply with requirements of the remaining planning sub-systems, namely, the forest roads management included on S1, the S6. Transportation Planning, the S10. Yards Planning and the S12. Supply Planning. Yet, the management of the forest roads integrated with harvesting was addressed by some research prototypes such as the Scandinavian RoadOpt (Karlsson, Ronnqvist et al., 2006). The ASICAM was successfully used to optimize transportation planning on several Chilean pulp and paper companies (Weintraub, Epstein et al., 1996). Consequently, the analysis suggested the adoption of SAGFLOR and SADPOF for forest planning as well as the development of specific decision support systems for Transportation Planning, Yards Planning and Supply Planning, incorporating the published research results. The technological requirements and development guidelines for the planning systems pointed out to multi-component web-based systems, with various combinations of models and optimization techniques, supported by Database Management Systems and accessed by spatial and graphical user interfaces (Marques, Borges et al., 2010). The open-source GIS and optimization solvers should be preferred.

There was a lack of operations control systems published in Portugal and abroad. The survey on computerized tools for forest planning in Portugal identified several unpublished information systems, often GIS-based, tailored to meet specific users requirements. The on-land information was usually collected on paper forms and added on the system afterwards. No mobile devices were usually used. Therefore, the analysis suggested the selection of versatile mobile devices to support several functionally-related sub-systems, as well as the development of adequate synchronization mechanisms to overcome the difficulties of mobile computation, mainly related with the frequent lack of internet connectivity on the forest sites. Accordingly, highly robust and autonomous PDA devices were chosen to support the S2., S4., S5., S8.1., S8.2. and S11. sub-systems. These devices should incorporate GPS features and enable GIS queries and remote edition. The device for stock control (S8.3) had similarities with the latter although it can be embedded on equipment used for wood movements inside the yard. The data synchronization between the mobile devices and the backoffices could occur at the end of the day, with the exception of the S8.1. whose information on the truck load must be deployed on real-time to the S8.2. sub-system. An embedded truck GPS-based tracking device was selected for transportation follow-up (S9). There were several standard embedded devices that could entirely address this sub-system requirements, such as the xTRAN solution commercialized by Tecmic (http://www.tecmic.pt/por/xtran/xtran_intro.html). Lastly, the already installed CICLOPE surveillance cameras network (www.inov.pt) provided information on forest fires detection. No solution was found to support the detection of forest diseases.

The analysis further suggested the internal development of the interoperability module, based on a Middleware software, such as the EAI (Enterprise Application Integration) often used for supply chain applications. The middleware software consisted of a set of technologies and services provided by the sub-systems, allowing its interactions while working simultaneously. It was considered a key component to support and simplify complex distributed applications (O'Brien & Marakas, 2009). The implementation of such a module would require:

- Complete specification of the data-services and business-services provided by the proposed sub-systems
- Agreement upon the data exchange formats and communication protocols to be used by all sub-systems
- Agreement upon technology standards
- Common ontology and common information exchange reference model

- Technologies to integrate existing legacy systems on the common iWS architecture

The proposed process and information architectures provided the baseline for identifying the unassociated and loose coupled services. Yet, these services should be properly specified and orchestrated in the course of a forthcoming Service-Oriented Architecture approach. Complementary, the syntactical and semantic interoperability were further addressed. The first related with the detailed specification of the data exchange formats and communication protocols to be used by the proposed sub-systems, often referred as interoperability by design. This should be complemented with technology standards and freely available for IT companies/end users involved on the development of commercial/proprietary systems through further detail of the proposed iWS architecture components. Additionally, interoperability was accounted for legacy systems trough the development of technological features for data conversion to the agreed data format. The second refereed to the ability of automatically interpret the information exchanged meaningfully and accurately in order to produce useful results as defined by the users of the sub-systems. Accordingly, a large group of supply-chain agents would agree upon a common ontology, and a common information exchange reference model, based on the information entities description and its high level entity-relationship model. This interoperability module should be managed by an independent IT team for continuous monitoring of the overall system functioning and coupling of legacy systems.

FUTURE RESEARCH DIRECTIONS

This research established the baseline towards complete cooperation and interoperability among the wood supply chain agents. Future initiatives should be promoted by a larger consultant committee, preferably including national and international experts/practitioners on all the wood supply chain activities. The work should be conducted in straight collaboration with other forest open standards initiatives such as the Papinet (www. papinet.org).

The semantic interoperability should be firstly addressed. A common *ontology* must be adopted among the supply chain agents. It will enable the definition of a common information exchange reference model. This will foster communication and interoperability among agents/systems. This ontology should be widely discussed among the Portuguese forestry community and represent a standard for cooperation, in parallel with the iWS architecture. The interoperability module should then be developed, starting on a *Service-Oriented Architecture* driven from the presented process and information architectures. It should specify the services to be implemented by the sub-systems to assure systems communication, data exchange and the support of the triggering events. It should be complemented with the definition of the *data exchange formats and communication protocols*.

Additionally, an iWS *governance model* for the overall solution should also be established. It includes the implementation of leadership and organisational structures, the definition of the role/permissions of each agent profile over the functions/data available on the overall solution and the activities performed by the Central for Operations Control. The issues related with the data ownership, data access and usability must be accounted in order to assure transparency and trust. These are critical aspects behind the acceptance and usage of these standards by the forestry community.

Both iWS governance model and integrated architecture should then be subjected to *validation under a real-life situation*. The involvement of representatives of the Portuguese wood supply chain across the entire iWS architecture process assured the adequacy of the results in respect to the forestry and logistics real-life context. Yet, a larger group of representants should be involved on building a future research prototype and testing it on a real-life case study in order to obtain a conclusive cost-benefit analysis for each sub-system as well as for the overall supply chain management solution. The interoperability model should be developed with the involvement of the IT team responsible for the Central for Operations Control. This team should also accompany the work conducted with the agents. In parallel, a thorough analysis should be conducted to clarify the status of each agent in respect to the iWS architecture. This analysis resembles the activities undertaken for each new agent adhering to the future iWS architecture. It includes:

- Detailing tasks and sub-tasks, based on the process elements presented on the Wood Supply Chain Process Architecture Framework.
- Mapping the information flows on existing data repositories: Identifying the relevance of information not yet collected. Quantifying the gap between the agents current situation and the ontology/ information exchange reference model.
- Mapping the current systems on the iWS applications architecture: Identifying legacy systems; adapting the sub-systems foreseen functional requirements to the agent real-life context.
- Documenting the legacy system interfaces and addressing its integration with the iWS platform trough the interoperability module.
- Undertake the necessary agent organization initiatives to promote the adoption of the iWS architecture (e.g. workers training, discussion forums)

Afterwards, the interoperability module specifications should be reviewed; especially its technological features for data conversion to the agreed format, assuring that the main legacy systems (proprietary or commercial) can be integrated into the iWS structure. The integration of legacy systems is potentially the bottleneck for the entire prototype since there must be a wide variety of legacy systems built in various technologies (some even outdated) often working like "black-boxes" and without sufficient documentation. An diagnose must be conducted prior to each integration and if there are low probabilities of success with satisfactory time-effort then a secondary plans should be foreseen and simple data sheets can be temporary used. Lastly, efforts must be made for iWS architecture and governance model continuous improvement and wide dissemination of its results.

CONCLUSION

In Portugal there was considerable experience on applying Enterprise Architecture to the design of Forest Decision Support Systems. This research was built on this experience. The proposed architecture approach addressed effectively the specification of the Integrated Wood Supply Management System in straight collaboration with the representants of the supply chain agents. The fourth stages of the Enterprise Architecture were instrumental to overtake the research underlying challenges. Specifically, both process and applications architecture assured the vertical integration among the supply chain agents. The proposed Wood Supply Chain Process Architecture Framework provided the hierarchical structure for standard processes performed by the agents involved on Forest Production, Wood Logistics and Plant Supply. This framework represented a best-practices reference guide, leading to individual agent efficiency improvements and enhancing its collaboration with the other supply chain counterparts. After the third level, the tasks must be detailed to address the agent specificities. Complementary, the sub-systems presented on the iWS applications

architecture were driven by the wood supply chain agents processes, thus enhancing the IT alignment with the business needs. They were adequate for concurrent agents, thus promoting cooperativism. It further enables easier and contextualized new system developments, thus reducing the overall IT costs. The architecture was based on functionally independent components, thus assuring adaptability and scalability. Similarly, both information and applications architecture contributed for vertical integration among the supply chain agents, though the definition of the data exchanged among sub-systems, the end-users of the sub-systems and the interoperability module main features (i.e. automating data exchange among sub-systems and with external systems, supporting the triggering events). Lastly, both applications architecture and technological architecture provided adequate solutions for planning systems, based on Decision Support Systems as well as operations control systems, based on mobile devices synchronized with central backoffices.

Results further show the relationship between the presented EA artifacts and the forthcoming Service-Oriented Architecture. The latter shall specify the services available by each sub-system as part of the interoperability module. Complementary work to achieve syntactic and semantic interoperability was also discussed. Emphasis was also the role of the agents on a future iWS governance model. Finally, an overall iWS research prototype was suggested in order to validate the proposed architecture under a real-life case study.

REFERENCES

AIMMP. (2008). *A fileira da madeira em Portugal - 2008. Caracterização estatística do sector da madeira e mobiliário* [The row of wood in Portugal - 2008. Statistical characterization of the wood and furniture sector]. Retrieved January 02, 2011, from www.aimmp.pt

Borges, J. G., & Falcão, A. Miragaia, C., Marques, P. &Marques, M. (2003). A decision support system for forest resources management in Portugal. In T. M. Barrett and G. J. Arthaud (Eds.) *System Analisys in Forest Resources: Managing Forest Ecosystems* (pp.155-164). Dordrecht, Netherlands, Kluwer Academic Publishers.

CAP. (2004). *Código de Boas Práticas para a Gestão Florestal Sustentável.*[Code of Practice for Sustainable Forest Management.] Retrieved January 02, 2011, from www.pefc-portugal.cffp. pt/pdfs/Boas_Prt_final.pdf

CELPA. (2008). *Boletim estatístico da Industria Papeleira Portuguesa.* [Statistical Bulletin of Portuguese Paper Industry.] Retrieved January 02, 2011, from www.celpa.pt

D'Amours, S., Ronnqvist, E. M., & Weintraub, A. (2008). Using Operational Research for Supply Chain Planning in the Forest Products Industry. *INFOR, 46*(4), 265–281.

Falcão, A., M. Próspero M. S. & Borges, J. G. (2006). A real-time visualization tool for forest ecosystem management decision support. *Computers and Electronics in Agriculture, 53*, 3–12. doi:10.1016/j.compag.2006.03.003

Falcão, A., & Borges, J. G. (2005). Designing decision support tools for Mediterranean forest ecosystems management: a case study in Portugal. *Annals of Forest Science, 62*, 751–760. doi:10.1051/forest:2005061

Falcão, A., Borges, J. G., & Tomé, M. (1999). SagFlor – an automated forest management prescription writer. *Faculty of Forestry Research Notes 97.* (pp. 211-218.) University of. Joensuu

Hetemaki, L., & Nilsson, S. (2005). *Information Technology and the Forest Sector* (*Vol. 18*). Vienna: IUFRO World Series.

IIBA. (2009). *A Guide to the Business Analysis Body of Knowledge (Babok Guide). Version 2.0.* Toronto, Canada: IIBA.

INE. (2007). *Estatísticas agrícolas 2007.* [Agricultural statistics 2007] Retrieved January 02, 2011, from www.ine.pt

ISO/IEC 2382-1:1993. *Information technology - Vocabulary - Part 1: Fundamental terms.* Retrieved January 02, 2011, from http://www. iso.org/iso

Karlsson, J., Ronnqvist, M., & Frisk, M. (2006). RoadOpt: A decision support system for road upgrading in forestry. *Scandinavian Journal of Forest Research, 21*, 5–15. doi:10.1080/14004080500487102

Marques, A., Borges, J. G., Pina, J. P., Lucas, B., & Garcia, J. (in press). A participatory approach to design a regional forest management planning decision support toolbox. *Annals of Forest Science.*

Marques, A. F., Borges, J. G., Sousa, P., Diaz, E., Moura, P., & Ferrinho, M. (in press). A hybrid approach for integrating harvest scheduling and product assortment and assignment to transformation centers. *Forest Science.*

Marques, A. F., Borges, J. G., Sousa, P., & Pinho, A. M. (2010). An enterprise architecture approach to forest management support systems design. An application to pulpwood supply management in Portugal. *European Journal of Forest Research.* doi:doi:10.1007/s10342-011-0482-8

O'Brien, J. A., & Marakas, G. (2009). *Introduction to Information Systems.* McGraw-Hill.

Reynolds, K. M., Twery, M., Lexer, M. J., Vacik, H., Ray, D., Shao, G., & Borges, J. G. (2007). Decision support systems in natural resource management. In Burstein, F., & Holsapple, C. (Eds.), *Handbook on decision support systems.* Springer Verlag International.

Ribeiro, R. P., Borges, J. G., Pereira, C., Sousa, P., & Lé, J. (2005). Designing an Integrated Forest Planning System for the forest industry: an application in Portugal. In: *Proceedings of the 2003 Symposium on Systems Analysis in Forest Resources.* Stevenson, WA, USA.

Ronnqvist, E. M. (2003). Optimization in Forestry. *Mathematical Programming, 97*(1-2), 267–284.

Schekkerman, J. (2009). *Enterprise Architecture Good Practices Guide: How to Manage the Enterprise Architecture Practice.* IFEAD / TOGAF Open Standards.

Sousa, P., & Pereira, C. (2005). Enterprise Architecture: Business and IT Alignment. In ACM. *Symposium on Applied Computing.* (pp. 1344-1345). New York, NY: ACM Press.

Spewak, S., & Hill, S. (1992). *Enterprise Architecture Planning: Developing a Blueprint for Data, Applications and Technology.* Wiley-QED Publication.

Supply Chain Council. (2008). *SCOR: The Supply Chain Reference Model.* Retrieved January 02, 2011, from www.supply-chain.org

Weintraub, A., Epstein, R., Morales, R., Seron, J., & Traverso, P. (1996). A truck scheduling system improves efficiency in the forest industries. *Interfaces, 26*(4), 1–11. doi:10.1287/inte.26.4.1

Chapter 2
Governance, Sociotechnical Systems and Knowledge Society:
Challenges and Reflections

Antonio J. Balloni
Center for Information Technology Renato Archer, Brazil

Paulo Henrique de Souza Bermejo
Federal University of Lavras, Brazil

Jeanne Holm
NASA/Jet Propulsion Laboratory, California Institute of Technology, USA

Adriano O. Tonelli
Federal University of Lavras, Brazil

ABSTRACT

This paper's objective is presenting some challenges and reflections about governance, knowledge society, and sociotechnical systems. Based on the Action Network Theory, Theory of Constraints, and others techniques, questions are discussed in a systematic and innovative way. Points like the synergism and collaborative ecosystem research efforts, knowledgeable organizations, and organizations as living beings, the involvement of people and others' IT resources regarding the questions, as well as others are discussed, while considering questions, challenges and future perspectives. In conclusion, points are made to offer governance the normative goals of sustainability, existing socio-technical systems, and to imply connecting and synchronizing changes among the knowledge society actors.

DOI: 10.4018/978-1-4666-1764-3.ch002

PANORAMA ON KNOWLEDGE SOCIETY AND SOCIOTECHNICAL SYSTEMS

Information Technology (IT) is redefining the business basis. Customer attendance, operations, products strategies, marketing and distribution and even the society of knowledge depend, sometimes even totally on information system (IS). IT and its costs are integral part of the enterprise day-by-day. However, many enterprises still believe that the simple act of computerizing, spreading computers and printers throughout departmental units, connecting them in a network and installing applications systems, can organize the same. Technology fortechnolog's sakey, without planning, management and effective action from knowledge workers and above all, without considering the sociotechnical systems, does not bring any contribution to the enterprise (Balloni, 2006).

The Knowledge Society

Knowledge societies are those in which knowledge becomes a major creative force, i.e., a major component of any human activity. Economic, social, cultural, and all other human activities become dependent on a huge volume of knowledge and information.

Knowledge societies are not a new occurrence: fishermen have long shared the knowledge of predicting the weather to their community and this knowledge gets added to the social capital of the community. What is new in a knowledge society (Storling & Vessuri, 2007)?

A. With current technologies, knowledge societies need not be constrained by geographic proximity. One example is the Internet cost per kilobit, that has decreased in the last years (Willinger, 2002; Laudon & Laudon, 2006);

B. Current technology offers greater possibilities for sharing, archiving and retrieving knowledge. Nowadays, everything about ourselves could be stored in a personal computer (Laudon, 2004; Chang, 2010);

C. Knowledge has become the most important capital in the present age, and hence the success of any society consists in controlling and making use of it.

Sociotechnical Systems

As we know, the implementation of a new technology has been associated with problems often linked to resistance by the work force and failure to achieve the expected benefits (Akbari, 2010).

Researchers, notably at the Tavistock Institute in London, suggested that it would be a fit between the technical system and the social system that together made up an organization (Akbari, 2010; Bostrom & Heinen, 1977; Warme & Hart, 1996). As detailed below (Laudon & Laudon, 2006; Wang, Pierce, Madnick & Fisher, 2005):

*   The social system - Organization comprises the employees (at all levels) and the knowledge, skills, attitudes, values and needs they bring to the work environment, as well as the reward system and authority structures that exist in the organization.
*   The technical system - Information system comprises the devices, tools and techniques needed to transform inputs into outputs in a way that enhances the economic performance of the organization.

The basis of the sociotechnical approach is: the fit is achieved by a design process aiming toward mutual optimization of all systems. Any organizational systems will maximize performance only if the interdependency of these systems is explicitly recognized (Lucas & Baroudi, 2010).

In support of this, one must examine both the real and perceived values of a system. The arguments that information has an inherent value independent of a system rely more heavily on long-term organizational views and perceived values, rather than on realistic or normative studies. The idea that information is valuable in and of itself relates not to the business value that an information object has today, but to the possibility that it will be valuable sometime in the future.

Most of the economic analyses techniques ignore the role of the user in the system. It is very difficult to predict the behavior of human beings within the boundaries of an IS—even harder these days to define the system's boundaries themselves! Nonetheless, the system is not valuable by itself, but only by the way in which the organization can use it. Consider that a user could synergistically combine information within a web-enabled, decision-support system with information from another system in order to reach a decision. The information within either system might be considered part of the data "junkyard" by that system's developers, but when combined in unexpected ways with unanticipated uses, the "valueless" information transforms into empowering knowledge.

One example of this is from the World Bank (Denning, 2000), which had deployed a web-based discussion forum for use by managers around the world. In June 1995, a health worker (not one of the intended users) accessed the site from a remote village in Zambia (not one of the intended user sites) and was able to effectively treat cases of malaria (not one of the intended uses) based on information he got from the people on the forum. The normal users of the site had tacit information in their minds, as well as explicit information published on the site; however, that information had little value to them—they were beyond the point of needing basic malarial information to make useful treatments. However, an unexpected usage of the system allowed a high return-on-investment that was not factored into the initial design or justification for the system.

Governance

The word governance is originated from the Greek verb "kubernân" and was used for the first time in a metaphorical sense by Plato to describe the act of governing men (European Commission, 2010). In the words of Cicero (Cadbury, 2002): governance "means either the action of governing or the method of governing and it is in the latter sense it is used with reference to companies . . ." A quotation which is worth keeping in mind in this context is: 'He that governs sits quietly at the stern and scarce is seen to stir'. Thus, in its strict meaning, governance involves actions related steering, guiding and acting as a pilot in monitoring and overseeing strategic direction, socio-economic and cultural context, externalities, and constituencies of the institution (Clarke, 2007; Mueller, 1981).

The essential meaning of governance could be defined as "the process of keeping under control". In this context, implementing overarching systems of governance can facilitate the achievement of desired outcomes through reliable and transparent decisions, controlled risks and focus on business or public value (ISACA, 2009). Governance can be classified into several themes. In its broadest form, governance applies to governments and societies, and can be categorized in themes such as environmental governance, collaborative governance and so on. In its narrow form (organizational and business environment), governance themes fall into three main domains: corporate governance, information technology governance and, more recently, enterprise governance. In the following sections, we will clarify environmental and collaborative governance and, in organizational context, corporate and IT governance.

Environmental and Collaborative Governance

Environment governance has become one of the main themes in global environmental politics.

It relates to political ecology and aims to define elements to achieve sustainability.

There are several definitions and controversies related to this theme. In this work we will define environmental governance, according to Bulkeley's work (Bulkeley, 2005), as both global institutions to manage global commons, transnational networks and new forms of civil societies. In this sense, treatment of global environmental problems could be considered environmental governance through worldwide atmospheric and oceanic regimes, combinations of market-based mechanisms, and actions and policies by the United Nations and local governments (Hempel, 1996).

The focus on "governance" for treating global environmental issues like biodiversity and climate change remains on the need to create deliberative mechanisms for making authoritative political decisions and choices about the future of environment. Through this approach, environment can became part of several (if not all) decisions made in our society, including choices made in economic, political and technological spheres.

Another common governance theme nowadays is collaborative governance. This form of governance emerge as a new strategy for governing organizations, societies and government based on multiple stakeholders together in common forums with public agencies to engage consensus-oriented decision making (Ansell & Gash, 2007).

Collaborative governance has emerged as a response to challenges in traditional policy making and government institutions (Ansell & Gash, 2007; Booher, 2005). We can point to several challenges that require greater focus on collaboration within governance. Some major challenges are:

- Increasing both specialization and decentralization of knowledge in societies, becoming institutional infrastructures become more complex (Ramesh and Tiwana, 1999);

- Creating new spaces for policy making, including greater collaboration of institutions outside the traditional political realm. This spaces are created as shared problems arise, requiring involvement and collaboration acrosssociety, communities, organizations and government (Booher, 2005);

- Embracing cultural diversity and the different perspectives it bringsposes the need to consider the extent to which all affected parties were included in decision making processes seeking mutual understanding and consensus (Booher, 2005).

There are several other challenges that we could list in this work. However, the three challenges above give us a good sense of the changes occurring in the world: increased importance and decentralization of knowledge, increasing problems of common interest (e.g. environmental problems) and increasing cultural diversity in societies, organizations and business initiatives.

Corporate and Information Technology Governance

The theme of corporate governance is strongly associated with top management of firms and centers around the way companies are managed and controlled.

Formally, we can define corporate governance in many ways. Several authors and institutions have provided definitions for this term. We present the following definitions offered by Cadbury (2002): "Corporate governance is concerned with holding the balance between economic and social goals and between individual and communal goals (…) to encourage the efficient use of resources and equally to require accountability for the stewardship of those resources. The aim is to align as nearly as possible the interests of individuals, corporations and society" (p. 1)

Through this definition, we can deduce that corporate governance has a critical role in both economic and social concerns, providing measures to achieve business success, transparency, stability and equity.

Corporate governance has its root on the success of capitalism. Specifically, on the opportunity for investors to fund extensive projects and large enterprises, becoming owners of shares (portions) of these organizations (Colley, Wallace, Doyle & Logan, 2005).

The growth of investment has created public owned companies, which has became one of the dominant forms of organizations from the 20th century. In these companies, one of the main characteristics is the separation between owners (shareholders) and management. This separation, or the agency problem, is the central point of the corporate governance emergence (Colley et al., 2005; Hoogervorst, 2009). Rather than acting in shareholder's interest, management usually acts according to its own agenda or interest, at least in shareholder's perception. In this sense, a system of corporate governance must be arranged to prevent management acting according to its own interest and encouraging that actions are taken based on shareholders' interests.

After this initial impulse for corporate governance, a second crisis gave additional impetus for corporate governance, related to government regulation of business activities. Rather than the first crisis associated with the agency problem, this second crisis has its causes on severe forms of fraudulent actions, corruptions, and appropriation of financial system of enterprises for vested interests. These events have served to focus the public eye on the crucial importance of corporate governance systems to ensure transparency, accountability and equity in public-owned enterprises.

Financial scandals in U.S companies (e.g. Enron, Tyco, Worldcom, and Adelphia) led to a governance reform strongly based on rules and legislation, among them the well-known Sarbanes-Oxley Act.

In addition to such U.S. efforts related to corporate governance reform, initiatives in other regions have arisen. In this sense, several corporate governance codes stand out, such as the Austrian Code of Corporate Governance, Dutch Corporate Governance Code, Cromme Code in Europe, Malaysian Code of Corporate Governance, Thai Code of Best Practices for Directors, and Indonesian Code of Corporate Governance in Asia Pacific context.

Although these initiatives deal with a similar theme, they differ substantially in how corporate governance is treated. Developed in distinct economic and cultural contexts, these corporate governance systems and practices have evolved differently in terms of ownership, regulatory structure and focus (insiders or outsiders). Different choices were made about the most efficient company structures to adopt, and the appropriate forms of regulation.

In the information technology / information systems area, governance has played an important role. Simply, IT/IS governance refers to a system of responsibilities that aims to coordinate all organizational activities aimed at IT/IS, referring to all involved (Hamaker, 2002). Broader definitions describe IT/IS governance as the specification of decision-making structures, processes and relational mechanisms to direct and control IT (Van Grembergen & De Haes, 2009; 2007).

IT governance is identified as an essential organization capability to strategically align IT and business with value creation (Weill & Ross, 2004; ITGI, 2007). Although not conclusive, studies have provided important evidence that IT governance is positively related to organizational performance. (Weill & Ross, 2004). In a worldwide study, researchers found that IT governance is the most important basis for IT value creation, and that organizations with superior IT governance have at least 20% higher profits than organizations with lower IT governance performance. In a Brazilian context, works have also been proposed in order to understand the performance and practical issues related to IT governance. In this vein, dealing with IT governance performance, Lunardi, Becker and Maçada (2009) found that IT governance can improve organizational performance, especially in profitability terms. Bermejo and Tonelli (2011), dealing with public organizations, proposed a method for IT governance implementations and illustrate some results of empirical verification of this method.

The concept of IT governance emerges in a context where information technology has become pervasive in a dynamic, competitive and turbulent business environment. In this sense, IT decisions and operational activities cannot be ignored or avoided. It is necessary that IT functions under adequate control, ensuring strategic alignment to the business, value delivery and control of risks associated with IT initiatives.

Given the role of IT in modern organizations, researchers and practitioners have led efforts to develop and improve norms (ISO, 2008), frameworks (Van Grembergen & De Haes, 2009; 2007; Weill & Ross, 2004; ITGI, 2007) and best practice models for IT governance (OGC, 2007).

The development of such works played an important role in the spread of IT governance among researchers and practitioners. According to Brown and Grant (2005), IT governance began to become prominent in the late 1990s when Sambamurthy and Zmud (1999) published their work describing an Information Technology Governance Framework.

The IT governance framework proposed by Sambamurthy and Zmud (1999) was based on a set of IT decisions and arrangement of responsibilities for such decisions (centralized, decentralized or hybrid). Later, this framework was enhanced by Peter Weil and Jeanne Ross (Weill and Ross, 2004). Based on studies of 250 organizations, these researchers developed a framework based on five decision domains and seven archetypes for decision making structure, together with a set of mechanisms (decision making structures, alignment processes and communication approaches) to implement IT governance. Additionally, they

developed an instrument for IT governance performance evaluation.

In the same vein, Van Grembergen and De Haes (2009; 2007) proposed an IT governance framework based on three main components: structures (for decision making), processes and relational mechanisms.

Other frameworks, like Cobit, RiskIT and ValIT (ITGI, 2007b), best practices models (ITIL) (OGC, 2007), management system (balanced scorecard) (Kaplan & Norton, 1997) and norms (ISO/IEC38500) (ISO, 2008) are available as sources for IT governance implementation in organizations. Except Cobit, defined as a complete framework for IT governance (ITGI, 2007), and ISO/IEC38500, designed specially to address issues of IT governance, the other tools have specific purposes: ITIL for IT service management, ValIT for IT investments, RiskIT for risk management and balanced scorecard for IT performance measurement.

In the arena of systems and services provided by the government, this governance is undergoing significant change. In 1993, the U.S. Government enacted the Government Performance and Results Act (GPRA) to ensure that the work funded by the Government made measurable progress toward practical outcomes. Under GPRA, applied research is subject to periodic reviews, outside peer reviews, relevance reviews (which includes users of the systems), and benchmarking. Even basic research is required to be measured in relation to quality, relevance, and leadership. Just recently, in December 2010, the U.S. Federal Chief Information Officer, Vivek Kundra, enacted a 25-point IT reform that speaks to the heart of governance, management (practices and training), and capabilities for information technology (Kundra, 2010). The focus is to strengthen IT governance "improve line-of-sight between project teams and senior executives, increase the precision of ongoing measurement of IT program health, and boost the quality and timing of interventions to keep projects on track."

Efforts such as these provide governments, corporations, and organizations the frameworks and oversight functions needed to help identify and mitigate risks early in programs, and allow corporations to align the business with value creation.

Governance and Microeconomic Stability: The Challenges

According to Cama ZJ (Economist Intelligence Unit – 2010), along with South Africa and India, Brazil has been a leading light in the G20 (group of 20 leading economies):

During the global economic crisis, the G20 superseded the G8 as the main platform for global governance, according large developing nations such as Brazil a greater voice at a time when the setting of global rules is dominating headlines. The consolidation of macroeconomic stability in the past decade has meant that the country's large internal market potential is finally being realized. Judged by its history, Brazil has done

well; judged by today's competition, however, the country still has much ground to make up. Although GDP growth this year is expected to approach Asian rates, such rates are far from sustainable given infrastructure deficiencies. Since GDP per head is significantly higher than in China – and especially India – comparisons to Asian rates of growth are not entirely appropriate; even so, Brazil's potential sustainable growth is much lower than it should be because of a failure to address structural reform. Swathes of its workforce are poorly educated; innovation is stunted; infrastructure unfit for purpose; and its companies' brands, having focused on home advantage are, with notable exceptions, little known abroad. In spite of this, Figure 1 presents what have been considered to be the main image of Brazil in the world.

Yet, Figure 2 shows several operational obstacles as the greatest challenges for business operations in Brazil. Weak governance has been pointed as the second greatest challenge.

Figure 1. The image of Brazil in the world in according to The Economist Intelligence Unit's survey. The survey has pointed to the "B" in BRICs (the oddball category of fast growing emerging giants comprising Brazil, Russia, India and China) rather than to the country's long-standing structural deficiencies. With Economist Intelligence Unit permission. Cama, ZJ (Economist Intelligence Unit – 2010).

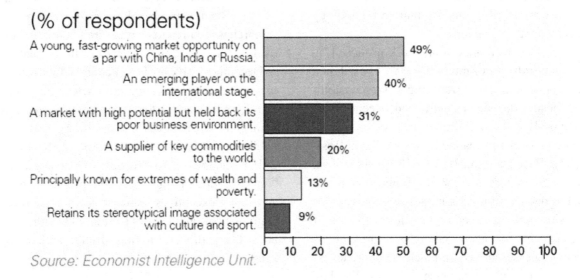

Figure 2. Weak corporate governance has been pointed as the main second principal operational obstacles against business operations in Brazil. With Economist Intelligence Unit permission. Cama, ZJ (Economist Intelligence Unit – 2010).

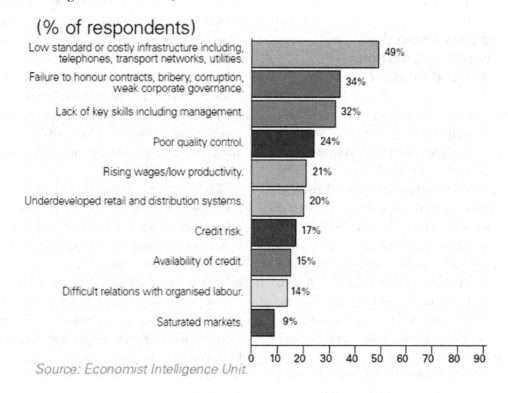

Challenges and Reflections

If we go back a little in history we shall remember that competitive advantage was marked by the ownership of capital and assets such as natural resources, estates, etc., but today we are experiencing a fourth great revolution, that of knowledge. The first revolution, the industrial age (initiated in 1750 until the mid 1960s) was marked by the evolution of the processes. A second moment took place in the 70s, marked by the expansion of the Japanese industry. The world was overtaken by a revolution in processes. Concepts such as Just in Time, Lean, Kam-bam, Six Sigma arose, defining quality as being "the differential". Today quality is just a basic requirement! In the 80s and 90s the third moment, marked by a technological revolution in the West, led by the Americans, commenced: the digital revolution via machines, software and

methodologies capable of controlling in detail the management of an organization, increasing their gains in productivity (Guevara, 2000).

Then from the mid 90s on, the investment for access to new technologies evolved into a non-impeditive factor in face of the vertiginous decrease on their prices, enabling organizations to compete in same levels (Laudon & Laudon, 2006; Gilheany, 2004).

In the present age, a great movement towards appreciation of the intellectual asset can be observed inside the organizations, focusing "people" as a great competitive differential. Here is the "Age of Knowledge" (Guevara, 2000).

At the present process of acceleration at the transition of Ages, we rapidly moved from the Age of Information to the Age of Knowledge and observed the emergence of an increasingly globalized and virtual culture, urged on by the development of computers and of communication in a very particular manner, which, consequently, is devastating for the social web and nature.

One asks How About the Social-Technical Question Involving IT and People?

A possible answer to such question could be provided by what is known as Action Network Theory: the emerging issue is linked to the complexity of the real, which shall not be able to be reduced since the great relations network (peer to peer) became evident through the technological development of ICT(s) (Aidemark, 2007; 2010). There is also the vision where the world is seem as an intricate fabric made up of connections, of several types, alternate, combined and juxtaposed, determinant of the structure of the whole (Capra, 1996). Other possible answers to the question could be provided by "knowing the organizations". Organizations are composed of complex organisms (people) who need to be understood through the knowledge of the nature of their relations and within a determined context. It is the treatment of the organization as a living being, through a systemic view (think globally but acting locally), that will enable the emergence of phenomena that shall enable the whole to be more than the sum of the parts of such a being or organism.

Treatment of the organization as a living being: Synergism!

On the other hand, the organizations can be known as relation networks, but not everything can be reduced and "systematized". Thus, the focus on people is not enough, it is necessary to connect and contextualize them in the organization's cause. So, by connecting and contextualizing the people in the organization's cause we hope to get the differential, that is, the full knowledge of the dynamics of the system as a whole!

How to Theorize Such Context?

An answer, perhaps, is in the Theory of Constraints (TOC), which possesses as one of its pillars the concept of Inherent Simplicity: "a deep understanding that there is always a simple explanation to any seemingly intractable problem. This leads one to use the intuition to find the core of the problem and develop a solution which both solves the immediate problem and doesn't create additional problems along the way". (Goldratt, 2000; Mabin, 1999)

The utilization of the Theory of Constraints (TOC), which considers the application of the exact science principles to human organizations, possesses as one of its pillars the concept of Inherent

Simplicity and, the difficulty, initially, is to believe in such a statement. Therefore, it is necessary to study the cause-and-effect relations from the system in question in order to discover such Inherent Simplicity. On the present causality map, the technological, psychological, environmental and political elements must be present, demonstrating all inevitable logical links between causes and effects (visible or not). Such logical maps, called "trees" in the TOC (from present reality, from future reality, etc.), aid us in obtaining an essential systemic view. The creator of the TOC, physicist Eliyahu Goldratt, applied the exact science principles to human organizations and demonstrated, amongst other things, that technology is necessary, but not sufficient. The personal factors, especially those linked to individual performance mensuration, generally exert a very strong influence in any context, which frequently frustrate any initiative for change (McMullen Jr., 1998).

But in the end, a simple answer to the previous question (How about the social-technical question involving IT and people?) could be the following: The social-technical question involves the people (obvious) and everything surrounding them, including the IT. It is a question of utility, of functionability, of usability for the consumer (if we are to discuss market) and for the user (if we are to discuss society).

How to Demonstrate This?

One of the aspects that is becoming important in everyone's everyday life has to do with the values changes in our society. As manual labor was the basis for the Agricultural Age, and capital and energy were basic at the Industrial Age, the computer networks and human beings are essential in the Age of Knowledge.

Therefore, how to deal with the social-technical questions in such an Age? A possible answer relates to the Facebook/Orkut phenomenon, with its 500+ million profiles and Twitter with its achievement of over 75 million active user accounts at the end 2009; id est. a good illustration for the social-technical questions from the new age. Its growth 'provoked' other social networks with specific purposes, but every network's dream is to become either Facebook, Orkut or Twitter. Today, organizations participate in such networks, not only using 'fakes' or aliases, but showing also under their true name in order to get closer to their consumers, to provide service, offer products and receive suggestions. Sales teams are being managed with the aid of Moodle, keeping the team informed of processes and procedures uniformly, distance training, study groups and collaborative works in real time. Chiefs of major organizations communicate with their personnel via blog (Wordpress, Blogger and alike) or micro-blog like Twitter. A small detail to be observed, not of little importance, is that teens of up to 18 years of age deal with e-mail the same way the rest of the post-teen humanity faces ID and Individual Taxpayers Registry ID: as ills necessary so as to take the compulsory bureaucratic measures.

Are Such Statements Facts, How Can We Prove This? Can We?

One possible answer is Yes: by 2008, blogging, photo- and video-sharing, social networking and on-line gaming had been embraced by half the Internet users worldwide. Some regional patterns seem to emerge: Asian countries are leading the adoption of these, followed by the US and Europe (Mutka et al., 2009).

We are living a unique moment in history, discovering that, while we think and live outside the holistic paradigm and are in the middle of a dehumanized digital economy, at the same time we are moving towards the development of a sense of unity and perception of the whole and, hopefully, towards a sustainable and solid economy.

In the Present Economic Crisis, What is the "Last Straw" in Order for Us to Finally Develop Such Sense of Unity and Perception of the Whole?

In order for such to take place, it is indispensable to learn new means of fomenting trust and the social and environmental responsibility, which means we need to organize our individual, social and political efforts in this new knowledge information society so as to develop a new conscience and new ethics. Figure 3 shows a representative model for such concern, identifying the 5 moral dimensions of a society across individual, social, and political levels of action (Laudon & Laudon, 2007; 2004).

Does the Solution for this Knowledge Information Society Go, Necessarily, Through the Social-Technical IT Questions?

One possible answer is: Yes! Again, according to what was previously showed about the concept of Inherent Simplicity (TOC), an answer could be: a deep understanding that there is always a simple explanation to any seemingly intractable problem, id est. this leads one to use intuition to find the core of the problem and develop a solution that both solves the immediate problem and doesn't create additional problems along the way. Following, it is necessary to study the cause-and-effect

Figure 3. The Relationship between Ethical, Social, and Political issues in an Information Society. This figure has been adapted from the original in Laudon & Laudon, (2007; 2004) and reproduced with PEARSON Education do Brazil permission.

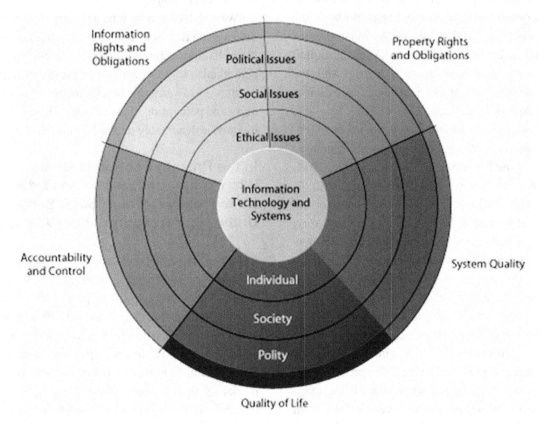

relations from the system in question in order to discover such Inherent Simplicity..."

The access to the Internet and television by all citizens is becoming essential for the participation in a real-time democratic life (Mutka et al., 2009).

Is it the Onset of a Negative Impact from the ITs Social-Technical Questions?

Maybe not! It could be the opposite: deals with the positive impact from the social-technical questions, now defined by the Ultimate Consumer. Not withdrawing the importance of TV and other means of mass communication, the consumer market on the Internet estimates the 'value' of products through clicks and, nowadays (and in

the future), this is what matters. The supplier who relates with such public square is able to estimate the impact of its product analyzing the number of clicks. Real mensuration, see Figure 4.

This is possible through the advance of Internet technologies. In the beginning of the popularization of the Internet, with Web 1.0, people accessed statics sites. Web 1.0 was the not-for-profit information age. After this, Web 2.0 can be seen as a result of technological refinements, such as broadband, improved browsers, and the rise of Flash application platforms. This has generally been regarded as the social Web. Web 3.0 refers to a third generation of Internet-based services (Mutka et al., 2009; Spivack, 2009).

This third generation of the Web has taken root and started to grow in a variety of environ-

Figure 4. As mentioned before, Web 3.0 refers to a third generation of Internet-based services. Web 4.0 must predict the management and the intelligent use of all available knowledge in the net with media convergence and more intuitive search mechanisms. Based on previous demands from Internet users as well in about the study of their behavior in the web, sites would start to deduce their next intentions... (Mutka et al., 2009; Spivack, 2009). What will this hold in the future? With Nova Spivack permission.

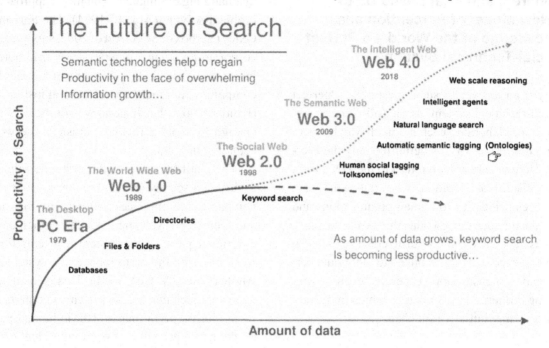

ments. Starting in the academic community, the semantic web efforts were focused on the creation of standards for open linked data that would allow machines to describe, access, and integrate data from multiple locations and services. They have matured into a wide variety of services from corporations and government (such as the U.S. governments' Data.gov, www.data.gov, effort). These use a combination of machine-readable services and ontologies that allow the categorization and organization of data without additional human insight, but are rendered in such a way as to allow humans to interact with, search, manipulate, and visualize the data for new findings, understandings, and knowledge.

THE FUTURE

Therefore, for countries in development, such as Brazil, to transform their condition, it is necessary, NOW, to advance their R&D and local Collaborative Ecosystem research efforts.

This R&D and local collaborative ecosystem (ecosystem refers to the combined components of an environment) research efforts must consider the principle of the Systemic View (thinking globally but acting locally), and it may be accomplished by the integration among one of these interdependent subjects: ecology, biology, communication, organizations, economy, education, communities, technology, culture and the human being (human, social, psychological, intellectual and mental ecology: social-technical systems).

How to Elaborate/Build a New Way of Development, Which Comprises the Social, Economical, Cultural and Environmental Spheres, and That Leads Us to a New Model of Perception and Knowledge of the World – a Perfect Social-Technical System?

Maybe an answer to such questioning "perfect social-technical system" is the following: many ways are elaborated each moment. Maybe there is no definitive way, as definitive only the Eternal. Here we are able to return to the TOC, from physicist Eliyahu Goldratt, who applied the exact sciences principles to human organizations and demonstrated, amongst other things, that technology is necessary, but not sufficient. The personal factors, especially those linked to individual performance mensuration, generally exert a very strong influence in any context, which frequently frustrate any initiative for change.

If Such New Systems had Already Been Developed, and Accepted, Would the Present Financial Crisis Have Occurred?

The run for money cannot be sustained for a long period and this was already common knowledge, as shown by the famous "pyramid schemes", where with the simple 'investment' of US $1,0 a citizen would receive several times more what had been invested without having to do anything—this is a crime. However, if I invest US $1,0 million, be it in stocks or a new enterprise, I expect, without having to actively work, to gain from my investment.

The present crisis, which has been announcing itself for a few years, is a symptom of a new Social-technical System (or symptom of a gigantic Information System), which is not yet well defined for a great parcel of the population, connected to the paradigms of the 19th century economy.

Today's crisis is the result of a catastrophic failure, primarily in the financial system, but also of our economic and political systems. It is the result of the reductionist, atomistic thinking that had long dominated humanity's approach to problem-solving (Ackoff, 1974). The Sarbanes-Oxley (Sarbox or SOX) Act of 2002, supported by corporate governance practices, was an important initiative of the U.S. Government to regulate companies after the drop of financial institutions (Lander, 2003), but it alone wasn't the effective enough to avoid a financial crash in the world economy in 2008.

The challenge now is the systemic thinking to design a society (regulator) that goes beyond companies' compliances and actually measures and focuses on systemic risks, rather than on the individual parts of the system. Systems thinking focuses on the performance of a system as a whole (Emery & Trist, 1981). This is in contrast to an approach that breaks systems into parts and focuses on the performance of the individual parts, on the assumption that if each individual part is improved then the sum of the parts will also be better. This assumption often proves wrong in practice: the only profession that he believed had truly embraced systems thinking is architecture, where the design process starts by asking what sort of building is desired, and then works backwards to focus on what individual parts are required. An architect never starts by saying, "Here are the parts, what can I build from them?

At this point governance could exercise its essential mean to extend its role to the whole society.

Contributing to Define a New Systematic Way of Managing Business, Society and Why Not the Individuals?

According to Balloni (Balloni/IJMIT/2010) the present economic model cohabits with the principle of shortage, of centralized production, of hierarchical relations, of private property. The model of the future has its sustentation in the non scarce goods, in collaborative production, in network relationships, in common or collective property and in ascent of the intangible goods!

Is Globalization at Risk with the 2008 Financial Crisis?, An Answer is Yes, the Need for a Gigantic Information System as Stated Before. Why?

The crisis has increased calls for a new "Bretton" to better regulate the global economy. World leaders, however, will be challenged to renovate the IMF (International Monetary Fund, special UN agency that was founded in 1944 to stabilize exchange rates and to facilitate international commerce) and devise a globally transparent and effective set of rules that apply to differing capitalisms and levels of financial institutional development. Failure to construct a new all-embracing architecture could lead countries to seek security through competitive monetary policies and new investment barriers, increasing the potential for market segmentation. Again, the sociotechnical concern of IT.

About Brazil (Balloni/IJMIT/2010), inserted in the world-wide context, the wide scale changes occurring in the environment business has compelled the enterprises to radically modify their organizational structures and productive processes: sociotechnical concerns. The main factors of these changes are: the products globalization, the wide scale of electronic processes use, the nature of the job (*shifting from industry to the services sector*) and the emergent markets as China, India and Brazil. Therefore, for the Brazilian enterprise, now and in the future, gets and keeps position in the world-wide market, it is vital to look forward the content proposed here. But, a question remain to be answered: "will management in IT, and the emergency of global partnerships allow Brazilian enterprises to compete more effectively in the global marketplace, or will they be undermined by greater global competition in their "home territory"? Indeed, is there such a thing as "home territory"?" Here it is important to remember what

Winston Churchill said (Balloni/IJMIT/2010): "We shape our buildings; thereafter they shape us." Therefore, *the collaborative work space and sociotechnical environment of tomorrow are being shaped today!*

Who is Willing to Take Responsibility for the Space Shaped?

How can we define many of the ethical and social dimensions that arise with connectivity and information privacy (sociotechnical concern), with an unfair shared leadership, information partnership and a collaborative relationship in this age of knowledge?

Finally, it is important to draw attention to new ways of organizations arising in the past few years and which provoked a reorganization of the social sectors. An important class of such new organizations is the so called Learning Community, promoting education and the social asset with the development of individual qualities. Such people networks are dynamized by the electronic networks, leading possibly to new ways of acquaintance and relationship, aiming essentially at the transformation of knowledge, circumstances, institutions, concepts, the Arts, the Sciences and values from the human being. However, the great challenge of the 21st century shall be to change the system of values behind the global economy, so as to make it compatible to the demands of human dignity and to the ecological sustainability in a system where the IT of information changes parameters every 24 months, lowering the income inequality.

Therefore, we must consider all technological possibilities available, not inventing the wheel, but, yes, improving bearing.

Innovation and the Future

While Brazilian industry can boast several centres of excellence—notably energy, aerospace, IT and agribusiness — education deficiencies hold back innovation in the wider economy. Innovation starts when people are able to speak their mind. On the other side, many investors regard their Brazilian staff to be "flexible and adaptable", quite probably because they have had to deal with a succession of economic crises that taught them how to succeed in the midst of instability: there is a tolerance for ambiguity that is much stronger in Brazil than in other countries. However, Brazilian managers are less able when it comes to creating the new and the different. In spite of recognizing that innovation is important, people do not necessarily behave that way.

An Economist Intelligence Unit innovation model that measures countries according to both their readiness and success in innovation ranks Brazil 52nd out of 82 countries, and notes that the country is likely to slip further down the rankings in coming years. More interestingly, the model shows that its ranking of the factors

that contribute to innovation (for example, the number of science graduates, education levels, the business environment, R&D spending, broadband penetration, etc.), although in itself low, is still higher than the measure for innovation successes (measured by the number of patents filed globally). This suggests that not only is Brazil insufficiently innovative compared with its peers, but that it is also inefficient with its resources, by failing to translate investments into practical innovation. Figure 5 presents several technological factors impacting our ability to innovate in Brazil.

PERSPECTIVES

Our world is fundamentally a sociotechnical world, id est. a world deeply characterized by human and technological interactions: human

Figure 5. The technological factors impacting our ability to innovate in Brazil Whether this is the result of a lack of inventiveness or systemic failures in the business environment is hard to gauge, but Brazil's weedy performance comes through in the views and experiences of companies surveyed. With Economist Intelligence Unit permission. Cama, ZJ (Economist Intelligence Unit – 2010).

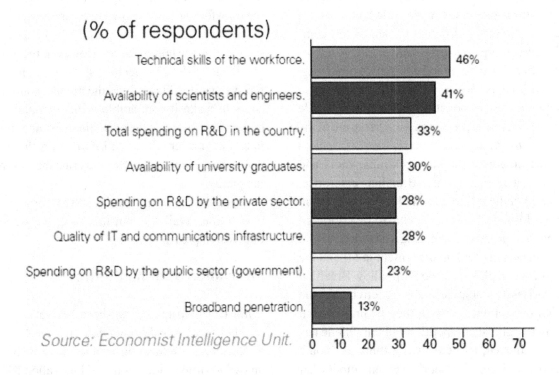

organizations are living systems and should be analyzed accordingly. Their interactions drastically affect people's relationships in space and time (Emery & Trist, 1981). Therefore, if we consider that the core knowledge is embodied in people's heads (tacit knowledge) (Balloni, 2004) and their ability to generate new knowledge, we cannot speak about a knowledge society without taking into account these interactions. Since the Internet brings together the computer, media, and the distributed intelligence of the family and the community, constituting a new basis for the effectiveness of socio-technical organizations, then in this way beyond the economic, organizational, cultural, and technological dimensions, the specific sociotechnical context characterizes every knowledge society initiatives: synergism and ubiquitously driven by the Internet!

The efforts to try and understand, measure, and share our work in tacit knowledge is extremely difficult, but clearly important in today's economy. Workers migrate easily from company to company and more and more of a company's "capital" is intellectual. However, not all KM efforts are so difficult to measure, and the ability for corporate customers and government citizens to use services (with a focus on explicit knowledge) to enhance their own knowledge and make actionable decisions can be measured in ways that show an improvement to the organization and it's partners. The organizations that will succeed tomorrow will be those that can leverage, measure, and manage their corporate intellectual capital.

However, management opposition persists because sociotechnical systems by nature enable collaborative decision-making and shared leadership. Management has been reluctant to give up the power and authority they have worked so hard to establish. Indeed, sociotechnical system challenges the traditional management taboos of sharing information and knowledge with subordinates on a need to know basis only (Balloni, 2004). The central cornerstone of a technocratic

bureaucracy is that decision-making is top-down and implementation is bottom up. The governance imposing normative goals of sustainability upon existing socio-technical systems implies connecting and synchronizing changes among these actors, institutions and artifacts at many different points in the system. Hereby, governance must consequently fulfill diagnostic, prognostic, prescriptive and coordination functions. The challenge is to bring appropriately resourced actors into the governance arrangements needed to steer socio-technical change (Smith & Stirling, 2006).

Finally, Brazil today seems better placed than ever to dispose of its frustrating, if clichéd, moniker "the country of the future". A decade of macroeconomic prudence has given the economy a sturdy platform for investment, growth and foreign expansion, and businesses have factored this change into their long-term strategies. A virtuous circle is turning. Sound policies and a growing domestic market have attracted foreign money, know-how, new skills and technologies, and unleashed the considerable pent-up energy of local business both at home and abroad. This, in turn, will help to fund investment into education and infrastructure, which will attract more investment and sustainable growth. That, at least, is the theory, and on Brazil's current trajectory there is no reason to think it cannot be achieved. It will take many years, but if recent successes are any guide, the prize will be worth the effort and, the innovation era for Brazil is coming.

This new scope is changing all our mentality about and, this chapter, in the section "Challenges and Reflections", tried to awake such feelings towards this new era of knowledge but, news questions remain to be answered: *who or what will be driving innovations in this new era? Which is the impact of the sociotechnical system in such innovations process? About SOX, it seems that it has not been to avoid a financial crash in the world economy in 2008- Why?*

ACKNOWLEDGMENT

This work is based on a previous publication at the CENTERIS Congress (Balloni and Bermejo, 2010), and has been chosen by the its committee to be reviewed and extended for publication as a book chapter. Sponsored by FAPESP.

REFERENCES

Ackoff, R. L. (1974). *Redesigning the Future: A Systems Approach to Societal Problems*. New York: Wiley.

Aidemark, J. (2007), *IS planning and sociotechnical theory perspectives - Växjö University*. *Retrieved* from: http://www.iseing.org/emcis/EM-CIS2007/emcis07cd/EMCIS07-PDFs/571.pdf

Akbari, H., & Land, F. (2010) *Socio-technical theory,* Retrieved from http://www.fsc.yorku.ca/york/istheory/wiki/index.php/Socio-technical_theory.

Ansell, C., & Gash, A. (2007). Collaborative Governance in Theory and Practice. *Journal of Public Administration and Theory Advance Access*, *18*(4), 543–571.

Balloni, A. J. (2004) *Why GESITI?: Why Management of System and Information Technology? Book Series IFIP International Federation for Information Processing*, Boston, Book Virtual Enterprises and Collaborative Networks: Springer

Balloni, A. J., (2006) *Por que GESITI?: Por que Gestão em Sistemas e Tecnologia da Informação?* Editora. Komedi, Livro I, 06-25. Retrieved April 21, 2012, from http://repositorio.cti.gov.br/repositorio/bitstream/10691/152/2/AJBLivro%20POR%20QUE%20GESITI.pdf

Balloni, A. J. (2010) Challenges and Reflections on Knowledge Society & Sociotechnical Systems. JMIT/2010 – International Journal of Managing Information Technology – Book /V.2, Nr.1, 06-26 Digital/IJMI: http://airccse.org/journal/ijmit/papers/0210ijmit3.pdf

Balloni, A. J., & Bermejo, P. H. S. (2010) Governance, Sociotechnical Systems and Knowledge Society: Challenges and Reflections. ENTERprise Information Systems -*Springer- International Conference, CENTERIS 2010, Part I,*(pp. 42-51.) Springer.

Bermejo, P. H. S., & Tonelli, A. O., (2011) Planning and Implementing IT Governance in Brazilian Public Organizations. *44th Hawaii International Conference on System Sciences*

Booher, D. E. (2005). Collaborative Governance Practices and Democracy. *National Civic Review*, *93*(4), 32–46. doi:10.1002/ncr.69

Bostrom, R., P, & Heinen, J. S. (1977). MIS Problems and Failures: A Socio-Technical Perspective, Part II: The Application of Socio-Technical Theory. *Management Information Systems Quarterly*, *1*, 345–349. doi:10.2307/249019

Brown, A. E., & Grant, G. G. (2005). Framing the frameworks: A review of IT Governance research. *Communications of the Association for Information Systems*, *15*, 696–712.

Bulkeley, H. (2005). Reconfiguring environmental governance: towards a politics of scales and networks. *Political Geography*, *24*(8), 875–902. doi:10.1016/j.polgeo.2005.07.002

Cadbury, A. (2002). *Corporate Governance and Chairmanship*. Oxford: Oxford University Press. doi:10.1093/acprof:oso/9780199252008.001.0001

Cama, Z. J. (2011)- *Brazil unbound - How investors see Brazil and Brazil sees the world. An HSBC report produced in co-operation with the Economist Intelligence Unit.* Retrieved from: http://www.hsbcculturalexchange.com/uploaded_files/HSBC_EIU_%20report_Brazil_Unbound.pdf or, http://www.globalautoindustry.com/images/HSBC_EIU_%20report_Brazil_Unbound.pdf or, http://www.100thoughts.hsbc.co.uk/downloads/Festival_Brazil_Report.pdf or, Brazil unbound: How investors see Brazil and Brazil sees the world download the report and watch the webcast or http://viewswire.eiu.com/report_dl.asp?mode=fi&fi=1857301570.PDF -Last access 01/08/2011.

Capra, F. (1996). *The web of life. A new scientific understanding of living systems.* New York: Anchor Books.

Chang, E. (2010) *Magnetic Data Storage and Nanoparticles.* Retrieved from http://www.eng.uc.edu/~gbeaucag/Classes/Nanopowders/Applications/ErnieChang_NaMagneticMemory.pdf. Last access 01/08/2011.

Clarke, T. (2007). *International Corporate Governance: A comparative approach.* New York: Routledge.

Colley, J., Wallace, S., Doyle, J., & Logan, G. (2005). *What is Corporate Governance?* New York: McGraw-Hill.

Denning, S. (1999), Enlisting Management Support for Knowledge Management, *Knowledge Management Symposium: Applications for Government and Non-Profit Organizations, World Bank Headquarters, Washington DC, October 2, 2000. Committee on Science, Engineering, and Public Policy, Evaluating Federal Research Programs,* Washington DC: National Academy of Sciences, National Academy Press

Emery, F. E., & Trist, E. (1981). Introduction to Volume 1, First Edition. Systems Thinking (Volume 1), selected readings. F. E. Emery. Harmondsworth, Penguin.

European Commission. (2010)*Étymologie du terme "gouvernance"[* The origin of the term "governance"], Retrieved 08/01/2011 from: http://ec.europa.eu/governance/docs/doc5_fr.pdf.

Gilheany, S. (2004)*Moore's Law and Knowledge Management,* Retrieved 01/08/2011 from: http://www.ee.ic.ac.uk/pcheung/teaching/ee4_asic/notes/Lec%201%20Moore%20Law%20and%20Knowledge%20Management.pdf.

Goldratt, A. Y. (2009) *The Theory of Constraints and its Thinking Processes,* http://www.goldratt.com/toctpwhitepaper.pdf. Last access 01/08/2011

Goldratt, M. V. (1999) *"Theory of Constraints" Thinking Processes: A Systems*

Guevara, A., & Catgarina Dib, V. (2000) *The Age of Knowledge and the growing relevance of human and social capital,* Retrieved 01/08/2011 from: http://in3.dem.ist.utl.pt/downloads/cur2000/papers/S26P05.pdf

Hamaker, S. (2003). Spotlight on Governance. *Information Systems Control Journal., 1,* 15.

Hempel, L. C. (1996). *Environmental Governance: The Global Challenge.* Washington, DC: Island.

Hoogervorst, J. A. P. (2009). *Enterprise Governance and Enterprise Engineering. Diemen.* Springer. doi:10.1007/978-3-540-92671-9

http://www.maoz.com/~dmm/complexity_and_the_internet/robustness_and_the_internet_design_and_evolution.pdf. Last access: 01/08/2011.

ISACA. (2009) Information Systems Audit and Control Association. In Summary: Taking Governance Forward Mapping Initiative. *ISACA Journal, 1:* 1-10

ISO, International Organization for Standardization. (2008). *ISO/IEC 38500 Corporate Governance for Information Technology.* Switzerland.

ITGI. Information Technology Governance Institute. (2007) *COBIT 4.1: Control objectives, Management guidelines, Maturity models.* Rolling Meadows: ITGI.

Kaplan, R. S., & Norton, D. P. (1997). *A Estratégia em Ação: Balanced Scorecard* [The Strategy in Action: Balanced Scorecard]. Rio de Janeiro, Brazil: Elsevier.

Kundra, V. (2010). *25 Point Implementation Plan to Reform Federal Information Technology Management.* White House Document.

Lander, G. (2003). *What Is Sarbanes-Oxley?* Blacklick, OH, USA: McGraw-Hill Trade.

Laudon, C. K., & Laudon, J. P. (2004). *MIS (Activebook).* Prentice Pearson.

Laudon, K. C., & Laudon, J. P. (2004) *Sistemas de informação gerenciais. (5th.ed.)* [Management information systems.] São Paulo: Pearson Prentice Hall.

Laudon, K. C., & Laudon, J. P. (2006). *Management Information Systems: Managing the Digital-Firm.* New Jersey: Prentice Hall.

Laudon, K. C., & Laudon, J. P. (2007) *Sistemas de informação gerenciais. (7th.ed).* [Management information systems.] São Paulo: Pearson Prentice Hall.

Leoni, W. Leoni, &Hart, D. (1996), *The Impact of Organizational Politics on Information Systems Project Failure - A Case Study*, Retrieved: 01/08/2011. from http://www.computer.org/plugins/dl/pdf/proceedings/hicss/1996/ 7333/00/73330191.pdf?template=1&loginState=1&userData=anonymous-IP%253A%253A201.82.72.62

Lucas, H. C. Jr, & Baroudi, J. (1994). The role of information technology in organization design. *Journal of Management Information Systems, 10*(4), 9–23.

Lunardi, G. L., Becker, J. L., & Maçada, A. C. G. (2009) The financial impact of IT governance mechanisms' adoption: an empirical analysis with Brazilian firms. *42nd Hawaii International Conference on System Sciences,* (pp. 1-10).

Mabin, V. J., & Balderstone, S. J. (2000). *The world of the theory of constraints: a review of the international literature.* The St. Lucie Press.

McMullen, T. B. Jr. (1998). *Introduction to the theory of constraints (TOC) management system.* The St. Lucie Press.

Methodology linking Soft with Hard, Retrieved from: http://www.systemdynamics.org/conferences/1999/PAPERS/PARA104.pdf. Last access: 01/08/2011.

Mueller, R. K. (1981). Changes in the wind of corporate governance. *The Journal of Business Strategy, 1*(4), 8–14. doi:10.1108/eb038907

Mutka, K. A., Broster, D., Cachia, R., Centeno, C., Feijóo, C., & Haché, A. (2009). *The Impact of Social Computing on the EU Information Society and Economy - European Commission.* Joint Research Centre Institute for Prospective Technological Studies.

OGC, Office of Government Commerce. (2007). *The Official Introduction to the ITIL Service Lifecycle.* London: The Stationery Office.

Ramesh, B., & Tiwana, A. (1999). Supporting Collaborative Process Knowledge Management in New Product Development Teams. *Decision Support Systems, 27,* 213–235. doi:10.1016/S0167-9236(99)00045-7

Sambamurthy, V., & Zmud, R. W. (1999). Arrangements for Information Technology governance: A Theory of Multiple Contingencies. *Management Information Systems Quarterly, 23*(2), 261–291. doi:10.2307/249754

Smith, A., & Stirling, A. (2006). *Moving Inside or Outside? Positioning the Governance of Sociotechnical Systems. Science and Technology Policy Research. Falmer*. UK: University of Sussex.

Sorlin, S., & Hebe, V. (2007). *Knowledge Society vs. Knowledge Economy: Knowledge, Power, and Politic*. New York, NY: Palgrave Macmillan. doi:10.1057/9780230603516

Spivack, N. (2009*)- Web Evolution Nova Spivack Twine,* Retrieved from: http://www.novaspivack. com/uncategorized/the-evolution-of-the-web-past-present-future or http://www.novaspivack. com/technology/powerpoint-deck-making-sense-of-the-semantic-web-and-twine or http://novaspivack.typepad.com/nova_spivacks_weblog/files/nova_spivack_semantic_web_talk.ppt

Van Grembergen, W., & De Haes, S. (2007). *Implementing Information Technology Governance: Models, Practices, and Cases*. Hershey, PA: IGI Publishing. doi:10.4018/978-1-59904-924-3

Van Grembergen, W., & De Haes, S. (2009). *Enterprise Govrernance of Information Technology: Achieving Strategic Alignment and Value*. New York: Springer.

Wang, R. Y., Pierce E. M., Stuart, E. M., & Fisher C. W. (2005). *Advances in Management Information Systems*.

Weill, P., & Ross, J. W. (2004). *Governança de tecnologia da informação: Como as empresas com melhor desempenho administram os direitos decisórios de TI na busca por resultados superiores. {Governance of information technology: As the best performers manage IT decision-making rights in the quest for superior results]*. São Paulo: M. Books do Brasil.

What is Actor-Network Theory? (2010), Retrieved 08/01/2011 from: http://carbon.ucdenver. edu/~mryder/itc_data/ant_dff.html

Willinger, W. &,Doyle J., (2002) *Robustness and the Internet: Design and evolution*. Retrieved from

Chapter 3
In Search of a Star Trek Affective State

Jonatan Jelen
Parsons The New School for Design, USA

Billy Brocato
Sam Houston State University, USA

Thomas Schmidt
University of Phoenix, USA

Stuart Gold
Walden University, USA

ABSTRACT

The authors' meta-analysis showed that leadership studies have ignored pioneering research into the heuristic tools people employ that affect decision-making and, subsequently, judgments regarding effective group performance in organizational settings. The chapter suggests a postmodern model superseding the modernist perspectives whose theoretical grounding remain mired in Frederick Taylor's (1911) scientific management theories. The authors' meta-analysis identified salient characteristics found in the selected leadership research, allowing for a disambiguation of the transformational and charismatic leadership operational traits. The meta-analysis comprised selected research studies from 1999 to 2008, and revealed distinctive intrapersonal (5 organizational referents) and interpersonal (5 social identity/ normative referents) icons that inform emergent leader and follower behaviors. The chapter proposes a postmodern evaluation matrix to reveal the structural biases and modernist conceptual ambiguities tied to the leader-worker dyadic in varying organizational contexts. The findings suggest that leadership researchers should consider complex behavioral decision-making processes that result in emergent group performances instead of focusing on a leader's ephemeral behavioral traits. A postmodern approach also helps leadership researchers identify a group's performance on a continuum that would demonstrate their willingness to act in a way that tests individual limits, stretches group boundaries, and exceeds company goals, what the authors term a Star Trek Affective State.

DOI: 10.4018/978-1-4666-1764-3.ch003

INTRODUCTION

Common leadership symbols embodied within films, novels, architecture, and art have typified modernist leaders who displayed transactional, transformative, or charismatic behavioral traits (Taylor, 1911; Lundberg, 1988; Handy, 1991; Ackoff, 1999; Pillai, Schriesheim, & Williams, 1999; Cantor, 2001; Hoyt & Blascovich, 2003; Kouzes & Posner, 2009). Modernist management studies have relied on these sweep-of-history-engulfing scopes, reinforcing Taylor's (1911) classical scientific management thesis in various organizational environments (Marcuse, 1964; Baudrillard, 1994; Travica, 1999; Gherardi, 2000; Gilovich & Griffin, 2002; Sillince, 2007; Albritton & Anderson, 2008; Herold, Fedor, Caldwell, & Liu, 2008; Hamel, 2009). In the selected literature reviewed for the past two decades, management techniques have mirrored changes in leadership symbolism, with the most recent leadership prescriptions focused on transformational or charismatic methods that motivated subordinates to act in a way that meet organizational goals. Some recent studies exemplify changing leadership perspectives that reflected a democratic, interpersonal, and contextualized leadership line of authority. Anonson et al. (2009) states:

Because leadership is dynamic, leaders and their traits should not be studied outside of context. Unlike traditional hierarchical models of leadership, in interprofessional leadership the platform on which member-leaders relate is horizontal, relational, and situational. Effective leadership combines both professional competency and the ability to foster team dynamics. (p. 19)

However, a question remains as to what direction leadership and group dynamics studies inform research efforts going forward if researchers derive their findings based on ambiguous leadership concepts. It seems a reasonable concern to ask what organizations will do as Baby Boomer leaders who learned these modernist's techniques exit the workforce, leaving a leadership culture unprepared for postmodern hiring, retention, resource-allocation, and succession-planning challenges and opportunities. Consequently, companies now and in the future require innovative management models and measurement solutions that would improve leadership understanding (Bolman & Deal, 2008) and address the multicultural contexts (Callan, 2003) that make up group interactions. This requires resolving, at the very least, the conceptual ambiguities that describe leadership traits (Nisbett, Borgida, Crandall, & Reed, 1982; Collins, 2001; Gross, 2009) and the epistemological complexities facing western moral imperatives. As we have illustrated in Figure 1, a great deal of modernists' management ambiguity remains mired in Immanuel Kant's reason versus nature paradigm. The Enlightenment perspective has relied on linear mental and socially evolving controls to explain civilization's inevitable progress. Reflective of the tumultuous *Ancien Régime* period, modernist or Enlightenment dogmatists have worked to legitimize power relations but from these earlier archaeological mistakes, have fostered conceptual ambiguities associated with leadership behaviors.

Because of this, we believe it is mindful to discover the epistemological elements of leadership mythology. Although there are researchers who claim that modernist management and leadership studies began with Mary Parker Follett and Elton Mayo (Wren, 2005), historically, it is clear that Taylor's (1911) *The Principles of Scientific Management*, was the first national thesis on the subject. Taylor provided a systematic, scientific, behavioral approach that heavily relies on identifying the components of management success and then teaching people who demonstrate enough ability to learn competent leadership behaviors. Interestingly, Taylor sounded chagrined in the opening pages to his book when he stated that businesses continued to seek out already well-trained competent men instead of "systemati-

Figure 1. Kant's Reason versus Nature Paradigm

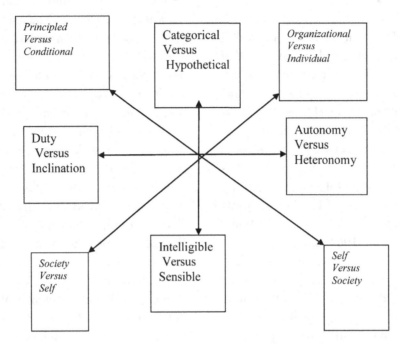

Principled Versus Conditional

Categorical Versus Hypothetical

Organizational Versus Individual

Duty Versus Inclination

Autonomy Versus Heteronomy

Society Versus Self

Intelligible Versus Sensible

Self Versus Society

cally cooperating to train to make this competent man" (p.6). Taylor believed that good managers and leaders were not simply born, but were a product of approved teaching methodologies. Not surprisingly, seventy-five years later, Tichy and DeVanna (1986) in the preface to their book *The Transformational Leader*, echoed Taylor's concerns and beliefs when they spoke about leadership as a systematic, behavioral process:

Transformational leadership is about change, innovation, and entrepreneurship. We agree with Peter Drucker that these are not the provinces of lonely, half-mad individuals with flashes of genius. Rather, this brand of leadership is a behavioral process capable of being learned and managed. It's a leadership process that is systematic, consisting of purposeful and organized search for changes, systematic analysis, and the capacity to move resources from areas of lesser to greater productivity. (p. 6)

THE POSTMODERN ORGANIZATIONAL CHALLENGE

As more companies employ advanced information and communications technologies to organize work in virtual environments, human resources managers need concrete metrics to evaluate the compatibility of strategic change initiatives, implementation costs, and group communication requirements, to name a few (LaRue, Childs, & Larson, 2006). Especially difficult is the development of leadership models that can lessen organization/stakeholders' cross-cultural, cross-gender, and cross-generational communication biases that lead to individual and group conflicts (Hine, 2000; Thompson, 2010). Law and Mol (2002) asserted a postmodern approach would re-examine organizations' systems designs, structure, and communication strategies without limiting analytical findings to simple, bounded rationality assumptions as found in contemporary organizational research (Travica, 1999; Bromiley, 2005; Barney & Clark, 2007; Davenport and Harris, 2007).

We suggest a postmodern perspective to eliminate conceptual ambiguities found in leadership studies (Pawar, 2003), by re-examining the leader-worker dyadic in varying organizational contexts found in a global work environment. Thus, we selected leadership studies published from 1999 to 2008 (see Table 1 in the Appendix) to investigate the conceptual ambiguities most often assigned to leadership traits in public and private organizations. Clarifying the conceptual ambiguity is important for two reasons: 1) To establish a firm theoretical foundation for future leadership research, and 2) encourage researchers to recast leader-worker interactions found in real and virtual environments (Hoyt & Blascovich, 2003).

Star Trek as a Postmodern Allegory

To describe the conceptual ambiguities derived from modernist leadership perspectives, employing an allegorical tool that represents the historical and sociological changes tied to modernist leadership studies seemed reasonable. Specifically, the *Star Trek* television and movies filmed during the Cold War and post-Cold War years was selected to highlight the similarities and differences in the social and psychological symbolism used. The generational success of *Star Trek*, first as a science fiction novel by the late Gene Roddenberry and then as a television and film success for more than three generations of viewers, demonstrated a resonance with inherited western democratic and leadership concepts. Cantor (2001) claimed that the television and movie successes particular to the United States were appropriate simulacra of the Americanization of global perspectives and social ideologies during the post-World War II era. Similarly, invoking the post-Cold War Star Trek television series *Star Trek: The Next Generation* as an allegorical referent would also help illustrate the changing complexity of leader-worker roles in the 21ˢᵗ century.

What is decidedly different between the two Star Trek's periods is the recent *Star Trek: The Next Generation* television series and movies illustrated a workforce made up of a central command leader, who more often than not, relied on subordinates to guide his policies and interactions. Gone was the earlier *Star Trek* captain as hero, charismatic as he may be, and in his place stood a transformational captain that cherished his subordinates' individuality (including an android seeking to become more human). This new starship crew as an allegory illustrated a significant change in the symbolic orientation found in contemporary leadership studies. We termed this leadership phenomenon A Star Trek Affective State in contrast to the Cold War-era Star Trek that went about Americanizing the galaxies by relying on the charismatic Captain Kirk to direct his crew to rise above their ordinariness. What we propose to demonstrate is that the key purpose of leadership research should re-examine the emergent salient social and psychological interactions among leaders and subordinates (Bolman & Deal, 2008), not on a leader's ephemeral behavioral traits.

Transformational and Charismatic Leadership Ambiguity

Would independent researchers or academics addressing charismatic or transformational leadership traits find clear distinctions between these two concepts as proposed on opposite ends of a behavioral continuum? From a meta-analysis of the published research devoted to these concepts as shown in Table 2, we would answer no. What was inferred from prior sociological and organizational literature (Katz & Kahn, 1978; Schneider, Gruman, & Coutts, 2005) was leadership traits were a consequence of a person's social and personal environments (Pillai, Schriesheim, & Williams, 1999; Bolman & Deal, 2008). Additionally, contemporary leadership studies *a posteriori* have located leaders' and workers' behaviors in a ad hoc structure or network (Latour, 2005) that included their companies' industry, their power position in the company, their responsibility to the company,

Table 1. Transformational and Charismatic Traits: A Content and Context Summary

Transformational	Charismatic	Context	Studies
	Interpersonal strength; magnetism; forceful; fair	Group perceptions, behaviors; exchange relationship	Scott, Colquitt, & Zapata-Phelan, 2007
	Symbolic, meaningful behavior; idealist; visionary; emotionally influential	Organizational fit of subordinates; organizational behaviors internalized	Huang, Cheng, & Chou, 2005
Idealized influence moral values; communication; role clarity; mission clarity	Ethical, moral consequences;	Affect subordinate behaviors; organizational effectiveness	Hinkin & Tracey, 1999
	Affects followers perceptions; emotional intelligence, social intelligence, social control; emotional displays	Organizational change management	Grover, 2005
	Affect attitudes; visionary; emotionally-charged; emotional contagion	Job satisfaction; group performance	Erez, Misangyi, Johnson, LePine, & Halverson, 2008
	Manipulative; ethical; visionary; empowerment	Organizational outcomes; change management	Tuomo, 2006
Idealized influence; inspirational; intellectual; vision, trust; respect; risk-taker; integrity; role model	(considered a component of transformational)	Organization-directed; group performance	Stone, Russell, & Patterson, 2004
Motivational; trust; charismatic; inspirational; intellectual, individualized communication	(Charisma as a central concept)	Exchange-oriented; organizational behaviors; group commitment	Pillai, Schriesheim, & Williams, 1999
Affective; motivational; empowering, role model, visionary; change agent; moral	Self-confident; visionary; unconventional; self-interested	Group performance needs; affect worker attitudes	McLaurin & Al Amri, 2008
Affect beliefs; values, visionary; moral; empowering	(Charismatic used synonymously)	Follower change commitment; change management	Herold, Fedor, Caldwell, & Liu, 2008
Role model; inspirational; intellectual; individualized consideration		Affect group performance; organizational commitment	Felfe & Schyns, 2004
Empowering, intellectual; vision-sharing; role model; mediator; emotionally intelligent	(Considered a component of transformational)	Relationship management; group performance in multicultural settings	Manning, 2003
Motivational; moral; social contagion; goal-directed; communicative	(Mainly a component of transformational, but case sensitive)	Organizational change process; inducing change in followers	Pawar, 2003
Authority; visionary; role model; problem solving; inspirational; idealism; risk taker; networking	(Considered a component of transformational)	Organizational power; legitimate authority; affect changes in followers; environment sensitive	Pearce, et al., 2003
Visionary, role model; inspirational; individualized consideration		Motivate change in others; aware of subordinates emotional/perceptions	Hautala, 2005
Stimulates; motivates; selfless; individualized consideration; inspirational; visionary; intellectual; fairness	(Idealized influences)	Organizational change; subordinate perceptions; group performance	Wu, Neubert, & Xiang 2007
Trustworthy; inspirational; communicative; intellectual; individual consideration; trust; moral; empowering, respect	(Considered a component of transformational, but can be different based on context)	Group satisfaction; group performance as a subjective assessment by followers; subordinates identify with group	Hoyt & Blascovich, 2003

Table 2. Content Analysis of Transformational and Charismatic Traits

	Organizational-related concepts	Personal/Self/Other Icons
Transformational/Transactional	1. Interpersonal skills aimed at organizational effectiveness 2. Multicultural competencies 3. Transcend role through internal drive to succeed 4. Powerful, 5. Knowledgeable 6. Respected 7. Change agents 8. Courageous 9. Empower others 10. Ethical 11. Life-long learners 12. Emotional Intelligence 13. Visionaries	1. Intrapersonal skills 2. Multiple Intelligences 3. Trustworthy 4. Powerful 5. Knowledgeable
Charismatic	1. Manipulative 2. Culture-specific 3. Trustworthy 4. Multiple Intelligences 5. Unconventional behavior 6. Visionaries/Idealists 7. Self-confident 8. High self esteem 9. Motivated by power 10. High Performers	1. Interpersonal skills aimed at empowering workers; spiritual; manipulative 2. Culture-specific competencies 3. Transcend role empathy, multiple intelligences 4. Trustworthy 5. Image building

their moral drive to succeed in general, and their specific culture or subcultures (Handy, 1995; Collins, 2001; Bolman & Deal, 2008).

A content analysis of the literature revealed that transformational leadership was conceptually a continuous intrapersonal practice that appeared simple on the surface; but as group complexity increased, so would the interpersonal dynamics involved (Felfe & Schyns, 2004; Konorti, 2008), increasing in our estimation the ambiguity in researchers' findings. For example, there was not a simple metric that could capture Becker's conceptual definition when he described transformational leadership as "…an art requiring the continual adaptation of interpersonal skills, situational analysis, and the involvement of many (if not all) organizational participants". (2007, p. 116). Additionally, Manning, (2003), Wren (2005), Erickson, et al, (2007), Scott, Colquitt and Zapata-Phelan (2007), and Erez, Johnson, Misangyi, and LePine (2008) have no less obscured attribu-

tional dynamics by describing varying leadership traits observed during periods of conflict, rationalization of resources, or the need for a leader to possess a blend of multicultural competencies.

So what does it mean to be a charismatic, transactional, or transformative leader? The literature remains opaque in this area (Pawar, 2003; McLaurin & Al Amri, 2008). For example, charismatic, transactional, transformational, or some combination of all three traits were found in various publications; although one study recast leadership traits into "directive", "transactional", "transformational", and "empowering" (Pearce, et al., 2002, p. 273). Similarly, charismatic operational definitions referred to leaders who possessed Rasputin-like qualities, an interpersonal force that drove followers' beliefs and actions (Den Hartog, De Hoogh, & Keegan, 2007). Some authors discussed charismatic traits as uplifting and inspiration-provoking, creating practically spiritual experiences in followers (Katz & Kahn,

1978). Researchers also described charismatic leaders as those who possess artful styles, promoting group cohesion and commitment to leadership goals, and at times exerting influences that were contradictory to social norms (Huang, et. al., 2005; Choi, 2006; Tuomo, 2006; Miller, 2007; Gehrke, 2008). There was also the work of Grover (2005), Hinkin and Tracey (1999), and Huang, et al, (2005) where charismatic qualities or traits portend some improvement in an organization through the willingness of followers to act on the wishes of their leader(s). Cranti and Bateman (2000) described charismatic traits as those that "include prosocial assertiveness, creativity and innovation, risk-seeking propensity, self-confidence, social sensitivity, and sensitivity to follower needs" (p. 64).

Transformational leaders who by the way were also charismatic on some dimension (and vice versa), added a bit more to the leadership soup with emotional intelligence that empowered group members, displayed "intellectual openness, vision-sharing, and role modeling" (Manning, 2003, p. 21). Transformational and transactional leadership traits were first conceptualized as two opposite poles but later were revised to apportion transactional leadership as a minor necessity (Felfe & Schyns, 2004) employed sparingly by transformational leaders who primarily demonstrated an ability to develop "organizational citizenship behaviors", including "conscientiousness, sportsmanship, civic virtue, courtesy, and altruism" (Pillai, Schriesheim, & Williams, 1999, p. 898). Some researchers described transformational leadership traits on a continuum that included a servant leader dimension. Stone, Russell, and Patterson (2003) explained the difference between transformational and a servant leader as one of leadership "focus", where transformational leaders were more concerned with "organizational objectives" and servant leaders focused more on "the people who are followers" (p. 349); another ambiguity linked to prior researchers' operational definitions.

Hoyt and Blascovich (2003) investigated transformational and transactional leadership traits in a face-to-face and virtual experimental setting. Their findings also demonstrated the conceptual ambiguity of leadership traits. For example, they arrived at a definition of transactional leaders as managers who set goals, provided feedback, and rewarded employees for accomplishing tasks, whereas, transformational leaders were charismatic, inspirational, intellectually stimulating, innovative, and "demonstrated a high degree of personal concern for the followers' needs" (p. 680).

Hautala (2005) examined the effects transactional and transformational leaders would have on employee ratings of superiors, employing the same operationalization of transactional versus transformational leadership as previously mentioned. Subjects were asked to rate an exchange-oriented leader or a leader who raised "subordinates' motivation" (p.85). The researcher operationalized transformational in this case as a leader's ability to motivate subordinates "to see deeper purposes behind their work, thus making them achieve high levels of (self) motivation" (p. 85). Characteristically, leaders and subordinates with similar extraversion and introversion traits comprised the sample, with the results indicating positive correlations between similar leader-worker traits. However, the findings did little to clarify transformational concepts. After all, transformational, transactional, and charismatic leaders can be extravorted at times, and introverted at other times. Thus, conceptual ambiguities remained.

Wu, Neubert, and Yi (2007) examined the effect transformational leaders' actions had on employee perceptions regarding justice or fairness in a large Chinese petroleum company. Similar to prior researchers' efforts, they operationalized transformational leadership on four dimensions: "individualized consideration, inspirational motivation, idealized influence (trait and behavior), and intellectual stimulation" (p. 331). These four dimensions helped them to explain transformational behavior, but they also found that subordinates perceptions were mediated based on "informational justice and interpersonal justice" (p. 338), where employees perceived their work group as cohesive, they were more in line with change management strategies. Of particular importance however, is the conclusion they came to: "A significant contribution of this study is that it uncovers the followers' psychological processes by which transformational leadership yields its influence on" employees (p. 345). Again, transformational leadership remains an amorphous endeavor. Instead, they linked psychological processes, group identity, and moral beliefs to outcomes. We in no way want to downplay the significance of the employee profiles, or related findings found in the literature we reviewed, but we do question the effectiveness attributed to a leader who possesses an ambiguously defined behavioral trait in each of these representative studies.

FINDINGS: RESOLVING THE AMBIGUITIES

In the selected literature reviewed, transformational and charismatic leadership conceptual traits selected demonstrated particular symbolic referents as given in Tables 1 and 2 in the Appendix. Transformational and charismatic concepts appeared synonymous in application, but appeared differentiated based on a pre-determined organizational or research setting. If researchers were investigating change management success, transformational leadership concepts came into play. In earlier studies cited in the research, charismatic leadership concepts differentiated a leader by his efforts to meet effectively organizational goals. No less than 26 traits were apportioned in the two categories. Not surprising, the conceptual ambiguity that plagues transformational leadership traits mirrored researchers' claims regarding charismatic traits. For example, transformational or charismatic concepts employed in leader-

worker exchanges implied responsibility for the success of organizational effectiveness lay with a leader. Thus, a causal link was established that demonstrated workers were malleable subjects who either abdicated much of their self in the process or had already aligned themselves psychologically with their particular leaders.

Essentially, the conceptual ambiguities operationalized in leadership studies were a result of subjective induction. As Popper (1959) stated, scientific objectivity can never be completely justified, but subjective operational definitions should be verifiable according to the theories employed; or in the case of leadership studies, by the operational definitions used. From the meta-analysis performed, it was apparent that leadership concepts changed more as a function of historical and sociological influence than from scientific induction. To remedy this induction problem, researchers should re-examine the interactive, complex, dynamic nuances that include management and worker relationships, and relinquish modernist pre-deterministic perspectives that rely on ambiguous leadership concepts. However, the research reviewed provided insightful results that illustrated the complex dynamics involved in work settings. Further, leadership studies should turn to examining emergent or evolving group behaviors from a postmodern perspective instead of relying on the philosophical foundations of Taylorism, where leaders hold a heroic position and workers remain well-tuned machines.

In the literature reviewed, charismatic traits remained linked to social-psychological theories that provided some clarity, and prescriptive rationales related to leader-worker dynamics, not whether a leader was actually transformational or charismatic. More importantly, these findings suggested quasi group heuristics linked to decisions about their perceptions regarding their leader's particular fit to their group ideal. To overcome the philosophical or modernists prejudices found in transformational and charismatic leadership approaches, researchers should consider the decision-making and judgement heuristics stakeholders employ that result in cooperative or failed relationships. For example, at least two key heuristics emerged from the literature reviewed: 1) stakeholders' interactions were a product of their social beliefs and 2) their willingness to meet organizational goals was a product of their intrapersonal beliefs about their position in a company, reflected as it were, in how well they rated leaders in the organization. Similar to Bolman and Deal's (2008) discussion of "espoused theories" and theories-in-use" (p. 169) that described two cognitive heuristics people used regarding interpersonal and group dynamics in an organizational setting. They said that people employ espoused theories to describe structural accounts of their behaviors, while people employ a theories-in-use decision-making heuristic or "implicit" (p. 169) program to explain the rules associated with how they chose to behave. A postmodern methodology would use these two components of decision-making based on individuals' organizational and personal projections, and thus mitigate conceptual ambiguities in leadership research.

A Postmodern Evaluation Model

In a technologically advanced communication environment, leaders and followers' interactions are qualitatively different, more complex and stretch beyond modernist organizational approaches (Hancock & Tyler, 2001). The guiding principles of one-dimensional man's rationality or enlightened instrumentality were far from appropriate in this new communications era (Marcuse, 1964). The *hamartia* of modernist research literature misses the mark by excusing or ignoring intrapersonal and group complexities arising from biased decision-making patterns that lead to emergent behaviors among participants. This methodology would investigate emergent leader-follower (or follower-leader) interaction as a consequence of personal biases, intuitive decision-making tools, and the cultural influences found in an organizational

milieu (Morris, 2006; Choi, 2006; Neuhauser, 2007; Taylor, 2007; Todorovic & Schlosser, 2007; Jacoby, 2008). As Rahim and Psenicka (2002) reported, multicultural studies in emotional intelligence have positively correlated mangers' responses to workers' perceptions regarding effective interaction skills, demonstrating far more about emergent behavior than describing a transformational or charismatic individual. Mapping the contextual influences between managers and subordinates was hypothesized based on two specific constructs: 1) organizational icons and 2) personal, social icons. Partitioning these intrapersonal and interpersonal biases would allow researchers to identify the underlying normative beliefs that lead to group performance in an organizational setting instead of wasting ink on transformational and charismatic leadership traits (McLaurin & Al Amri, 2008). Further, addressing symbolic referents and heuristic biases would promote an understanding of the "intuitive judgments" (Kahneman & Frederick, 2002, p. 50) or philosophical grounding (Sandel, 2009) that give rise to emergent behaviors based on decisions in leader-directed or worker-directed group settings.

Thus, from the meta-analysis, important clues as to the interactions that comprised management and subordinates relationships emerged. For example, two distinct modernist contextual influences surfaced from the literature reviewed, organizational or institutional icons and individual, quasi-group icons. In most cases, transformational traits were associated with behaviors that primarily reinforced organizational goals through benevolent manipulation of worker concerns. Charismatic concepts were associated with a leader's personality, or interpersonal characteristics that would lead to effective control or manipulation of workers for a singular, but higher purpose. However, when we examined the leadership traits presented in the literature, we found that at least five salient constructs that were associated with organizational structure and five constructs linked to social psychological or perceptual influences as shown in Table 2 found in the Appendix.

Charismatic leaders were mapped as people, who led by example, were team focused, fair/just/ethical, has emotional intelligence, and was innovative, manipulative, or artfully persuasive. Upon closer examination, these phrases appeared derived from subjects' responses that in our estimation revealed their heuristic biases in terms of how well their beliefs matched those of their superiors; their *quasi* group intuitions (Kahneman & Frederick, 2002) that give rise to their decisions in leader-directed or team-directed group performances. Transformational concepts were associated with organizationally directed characteristics or phrases. In those cases investigated, transformational leaders were individuals who

have expert knowledge, have a primary ownership or a personal investment in the company, recognized as prestigious, have networking capabilities or specific industry knowledge, and were trustworthy, a veteran in the industry who other industry leaders trusted. In our estimation, these phrases resembled a systematic procedural tool people employed (Sloman, 2002) in organizational settings that allowed them to judge how well their leaders matched their beliefs about organizational outcomes based on how those outcomes would affect their professional lives. Identifying the cognitive tools used provided insight into how environmental contexts effect various stakeholders' actions (see hypothesized heuristic model presented in Figure 2).

Figure 2. Organizational Power and Social Beliefs Leadership Matrix

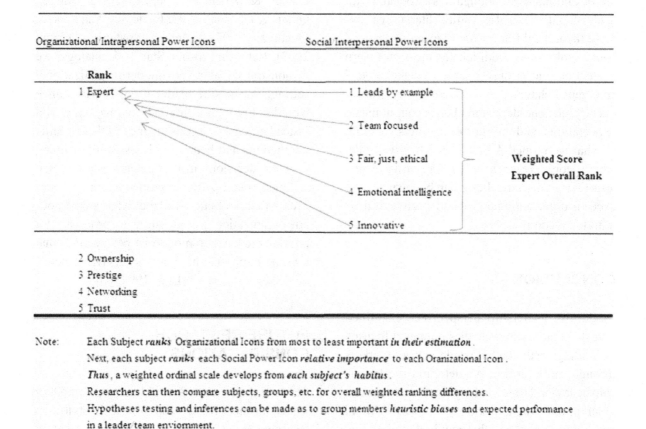

Note: Each Subject *ranks* Organizational Icons from most to least important *in their estimation*.

Next, each subject *ranks* each Social Power Icon *relative importance* to each Oranizational Icon.

Thus, a weighted ordinal scale develops from *each subject's habitus*.

Researchers can then compare subjects, groups, etc. for overall weighted ranking differences.

Hypotheses testing and inferences can be made as to group members *heuristic biases* and expected performance in a leader team enviornment.

Relevance of Findings

Examining leaders and workers on the 10 operational heuristics culled from the leadership traits found in the literature, provided a simpler metric of the dynamic interaction that leads to emergent group behaviors, instead of focusing simply on a leader's behavioral traits or an organization's associational power (Gilovich, Griffin, Kahneman, 2002; Fiedeldey-Van Dijk & Freedman, 2007; Albritton, Oswald, & Anderson, 2008). These findings are important for two reasons. First, our postmodern performance metric accepts *a posteriori* that complex personal, cultural, and institutional biases appear in the context of social or work settings (Gardner, 1983; 2006; 2007; Engen, Leeden, & Willemsen, 200; Mintzberg, Lampel, Quinn, & Ghoshal, 2003; Fiedeldey-Van Dijk, & Freedman, 2007; Anderson, Spataro, & Flynn, 2008). Secondly, adopting a postmodern metric eliminates the ambiguities associated with leadership studies that rely on a utilitarian or a Taylorist theoretical framework to examine leaders' behavioral virtues. Additionally, the postmodern evaluation matrix makes sense of stakeholders' emergent behaviors in a concrete way. Subsequently, stakeholders could better communicate expectations and minimize conflicts, leading to what we termed A Star Trek Affective State, where people are *free to act willingly* in a way that tests their limits, stretches group boundaries, and exceeds organizational goals, respective of their individual contributions.

CONCLUSION

Modernist leadership perspectives examined revealed that research studies remained focused on finding methods that would control workers through some form of pre-deterministic leadership behavioral trait. Underlying these modernist assumptions was a workforce limited in mind and behavioral scope that required leaders that taught normative behaviors and closely monitored employee responses (Wren, 2005; Kilduff & Krackhardt, 2008). Perhaps, not so surprising, Taylor's (1911) *The Principles of Scientific Management* haunts modernist perspectives in the cases examined, fostering the conceptual ambiguities that undermine organizational research. From the literature reviewed, 10 salient psychological and social simulacra were identified that provided a plausible theoretical framework. The key factors identified demonstrated associations among social icons or organizational factors and individual, perceptual icons that represent an individual's underlying belief structures and their decision-making and judgement heuristics in organizational settings (Albritton, Oswald, & Anderson, 2008).

The postmodern performance metric presented accepted *a posteriori* that each group brings complex personal, cultural, and institutional biases to a work setting (Gardner, 1983; 2006; 2007; Engen, Leeden, & Willemsen, 200; Mintzberg, Lampel, Quinn, & Ghoshal, 2003; Fiedeldey-Van Dijk, & Freedman, 2007; Anderson, Spataro, & Flynn, 2008). Returning to our Star Trek analogy, we demonstrated that in a postmodern organizational setting, successful leader-group performance would not rely on utilitarian notions, but would instead emerge as a consequence of the dynamic interactions and heuristic biases people employ to make decisions in particular group-oriented settings. Specifically, we coined a term—A Star Trek Affective State—to label what a postmodern organization would aspire to promote, not provide credence to modernist perspectives that *a priori* imply that humanity's survival depends on a "heroic agency" (Law, 1994, p.66).

FUTURE RESEARCH CONSIDERATIONS

Leadership researchers could use a postmodern leadership model to develop empirical tests to map emergent group behaviors and provide mitigation of subdued company performance or promote the salient characteristics that result in A Star Trek Affective State (Branden, 1969; Hines, 2000; Frith, 2007; Ariely, 2008; Goleman & Boyatzis, 2008). In particular, we believe researchers should borrow from decision-making theory (Kahneman & Tversky, 1982; 2000; Gilovich, Griffin, & Kahneman, 2002) and actor-network theories (Latour, 2005) to find common linkages among complex dynamics displayed by leaders and workers in their particular settings (Wu, Neubert, & Yi, 2007), not rely on a single, powerful person's behavioral traits to explain group behaviors. Although researchers have associated transformational or charismatic traits with historical figures, their findings have failed to demonstrate which came first, Adolph Hitler's form of Nazism, or the German nation's willingness to follow a Nazi vision. Similarly, was acceptance of the Vietnam War a consequence of a single U.S. president's rhetoric, or were the American people willing to view the world as an American surrogate? In either case, the answer should result in an investigation into the underlying biases that guide leader-follower communication and how these internalized and externalized symbols affect group communication, interaction, acceptance, and performance (Tarde, 1899; Green, 2007; Kearney, 2008).

REFERENCES

Ackoff, R. L. (1999). Transformational leadership. *Strategy and Leadership, 2*(1), 20–25. doi:10.1108/eb054626

Albritton, M., Oswald, S., & Anderson, J. (2008). Leadership quality and follower affect: A study of U.S. presidential candidates. *The Journal of Leadership Studies, 1*(4), 6–22. doi:10.1002/jls.20035

Anderson, C., Spataro, S., & Flynn, F. (2008). Personality and organizational culture as determinants of influence. *The Journal of Applied Psychology, 93*(3), 702–710. doi:10.1037/0021-9010.93.3.702

Anonson, J. M., Ferguson, F., MacDonal, M. B., Murray, B. L., Fowler-Kerry, S., & Bally, J. M. (2009). The anatomy of interprofessional leadership: An investigation of leadership behaviors in team-based health care. *The Journal of Leadership Studies, 3*(3), 17–35. doi:10.1002/jls.20120

Ariely, D. (2008). *Predictably irrational: The hidden forces that shape our decisions.* New York: HaperCollins.

Barling, J., Christie, A., & Turner, N. (2008). Pseudo-transformational leadership: towards the development and test of a model. *Journal of Business Ethics, 81*(4), 851–861. doi:10.1007/s10551-007-9552-8

Barney, J. B., & Clark, D. N. (2007). *Resource-based theory: Creating and sustaining competitive advantage.* Oxford: Oxford University Press.

Baudrillard, J. (1994). *Simulacra and simulation* (Glaser, S. F., Trans.). Ann Arbor: The University of Michigan Press.

Becker, G. F. (2007). Organizational climate and culture: Competing dynamics for transformational leadership. *Review of Business Research, 7*(6), 116–123.

Bolman, L. G., & Deal, T. E. (2008). *Reframing organizations: Artistry, choice, and leadership.* San Francisco: Jossey-Bass.

Branden, N. (1969). *The psychology of self-esteem.* San Francisco: Jossey-Bass.

Bromiley, P. (2005). *The behavioral foundations of strategic management.* Malden, MA: Blackwell Publishing.

Callan, S. (2003). Charismatic Leadership in Contemporary Management Debates. *Journal of General Management*, *29*(1), 1–14.

Callon, M. (2002). Writing and re(writing) devices as tools for managing complexity. In Law, J., & Mol, A. (Eds.), *Complexities: Social studies of knowledge practices* (pp. 191–217). Durham: Duke University Press.

Cantor, P. A. (2001). *Gilligan unbound: Pop culture in the age of globalization*. London: Rowman & Littlefield Publishers, Inc.

Chia, R. (1996). The problem of reflexivity in organizational research: Towards a postmodern science of organization. *Organization*, *3*(1), 31–59. doi:10.1177/135050849631003

Chisnall, P. S. (2001). Virtual ethnography [Review of the book Virtual ethnography]. *International Journal of Market Research*, *43*(3), 354–356.

Choi, J. (2006). A motivational theory of charismatic leadership: envisioning, empathy, and empowerment. *Journal of Leadership & Organizational Studies*, *13*(1), 24–43. doi:10.1177/10717919070130010501

Collins, J. (2001). *Good to great: Why some companies make the leap and others don't*. New York: HarperCollins Publishers, Inc.

Covey, S. M. R. (2006). *The speed of trust: The one thing that changes everything*. New York: Free Press.

Cranti, J., & Bateman, T. (2000). Charismatic leadership viewed from above: The impact of proactive personality. *Journal of Organizational Behavior*, *21*(1), 63–75. doi:10.1002/(SICI)1099-1379(200002)21:1<63::AID-JOB8>3.0.CO;2-J

Davenport, T. H., & Harris, J. G. (2007). *Competing on analytics: The new science of winning*. Boston: The Harvard Business School Press.

DeLanda, M. (2006). *A new philosophy of society: Assemblage theory and social complexity*. London: Continuum.

Den Hartog, D., De Hoogh, A., & Keegan, A. (2007). The interactive effects of belongingness and charisma on helping and compliance. *The Journal of Applied Psychology*, *92*(4), 1131–1139. doi:10.1037/0021-9010.92.4.1131

Denning, S. (2005). Transformational innovation: a journey by narrative. *Strategy and Leadership*, *33*(3), 11–16. doi:10.1108/10878570510700119

Derrida, J. (1976). *Of grammatology* (Spivak, G. C., Trans.). Baltimore: The Johns Hopkins University Press.

Doolin, B. (2003). Narratives of change: Discourse, technology and organization. *Organization*, *10*(4), 751–770. doi:10.1177/13505084030104002

Drucker, P. F. (1997). Toward the new organization. In Hesselbein, F., Goldsmith, M., & Beckhard, R. (Eds.), *The organization of the future* (pp. 1–5). New York: The Peter F. Drucker Foundation for Nonprofit Management.

Ehin, C. (2008). Un-managing knowledge workers. *Journal of Intellectual Capital*, *9*(3), 337–350. doi:10.1108/14691930810891965

Engen, M. L., Leeden, R., & Willemsen, T. M. (2001). Gender, context and leadership styles: A field study. *Journal of Occupational and Organizational Psychology*, *5*(74), 581–598. doi:10.1348/096317901167532

Erez, A., Misangyi, V., Johnson, D., LePine, M., & Halverson, K. (2008). Stirring the hearts of followers: Charismatic leadership as the transferal of affect. *The Journal of Applied Psychology*, *93*(3), 602–616. doi:10.1037/0021-9010.93.3.602

Erickson, A., Shaw, J., & Agabe, Z. (2007). An empirical investigation of the antecedents, behaviors, and outcomes of bad leadership. *The Journal of Leadership Studies*, *1*(3), 26–43. doi:10.1002/jls.20023

Felfe, J., & Schyns, B. (2004). Is similarity in leadership related to organizational outcomes? The case of transformational leadership. *Journal of Leadership & Organizational Studies, 10*(4), 92–102. doi:10.1177/107179190401000407

Fiedeldey-Van Dijk, C., & Freedman, J. (2007). Differentiating emotional intelligence in leadership. *The Journal of Leadership Studies, 1*(2), 8–20. doi:10.1002/jls.20012

Frith, C. (2007). *Making up the mind: How the brain creates our mental world*. Malden: Blackwell Publishing.

Gardner, H. (1983). *Frames of mind: The theory of multiple intelligences*. New York: Basic Books.

Gardner, H. (2006). *Multiple intelligences: New horizons*. New York: Basic Books.

Gardner, H. (2007). *Five minds for the future*. Boston: Harvard Business School Press.

Gehrke, S. J. (2008). Leadership through meaning-making: An empirical exploration of spirituality and leadership in college students. *Journal of College Student Development, 49*(4), 351–359. doi:10.1353/csd.0.0014

Gherardi, S. (2000). Practice-based theorizing on learning and knowing in organizations. *Organization, 7*(2), 211–223. doi:10.1177/135050840072001

Gilovich, T., & Griffin, D. (2002). Introduction – Heuristics and biases: Then and now. In Gilovich, T., Griffin, D., & Kahneman, D. (Eds.), *Heuristics and biases: The psychology of intuitive judgment* (pp. 1–18). Cambridge: Cambridge University Press.

Glaser, B. G., & Strauss, A. L. (1967). *The discovery of grounded theory: Strategies for qualitative work*. New Brunswick: Aldine Transaction.

Goffman, E. (1959). *The presentation of self in everyday life*. New York: Anchor Books.

Goffman, E. (1974). *Frame analysis: An essay on the organization of experience*. Boston: Northeastern University Press.

Goldman, A. I. (1999). *Knowledge in a social world*. Oxford: Oxford University Press. doi:10.1093/0198238207.001.0001

Goleman, D., & Boyatzis, R. (2008). Social intelligence and the biology of leadership. *Harvard Business Review*, (September): 1–8.

Green, D. D. (2007). Leading a postmodern workforce. *Academy of Strategic Management Journal, 6*, 15–26.

Gross, N. (2009). A pragmatist theory of social mechanism. *American Sociological Review, 74*(3), 358–379. doi:10.1177/000312240907400302

Grover, K. S. (2005). Linking leader skills, follower attitudes, and contextual variables via an integrated model of charismatic leadership. *Journal of Management, 31*(2), 255–277. doi:10.1177/0149206304271765

Guzman, P. M. (2007). *Strategic leadership: Qualitative study of contextual factors and transformational leadership behaviors of chief executive officers*. Unpublished doctoral dissertation, University of Phoenix, Phoenix, Arizona.

Hamel, G. (2009). Moon shots for management. *Harvard Business Review, 2008*(February), 91–08.

Hancock, P., & Tyler, M. (2001). *Work, postmodernism and organization: A critical introduction*. Thousand Oaks: Sage Publications.

Handy, C. (1991). *Gods of management: The changing work of organizations*. Oxford: Oxford University Press.

Hautala, T. (2005). The effects of subordinates' personality on appraisals of transformational leadership. *Journal of Leadership & Organizational Studies, 11*(4), 84–92. doi:10.1177/107179190501100407

Herold, D., Fedor, D., Caldwell, S., & Liu, Y. (2008). The effects of transformational and change leadership on employees' commitment to a change: A multilevel study. *The Journal of Applied Psychology, 93*(2), 346–357. doi:10.1037/0021-9010.93.2.346

Hesselbein, F., & Goldsmith, M. (2009). *The organization of the future 2*. San Francisco: Jossey-Bass.

Hine, C. (2000). *Virtual ethnography*. London: Sage Publications.

Hinkin, T., & Tracey, J. B. (1999). The relevance of charisma for transformational leadership in stable organizations. *Journal of Organizational Change Management, 12*(2), 105–119. doi:10.1108/09534819910263659

Hoopes, J. (2003). *False prophets: The gurus who created modern management and why their ideas are bad for business today*. New York: Basic Books.

Hoyt, C. L., & Blascovich, J. (2003). Transformational and transactional leadership in virtual and physical environments. *Small Group Research, 34*(6), 678–715. doi:10.1177/1046496403257527

Huang, M., Cheng, B., & Chou, L. (2005). Fitting in organizational values: The mediating role of person-organization fit between CEO charismatic leadership and employee outcomes. *International Journal of Manpower, 26*(1), 35–49. doi:10.1108/01437720510587262

Huber, G. (1990). A Theory of the effects of advanced information technologies on organizational design, intelligence, and decision making. *Academy of Management Review, 15*(1), 47–71.

Jacoby, R. (2008). The CIO's Role in Enabling Innovation. *Thoughtleaders, 2007*(4), Retrieved April 22, 2008, from http://www.bmighty.com/printableArticle.jhtml;jsessionid=VNC2O21E3AHJCQSNDLOSKH0CJUNN2JVN?articleID=205208507

Jamrog, J., & Overholt, M. (2005). The future of HR metrics. *Strategic HR Review, 5*(1), 3–3. doi:10.1108/14754390580000837

Jung, D., & Sosik, J. (2006). Who are the spellbinders? Identifying personal attributes of charismatic leaders. *Journal of Leadership & Organizational Studies, 12*(4), 12–26. doi:10.1177/107179190601200402

Kahneman, D., & Frederick, S. (2002). Representativeness revisited: Attribute substitution in intuitive judgement. In T. Gilovich, D, Griffin, & D. Kahneman (Eds.) *Heuristics and biases: The psychology of intuitive judgment* (pp. 49-81). Cambridge: Cambridge University Press.

Kahneman, D., Slovic, P., & Tversky, A. (Eds.). (1982). *Judgment under uncertainty: Heuristics and biases*. Cambridge: Cambridge University Press.

Kahneman, D., & Tversky, A. (1982). Causal schemas in judgments under uncertainty. In Kahneman, D., Slovic, P., & Tversky, A. (Eds.), *Judgment under uncertainty: Heuristics and biases* (pp. 117–128). Cambridge: Cambridge University Press.

Kahneman, D., & Tversky, A. (Eds.). (2000). *Choices, values, and frames*. Cambridge: Cambridge University Press.

Kallinikos, J. (2009). On the computational rendition of reality: Artifacts and human agency. *Organization, 16*(2), 183–202. doi:10.1177/1350508408100474

Katz, D., & Kahn, R. L. (1978). *The social psychology of organizations*. Hoboken: John Wiley & Sons, Inc.

Kearney, E. (2008). Age differences between leader and followers as a moderator of the relationship between transformational leadership and team performance. *Journal of Occupational and Organizational Psychology, 81*(4), 803–811. doi:10.1348/096317907X256717

Kilduff, M., & Krackhardt, D. (2008). *Interpersonal networks in organizations: Cognition, personality, dynamics, and culture.* New York: Cambridge University Press. doi:10.1017/CBO9780511753749

Konorti, E. (2008). The 3D transformational leadership model. *Journal of American Academy of Business, Cambridge, 14*(1), 10–20.

Kotlyar, I., & Karakowsky, L. (2007). Falling over ourselves to follow the leader: conceptualizing connections between transformational leader behaviors and dysfunctional team conflict. *Journal of Leadership & Organizational Studies, 14*(1), 38. doi:10.1177/1071791907304285

Kouzes, J. M., & Posner, B. Z. (2009). To lead, create a shared vision. *Harvard Business Review, 2009*(January), 20–21.

LaRue, B., Childs, P., & Larson, K. (2006). *Leading organizations from the inside out: Unleashing the collaborative genius of action-learning teams.* New York: Wiley.

Latour, B. (2005). *Reassembling the social: An introduction to actor-network-theory.* Oxford: Oxford University Press.

Law, J. (1994). *Organizing modernity.* Oxford: Blackwell Publishers.

Law, J. (2004). *After method: Mess in social science research.* New York: Routledge.

Law, J., & Mol, A. (2002). Complexities: An introduction. In Law, J., & Mol, A. (Eds.), *Complexities: Social studies of knowledge practice* (pp. 1–22). Durham: Duke University Press.

Lepelley, D. M. (2001). *Exploring the adaptability of leadership styles in senior business executives: Life narratives and self discovery of factors contributing to adaptability.* Unpublished doctoral dissertation, Fielding Graduate Institute, California). Retrieved January 28, 2009, from ABI/INFORM Global database. (Publication No. AAT 3037966).

Lundberg, C. (1988). Working with culture. *Journal of Organizational Change, 1*(2), 38–47. doi:10.1108/eb025598

Manning, T. T. (2003). Leadership across cultures: Attachment style influences. *Journal of Leadership & Organizational Studies, 9*(3), 20–30. doi:10.1177/107179190300900304

Marcuse, H. (1964). *One-dimensional man.* Boston: Beacon Press.

McLaurin, J. R., & Al Amri, M. B. (2008). Developing an understanding of charismatic and transformational leadership. *Allied Academies International Conference. Academy of Organizational Culture, Communications and Conflict. Proceedings, 13*(2), 15–19.

Middlebrooks, A. E., & Haberkorn, J. T. (2009). Implicit leader development: The mentor role as prefatory leadership context. *The Journal of Leadership Studies, 2*(4), 7–22. doi:10.1002/jls.20077

Miller, M. (2007, July). Transformational leadership and mutuality. *Transformation, 24*(3/4), 180–192.

Mintzberg, H., Lampel, J., Quinn, J.B., & Ghoshal, S. (2003). *The strategy process: Concepts, contexts, cases.* Edinburgh Gate: Pearson Education Limited.

Morris, L. (2006). *Top-down innovation: leaders define innovation culture.* Retrieved April 26, 2008 from http://www.realinnovation.com/content/c070528a.asp

Neuhauser, C. (2007). Project manager leadership behaviors and frequency of use by female project managers. *Project Management Journal, 38*(1), 21–31.

Nisbett, R. E., Borgida, E., Crandall, R., & Reed, H. (1982). Popular induction: Information is not necessarily informative. In Kahneman, D., Slovic, P., & Tversky, A. (Eds.), *Judgment under uncertainty: Heuristics and biases* (pp. 101–116). Cambridge: Cambridge University Press.

Pastor, J., Mayo, M., & Shamir, B. (2007). Adding fuel to fire: the impact of followers' arousal on ratings of charisma. *The Journal of Applied Psychology*, *92*(6), 1584–1596. doi:10.1037/0021-9010.92.6.1584

Pawar, B. (2003). Central conceptual issues in transformational leadership research. *Leadership and Organization Development Journal*, *24*(7), 397–406. doi:10.1108/01437730310498596

Pearce, C. L., Sims, H. P. Jr, Cox, J. F., Ball, G., Schness, E., Smith, K., & Trevino, L. (2003). Transactors, transformers and beyond: A multi-method development of a theoretical typology of leadership. *Journal of Management Development*, *22*(4), 273–307. doi:10.1108/02621710310467587

Pillai, R., Schriesheim, C. A., & Williams, E. S. (1999). Fairness perceptions and trust as mediators for transformational and transactional leadership: A two-sample study. *Journal of Management*, *25*(6), 897–933. doi:10.1177/014920639902500606

Popper, K. (1959). *The logic of scientific discovery*. London: Hutchinson and Company.

Rahim, M. A., & Psenicka, C. (2002). A model of emotional intelligence and conflict management strategies: A study in seven countries. *The International Journal of Organizational Analysis*, *10*(4), 302–326. doi:10.1108/eb028955

Rizzolatti, G., & Sinigaglia, C. (2006). *Mirrors in the brain: How our minds share actions and emotions* (Anderson, F., Trans.). Oxford: Oxford University Press.

Sandel, M. J. (2009). *Justice: What's the right thing to do?* New York: Farrar, Straus, and Giroux.

Scheider, F. W., Gruman, J. A., & Coutts, L. M. (Eds.). (2005). *Applied Social Psychology: Understanding and addressing social and practical problems*. Thousand Oaks: Sage Publications.

Scott, B., Colquitt, J., & Zapata-Phelan, C. (2007). Justice as a dependent variable: Subordinate charisma as a predictor of interpersonal and informational justice perceptions. *The Journal of Applied Psychology*, *92*(6), 1597–1609. doi:10.1037/0021-9010.92.6.1597

Sillince, J. A. (2007). Organizational context and the discursive construction of organizing. *Management Communication Quarterly*, *20*(4), 363–394. doi:10.1177/0893318906298477

Sloman, S. A. (2002). Two systems of reasoning. In Gilovich, T., Griffin, D., & Kahneman, D. (Eds.), *Heuristics and biases: The psychology of intuitive judgement* (pp. 379–396). Cambridge: Cambridge University Press.

Soulsby, A., & Clark, E. (2007). Organization theory and the post-socialist transformation: Contributions to organizational knowledge. *Human Relations*, *60*(10), 1419–1442. doi:10.1177/0018726707083470

Stone, G. A., Russell, R. F., & Patterson, K. (2004). Transformational versus servant leadership: A difference in leader focus. *Leadership and Organization Development Journal*, *25*(4), 349–361. doi:10.1108/01437730410538671

Tarde, G. (1899). *Social laws: An outline of sociology* (Warren, H. C., Trans.). New York: The Macmillan Company.

Taylor, F. (1911). *The principles of scientific management*. New York: Harper & Brothers Publishers.

Taylor, V. (2007). Leadership for service improvement: part 3. *Nursing Management*, *14*(1), 28–32.

Tekleab, A. G., Sims, H. P., Yun, S., Tesluk, P. E., & Cox, J. (2008). Are we on the same page? Effects of self-awareness of empowering and transformational leadership. *Journal of Leadership & Organizational Studies*, *14*(3), 185–201. doi:10.1177/1071791907311069

Thaler, R. H. (2000). Mental accounting matters. In Kahneman, D., & Tversky, A. (Eds.), *Choices, values, and frames* (pp. 241–268). Cambridge: Cambridge University Press.

Thompson, C. (2010). Group think: When it comes to what we say we like, often we're just following the herd. *Wired,* 18.01.

Thompson, C. J. (1995). A contextualist proposal for the conceptualization and study of marketing ethics. *Journal of Public Policy & Marketing, 14*(2), 177.

Tichy, N. M., & Devanna, M. A. (1986). *The transformational leader.* New York: John Wiley & Sons, Inc.

Todorovic, W., & Schlosser, F. (2007). An entrepreneur and a leader! A framework conceptualizing the influence of leadership style on a firm's entrepreneurial orientation--performance relationship. *Journal of Small Business & Entrepreneurship, 20*(3), 289–307.

Travica, B. (1999). *New organizational designs: Information aspects.* Stamford: Ablex Publishing Corporation.

Tuomo, T. (2006). How to be an effective charismatic leader: lessons for leadership development. *Development and Learning in Organizations, 20*(4), 19–21. doi:10.1108/14777280610676963

Varner, I., & Beamer, L. (2005). *Intercultural communications in the global workplace.* New York: McGraw-Hill/Irwin.

Walumbwa, F. O., Avolio, B. J., & Zhu, W. (2008). How transformational leadership weaves its influence on individual job performance: the role of identification and efficacy beliefs. *Personnel Psychology, 61*(4), 793–825. doi:10.1111/j.1744-6570.2008.00131.x

Wren, D. A. (2005). *The history of management thought.* New Jersey: John Wiley & Sons.

Wu, C., Neubert, M., & Xiang, Y. (2007). Transformational leadership, cohesion perceptions, and employee cynicism about organizational change: The mediating role of justice perceptions. *The Journal of Applied Behavioral Science, 43*(2), 327–351. doi:10.1177/0021886307302097

Chapter 4
The Role of Social Networks in Distributed Informal Information Systems for Innovation

Vasco Vasconcelos
EGP- University of Porto Business School, Portugal

Pedro Campos
LIAAD - INESC TEC,FEP and University of Porto Business School, Portugal

ABSTRACT

Web 2.0 and Enterprise 2.0 concepts offer a whole new set of collaborative tools that allow new approaches to market research, in order to explore continuously and ever fast-growing social and media environments. Simultaneously, the exponential growth of online Social Networks, along with a combination of computer-based tools, is contributing to the construction of new kinds of research communities, in which respondents interact with researchers as well as with each other. Furthermore, by studying the networks, researchers are able to manage multiple data sources - user-generated contents. The main purpose of this paper is to propose a new concept of Distributed Informal Information Systems for Innovation that arises from the interaction of the accumulated stock of knowledge emerging at the individual (micro) level. A descriptive study unveils and reports when and how market research professionals use Social Networks for their work and therefore create distributed information systems for Innovation.

INTRODUCTION

Networks play an important role in economics. Firms set up connections with other firms in order to establish production relationships, cooperation, etc. Therefore, firms expect to in-crease their profits and survival. Innovation is essential to competitiveness and represents the way in which to anticipate, live with, or react to change (Ratti, 1991). Innovation capabilities and technological advance have been enhanced by strategic alliances and Collaboration networks that have proliferated in recent years, particularly in

DOI: 10.4018/978-1-4666-1764-3.ch004

information technology sectors (Gordon, 1991). Information and Communication Technologies are frequently seen as an important enabler for such networks and a key factor in Economy. With the fast diffusion of technologies, companies and individuals unable to face the challenge can rapidly become uncompetitive (Solé & Valls, 1991). If they are not able to preserve their advantage on the long term, technological cooperation may be a possible course of action. Hakansson (1987) suggests a new perspective that sees Innovation (and technological development in general), as a product of exchange among different agents (firms, individuals, in the network). The former view treated Innovation either as an individual fact (like a Nobel Prize) or as a secret process in a firm. Innovation systems include the interaction between the individual (or actors) who are needed in order to turn an idea into a process, product or service on the market (Freeman, 1982).

Most of the information technologies that are used for communicating and spreading Innovation fall into two categories: (i) direct channels (person-to-person communication by email or instant messaging), having low share and low commonality of information for the other agents involved and (ii) platforms, like intranets, corporate Web Sites and corporate portals (McAfee, 2006). Knowledge management systems have tried to elicit tacit knowledge, best practices and relevant experience from people throughout a company and put this information available to other in databases.

Nowadays, Enterprise 2.0[1] provides business managers with access to the right information at the right time through a web of inter-connected applications, services and devices. By providing such a wide quantity of resources to firms and individuals, Enterprise 2.0 makes the collective intelligence of many accessible, translating into a huge competitive advantage in the form of increased Innovation, productivity and agility (Wylie, 2009). Within the concept of Enterprise 2.0, information systems are emergent. One of the most challenging examples of such an emergent information system is Wikipedia (www.wikipedia.org). Articles in this online encyclopaedia are assembled by ad hoc virtual teams. The social engineering of the wiki model is aimed at creating a cooperative and networked culture (Giles, J, 2005; McAfee, 2006).

In this chapter, we study the use of Social Networks by individuals with the aim of creating Innovation. Knowledge capture through the interaction of individuals is therefore accumulated in Social Networks. Informal structures of knowledge that is shared by firms or individuals (or both) can be seen as Distributed Informal Information Systems for Innovation. Our main research hypothesis is that Social Networks are used as Distributed Informal Information Systems for Innovations by market research professionals.

In order to capture the use of Social Networks, a survey was made in which a set of market research professionals (our target population) was analyzed, taking in consideration four Social Networks: Linkedin, Hi5, The Star Tracker and Twitter. To capture the Innovation capabilities inherent to market research professionals, information was gathered concerning eight main concepts: Finding Business Partners, Academic, New Business, Benchmarking, Find Human resources, Costumer experience, Concept testing and Product development. According to previous research conducted by Chadwick (2006) and Day & Schoemaker (2006), these concepts define the most common goals for the use of Social Networks by our target population. These are the main components for the creation of an Information System for Innovation.

The rest of the chapter is organized as follows: in Section 2 the main concepts are presented. Section 3 contains the study design and the results and, finally, in Section 4 the concluding remarks are presented.

DISTRIBUTED INFORMAL INFORMATION SYSTEMS FOR INNOVATION (DIISI)

Markets, Collaborative Networks, and Innovation

In Economics, an inter-firm network is a set of firms (nodes) that interact through inter-firm relations (connections or links). These links are contracts or correspond to informal exchange of information in order to produce Innovation. Based on the origin of an Innovation, three types of network relations can be distinguished (Kamann & Strijker, 1991): (1) the supplier-dominated relation; (2) the user-dominated relation; (3) the research-dominated network. The question of the origin of the Innovation (who gave the impetus) was studied by Laage-Hellman (Kamann & Strijker, 1991) that supported that Innovations are the result of the joint effort of various actors. As Innovation involves learning, Hakansson et al. (1999), stress the importance of the business relationships in the diffusion of learning through the network. The more complementary are the organizational competences, the more advantage the firms get from each other. The authors mention, that *"there are reasons to believe that the more connections a relationship has, the greater are the possibilities to learn. [...] The argument for this is that if a relationship has a number of connections there are also a number of interfaces where learning could appear: between products, between production facilities and between different backgrounds and competences. A large number of interfaces increase the variation, which is one basic condition for learning"*.

Collaboration is a fundamental concept in the theory of networks (Campos, 2006). It can be considered as the complementary action between the elements of a network. Collaborative strategies permit firms to specialize in certain activities where they can be more efficient, letting other activities to be accomplished by other members

of the network. Consequently, economies of scale can be attained and costs can be reduced. According to Ebers (1997) Collaboration permits firms to enter in inter-organizational networks with the purpose of: (i) increasing their revenue by binding competitors as allies and accessing complementary resources and/or capabilities; (ii) reducing their costs as the result of economies of scale that can be achieved, for example, through joint research, marketing or production (Hakansson & Snehota, 1995). Inter-organizational networking represents a cost-efficient way of gaining access to crucial know-how that can neither be made available internally nor be easily transferred by licensing.

Collaborative networked organizations (CNO) are a new concept that is emerging in electronic business models. In addition to the rapid evolution of traditional supply chain and outsourcing practices, a growing trend consists of tasks performed by autonomous teams of a small number of people or small and medium enterprises (Camarinha-Matos & Afsarmanesh, 2004). The autonomous teams can be formed by independent firms that are linked by a network, coming together to tackle various projects. They may dissolve once the work is done. Information and Communication Technologies are frequently seen as an important enabler for CNO's. However, in order to initiate a CNO, the environment where it operates (as well as the organizations and involved individuals) must be previously prepared. Therefore, a long-term base cooperation agreement should be established: it requires the virtual organization breeding environment (VBE). The breeding environment is a long-term networked structure, having an adequate base environment for the establishment of cooperation agreements, common infrastructures, common ontologies and mutual trust. The establishment of cooperation agreements between firms is not a new phenomenon, but rather belongs to the very nature of the business world. But, as Camarinha-Matos and Afsarmanesh (2004) indicate, "the use of communication and information technologies to support agile communication as one key characteristic of the virtual concept, brings this approach to a new level of effectiveness. Cooperation on a global scale (intercontinental) is expected to substantially increase, as distance will no longer be a major limiting issue".

Organizational networks can be viewed as Virtual Enterprises. Industry clusters or industrial districts are examples of breeding environments in which the cluster is formed by organizations located in the same region, although the physical distance is not the major attribute when cooperation is supported by computer networks. In addition and according to Osterle et al. (1991 p. 2) *"The introduction of transportation technologies and IT, are pushing the physical disintegration of markets and enterprises to its global limits and thus enabling the maximal specialization of enterprises"*.

Information is Distributed

Nowadays, the way firms communicate is distributed. The same happens with individuals. The Internet and the Web evolved to a platform for Collaboration, sharing, Innovation and user-created content - the so-called Web 2.0 environment. This environment includes social and business networks, and it is influencing what people do on the Web and intranets, individually and in groups. One of the main advantages of the Web 2.0 is the ability to tap into the collective intelligence of users. It is known that the more users contribute the more popular and valuable a Web 2.0 site becomes. Enterprise 2.0 is a direct consequence of what Web 2.0 has introduced in firms: the socialization of business applications – moving from data☐centric models to people☐driven applications. Exploiting the analysis from the use of on line information services, Lamb and Kling developed an institutionalist concept of a social actor whose everyday interactions are infused with ICT use (Lamb & Kling, 2003). The authors changed the concept of the user to the concept of social actor in Information Systems, taking into

consideration the complexity and multiplicity of the roles that people fulfill while adopting, adapting, and using information systems.

Frequently we try to use what is known about individual actions to predict the social aggregate phenomena produced by the group. There are cases in which the aggregate is merely an extrapolation from the individual: if we know, for instance that every driver turns his lights on at sunset, we can guess that the street could appear illuminated almost suddenly. But if most people turn their lights on when some proportion of oncoming cars already have their lights on, we would get a different picture. In this latter case, drivers would be influencing each others' behavior and responding to each others' behaviour.

This example was given by Schelling (1978), who was interested in studying the macro behaviour that emerged from micro decisions. Some of these micro decisions are influenced by the system of interaction between those individuals and their environment. The notion of behaviour is an important issue. Belew and Mitchell (1996) describe behaviour, as something that "closes the loop" between an organism and its environment. The kind of behaviour in Shelling's drivers example is contingent, that is, the behaviour of some depends on what the others are doing. But this notion of behaviour cannot be isolated from another important concept - the purpose. In general, individuals pursue goals, try to minimize his/her effort and maximize his/her comfort. The goals, purposes or objectives relate directly to other individuals and their behaviour. This micro-macro vision strengthened the rise of Innovation through the exponential growth of online Social Networks. A combination of computer-based tools, forced new kinds of research communities to appear, in which respondents interact with researchers as well as with each other.

Distributed Information Systems arose, consisting of multiple autonomous entities (individuals, organizations, computers, etc.) that communicate through various means, usually computer networks. In fact, information systems are fed by the Internet (Komninos, 2009). Digital services referring to R&D (Reseach and Development), technology and transfer allow for the acquisition of best practice, by comparing and testing new concepts or new businesses or products, and increase the problem solving capabilities in all organizations and involving all the collaborators: that is when Information Systems for Innovation are created (see Figure 1). These "Distributed Informal Information Systems for Innovation" (DIISI), are "distributed" because the stock of knowledge is created through the interaction of the distributed agents at the micro-level (individuals) and spread at the macro level, with feedback to all agents in the network. They are also informal because, in many situations, there is no intention a priori of creating a formal information system. Furthermore, and taking in consideration the concept of Enterprise 2.0, information systems are emergent, and therefore this micro-macro mechanism promotes the creation of DIISI. Af-

filiations comprise networks of relationships that link organizations and individuals within and across industries. Within this network of relationships, the use of online databases by organization members is best explained from a perspective that understands these ICTs as interaction technologies. Organization members, like attorneys, commercial real estate brokers or members of biotechnology companies, use online services to exchange information and interact with affiliated organizations, such as clients or regulators, in ways that are considered legitimate within the industry. When ICTs are used as part of those interactions—to package, present, and exchange information—they also construct identities for firms and their members (Lamb & Kling, 2003).

Previous Works

Several works use the "distributed-agents" metaphor to explore the emergence of Innovation, partner selection and use of information systems.

Figure 1. The creation of Distributed Informal Information Systems for Innovation as emergent processes of the interaction in Social Networks

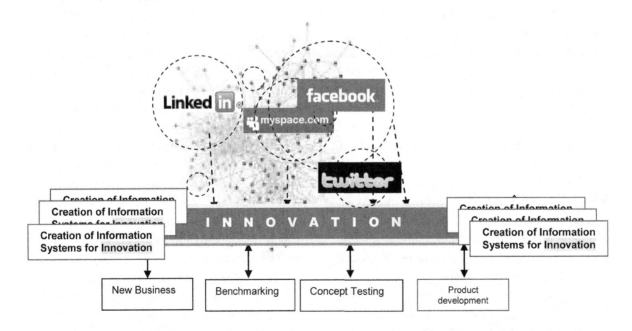

We separate those studies in two different areas: (i) organizational collaborative networks, and (ii) individual collaborative networks. Only few examples are cited.

(I) Organizational collaborative networks

Some authors have related the process of Innovation with the creation of networks of firms, using simulated environments: Carayol and Roux (2003) study Innovation as a collective and interactive process that generates the formation of networks of organizations. Wersching (2005) uses an Agent-Based model to study the technological development, the economic performance of firms and the evolution of agglomerations in differentiated industry. In a previous work (Campos, Brazdil, & Brito, 2006) proposed an Agent-Based approach to analyze the dynamics of network formation resulting from the Collaboration between firms. Firms (the agents) contain cognitive attributes that help them build their own decisions. Four Collaboration strategies have been compared and it was concluded that profit is associated with stock of knowledge and with small diameter of the networks. In addition, it has been proved that concentration strategies are more profitable and more efficient in transmitting knowledge through the network, and that the stock of knowledge is determinant for the growth of networks.

Hinttu, Fosman, and Kock (2004) explored the impact of Social Networks in international business partner selection. Authors pursued a qualitative study with semi-structured interviews with key actors and selected firms. The effect of (on line) Social Networks on the internationalization of small and medium enterprises is clear and increasing in the last decades.

(II) Individual collaborative networks.

In a different perspective, Yu, Venkatamaran and Singh (2003) consider a social network of software agents who assist each other in helping their users find information. The architecture is fully distributed and includes multiagent learning heuristic who preserve the privacy and autonomy of their users. These agents learn models of each other in terms of expertise (ability to produce correct domain answers) and sociability (ability to produce accurate referrals). The authors studied their framework experimentally in order to study how the social network evolves. Under the multiagent learning heuristic, the quality of the network improves with interactions; the quality is maximized when both expertise and sociability are considered; pivot agents further improve the quality of the network and have a catalytic effect on its quality even if they are ultimately removed. In addition, the quality of the network improves when clustering decreases, reflecting the intuition that you need to talk to people outside your close circle to get the best information.

The previously referred work of Lamb and Kling (2003) changed the concept of the user to the concept of social actor in Information Systems. The authors believe that the social-actor framework provides a way to conceptualize ICT research and design: it can move the research in information systems (IS) beyond the concept of users. The actor metaphor reinforces the researchers' imagination to ask with whom an actor is interacting, about what issues, under what conditions, for what ends, with what resources, etc. It is a metaphor that really expands the scope and scale of the social space of people's interactions with ICT's with other people, groups and organizations.

STUDY DESIGN

Research Problem, Information Sources and Sample Characterization

Traditional market research has been accused of not being able to satisfyingly deliver answers for the client's needs and are, in an ever more complex society, challenged to embrace new mental models, based on different principles (Chadwick, 2006). The corporate use of social media is quickly changing from an adoption stage – where companies use it as a channel to promote and manage brand awareness, products and services – to a paradigm focused on the comprehension of how people and institutions take advantage of it (Lenhart, 2009).

Chadwick, (2006) and Day, and Schoemaker, (2006) define the concepts associated with the most common goals for the use of Social Networks for market research purposes: Finding Business Partners, Academic, New Business, Benchmarking, Find Human resources, Costumer experience, Concept testing and Product development. According to previous research by those authors, these concepts define the most common goals for the use of Social Networks by our target population, and enabled by new "arenas" opened up by these communities, backed-up by the Web 2.0 concept of Collaboration and user-generated content. These are the main components for the creation of a DIISI.

In this study, the research problem is specified by the question: how are Social Networks being used by market research professionals for Innovation purposes. The components of this question are: (a) professionals and businesses that use social network for market research, (b) frequency of use of this type of tool, (c) objectives of use (d) Social Networks most used for market research, (e) relevance of Social Networks as information sources and (f) main advantages and disadvantages of using this type of market research tool.

A non-documental indirect observation methodology was chosen through the form of an online survey, which was created using an online survey tool[2]. The questions were designed considering the objectives of the descriptive study and supported by information gathered through scientific literature review. The survey includes independent and dependent (both qualitative) variables, the latter being filter-origined. Which Social Networks are

used the most used and with which objectives constitute the dependent variables of the study. The sample was designed using a convenience-based sampling methodology (Cochran, 1977), following two steps: (1) selection of four Social Networks: Linkedin (www.linkedin.com), Hi5 (www.hi5.com), Thestartracker (www.thestar-tracker.com) and Twitter (www.twitter.com) and (2) selecting individuals within these networks. The dimension of the sample is, therefore, difficult to determine a priori, as the number of members of the discussion groups and blogs grows on a daily basis. A great difficulty that contributed for the sample's size non-determination is the fact that the URL posted on Twitter has been "retwitted" by the authors' followers. All the contacted individuals are somehow related or interested in market research and are members of Social Networks, whose habits of use of Social Networks for market research are intended to be studied, having been obtained 63 answers to the survey. Considering this is a convenience-designed sample, no inferences or conclusions were drawn to the whole market researchers' population, nor Social Networks studied. The restricted number of answers is a limitation of our study, but taking into account that this convenience-designed sampling was applied to a study that is based on professional networks (not completely opened to a wide audience), the dimension of the sample is to be considered as adequate. The respondents were contacted either by direct messaging through the chosen social network platforms and by posting the survey on discussion groups and forums available in the very same networks. This way of contact allowed the sample to overcome geographical boundaries as well as faster distribution of the survey and data collection. The survey was designed and formatted so that each respondent could answer only once, in order to better control the answers and narrowing chances of multiple responses per respondent, enabling more reliable results. The data were gathered between November 17 and

Figure 2. Sample composition (by nationality)

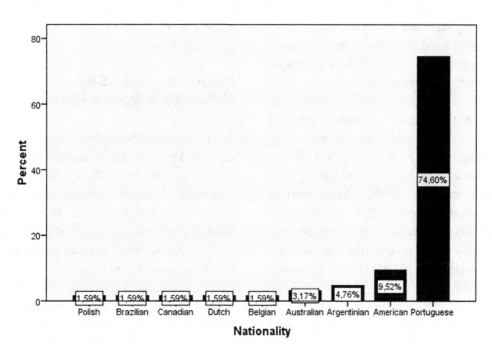

December 30, 2009 and then exported to SPSS Statistics (SPSS, 2007), for the statistical analysis.

In the sample, 74,60% of the individuals are Portuguese. From a total of nine different nationalities, the second most represented country is the United States of America, with 9,52% of the respondents, followed by Argentina (4,76%) and Australia (3,20%).

Several industries (15) are present in the sample: Information Technologies (IT) is the most represented (26,98%). Marketing and Information Management is second, with 14,29% of the answers. In the bottom end are Pharmaceutical Industry, Food and Beverages, Non-profit Organizations (NPO's), Publishers and Energy (1,59%).

58,73% of the respondents have a University Degree and 31,75% possess a Master's Degree of PhD. These results demonstrate a high level of literacy of the subjects within the sample.

Regarding professional headlines, 17,34% of the sample is composed by Marketers and 11,29%

CEO's. Business Managers represent 9,68% and Market researchers 8,06%. Public Relations Manager, Inventor, Engineer, Marketing Consultant, Marketing Director, Teacher, Information Technologies Consultant and Competitive Intelligence Expert are some of the 20 professional headlines included in the sample.

Social Network Use

The analysis of the gathered data allows us to verify that, on what concerns Social Networks for market research, 22,22% of the respondents claim never to use it, whereas only 11,11% uses Social Networks for such a purpose either frequently or all the time (the remaining professionals fit in the other classes).

Amongst the non-users we find the Pharmaceutical Industry and Non-profit Organizations (NPO'S), both of which claim never to use Social Networks in the studied context.

Among the Building Materials Industry, 50% of the respondents claim not to use Social Networks; 42,86% in Consulting and 40% of the Consumer Goods Industry have the same answer.

On the other hand, Web Development claims a continuous/permanent use (100%). The Import/Export Industry also shows a frequent use of Social Networks for the studied purpose. 60% of the respondents of the Education Industry use Social Networks all the time, while the remaining 40% use them frequently. The consumer Services Industry also uses Social Networks frequently, with a 66,67% use rate. Only 11,11% of Marketing and Information Management professionals never use Social Networks, whereas the other respondents in this industry reveal diverse use rates: seldom (22,22%), sometimes (44,44%) and frequently (22,22%) (Table 1).

All of these results are consistent with the 2009 Business Social Media Benchmarking Study (Business.com, 2009).

Overall, and considering the whole sample, over one third of the respondents use Social Networks for market research purposes either frequently or all the time, whereas 22% never use it at all.

Frequently Used Social Networks in Market Research

With the array of Social Networks available these days (and more being created each day), market researchers can select those where they believe their research targets are present, and so the information they seek. Therefore, different industries use different networks/combinations of networks.

The data reveals Linkedin as the most commonly used social network for market research (58,73% of the respondents), being the only one used in the Building Materials Industry. Such fact may be explained for being the only professional network in the study. In fact, according to the "2009 Business Social Media Benchmarking Study"

Table 1. Use of Social Networks by Industry

		Use of Social Networks				
		Never	Seldom	Sometimes	Frequently	All the time
Industry	Food & Beverages	,0%	100,0%	,0%	,0%	,0%
	Trade Publisher	,0%	100,0%	,0%	,0%	,0%
	Mkt & Information Management	11,1%	22,2%	44,4%	22,2%	,0%
	Consumer Services	,0%	33,3%	,0%	66,7%	,0%
	IT	11,8%	11,8%	35,3%	35,3%	5,9%
	Import/Export	,0%	,0%	,0%	100,0%	,0%
	Banking	33,3%	50,0%	16,7%	,0%	,0%
	Education	,0%	,0%	,0%	40,0%	60,0%
	Construction Materials	50,0%	,0%	25,0%	25,0%	,0%
	Pharmaceutical	100,0%	,0%	,0%	,0%	,0%
	Consumer Goods	40,0%	,0%	40,0%	20,0%	,0%
	Web Development	,0%	,0%	,0%	,0%	100,0%
	Consulting	42,9%	14,3%	,0%	14,3%	28,6%
	Energy	,0%	,0%	100,0%	,0%	,0%
	Non-profit organisation	100,0%	,0%	,0%	,0%	,0%
Total		22,2%	17,5%	23,8%	25,4%	11,1%

(Business.com, 2009), 38% of the professionals have an active profile in this network. However, it is never used by 16,66% of the industries included in the sample and that use Social Networks as a market research tool.

According to our data, the distribution of the Social Networks by type of industry is as follows: Food and Beverages (Facebook (50%) and Hi5 (50%)), Trade Publishing (Facebook (50%) and Secondlife (50%)), Import/Export (Facebook (50%) and Twitter (50%)). Education professionals mainly use Twitter (26,67%) and Linkedin (33,33%).

The Star Tracker (20%) and Linkedin (37,50%) are the most commonly used Social Networks by the Marketing and Information Management Industry, being this the industry with the largest number of users of different Social Networks (6), including Orkut.

Apart from Food and Beverages (which only uses Facebook), all industries use two or more Social Networks for market research purposes.

Overall, Facebook is used by 46,03% of the professionals in the sample and Twitter, by 31,75%.

Given the number of registered users on these platforms (over 600 million on Facebook and 106 million on Twitter), it is more than natural that market research professionals use these networks as research platforms/labs. In fact, and according to the "2010 Social Media Marketing Industry Report" (socialmediaexaminer.com, 2010) 88% of American companies have a Facebook page. Twitter (88%), Linkedin (78%) and Blogs (70%) complete the Top 4 most used tools by marketers.

Goals of Using Social Networks for Market Research

For this study, and considering the work of Chadwick (2006) and Day & Schoemaker (2006), six concepts were associated with the most common goals on the use of Social Networks for market research purposes: Finding Business Partners, Academic, New Business, Benchmarking, Find

Human resources, Costumer experience, Concept testing and Product development, being these the main components for the creation of an Information System for Innovation (as stated earlier in this chapter),

The main goals appointed by the sample in the use of Linkedin are: Idea Generation (27,78%), Concept Testing (13,39%), Product Development (13,39%) and Test Methodology (2,78%) being, in fact, the only social network used to find human resources and new business partners. Again, this result is no stranger to the fact that Linkedin is a prominently professional network.

All of the respondents that use Hi5 claim to use it with the goal of Generating Ideas.

The goals of using Facebook concern specially Idea Generation and Consumer Experience (33,33% each).

Among the respondents that use Twitter as a market research tool, 30% do it for Idea Generation, whereas 33% has Consumer Experience in mind, 14,81% Concept Testing and 11,11% for Product Development purposes. The only social network exclusive to Portuguese users (The Star Tracker) is used for Generating Ideas, Product Development and Consumer Experience (33,33% each). Within the sample, the concept of Benchmarking is explored through Myspace (25%), Twitter (5%), Delicious (100%) and Facebook (3,70%) (Relative percents of goals of use given to each social network).

Overall, the goals Finding New Business Partners (4,76%) and New Business Opportunities (1,5%) are poorly mentioned.

All Social Networks considered, the most mentioned goals are Customer Experience (28,10%) and Idea Generation (26,30%).

Perceived Advantages of the Use of Social Networks for Market Research

As seen on Figure 3, the main advantage perceived by the sample of this research study is the fact that the" information is *pulled* by the consumers", with

Figure 3. Frequently used Social Networks in market research

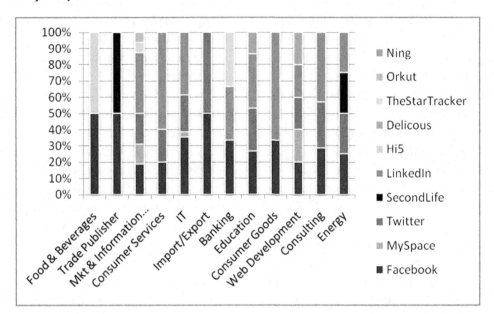

Figure 4. Goals of using Social Networks for market research

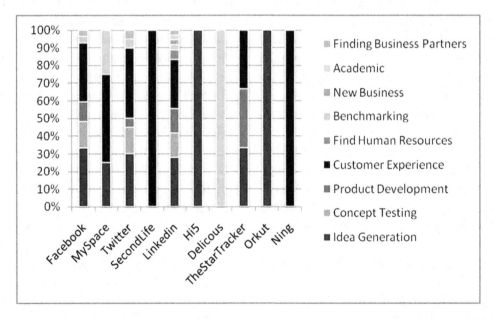

nearly fourty percent of the answers collected, followed by "Rich Consumer Insights" (26,98%). More than 14% of the respondents mention the possibility of seeing the consumers as "part of a tribe". We can then perceive the influence of networks around friendship relations or common interests as an important factor in individual's life, as it was previously defended by Cooke & Buckley (2008).

The ability of Social Networks to identify weak signals from the market is mentioned by 12,70% of the sample. These signals are traditionally difficult to identify by more "mainstream" research methods (idem).

Table 2. perceived advantages of the use of Social Networks for market research

Advantage	Percent	Cumulative Percent
No advantage	1,59	1,59
Information "pulled" by consumers	39,68	41,27
View the customer as part of a tribe	14,29	55,56
Rich consumer insights	26,98	82,54
Identify weak signals	12,70	95,24
Relevant audience	1,59	96,83
Find employees of target	1,59	98,41
Easy to use	1,59	100,00
Total	100,00	

Other mentioned advantages include: "Relevant audience", "Find Employees of Target" and "Easy To Use". 1,59% of the respondents find no advantage on the use of Social Networks for market research.

Perceived Disadvantages of the Use of Social Networks for Market Research

About 31,75% of the respondents point out the inability to cover all relevant types of individuals as the main disadvange of Social Networks, on what market research is concerned. The reason behind this answer is the fact that not all consumers – at least not all considered relevant for any given research – are members of Social Networks. The same percentage of our sample refers to poor control of the respondents as the main disadvantage. Another great disadvantage of this type of open and collaborative tool is the array of data one can collect from it. However, and by definition, this whole mechanism is out of the control of any entity, researchers included, thereby endangering the usual control procedures (Chadwick, 2006). Simultaneously, this very same array of data, implies "fuzzy data" (idem), pointed out as the biggest disadvantage by 15,87% of the respondents of our research(Table 3).

FUTURE RESEARCH DIRECTIONS

Distributed Informal Information Systems for Innovation (DIISI) have been introduce and discussed here. However, the concept do DIISI lacks further formalization and systematization in order to be measured, validated and compared. The

Table 3. perceived disadvantages of the use of Social Networks for market research

Disadvantage	Percent	Cumulative Percent
Fuzzy data	15,87	15,87
Difficulty to identify significant findings	17,46	33,33
Poor control of the respondents	31,75	65,08
Doesn't cover all relevant types of individuals	31,75	96,83
weak personal relationships	1,59	98,41
All of the above	1,59	100,00

authors aim at introducing a mathematical model so that the flow of knowledge can be computed. In Campos, Brazdil, and Brito, (2006), an Agent-Based model has been created where links between firms allow for the diffusion of the knowledge among the firms in the network. Therefore, it is possible to measure and follow the evolution of networks and to register the effects of the aggregate knowledge starting from the individual contributions of the distributed agents. In the future, we aim at applying the same methodology to individuals (for example market researchers, or other professionals), that collaborate for Innovation purposes. As a consequence of this, another issue that we aim at exploring in the future is the phenomenon of *emergence*. In the view of Holland (2001 [1975]) and Holland & Miller (1991), emergence is one of the effects of complex systems. The author argues that Multi-Agent organizations are complex systems, and many economic systems can be classified as complex adaptive systems. Such a system is complex in a special sense, because (i) it consists of a network of interacting agents (processes, elements); (ii) it exhibits a dynamic aggregate behaviour that emerges from the individual activities of the agents; (iii) its aggregate behaviour can be described without a detailed knowledge of the individual agents.

CONCLUSION

In conclusion, one can verify that the social network phenomenon is seen by market research professionals in the most diverse industries and businesses as a new market research tool. The Web 2.0 and its collaborative tools bring new approaches and ways of seeing the professionals as social actors, a mechanism which promotes the creation of Distributed Informal Information Systems for Innovation. For the studied sample, one can conclude that: (i) nearly 80% of the respondents use one or more Social Networks

for market research purposes. These numbers indicate the importance and dimension of this phenomenon in which Social Networks are seen as a new market research tools, even though its use is not always consistent; (ii) several Social Networks are used, with clear tendency towards professional networks, namely Linkedin, the most commonly used by Marketing and Information Management professionals; (iii) the professional network Linkedin presents the broadest scope of different uses and it is the most commonly used for Finding Human Resources, which can be easily explained by its own definition: a professional network with over 80 million members (and growing rapidly), which connects people to their trusted contacts and helps you exchange knowledge, ideas, and opportunities with a broader network of professionals.

The main goals pointed out by the professionals in the sample concerning the use of Linkedin are: Idea Generation (27,78%), Concept Testing (13,39%), Product Development (13,39%) and Test Methodology (2,78%); (iv) Social Networks, while market research tools pass up some gaps or weaknesses found in more "traditional" research methodologies. According to the sample studied, Social Networks allow a vision of the consumer as a dynamic entity, inserted in mutually influential groups, providing richer information on the consumers, mainly due to the fact that all data and contents are created by the consumers themselves, rather than by the researchers. On the other hand, there is poor control of the respondents, making the "traditional" control methods completely ineffective translating into fuzzy and not so clear data, making its analysis difficult. The fact that Social Networks do not include all types of relevant audiences is one of the most mentioned disadvantages by the professionals in the sample of this research study. Therefore, this sample is restricted to the groups of consumers that have (a) access to the Internet, (b) some computer skills and (c) are registered in Social Networks;

(v) as mentioned above, the restricted number of answers is a limitation of our study, but taking into account that this convenience-based sampling method was applied to a study that is based on professional networks (not completely opened to a wide audience), the dimension of the sample is to be considered as reasonable.

The use of Social Networks (and social media) allows professionals to create and develop relationships and networks from which they can extract, mash-up and analyze data from several relevant sources, and maintain contact with those sources for long-term useful information for their business, in the same way intranets do inside companies and, therefore, working as DIISI: "(…) the people I follow provide me with more relevant links and information than any other tool." (Business.com, 2009).

Bearing in mind the objectives defined for this study, as well as the results and analysis reported, and considering that the sample has been designed using a convenience methodology, it does not allow us to make any inferences or to take any conclusions for the whole population of market researchers, nor to the Social Networks studied. Anyway, we consider that the goals set were achieved, since it was possible to analyze how Social Networks are being used by our target population for Innovation purposes. Within this community of users, and due to the interaction of the accumulated stock of knowledge emerging at the individual (micro) level, a new DIISI was observed in the sample. In this case, the scope of the DIISI was limited to the sample of market research professionals that use Social Networks for Innovation purposes such as the ones stated by Chadwick (2006) and Day & Schoemaker (2006). In the future, we aim at computing the exchange of knowledge between partners in the networks by introducing a mathematical model.

REFERENCES

Belew, R., & Mitchell, M. (1996), "Introduction", in R. Belew and M. Mitchell (editors), *Adaptive Individuals in Evolving Populations: models and algorithms, Chapter 1, Proceedings volume XXVI*, Santa Fe, CA: Addison Wesley

Business.com (2009): *Business Social Media Benchmarking Study.*

Camarinha-Matos, L., & Afsarmanesh, H. (2004). *Collaborative Networked Organizations - A research Agenda for emerging Business Models.* Springer. doi:10.1007/b116613

Campos, P., Brazdil, P., & Brito, P. (2006). Organizational survival in cooperation networks: the case of automobile manufacturing. In Camarinha-Matos, L., Afsarmanesh, H., & Ol-lus, M. (Eds.), *Network-Centric Collaboration and Supporting Frameworks* (pp. 77–84). Heidelberg: Springer. doi:10.1007/978-0-387-38269-2_8

Chadwick, S. (2006): Client-driven change: The impact of Changes in Client Needs on the Research Industry. *International Journal of Market research 48*, 391–414.

Charron, C., Favier, J., & Li, C. (2006). *Social Computing.* Forrester Research.

Cochran, W. G. (1977). *Sampling Techniques* (3rd ed.). Chichester: Wiley.

Cooke, M., & Buckley, N. (2008): Web 2.0, Social Networks and the Future of Market research. *International Journal of Market research 50*(2).

Day, G. S., & Schoemaker, P. J. H. (2006). *Peripheral Vision: Detecting the Weak Signals that will Break or Make your Company.* Cambridge: Harvard Business School Press.

Ebers, M. (1997). Explaining Inter-Organizational Network Formation. In Ebers, M. (Ed.), *The Formation of Inter-Organizational Networks* (pp. 3–40). New York: Oxford University Press.

Freeman, J. (1982). Organizational life cycles and natural selection processes. In Staw, B., & Cummings, L. (Eds.), *Research in Organizational Behavior* (pp. 1–32). JAI Press Inc.

Giles, J. (2005): Internet Encyclopedias Go Head to Head. *Nature* (December).

Gordon, R. (1991). Innovation, Industrial Networks and High-technology Regions. In Camagni, R. (Ed.), *Innovation Networks: Spatial Perspectives* (pp. 174–195). London: Belhaven Press.

Hakansson, H. (1987). *Industrial Technological Development: a Network Approach.* London: Croom Helm.

Hakansson, H., Havila, V., & Pedersen, A.-C. (1999). Learning in Networks. *Industrial Marketing Management, 28*, 443–452. doi:10.1016/S0019-8501(99)00080-2

Hakansson, H., & Snehota, I. (1995). *Business Networks.* London: Routledge.

Hinttu, S., Fosman, S., & Kock, S. (2004). A network perspective of international entrepreneurship. In Dana, L.-P. (Ed.), *Handbook of research on International Entrepreneurship.* USA: Edward Elgar Publishing Limited.

Holland, J. (2001). *Adaptation in Natural and Artificial Systems - an Introductory Analysis with Applications to Biology, Control and Artificial Intelligence, 6th printing.* The MIT Press. (Original work published 1975)

Holland, J. H., & Miller, J. (1991). Artificial Adaptive Agents in Economic Theory [AEA papers and proceedings]. *The American Economic Review, 81*, 365–370.

Kamann, D. J. F., & Strijker, D. (1991). The Network Approach: concepts and Applications. In Camagni, R. (Ed.), *Innovation Networks: Spatial Perspectives* (pp. 145–172). London: Belhaven Press.

Komninos, N. (2009). Intelligent Cities: towards interactive and Global Innovation Environments. *International Journal of Innovation and Regional Development, 1*(4), 337–355. doi:10.1504/IJIRD.2009.022726

Lamb, R., & Kling, R. (2003). Reconceptualizing Users as Social Actors in Information Systems Research. *Management Information Systems Quarterly, 27*(2), 197–235.

McAfee, A. (2006). Enterprise 2.0: The Dawn of Emergent Collaboration, *MIT Sloan Management Review, 47*(3).

Osterle, H., Fleisch, H., & Alt, R. (2001). *Business Networking - shaping Collaboration between enterprises* (2nd ed.). Berlin, Germany: Springer.

Ratti, R. (1991). Small and Medium-Size Enterprises, Local. Synergies, and Spatial Cycles of Innovation. In Camagni, R. (Ed.), *Innovation Networks: Spatial Perspectives* (pp. 71–88). London: Belhaven Press.

Schelling, T. (1978). *Micromotives and Macrobehaviour.* New York: Norton.

Solé, F., & Valls, J. (1991), "Networks of Technological Cooperation between SMEs: Strategic and Spatial Aspects", in Camagni (ed.) *Innovation Networks: Spatial Perspectives,* (pp. 174-195) London: Belhaven Press

SPSS for Windows. (2007). *Rel. 15.0.* Chicago: SPSS Inc.

Stelzner, M. (2010): *2010 Social Media Marketing Industry Report: how marketers are using social media to grow their businesses.*

Wersching, K. (2005), "Agglomeration in an Innovative and Differentiated Industry with Heterogeneous Knowledge Spillovers", Workshop Regional Agglomeration, growth and multilevel governance: the EU in a comparative perspective", Ghent (Belgium), 24-25 Nov.

Wylie, S. (2009), *Enterprise 2.0: What, Why and How, White paper for the Enterprise 2.0 Conference, Boston, 2009*, Retrieved from: http://www.e2conf.com/whitepaper

Yu, B., Venkatamaran, M., & Singh, M., P. (2003). An adaptive social network for information access: theoretical and experimental issues. *Applied Artificial Intelligence, 17*, 21–38. doi:10.1080/713827056

ENDNOTES

[1] According to Wylie, S. (2009), the premise of Enterprise 2.0 is that the more easily people can communicate – with other workers, team members, customers, vendors, clients – the less information will be siloed. When information is free, people can get more feedback and input (collaborate), react more quickly (agility), and make better decisions. This is the opportunity inherent in Enterprise 2.0: a more efficient, productive and intelligent workforce through the use of participative means such as Social Networks, blogs, open source software, etc..

[2] The survey tool used in this study is eSurveyspro, from Outside Software Inc. (2009), available at www.esurveyspro.com

Chapter 5
Adaptive Learning Cycle to Improve the Competence–Building for Enterprise Systems in Higher Education

Dirk Peters
Carl von Ossietzky Universität Oldenburg, Germany

Liane Haak
Carl von Ossietzky Universität Oldenburg, Germany

Jorge Marx Gómez
Carl von Ossietzky Universität Oldenburg, Germany

ABSTRACT

Higher education institutes like universities cannot ignore the need to teach well known information systems, like ERP systems. Case studies are the most chosen way to introduce the handling of these systems to fulfill the needs of the international employment market and to provide a practical focus within the education. Effective teaching concepts have to improve this situation by considering the pedagogical aspects, which support the individual learning process of each student. This chapter discusses the changes and challenges of enterprise systems in higher education and provides an overview about the learning theory and the actual learning supporting technology as a basis for our concept. The approach considers actual needs of higher education, e.g. present learning in a lab as well as e-Learning courses supported by new methods in technology-enhanced learning by recording students' behavior to guide them through the system. Therefore the authors introduce an Adaptive Learning Cycle which considers tracking and analyzing results deduced with mining methods to improve the learning progress. The aim is to achieve positive influences on the progress of the learning process to build up professional competence.

DOI: 10.4018/978-1-4666-1764-3.ch005

INTRODUCTION

The actual situation in higher education is affected by universities with high drop-out rates, shoestring resources and increasing pressure of competition. Besides, they are fighting with manifold public criticism. Concurrently the change from the industry to a knowledge society enhances the relevance of universities as knowledge imparting institutions. Especially for the productivity of countries like Germany, education is an important factor for future and sustainable development: "The academic system in higher education accomplishes an important and long-lasting effective contribution for the advancement of growth an innovation and therefore for the dealing with the challenges of the demographic and economic change." (German Science Council, 2006). So investments in education have a high Return on Investment. But the increasing amount of students and the enormous costs of this education bare the need to more efficiency and effectiveness in teaching. The classic lecture without the interaction with students has no cheaper alternative, because more interaction causes more effort in time and resources. Individuality and attractive learning offers could be only realized, if they compete in economic aspects. So, high-quality teaching stands in tension with economic aspects. The aim is to receive an increase in productivity of the teaching through the rise of the output (i.e. satisfaction and learning success) under concurrently reduction of the input (teaching effort).

To achieve an acquirement in factual and practical knowledge as well as in specific professional comprehensive competencies, a learning progress with interaction between the instructor and the learner is necessary. But the result is difficult to measure and depends much on the input and engagement of the learner. Both, instructor and learner have to invest in the teaching process, which makes it important to consider the input and output within the learning process. Exemplarily, the usage of multimedia input could be useful from the didactical perspective: different learning types need different learning material or learning environment (Kahiigi, Ekenberg, & Hansson, 2007). Also it offers the possibility to repeat sections, which are not clear and understood yet. And of course this material could be provided independent from time and place, which offers more possibilities for self-directed learning and flexibility for the learner (Zangh, Zhao, Zhou, Jay, & Nunamaker, 2004).

The actual conversion of the degrees to the bachelor and master system following the bologna process and the resulting demand on competence orientation entail new requirements for the higher education system. They contain a change of the objectives in academic teaching from the primary scientific education to a professional oriented competence-building. This requires new teaching and learning forms to build up competence. Basically, academic teaching can be differentiated in three major tasks: the knowledge transfer, the knowledge application, expanding and deepening and the knowledge revision. The offer of praxis-relevant tasks in form of e-Learning or technology-enhanced is mainly focusing on the application and revision of the teaching issues. Internet-based e-Learning systems offer the students the possibility to learn and get practice independent from time and place. This self-directed learning is the most efficient learning (Kerres & Jechle, 2002). An interactive e-Learning-system will provide demanding and interactive practice for the students. The aim should be to utilize the knowledge and to build up problem-solving competence. But the initial euphoria about the potentials of pure e-Learning disappeared (Gabriel, Gersch, Weber, & Venghaus, 2006) and we need methodic foundered instruments of evaluation for specific teaching and learning situations to build up this specific competence.

This contribution introduces an approach for a concept for new learning environments for enterprise systems. The concept focuses on the needs of teaching and learning in higher education institutes. After the motivation, a short introduction in the background of enterprise systems in higher education will be given in the next section, followed by essentials in learning and teaching theory. Afterwards an overview about the state of the art in enterprise system education and the resulting requirements is given before our approach for supporting the learning process using mining technologies is explained in detail. The chapter closes with future research directions and conclusions.

BACKGROUND

After this short introduction of our research approach, we want to describe the relevant technologies and the adjoined topics to enterprise system learning environments in a more detailed way. Therefore we are firstly going to introduce enterprise systems as the domain, which delivers the "content" for learning environments in the higher education institutes. Secondly, we are defining the essentials in the competence-building theory and as the third part of this section we give an overview of the actual state-of-the-art including the existing approaches in teaching Enterprise Systems with focus on ERP systems showing examples like ERPsim, ERPlearn, etc.

ENTERPRISE SYSTEMS IN HIGHER EDUCATION

Business informatics and business information systems deal with the development and application of theories, concepts, models, methods and tools for the analysis, design, and usage of information systems (Kurbel, 2009). Enterprise systems, like enterprise resource planning (ERP) systems represent an automated partly system of a comprehensive operational information system in form of integrated application systems. They support nearly all operational business processes and

are highly complex. Higher education institutes, like universities or universities of applied science, can not ignore the need to teach these well know application and information systems, like ERP systems e.g. Though, interferences and complexity of the different perspectives in computer science, business economics and the technology aspects make teaching and learning quite difficult in this field. Students need to be taught on practically approved systems to develop their own practical experience besides the theoretical lectures. Therefore ES offer the capability for future pedagogic innovation within higher education, which results from the possibilities in illustration, visualization and simulation of business and decision-making processes to students (Ask, Juell-Skielse, Magnusson, Olsen Dag, & Päivärinta, 2008).

The main goal of using enterprise systems, such as ERP systems, Business Intelligence, etc., in higher education is to prepare the students for real work life and to give them practical experience in the application of these technologies. Although many studies have shown that graduates with experience with ERP systems have better chances on the job market (Boyle, 2007; Johnson, Lorents, Morgan, & Ozmun, 2004; Rang, Hohn, & Rühl 2008; Strong, Fedorowicz, Sager, Stewart, & Watson, 2006). Hence, it is not a question anymore, that skills and knowledge in the development and application of enterprise systems are highly recommended and a component of a modern academic education. But especially Strong (2006) has shown in his study, that the successful integration of ERP systems in the actual teaching is not that easy and requires a detailed planning. The different needs of instructor and learner have to be considered as well as the business process context within the systems to achieve a progress in learning.

In order to proof the before mentioned motivation we conducted our own survey within one of our courses at the University of Oldenburg in the winter term in 2009/2010. The main objective of the survey was the empirical analysis of the course quality. Therefore we decided to use formative and summative evaluation methods. The investigated course was the block seminar "Business Intelligence - Data Warehousing" which includes theoretical lectures as well as a practical case study. 48 master students coming from different fields of studies, such as business informatics, informatics and economics, took part in the course and according to that also in the survey.

The "Business Intelligence"-case study (BI case study) that was handed out to the students, was created on the basis of the SAP IDES case studies by a research assistant and improved teacher. The aim of the BI case study in general is to deliver a practical insight into the SAP Business Intelligence (SAP BI) 7.0 component, which is data warehouse-solution of the SAP AG and part of SAP NetWeaver. Case studies are a common way to teach and learn the handling of SAP systems or software systems in general. They are often used to illustrate the theoretical knowledge in a practical case. Furthermore they conduce to the competence promotion of students. Phases of classroom teaching are alternating with phases of independent work of the students with the system. But in our expertise, regarding the execution of case study in several lectures, the SAP IDES case studies meet with criticism by students: They often describe them as "click instructions" and rate their intended learning effect as quite low. The connection between theory and practice is not readily identifiable and the learning matter is forgotten very fast.

Teaching- and Learning-Theory

Learning theories are scientific theories that are needed to clarify, which conditions and which reasons effect processes of learning. In other words: Those theories describe the internal discourses learners use to justify their learning or non-learning in order to decide – as an expression of autonomous action – for or against learning (Müller, 2006). On the other hand, teaching

theories have to be based on learning theories in order to enable meaningful conclusions about instruction, lecturing and teaching at all (Müller, 2006; Weinert, 1996). Teaching theories include common didactic models, but also the more technological discipline of instructional designs. The didactic models as well as the instructional design models are founded more or less on psychological findings. Teaching-learning theories intend to systematize and summarize findings about teaching and learning. They describe conditions for learning and teaching processes. Seeking for general principles for teaching and learning has a long tradition; it already began in the 19th century (Reinmann & Mandl, 2006; Reinmann-Rothmeier & Mandl, 1997). All in all there are three big approaches for explaining teaching and learning: the behaviorism, the cognitivism and the constructivism.

Constructivist Learning Paradigm

With the constructivist approach a fundamental subject-related perspective on learning and teaching entered the whole discussion since the 1980s. This perspective is released from obsolescent conceptions of teaching and learning, as they were in particular carried out by the behaviorism and the cognitivism. Obsolescent conceptions of teaching and learning are mostly based on an objectivist cognitive science. Thus, our world can – at least in basic principles – be described reliably and completely by knowledge. This world exists independently from our own experiences and perceptions, and the knowledge about that world is relative stable.

In contrast, there are subject-related perspectives on teaching and learning (Rebmann, 2001). In those perspectives each individual constructs its own knowledge about the world in its own way. Strictly speaking, it implies, knowledge cannot be submitted from the teacher's head into the learners' heads. But rather, knowledge acquisition respectively learning is a highly individual construction activity: each individual creates its own knowledge based on previous experiences, and in a social context: "Knowledge is socially and interpersonally constructed" (Streibel, 1993). What we call reality is therefore diverse for each individual; it is as different as the previous experiences and social interactions are.

The constructivist approach of learning and teaching emanates from the primacy of construction. Learners are considered as self-directed and self-organized creators of knowledge (Müller, 2006). In other words: the regularities of learning are considered as more or less depending on the learners and their individual differences (Weinert, 1996; Weinert & Helmke, 1995). With this perspective finally the learner is put at the centre of theory building: learners, who construct self-directed their own world and their knowledge about the world. Summarized, with this theoretic understanding learning can be conceptualized as cognitive processes of percipience, making experiences, acquisition and structuring of knowledge, acting and the use of language.

The constructivist learning paradigm leads to shifted roles of teachers and learners. Teachers create learning situations together with learners. That means (Fosnot, 1996; Krüssel, 1996; Rebmann 2001):

- Learners can follow up their own action objectives,
- Processes of negotiating meaning, content and objectives in the learning-teaching-process gain a bigger weight and should be supported therefore in the lecturing,
- Learners take the responsibility for their thinking, knowledge and acting,
- Options to design learning environments should be offered to learners,
- The learners' activity should be demanded,
- Mutual respect and esteem for different constructions of the reality are supported,

- Lecturers and teachers respectively become sensitive for different learning biographies and learning pre-conditions, learners have,
- Lecturers and teachers respectively act like researchers: they ask questions, express and develop opinions and assumptions and evaluate them for its viability,
- Sufficient possibilities for reflections are offered, so that learners learn to observe and evaluate themselves,
- Dialogues and interactions take place,
- The qualified lecturer and teacher respectively should not behave like a know-it-all, but as a "know-it-different".

Following those suggestions for creating learning environments, learners will acquire and develop professional competence. In this context of higher education professional competence means a constructive bundling of single competences that people need to cope with specific job-specifications (Rebmann, Tenfelde, & Uhe, 2005). In the following section a competence model – based on the previously presented learning theory – will be introduced.

Professional Competence

In our understanding six competence dimensions constitute professional competence. They are related in a circular connection (Kastrup & Tenfelde, 2008; Rebmann, Tenfelde, & Uhe, 2005; Rebmann & Tenfelde, 2008; Schlömer, 2008). Due to that circular structure it is not possible to promote only a single competence, professional competence can only be developed as a whole (see Figure 1). The main components of professional competence are the knowledge-competence (know-that), the creative-competence and the social-competence. The methodical-competence (know-how), the moral-ethical-competence and the abstraction-competence bring in bridging

Figure 1. Model of Professional Competence (Rebmann, Tenfelde, & Uhe, 2005).

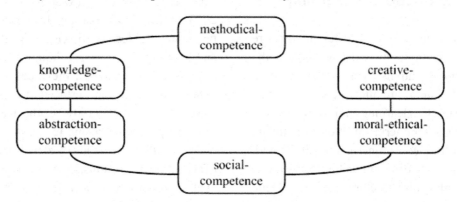

functions: they connect the three components and create the circular structure of the model.

First of all, professional competence means to have knowledge-competence. It includes task-, organization-, process- and workplace-related knowledge (Kauffeld, 2003). Employees develop their individual knowledge-competence by gaining new experiences and connecting them with previous experiences. This cognitive process of construction is marked by individual percipience and experiencing (von Foerster, 1985; Schmidt, 1992). Another important core competence is the creative-competence: it describes the transformation of own ideas and concepts in order to deal with job-specific tasks and issues in business (Kehl, Kunzendorf, & Wolf, 2006). An essential pre-condition for vocational creating is that employees get an appropriate scope for following up their own ideas. The social competence represents the skills for a situation-adequate interaction with other people. Social-competence is expressed in the capacity for teamwork, the ability to cooperate, professional communicative skills and also the ability to solve conflicts (Reetz, 1999).

The methodical-competence (know-how) bridges the knowledge-competence with the creative-competence in the circular model of professional competence. Methodical-competence enables the strategically planned and task-oriented transformation of existing knowledge, behavior patterns and skills when diverse tasks and prob-

lems have to be managed (Jäger, 2001). Through the connection of the creative-competence with the social-competence, the moral-ethical-competence is generated: it is regularly demanded in social contexts when there is a need to solve a problem conjointly. Many companies declare code of conducts that are based on ethical values such as equity, solidarity, responsibility and fairness. Those values offer a normative orientation for employees and they help them to create convincing proposals that make sense for all involved individuals (Lempert, 2002). Finally, the abstraction-competence is a result of bridging social competence with knowledge-competence: firstly, it is expressed as the ability to generalize (abstract) the own knowledge and the own experience in a way that other people can understand it. Secondly, abstraction competence is the ability to understand the conceptions other people bring into a social context, e. g. the context of a common problem-solving.

For the development of professional competence adequate concepts for teaching and learning have to be offered. The above listed suggestions that were derived from the constructivist learning paradigm need to be applied to the specific circumstances, learning environments for enterprise systems demand. In the following chapters the unfolded learning theory will be taken into account.

Technology Supported Learning

Nowadays a large variety of different software systems and technologies exist to support the learning process and its integration. Learning management systems are often the basis systems supporting a modern learning environment (Kuechler, Thissen, & Zimmermann, 2009; Grohmann, Kraemer, Milius, & Zimmermann, 2007) with the aim to integrate different technologies into a common learning infrastructure. Following Helic (2006) learning management systems primarily focus on the management of learning and training processes, distributing the learning content, supporting the learning process, and serving as a shared communication point and interface between the learners and teachers. It allows to fulfill the compliance needs and to manage an efficient education and training process.

Nevertheless there are many dependencies between the possibilities of software-supported learning activities and the reality in learning processes (Leyking et al., 2010). The software products in this field need to fulfill a lot of tasks like analyzing the learning progress and behavior, improving the learning design etc. The dimensions of learning management systems are wide: from learner self-service, training workflow, online learning and assessment to the complete management of the continuous professional education, collaborative learning and training resource management. Due to this, there are in the evolution three generations of learning management systems: monolithic, modular and service (Dagger, 2007).

One actual idea is to make learning management systems more and more open and extensible, allowing developers to integrate new learning functionality and vice versa allowing learning functions to be integrated into employee portal or collaboration systems (Leyking et al., 2010). This approach is based on the service-oriented architecture (SOA) concept and is called service-oriented learning architecture (SOLA) and in-troduced initially 2003 (Westerkamp & Vossen, 2003). While SOA is aligned with the business processes, the idea of SOLA is to align the teaching and learning processes. Although SOLA allows service providers to sell the access to learning content and learning services (Leyking et al., 2010). But focusing only on the teaching and learning processes seems to be so narrow and does not fulfill the needs of actual requirements of academic institutions. Because of this, Leyking et al. (2010) proposed a wider SOA for Learning Architecture and based on this a set of learning management services and it is part of the PROLIX project. Actually it is a first conceptual blueprint, but it is an interesting outlook in future learning management system architectures.

Besides learning management system, technology-enhanced learning (TEL) and e-Learning are terms used when we are talking about how technology supports the learning process. TEL and e-Learning are used in the same way, but there are some differences. E.g. the term of TEL is the wider expression, which means that TEL is focusing on the technological support of any pedagogical approach that utilizes technology. That is maybe one reason why the existing definitions for TEL broadly spread and change continuously due to the dynamic nature of this evolving research field.

Anyway, the definition of TEL must be as general as possible in order to capture all aspects: TEL encompasses virtual and physical technology-enhanced learning environments (incorporating physical learning spaces, institutional virtual learning environments, personalized learning environments and mobile and immersive learning environments). And the aim is to explore and develop effective practice in the delivery of flexible, seamless and personalized services to learners, focusing on the technological interface between the learner and their learning environment. Learning activity consists of learning resources, actions, context, roles and the learning objective to support the learner to his learning goals, respecting individual as well as organizational learning preferences. Technologies play an important role in supporting these activities. That is surely one reason why the European Union support a number of project in this area, e.g. within in the 6th framework the Network of Excellences PROLEARN and Kaleidoscope which have the main objective to have shape the research area around TEL.

Our approach is technology-enhanced and combines several technologies to support the learning progress during the learning process. Besides the consideration of business processes and the functional and technical aspects of the ERP system the learner behavior will be focused. The aim is to introduce a kind of learning life cycle technical supported to improve the learning process constantly.

STATE-OF-THE-ART

Currently, there are several solutions available at the market or as part of actual research interest to transfer the knowledge in the field of enterprise systems in higher education. Some of the most common or maybe successful solutions are introduced in this chapter. After a short description about the main characteristics, the major assets and drawbacks of each solution are discussed.

Software Vendor-oriented Education Programs

Nowadays almost every international software vendor offers education programs or training courses for their software products. This is more popular, when the complexity of these systems is high and the educational training give an advantage in professional life for students. The main idea of companies is to decrease the fear of their complex products and increase the number of users, which are familiar with it. Furthermore, the vendors expect to improve the diffusion rate of

their software products, because today's students can be the decision makers of tomorrow.

One of the most common ERP systems that is used in practice, as well as in teaching at higher education institutes, is the SAP ECC (SAP ERP Central Component) system. Especially for teaching purposes, the German software producer SAP founded the SAP University Alliance (UA) Program, which has nowadays around 270 associated German higher education institutes. According to this number, around 86,000 students are getting in contact with SAP products and solutions within the SAP UA Program only in Germany (Winkelmann, Leyh, & Frick, 2010). Furthermore, the SAP UA Program is cooperating with a lot of other higher education institutes in other countries especially in Europe, the Middle East and Africa (EMEA). In order to support the connected universities or universities of applied sciences with the necessary IT infrastructure, so called University Competence Centers (UCC) were founded, which allow the connection to the SAP systems from an application service provider. In Germany, there is one UCC in Magdeburg and one in Munich. The UCCs are responsible for services, like maintenance and support for the connected institutes.

For educational purposes SAP offers different kinds of learning material (primarily case studies), which help the students or learners to understand the practical handling of the system as well as the underlying integrated business processes. Besides the acquirement of the navigation and process execution at the pre-configured SAP system, the students also gain theoretical knowledge. The case studies are based on a virtual model enterprise called "Internet Demonstration and Evaluation System" (IDES). It contains real-life application data for different business scenarios, such as production planning (IDES-PP) or logistics (IDES-LO) that can be run in the SAP system. Thus, the case studies have realistic characteristics.

Besides these specific case studies, SAP offers random material in form of presentation, documentations, videos or webinars on their developer network platform: the SAP SDN (http://www.sdn.sap.com). This e-Learning platform is based on product details and acts as an exchange platform for the community. Started as a portal for developers, it is actually open to everyone and contains material for beginners as well as for IT professionals.

SAP has a leading role in this area of education, especially the international acting SAP UA Program, which has spread out on each continent. Nevertheless other software vendors like Microsoft offer similar but smaller programs for their ERP system Dynamics NAV or Oracle for the Oracle E-Business Suite to train teachers and students. But at least they all recognize the need for an education offering and provide a more or less specific set of solutions for different education purposes. The most consequent offer is probably the one from SAP who built up an international education network within the SAP UA. They provide worldwide access to the SAP systems for trainings through the University Competence Center. Anyway, the most critical factor in this trainings, material providing and education is maybe the very strong focus on the software product itself. All measures are taken to insure the right usage of the specific software function and an overall focus at the environment and business and process needs is mainly missing.

ERPsim

The ERP Simulation Game (ERPsim) is a Learning by doing-approach to teach ERP concepts. It offers a continuous-time simulation to students, in order to put them into a real business situation by using an existing ERP system. During the execution of business processes the simulation can initiate new actions, on which the learners have to react appropriately. ERPsim was developed by (Léger, 2006) at the Hautes Études Commerciales (HEC) Montreal in Canada in 2004 and its architecture consists substantially of two major components: First of all, there is a regular SAP

ECC 6.0 standard system for real-life transactions and secondly, there is a specially developed Java web application, which initiates specific events in the SAP system. The web application also stores the system of rules, which causes different actions and disturbing factors (Konstantinidis, Kienegger, Wittges, & Krcmar, 2010). This technology allows the creation of realistic interactions between learner and ERP system.

Different business processes (e.g. procurement, production, etc.) can be automatically executed by the simulation depending on the given inputs of the learner. In this way, the learners are able to understand the capacity limitation within the production or delays within a procurement process. As a concrete example, ERPsim can control the demand for a product according to the defined price the learner has chosen. On the basis of this demand, the learner has to plan the procurement and production of needed materials. Through the influence of the environmental factors on which the learners have to react, there is not only practical knowledge imparted. Moreover, additional competencies like soft skills are also needed. In ERPsim the learners have to act independently and are able to assume different roles. On the basis of the results of their reactions, the participants are able to identify the impact of their actions at the system.

In the context of gaining hands-on experience, ERPsim delivers a reasonable extension to an ERP curricular by allowing students to learn about the influences of environmental factors on a real system. It encourages the participants to act in a team with different roles and positions. However, the educational quality is heavily depending on the lecturer and the students need to have a specific degree of basic knowledge in business functions and processes before they can successfully attend to the course.

PROBAS

In comparison to the SAP UA Program and ERP-sim the "Projektseminar betriebswirtschaftliche Anwendungssysteme" (PROBAS) is a concrete ERP course established by the Technical University Ilmenau (Büsch, Nissen, & Schmidt, 2010). The project seminar is an extension to the regular ERP lectures at the university and also focuses on the SAP ECC system. According to the characteristics of a seminar, it imparts competencies in project management, which also includes aspects of soft skills, such as communication, time management and presentation skills. PROBAS involves other associated topics like SAP Business Intelligence (SAP-BI), SAP Process Integration (SAP-PI) and Advanced Business Application Programming (ABAP) with the SAP NetWeaver technology platform. The course is executed by the students in groups and during one semester.

At the beginning of the course, the participants study the basic theoretical knowledge about ERP and SAP systems. In the following, the first exercises are carried out in smaller workshops together with the lecturer. During the semester the groups are working more and more independent. For the practical parts of the course, PROBAS uses mainly case study material, which contains typical business scenarios and a related dataset. Therefore the Technical University Ilmenau operates an own model enterprise in a SAP system including all relevant business processes and data. Besides the competition of explicit tasks within business processes, it also consists of exercises in the field of customizing. Furthermore, in PROBAS different teaching methods are utilized: Through a so called "job rotation" for example, the students are able to understand the process from different perspectives. Each student changes his "job" (role) several times during the semester. The exercises in general, shall impart knowledge through a more independent learning. Moreover, the students are organized in groups, which are well-balanced with respect to their previous knowledge and personal background.

The diversity of the supported teaching and learning methods of the project seminar PROBAS offer several advantages. Besides the theoretical knowledge and the practical hands-on experience with SAP systems, the learner gains knowledge about project management and additional soft skills within the group work. The heterogeneity or balance in the groups assists a lively exchange of knowledge. Due to its structure as a seminar PROBAS doesn't want to deliver an integrated learning environment to its students. It is necessary to have a specific expertise in the field of business information systems and a plenty of experience in teaching this course. The single exercises are not technologically supported by a tool, which could enable the students to follow and organize their learning process by themselves.

ERP-Elearn

In contrary to the before mentioned solution the ERP-ELearn solution is a pure e-Learning based approach. Developed at the University of Applied Science in Osnabrück/Germany it focuses on a web based support in the ERP education (Eiker, Kress, & Mense, 2007). The main idea is to support the student in his repetitions of the course material and the learning at the SAP System independent from place and time. Therefore the ERP-Elearn system was invented to improve the learning on the SAP System.

Basis is the well-known ERP infrastructure given from the University Competence Center in Magdeburg in form of an application service providing solution. Additionally the system is integrated in the open source learning management system StudIP, used at this university of applied science. Together with the installed SAP GUI software on side of the client, i.e. a student's laptop or desktop at home, and an internet connection this is the setting of the environment of this solution.

Besides the content requirements on ERP education, like focusing on extended functions, integration of business processes, data integration issues and the customizing aspects concerning ERP Systems, the approach wants to reach some didactical objectives. Therefore besides the traditional case study material additional reading sections, glossaries, online help and multimedia content like videos are provided within this solution. Short test in form of quiz should help the student to check his knowledge and learning forthcoming and provides a feedback to the teacher about the learning progress.

ERP-Elearn was prototypically implemented at this institution and used in several courses and the afterwards evaluations of the courses were successful and positive. The main difference to the other solutions is first of all that this offer is "only" an additional e-Learning possibility and second that it covers at that status with only 15-16 hours just a small part of the whole course unit. The rest is given in a very traditional way. Therefore the developing cost (approximately 16,000€) and the time for maintenances, i.e. for new software releases, are a high effort for one institution. For this reason a further development and usage in a higher education network is useful and necessary.

REQUIREMENTS ANALYSIS

On the basis of the state-of-the-art and the results coming from our literature review, we want to elaborate the requirements for our concept, which will form the initial point for the intended learning environment. The requirements are coming from two perspectives. At first we need to describe the content which needs to be taught to learners. Due to the specific domain of enterprise systems, these content requirements are concentrating on knowledge coming from the ERP education in general. Secondly, we are going to derive the didacatical aspects in order to meet the requirements of todays higher education learning standards and the changing development in the field of learning with new technologies.

Content Requirements

In the field of enterprise systems we have different learning targets coming from different perspectives. A number of researchers have discussed methods and topics regarding the implementation and the content structure of an ERP curriculum. These relevant skills are the basis for the definition of learning targets in an enterprise systems learning environment. In literature several research results regarding so called "ERP skills" or "required key skills for ERP students" exist. Peslak (2005) for example, proposes a 12-step ERP curriculum, where he defines key skills such as knowledge of different business function, business processes, required hardware and software, reporting functionality of an ERP system, different programming languages and hands-on experience to the ERP navigation. Watson and Schneider (1999) present a KnowDule curriculum to impart knowledge in the field of enterprise systems in general, process-centered systems, ERP planning and implementation, system administration, network resource planning and also an exposure to an ERP programming language like ABAP for example. Furthermore Boyle and Strong (2006) define specific key skills organizations expect from ERP graduates. They conducted a survey on the basis of five, from Lee, Trauth, and Farwell (1995) adapted categories of ERP skills, which are ERP Technical Knowledge, Technology Management Knowledge, Business Functional Knowledge, Interpersonal Skills and Team Skills and Knowledge. In order to determine these ERP skills in a quantitative way, they involved IT specialists to measure the importance of single competencies coming from these five categories.

On the basis of the above mentioned literature review and in combination with the results coming from the state-of-the-art of existing solutions available at the market, we determined the content requirements for an enterprise system learning environment. Due to the fact, that we don't want to establish another suggestion for an

ERP curriculum, we are focusing on the content requirements, which can be met by an adaptive, hands-on enterprise system learning environment. These requirements are the following:

Business Functional Knowledge: According to Boyle and Strong (2006) detailed knowledge of traditional business functions (accounting, finance, human resources, etc.) is still a critical factor. Furthermore, in their survey they figured out, that the ability to understand the business environment and the ability to interpret business problems are also relevant in the ERP context.

Business Process Knowledge: How the business functions are adapted to business processes in an information system is another important criterion. "By focusing on business processes, rather than on specific business functions, students can gain an understanding of the complex relationships between the various business functions and how these relationships impact business decision making in general" (Boyle & Strong, 2006, p. 109). Related skills to this domain are business process design, modeling and implementation (Becerra-Fernandez, Murphy, & Simon, 2000) and the possibility to focus on business processes but use the ERP system to assist in the presentation of information and skills development (Hawking & McCarthy, 2000).

Role Concepts: Business processes, which are implemented in an ERP system, have several people involved. In order to understand a complete business processes and the impact of its single tasks on other business areas, it is necessary to teach the underlying role concepts. This is according to the Multiple Perspectives, as a part of the following didactical requirements. Typical roles in an ordering process can be telephone operator, warehouse clerk and accountant.

Integration Aspects: Besides the knowledge of business functions and processes it is also necessary to have the ability to integrate across business functions (areas: accounting, finance, marketing, information systems, operations, and management) (Becerra-Fernandez, Murphy, & Simon, 2000). These integration aspects can be in connection with the role concepts, if there are different responsibilities between business functions, which are mapped to concrete roles within an ERP system.

Technical Knowledge: Ranked with the lowest group mean among the five skill categories in the survey of Boyle and Strong (2006), a learning environment also needs to impart knowledge of systems analysis, systems design and data management (e.g. data modeling). Other researches emphasize the necessity of knowledge transfer in the field of enterprise computing architectures, process management and systems development and information abstraction, representation, and organization (Hawking & McCarthy, 2000).

Technology Knowledge: Boyle (2007) argues that three key areas of ERP systems (mySAP ERP in his specific case) have to be considered as emerging technologies for IT students. This knowledge of technologies would be a key skill for future ERP developers and therefore also an important content requirement for a learning environment. These technologies are Netweaver (including the creation of web portals and the linkage of separate system with single sign-on), Customer Relationship Management (CRM) and Business Warehouse (BW).

Navigation and Handling: The instruction or training in a particular ERP system (Hawking & McCarthy, 2000) is a major content requirement. In connection with the didactical requirements (Learning by Doing) it is necessary, the offer the learners a hands-on experience with ERP systems. Therefore they need knowledge of the navigation possibilities within a specific ERP system.

Personal/Interpersonal Knowledge: Besides the domain knowledge in the field of business functions, business processes and its integration aspects in connection with the role concepts, there are several soft skills an ERP learner needs to have. On the personal side these are system-thinking skills, problem-solving skills, critical-thinking skills, risk-taking skills, personal-discipline skills, persistence, and curiosity. On the interpersonal side there are collaborative skills, conflict resolution skills and communication skills (oral, written, listening, and group) (Hawking & McCarthy, 2000). Boyle and Strong (2006) and Lee, Trauth, and Farwell (1995) also discuss abilities which correspond to the above mentioned (ability to accomplish assignments, ability to deal with uncertainty, etc.).

Team Skills and Knowledge: Moreover, Lee, Trauth, and Farwell (1995) identified additional team skills and knowledge such as the ability to work cooperatively in a team environment and the ability to work in a collaborative environment. Boyle and Strong (2006) evaluated, that the ability to plan and lead projects is also relevant in the field of teaching enterprise systems.

Didactical Requirements

In independence of the learning content it is also necessary to think about the didactical perspective and the resulting didactical requirements of an intended learning environment. In accordance to the constructivist learning approach (section 2.2.1), we identified the following list of requirements (Mandl, Gruber, & Renkel, 2002):

Learning by Doing: One of the most important requirements from a didactical perspective is the necessity of a practical education and knowledge transfer of the learning content. Therefore the intended learning environment has to allow an experimental exploration to the learner. The practical work has to be integrated into an ERP system or enterprise system in general. Hands-on working in realistic situations serves the acquirement of professional decision-making and responsibility.

Authenticity: The learning environment has to be designed in the way, that it offers the learner the contact with realistic, job-relevant problems and authentic situations. Authenticity ensures an applied approach in the learning context.

Case-based and Problem-oriented Learning: Authenticity can be reached through case-based or problem-based learning. Thus, the starting point of the learning process should be a complex, interesting, intrinsic problem, which motivates the learner to deal with the subject and inspires him/her to solve the problem.

Multiple Perspectives: The learning environment should provide the possibility to adopt different perspectives with a view to the ERP system (user-, consultant-, developer- and analyst perspective). From these different points of view the learner gains a higher flexibility to apply the new knowledge.

Structuring: In order to prevent the learner against disorientation, elements of knowledge and learning units have to be prepared in a structural way.

Differentiation: The learning environment should be able to deliver differentiated learner assistance due to individual learning status, learning speeds and learning strategies. Furthermore, it should deliver variable learning paths in order to bring forward each individual learner.

Self-Control: The learn processes should be organized in a self-controlled and self-organized way. This means that the learner, as the initiator and organizer of his own learn process is able to control basic decisions about if, what, when and whereupon he/she learns. These decisions seriously affect the success of the learning environment (Weinert, 1982; Deithering, 1995; Müller 2006).

Learning by Demand/Instructional Support: However, self-controlled learning doesn't mean that the learning is carried out autonomously and without any assistance from the outside. The learning in a higher educational context is often self- and externally controlled. Konrad and Traub (1999) describe the "absolute autonomy" (self-controlled learning) and the "entire external control" (externally controlled learning) as extremes wherein the learners range in between. Therefore the learning environment has to support the learn process with the allocation of the needed information, in the case of the learner needs assistance for solving a specific problem.

Social Interaction: Within the intended learning environment a social and cooperative learning and problem solving should be possible. The constructivist learning paradigm also shows how important dialogues and interactions are (Fosnot, 1996; Krüssel, 1996; Rebmann, 2001).

Motivation: The design of the learning environment should promote the learners to an active participation with the learning content.

Visualization: The illustration of complex and dynamic relationships should be supported by animations, simulations, pictures, models or videos.

Orientation towards the Future: The learning environment should contain trendsetting technologies such as e-Learning or web 2.0 applications (wikis, podcasts, weblogs, etc.).

These didactical requirements for a learning environment in the field of enterprise systems of higher education can be enriched by criteria coming from additional requirements of multimedia-based learning environments in general (Mandl, Gruber, & Renkel, 2002):

Multiple Contexts: In order to ensure a flexible handling with the new gained knowledge, the knowledge should be transferred to other contexts as well. Therefore, the intended learning environment should be able to offer multiple contexts, where specific content can be embedded into different scenarios.

Articulation: Problem solution processes should be articulated and reflected, so that learners learn to observe and evaluate themselves.

After defining these requirements from the content and didactical perspective, we are going to present our concept of an Adaptive Learning Cycle, which builds the basis for a future architecture of an enterprise system learning environment.

CONCEPT OF AN ADAPTIVE LEARNING CYCLE

As already introduced in the first parts of this contribution, the focus of the new approach is primarily on the learner itself. This learner-oriented view assumes that an improved learning environment is based on the individual and his specific qualification (cf. Peters, Haak, & Marx Gómez, 2010). This approach describes an adaptive learning environment based on the concept of an Adaptive Learning Cycle (ALC), which is visualized in Figure 2. The basic idea of the concept for an adaptive learning environment comes from Brusilovsky's Adaptive Hypermedia Systems-approach (Brusilovsky, 1996). Within the ALC, exercises and tasks are adapted to the individual state of the learner under the consideration of the before mentioned content and didactical requirements.

The ALC is subdivided into four areas: Initially, it starts with the tracking of the learner's behavior or his interaction with the system. Corresponding to the Learning by doing requirement

Figure 2. Adaptive Learning Cycle

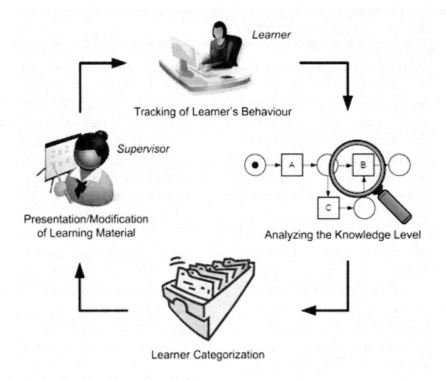

the tracking is executed while he is performing a specific task directly at the system. On the basis of the information coming from the tracing algorithm, it is possible to analyze the learner's behavior and derive some detailed information about his way of interaction, the knowledge level, strengths and weaknesses or general information about the learner and his familiarity with the system. This leads to a categorization of the learner as a result of the analyzing phase. Depending on the assigned category, the learning material can be modified by an advising entity (a lecturer e.g.) and presented to the learner. The content depends on the desired learning target, which needs to be defined before starting the lecture. The effectiveness of this new advisement of learning content can also be measured by our intended learning system. More precisely, the success of the new modified learning material, which was presented to the learner, can be analyzed via a second run through the ALC. If applicable,

a new categorization of the learner can be made. Every single step of the ALC is described in more detail in the following subsections.

Tracking the Learner's Behavior

The tracking of learner's behavior is the initial phase of the ALC-concept. Here, the learner is performing a specific exercise according to his exercise in the system. Following the results of the requirements analysis, it is important that the learner acts in his working environment in order to maintain a familiar working and also learning atmosphere. The exercise can be a single task within a broader business scenario context, like executing a transaction in a SAP ERP-system for example. The content of the learning material has also to be defined in accordance to the content requirements, which were discussed before.

Regarding the way of tracking the learner's interaction with the system, there are several techniques existing. The most obvious solution is the logging of transaction data via trace-files and protocols. Most systems already deliver this possibility more or less. In a SAP R/3-system for example, a huge amount of data is collected while the system is used. In so-called user-trace-files detailed information (e.g. name of the performing user, transaction codes, input values, time duration, etc.) about the performed interaction between the user and the system is stored. This allows to deduce detailed information concerning the learner's interaction with the system. (Kassem, 2007) uses this technique in the Application Usage Mining (AUM)-approach. In his work, he achieves an optimization of business processes on the basis of the described tracking information. Hence, his focus is on the identification of unused business processes in an enterprise system in order to optimize them. This approach can be modified for the specific content and didactical requirements in an educational context as well.

Analyzing the Knowledge Level

The biggest challenge is, to find out the individual state of each learner in order to categorize these types for a most effective learner support. Therefore, the tracking information from the previous step has to be analyzed in a meaningful way. The superior aim of the analyzing phase is to find out meaningful information about the knowledge level of the learner on basis of his transaction data. In this field a widespread experience regarding mining techniques exists. Some of these techniques, which play an important role within the ALC-context, will be explained in the following. Data Mining is the major discipline for generating information or detecting patterns in a huge amount of unstructured and raw data (Peterson, 2005). The use of this information is depending on the domain in which the Information is needed. Data Mining is the basis of all mining technologies, but in the field of higher education, it is necessary to take different specific mining technologies into account.

Process Mining is one specific area of Data Mining and aims on process knowledge in general. Therefore, Process Mining extracts data, which describes the execution of processes in order to store, transfer and reuse the process knowledge in form of models or schemas (Schimm, 2003). A very close related technique to Process Mining is the method of Workflow Mining. It is used to control, optimize, execute and monitor business processes (zur Mühlen, 2005). As an example, enterprises often run different business processes which are not really needed in practice. Via Workflow Mining these processes can be identified and displace or changed. In contrast to this, some other business processes which are used very frequently can also be identified with Workflow Mining and optimized later on (Remberg, 2009). All these processes can be identified from transaction data or event logs of an enterprise software system in order to generate the described effects. An approach which aims on the identification and optimization of business process in an enterprise is the already mentioned AUM-approach by Kassem. Data, Process and Workflow Mining are not directly addressed to the field of analyzing the knowledge level of a learner. They can only help with the identification of patterns in unstructured data belonging to different application areas. Therefore, other approaches have to be taken into account. One idea, which deals with educational data, is the Educational Data Mining (EDM). It is used to convert raw data from educational systems like interactive learning environments, computer-supported collaborative learning or administrative data from schools and universities, to meaningful information to better understand the learner. This emerging discipline is primarily used by educational software developers, learners, teachers, parents and other educational researchers (Baker, Barnes, & Beck, 2008).

Learner Categorization

For the learner categorization, as the third step in our ALC, the usage of different mining techniques is not sufficient enough. The challenge for the categorization is to integrate the intended learning target of the actual task the learner performs in the system into the applied mining technique, like EDM for example. Therefore the target state of the learning process has to be compared with the results of the analysis of the learner's interaction (actual state). In this phase it is possible to consider other information than just the tracking information. The categorization can also depend on the specific university program the student takes part in. So, several contexts playing a role in this categorization phase, which have an effect for the future execution of his learning progress.

Modification of the Learning Material

The result of the categorization phase will affect the future learning material, which is presented to the learner. Because of the adaptive individuality of this approach, the learning material is specific to each learner. According to the category, the learner has been classified before, the following tasks are more or less difficult then the task assigned before or coming from another context. Especially in this phase of the ALC the advising entity, like a supervisor, lecturer or teacher, can influence the assignment of tasks. For example, if the majority of the learners were categorized on a very low knowledge level, the lecturer has to rethink the initial curricular situation. This can lead to the necessity of an additional theoretical discussion or lecture in order to respond to specific shortfalls of the students. Furthermore, the way how the learning material is presented can be influenced by the lecturer as well. The adequacy of the presented learning material or future tasks can be measured in the following analysis within the ALC with regard to the state of the learners. If the learning material was adequate, the next categorization will provide information of a successful knowledge increase. The learning material itself is following the content and didactical requirements as described in section four.

FUTURE RESEARCH DIRECTIONS

After identifying the major requirements for an intended enterprise system learning environment, a concept on how these requirements could be integrated into a future learning system were introduced. The further research directions will be, to think about an architectural design of an enterprise system learning environment, which meets the discovered requirements in accordance to the presented ALC concept. Therefore it is necessary, to define concrete components of this architecture and to describe how these components are interconnected. After the architectural design, technical requirements can be defined for a first prototypical implementation. On the basis of this prototype, some evaluations can be executed in order to measure the success of the proposed idea. These evaluations in form of surveys for example, can be carried out in the higher education context at a university. After a critical reflection of the results, the architecture and its components may be corrected in accordance to the occuring problems. Finally, the evaluated architecture of the enterprise system learning environment and its prototype can be introduced into a real curriculum in order to let students benefit from the research results.

CONCLUSION

Enterprise systems are an important part of the actual curricula in higher education institutes. Therefore a professional oriented competence-building is one of the major challenges universities and universities of applied sciences are facing today. But enterprise systems like ERP systems are also highly complex software products and have a variety of specific educational needs. An adequate education requires, besides good trained teachers and actual materials, specific environments, and business and process knowledge.

Within this chapter we introduced our approach about an adaptive learning cycle for enterprise systems in higher education. After a short reflection of the actual situation in the field of higher education institutes in the introduction, we pointed out the background of our concept. Therefore we introduced to the fields of enterprise systems, teaching and to the area of learning theories and technology supported learning. Based on this, the state of the art is given in the next section. Hereby, different actual approaches and scenarios used for the teaching on ERP systems and their differences are presented and their lacks and advantages are given. Consequently followed from the section requirements, content and didactical requirements for a modern teaching and learning approach are differentiated and are forming the basis of our main concept, the Adaptive Learning Cycle, which is in detail explained in the forthcoming section. The chapter finally closes with an outlook to future research directions and these conclusions.

In our research, we found out that there are new needs for teaching and learning and new requirements for the higher education system at all. A professional oriented competence-building is one of the major challenges universities and universities of applied sciences are facing today. On this problem, we developed the introduced the Adaptive Learning Cycle, which describes the concept of our idea and contains an approach how exercises and tasks are adapted to the individual state of the learner. Using the learners' behavior to get an overview of his results and status allows the teacher to provide more specific help, i.e. through specific exercise. Additionally modern media could be used to annotate the material in a proper way. Considering the business process behind the case study or learning material gives the learner an overall advantage in process knowledge. Finally the teacher has a basis for the improvement of the learning material because he knows based on the results of the tracking where are the most critical points in the material, which steps are not clear and lead the learner in the wrong direction. This feedback is possible during the learning process and as a summary at the end.

For future research we focus on the conception and realization of a technical solution of this approach. The idea is to implement an adaptive learning environment using the before mentioned parts of the Adaptive Learning Cycle. This interactive software product could be used in different learning contexts and would be a revolutionary solution in the enterprise system education. Our research has shown that the needs for a new teaching and learning approach is ripe for a change and necessary to fulfill the needs of the nowadays enterprises and of the students.

REFERENCES

Ask, U., Juell-Skielse, G., Magnusson, J., Olsen Dag, H., & Päivärinta, T. (2008). Enterprise Systems as Vehicles of Pedagogic Innovation - Enterprise System Inclusion in Higher Education. *Proceedings of the 5th International Conference on Enterprise Systems, Accounting and Logistics (5th ICESAL '08)*, 7-8 July 2008, Crete Island, Greece.

Baker, R. S. J. d., Barnes, T., & Beck, J. E. (Eds.). (2008). Educational Data Mining 2008: 1st International Conference on Educational Data Mining. *Proceedings*, Montreal, Quebec, Canada.

Becerra-Fernandez, I., Murphy, K., & Simon, S. (2000). Integrating ERP in the business school curriculum. Association for Computing Machinery. *Communications of the ACM, 43*(4), 39–41. doi:10.1145/332051.332066

Boyle, T. A. (2007). Technical-Oriented Enterprise Resource Planning (ERP): Body of Knowledge for Information Systems Programs: Content and Implementation. *Journal of Education for Business*, (May/June): 267–274. doi:10.3200/JOEB.82.5.267-275

Boyle, T. A., & Strong, S. E. (2006). Key Skills Organizations Expect from ERP Graduates. Proceedings of the 2006 Conference, Production and Operations Management Division. *Administrative Sciences Association of Canada, 27*(7), 109-124.

Brusilovsky, P. (1996). Methods and Techniques of Adaptive Hypermedia. *User Modeling and User-Adapted Interaction, 6*(2-3), 87–129. doi:10.1007/BF00143964

Büsch, S., Nissen, V., & Schmidt, L. (2010). Praxisnahe und effiziente ERP-Ausbildung am Beispiel der TU Ilmenau. In M. Schumann, L. M. Kolb, M. H. Breitner, & A. Frerichs (Eds.), *Multikonferenz Wirtschaftsinformatik 2010 [Multi-Industry Computer Science Conference, 2010]* (pp. 1697-1708). Göttingen: Universitätsverlag.

Dagger, D. (2007). Service oriented e-Learning platforms: From monolithic systems to flexible services. *IEEE Internet Computing, 11*(3), 28–35. doi:10.1109/MIC.2007.70

Deithering, F. G. (1995). *Selbstgesteuertes Lernen* [Self-directed learning.]. Göttingen: Verlag für Angewandte Psychologie.

Eicker, S., Kress, S., & Mense, L. (2007). ERP-ELearn – e-Learning für ERP-Systeme im Hochschulbetrieb am Beispiel von SAP R/3. In Breitner, M., Bruns, B., & Lehner, F. (Eds.), *Neue Trends im E-Learning* [New Trends in E-Learning]. (pp. 59–74). Physica. doi:10.1007/978-3-7908-1922-9_5

Fosnot, C. T. (1996). Constructivism: A Psychological Theory of Learning. In Fosnot, C. T. (Ed.), *Constructivism: Theory, Perspectives and Practice* (pp. 8–33). New York: Teachers College Press.

Gabriel, R., Gersch, M., Weber, P., & Venghaus, C. (2006). Blended Learning Engineering: Der Einfluss von Lernort und Lernmedium auf Lernerfolg und Lernzufriedenheit - Eine evaluationsgestützte Untersuchung. [The influence of place of learning and learning medium of learning success and learning satisfaction - An evaluation based study] In Breitner, M. (Ed.), *Technologiebasiertes Lehren und Lernen* [Technology-based teaching and learning]. Passau.

German Science Council. 2006 (Wissenschaftsrat (2006)) Empfehlungen zum arbeitsmarkt- und demographiegerechten Ausbau des Hochschulsystems. [Recommendations to the labor market and demographic requirements of the expanding higher education system], Berlin: Wissenschaftsrat.

Grohmann, G., Kraemer, W., Milius, F., & Zimmermann, V. (2007). Modellbasiertes Curriculum-Design für Learning Management Systeme: Ein Integrationsansatz auf Basis von ARIS und IMS Learning Design. [Model-Based Curriculum Design for Learning Management Systems: An approach to integration based on ARIS and IMS Learning Design] In A. Oberweis, C. Weinhardt, H. Gimpel, A. Koschmieder, V. Pankratius, & B. Schnitzler (Eds.), *Tagungsband 8. Internationale Konferenz Wirtschaftsinformatik* [Proceedings of 8th International Conference economy computer science,], Karlsruhe.

Hawking, P., & McCarthy, B. (2000). Industry Collaboration: A Practical Approach for ERP Education. *Australasian Conference on Computer science education. 8*, 129-133.

Helic, D. (2006). *A Didactics-Aware Approach to Management of Learning Scenarios in E-Learning Systems*. Graz University of Technology.

Jäger, P. (2001). Der Erwerb von Kompetenzen als Konkretisierung der Schlüsselqualifikationen, [*The acquisition of skills as a specification of the key skills*] Universität Passau.Retrieved from: http://www.opus-bayern.de/uni-passau/voll-texte/2003/17/pdf/jaeger.pdf [24.02.2010]

Johnson, T., Lorents, A. C., Morgan, J., & Ozmun, J. (2004). A Customized ERP/SAP Model for Business Curriculum Integration. *Journal of Information Systems Education, 15*(3), 245–253.

Kahiigi, E., Ekenberg, L., & Hansson, M. (2007). Exploring the e-Learning State of art. *Proceedings of the Conference on E-Learning.*

Kassem, G. (2007). *Application Usage Mining.* Aachen: Grundlagen und Verfahren. Shaker Verlag.

Kastrup, J., & Tenfelde, W. (2008). *Werkstattbericht Lern- und Testaufgaben für die Konstruktion von Lehr-Lernarrangements und die Diagnose von Kompetenzentwicklung im Modellversuch Ha-BiNa* [Workshop report, learning and assessment tasks for the design of teaching-learning arrangements and the diagnosis of skills development in the pilot HaBiNa], Universität Hamburg, URL: http://www.habina.de/files/downloads/Werkstatt-bericht%201_Endversion.pdf [14.02.2010]

Kauffeld, S. (2003). Weiterbildung: eine lohnende Investition in die berufliche Zukunft? [Training: a worthwhile investment in their future careers?] In A. Frey, R. S. Jäger, & U. Renold (Eds.), *Kompetenzmessung – Sichtweisen und Methoden zur Erfassung und Bewertung von beruflichen Kompetenzen [*Measuring competence - perspectives and methods for evaluation and assessment of professional competence], (pp. 176–195) Landau: Empirische Pädagogik Verlag.

Kehl, V., Kunzendorf, M., & Wolf, M. (2006). Die berufliche Handlungskompetenz im Zeichen visualisierter Arbeitskontexte. [The professional competence in work contexts visualized characters] In Ott, B. (Ed.), *Eigene Kompetenzen erkennen und fördern* [Own skills to recognize and promote]. (pp. 47–70). ChangeX-Edition, Erding.

Kerres, M., & Jechle, T. (2002). Didaktische Konzeption des Telelernens. [Instructional design of telelearning] In Issing, L. J., & Klimsa, P. (Eds.), *Information und Lernen mit Multimedia und Internet* [Information and learning with multimedia and Internet]. (pp. 267–281). Weinheim: BeltzPVU.

Konrad, K., & Traub, S. (1999). *Selbstgesteuertes Lernen in Theorie und Praxis* [Self-directed learning in theory and practice]. München: Oldenbourg Verlag.

Konstantinidis, C., Kienegger, H., Wittges, H., & Krcmar, H. (2010). Planspiele in der ERP-Lehre: Eine empirische Untersuchung deutscher Bildungseinrichtungen.[Simulation games in ERP Education: An Empirical Investigation of German educational institutions.] In M. Schumann, L. M. Kolb, M. H. Breitner, & A. Frerichs (Eds.), *Multikonferenz Wirtschaftsinformatik 2010 [Multi-Industry Computer Science Conference, 2010]* (pp. 1709-1721). Göttingen: Universitätsverlag.

Krüssel, H. (1993). *Konstruktivistische Unterrichtsforschung [Constructivist teaching research].* Frankfurt am Main: Lang.

Krüssel, H. (1996). Unterricht als Konstruktion. [Lessons as a design] In Voß, R. (Ed.), *Die Schule neu erfinden* [Reinventing the School]. (pp. 92–104). Luchterhand, Neuwied.

Kuechler, T., Thissen, D., & Zimmermann, V. (2009). Into the great wide open: Responsive Learning Environments for Personalised Learning. In O'Donoghue, J. (Ed.), *Technology Supported Environment for Personalised Learning: Methods and Case Studies.* London: IGI Global.

Kurbel, K. (2009). Das Studium der Wirtschaftsinformatik. [The study of the computer science industry] In Kurbel, K., Brenner, W., Chamoni, P., Frank, U., Mertens, P., & Roithmayer, F. (Eds.), *Studienführer Wirtschaftsinformatik 2009/2010* [Business computer science study guide 2009/2010]. (pp. 17–23). Wiesbaden: Gabler. doi:10.1007/978-3-8349-8057-1_3

Lee, D., Trauth, E., & Farwell, D. (1995). Critical skills and knowledge requirements of IS professionals: A Joint Academic/Industry Investigation. *Management Information Systems Quarterly, 19*(3), 313–340. doi:10.2307/249598

Léger, P.-M. (2006). Using a Simulation Game Approach to Teach ERP Concepts. *Journal of Information Systems Education, 17*(4), 441–447.

Lempert, W. (2002). Prinzipien der Auswahl, Entwicklung und Verwendung moralischer Dilemmata als Materialien für die berufliche und berufspädagogische Aus- und Weiterbildung, [Principles of selection, development and use of moral dilemmas as materials for the professional and vocational education and training] *Zeitschrift für Berufs- und Wirtschaftspädagogik, 98* [Journal of Vocational and Business Education], 330-353.

Leyking, K., Angeli, R., Faltin, N., Giorgina, F., Martin, G., Siberski, W., & Zimmermann, V. (2010). Towards an Open SOA for Learning Management. In Schumann, M., Kolbe, L. M., Breitner, M. H., & Frerichs, A. (Eds.), *Multikonferenz Wirtschaftsinformatik 2010* [Multi-industry computer science conference]. (pp. 355–368). Universitätsverlag Göttingen.

Mandl, H., Gruber, H., & Renkl, A. (2002). Situiertes Lernen in multimedialen Lernumgebungen. [Situated learning in multimedia learning environments] In Issing, L. J., & Klimsa, P. (Eds.), *Information und Lernen mit Multimedia und Internet* [Information and Learning with Multiedia and the Internet]. (pp. 139–148).

Müller, K. R. (2006). Berufliches Lernen und Lerntheorie. [Vocational learning and learning theory] In Kaiser, F.-J., & Pätzold, G. (Eds.), *Wörterbuch Berufs- und Wirtschaftspädagogik* [Dictionary of Professional and Business Education]. 2nd ed., pp. 86–89). Klinkhardt, Bad Heilbrunn.

Peslak, A. (2005). A twelve-step, multiple course approach to teaching enterprise resource planning. *Journal of Information Systems Education, 16*(2), 147–155.

Peters, D., Haak, L., & Marx Gómez, J. (2010). Learner-oriented Approach for Enterprise Systems in Higher Education using TEL-based Concepts. In J. Cordeiro (Ed.), *Proceedings of the 2nd International Conference on Computer Supported Education* (pp. 521-526), INSTICC Press, Setúbal, Portugal.

Peterson, H. (2005). *Data Mining. Verfahren, Prozesse, Anwendungsarchitektur*. Oldenbourg. doi:10.1524/9783486593334

Rang, M., Hohn, B., & Rühl, O. (2008). *Wirtschaftswissenschaftler: Neue Chancen auf dem Europäischen Arbeitsmarkt?* [Economists: New Opportunities in the European labor market?]. (pp. 283–287). Wirtschaftsstudium. [Business studies]

Rebmann, K. (2001). *Planspiel und Planspieleinsatz* [Simulation and simulation applications]. Hamburg: Kovac.

Rebmann, K., & Tenfelde, W. (2008). *Betriebliches Lernen* [Workplace learning]. München: Hampp.

Rebmann, K., Tenfelde, W., & Uhe, E. (2005). *Berufs- und Wirtschaftspädagogik* [Vocational and Business Education]. Wiesbaden: Gabler.

Reetz, L. (1999). Zum Zusammenhang von Schlüsselqualifikationen – Kompetenzen – Bildung. [On the relationship of key skills - skills – Education] In Tramm, T., Sembill, D., Klauser, F., & John, E. G. (Eds.), *Professionalisierung kaufmännischer Berufsausbildung* [Professional commercial training]. (pp. 32–51). Frankfurt am Main: Lang.

Reinmann, G., & Mandl, H. (2006). Unterrichten und Lernumgebungen gestalten. [Teaching and learning environments.] In Krapp, A., & Weidenmann, B. (Eds.), *Pädagogische Psychologie* [educational Psychology]. 5th ed., pp. 613–658). Weinheim: Beltz.

Reinmann-Rothmeier, G., & Mandl, H. (1997). Lehren im Erwachsenenalter.[Lessons in adulthood.] In F.E. Weinert, & H. Mandl (Eds.), *Psychologie der Erwachsenenbildung* [Psychology of Adult Education] 4 (pp.355-403). Hogrefe, Göttingen.

Remberg, J. (2009). *Grundlagen des Process* [Fundamentals of Process]. Mining. GRIN Verlag.

Schimm, G. (2003). Mining most specific Workflow Models from Event-based Data. In W. van der Aalst, A. ter Hofstede, & M. Weske (Eds.), *Proceedings of the International Conference BPM* (pp. 25-40), Springer-Verlag, Berlin.

Schlömer, T. (2008). Die Sustainability Balanced Scorecard als Lerngegenstand in der Berufsbildung für eine nachhaltige Entwicklung. [The Sustainability Balanced Scorecard as a learning object in professional education for sustainable development.] In Duensing, M., Schwithal, T., & Tredop, D. (Eds.), *Kapital, Kompetenz, Konflikte* [Capital, expertise, conflicts]. (pp. 175–193). Oldenburg: BIS.

Schmidt, S. J. (1992). *Der Kopf, die Welt, die Kunst. Konstruktivismus als Theorie und Praxis* [The head, the world of art. Constructivism as a theory and practice]. Wien: Böhlau.

Streibel, M. J. (1993). Queries About Computer Education and Situated Critical Pedagogy. *Educational Technology, 33*(3), 22–26.

Strong D. M., Fedorowicz J., Sager J., Stewart G., & Watson E. (2006). Teaching with Enterprise Systems. *Communications of AIS*, (17), article 33.

Unterrichts. [Self-directed learning as a prerequisite, method and aim of teaching] *Unterrichtswissenschaft*, [Teaching Science] *10*(2), 99-110.

Von Foerster, H. (1985). *Sicht und Einsicht* [Perspective and insight]. Braunschweig: Vieweg.

Vossen, G., & Westerkamp, P. (2003). E-learning as a web service. In *7th International Database Engineering and Applications Symposium (IDEAS 2003)* (pp. 242-249). IEEE Computer Society.

Weinert, F. E. (1982). *Selbstgesteuertes Lernen als Voraussetzung*. Methode und Ziel des.

Weinert, F. E. (1996). Lerntheorien und Instruktionsmodelle. [Learning theories and instructional models] In Weinert, F. E. (Ed.), *Psychologie des Lernens und der Instruktion* [Psychology of learning and instruction]. (pp. 1–48). Göttingen: Hogrefe.

Winkelmann, A., Leyh, C., & Frick, N. (2010). ERP-Systeme in der Lehre - ein vergleichendes hochschulübergreifendes Seminar mit mittelgroßen ERP-Systemen. [ERP systems in education - a comparative inter-university seminar with medium-sized ERP systems.] In Schumann, M., Kolb, L. M., Breitner, M. H., & Frerichs, A. (Eds.), *Multikonferenz Wirtschaftsinformatik 2010* [Multi-industry computer science conference]. (pp. 1625–1636). Göttingen: Universitätsverlag.

Zhang, D., Zhao, J. L., Zhou, L., Jay, F., & Nunamaker, J. (2004). Can e-learning replace classroom learning? *Communications of the ACM, 47*(5), 75–79. doi:10.1145/986213.986216

ADDITIONAL READING SECTION

Adelsberger, H., Bick, M., Kraus, U., & Pawlowski, J. (1999). A simulation game approach for efficient education in enterprise resource planning systems. *Proceedings of the European Simulation Multiconference*. Warschau, Poland.

Back, A., Bendel, O., & Stoller-Schai, D. (2001). *E-Learning im Unternehmen: Grundlagen – Strategien – Methoden – Technologien*. Zurich: Orell Fussli.

Becerra-Fernandez, I., Murphy, K., & Simon, S. (2000). Enterprise resource planning: integrating ERP in the business school curriculum. *Communications of the ACM, 43*(4), 39–41. doi:10.1145/332051.332066

Corbitt, G., & Mensching, J. (2000). Integrating SAP R/3 into a college of business curriculum - lessons learned. *Information Technology Management, 1*(4), 247–258. doi:10.1023/A:1019181210298

Dittler, U. (2003). E-Learning in der betrieblichen Aus- und Weiterbildung. [E-learning in corporate training and education] In Dittler, U. (Ed.), *E-Learning - Erfolgsfaktoren und Einsatzkonzepte des Lernens mit interaktiven Medien* [E-learning - success factors and operational concepts of learning with interactive media]. München: Oldenbourg.

Gable, G., van Den Heever, R., Erlank, S., & Scott, J. (1997). Using large packaged software in teaching - The case of SAP R/3. In *AIS American Conference*, Indianapolis.

Gronau, N. (2004). *Enterprise Resource Planning und Supply Chain Management*. Munchen: Oldenbourg. doi:10.1524/9783486593266

Hawking, P., & McCarthy, B. (2000). Industry collaboration: a practical approach for ERP education. *Proceedings of the Australasian conference on Computing education*, Melbourne.

Hawking, P., & McCarthy, B. (2001). The ERP e-Learning model for the delivery of ERP (SAP R/3) curriculum into the asian region. *Proceedings of the Informing Science Conference*, Krakau, Poland.

Lee, H., Chen, K., & Yang, J. (2006). Teaching enterprise resource planning (ERP) systems in the supply chain management course. In *Communications of The IIMA 6(3)*, 77-86.

Léger, P.-M. (2007). Using a simulation game approach to teach enterprise resource planning concepts. *Journal of Information Systems Education, 17*(4), 441–447.

Maurizio, A., & Rosemann, M. (2005). SAP-related education - status quo and experiences. *Journal of Information Systems Education, 16*(4), 437–453.

McCarthy, B., & Paul, H. (2004). ERP e-Learning - if you can't take mohammed to the classroom, take the classroom to mohammed. *Proceedings of the Australasian Conference on Information Systems*.

Murphy, K. (2007). Critical success factors for implementing ERP systems as a vehicle for business curriculum integration at large state university. In Targowski, A., & Tarn, J. (Eds.), *Enterprise Systems Education in the 21st Century*. Hershey: Information Science Publishing. doi:10.4018/978-1-59904-349-4.ch001

Noguera, J., & Watson, E. (2004). Effectiveness of using an enterprise system to teach process-centered concepts in business education. *Journal of Enterprise Information Management, 17*(1), 56–74. doi:10.1108/09576050410510953

Scott, J. (1999). ERP effectiveness in the classroom - assessing congruence with theoretical learning models. *Proceedings of Americas Conference on Information Systems*, Milwaukee, USA.

Stewart, G., Gable, G., Andrews, R., Rosemann, M., & Chan, T. (1999). Lessons from the field - a reflection on teaching SAP R/3 and ERP implementation issues. *Proceedings of Americas Conference on Information Systems*.

Watson, E., Rosemann, M., & Stewart, G. (1999) An overview of teaching and research using SAP R/3. *Proceedings of Americas Conference on Information Systems*, Milwaukee, USA.

Chapter 6
Organization Identity:
The Business Model

Carlos Páscoa
Air Force Academy, Portugal & Instituto Superior Técnico, Technical University of Lisbon, Portugal

Pedro Leal
Air Force Academy, Portugal

José Tribolet
Instituto Superior Técnico, Technical University of Lisbon, Portugal & CODE - Center for Organizational Design & Engineering, INOV, Portugal

ABSTRACT

Organizations not only play an increasingly active role in today's society but also address everyday necessities and concerns of individuals. To achieve a competitive advantage, it is becoming more and more necessary that organizations perform efficiently in order to survive. As organizations can be defined as a group of people who work together to obtain common results, it is imperative that all its constituents represent themselves as part of the whole. Essential issues belonging to self-identity such as: who is the organization, what it does, for whom it operates, and what its core values are can be answered by building a Business Model. In this context, the Business Model and artifacts like the Business Motivation Model, which help to specify the enterprise business architecture, can be complementary. This paper shows how the Portuguese Air Force developed its generic Business Model and describes two example of application in the strategic and operational levels.

INTRODUCTION

Organizations appear as a response to the needs that society presents. Since their appearance, their business practice, irrespective of their activity, should produce something in order to receive value in return.

In order to identify the feasibility of a particular business, concepts such as Mission, Objectives and Strategy (BRG, 2007), should be clearly presented and should also identify the final state seeking to be achieved and how to obtain it.

All organizations are situated in dynamic environments. It is important that both internal and external participants clearly understand

DOI: 10.4018/978-1-4666-1764-3.ch006

the information about the substance of "Being" (Páscoa & Tribolet, 2008).

A Business Model responds to a number of important questions about the organization, such as: "who we are", "what we do", "how we behave", "what are our values".

From the combination of Enterprise Architecture (EA) with the Business Model arises, not only the definition of the executable internal business (Páscoa & Tribolet, 2008), but also the presentation of substantial information about the organization allowing its classification, internally and externally. In fact, by way of example, it is worth mentioning that the presentation of the EA of a complete and well structured organization, together with a Business Model can answer questions about identity, regarding: (1) an understanding of the contribution of each of the internal actors to achieve the objectives, (2) an understanding of the flight plan of the organization, (3) an understanding of identity, resources and values.

Accordingly, this paper presents the concepts necessary for the definition of EA in an organization, taking as reference the Business Motivation Model (BMM) (BRG, 2007) and also the concepts that underpin the creation of a Business Model. In addition, a generic Business Model for the Portuguese Air Force and two examples of application are proposed.

The document is divided into four paragraphs. The first paragraph introduces the document. The second paragraph presents relevant literature on the mentioned concepts. The third paragraph focuses on the creation of the proposed Business Model for the Air Force. The final paragraph is a brief conclusion of all the work.

ENTERPRISE CONCEPTS

When a person meets another he introduces himself by stating what his name is. The same should be valid for organizations, which should introduce themselves by stating who they are.

Areas of scientific knowledge are seeking to understand the organization, developing models and methodologies to apply in order to gain situational awareness.

The Center for Organizational Design and Engineering, the Technical University of Lisboa and the Portuguese Air Force (represented by the Air Force Academy) have been working together, using organizational and design engineering to further investigate and consolidate organizational concepts.

In this paragraph brief references will be made to the concepts used by organizational and design engineering while studying the organization: Business Motivation Model, Business Model, Business Strategy, Nonprofit Organizations and Values.

Organizational and Design Engineering

An organization can be defined as a group of people working together to achieve a common goal. This, too, can be seen as an aggregate of two or more people who carry out joint activities individually or coordinated and controlled within a certain environment in order to achieve a common result.

All organizations, knowing the environment in which they are inserted, must have their fundamental principles and objectives coordinating the human and material resources needed to carry out its business. Organizations should also seek excellence through efficiency and effectiveness in pursuit of quality in the services they provide, because only in this way they can continue their existence.

Universities and Institutes in the civilian world are currently going deep into investigating the integration of knowledge coming from different fields and paradigms. One of these fields of interest is Organizational Design and Engineering (ODE), a multidisciplinary research project born at the Department of Computer Science and Engineering of the Instituto Superior Técnico in Lisboa, Portugal, and now established at the Centre for Organizational Design and Engineering (CODE).

ODE is defined as "the application of social science and computer science research and practice to the study and implementation of new organizational designs, including the integrated structuring, modeling, development and deployment of artifacts and people" and its *"mission is to help organizations make better use of existing human, information and computer-based resources in order to build up the organization's knowledge and intelligence in a sustainable fashion"* (Magalhães & Silva, 2009).

ODE describes organizations as complex adaptive systems whose components are networks of people, processes, machines and other organizations. This has numerous implications:

- The first implication is that a clear assumption is made that it is possible to apply principles of decomposition to the organization (system classification);
- The second implication is that it is assumed that these systems change and are self-managing (the adaptive classification); and
- Other implications come from classifying enterprises as social and complex, meaning that enterprises will have particular properties namely: (1) System Properties such as scalability, flexibility, stability, accuracy, robustness, among others, which may be selectively targeted and most of the time imply the favoring of certain aspects over others (tradeoffs); (2) Emergent Values or Soft Properties that are related to categories of social systems and result from the human dimension inherent to any enterprise.

ODE talks about properties such as *trust, motivation, loyalty, dedication,* and others. The last matter of relevance about ODE positioning, and that cannot be directly inferred by its ontological position is that a clear assumption is made that it is possible to apply the rigour of engineering sciences to approach organizational problems such as design and change (Matos, 2007).

Without having the tools to do so, organizations have to adapt to external and internal changes almost on a daily basis. Hence, today's organizations – profit-making and not-for-profit – have to develop new capabilities for continuous sensing, learning and adapting to ever-changing environments (Magalhães & Silva, 2009).

The CODE's Mission, based on ODE principles, is to help organizations make better use of existing human, information and computer-based resources in order to build up the organization's knowledge and intelligence in a sustainable fashion. In this environment "Intelligence" is the term usually referring to a general mental capability to reason, solve problems, think abstractly, understand new information, learn from past experience and adjust to new situations (Magalhães & Silva, 2009).

When applied to organizational settings, the representational technologies that Youngjin et al (2006) talk about are crucial sources of self-awareness. Organizational self-awareness is part of the organization's knowledge creation process. It comprises a number of capabilities that jointly give the organization greater power to know itself. Self-awareness is of course a human capability, which can be greatly enhanced or diminished by the existing organizational designs combined with the existing computer-based artifacts (Tribolet, 2005). The concept is obviously important because the larger the degree of self-awareness of any organization, the more cohesive it will become and the readier it will be at reacting to environmental change (external or internal). Organizational self-awareness and organizational agility go hand-in-hand.

The discipline of ODE is different from the traditional disciplines of Organizational Engineering because it tries to combine knowledge of social sciences with engineering sciences, enabling that the design of the social component of the organization (individuals, groups, values, culture, etc.) is combined to the rigor and the tools of the engineering disciplines (Matos, 2007).

Using the computer in the organization, as an essential tool to achieving strategy and managing own information and decision support elements, requires the determination of the Information Systems Architecture (ISA), which consists of five architectures (Abreu & Tribolet, 2008).

- Enterprise Architecture (EA). Deals with aspects of the organization that are not directly related to the specific business and its operations, such as 'Mission', 'Vision', 'Strategy', and 'Organizational Goals';
- Business Architecture (BA). Relates with the materialization of the business strategy, implemented by business processes, representing the objects 'business process' and 'business purpose';
- Information Architecture (IA). Focus on what is that the organization needs to know to perform the operations, as defined in BA, characterized in EA and provides an abstraction of the organization's information needs, regardless of technology; it contemplates the objects 'feature', 'actor', 'observable state 'and 'activity';
- Application Architecture (AA). Deals with the needs of applications in data management and support of business, being independent of the software used to implement the different systems and includes the objects 'component SI' ('block IS') and 'service';
- Technological Architecture (TA). Handles all the technology behind the implementation of the applications as defined in the AA, as well as the necessary infrastructure for the production of support systems, business processes, and it considers concepts

such as 'Information Technologies (IT) component', ('IT block') and 'IT service'.

One of the ISA components encompasses the definition of Business Processes, which can be defined as the "*set of interrelated and inter-performing activities that transform inputs into outputs*" (IPQ, 2000). The Business Process embody the generation of value-added businesses and is decomposed into activities that require a set of resources, human and material, in a defined time, which could contribute to their achievement.

The inability to run the processes, depending on its nature, leads to impairment of the success of an organization resulting in a set of incalculable damage that may even lead to loss of competitiveness and consequent market exit.

Enterprise Architecture and Enterprise Governance

"Architecture" when applied to the enterprise is denominated by Enterprise Architecture. Within this context is also important to define what an enterprise is and what enterprise architecture is. Enterprise can be defined as "*any collection of organizations that has a common set of goals and/or a single bottom line*" (Open Group, 2007).

While enterprise architecture provides a holistic view and captures the essentials of the business, and its evolution is very helpful in keeping the essentials of the business, so allowing for maximal flexibility and adaptability towards business success, good enterprise architecture provides the insight needed to balance these requirements and facilitates the translation from corporate strategy to daily operations (Lankhorst et al, 2005).

A definition of EA can be "*a coherent set of descriptions, covering a regulations-oriented, design-oriented and patterns-oriented perspective on an enterprise, which provides indicators and controls that enable the informed governance of the enterprise's evolution and success*" (Op 't Land et al, 2009).

Theories exist, today, to help to develop the Architecture. For instances, the Enterprise Ontology, can be defined "*as the realization and implementation independent essence of an enterprise, in short, as the deep structure behind its observable surface structure*" (Dietz, 2006).

Enterprise Governance is a recent term that introduces the governance perspective that includes the strategic and operational performance with focus on compliance and performance concerns. Enterprise governance is considered as "*the set of responsibilities and practices exercised by the board and executive management with the goal of providing strategic direction, ensuring that objectives are achieved, ascertaining that risks are managed appropriately and verifying that the organization's resources are used responsibly*" (Hoogervorst, 2009).

The Business Motivation Model

The BMM (BRG, 2007) is a framework to develop the architecture of the Business in an organized way. BMM provides a scheme or structure for developing, communicating, and managing business plans in an organized manner. The Model does all of the following:

- It identifies factors that motivate the establishing of business plans.
- It identifies and defines the elements of business plans.
- It indicates how all these factors and elements inter-relate.

Among these elements are ones that provide governance for and guidance to the business, Business Policies and Business Rules.

BMM has five major distinct areas: "Ends", "Means", "Influencers", "SWOT" and "Potential Impact".

- "Ends", state what the organization wants to achieve and is composed by "Vision", "Goals" and "Objectives";
- "Means", the way the organization uses to achieve its "Ends" includes the "Course of Action" and within, the "Strategy" and "Tactics", and also "Directives" which can be "Business Policies " and "Business Rules";
- Internal and external "Influencers" perform actions that could significantly impact both the "Ends" and the "Means";
- The "Strength, Weakness, Opportunities and Threats (SWOT) Analysis" lets one know what impact these influencers have in the "Means" and in the "Ends";
- "Potential Impact" can limit or jeopardize the activities of the organization.

Although it is a model revealing the behavior of the organization pursuing what it wants to be achieved, and how it will be accomplished, the BMM also has as a main idea: to motivate the components of the organization. Through this model the elements understand the desired outcomes of the organization and how they are achieved, so there is a greater motivation on the part of its constituents. The following text describes the model components adopting, in most of the cases, the Business Rules Group description.

Mission indicates the main activities of the organization, while the Vision indicates the state that is sought and amplified by Goals and Objectives.

Ends

An End is something the organization seeks to accomplish. An End does not include any indication of how it will be achieved. Ends encompass Vision and Desired Results which, in turn, encompass Goals and Objectives (BRG, 2007).

- **Vision:** Describes the future state of the organization, without regard to how it will be achieved. A Vision is the ultimate, preferably attainable, state the enterprise would like to achieve. A Vision should focus all aspects of the business problem. A Goal, in contrast, should generally be attainable and should be more specifically oriented to a single aspect of the business problem. A Vision is supported or made operative by Missions and it is amplified by Goals (BRG, 2007).

- **Desired Result:** An End that is a state or target that the enterprise intends to maintain or sustain. Comprehends the Goal and Objective concepts and is supported by Courses of Action. Desired Results are supported by Courses of Action, which can be either Strategies or Tactics. One Desired Result can include other Desired Results; a Desired Result can be included in some other Desired Result (BRG, 2007).
- **Goal:** A statement about a state or condition of the enterprise to be brought about or sustained through appropriate Means. A Goal amplifies a Vision – that is, it indicates what must be satisfied on a continuing basis to effectively attain the Vision. A Goal should be narrow — focused enough that it can be quantified by Objectives. A Vision, in contrast, is too broad or grand for it to be specifically measured directly by Objectives. Compared to an Objective, a Goal tends to be longer term, qualitative (rather than quantitative), general (rather than specific), and ongoing. Compared to a Goal, an Objective tends to be short term, quantitative (rather than qualitative), specific (rather than general), and not continuing beyond its timeframe (which may be cyclical). Generally, Goals are supported by Strategies (BRG, 2007).
- **Objective:** A statement of an attainable, time-targeted, and measurable target that the organization seeks to meet in order to achieve Goals. Objectives should be: (1)

Attainable in the meaning that if business plans are unrealistic they will likely fail; (2) Time-targeted set in either an absolute timeframe (e.g., "by January 15, 2007") or relative timeframe (e.g., "within one year") indicating when the Objective is to be met; (3) Measurable, meaning they must include some explicit criteria for determining whether the Objective is being met in practice. An Objective quantifies a Goal is achieved by Tactics (BRG, 2007).

Means

Means represents any device, capability, regime, technique, restriction, agency, instrument, or method that may be called upon, activated, or enforced to achieve Ends. They may be either a Mission, a Course of Action (a Strategy or Tactic), or a Directive (Business Policy or Business Rule) (BRG, 2007).

- **Mission:** Indicates the ongoing operational activity of the enterprise. The Mission describes what the business is or will be doing on a day-to-day basis making Vision operative. A Mission is planned by means of Strategies and indicates a correspondingly long-term approach. Like Vision, Mission is not very specific; it is something broadly stated, in terms of the overall functioning of the enterprise. The Mission statement should be focused on day-to-day operations, generic enough to cover all Strategies, and broad enough to cover the complete area of operations (BRG, 2007).
- **Course of Action:** A Course of Action is an approach or plan for configuring some aspect of the enterprise involving things, processes, locations, people, timing, or motivation, undertaken to achieve Desired Results. Courses of Action channel efforts towards Desired Results and are governed

by Directives, which include both the Strategy and Tactics (BRG, 2007).

- **Strategy:** One component of the plan for the Mission. A Strategy represents the essential Course of Action to achieve Ends — Goals in particular. A Strategy usually channels efforts towards those Goals. It is more than simply a resource, skill, or competency that the enterprise can call upon; rather, a Strategy is accepted by the enterprise as the right approach to achieve its Goals, given the environmental constraints and risks. Compared to Tactics, Strategies tend to be longer term and broader in scope. A Strategy is implemented by Tactics. Strategies usually channel efforts towards Goals, rather than Objectives (BRG, 2007).
- **Tactic:** A Course of Action that represents part of the detailing of Strategies. A Tactic implements Strategies and generally channels efforts towards Objectives. Compared to a Strategy, a Tactic tends to be shorter term and narrower in scope. Tactics implement Strategies; they are courses of action that will support those Strategies. Tactics generally channel efforts towards Objectives, rather than Goals (BRG, 2007).
- **Directive:** Govern Courses of Action. Specifically, a Directive defines, constrains or liberates some aspect of an enterprise. It is intended to assert business structure or to control or influence the behavior of the business, and is stated in declarative form. It is expected that all Courses of Action should be governed by some Directive, especially as the business plans evolve and become more coherent and complete. Any Course of Action not governed by a Directive should be examined carefully to discover potential omissions. Directives include Business Policy and Business Rule concepts. A Directive may act as some other Organization Unit's Regulation. The Business Rules and Business Policies de-

termined at one level in an organization may be effectively the law (Regulation) for lower-level organizations (BRG, 2007).

- **Business Policy:** A non-actionable Directive whose purpose is to govern or guide the enterprise. Business Policies provide the basis for Business Rules and govern Business Processes. They exist to govern – that is, control, guide, and shape – the Strategies and Tactics. The formulation of a Business Policy, which is always under the enterprise's control, is by some party who is authorized to manage, control, or regulate the enterprise by selecting from a variety of alternatives in response to one or more Assessments. Business Policies are, in comparison with the Business Rules, less structured, less discrete and not so small. On the other hand, Business Rules are highly structured, very thorough, presenting the standard vocabulary of the business, authorizing, restricting or guiding the work of the organization in specific areas (BRG, 2007).
- **Business Rule:** A Directive, intended to govern, guide or influence business behavior, in support of Business Policy that has been formulated in response to an Opportunity, Threat, Strength, or Weakness. It is a single Directive that does not require additional interpretation to undertake Strategies or Tactics. Often, a Business Rule is derived from Business Policy. Business Rules guide Business Processes (BRG, 2007).

Influencers

An Influencer can be anything that has the capability to 'produce an effect without apparent exertion of tangible force or direct exercise of command, and often without deliberate effort or intent.' The Influencers specifically of concern to business plans are those that can impact the enterprise in its employment of Means or achievement of its Ends. This impact has influence that is judged in Assessments (BRG, 2007).

The external influencers are those that stand outside the organization and create an impact on the application of Means or achievement of Ends. The internal influences come from within the organization and have an impact on employment of Means and in the achievement of Ends. Influencers have two categories: external and internal.

- **External Influencer:** Those outside an enterprise's organizational boundaries that can impact its employment of Means or achievement of Ends. Categories include the following: Competitor, Customer, Environment, Partner, Regulation, Supplier and Technology. The enterprise may choose to add additional categories or even introduce its own categorization scheme (BRG, 2007).
- **Internal Influencer:** Those from within an enterprise that can impact its employment of Means or achievement of Ends. Categories include the following: Assumption, Corporate Value, Explicit Value, Habit, Infrastructure, Issue, Management Prerogative and Resource. A particular instance of Internal Influencer actually may have more than one of these categories (BRG, 2007).

A SWOT analysis, according to the BMM, is a judgment on an Influencer, which affects the organization in its work to implement its Means or achieve its Ends, that is, an analysis of strengths and weaknesses, opportunities and threats (BRG, 2007).

With the development of the SWOT analysis the potential impact can be anticipated, that is, to anticipate what impact the Influencers will have on Means or Ends, positively or negatively. While negative influencers present a high Risk to the activity of the organization, positive influenc-ers could, in turn, be used as a way to Potential Reward (BRG, 2007).

Risk arises from negative impacts indicating the probability of loss; naturally, without an analysis on the influencers, one cannot know the risk associated. The Potential Reward comes from positive results, indicating the winning probability. Like in the Risk, the absence of an analysis on Influencers, the organization will not know what good could draw from them (BRG, 2007).

The Business Model

The term Business Model can be defined as a logical summary of the value creation of an organization or a network of companies, including assumptions about their partners, competitors and customers. It is a very complex term that appeared on the Internet in the 90s, which advocates, in its beginnings, that the organization not only needs a strategy, a special competence and customer needs, but also a Business Model that promises big gains for the organization in its future.

"*A business model describes the rationale of how an organization creates, delivers and captures value*" (Osterwalder & Pigneur, 2010). The concept Business Model is used in many areas, including traditional theories, strategies, general management, innovation and management literature information. As a result, the concept of Business Model has different ideas, different assumptions and values. Some have a central vision of the organization, others are focused on the value of ends, a focus on Strategy, other on operational aspects; some are looking for innovation, others to technology aspects (Jägers et al, 2007).

The Business Model serves as a competitive advantage when facing competition. If the organization clearly knows what its goal is, it can respond to external and internal organizational issues such as: "Who is?", "What does?", "To whom?" and "What values does it practice?".

Business Model and Business Strategy are different concepts and can be easily confused.

Business Models show the organization's system and how its elements come together and interact. However, it does not take into account components that can influence the organization (Candeloro, 2009).

Business Strategy

Nowadays, due to dynamic markets and changing technologies, Strategy cannot be static. According to the new paradigm, the rivals can quickly steal any market position, and the apparent advantage is purely temporary (Porter, 1996).

Ernst & Young (1998) cited by Kaplan & Norton (2000) *"reported that the ability to execute strategy was more important than the quality of strategy itself"*. Kaplan & Norton (2000) articulated the principles for the strategy-focused organizations: (1) translate the strategy to operational terms; (2) align the organization to the strategy; (3) make strategy everyone's everyday job; (4) make strategy a continual process; (5) mobilize change through strong, effective leadership.

In order to formulate a Strategy, the organization needs to find or create a structure in which the Strategy can be organized, determining what information is needed to apply it, identifying, then, how to capture the information and, ultimately, decide how this information should be processed within the structure to create, evaluate and optimize the Strategy or solution (Ulwick, 1999).

"The strategy should be the main focus of cooperation, overlap the growth is a mistake that many organizations keep on committing" (Porter, 1996).

Thus, it may be that the organization's Strategy is very important and, so it should remain constant over time, as it is fundamental to achieve its "Ends".

In the organization, the existence of a Business Strategy is a plus, as it answers questions such as *"Where is it done?"*, *"How is it done?"* And *"When is it done?"*. Therefore, Business Strategy development is essential to obtain results since it

allows identifying, during execution, failures or missed opportunities (Candeloro, 2009).

Strategic Management of Nonprofit Organizations

On the context of a military organization, this theme appears to be relevant because the Air Force is a public, nonprofit organization. However, like any other, non-profit organizations should optimize its resources in a way that can achieve its objectives with utmost effectiveness, using fewer resources.

Non-profit organization exists primarily to bring about changes in individuals and in society and therefore, the figure of "profit", in theory, is not a key word on the organization's strategy. Typically, these organizations exist to perform righteous or moral acts or causes to serve. However, like in profitable organizations, they should optimize their resources in order to add efficiency and effectiveness to their processes.

Strategy implementation in this type of organization differs from the others. While the Strategy of the organization that seeks to profit leads to produce the maximum profit as a result of its operation, Strategy in the nonprofit organization is merely a means of maximizing resources.

"Non-profit" organizations need to be well managed because they do not have a "conventional" profit. They know they need it so they can concentrate on their mission (Drucker, 1989).

The application of a strategy in such organizations cannot be seen in equal terms when comparing with a "profit" organization. While in a profit organization, Strategy takes the organization to produce the greatest possible profit, in non-profit, Strategy makes the organization to maximize resources usage in order to spend as little as possible.

Strategy makes the organization to evolve and change, fulfilling the goals it has set for itself. In an organization that tries to create profits, Strategy will use organization's resources in such a way that it achieves minimizing costs and maximizing profits. In non-profit organizations, resources maximization will lead the organization to conduct its activities, but with the least possible cost, ensuring that its work continues to be conducted with minimal resources.

Values of an Organization

The core values of an organization should reflect the deep beliefs people embrace and must be totally independent from industry standards or management topics. Values can adjust the organization to the competition market, clarify its identity, limit its strategy and operational freedom and regulate the behavior of its employees. Values that the organization undertakes to achieve its purpose, should be few in number, but can be expressed in long sentences (Marr, 2006).

Values also reflect the way of being of the organization and the people who work in it, determining how they operate and behave towards the business. The value statements come from the people and values of their chiefs. Values are things that people within the organization believe blindly. They determine how people act, what ethics they use and what their behaviors are, all of this in relation to the business (Person, 2009).

In an organization values form a kind of immaterial frame that surrounds all the interactions of individuals within it. The values and beliefs related to them, determine how the events and communications are interpreted and given meaning. So are the key to motivation and culture. Shared values and beliefs are the "glue" that holds together an organization. Conflicts of values are a source of disharmony and distension.

The set of values and beliefs can help to discern the deeper assumptions and assumptions on which an organization is based. In a functional system, values and beliefs align with the identity and the organization's environment. The objectives and actions to support individual functional objectives and strategy related to the roles which, in turn, are congruent with the organization's culture and identity, and the mission on its upper atmosphere (Dilts, 2001).

It is important to understand that there are different kinds of values, which exert different influences and functions on the organization. The "core values" are those that most closely express and support an organization's identity. Core values are usually expressed through "strategic assets" and "process values." The strategic values are expressed, externally, about the environment and customers, organization, etc. Usually, denoting the way the organization presents itself and acts in the outside world. The process values are expressed internally and relate to the way organization members relate and behave towards their colleagues and collaborators.

THE AIR FORCE BUSINESS MODEL DEVELOPMENT

Based on the concepts previously described, this paragraph proposes and develops the Business Model that is thought to be the most appropriate for the Portuguese Air Force in general, instantiating it, then, to one of the Air Units.

During the development of the Business Model, several Air Force officers were interviewed. The questions received several responses that denote some dispute at the judgment cross this theme. It should be noted, though, that the concept of "business" engaged in a military organization generates discomfort. However, all the interviewed agreed that, since financial resources are needed to the operation of the Air Force on a daily bases, it is also a business but in a non-profit way.

Moreover, there is still the opinion of some of the interviewed who affirm that there is an implicit business model in what the organization performs. However, there is a group that agrees that a Business Model would certainly influence the Strategy and further improve the organization, whose current output is already of high quality.

In order not only to identify parallels, but also to be able to find new ways to improve the Air Force's EA, a comparison was made between the current institutional artifacts that compose the Air Force's EA and the BMM concepts.

In this sense, there were found some substantial common points between BMM and the Air Force in the areas of Ends and Means, and it was concluded that a direct application of the BMM could improve the mainstream of concepts used by the organization, grouping them by relating and aligning them with a derived view from the "Mission", published by a Government Law and the Vision of the General Chief-of-Staff: *"In the multi-faceted coverage of the mission, I envision an Air Force with a highly deployable nature, while maintaining a high degree of interoperability with other national and multinational forces, supported by the use of equipment that incorporate new technologies, served by a deployable command and control that enables operation in different environments, and a streamlined logistics, based on a modular structure, that eases expedited activation process."* (Araújo, 2008).

Down in detail, from the various concepts compared, it can be concluded that the process of studying external and internal influencers, and its relation to the SWOT analysis could be improved by adding effectiveness to the overall organization's EA.

Other of the conclusions stood on the need of introducing the organization and characterizing it in and out, answering questions such as: *"Who are we?"*, *"What do we do?"* and *"What are our values?"*.

Since the Business Model answers questions such as those identified in the previous paragraph, it became important to complement the Business Architecture and add information about the organization itself, seeking to develop a generic Air Force Business Model.

The following sections identify the principles and the development of the generic Air Force Business Model and its application to: (1) the stra-

tegic level of the Air Force within the operational context; (2) the operational level in the context of an operational Air Unit.

Generic Model Development

A survey was done by the Portuguese Air Force Academy students in which they enquired a selected set of people about if they knew what the contribution was of the work that they were developing to a greater achievement. In general, the selected people, working in the strategic and operational level knew what they were working for in terms of strategic objectives. However, when asked about if they knew everything that the Air Force was doing, the answer was negative.

One very important aspect of organization is that every human member understands what he or she is contributing with his or her individual work. Answering questions such as: "Who are we?", "What do we do?", "What are our values?" can be done by the Business Model (Jägers et al, 2007; Candeloro, 2009; Porter, 1996; Ulwick, 1999). Therefore, it became important to complement Business Architecture Concepts by adding information about the organization itself. The Air Force Business Model development had to follow specific requirements:

- To appeal to patriotism, given the highly patriotic nature of armed forces;
- To be made into an easy and readable symbol, an image easy to understand;
- To be able to represent any level (strategic, tactic and operational) of the Organization;
- To represent the Organizational Structure;
- To show the corporate values and mission;
- To reflect areas (local) of employment.

Figure 1 shows the generic Business Model (Páscoa & Tribolet, 2010)

The graphic representation of the Business Model complies with all the requirements previously described. The next two sections show the

Figure 1. Generic Business Model

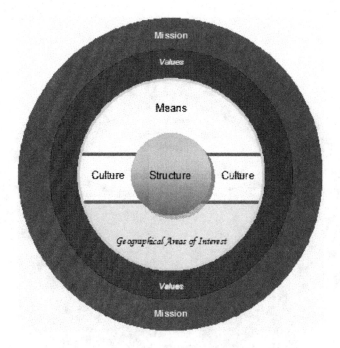

direct application of the generic model to the strategic level (within the Air Units context) and to the operational level (also within the same context).

Strategic Level Business Model

The Portuguese Air Force was established on 1952 as an independent branch, integrating the air forces formerly embedded in the Army and the Navy.

The Portuguese Air Force is an element of the national defense system. It has the mission of cooperating in an integrated way in the military defense of the Republic, through air operations. It is also responsible for Missions derived from international commitments and for Missions of civilian interest.

To better manage the flexible features of the weapons systems, the Air Force has a centralized Command and Control and a decentralized execution represented by its Air and Functional Commands. The Air Force is organized according to Figure 2 (source: http://www.emfa.pt/www/organizacao.php?lang=pt&cod=*).

The Air Force structure is defined in the Organic Law for the Air Force, published by the Portuguese Government, and is composed of:

- Chief of Staff (CEMFA), the Air Force Commander, also designated as the Chief-of-Staff.
- Air Force Headquarters (EMFA), the entity responsible for studying, conceiving and planning the Air Force activities, supporting the CEMFA's decisions.
- The Finance Directorate (DFFA) administers the Air Force finance resources in accordance with the CEMFA´s plans and directives.
- The Organs of Cultural Nature (ONC) preserve and display the historical and museum heritage of the Air Force. They are the Air Museum (MUSAR), the Air Force Band and the Air Force Magazine.

Figure 2. Graphic representation of the Business Model for the Portuguese Air Force (Leal, 2010; Leal et al, 2010).

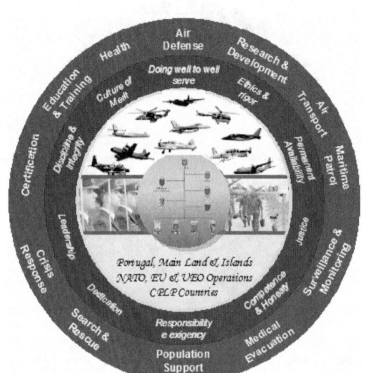

- The Counseling Organs (ÓRGÃOS DE CONSELHO) advise the CEMFA on matters related to the administration, discipline and historical. They are the Superior Council, the Discipline Council, the Historical and Cultural Committee and the Council of Health.
- The Inspection (IGFA) supports the CEMFA in the evaluation and control of the Air Force.
- The Logistics Command (CLAFA) manages the material resources and infra-structure of the Air Force in order to accomplish the Chief of Staff's plans and directives while complying with the requirements of airworthiness of military aircraft.
- The Personnel Command (CPESFA) administers the human resources in accordance with the CEMFA´s plans and directives.

- The Training and Formation Command (CIFFA) manages training and formation activity on the academic and professional domains, including the draft and preparation of the personnel.
- The Air Command (CA) is responsible for planning, directing and controlling the efficiency of the air power, the air activity and the defense of the national air space.

In its normal activity Air Force relates to the various entities including: the Portuguese Government, a regulatory element that ensures also a financial component, other state organs, such as the Presidency and the various Ministries and the Regional Governments, the military, for example, the General Staff of the Armed Forces, Army, Navy, Portuguese Official Language's African Countries (PALOP), and International Organizations such as the European Union and

NATO, the Universities, the Media, Hospitals and cultural entities.

As part of its mission, the organization provides a range of services to entities described above, being the most relevant: the defense of national airspace, air transport operations, patrol, search and rescue, maritime surveillance and medical evacuation, formation, university and professional, research and development, health, courses of command and leadership and uses of the wind tunnel.

The Air Force is a military institution that practices noble values, such as the following: *"Do well to well serve"*, *"Ethics of Rigor"*, *"Responsibility"*, *"Demand"*, *"Culture of Merit"*, *"Integrity"*, *"Dedication"*, *"Competence"*, *"Justice"*, *"Permanent availability"*, *"Honesty"*, *"Leadership"* and *"Discipline"* (Araújo, 2008).

In carrying out its specific mission, the Organization operates around the Globe specially Portugal, Main Land and Islands, the area of influence of NATO, the European Union and the Western European Union and also within the Community of Portuguese Speaking Countries, having recently participated in several national and international operations of which stands out Afghanistan.

In Figure 2, the concepts presented above are illustrated in the representation of the Business Model for the Portuguese Air Force at the strategic level.

In a clear reference to patriotism and the highest values of the Nation, the colors of the National Flag can be observed in the two outer circles and in the small inner circle.

In the center there is the organizational structure of the Air Force and various images. On left there are shown the students of the Air Force Academy, representing the essential training for any organization and on the right F-16 personnel, representing the operational field.

Also in the center at the bottom there are the local activities of that organization, at the top are the operational means of the Air Force, in a set-

ting that enhances the Air Force flies in all ways and directions.

In the green circle are observed values of all the Portuguese Air Force and in the red circle there are the various actions that the Air Force plays in civil and military components, in strict compliance with its mission.

On the overall, the picture combines all the attributes needed to represent the Business Model of achieving the purpose for which it is intended, namely the easy understanding of who you are, what you do, to whom you do it and what values are practiced, fulfilling all the requirements.

Operational Level Business Model

The ability of specification of the model is measured by the development of the Business Model of the Air Units. In this case, for example (see Figure 3) it is shown the Business Model for Squadron 504, which operates the FALCON 50.

The Model of the Fleet 504 shows in the center, above, the image of three FALCON 50 aircraft; still at the center, there are images of the aircraft in flight and an aspect of its interior; instead of the organizational structure of the Air Force there is the patch of the Air Unit: the "Linces" and, finally, in the center there are referred the places of action (in this case, the same as the Air Force).

In the green circle remain the "Values" of the Organization while the outer circle describes the tasks that the Fleet 504 can do, such as: air transport, medical evacuation, special transportation, crisis response, VIP transport and organs transport.

The example shows that the model can be instantiated to any organization at any level while informing the stakeholders what the organization is, what it does, to whom it does and what values it uses.

Figure 3. Graphic Representation of the Business Model for Squadron 504 (Leal, 2010).

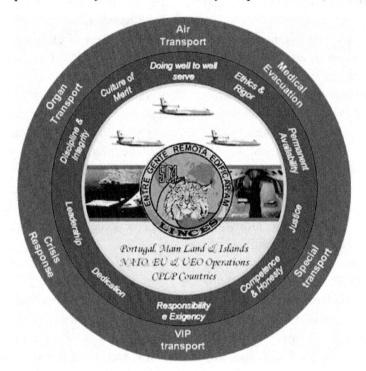

CONCLUSION

The Business Model complements the enterprise architecture of the organization, allowing the characterization and understanding not only of its business but also its identity and values, resulting in a better understanding by stakeholders, both internal and external.

In the process of understanding of what would be the best Business Model for the Air Force, it has been studied the formulation of its EA, compared with the BMM (BRG, 2007). It was concluded that, considering that there is always room for improvement, implementation of the BMM, and SWOT analysis of influencers could add effectiveness to the activities related to the achievement of the Mission.

One also sought to understand what the various internal stakeholders thought about the "Business Model" and its suitability to the organization. Several interviews were conducted that showed that most human resources think this model would be appropriate provided that it showed immediate

gains in understanding the organization and how it relates with the outside.

After a thorough investigation, it was concluded that the Business Model most suited to Air Force, would be an artifact that clearly answered the questions "Who are we?", "What do we do" and "To whom we do it?" and "What are our values?", recognizable throughout the organization, being identified a set of requirements that the development should conform.

In addition to clearly explain what the organization does and how, the Business Model proposed for the Air Force at the strategic level (see Figure 2), reflects the its values, the air assets operated, what its top-level structure, in which areas of the globe it acts and provides services, having some room for the representation of high patriotic values as the colors of the National Flag.

The proposed Business Model is also specific and can be adapted to represent any unit inside the Air Force through the modification of some elements of its structure. Two examples were done designing the Business Model for the Air

Force strategic level and for the operational level (Squadron 504).

The Business Model, providing information to stakeholders about the identity and values of the organization, complements the enterprise architecture that defines the Mission, Vision, Objectives and Strategy. Thus, there is a complementary relationship between them.

The structure of the Business Model, shown in the image, is also suitable for the purpose intended, since it allows understanding of the relationship of a set of concepts in an immediate and easy way.

Future studies will be able to better identify the complementarities of the architecture of business and the Business Model, designing and proposing new artifacts that allow their composition.

REFERENCES

Abreu, M., & Tribolet, J. (2008). *Considerações Sobre a Medição de Factores Soft nas Organizações* [Considerations on the Measurement of Soft Factors in Organizations]. Portugal: Center for Organizational and Design Engineering, INESC-INOV.

Araújo, L. (2008). *Portuguese Air Force Chief-of-Staff Speech*. Portugal: Portuguese Air Force.

Candeloro, R. (2009). *Modelo de Negócio e Estratégia. Você tem?* [Business Model and Strategy. Do you?] Retrieved October 2009 from: http://www.gestaoetc.com.br/213/modelo-de-negocio-e-estrategia-voce-tem/

Dietz, J. (2006). *Enterprise Ontology: Theory and Methodology*. Delft: Springer. doi:10.1007/3-540-33149-2

Ernst & Young. (1998). *Measures that Matter*. Boston, USA.

Hoogervorst, J. (2009). *Enterprise Governance & Enterprise Engineering*. The Netherlands: Springer. doi:10.1007/978-3-540-92671-9

Instituto Português da Qualidade [Portuguese Institute for Quality](2000). ISO 9000:2000, *Quality Management Systems – Fundamentals and Vocabulary*, Lisboa.

Jägers, H., Jansen, W., & Steenbakkers, W. (2007). *New Business Models for the Knowledge Economy*. Hampshire: Gower Publishing Limited.

Kaplan, R., & Norton, D. (2000). *The Strategy-Focused Organization: How Balanced Scorecard Companies Thrive in the New Business Environment*. Harvard Business School Press.

Lankhorst, M. (2005). *Enterprise Architecture at Work - Modelling, Communication and Analysis*. Springer-Verlag Berlin Heidelberg.

Leal, P. (2010). *Definição do Modelo de Negócio da Força Aérea*. [Definition of Business Model of the Air Force] Master Thesis, Portuguese Air Force Academy, Department of University Education, Sintra

Leal, P., Páscoa, C., & Tribolet, J. (2010), *A Business Model for the Portuguese Air Force*, Springer CCIS Series on Minutes of the CENTERIS 2010 Conference on ENTERprise and Information Systems, Viana do Castelo, Portugal.

Magalhães, R., & Silva, A. (2009). A White paper on Organizational and Design Enginering, Center for Organizational and Design Engineering, *INESC INOV*, Portugal.

Marr, B. (2006) *Strategic Performance Management. 1.ª ed*. Oxford: Elsevier Ltd.

Matos, M. G. (2007), *Organizational Engineering: An Overview of Current Perspectives*, Master Thesis in Computer Science, IST/UTL, Lisboa.

Op 't Land, M, Proper, E., Maarten, W., Cloo, J., & Steghuis, C. (2009): Enterprise Architecture – Creating Value by Informed Governance, Springer – Verlag Berlin Heidelberg.

Osterwalder, A., & Pigneur, Y. (2010). *Business Model Generation – A Handbook for Visionaries, Game Changers, and Challengers*. Hoboken, NJ: John Wiley and Sons, Inc.

Páscoa, C., & Tribolet, J. (2010). Organizational and Design Engineering of the Operational and Support Components of an Organization: the Portuguese Air Force Case Study, Practice-driven Research on Enterprise Transformation (PRET) *Conference on Enterprise Engineering, Springer Lecture Notes in Business Information Processing (LNPIB) Series*, Delft University, The Netherlands.

Person, R. (2009). *Balanced Scorecards and Operational Dashboards with Microsoft Excel*. Indianapolis, IN: Wiley Publishing, Inc.

Porter, M. (1996). *What is Strategy?* Harvard Business School Publishing Corporation.

The Business Rules Group. (2007). *The Business Motivation Model: Business Governance in a Volatile World. Version 1.3* Retrieved October 2009 from: http://www.businessrulesgroup.org/bmm.shtml.

The Open Group. (2007). *The Open Group: A Pocket Guide to TOGAF Version 8.1.1 Enterprise Edition*. Retrieved from: http://www.opengroup.org/togaf.

Tribolet, J. (2005). Organizações, Pessoas, Processos e Conhecimento: da Reificação do Ser Humano como Componente do Conhecimento à "Consciência de Si Organizacional. [Organizations, People, Processes and Knowledge: from the reification of the human being as a component of knowledge to the knowledge of the organizational self] In Amaral, L., Magalhães, R., Morais, C. C., Serrano, A., & Zorrinho, C. (Eds.), *Sistemas de Informação Organizacionais* [Organizational Information Systems]. Portugal: Sílabo Editora.

Tribolet, J., & Páscoa, C. (2008). *Apontamentos das aulas de Engenharia Organizacional I*. Academia da Força Aérea. [Lecture notes and Organizational Engineering, Air Force Academy.]

Ulwick, A. (1999). *Business Strategy Formulation: Theory, Process, and the Intellectual Revolution*. Westport: Quorum Books.

Youngjin, Y., Boland, R., & Lyytinen, K. (2006). From Organization Design to Organization Designing. *Organization Science, 17*(2), 215–229. doi:10.1287/orsc.1050.0168

Chapter 7
The Use of Experts Panels in ERP Cost Estimation Research

Ahmed Elragal
German University in Cairo, Egypt

Moutaz Haddara
University of Agder, Norway

ABSTRACT

This chapter is an effort towards illustrating the use of expert panels (EP) as a means of eliciting knowledge from a group of enterprise resource planning (ERP) experts in an exploratory research. The development of a cost estimation model for ERP adoptions is very crucial for research and practice, and that was the main reason behind the willingness of experts to participate in this research. The use of EP was very beneficial as it involved various data collection and visualization techniques, as well as data validation and confirmation. Arguments for using EP over other group techniques are presented in this chapter. Experts modified and enhanced the initial cost drivers list and their sub-factors significantly, as they added, modified, merged and split different costs. Moreover, they ranked the cost drivers according to their weight on total costs. All of this helped the authors to better understand relationships among various cost factors.

INTRODUCTION

As they say, *"it's about the journey, not the destination"*, research techniques are very crucial for any research endeavour. They can lead researchers to the right path, or deviate them away from the desired destination. Moreover, the significance of any research results is determined by several measures, and the data collection and analysis techniques are on top of them.

In our proposed research phases, different data collection techniques are *used* and proposed. Some of those techniques are qualitative in nature, some are quantative, and some are mixed approaches. The variety of methods chosen should help in identifying the different costs and factors that influence costs in the Enterprise Resource Planning systems (ERP) adoption processes, in order to establish a cost estimation model. In addition, these

DOI: 10.4018/978-1-4666-1764-3.ch007

techniques should provide a multi-perspective on costs through involving various key stakeholders from beneficiaries, independent consultants, and vendors that participate in Enterprise Resource Planning adoption projects. The focus of this research is on *ERP cost factors* within the small and medium enterprises (SMEs) domain. The *Egyptian context* was chosen as a research kick-off, as it was convenient to the authors due to the availability and access to data. Moreover, based on preliminary pilot interviews with ERP consultants, many of them assured that the current cost estimation methods are *not valid* or applicable for ERP settings. In addition, some experts argued that the usual European or American cost factors weight distributions (e.g. labours' rate/hour) are not appropriate in the Egyptian context. The results presented in this chapter could supplement ERP literature and practice if further validated, extended, and compared with other research in other countries or contexts.

In particular, this chapter discusses the Experts Panel approach that was used as a part of our "initial model development phase" *(see Figure. 2)*. The chapter is an effort on arguing why *group discussions and interviewing* techniques are proposed in our initial exploratory research phase, and why we preferred the term "Experts Panels" over Delphi and Focus Groups.

In this chapter, the experts panel (EP) is contrasted with other group techniques. In general, *group techniques* are recommended for use when the phenomenon studied is emerging, or doesn't have clear boundaries. Moreover, group techniques benefits from participants' (field experts) brainstorming and field expertise. Furthermore, these techniques are recommended for initial exploratory research, or when it is hard to find a statistically valid sample.

The remainder of the chapter is organized as follows: the next section presents the chapter overview, cost estimation background and research motivation, followed by research scope and researchers' perspective of costs. Followed by a description of the experts panel conducted. Moreover, a brief comparison between the experts panel and other related techniques followed by a conclusion.

CHAPTER OVERVIEW

In the next sections, cost estimation background and motivation, scope, perspectives, and research methods are discussed.

Cost Estimation Background

ERP system implementation is a significant project that requires commitment, and consumes a substantial amount of resources, and requires organisational changes and fits (Moon, 2007). Many variables affect ERP implementations, size and structure of organisations are not the only variables within the ERP project. Its specific context factors, industry, existing system reuse, and the adoption of a specific vendor ERP implementation method are also important factors (Daneva, 2007). Furthermore, cultural context can radically influence an ERP project (Soh, Kien, & Tay-Yap, 2000).

Given the high costs of ERP systems and their complexity, when organisations take the first step towards adopting an ERP system, they need to think about various things, foremost among which is the adoption cost (Van Everdingen, Van Hillegersberg, & Waarts, 2000). Costs in this research are defined as the budget expenditures needed for the attainment of the ERP adoption goal. Besides direct costs and system price, costs can have other forms that can be mapped to a monetary value, like search for vendors, time, and human resources costs related to the ERP adoption project.

With the scarcity of proper cost estimation methods, ERP systems implementation projects are facing difficulties in estimating costs, size, time, effort, productivity and other cost factors (Daneva, 2004; Seddon, 2003; Stensrud, 2001).

Furthermore, costs could cross their estimated budgets, which could be critical for small and medium size organizations with limited resources.

Because SMEs do not possess similar amount of resources other large enterprises have, thus they are vulnerable when costs rise. Moreover, any cost increase or project latencies could seriously affect SMEs' survival in the market. Even some large enterprises have filed bankruptcy because of a flawed ERP implementation projects. Since ERP adoption within SMEs is still in its infancy, researchers need to pore over and identify the basic drivers that influence ERP adoption decision (Van Everdingen, et al., 2000), specially ERP adoption costs.

Why Cost Estimation for ERP in SMEs?

Most ERP systems implementations fail due to erroneous budget and schedule estimations (Holland & Light, 1999; Jones, 2007; Martin, 1998). With the lack of empirical research on specific ERP cost drivers and models to estimate costs related to ERP systems adoptions (Haddara & Zach, 2011); ERP systems adoption faces a high threat of failure.

According to (Holland & Light, 1999; Martin, 1998), around 90% of ERP implementations are behind schedules, crossed their budgets, or utterly cancelled due to stern underestimations during the requirements phase (Jones, 2007), in which gratuitous optimism in cost and schedule estimations could be the cause, rather than project management drawbacks (Holland & Light, 1999; Jones, 2007). Failures within ERP adoptions in some cases have lead to the departure of some companies (Al-Mashari, 2002; Moon, 2007; Newman & Zhao, 2008).

As a result, the main aim of this research is to explore and identify the factors that can explain the costs resulting from an ERP adoption in SMEs in order to develop a cost estimation model. This model will give SMEs, consultants, and vendors

a more realistic view on the expected budget expenditures within the ERP adoption process. As an initial step, an experts panel have been conducted and presented in details in this chapter.

Research Scope

As previously mentioned, this research focuses on identifying costs and the factors that influence costs within the adoption process in SME's in order to develop a cost estimation model (CEM). *Adoption* in this research starts prior to phase 1, and ends at phase 5 *(see Figure 1)*. In other words, the focus starts with the cost drivers occurring during the feasibility study, consultant selection, vendor selection, contracting, etc till the Go-live phase. Post installation costs are often recurring within the ERP system lifetime. These costs are hard to take account of within this research. Thus, costs that occur after ERP installations are off boundaries of this research effort and maybe left for future research, yet the standard agreed-upon maintenance costs in contracts fall within this research's boundaries.

Authors' Perspective *(The Cost Lens)*

This research is not concerned with cost/benefit analysis; it is more focused on the relation (or difference) between estimated ERP budgets with actual spending on completed projects. The cost lens proposed in this research is because sometimes benefits in relation to costs are not important or unattainable. For example, when an SME's budget is crossed, it does not matter how much benefits it will gain through devoting more money to the project, as it might be out of the required resources already. In addition, benefits and their associated costs should be projected correctly from the beginning, as many companies implementing ERP systems filed for bankruptcy e.g. FoxMeyer Drug (Al-Mashari, 2002; Moon, 2007; Newman & Zhao, 2008), and this was mainly due to a faulty ERP

Figure 1. SAP's accelerated methodology (ASAP) – Adapted from www.sap.com

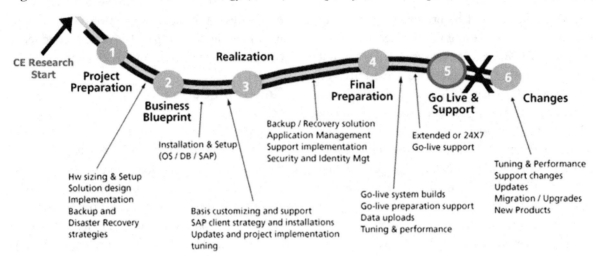

budget and schedule estimations (Al-Mashari, 2002; Moon, 2007; Newman & Zhao, 2008). Thus, in the previous example, the costs view is more crucial despite the potential benefits, as you can usually gain more benefits when you pay more money, but it is all about your resources availability. Moreover, the CEM should be used in order to project more realistic cost estimates, while benefits should be the motive for implementing an ERP in first place. Furthermore, a research conducted in Egyptian SMEs shows that, the expected benefits are usually having an up-and-running system, that doesn't negatively affect the firm's operations (Haddara & Päivärinta, 2011), or based on the system requirements included within the *request for proposal* (RFP) invitation.

Research Methods and Design

It is hard to predict the future without studying the past. Hence, this research will be based on data collected from experts panels along with actual data from organisations that already completed their ERP adoption process. And this will be done through a multiple case study design, as it has more investigative recompense compared to single case study, as well as it provides a flexible approach for Information Systems research (Cavaye, 1996;

Eisenhardt, 1989; Yin, 2003). This research will apply a multi-method research technique, encompassing multiple case studies, empirical literature findings, experts panels, documents analysis, interviews, as well as surveys. Furthermore, in order to build strong substantiation of constructs, data triangulation as a mixture of qualitative and quantitative data collection methods will be used (Eisenhardt, 1989).

To reach the goal of developing a CEM, this research project will tackle different research questions and aspects within the very domain of ERP cost estimation within SMEs. These aspects will require different perspectives, methods, and tools within its development cycle. After identifying relevant perspectives through inductive methods that can assist in identifying factors that influence costs and cost driver to be included in a priori CEM within phase one. Then phase two will start, and in this phase, an empirical test of the cost model will be conducted in order to identify the relative contribution of the different cost concepts in understanding the resulting costs of ERP adoption in SMEs. While phase one will be qualitative and inductive in nature, phase two will be deductive and quantitative.

This research will conduct *multiple case studies*. Fig 2 presents an initial map of the proposed

Figure 2. Proposed research design: Adapted from (Eikebrokk, Iden, Olsen, & Opdahl, 2008)

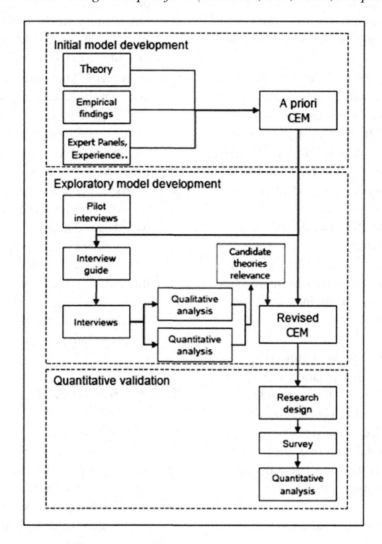

research design. Within the initial model development, theory, literature review of empirical research and the researchers' experience will be used in order to develop an *a priori* CEM. In addition to that, several experts panels with vendors, consultants, and beneficiaries are going to be held in order to direct the a priori CEM development into the right direction.

The theory to be used in this phase is the stakeholder theory (ST), which plays a role in identifying the stakeholders and cost associated with them in these ERP adoption process using its stakeholder identification instruments. Besides ST, the empirical findings and data collected will compliment ST in cost drivers' identification. The a priori CEM will be used in the second stage as an initial guide for pilot interviews. Then an interview guide will be developed, and interviews will be conducted to the cases selected.

In the following stage, a mixture of qualitative and quantitative analysis will be undertaken. As the ST has a very good technique to identify stakeholders and respondents, still it lacks relevance to information and technological aspects. Thus, a complementary theory(ies) will be considered after this initial research step. The findings from the analysis are crucial, because they will be used in mapping candidate theories to these findings, in other words, an iterative theory relevance check will be conducted.

In case of not finding a relevant theory, a grounded approach will be an alternative for theory building from case study data as advised by Eisenhardt (1989). After theory mapping or building, the research design will be modified to accommodate the chosen theory. Then a survey will be conducted followed by quantitative analysis.

Sources of Data and Data Collection Methods

In order to develop an effectual CEM, this research will collect actual data from the industry. The data required is as follows:

1. *Data* is based on finished projects.
2. *Data Sources:* Beneficiaries, consultants, vendors, and any stakeholder identified through the stakeholders analysis.
3. *Type of data:* Company size, industry type, cost factors and drivers (e.g. Business process reengineering, vendor selection costs, new hires, contracts, etc).

A further description of each data collection technique is as follows:

a. **Experts Panel:** incorporates different techniques and data collection methods. The panels includes various key experts in the ERP adoption field, including consultants, vendors, and key project representatives from beneficiaries.
b. **Interviews:** s*emi-structured* interviews will be conducted with beneficiaries, consultants, and vendors, and guided by (Myers & Newman, 2007) 'recommendations for qualitative interviewing'. The interviews will be carried out with diverse employee positions within the organisations in accor-

dance to 'triangulation of subjects' strategy proposed by Rubin & Rubin (2005), and based on the initial interviewee's sample plan identified by the stakeholder analysis.

c. **Document Analysis:** analysis of project documentations including feasibility studies, project plan, project schedule, cost estimations, actual project expenses, as well as any documents recommended by the people involved in the project.
d. **Surveys:** some are conducted as a part of the experts panel in order to collect preliminary data about cost factors and cost drivers within SMEs. Other proposed surveys will be conducted in order to get feedback on the adequacy of the *a priori* cost estimation model developed. As mentioned earlier in the chapter, the survey will be only used if a representative sample was identified.

THE EXPERTS PANEL

Due to the implications of this research into practice, an experts panel has been conducted. The experts panel recommendations and insights would be very valuable to this research within its exploratory stage, as experts would provide more inputs that would help the researchers to understand the phenomena or the problem they are studying.

The experts panel serves as an initial research kick off, that will ensure the mapping of the researcher's ideas and research problems with practice. Moreover, the experts panel is used as a mean of eliciting knowledge from ERP experts.

The panel included key persons involved in ERP implementations in Egypt. The participants were from selected ERP consultants, vendors' representatives and implementation project managers in Egypt. The expertise of the participants represents various knowledge in a broad range of national/multinational corporations and industrial sectors. The potential participants were chosen according to their number of clients and market share in the Egyptian ERP market. Twelve potential participants were contacted by phone and via e-mail, and eight experts responded and participated. The panel included vendor consultants from SAP, JD Edwards, Focus ERP, independent ERP consultants, and project champions and managers from different industrial beneficiaries. The variety of experts was to ensure that the researcher captures different views and perspectives on *costs factors*.

The Briefing

Prior to the actual panel discussion, a research briefing was sent by email to participating experts. It contained information about the research, the panel setting, the research objectives, as well as the expected implications for practice.

The Experts Panel Discussion

On the first panel meeting, an explanation (reminder) about the research objectives was provided. A set of presentations took place to explain the CEM, and what is needed from them in order to develop a model for estimating costs within the ERP adoption phase. Additionally, we illustrated the importance and need for such a model by beneficiaries, consultants, and vendors. Moreover, a less formal discussion was held at the beginning of the panel regarding their experiences with ERP projects in SMEs. Participants were asked predefined questions centred on the features of ERP adoption cost estimations within SMEs in Egypt, and its success rate of finishing projects at hand within budgets. Moreover, they were asked about the challenges facing implementers and costs' impact on ERP adoptions in SMEs. Some participants from major ERP vendors mentioned that they use CEMs to estimate budgets needed from beneficiaries to cover their part of costs, but they said that these models are not accurate, nor give a realistic view for beneficiaries about all the dimensions of costs needed for the whole ERP

adoption project. One major note from several experts was that organisations regularly do not face cost problems in selection nor post-adoption phases, the majority of ERP problems and costs pop-up during the adoption phase, and that the research should focus and start with these costs.

The First Round

In the first panel round, the participants were provided with an initial cost drivers conceptual model (mind map). The initial mind map (Figure 3) was a visualisation of cost factors gathered through literature and researchers' own experience with previous ERP adoption projects. The visualising of cost drivers and factors in a mind map (tree-like) format is believed to enhance the participants' insights and interpretations.

While the mind map was presented to the participants, group discussions took place and were managed by two moderators. One moderator's role was to ensure that the session advances smoothly, and the other's role was to ensure that all the topics are covered. Both of them were taking notes. The moderator had predefined list of questions for group interviewing, and these questions evoked the discussion and brainstorming among participants. The discussions were about which cost drivers and factors should be merged or split, change their naming, cost factors' approximate weight on total costs, and their priority pertaining to SMEs, etc.

Although some debates on some specific cost drivers' importance took place, the moderator reminded the group about the focus of discussion, and that they should adopt a *costs view* within an SME setting, and this minimised the level of debates between them. From our point of view, the discussion between participants was very fruitful, as it initially consolidated their views, and made the participants brainstorm together and start to provide valuable suggestions and remarks.

Further, each participant was provided with a questionnaire in a table (list) format that contained

Figure 3. Initial Cost Drivers mind map

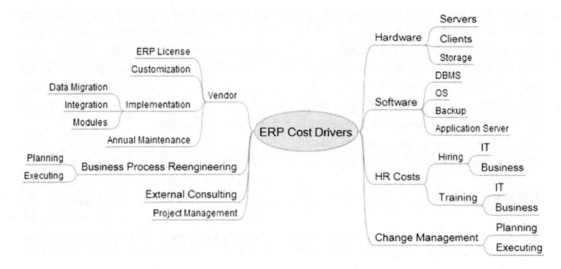

the compiled ERP costs. Their task was to verify if the listed cost drivers were appropriate to build a CEM, and to ensure whether there are missing cost drivers or existing ones that should be apart or combined, according to their relevance to the adoption process in SMEs. The questionnaire contained four main parts:

1. A list of cost drivers;
2. A column to associate them with other cost drivers that can influence these factors;
3. A column to cost factors according to impact on SMEs' ERP adoption projects;
4. A space to comment or add additional cost drivers or factors that can influence these costs, which should be considered and were over looked.

The cost drivers list was gathered through literature and the author's personal experience in the field. This was to ensure the relevance of the data collected through research and experience in the field with practice. The questionnaire was a combination of open and closed ended questions. The open-ended questions were to help the experts provide their insights, recommendations

or suggestions about which additional cost factors to include, exclude, combine, or split. The costs factors column contained cost items compiled from literature and researchers' previous experience with ERP adoption projects. The cost items scale was from very high to very low in relevance to overall costs in an SME setting. The main initial cost drivers were vendors, change management, business process reengineering, project management, hardware, software, human resources costs.

The participants' feedback helped in further developing cost drivers, adding new factors, merging some factors, decomposing some factors to include important sub-factors, and identifying cost drivers that can influence other cost factors. This brought us to a better understanding of cost drivers that should affect an ERP adoption process.

The Second Round

In the second round, an updated list of cost drivers was provided for participants. The list contained the new updated cost factors and drivers captured during the first round's questionnaire, interviews, and discussions. The updated list was presented in a table format as well as a mind map. The

Figure 4. Updated mind map

moderator initiated a discussion about the comprehensiveness of this list, and this stimulated group discussions and interactions. During this round, the participants have agreed upon some slight modifications to the cost factors' list, and the list was directly updated accordingly. At the end of this round, the participants were provided with the reviewed cost factors list and were asked to rank them *independently*. Their task was to re-rank the costs and to make sure that all the presented cost factors and our interpretations are complying with their suggestions and recommendations. The provided rankings of cost drivers were: very high, high, medium, low, and very low. The participants were alerted that cost drivers should be ranked to their importance to the adoption phase within SMEs and from a cost perspective.

The data was analysed and showed that the experts has reached consensus. Moreover, the updated and consolidated mind map was sent electronically to the participants in order to confirm the validity of the cost drivers presented. The updated mind map is in Figure 4.

EXPERTS PANEL IN CONTRAST WITH DELPHI AND FOCUS GROUPS TECHNIQUES

As researchers should choose the best method *they think* satisfies their research objectives, the method used and proposed in this research is a combination of several techniques. Although it is difficult to establish clear boundaries between the experts panel conducted in this research, and Delphi and Focus Groups, but we will try in the following section to illustrate the main common similarities and differences between them. Part of this difficulty or confusion comes from literature itself, as the Delphi and Focus Groups studies have various variations which sometimes conflict with their own main principals, like incorporating fact-to-face group discussions in Delphi studies for example (Dick, 2000). Moreover, while writing this chapter, we have discussed it and consulted several colleagues in order to obtain their opinions about categorising the method used in this research. Some of them viewed it as a Delphi style research technique, and others viewed it more of Focus Groups research. These different views made us affirmative that the research technique used here is none of them; it is actually a combination of them whilst incorporating other techniques from other research methods as well.

As mentioned above, the next part will discuss the technical and conceptual differences between the experts panel in comparison with other "similar" techniques. In addition, we will provide arguments about why the technique used is more adequate than these techniques.

Similarities and Differences

The experts panel technique used in this research shares similarities with Delphi, Focus Groups and NGT research methods.

Although Delphi and Focus Groups techniques are considered data collection techniques through group interviewing or surveying, still they have basic differences.

Experts Panel and Delphi

Similarities

In literature, the Delphi method has been used to acquire knowledge from single or multiple experts (Roth & William C. Wood, 1990). The Delphi technique serves as a systematic method to collect ideas, opinions, and judgments on a particular topic at stake through the use of sequential questionnaires combined with feedback and summaries derived from previous responses (Delbecq, Van de Ven, & Gustafson, 1975). The Delphi method is primarily used when the problem at stake does not suit itself with precise analytical techniques but can benefit from collective subjective judgments and opinions (Linstone & Turoff, 1975). Moreover, one of the main goals of the Delphi technique is to reach consensus position from experts (Delbecq, et al., 1975; Nevo & Chan, 2007). Some Delphi studies use sound ranking measurement techniques (e.g. Kendall's W) through its iterations in order to measure the degree of consensus (Brancheau & Wetherbe, 1987; Schmidt, 1997).

Differences

Although the above-mentioned characteristics and goals match with those of experts panels, yet there are basic differences between both techniques. The typical Delphi method is asynchronous and does not incorporate face-to-face interactions between participants or experts (Van de Ven & Delbeco, 1971), as the anonymity of respondents is believed to give the method positive recompenses over face-to-face interactions (Linstone & Turoff, 1975).

In order to reach consensus, there have been rounds in the experts panel that are similar to those of Delphi; on the other hand, these rounds incorporated surveys, rankings, *plus* group discussions and interviews. Furthermore, the experts panel incorporated ideas and suggestions from the experts' group discussions, as group interaction and brainstorming would enhance the amount and quality of responses, and would initiate new ideas in contrast with individual brainstorming (Osborn, 1957; Parnes & Meadow, 1959) in (Van de Ven & Delbeco, 1971). Moreover, group interactions can be used to examine not only what individuals think, but also how they think and why they think that in a particular way (Kitzinger, 1995). In our point of view, face-to-face interactions are better when there is a group of experts that represents clients' side and vendors' side in order to decrease bias through objective discussions. In addition, group discussion would enable participants to exchange ideas and point-of-views, which would help in narrowing down and reaching consensus. Furthermore, Delphi presents data, key issues, and items in a *list* format to participants (Brancheau & Wetherbe, 1987; Van de Ven & Delbecq, 1974). On the other hand, during the experts panel rounds, lists and mind maps were used. Instead of presenting cost factors in lists only, mind maps were used to visualise information and to help participants grasp the full picture of the factors and the relationships among them. A mind map is an information construction tool represented as a graphical illustration of connections between concepts and ideas that are related to one core subject, and the process of constructing mind maps engages the participants with the content (Willis & Miertschin, 2006). Mind maps are useful in situations where developing understanding, problem solving, brainstorming, delivering information, and evaluation of participants understanding are needed (Willis & Miertschin, 2006). Moreover, mind maps are very similar to the notion of *cognitive maps,* which are used to record and graphically present qualitative data (Eden & Ackermann, 2004). The mind map used was dynamic; as we modified the map instantaneously according to their recommendations and suggestions to enable the experts to view the changes and re-evaluate them.

Experts Panels and Focus Groups

Similarities

A focus group is a qualitative data collection technique through conducting organised group discussions and interactions, moderated by one or more moderators. In addition, Focus Groups are a form of group interview that relies on communication between group participants in order to generate data (Kitzinger, 1995). The participants in this group are selected and assembled by researchers in order to discuss and reflect on, from their personal experiences, the topic of researchers' interest (Powell & Single, 1996). Focus Groups can be used at the initial or exploratory stages of a research (Hines, 2000; Kreuger, 1988). The chief purpose of Focus Groups research is to draw upon respondents' beliefs, experiences, and responses in a way in which would not be suitable using other techniques like one-to-one interviewing or questionnaires (Gibbs, 1997). Moreover, several researchers have also indicated that group discussions can generate more significant comments than usual interviews (Hines, 2000; Watts & Ebbutt, 1987).

Differences

Focus Groups are usually conducted in one rounds and do not capture comprehensive reflections from participants (Frankfort-Nachmais & Nachmais, 2008), on the other hand the experts panel was conducted in two rounds in order to reach consensus. In Focus Groups, data collection relies on the group interaction, interviews, and discussions solely, while in experts panel, those techniques were incorporated with surveys, mind maps, and rankings in order to ensure data validity and reliability. One of the core differences between the experts panel and focus groups is that, focus groups research is not considered a consensus oriented technique, and it is typically conducted in social research in order to observe the behaviour, reactions, and interactions among the group (Hines, 2000; Kitzinger, 1995). On the contrary, the primary goal of the experts panel was to reach *consensus* about the ERP cost factors and cost drivers within SMEs.

CONCLUSION AND FUTURE RESEARCH AVENUES

This chapter is primarily an effort towards illustrating the use of experts panel technique as a mean of eliciting knowledge from a group of ERP experts as an exploratory research. The area of cost estimation in ERP is rarely discussed in literature. Thus developing of a CEM for ERP adoptions is very crucial for research and practice, and that was the main reason behind the willingness of experts to participate in this research. In our point of view, the use of experts panel was very beneficial, as it involved various data collection and visualisation techniques, as well as data validation and confirmation. Beside its advantages, one of the main motives for using a group technique is that it is difficult to find a representative sample for a casual survey method, as ERP experts and consultants are rare to find, especially in the scope of SMEs'

ERP implementations. The experts modified and enhanced the initial cost drivers list largely, as they added, modified, merged and split different costs drivers. In addition, the experts added cost factors (sub-factors) that could influence or affect each cost driver. Moreover, they ranked the cost drivers according to their weight on total costs. All of this helped the authors to better understand relationships among various cost factors. It worth noting that the panel reached consensus regarding the results of the experts panel, which gave extra rigor to the list presented in this chapter.

As this is an initial phase of cost estimation research, more research efforts are needed to operationalize the *costs list* presented here into a practical cost estimation model. Moreover, because of the significance of this model for practice and research, the assessment of this model and its generalizibilty would be important research avenues.

REFERENCES

Al-Mashari, M. (2002). Enterprise resource planning (ERP) systems: a research agenda. *Industrial Management & Data Systems, 102*(3), 165–170. doi:10.1108/02635570210421354

Brancheau, J. C., & Wetherbe, J. C. (1987). Key Issues in Information Systems Management. *Management Information Systems Quarterly, 11*(1), 23–45. doi:10.2307/248822

Cavaye, A. L. M. (1996). Case study research: a multi-faceted research approach for IS. *Information Systems Journal, 6*(3), 227–242. doi:10.1111/j.1365-2575.1996.tb00015.x

Daneva, M. (2004). ERP Requirements Engineering Practice: Lessons Learnt. *IEEE Software, 21*(2), 26–33. doi:10.1109/MS.2004.1270758

Daneva, M. (2007). *Approaching the ERP Project Cost Estimation Problem: an Experiment.* Paper presented at the Proceedings of the First International Symposium on Empirical Software Engineering and Measurement.

Delbecq, A., Van de Ven, A., & Gustafson, D. (1975). *Group techniques for programme planning: a guide to nominal group and Delphi processes.* Glenview, Illinois: Scott, Foresman & Company.

Dick, B. (2000). *Delphi face to face* Retrieved December 4, 2009, from http://www.scu.edu.au/schools/gcm/ar/arp/delphi.html

Eden, C., & Ackermann, F. (2004). Cognitive mapping expert views for policy analysis in the public sector. *European Journal of Operational Research, 152*(3), 615–630. doi:10.1016/S0377-2217(03)00061-4

Eikebrokk, T. R., Iden, J., Olsen, D. H., & Opdahl, A. L. (2008). Validating the Process-Modelling Practice Model. *EMISA, 3*(2), 3–17.

Eisenhardt, K. M. (1989). Building theories from case study research. [AMR]. *Academy of Management Review, 14*(4), 532–550.

Frankfort-Nachmais, C., & Nachmais, D. (2008). *Research methods in the Social Science* (7th ed.). New York, NY: Worth Publishers.

Gibbs, A. (1997). Focus groups. *Social Research Update, Department of Sociology, 19*. Retrieved from www.soc.surrey.ac.uk/sru/sru19.html

Haddara, M., & Päivärinta, T. (2011). *Why Benefits Realization from ERP in SMEs Doesn't Seem to Matter?* Paper presented at the HICSS 44, Kauai, Hawaii.

Haddara, M., & Zach, O. (2011). *ERP Systems in SMEs: A Literature Review.* Paper presented at the HICSS 44, Kauai, Hawaii.

Hines, T. (2000). A Evaluation of Two Qualitative Methods (Focus Group Interviews and Cognitive Maps) for Conducting Research into Entrepreneurial Decision Making. *International Journal of Qualitative Market Research, 3*(1), 7–16. doi:10.1108/13522750010310406

Holland, C. R., & Light, B. (1999). A critical success factors model for ERP implementation. *Software, IEEE, 16*(3), 30–36. doi:10.1109/52.765784

Jones, C. (2007). *Estimating software costs Bringing realism to estimating* (2nd ed.). New York: McGraw-Hill Companies.

Kitzinger, J. (1995). Qualitative Research: Introducing focus groups. *BMJ (Clinical Research Ed.), 311*(7000), 299–302. doi:10.1136/bmj.311.7000.299

Kreuger, R. (1988). *Focus groups: a practical guide for applied research*. London: Sage.

Linstone, H., & Turoff, M. (1975). *The Delphi Method: Techniques and Applications*. London: Addison-Wesley.

Martin, M. H. (1998, Feb. 2). An ERP Strategy. *Fortune*, 95–97.

Moon, Y. (2007). Enterprise Resource Planning (ERP): A review of the literature. *International Journal of Management and Enterprise Development, 4*(3), 200. doi:10.1504/IJMED.2007.012679

Myers, M. D., & Newman, M. (2007). The qualitative interview in IS research: Examining the craft. *Information and Organization, 17*(1), 2–26. doi:10.1016/j.infoandorg.2006.11.001

Nevo, D., & Chan, Y. E. (2007). A Delphi study of knowledge management systems: Scope and requirements. *Information & Management, 44*(6), 583–597. doi:10.1016/j.im.2007.06.001

Newman, M., & Zhao, Y. (2008). The process of enterprise resource planning implementation and business process re-engineering: tales from two chinese small and medium-sized enterprises. *Information Systems Journal, 18*(4), 405–426. doi:10.1111/j.1365-2575.2008.00305.x

Osborn, A. F. (1957). *Applied Imagination* (revised ed.). New York: Scribners.

Parnes, J., & Meadow, A. (1959). Effects of Brain-Storming Instruction on Creative Problem-Solving by Trained and Untrained Subjects. *Journal of Educational Psychology*, 50.

Powell, R., & Single, H. (1996). Focus groups. *International Journal for Quality in Health Care, 8*(5), 499–504. doi:10.1093/intqhc/8.5.499

Roth, R. M., & William, C. Wood, I. (1990). *A Delphi approach to acquiring knowledge from single and multiple experts*. Paper presented at the Proceedings of the 1990 ACM SIGBDP conference on Trends and directions in expert systems.

Rubin, H. J., & Rubin, I. S. (2005). *Qualitative interviewing: The art of hearing data* (2nd ed.). Thousand Oaks, CA: Sage.

Schmidt, R. C. (1997). Managing Delphi Surveys Using Nonparametric Statistical Techniques. *Decision Sciences, 28*(3), 763–774. doi:10.1111/j.1540-5915.1997.tb01330.x

Seddon, P. (2003). *Second-Wave Enterprise Resource Planning Systems*. New York, NY: Cambridge University Press.

Soh, C., Kien, S. S., & Tay-Yap, J. (2000). Enterprise resource planning: cultural fits and misfits: is ERP a universal solution? *Communications of the ACM, 43*(4), 47–51. doi:10.1145/332051.332070

Stensrud, E. (2001). Alternative Approaches to Effort Prediction of ERP Projects. *Information and Software Technology, 43*(7), 413–423. doi:10.1016/S0950-5849(01)00147-1

Van de Ven, A., & Delbeco, A. (1971). Nominal versus Interacting Group Processes for Committee Decision-Making Effectiveness. *Academy of Management Journal, 14*(2), 203–212. doi:10.2307/255307

Van de Ven, A., & Delbecq, A. (1974). The Effectiveness of Nominal, Delphi, and Interacting Group Decision Making Processes. *Academy of Management Journal, 17*(4), 605–621. doi:10.2307/255641

Van Everdingen, Y., Van Hillegersberg, J., & Waarts, E. (2000). Enterprise resource planning: ERP adoption by European midsize companies. *Communications of the ACM, 43*(4), 27–31. doi:10.1145/332051.332064

Watts, M., & Ebbutt, D. (1987). More than the sum of the parts: research methods in group interviewing. *British Educational Research Journal, 13*, 25–34. doi:10.1080/0141192870130103

Willis, C. L., & Miertschin, S. L. (2006). Mind maps as active learning tools. *J. Comput. Small Coll., 21*(4), 266–272.

Yin, R. K. (2003). *Case study research: Design and methods* (3rd ed., *Vol. 5*). Thousand Oaks, CA: Sage.

Chapter 8
Evaluating the Success of ERP Systems' Implementation:
A Study About Portugal

Ricardo Almeida
Faculdade de Engenharia da Universidade do Porto, Portugal

Miguel Nuno de Oliveira Teixeira
Universidade Trás-os-Montes e Alto Douro, Portugal

ABSTRACT

Information management has assumed an increasing importance at business organizations, over the last decades. Such trends lead companies to promote enormous efforts on organizing and optimizing their business processes, acquiring expensive enterprise information systems, aiming to promote an accurate answer to market uncertainty. Unfortunately, traditional software implementations have revealed low levels of satisfaction by Enterprise Resource Planning (ERP) systems' customers. This study aims to evaluate the reasons for success and failure of ERP systems implemented in Portugal and the methodologies taken by consulting teams. To achieve such a goal, it has been submitted a web survey to Portuguese companies and consulting teams, in order to confirm major errors, ERP systems' coverage and quality's response for business processes, and assessment of engineering requirements as a major concern. This study is concluded with the presentation of the web survey results and some conclusions about ERP systems' implementation at Portugal.

INTRODUCTION

Some authors believe that ERP systems implementation' process should be considered as an information system development project, due to complexity and project management needs; which involves the use of skills and knowledge in coordinating the scheduling and monitoring of defined activities, to ensure that the stated objectives of implementation projects are achieved. Several steps should be taken in targeting full enterprise fitting by the ERP solution implementing team (Nah, J Lau, & Kuang, 2001, Akkermans & van Helden, 2002), resulting in a extended high risk

DOI: 10.4018/978-1-4666-1764-3.ch008

process that often results in great expenditures of both time and money, while arising as an unfinished and/or failed project, both completely or partially (Bingi, Sharma, & Godla, 1999, Guang-hui, Chun-qing, & Yun-xiu, 2006, Kang, Park, & Yang, 2008). The reasons for not accomplished implementation processes have been discussed since the mid of 90's; with special focus on the key factors leading to failure or success and entailing the notion that there is a spectrum of factors that either combined or individually can lead to ERP failure; being it due time overruns, cost overruns or both, or ultimately the solution adopted falling short in the expectations. To complement this, it's often found that the Requirements Engineering somewhat seems to either overlook certain aspects of the whole project or apply generic formulas to not so generic customers, with special notice to often mismatched choice of the solutions or the natural fitting of the latest to the customer's specific demands.

Parallel to this, most applications are built by software houses to become modular, whereas one enterprise will only acquire and implement those in need of (or at least the perceived need of) by choosing the product following a complex and multi-factor influenced decision (Verville, 2000, Verville & Halingten, 2002). The acquisition process often broadens the whole time span of the process for its very own beginning, with particular expression in larger corporations (Bernroider & Koch, 2001). Such processes often result in a 12 and plus months implementation process due to several facts, namely the number of modules to be implemented, the geographical extent of the facilities where the implementation and training takes place, the extent and difficulty of customization (Bingi et al., 1999, Almeida & Azevedo, 2009). To cut down on the implementation time-span, ERP vendors and producers are developing less customizable solutions, to whom Bingi et. al refer to as 'plain vanilla', as in reference to bland, not fully fitted or customizable solutions that somewhat tend to fall short in replying the enterprise

demands, even more so within this new global fast reaction economy. This phenomena also clashes with the motivation and the cultural constraints as we will look in further detail later in this work, further increasing the obstacle to successful implementations (Bingi et al., 1999, Almeida & Azevedo, 2009). Alternatively, software houses also develop vertical solutions, geared towards specific industry sectors or markets, leaving short flexibility to the buyer which only can customize/configure some personal requirements (which, in some cases, could respond to important specific needs, that reflect ultimately each organizations competences, more than the sector overall needs).

RESEARCH METHODOLOGY

The professional experience of both authors on ERP systems' implementations has raised some questions which require a consistent theoretical validation, gathering important scientific contributions (from scientific papers, Msc and PhD thesis) that could ensure a conceptual evaluation. To provide a practical approach and ensure veracity to our conclusions, it has been realized a web-survey to ERP systems' companies and consulting teams.

This study has been organized and divided in 4 main phases, as resumed on Figure 1.

The first step was to resume some questions that always remain as major doubts on ERP systems' implementation (presented on the next chapter). The following step was a detailed work on the analysis of bibliographic and scientific papers, which could validate and present the theoretical concepts of the main theme.

One major concern from authors was the practical appliance and validation of this study, which lead to the development of a web survey (using *SurveyMonkeys* platform – www.surveymonkeys.com) to Portuguese companies, from different business sectors.

Figure 1. Steps taken for the research methodology

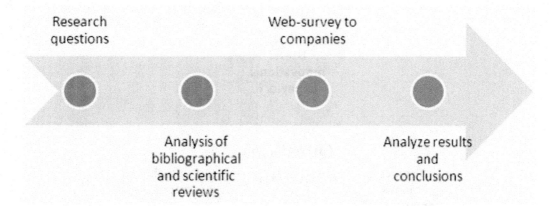

This methodology allowed us to explore some *cause & effect* topics arise from the research questions and raised us the concern of the theme at Portugal, regarding inefficiency and failure of implementation projects. The work finishes with survey's data dissemination and conclusions (which include some statements and advices).

RESEARCH QUESTIONS

This chapter resumes the main questions raised by the authors concerning the subject of this scientific work. The questions were carefully defined and classified in four areas (user's behavior/acceptance, team's competence, ERP's flexibility and dynamic organizational cycle), presented graphically on Figure 2.

Question: Are Users Considered as a Barrier to Implementation (Due to Their Motivational Behavior)?

We believe that one constraint to be considered is the motivational approach of users when facing the usage of a new information system. According to (Frank Crewe, 2009), the implementation of a new ERP system can cause fears and concerns for many employees. Some of these employees never have been involved in an ERP implementation

before, and it will be unclear about the implications the project will have for them and their roles in the organization.

As mentioned on the well known Fox Meyer Drug's bankruptcy case study (Scott, 1999), one strategy that should be conducted to avoid the morale problem would be a better training of the employees, helping them to develop new skills, putting some of them on the implementation team and using other change management techniques. More recently the Lumber Liquidators ERP' failure case study was credited to user acceptance constraints, which arose from lack of IT skills of end users and poor communication of objectives. These examples further increase the evidence of the needed education and training of users across the organization's hierarchy as a tactical factor (as evidenced by several authors who have addressed the training and organization overall involvement as a critical success factor for ERP success (Bingi et al., 1999, Al-Fawaz, 2009, Yanhong, 2009)).

This phenomenon is amplified whenever the ERP implementation to be undertaken does not possess clear objectives aligned with the company's transversal operations. Subsequently, people which work is those areas where research conducted observed a clear objective have demonstrated that is highly influential in the positive alignment of the ERP with the organization and the outcome of the IT investment (Kang et al.,

Figure 2. Research questions major areas

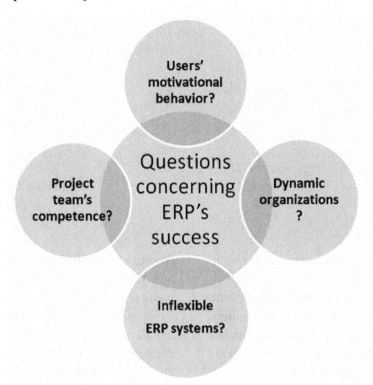

2008) and a user participated and committed action, is of major importance in achieving success. This can be achieved by involving the users in the implementation, co-working with change agents and addressing their concerns with regular communication (Nah et al., 2001, Akkermans & van Helden, 2002). The overall benefit of ERP systems' implementation which affects the whole organization, is better achieved by introducing a factor of re engineering of business process (Holland & Light, 1999) where *"various levels of the organization engage is a series of dialogues"* (Buckhout, Frey, & Nemec JR., 1999) in order to define the relations between what is operational and strategic priorities and what trade-offs must be made. To consider an ERP implementation as successful, it must be accepted by all workers, independently of their position in the hierarchy. These users' input should be considered as an important source for requirements, reactions and approval (Fiona Fui-Hoon Nah et al., 2001,

Kimberling, 2010, Rosario, 2000). Several ERP systems' deployment success factors studies have identified users' acceptance of the systems as critical success factor (Nah et al., 2001, Bingi et al., 1999, Al-Mashari, Al-Mudimigh, & Zairi, 2003).

Shanks (Wee, 2000) referred that resistance can be destructive since it can create conflicts between actors and it can be very time consuming. To implement an ERP system successfully, the way organizations manage their business will need to change and ways people perform their jobs will need to change as well. This author also referred that training concern are not only using a new system, but also in new processes and in understanding the integration within the system – how the work of one employee influences the work of others. This trend further enhances the need of the enterprise top management to "establish the guidelines of user involvement" (Buckhout et al., 1999).

Panorama Consulting has developed a worldwide ERP system's survey and, as results, it stated that an impressive 53% of implementing organizations perceive their ability to deal with change as fairly poor or very poor. Additionally, 47% believe that communication between management and employees is poor. These types of environments are, as previously stated, not conducive to successful ERP systems' implementations. Organizational change management tools, however, help address such barriers to make the rollouts more successful.

Question: Does a Project Team Competence Become Crucial for a Successful ERP Systems' Implementation?

The research conducted in the critical success factors regarding ERP system's implementations takes notice also on the fact that having a competent team in the area of expertise (for both the business undergoing the implementation and the solution itself) provides a solid leverage to sustained and successful implementations (Akkermans & van Helden, 2002, Bingi et al., 1999) and is recognized by business owners and involved actors as a key factor for goal achievement (Bingi et al., 1999, Buckhout et al., 1999, Rosario, 2000).

In the past years, several authors studying the critical success factors for ERP implementation processes have defined and established different approaches and terms, but yet all leading to this very same concept: the importance of the actors involved in the implementation (Nah et al., 2001, Akkermans & van Helden, 2002, Bingi et al., 1999, Guang-hui et al., 2006, Buckhout et al., 1999, Yanhong, 2009), with a special interest in the ERP team and its composition, personal and professional skills and competences (Bingi et al., 1999, Buckhout et al., 1999, Rosario, 2000). This becomes more evident since most ERP implementation projects have a time frame of several months or even years and the general consensus of the authors who have developed studies in the

subject is that the team competences is a CSF that impacts the whole span, i.e. from early stages of the chartering phase to the later maintenance stages (Nah et al., 2001, Umble, Haft, & Umble, 2003).

Not accidentally, there is also a common perception that the growth of ERP markets led to the shortage of skilled personal and such challenges are further aggravated by difficulties on maintaining those skilled elements for at least the time-span of the project (Bingi et al., 1999), due to several reasons, with focus on the fact that these highly skilled consultants are sought after. Therefore, opening the market to the less skilled at one and tremendously increasing the implementation costs for those who want "nothing but the best". In addition, the fact that the team set of competencies is wider than mere technical skills (Bingi et al., 1999), ranging from technical and business functional skills to more importantly in this case, interpersonal skills, namely communicational ones which can be a main weapon to prevent implementations stalling and crisis (Akkermans & van Helden, 2002), can furthermore enhance the critical need to allocate the best employees to the ERP systems' implementations (Bingi et al., 1999) in order to minimize the risk.

As already referred, one important aspect is the communication between all agents, which has to be promoted by project managers as a vital competency. According to Shanks (Wee, 2000) it is essential for creating an understanding, an approval of the implementation and sharing information between the project team and communicating to the whole organization the results and the goals in each implementation stage. The communication should start early in the ERP implementation project and can include overview of the system and the reason for implementing it be consistent and continuous.

The latest trends states the growing importance given to enterprise maturity capacity models (like CMMI) and PMI certifications for project managers, as important elements when choosing a team/company for ERP systems' implementation.

Question: Are ERP Systems Inflexible? What Should I Develop, Instead?

In recent years, ERP systems have been increasing their configuration capabilities, in order to promote a better adaptation to the business processes of any organization. This trend can be confirmed with the raising activity of *package software development* against *customized software development* (leaving this option as only affordable when facing a distinct business processes). In addition, the predicted changes on governmental and fiscal impositions to occur (in the coming times) will further undermine the internal (indoors) development systems by imposing normalization of procedures and systems certification; it will, probably, impose a shift in many companies to leave the indoors development solutions to packaged ERP solutions. This will lead companies to a *choice trap* where they need to choose between the costly packaged software customization and the internal process re-engineering in order to adapt to the chosen ERP's demands. Verville & Halingten (2002) have addressed this question in the study of the influencing factors on the decision process of ERP acquiring, where the authors note a strong influence of the development vs. adaptation dilemma, in which the economical factors of internal development plays an important role in shifting the gear from total or partial customization to total or partial adaptation of the companies' business processes.

The reasons for requesting such high levels of customization are not a courtliness of companies. In fact, the current markets are characterized by greater turbulence and demand of new products of higher complexity which, combined with a delivery time greatly reduced, forced companies to extreme efforts to adapt their businesses processes (Almeida & Azevedo, 2011), which affect, consequently, information systems. Therefore, companies demand for an extraordinary agility and quick responses to development teams

which, sometimes, not adjusted to the financial investments dedicated for information technology' departments. Two decades ago, software houses started to offer a wider coverage (in terms of functional areas) of their applications and also some powerful benefits, like constant updates for Government regulations adoption and software localization, vertical solutions, etc. Software houses like SAP, Baan and JD Edwards (to mention just a few) become popular in a worldwide scale, being SAP the most recognized nowadays.

As with regards to major players in the Portugal information system market, there a few international software houses and a larger number of national producers, being all of them centered in packaged development (yet to a certain degree, customizable solutions). On a worldwide scale, SAP assumes the leadership of ERP market, with implementations on the major companies (like Sonae, Cimpor, etc). On a national scale, market is mainly shared by PHC Software, Primavera Software and Sage. Due to the small Portuguese' SMEs scale, these 3 vendors have developed ERP's versions specific to small companies (achieving prices less than 2000€ for a *small* ERP system).

Although with different nomenclatures, all these ERP systems response to the same functional areas, being stated that the major differences exist on their configurations' capability. (Almeida & Azevedo, 2009) identified three parameterization levels to represent the existent functional structure for ERP systems (Almeida & Azevedo, 2009). It was defined a first level for *ERP internal business development*, which includes all the business rules developed by the software house as standard operation routines. The second level is defined as the *Business Process customization level*, which concerns the entire advanced configuration promoted by consultants and implementers, in order to guarantee system's adaptation to companies' requirements. Finally, the third level is dedicated to *Low level customization*, which includes the entire parameterization available for ERP's users. We consider that the Business Process customization level is the "distinguish element" between the current ERP system available at Portugal.

Question: Do Organizations Have Such Dynamic Business Models Impossible to be "Tame"?

The global market is in constantly changes and companies desire for agility and flexible strategies, in order to react accurately and with a reduced risk. Such trend asks for flexible information systems but also flexible organizations, available to re-engineer quickly their business models.

In this "not so new" digital economy that seems to raise the greatest challenges to business leaders and the organizations, the contemporary manufacturing practices are contextualized in light of digital economy practices and entailed to synthesize the development towards the enterprise adapted to a global information society (Parr & Shanks, 2000). This economical and technological turmoil has been shifting the gear of the organizations from a product/process based activity to a more information based business, imposing a new supply chain relation based on information exchanges via IT, albeit the core business remaining the same i.e. producing and/or selling a certain product or service (LAZARICA, 2009, Machado, Costa, & Gomes, 2008). This is forcing a new perception that certain IT rationality is the critical path, rather than the focal point itself, imposing the ERP implementations to remain focused in developing/fitting the information flows as per prioritized demands. The argument for this option is, as Buckhout (Buckhout et al., 1999) mentioned that such ever-changing economical landscape inputs constant changes and updates in such terms that the financial and schedule overruns more often than not, and can ultimately obscure and consume much of the ERP's original perceived benefits.

A possible approach to avoid such mismatches is to define top business vertical priorities and postpone the more *in-depth* developments required by local units or functional areas, eventually by

partially re-engineering the internal processes. This would allow reaching a compromise solution and as a result dramatically reduce the implementation time as mentioned in the Autodesk and the Owens Corning case studies to name just a couple (Buckhout et al., 1999).

This compromise can be achieved by re-thinking the business itself as a supply chain customer centered operation (Buckhout et al., 1999) and hunting for solutions that address these *"extra-organizational ties"* (Bernroider & Koch, 2001).

Additionally, Umble *et. al.* have defended that buying an ERP suite goes beyond selecting a software, and that it *"means buying into the software vendor"* (Aladwani, 2001), therefore assuming the vendors views of the business best practices as their own. Furthermore, the authors defended that in order to succeed, the ERP must underscore *"its unique competitive strengths while helping to overcome competitive weaknesses"*.

STUDY RESULTS

Sample and Questions Management

The web survey has been conducted, for some weeks over, almost 2000 Portuguese companies from distinct business sectors. The major content of this survey was to evaluate ERP system's implementation (level of satisfaction, constraints, problems, etc) according to user's perceptions of functionalities provided and the impact of changes on their daily management. To achieve this goal, it has been prepared 17 questions resumed on Table 1.

RESULTS

The survey results were analyzed and classified according the following phases (presented on Figure 1), for a better evaluation and conclusions dissemination.

Table 1. Questions included on the survey

Question role	Possible answers	Goal
Actual status of ERP system implementation	• Running; • Finished less than 1 year ago; • Finished less than 3 years ago; • Finished more than 3 years ago;	Evaluate if some answers (related with requirements' coverage) could be affected by the execution of implementation plan.
Most important factors in the decision of a ERP system	• Increase efficiency of business processes; • Increase companies' market competiveness; • Increase communication/integration with customers; • Increase communication/integration with suppliers; • Ensure Government legislation's compliance (financial and/or accountable); • Strategic option (integration on a major group); • Other reasons;	Evaluate the main reasons for decision of choosing an ERP system to the company.
Software classification	• 100% customized developed software; • Package software (high parameterization level); • Package software (low parameterization level);	Evaluate the chosen type of software implemented.
Expectation level	• 100% fulfilled; • Above 75%; • Between 25 and 50%; • Bellow 25%;	Evaluate the expectation level of the ERP system's implementation executed.
Main reasons for fulfilled ERP system's implementations	• Implementation's project has been well conducted; • ERP system is very complete; • Company's business processes weren't complex; • Users participated actively in the implementation; • Other reasons;	Evaluate major reasons to a successful ERP system's implementation.
Functional areas which have benefit with the ERP system's implementation	• Commercial; • Accountable/Financial; • Marketing; • Purchasing; • Production; • Expedition;	Evaluate major appliances (functional areas) of ERP system's implementation.
Main reasons for an unfulfilled ERP system's implementations	• ERP system didn't provide enough business coverage; • Implementer wasn't aware of companies business; • Implementer didn't performed a complete requirement analysis; • Implementer didn't had the knowledge capacities; • Companies businesses processes are very dynamic; • Users have not adapted to the ERP system; • Other reasons;	Evaluate major reasons to an unsuccessful ERP system's implementation.
Major deviations on ERP system's implementation	• Costs; • Timings; • Business processes' implementation coverage; • Expectations related with business processes' timing execution; • Increase customers' "proximity"; • Increase suppliers' "proximity"; • Other reasons;	Evaluate major deviations according to implementations' initial plan.
Project's status communication (of implementers with users)	• Communicate, often, the status to Administration; • Communicate, often, the status to Administration and senior staff; • Communicate, often, the status to all users; • No communication;	Evaluate the involvement of users (and their roles) in the implementation's process;
Level of adaptability of the ERP system to company's business processes.	• Yes! Company had to change, without benefits; • Yes! Company had to change, with benefits; • No! ERP system has adapted to our business processes;	Evaluate the impact of the ERP system over the company's current business processes.

continued on following page

Table 1. Continued

Question role	Possible answers	Goal
Users' involvement in ERP system's implementation	• Users never been consulted by implementers; • Users were consulted, only, at an initial period; • Users had participated, actively, on implementation meetings; • Users have implemented the ERP system;	Evaluate the involvement of users in the implementation's process;
How users evaluate the new ERP system	• Considered a useful and easy to use tool; • Considered a useful tool, but requires a huge effort to learn; • Considered a useful tool for the company, but not for your daily work; • Not considered a useful tool for your daily work	Evaluate user's opinion about the practical utility of the ERP for their daily work.
Does the company consider the ERP system as a tool which provide flexibility	• Yes! It allows adaptation, by my internal team; • Yes! It allows adaptation, for implementers; • No! It doesn't allow adaptation and it's a constraint for business processes' evolution; • No! The ERP system is very limited on the available configurations; • No! The system is going to be replaced;	Evaluate the perception of the users of the ERP system's adaptation capabilities.
It was performed any requirement analysis?	• Yes • Only the first meetings (before the presentation of the implementation plan); • No	Confirm if any requirement analysis study was made.
The implementation plan included any business processes representation?	• No!; • Yes! Included WBS, Gantt chart, costs, resources; • Yes! Included UML diagrams; • Yes! Included IDEF diagrams; • Other;	Evaluate if the requirements analysis phase was documented.
Do you believe that a better engineering requirement phase would result on a better implementation project	• Yes! No doubts about that; • Yes! That's what we have done; • Not necessary; as long requirements are gathered, are also implemented; • This stage is unnecessary;	Evaluate user's perception of the importance of a engineering requirement phase
ERP system implemented on the company	• SAP R/3; • SAP Business One; • Microsoft Dynamic (Navision); • PHC Software; • Primavera Software; • Totvs; • JD Edwards; • Sage; • Baan; • Other;	Evaluate the ERP systems included on the survey.

Figure 3. Classification of survey's questions

Figure 4. Most important factors in the decision of an ERP system (results from survey)

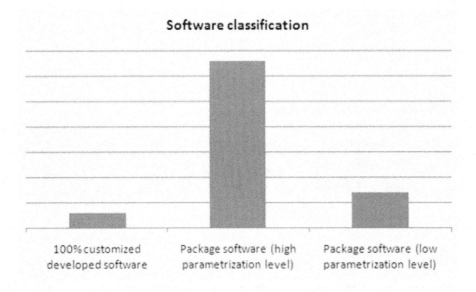

Almost 45% of the overall companies which have answered to the survey have already finished their implementation, while only 30% still are on the implementation phase. The fact of having a high percentage of companies already finished their ERP system's implementation gave us a higher confidence on the answers retrieved from the subsequent questions.

With regards to the conclusions extracted from the descriptive statistics we found that there is a major concern with the business processes' efficiency and increasing market competitiveness, which are considered as the major reasons for decide for an ERP system. The data gathered also raised the need of companies to ensure Government's legislation compliance, representing almost 13% of inquired answers. A graphical representation of these factors (which affect the decision when choosing an ERP system) is resumed on Figure 4.

It has been also stated that most of respondent companies use packaged software with flexible frameworks (reaching almost 77%), which has

Figure 5. Software classification (results from survey)

Figure 6. Level of fulfillment (results from survey)

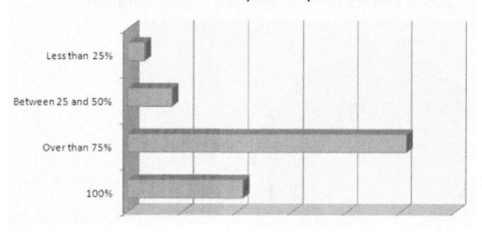

confirmed the overall trend of the last decades of leaving the 100% customized software (data presented, graphically, on Figure 5).

Despite the expected general opinion that ERP systems don't achieve full expectations prior to implementation, there is a general consensus (60% of the respondents) that it did meet at least 75% of the expected goals, like presented on Figure 6.

In fact, these results make us believe that most of the negative opinions are totally unfounded.

One of the major objectives of the survey was to evaluate which functional areas benefit most from an ERP system's implementation. The survey has showed that Commercial and Financial areas are the most benefits functional areas from ERP system utilization, probably, by the importance of Orders and Invoice management pro-

Figure 7. Functional areas which benefit with ERP systems (results from survey)

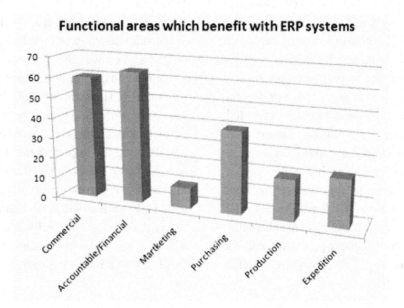

Figure 8. Major reasons for success of ERP system's implementations (results from survey)

Success factors on ERP system's implementations

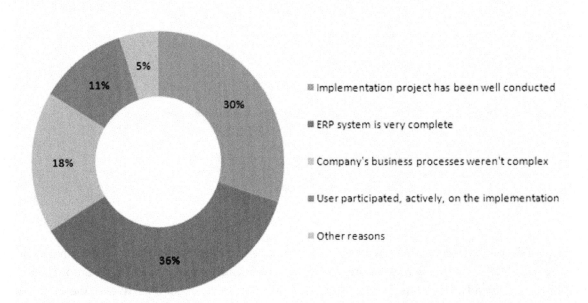

cesses, customer relationship management and legacy procedures (Government taxes, etc) on the daily business management of companies. These conclusions were gathered by the analysis of the graphic presented on Figure 7.

One major concern of this research study was to evaluate some of the factors that could be lead to successful ERP system's implementations. The study gathered information from companies which claim for a positive final result on the use of ERP systems, pointing the implementation project management and ERP systems' coverage as the crucial factors for the success (data presented, graphically, on Figure 8). The two factors were validated on subsequent questions, in order to detail user's perception of each one.

One the other hand, unsatisfied users claimed that two major reasons for unsuccessful ERP system's implementation: the dynamic characteristic of companies' business processes and the uncompleted coverage of them by these systems.

The major unsuccess factors detected are resumed, graphically, on Figure 9.

Most of the overruns occurred in the time-schedule rather than the overall cost, therefore increasing the notion that the ERP systems implementations are becoming rather "economical" either for its license price or overall project cost. These data is presented, graphically on Figure 10.

Also a major factor concluded from the conducted survey was the importance of user's involvement on the implementation process. When users participate (actively) on requirements engineering processes, a high percentage of errors or misunderstandings are solved on earlier stages, not affecting the implementation stage.

Also 60% of the organizations recognize having benefited from process re-engineering in order to adapt to some of the ERP's standard processes, rather than choosing to fully adapt the ERP. This notion seems to be in agreement to the idea that there is a need of compromise between ERP's

Figure 9. Major reasons for unsuccess of ERP system's implementations (results from survey)

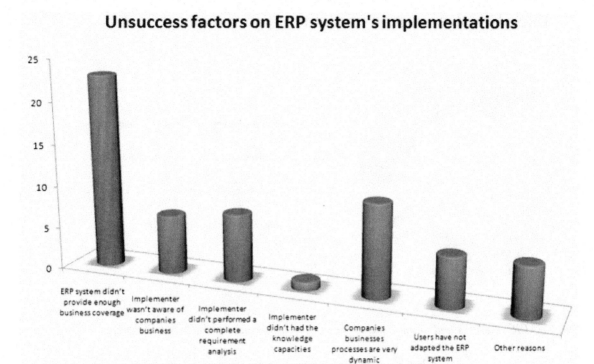

Figure 10. Major deviations concerning implementation plan (results from survey)

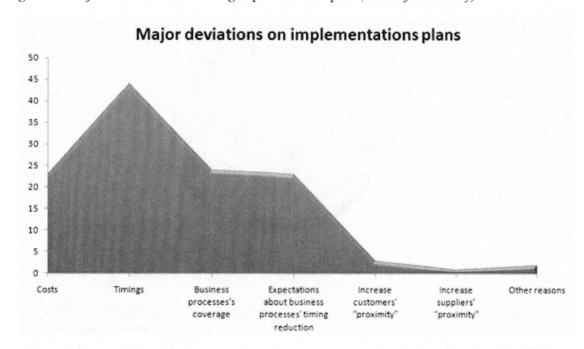

Figure 11. User's involvement on implementation process (results from survey)

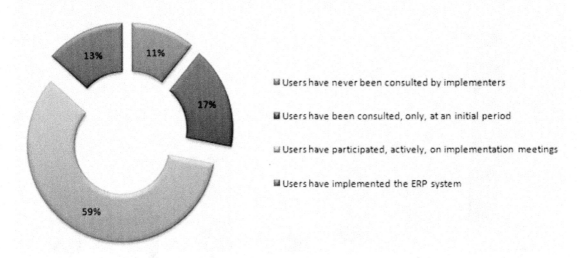

Figure 12. ERP systems and change management for companies (results from survey)

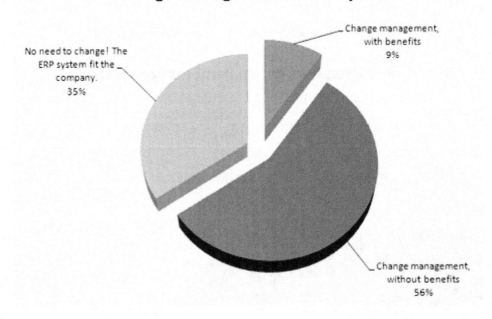

configuration and Business Process Re-engineering (BPR).

The grand majority, some 85% of the respondent organizations, believes that there is a major advantage in choosing adaptable ERP system, which promotes organizational scalability providing autonomy to both internal and external implementation teams. Additionally, we found there

Figure 13. ERP systems included on the study (results from survey)

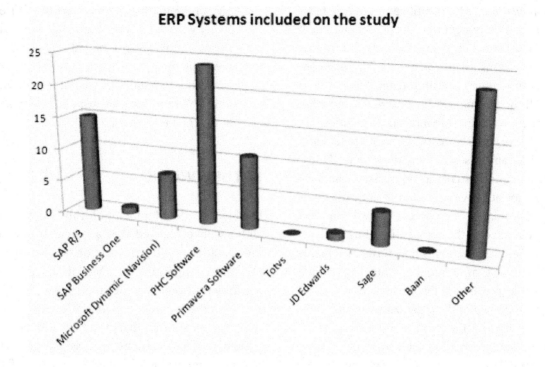

was a majority of implementation processes (65%) that were conducted having a requirements analysis, and from these, nevertheless there is a 25% ERP implementations that did not result in a proper requirements engineering report handed/delivered prior or during the implementation to the organization.

Concerning the ERP systems included on the study, a high relevance should be made to PHC Software and SAP R/3 as the leading ERP systems presented on Portuguese market (according to the results from the survey conducted).

CONCLUSION

In the process of literary research for this paper, several authors lead us to believe that there were 4 relevant clusters of phenomena to observe with regards to ERP & Organizational alignment for successful implementation of ERP's in general and there was no reason to suspect that Portuguese

organizations to be otherwise. Those 4 clusters, rather than focused in the technical aspect of the acquired software (which are, undoubtedly important, but have been "scrutinized" many times) are to be found revolving around personal and organizational issues as well as the interaction of the actors involved in the whole project; being those actors the implementing team: the organizations workers (from top management to low end users throughout all of the ERP adoption phases, i.e. from the very moment of choosing the best suited solution to the project conclusion).

In light of these conclusions, and following the general consensus of several authors reviewed in this paper, we find that there is a number of traits be taken in consideration when choosing to change and implement a ERP in any given organization, in order to minimize the risk of failure or leverage the success of the process itself, and that can be resumed in the following points, each one related to one of the 4 areas previously researched.

- *Focus on business processes and requirements first:* The identification of key business requirements and the proper alignment of software implementation with business operations assume a major role. Such concern requires a skillful team that can raise all the Businesses Requirements and align them with the software's potentialities.
- *Do not rush the decision!* Such a potentially risky and costly activity must be well measured, and usually a bad decision can have major negative impact in the organizations performance. The pace of a decision must be related to the complexity of its processes and requirements and further increases the need of a requirements engineering work to evaluate the best solution to meet the demand of the organization itself, without causing the price or time schedule of the implementation itself overrun
- *Provide adequate training and Organizational commitment:* The degree of change in the daily life of the employees can become tremendous, so it's demanding attitude to communicate the objectives, new jobs and task to those re-engineered processes and adequate training in terms of end user. Avoiding these steps can increase the level of personnel resistance to change and as stated prior in the study, turn what would be a technological leap forward into a tremendous financial drawback.
- *Commit between customization and process adaptation:* Fully fitting the software is not always the wiser choice, since some customizations involves too much time and money, and have such little impact in the overall perception of the ERP's benefits to the organization; the most rational choice is to find a midway solution! Changes to software source code can increase implementation cost and risk, so it is necessary to refrain from small precious iniquities and "must-have" competitive advantages

to your organization. Nevertheless, the chosen ERP must be able to respond effectively whenever a new challenge or priority arises at any given moment, either during the implementation of after going live, thus rendering inevitable choice of a customizable solution that can respond adequately at any given moment.

FUTURE WORK

During the development of this work, both authors have realized that a potential detailed investigation could start (base on this first study) for future opportunities. One of the possible research dimensions to be studied, for example, is the evaluation of companies' hierarchy levels different perceptions that might exist of the ERP system's implementations (successful or not). This research could potentially address some of the issues in how (and why) is perceived the success of an ERP system's implementation according to the user role in the company's hierarchy; and find potential relations to the Implementation team and Top management communication to end users.

Another dimension to be evaluated would the positive impact of the ERP implementation in the companies' overall business performance, by identifying if such positive alignment could have (or not!) a direct consequence of a thoroughly developed business requirements mapping or a C-CEI process. This investigation could deal with the concept of how important is a successful ERP system's implementation in terms of overall business performance. Also would be considered as a result of a objective and purposeful buying process and thoroughly explored requirements in the span of the implementation, thus finding the conditions of acquisition and requirements engineering under which an implementation has a positive impact on the business performance.

REFERENCES

Akkermans, H., & van Helden, K. (2002). Vicious and virtuous cycles in ERP implementation: a case study of interrelations between critical success factors. *European Journal of Information Systems, 11*, 35–46. doi:10.1057/palgrave/ejis/3000418

Al-Fawaz, K. (2009) *An Investigation of The Factors That Impact Users Satisfaction In ERP Implementations* Paper presented at Ph.D. Symposium, Brunel University, UK.

Al-Mashari, M., Al-Mudimigh, A., & Zairi, M. (2003). Enterprise resource planning: A taxonomy of critical factors. *Elsevier - European Journal of Operational Research*, (146): 352–364. doi:10.1016/S0377-2217(02)00554-4

Aladwani, A. M. (2001). Change management strategies for successful ERP implementation. *Emerald - Business Process Management Journal, 7*(3), 266–275. doi:10.1108/14637150110392764

Almeida, R., & Azevedo, A. (2009). The needed adaptability for ERP systems. In Cruz-Cunha, M. M. (Ed.), *Enterprise Information Systems Design, Implementation and Management: Organizational Applications*. Hershey, PA: IGI Global.

Almeida, R., & Azevedo, A. (2011) Collaborative business networks - Evaluation of technological tools for decision support making. *e-LP Engineering and Technology Journal*.

Bernroider, E., & Koch, S. (2001) ERP selection Process in Mid-size and Large Organizations. *Business Process Management Journal 7* (3) 251, 257.

Bingi, P., Sharma, M., & Godla, J. (1999). Critical Issues Affecting an ERP Implementation. *Information Systems Management, 16*(3), 7–14. doi:10.1201/1078/43197.16.3.19990601/31310.2

Buckhout, S., Frey, E., & Nemec, J., Jr. (1999) *Making ERP Succeed: Turning Fear into Promise*. Retrieved from: http://www.strategy-business.com/article/16678?gko=49d43

Crewe, F. (2009). *Shock of the Old*. Evaluation Centre.

Guang-hui, C., Li, C., & Sai, Y. (2006)... *Critical Success Factors for ERP Life Cycle Implementation International Federation for Information Processing Digital Library, 205*, 553–562.

Holland, C. P., & Light, B. (1999). A critical success factors model for erp implementation. In *IEEE Software*. Washington, DC: IEEE Press. doi:10.1109/52.765784

Kang, S., Park, J. H., & Yang, H. D. (2008). ERP alignment for positive business performance: Evidence from Korea's ERP market. *Journal of Computer Information Systems, 48*(4), 25–39.

Kimberling, E. (2010) *What Was the Cause of the SAP Failure at Lumber Liquidators?* 360° ERP Blog. Retrieved from: http://panorama-consulting.com/erp-blog/

Lazarica, M. *The Virtual Enterprise – Opportunity for SMES in the Digital Economy*.

Machado, R. J. M., Costa, L. A. A. F., & Gomes, J. L. F. (2008). *Processo de implementaçao de ERPs: um método para o ajuste de requisitos e optimizaçao de funcionalidades* [Process of implementing ERP: a method for setting requirements and sparing use of features]. Portugal: Universidade do Minho.

Nah, F. F., Lau, J. L., & Kuang, J. (2001). *Critical factors for successful implementation of enterprise systems*. Emerald - Business Process Management Journal.

Parr, A., & Shanks, G. (2000). A model of ERP project implementation. *Emerald - Journal of Information Technology, 15*(4), 289–303. doi:10.1080/02683960010009051

Porter, M. (1996) *What is strategy?* Harvard Business Review

Rosario, J. G. (2000). *On the leading edge: Critical sucess factors on ERP implementation projects.* Business World.

Scott, J. E. (1999) The FoxMeyer Drugs' bankruptcy: Was it a failure of ERP. In *Americas Conference on Information Systems, August,* 13–15.

Umble, E. J., Haft, R. R., & Umble, M. M. (2002). *Enterprise resource planning: Implementation procedures and critical success factors* (pp. 241–257). Elsevier.

Verville, J. C. (2000) *An empirical study of organizational buying behavior: a Critical investigation of the acquisition of ERP software,*.

Verville, J.C. & Halingten, A. (2002) A Qualitative study of the influencing factors on the decision process for acquiring ERP software. *Qualitative Market Reasearch: An International Journal 5*(3) 188, 198.

Wee, S. (2000) Juggling toward Erp Sucess: Keep key success factors high. *ERP News,* (February).

Yanhong, Z. (2009) ERP Implementation Process Analysis Based on the Key Success Factors. *Information Technology and Applications, IFITA '09.*

Chapter 9
Two Case Studies on RFID Initiatives:
Testing the Impact of IT Infrastructure Integration and Supply Chain Process Integration

Rebecca Angeles
University of New Brunswick Fredericton, Canada

ABSTRACT

This paper features the results of an empirical online survey focusing on radio frequency identification initiatives and the revalidation of these results using brief case studies on Charles Voegele and Vail Resorts. The empirical study investigates the ability of information technology (IT) infrastructure integration and supply chain process integration to moderate the relationships between the importance of the perceived seven adoption attributes and system deployment outcomes, operational efficiency and market knowledge creation in radio frequency identification (RFID)-enabled supply chains. Using the online survey method, data was collected from members of the Council of Supply Chain Management Professionals in North America. The moderated regression procedure suggested by Aguinis (2004) was applied. The three adoption attributes, relative advantage, results, and images turned out to be the most important attributes in these RFID systems. Indeed, both IT infrastructure integration and supply chain process integration moderate the relationships between these three adoption attributes and the RFID system outcomes.

INTRODUCTION

Studying RFID adoption attributes will be a continuing exercise as research uncovers more issues that need to be addressed. Using the online survey method, this study focuses on the seven

adoption attributes that are very likely to impact the executive decision to deploy RFID to pursue either operational efficiency or market knowledge creation or both in their supply chains. This study also investigates the influence of information technology (IT) infrastructure integration and supply chain process integration on the relationships

DOI: 10.4018/978-1-4666-1764-3.ch009

between each of the RFID adoption attributes and the two dependent variables, operational efficiency and market knowledge creation. Moderated regression analysis (MRA) is used to undertake this determination. After establishing the findings of the MRA statistical procedure, two case studies will be presented to confirm the findings of the empirical study. Practical lessons for corporate executives will also be offered based on the learning experiences of the two firms, Charles Voegele and Vail Resorts.

BACKGROUND

This study is part of larger exploration on the importance of RFID in the supply chain on account of its potential to render information visibility that will, in turn, solve a number of supply chain problems such as the "bullwhip effect" or distortion of signals down the value chain due to lack of accurate information. Previous published work on the larger study has featured the relationships between the elements that constitute IT infrastructure integration and supply chain process integration and four system deployment outcomes that are typical of a supply chain: exploitation, exploration, operational efficiency, and market knowledge creation (Angeles, 2009; Angeles, 2008). In another related study, the relationships between absorptive capacity attributes or organizational routines and business processes used by firms to acquire, assimilate, transform, and exploit knowledge, and two system outcomes, operational efficiency and market knowledge creation were explored (Angeles, 2010). In this second study, the ability of IT infrastructure integration and supply chain process integration to moderate the relationships between the independent and dependent variables was also tested. The study presented in this paper is a piece of the aforementioned more comprehensive inquiry, that focuses on the relationship between the perceptions of study respondents of the importance of seven adoption

attributes of RFID and two system outcomes, operational efficiency and market knowledge creation. More importantly once again, the ability of IT infrastructure integration and supply chain process integration to moderate these relationships was investigated.

Independent Variables: RFID Adoption Attributes

Rogers' (Fichman, 1992; Rogers, 1983) review of more than 3,000 studies on diffusion of innovations has resulted in the identification of five general adoption attributes: relative advantage, compatibility, complexity, observability, and triability. Numerous attempts early on at conceptualization and empirical testing resulted in mixed and inconclusive findings, attributed mainly to the lack of a solid theoretical foundation. To improve on this situation, Moore and Benbasat (1991) developed a refined instrument intended to measure individual and organizational perceptions of adopting an IT innovation. Two more attributes, image and voluntariness of use, were added to the original five constructs by Moore and Benbasat (1991). "Image" refers to "...the degree to which use of an innovation is perceived to enhance one's image or status in one's social system" (Angeles, 2010, p. 195) (and "voluntariness of use" refers to "... the degree to which the use of the innovation is perceived as being voluntary or of free will" (Moore & Benbasat, 1991, p. 195). In this study, the Moore and Benbasat formulation was chosen over other rival frameworks such as the "technology acceptance model" (TAM) because of the former's breadth of coverage of adoption attributes. TAM, an adaptation of the Theory of Reasoned Action, puts forth that perceived usefulness and perceived ease of use determine a person's intention to use a system with intention to use mediating the relationship with another variable, actual system use. These two TAM concepts are included in the Moore and Benbasat model as well. Davis et al. (1989) referred to the concept of "relative advantage" as "perceived usefulness" within the context of the technology acceptance model, where "perceived usefulness" is understood to mean an end users' perception of the degree to which the new technology could raise their job performance level within their organizations.

In this study, selected items from the instrument of Moore and Benbasat (1991) were used and modified to reflect perceptions of representatives who may be involved in the RFID implementation for firms that intend to use RFID in their supply chains. The seven RFID adoption attributes used in this study are the following: (1) relative advantage: the superiority of the new technology over the one it is replacing; (2) compatibility: congruence of the perceptions of the new technology with the existing values, needs, and experiences of potential end users; (3) ease of use: how easy or difficult it is for end users to learn to use the new technology; (4) visibility: how evident the results of using the new technology will be to observers; (5) triability: ability to test the new technology on a pilot basis; (6) image; and (7) result demonstrability (i.e., the ability of the technology to deliver actual results).

Dependent Variables: RFID System Deployment Outcomes: Operational Efficiency and Market Knowledge Creation

In this study, the construct "operational efficiency" was measured as the mean of the following items: (1) meeting agreed upon costs per unit associated with the trading partner; (2) meeting productivity standards associated with the trading partner; (3) meeting on-time delivery requirements with respect to the trading partner; (4) meeting inventory requirements (finished goods) associated with the trading partner; and (5) responding to the trading partner's other requests. On the other hand, "partner-enabled market knowledge creation" was measured as the mean of the following items: (1) better understand the needs of customers; (2) find better ways of distributing/selling the products; (3)

improve service for the end customers; (4) better understand the market segments being served; (5) better understand new and emerging markets; (6) better understand intentions and capabilities of competitors; and (7) develop strategies to compete in the market, that would not have been possible otherwise (Malhotra, Gosain, & El Sawy, 2005).

Moderator Variables: IT Infrastructure Integration and Supply Chain Process Integration

IT Infrastructure Integration. IT infrastructure integration is defined as the degree to which a focal firm has established IT capabilities for the consistent and high-velocity transfer of supply chain-related information within and across its boundaries. The formative construct introduced by Patnayakuni, Rai, and Seth (2006) was adopted in this study and used both conceptually and in the instrumentation as well. They define IT infrastructure integration in terms of two sub-constructs, data consistency and cross-functional SCM application systems integration. The extent to which data has been commonly defined and stored in consistent form in databases linked by supply chain business processes is referred to as data consistency (Patnayakuni, Rai, & Seth, 2006). Data from legacy systems of supply chain trading partners need to be accessed to produce useful, integrated data, and to be able to transport this data into various datawarehouse structures. Cross-functional supply chain management applications systems integration is defined as the level of real-time communication of a hub firm's functional applications that are linked within an SCM context and their exchanges with enterprise resource planning (ERP) and other related inter-enterprise initiatives like customer relationship management (CRM) applications as well (Malhotra, Gosain, & El Sawy, 2005).

Supply Chain Process Integration. In this study, supply chain process integration is defined following the construct used by Malhotra et al. (2005):

the degree to which a hub firm has integrated the flow of information (Lee, Padmanabhan, & Whang, 1997), physical materials (Stevens, 1990), and financial information (Mabert & Venkatraman, 1998) with its value chain trading partners. This formative construct has three subconstruct components: information flow integration, physical flow integration, and financial flow integration (Mangan, Lalwani, & Butcher, 2008). Information flow integration refers to the degree to which a firm exchanges operational, tactical, and strategic information with its supply chain trading partners (Malhotra, Gosain, & El Sawy, 2005). The instrument used in this study measures the sharing of production and delivery schedules, performance metrics, demand forecasts, actual sales data, and inventory data, for information flow integration. Physical flow integration refers to the level to which the hub firm uses global optimization with its value chain partners to manage the flow and stocking of materials and finished goods, and is measured in terms of multi-echelon optimization of costs, just-in-time deliveries, joint management of inventory with suppliers and logistics partners, and distribution network configuration for optimal staging of inventory (Malhotra, Gosain, & El Sawy, 2005). Financial flow integration is defined as the level to which a hub firm and its trading partners exchange financial resources in a manner driven by workflow events (Malhotra, Gosain, & El Sawy, 2005). In this study, the financial flow integration items measure the automatic triggering of both accounts receivables and accounts payables (Malhotra, Gosain, & El Sawy, 2005).

MAIN FOCUS OF THE CHAPTER

Hypotheses to be Tested

This study purports to test the following four hypotheses:

H1: The positive relationship between each of the RFID adoption attributes and operational efficiency will be moderated by IT infrastructure integration --- i.e., the higher the level of IT infrastructure integration, the greater the positive relationship between each of the RFID adoption attributes and operational efficiency.

H2: The positive relationship between each of the RFID adoption attributes and market knowledge creation will be moderated by IT infrastructure integration --- i.e., the higher the level of IT infrastructure integration, the greater the positive relationship between each of the RFID adoption attributes and market knowledge creation.

H3: The positive relationship between each of the RFID adoption attributes and operational efficiency will be moderated by supply chain process integration --- i.e., the higher the level of supply chain process integration, the greater the positive relationship between each of the RFID adoption attributes and operational efficiency.

H4: The positive relationship between each of the RFID adoption attributes and market knowledge creation will be moderated by supply chain process integration --- i.e., the higher the level of supply chain process integration, the greater the positive relationship between each of the RFID adoption attributes and market knowledge creation.

METHODOLOGY

Data for this research study were collected using an online survey questionnaire intended for a more comprehensive study of RFID that covered the following topics: 1) critical success factors for RFID implementation; 2) RFID adoption motivation --- exploitation versus exploration; 3) absorptive capacity attributes associated with RFID use; 4) RFID system outcomes --- operational efficiency versus market knowledge creation; and 5) IT infrastructure integration and supply chain process integration requirements of RFID. Only the section of the study that focuses on RFID adoption attributes and system deployment outcomes is featured in this paper. Members of the Council of Supply Chain Management Professionals (CSCMP) were contacted and invited to participate in the study. A total of 126 firms responded to the relevant section of the study. The low response rate is due to the length and depth of the questionnaire that covered an extensive range of topics.

Moderated Regression Procedure

Moderated regression analysis tests whether the relationship between two variables changes depending on the value of another variable (i.e., interaction effect) (Aguinis, 2004). Regression analysis was conducted to test the hypotheses presented in this study. The moderated regression procedure requires testing first order effects, which in this study, will be referred to as "model 1." A model 1 simple regression tests the direct effects of a predictor variable on a dependent variable. As the independent variable, each of the RFID adoption attributes was regressed against each of the dependent variables, operational efficiency and market knowledge creation. The variance in the dependent variable on account of the independent variable is noted using the R^2 value. Then, the regression procedure testing second order effects is conducted, which will be referred to as "model 2" in this study. A model 2 regression duplicates the model 1 regression equation and adds the product term which includes the hypothesized moderator variable.

It is important to determine how large the change in R^2 should be in order to qualify as "practically significant" or one that should merit serious attention (Aguinis, 2004). After conducting a Monte Carlo simulation, Evans (1985) stipulated that "...a rough rule would be to take 1% variance explained as the criterion as to whether or not a

significant interaction exists in the model...." (p. 320). Empirical and simulation results appear to indicate that a statistically significant R^2 change of about 1 percent to 2 percent demonstrates an effect size worthy of consideration. The results in this study include significant R^2 change values within the range with a maximum value of 6.9 percent and a minimum value of 1.0 percent, which indicate considerable significant moderating effects of IT infrastructure integration and supply chain process integration.

ISSUES, CONTROVERSIES, PROBLEMS

Findings

Moderated Regression Analysis (MRA) Findings

As a first step prior to the actual moderated regression procedure, separate multiple regression runs were conducted with all seven adoption attributes as independent variables for each of the two dependent variables, operational efficiency and market knowledge creation. There were serious multicollinearity issues with all seven independent variables in the two multiple regression models. To solve this problem, the number of independent variables was reduced until the multicollinearity issue disappeared. Only three adoption attributes made it to the final regression models: relative advantage, result demonstrability, and image. Only these three adoption attributes were, therefore, used in the MRA procedure.

The four other adoption attributes, compatibility, ease of use, visibility, and triability were not included in the MRA procedure because of the multicollinearity they introduced in the models. It is interesting to note that in testing an earlier instrument developed by Hurt and Hubbard (1987), the authors arrived at the finding that triability and observability, which corresponds to visibility

Table 1. MRA for Operational Efficiency with IT Infrastructure Integration as Moderator

Independent Variables: Selected RFID Adoption Attributes (N=126)					
Dependent Variable: Operational Efficiency					
Moderator: ITIntegrateCat1 (Nominal variable for product term)					
RFID Adoption Attributes	Model 1: R^2 Without Product Term	Model 2: R^2 With Product Term	% Variance Explained by Moderator with Product Term	F Value of Model 2 (degrees of freedom)	Significance of F Change
Relative Advantage	.780	.804	2.4%	166.351 (3, 122)	$p<.000$
Result Demonstrability	.730	.760	3.0%	126.405 (3, 120)	$p<.000$
Image	.624	.693	6.9%	90.436 (3, 120)	$p<.000$

in this study, did not emerge as separate factors. They explained this outcome as having two possibilities: 1) perhaps, there was an instrumentation flaw that resulted in not clearly delineating the two concepts and 2) it is possible, too, that the study participants treated the two attributes as a single concept. Compatibility and ease of use appear to be somewhat related issues also. In the study, compatibility is defined as the congruence of perceptions of the new technology with existing values, needs and experiences of the end users. The familiarity of the users could naturally lead to ease of use of the new technology.

IT Infrastructure Integration Capability as Moderator Variable with Operational Efficiency as a System Outcome. More substantial results are shown here in descending order of importance based on the percent R^2 change resulting from the introduction of a product term, ITIntegrateCat1, in the multiple regression equation. This is the nominal variable that represents the mean of data consistency

and cross-functional process integration, the two components of IT infrastructure integration. Tables 1 and 2 show the results of running two regression models: model 1 showing the relationships between the predictor variables and operational efficiency, without the product term and

model 2, the regression results with the inclusion of the product term.

Table 1 shows the results with operational efficiency as the dependent variable and IT infrastructure integration capability as a moderator variable. IT infrastructure integration significantly moderates the relationship between the following predictor variables (i.e., RFID adoption attributes) and operational efficiency in descending order of importance: 1) image; 2) result demonstrability; and 3) relative advantage. The table column labelled "% Variance Explained by Moderator with Product Term" indicates the contribution of the product term --- which is the product of the moderator variable, in this case, IT infrastructure integration and the specific predictor variable. And so, for instance, in the case of image, for instance, the product term would be the product of image and IT infrastructure integration (i.e., Image3XIntegrate1). The next column label shows "F Value of Model 2 (degrees of freedom), which means that the F value of model 2 which includes the product term is shown along with the degrees of freedom for that regression model. The significance of the F change from model 1 to model 2 is indicated by the last column.

The relationships between the predictor variables and operational efficiency as moderated by IT infrastructure integration should be interpreted

Table 2. MRA for Operational Efficiency with Supply Chain Process Integration as Moderator

Independent Variables: Selected RFID Adoption Attributes (N=126)					
Dependent Variable: Operational Efficiency					
Moderator: SCMIntegrateCat1 (Nominal variable for product term)					
RFID Adoption Attributes	Model 1: R^2 Without Product Term	Model 2: R^2 With Product Term	% Variance Explained by Moderator with Product Term	F Value of Model 2 (degrees of freedom)	Significance of F Change
Relative Advantage	.778	.788	1.0%	151.343 (3,122)	p<.000
Result Demonstrability	.733	.751	1.8%	120.396 (3,120)	p<.000
Image	.627	.669	4.2%	80.910 (3,120)	p<.000

accordingly. Let's take the case of image, again, the predictor variable whose relationship with operational efficiency is significantly moderated to the greatest extent by IT infrastructure integration. About 62.4 percent of the variance in operational efficiency is explained by image and IT infrastructure integration as indicated by model 1 in Table 1. Model 2 is, then, introduced by including the product term (i.e., Image3XIntegrate1) which represents the interaction between image and IT infrastructure integration. As shown on Table 1, the addition of the product term resulted in an R^2 change of .069, F(3,120) = 90.436, p<.000. This result supports the presence of a moderating effect. In other words, the moderating effect of IT infrastructure integration explains 6.9 percent of the variance in the increase of operational efficiency over and above the variance explained by image and IT infrastructure integration as separate independent variables.

Supply Chain Process Integration as Moderator Variable with Operational Efficiency as a System Outcome: Table 2 shows the results with operational efficiency as the dependent variable and supply chain process integration capability as the moderator variable. Supply chain process integration significantly moderates the relationship between the following predictor variables

and operational efficiency in descending order of importance: (1) image; (2) result demonstrability; and (3) relative advantage.

About 62.7 percent of the variance in operational efficiency is explained by image and supply chain process integration as indicated by model 1 in Table 2. Model 2 is, then, introduced by including the product term (i.e., Image3XIntegrate2) which represents the interaction between image and supply chain process integration. As shown on Table 2, the addition of the product term resulted in an R^2 change of 4.2 percent, F(3,120) = 80.910, p<.000. This result supports the presence of a moderating effect. In other words, the moderating effect of supply chain process integration explains 4.2 percent of the variance in the increase of operational efficiency over and above the variance explained by image and supply chain process integration as separate independent variables.

IT Integration Capability as Moderator Variable with Market Knowledge Creation as a System Outcome: Table 3 shows the results with market knowledge creation as the dependent variable and IT infrastructure integration as the moderator variable. IT infrastructure integration significantly moderates the relationship between the following predictor variables and market knowledge in

Table 3. MRA for Market Knowledge Creation with IT Infrastructure Integration as Moderator

Independent Variables: Selected RFID Adoption Attributes (N=126)					
Dependent Variable: Market Knowledge Creation					
Moderator: ITIntegrateCat1 (Nominal variable for product term)					
RFID Adoption Attributes	Model 1: R^2 Without Product Term	Model 2: R^2 With Product Term	% Variance Explained by Moderator with Product Term	F Value of Model 2 (degrees of freedom)	Significance of F Change
Relative Advantage	.670	.697	2.7%	93.500 (3,122)	p<.000
Result Demonstrability	.680	.716	3.6%	100.982 (3,120)	p<.000
Image	.607	.660	5.3%	77.602 (3,120)	p<.000

descending order of importance: (1) image; (2) result demonstrability; and (3) relative advantage.

About 60.7 percent of the variance in market knowledge creation is explained by image and IT infrastructure integration as indicated by model 1 in Table 3. Model 2 is, then, introduced by including the product term (i.e., Image3XIntegrate1) which represents the interaction between image and IT infrastructure integration. As shown on Table 3, the addition of the product term resulted in an R^2 change of .053 or 5.3 percent, F(3, 120) = 77.602, p<.000. This result supports the presence of a moderating effect. In other words, the moderating effect of IT infrastructure integration explains 5.3 percent of the variance in the increase of market knowledge creation over and above the variance explained by image and IT infrastructure integration as separate independent variables.

Supply Chain Process Integration as Moderator Variable with Market Knowledge Creation as a System Outcome: Table 4 shows the results with market knowledge creation as the dependent variable and supply chain process integration as the moderator variable. Supply chain process integration significantly moderates the relationship between the following predictor variables and market knowledge in descending order of importance: (1) image; (2) result demonstrability;

and (3) relative advantage. About 63.5 percent of the variance in market knowledge creation is explained by image and supply chain process integration as indicated by model 1 in Table 4. Model 2 is, then, introduced by including the product term (i.e., Image3XIntegrate2) which represents the interaction between image and supply chain process integration. As shown on Table 4, the addition of the product term resulted in an R^2 change of .034 or 3.4 percent, F(3,120) = 80.678, p<.000. This result supports the presence of a moderating effect. In other words, the moderating effect of supply chain process integration explains 3.4 percent of the variance in the increase of market knowledge creation over and above the variance explained by image and supply chain process integration as separate independent variables.

SOLUTIONS AND RECOMMENDATIONS

Case Studies and Lessons Learned

Two case studies will be featured here to showcase the suggested solutions and recommendations in the use of RFID to gain either operational efficiency or market knowledge creation or both. The

Table 4. MRA for Market Knowledge Creation with Supply Chain Process Integration as Moderator

Independent Variables: Selected RFID Adoption Attributes (N=126)					
Dependent Variable: Market Knowledge Creation					
Moderator: SCMIntegrateCat1 (Nominal variable for product term)					
RFID Adoption Attributes	Model 1: R^2 Without Product Term	Model 2: R^2 With Product Term	% Variance Explained by Moderator with Product Term	F Value of Model 2 (degrees of freedom)	Significance of F Change
Relative Advantage	.682	.694	1.2%	92.084 (3,122)	$p<.000$
Result Demonstrability	.703	.716	1.3%	100.744 (3, 120)	$p<.000$
Image	.635	.669	3.4%	80.678 (3,120)	$p<.000$

importance of the key RFID adoption attributes, relative advantage, results demonstrability, and image will be highlighted in the lessons learned in the two case studies, which also indicate actions recommended to firms thinking of implementing RFID in their supply chains.

Charles Voegele (CV) Group

IT infrastructure integration as an important moderator for achieving operational efficiency will be illustrated by the Charles Voegele (CV) case study. CV is a major purveyor of fashion goods for men, women, and children at 851 European retail outlets, with a reported earnings of 1.5 billion Swiss francs (US$1.3 billion) (Swedberg, April 29, 2009). What is notable about CV is that the firm decided to deploy RFID at the item-level at its first pilot, skipping the regular stages of tagging at the case and pallet levels as is typical of most firms experimenting with the technology. CV implemented item-level RFID tagging right away as it integrated RFID use through various points in its supply chain. CV achieved incrementally increasing levels of data consistency and cross-functional application integration.

Lesson: Plan well in advance for achieving data consistency especially when the supply chain is long, complex, and involving multiple trading partners.

Data consistency would be difficult to achieve especially with item-level tagging as granular data need to be captured at the following points that span the globe from Asia all the way to Slovenia. CV implemented RFID with its "A" suppliers involved in eight production sites, which were required to use hand-held RFID interrogators through the picking and packing processes to improve packing accuracy (Edwards, July 27, 2009). From the supplier node, the goods are transferred to a container freight station near the Shanghai Harbor in China. RFID interrogators at each of the 34 freight stations read the tags attached to each piece of garment and verify the item against a virtual packing list. Once approved, the shipment proceeds to CV's European hub near Hanover, Germany where the goods are subjected to quality checks. Garments that do not pass muster are returned to their respective suppliers. Approved garments, however, proceed to CV's distribution center (DC) near Graz, Austria where employees either keep them for short-term storage or repackaging. Once again, at the DC,

RFID is relied upon to check packing and delivery accuracy. The next stop is the value-added logistics service provider station where the garments are subjected to a "tunneling" process that uses both heat and humidity to steam out wrinkles and creases. Finally, the garments are sent to the five Slovenian retail stores designated for this RFID pilot project, where point-of-sale (POS) terminals have been configured to read the tags. At the stores, RFID is used primarily, again, to reduce manual counting and out-of-stock scenarios. In addition, RFID is the basis for the stores' shelf management systems, fitting room data gathering processes, and conduct of customer surveys (RFID Journal, 2009).

Lesson: Address technical challenges with the RFID hardware environment that will directly impact the ability to gain data consistency.

Achieving data consistency through the different CV supply chain nodes was a challenge on account of the technical issues CV faced. Item-level tagging presented its own tag reading challenge since hundreds of garment pieces are stored in flat pallets. RFID readers would occasionally generate double or triple tag reads. The problem was addressed and eventually solved by a combination of modifying the software, adjusting RFID reader positions, and changing tag antennas. Ensuring that captured RFID data from all points of the global CV system was accurate, consistent, synchronized, and current was quite a feat. All RFID data gathered from all nodes of CV's supply chain is stored in its Web-based central enterprise resource planning (ERP) system (Swedberg, April 29, 2009).

Lesson: RFID is not just a hardware issue. Integration of all affected internal cross-functional business applications is key and is a critical software issue as well.

The other aspect of IT infrastructure integration, "cross-functional application" integration was another hurdle as well. The effectiveness of "cross-functional application" integration hinges heavily on both the accuracy and consistency of the data flows being exchanged among interrelated business applications. The following are the business applications designed to interact with the RFID system: (1) goods entry and departure tracking --- handheld RFID readers both record newly arrived garments and clearance of unsold items; (2) stock-out management --- handheld RFID readers inform store employees of garments that need replenishment; (3) POS transactions --- RFID readers mounted under the counters record sales and update the store's inventory database; and (4) front store/back store stock booking --- each garment item status is updated as it is brought out from stock and delivered to the sales floor for display (Edwards, July 27, 2009).

Lesson: Track results both to establish result demonstrability and to build a business case for a continuing RFID implementation.

CV gained the following operational efficiency benefits as a result of the RFID deployment: (1) recording store and warehouse inventories: time savings of at least 70 percent for both; (2) fewer instances of out-of-stock items; and (3) accuracy in picked orders from supplier factories: at least 7 percent accuracy increase. Benefits gained that are more related to market knowledge creation include gathering better quality data for tracking and tracing, using more accurate planning information, and garnering increased sales (Hardgrave, July 2009; Edwards, July 27, 2009).

Lesson: Optimize RFID business applications that can enhance the firm's "image."

Another application that CV has implemented to gained market knowledge creation is the production of "heat maps" generated at the retail outlets using KooBra Software (Swedberg, April 29, 2009). These "heat maps" display icons representing customers and their locations in the store as they go around shopping for garments. In order to do this, customers agree to be tagged as they window shop around the store. "Hot" spots in the store indicate where customers tend to spend more of their time window shopping and where, ultimately, sold items come from.

Vail Resorts (VR) Case Study

The importance of IT infrastructure integration in pursuing market knowledge creation will, in turn, be illustrated using the case study on Vail Resorts (VR). VR gathers data basically from two key locations in its resorts: first, from the base of the mountains as the skiers or snowboarders are mounting the ski lifts and second, from further up the mountain slopes. VR issued RFID enabled passes to its season pass holders in the 2008-2009 season as part of its EasyScan program (Microsoft, June 2009). At the first level --- the entrance to the 89 ski lifts at any of VR's five resorts --- EPC Gen 2 RFID readers and antennas mounted on bars or gantries above the loading areas pick up signals from visitor's tags, which are, then, transmitted to a Microsoft backend platform developed by VR's IT staff (O'Connor, September 2, 2010). The application that runs the attendants' handheld computers is supported by the Windows Mobile 5.0 operating system. ODIN, a systems integrator VR worked with, developed the EpicMix RFID infrastructure whose EasyEdge operating system performs data filtering and acts as middleware between the RFID readers and the backend system software. ODIN also provides EasyMonitoring software used to monitor and maintain the RFID readers.

VR also uses the Resort Management System (RMS), which was customized from Resort Technology Partners' RPOS 5.5 software (Gambon, June 1, 2009). The information in a skier's pass is

checked by RMS against an SQL database server to validate the person's identification. A validated skier personal profile is indicated by a digital image and personal information of the skier, which are shown in the handheld computer. Equipped with Intermec's ruggedized CN3 handheld computer with a snap-on IP30 RFID reader and integrated barcode scanner, resort attendants aim the device at the skier's mid-torso while standing 1 to 2 feet away. They, then, compare the digital image with the skier's face, and if there is some uncertainty about the person's identity, they proceed to ask personal profile information.

Lesson: Plan well and test thoroughly for the exchange of data at all points of the physical environment that will involve RFID technology as this will affect the ability to gain data consistency.

After entry into the resort, skiers continue to be tracked further up the slopes throughout the resort properties. Skiers' RFID tag information is continuously captured and sent to the backend system. Specialty ski lifts have mounted on them Intemec's IF61 Enterprise RFID readers and antenna arrays, which are capable of reading multiple tags simultaneously. These readers use the Microsoft BizTalk Server RFID feature of BizTalk Server 2006 R2 to gather radio frequency data. VR acknowledges that it relies heavily on this product to be able to manage the enormous volumes of data generated by the RFID system. The system also uses the BizTalk Server Enterprise Edition and Branch Edition as the main application integration broker for data and reporting purposes, including Microsoft SQL Server 2005 Standard Edition data management software and its SQL Server 2005 reporting services (Microsoft, June 2009). Should downstream systems in VR's enterprise application need specific RFID data attributes, VR uses Windows Communication Foundation for messaging purposes. All integration services needed by VR's systems that need to coordinate with the RFID application sits on the Microsoft. NET framework version 3.5, using the Microsoft Visual Studio 2008 development system (Microsoft, June 2009). All this IT infrastructure was to become the basis of VR's EpicMix application.

Lesson: Leverage all related business applications that can take advantage of the RFID data generated by the system in order to boost the firm's "image" in the marketplace.

VR has launched EpicMix for "market knowledge creation" and eventually, for "market knowledge conversion to sales" by rewarding skiers with special "pins" for things like riding the first chairlift of the day or skiing a specific number of feet over a period of time (Tsai, November 4, 2010; Indvik, 2010; www.mashable.com). In addition to tracking skiers on the resort properties, the RFID system aggregates the total number of feet a skier or snowboarder travels based on distances between chairs

(O'Connor, September 2, 2010). This distance is calculated based on the difference in elevation at the top of the lift that the skier rode, and the elevation at the bottom of the next lift where his or her RFID tag is read. The system accumulates the distance figures throughout a skier's stay in the property and say, at the end of a day, the daily totals are automatically logged in the skier's profile and are expressed in terms of "electronic pins." Examples of electronic pin rewards are the "Echo pin" awarded to a skier who accumulates 350,000 vertical feet, or the "Nightrider pin" given to visitors who board three different chairlifts in a given night's visit.

Lesson: Address technical challenges with the RFID especially when deployed under "ruggedized" physical conditions as this will directly impact the ability to gain data consistency.

The challenges for achieving IT infrastructure integration are related to the technical issues of physically dealing with RFID tag technology subject to extreme resort conditions. For instance, the ability to gain data consistency is affected by the quality of the RFID data captured. Using handheld devices to gather tag data from skiers sometimes resulted in multiple tag reads due to the proximity of skiers or snowboarders when lining up to get on board lifts (Gambon, June 1, 2009). Initially, for instance, VR used a 751 handheld device which contributed to the multiple reads. VR, then, switched to the Intermec CN3 handheld with an IP30 reader attached to enable linear polarization, which reduced the multiple tag reads. Also, in the case of the passive RFID readers mounted on the gantries, the technical challenge VR dealt with had to do with the configuration needed to accommodate various possible positions of skiers or snowboarders as they prepare to board the lifts. VR decided to use circular, polarized antennas to anticipate all sorts of visitor positions and the radio frequency signal strength was also maximized. The presence of moisture from snow and other harsh winter conditions were also issues VR had to deal with since it could affect radio frequency signal transmission (O'Connor, September 2, 2010). Another technical issue involved the choice of the tag itself considering that fact that it needed to be read while worn under a visitor's clothing (Zebra Technologies, 2009). Zebra Technologies assisted VR in choosing a tag that maximized read range and read speed even as the tag could be hidden under a number of clothing layers and could be close to the person's skin. VR eventually chose to use Zebra's inlay design and chip from NXP Semiconductors, and since it is a UHF card, it has superior security features as well and has longer read ranges than regular HF tags.

Lesson: Optimize the relative advantages of RFID technology over older technologies such as bar codes in order to maximize organizational benefits.

The VR case study also clearly illustrates "relative advantage" as a key adoption attribute. The RFID tags replaced bar codes that required line-of-sight scanning that inconvenienced guests who had to unzip their jackets to retrieve the passes for inspection (Microsoft, June 2009).

FUTURE RESEARCH DIRECTIONS

All four proposed hypotheses were partially supported in this study. Both variables, IT infrastructure integration and supply chain process integration, moderate the relationships between selected RFID adoption attributes and the two dependent variables examined in this study, operational efficiency and market knowledge creation. Between the two moderator variables, however, IT infrastructure integration tempered a greater degree of the variance between selected RFID adoption attributes (i.e., image, result demonstrability, and relative advantage) in a fairly consistent pattern and the dependent variables, operational efficiency and market knowledge creation. The case studies on Charles Voegele and Vail Resorts illustrate the study's findings in action and lessons learned are offered to firms contemplating future RFID deployment in their supply chains.

Future research efforts involving an empirical study looking into the experience of many firms in the sample pool should investigate firms that have implemented RFID in their supply chains and validate the actual impact of IT infrastructure integration and supply chain process integration.

REFERENCES

Aguinis, H. (2004). *Regression Analysis for Categorical Moderators. New York, NY*. New York: Guilford Press.

Angeles, R. (2008). Anticipated IT Infrastructure and Supply chain Process Integration Capabilities for RFID and Their Associated Deployment Outcomes. In *Proceedings of the ACMiiWAS Workshops: ERPAS 2008: Business and Service Model* (pp. 634-646).Springer.

Angeles, R. (2009). Anticipated IT Infrastructure and Supply Chain Integration Capabilities for RFID and Their Associated Deployment Outcomes. *International Journal of Information Management, 29*(3), 219–231. doi:10.1016/j.ijinfomgt.2008.09.001

Angeles, R. (2010). Moderated Multiple Regression of Absorptive Capacity Attributes and Deployment Outcomes: The Importance of RFID IT Infrastructure Integration and Supply Chain Process Integration. *International Journal of Information Systems and Supply Chain Management, 3*(2), 25–51. doi:10.4018/jisscm.2010040102

Davis, F. D. (1989). Perceived Usefulness, Perceived Ease of Use, and User Acceptance of Information Technology. *Management Information Systems Quarterly, 13*(3), 319–339. doi:10.2307/249008

Davis, F. D., Bagozzi, R. P., & Warshaw, P. R. (1989). User Acceptance of Computer Technology: A Comparison of Two Theoretical Models. *Management Science, 35*, 982–1003. doi:10.1287/mnsc.35.8.982

Edwards, J. (2009, July 27). An RFID Fashion Statement. *RFID Journal*. Retrieved November 1, 2010, from http://www.rfidjournal.com/article/view/5081

Evans, M. G. (1985). A Monte Carlo Study of the Effects of Correlated Method Variance in Moderated Multiple Regression Analysis. *Organizational Behavior and Human Decision Processes, 36*, 302–323. doi:10.1016/0749-5978(85)90002-0

Fichman, R. G. (1992). Information Technology Diffusion: A Review of Empirical Research. In *Proceedings 13ᵗʰ International Conference on Information Systems* (pp. 195-206). Dallas, TX: ICIS.

Gambon, J. (2009, June 1). Benefits Up and Down the Ski Slope. *RFID Journal*. Retrieved November 10, 2010, from http://www.rfidjournal.com/article/view/5120

Hardgrave, B., Langford, S., Waller, M., & Miller, R. (2008). Measuring the impact of RFID on out of stocks at Wal-Mart. *MIS Quarterly Executive*, *7*(4), 181–192.

Hardgrave, B. C. (2009, July). Charles Vogele: Reaping the Benefits of Source-to-Store RFID. *Apparel Magazine*, *50*(11), 17–20.

Hurt, H., & Hubbard, R. (1987, May). The Systematic Measurement of the Perceived Characteristics Of Information Technologies: Microcomputers as Innovations. In *Proceedings of The ICA Annual Conference*. Montreal, Quebec.

Indvik, L. (2010). *Nike+ Meets Gowalla in Vail Resorts App for Skiers and Snowboarders*. Retrieved November 12, 2010, from http://mashable.com/2010/08/30/epicmix-app/

Journal, R. F. I. D. (2009). RFID Journal's Best RFID Implementation of 2009: Source-to-Store Visibility at Charles Vögele (Part 1). *RFID Journal*. Retrieved November 3, 2010, from http://www.rfidjournal.com/videos/view/120

Lee, H. L., Padmanabhan, V., & Whang, S. (1997). The Bullwhip Effect in Supply Chains. *Sloan Management Review*, *38*(3), 93–102.

Mabert, V. A., & Venkatraman, M. A. (1998). Special Research Focus on Supply Chain Linkages: Challenges for Design and Management in the 21ˢᵗ Century. *Decision Sciences*, *29*(3), 537–550. doi:10.1111/j.1540-5915.1998.tb01353.x

Malhotra, A., Gosain, S., & El Sawy, O. A. (2005). Absorptive Capacity Configurations in Supply Chains: Gearing for Partner-Enabled Market Knowledge Creation. *Management Information Systems Quarterly*, *29*(1), 145–187.

Mangan, J., Lalwani, C., & Butcher, T. (2008). *Global Logistics and Supply Chain Management*. Hoboken, NJ: John Wiley & Sons.

Microsoft Corporation. (2009, June). Resort *Streamlines Skier Check-In, Improves Data Collection with RF Technology*. Retrieved November 10, 2010, from http://www.microsoft.com/casestudies/Case_Study_Detail.aspx?CaseStudyID=4000004666

Moore, G. C., & Benbasat, I. (1991). Development of an Instrument to Measure the Perceptions of Adopting an Information Technology Innovation. *Information Systems Research*, *2*(3), 192–222. doi:10.1287/isre.2.3.192

O'Connor, M. C. (2010, September 2). Vail Resorts Links RFID with Social Media. *RFID Journal*. Retrieved November 10, 2010, from http://www.rfidjournal.com/article/view/7845

Patnayakuni, R., Rai, A., & Seth, N. (2006). Relational Antecedents of Information Flow Integration for Supply Chain Coordination. *Management Information Systems Quarterly*, *23*(1), 13–49. doi:10.2753/MIS0742-1222230101

Robert, M. (2010, March 22). The Age of RFID Pilots is Over --- Deployments Crank Up. *RFID Journal*. Retrieved November 13, 2010, from http://www.rfidjournal.com/article/view/7471

Roberti, M. (2009, May 11). RFID Moves Beyond Tracking. *RFID Journal*. Retrieved November 10, 2010, from http://www.rfidjournal.com/article/view/4860

Roberti, M. (2010, August 2). Putting Wal-Mart's Apparel Tagging in Context. *RFID Journal*. Retrieved November 13, 2010, from http://www.rfidjournal.com/article/view/7769

Roberti, M. (2010, July 26). Wal-Mart Takes a New Approach to RFID. *RFID Journal*. Retrieved November 13, 2010, from http://www.rfidjournal.com/article/view/7756

Roberti, M. (2010, January 11). The Decade Ahead. *RFID Journal*. Retrieved November 13, 2010, from http://www.rfidjournal.com/article/view/7308

Rogers, E. M. (1983). *Diffusion of Innovations*. New York, NY: Free Press.

Stevens, G. C. (1990). Successful Supply Chain Management. *Management Decision, 28*(8), 25–30. doi:10.1108/00251749010140790

Swedberg, C. (2009, April 29). Charles Voegele Group Finds RFID Helps It Stay Competitive. *RFID Journal*. Retrieved November 2, 2010, from http://www.rfidjournal.com/article/view/4836

Tsai, C. (2010, November 4). Ski resorts storm the slopes with new apps. *Taiwan News Online*. Retrieved November 11, 2010, from http://today.msnbc.msn.com/id/39892850/ns/today-todaytravel

Visich, J. K., Li, S., Khumawala, B. M., & Reyes, P. M. (2009). Empirical evidence of RFID impacts on supply chain performance. *International Journal of Operations & Production Management, 29*(12), 1290–1315. doi:10.1108/01443570911006009

Zebra Technologies. (2009). *Vail Resorts: Zebra Technologies Case Studies*. Retrieved November 10, 2010, from www.zebra.com/.../zebra/.../vail_resorts.../CS_P1011336_VailResorts2010.pdf

Chapter 10

EX–ANTE and EX–POST Model Applied to the Portuguese Air Force Flying Regime

Carlos Páscoa
Air Force Academy, Portugal & Instituto Superior Técnico, Technical University of Lisbon, Portugal

António Alves
Air Force Academy, Portugal

José Tribolet
Instituto Superior Técnico, Technical University of Lisbon, Portugal & CODE - Center for Organizational Design & Engineering, INOV, Portugal

ABSTRACT

In order to be able to plan, execute, and control its activities to achieve the desired results, it is essential that organizations tie together the academic knowledge and the operational experience by utilizing proven scientific theories in the organization executables. There are several theories about how to frame the models of corporate governance according to different perspectives; there are advantages and disadvantages in the adoption of each of them. The more or less complete dimension when related to the scope of each model is also an important aspect in its use and disclosure. The EX-ANTE and EX-POST model proposes a set of concepts that allow for the co-existence of mechanisms of access control and registration and validation, being the governance of the system based on four architectures: strategic, business, applications and technology. The model that the Portuguese Air Force uses for the definition of its annual flying hours regime includes five well-defined phases that may improve the level of coverage if the listed security mechanisms, control and audit, recommended in the Model EX-ANTE and EX-POST, are considered.

DOI: 10.4018/978-1-4666-1764-3.ch010

INTRODUCTION

The indicators that support strategic decisions are essential for the current organizations to monitor the strategy outlined for the attainment of the organizational goals.

To fulfill its mission, the Portuguese Air Force (PoAF) identifies each year the number of flying hours needed to be accomplished by the various Air Units by establishing the Flying Regime (FR). This is an annual essential tool for the optimal management of the air activity in the medium and short terms.

The Flying Regime Calculation and Monitoring Model (FRCMM), aligned with the doctrinal framework, objectives and methodology (to be included in the development of the Annual FR planning), defines the authority, responsibilities and coordination instructions covering the PoAF areas directly related to the planning, programming, execution, control and monitoring of the FR.

The inclusion of the EX-ANTE and EX-POST mechanisms, a model proposed by the Center for Organizational Design and Engineering (CODE), reinforces the FRCMM, making it safer and also more flexible and dynamic, allowing for a better adaptation of the Air Force to the current days.

To describe the use of the EX-ANTE and EX-POST Model on the FRCMM, this article is divided in four paragraphs: paragraph one, introduces the subject and defines the domain; paragraph two presents the concepts and describes the EX-ANTE and EX-POST Model; paragraph three states how the integration between the two Models was made; paragraph four presents the conclusion.

THE EX-ANTE & EX-POST MODEL

In the current scenario, the concepts of flexibility and adaptability are directly applied to the organizations that need to monitor the changes in the environment in which they operate.

In this context, it is stated that *"the search for flexibility can be considered as the main driving force behind the management of business processes, both at the organizational level, where the strategy of business processes is investigated, and at the operational level, where the work-flow of the people and the system are important concepts for the definition of the business processes."* (Weske, 2007).

For organizations to be aware of what is happening in their surrounding environment, and even within their own organization, they need technology to enable them to know how their actions are leading to compliance with the strategy.

"A successful organization identifies new technologies, introduces them quickly and sells them next. An organization that does not have this behavior will be absorbed by a competitor. Thus, top managers require their employees to develop and implement an enterprise architecture that ensures a superior position over its competitors." (Chorafas, 2007).

The indicators appear due to the emergence of information systems, databases and data warehousing, the use of which has established themselves as essential for the survival of businesses and organizations in a context of competitiveness, as they now deal with an amount of complex data without precedents. Working the amount and complexity of information in a useful way is a challenge. One can then conclude that *"providing quality information adds value as it helps managers to make better decisions, contributing to a consequent improvement of the business performance."* (Neves, 2007).

It can be argued that *"well designed performance indicators help the organization to spend more time on important activities that are relevant for its performance and less time on activities that are not so relevant."* (Rasmussen et al, 2009).

It is through the indicators the *"information systems provide that we are aware of what is essential for the functioning of the organization, allowing us to gain an insight and knowledge of the organization"*. (Tribolet, 2005; Magalhães, Zacarias & Tribolet, 2007; Aveiro, 2010). The Organizational Self-Awareness (OSA) represents an evolution from the traditional view, since it brings in the need for capturing the static and dynamic aspects of the interactions of the organization's agents with the organization's activities and resources and enabling the construction of models exhibiting non-deterministic interaction patterns.

"Organizational self-awareness has to be constructed, and maintained, through a continuous interaction between the members of the organization so it can be applied to the entire organization" (Vicente, 2005). This also agrees with the assumption that the knowledge *"of persons is the basic definition of this concept, due to the fact that this is the way to have a common sense of the organization"* (Macedo et al, 2005).

For the organization to evolve, it "needs to increase the capacity of continuous sense, to learn and adjust to the dynamic environment that surrounds it." (Vicente, 2005).

If the results are not in agreement with the organization's objectives, it has to develop a plan that allows for the introduction of change and restructuring.

A competitive environment, as changing as it is today, requires planning. To support innovation, planning can't be limited by financial objectives.

"A plan has objectives that must be measurable, responds to the demands required by the stakeholders, builds options and contingencies, identifies and quantifies risks, defines how to minimize those risks or the adverse consequences which may arise from them and allows for progress to be measured. In this context, planning involves management time and executive commitment, cost, research, and assumptions. Consequently, it is important to do it well (or less bad than the competition) because it gives certainty, measures,

confidence, the way forward and, to others, evidence of premeditation." (Russel-Jones, 1998).

Planning, after being made and implemented, will lead the organization to adapt to the new environment. In this respect, it ensures that *"much of the work of a new organization can be characterized as having a perspective of institutional changes."* (Poole & Van de Ven, 2004).

In turn, the adaptation will require change and restructuring because in these days, the organizations are subject to constant change. Most of the changes are imposed by the need to adapt the business management to the market. To plan and implement these changes, it is necessary to understand the current state of the organization and the only way to make it possible is to conduct a proper needs analysis (Vicente, 2005).

Institutional change is defined *"as the difference in form, quality, or state over time in the institution. This change in institutional settlement can be determined by observation or agreements of two factors at a given time in a certain dimension (eg, cognitive and normative) and then you can estimate the differences over time in these dimensions. If there is one big difference, we can express that the agreement has had an institutional change."* (Poole & Van de Ven, 2004).

It is said that *"sooner or later all structures must be redesigned as a result of internal and external changes."* (Bolman & Deal, 2003).

There is no doubt that the organization should have mechanisms, dynamic and flexible, to allow its adaptation, not only to the outside word but also to help to design, implement and maintain artifacts that can help its day-to-day operations.

In this context, the EX-ANTE and POST-EX Model, developed by the Center for Organizational and Design Engineering (CODE), as an example of the framing of an essential tool with a scientific reference, was chosen and implemented by the Portuguese Air Force for managing its flying activity.

Figure 1. EX-ANTE and EX-POST Architecture Model (source: CODE, 2009).

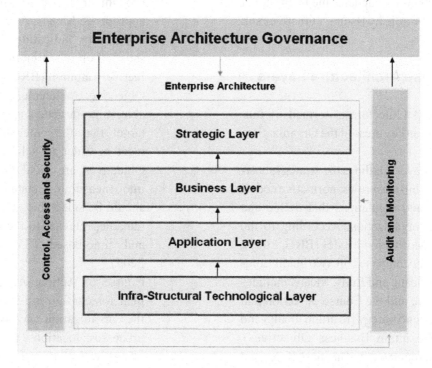

The EX-ANTE and EX-POST Model includes a central structure, embedded in the Corporate or Enterprise Architecture, aiming to describe the elements of an organization and with the intent of normalizing, integrating and enhancing its automation in regard to the organization's operations.

The elements of the organization, considered in the architecture include:

- Information management, for example: objectives and strategic indicators;
- Organizational elements, for example: people, skills, units;
- Operational elements, for example: flows, business rules and operating procedures;
- Applicational elements, for example: business services;
- Elements of the infrastructure.

The Model components are: the Enterprise Architecture Governance layer, the Enterprise Architecture (divided in four layers), the Access

Control and Security layer and the Audit and Monitoring layer. Figure 1 shows the generic model.

The model components are described next.

The Governance Layer

Enterprise Governance is a recent term that introduces the governance perspective that includes the strategic and operational performance with focus on compliance and performance concerns (Páscoa & Tribolet, 2010).

Enterprise governance is considered as "*the set of responsibilities and practices exercised by the board and executive management with the goal of providing strategic direction, ensuring that objectives are achieved, ascertaining that risks are managed appropriately and verifying that the organization's resources are used responsibly*" (Hoogervoorst, 2009).

Within the context of the EX-ANTE and EX-POST Model, there is a Board of Governance that defines authority, responsibilities and processes. It also manages, plans and updates the institutional architecture as a whole by issuing Directives and Orders.

The Enterprise Architecture Layers

The Enterprise Architecture is formed of four layers that focus on key areas of the Organization.

- Strategic Layer. Outlines the strategy, business goals, business rules, normative codes, standards and regulations that define and frame the organization. According to the Business Motivation Model (BRG, 2007), those are decomposed in two main components: Means and Ends. Means includes the Mission, and the Course of Action that encompasses Strategy (to attain Goals) and Tactics (to attain Business Objectives). Those are regulated by Business Rules and Business Objectives. An End is something the business seeks to accomplish. An End may be either a Vision or some Desired Result (a Goal or an Objective) and it encompasses the Vision, Goals and Objectives concepts (BRG, 2007; Lankhorst et al, 2005):
  - Vision. An overall image of what the organization wants to be or become describing its future state, without regard to how it will be achieved. A Vision is the ultimate, possibly unattainable, state the organization would like to achieve, supported (or made operative) by Missions and amplified by Goals (BRG, 2007).
  - Desired Result. End that is a state or target that the organization intends to maintain or sustain. A Desired Result is supported by a selected Course of Action and includes the following concepts: Goals and Objectives (BRG, 2007).
  - Goal. A statement about a state or condition of the enterprise to be brought about or sustained through appropriate Means. A Goal amplifies a Vision by indicating what must be satisfied on a continuing basis to effectively attain it (BRG, 2007).
  - Objective. A statement of an attainable, time-targeted, and measurable target that the enterprise seeks to meet in order to achieve its Goals. Objectives are Goal decomposition into measurable states. Objectives should be selectable, measurable, attainable, relevant to the organization and time-based (SMART) (BRG, 2007).
  - Course of Action. An approach or plan for configuring some aspect of the organization involving things, processes, locations, people, timing, or motivation, undertaken to achieve Desired Results. Courses of Action, representing the basic elements of a general plan or overall solution, are governed by Directives and include Strategies and Tactics. Courses of Action are realized by Business Processes (BRG, 2007).
  - Strategy. One component of the plan for the Mission. A Strategy represents the essential Course of Action to achieve Ends — Goals in particular. A Strategy usually channels efforts towards those Goals. A Strategy is more than simply a resource, skill, or competency that the enterprise can call upon; rather, a Strategy is accepted by the enterprise as the right approach to achieve its Goals, given the environmental constraints and risks (BRG, 2007). Ernst & Young (1998) cited by Kaplan & Norton (2000) *"reported that the ability to execute strategy was more important than the quality of strategy itself"*. Kaplan &

Norton (2000) articulated the principles for the strategy-focused organizations: (1) translate the strategy to operational terms; (2) align the organization to the strategy; (3) make strategy everyone's everyday job; (4) make strategy a continual process; (5) mobilize change through strong, effective leadership.

- Tactic. Course of Action that represents part of the detailing of Strategies. A Tactic implements Strategies (BRG, 2007).

- Directive. Indicate how the Courses of Action should, or should not, be carried out, governing Courses of Action. Specifically, a Directive defines or constrains or liberates some aspect of an enterprise. It is intended to assert business structure or to control or influence the behavior of the business, and is stated in declarative form (BRG, 2007).

- Business Rule. Governs (controls, guides, and shapes) Strategies and Tactics. Highly structured and very thorough, they present the standard vocabulary of the business, authorizing, restricting or guiding the work of the organization in specific areas (BRG, 2007).

- Business Policy. Governs (controls, guides, and shapes) Strategies and Tactics. Unlike the Business Rule, they are less structured and convey broad statements (BRG, 2007).

- Business Layer. Describes how the organization conducts its business, ie how the organization uses its resources in pursuing its strategic objectives and responds to their internal and external customers. It is decomposed into:
  - Organization. Focuses on the organizational structure, including the description in terms of positions and functions. Usually the definition of the organizational structure is partially the organization's responsibility (e.g. definition of specific working groups). It also includes the identification of standards and laws outside the organization. The concepts that define the organization are not static, meaning that all settings and types of relationships may vary over time due to external or internal causes.

  - Information. Describes the informational entities, ie information relevant to the organization. The structure of information has an intrinsically long duration because it derives from the business area of the organization and its objectives and not from a specific mode of operation (ie business processes). As such, the identification of the relevant information is of particular importance. The concepts described in this view are used in the specification of business processes and are implemented by one or more applications.

  - Business Processes. Specify the mechanisms used by the organization to respond, with products or services, to client requests. This specification shows how the business is actually operated, by whom and where. From the business processes and their respective flows of activities are derived requirements for applications designed to support them.

- Application Layer. Identifies applications and services rendered by them to support business processes and related information in a totally independent view from technology, thus separating the applications business layer from the technology systems layer. An application, in this layer, does not correspond to a software package or a "program" in a given technological environment, but to the services provided by this application. This view thus has a dual purpose: on the one hand, it aims to separate the implementation of the technological applications from its non-technologic specification; secondly, it seeks to align the business layer with the technological layer designed for its support.

• Infra-structural Technological Layer. Describes how the applications are physically concretized through specifying the computational infrastructure for processing, for storage and for communications.

These four layers are crossed by two further layers to ensure security and access control as well as the observability of the organization, while the architecture is managed by governance mechanisms.

Control, Access and Security and Audit and Monitoring Layers

The Access Control and Security mechanisms are called EX-ANTE and the Audit and Monitoring mechanisms are called EX-POST and they are actually the ones that give the name to the EX-ANTE & EX-POST Model.

The Access Control and Security and Audit are key components in the institutional structure due to the confidentiality of information, as well as, to the need to make the system observable with regard to external scrutiny and evaluation.

The Access Control and Security describes the requirements that all the elements in the architecture need to respond to, from the perspective of access control (ie which applications or persons are authorized to use what resources and in what context) and security (eg how is data shown, what level of encryption will it need, etc.).

In this context, Security is to make the system capable of hiding information via encryption

mechanisms. The Access Control System aims to provide the ability to allow or deny access of a specific entity (person or application) to a resource in the system.

The Audit and Monitoring aims to enable the system with mechanisms for evaluation of status changes of any of its resources and activities, allowing for the verification of the validity and reliability of the information as well as for the tracking of activities and changes in the system.

The EX-ANTE and EX-POST mechanisms are specified by a Governance Committee that defines the access control, the security level and the audit & monitoring policy and rules.

Control, Access and Security layer

The Control, Access and Security layer is based on several aspects related to security:

• Access controls. Includes policy definition that grants user access to data in accordance with given authority. Includes definition of: i) role based access clarifying role usage and access to data on a need-to-know basis (users should have privileges based on roles or levels and only access to the data required and cannot view data in other business units even if they have the proper security level); ii) user group support embedded on sodtware (the software must support use of user groups to help control permissions); iii) password controls including minimum password complexity rules, maximum password age, and minimum password age; iv) account lockout controls.

• Privilege control. Policy requirements related user's ability to use privileges such as reading, writing and modifying files and directories (including users privileges to modify permissions or attributes of other objects such as giving another user access to other files, changing their group, deleting them, or adding users), have to be defined.

- Logging. User logging policy that helps ensure data integrity has to be defined on the several aspects such as: i) logging of records and changes; ii) change of data security level; iii) change of data from one functional area to another; iv) change of user security access level; v) change of user functional area access either removed or added; vi) adding a user to a group or removing a user from a group; vii) user access of any sensitive data; viii) user modification to data; ix) all logs must contain a time and date stamp; x) system logs must be protected from users who do not have privileges to view them.

- Data security categorizations. Refers to how data is categorized according to security needs such as confidentiality, integrity, and availability. This categorization determines how it should be stored and transmitted and includes policy definition for: i) data encryption for stored sensitive data; ii) data encryption for transmitted sensitive data; iii) data encryption/hashing/truncation for account information (such as passwords) during storage; iv) data encryption/hashing for account information (such as passwords) during transmission; v) caching pages with sensitive data or passwords (for internet and intranet applications).

- Quality assurance policy must be defined including: i) buffer overflow errors checking; ii) user input checking; iii) output to the user checking; iv) configuration files and library files checking; v) environment variables or file names modification error checking; vi) error checking in file, registry and database failure or configuration or library files unavailability.

Audit and Monitoring Layer

The Audit and Monitoring layer is based on several aspects related to the integrity and quality of the system. Not only is must assure that the system is working properly as to the governance rules designed but also that all the data maintains traceability and integrity.

THE EX-ANTE AND EX-POST MODEL APPLICATION

This section briefly describes the terms of the application of EX-ANTE and EX-POST, described earlier to the Air Force FRCMM, presenting the resulting instantiation Model. The first section introduces a brief description about the Portuguese Air Force and its structure and the second section highlights the importance of the FR calculation. Lastly, section three describes EX-ANTE & EX-POST application.

The Portuguese Air Force

The Portuguese Air Force was established on 1952 as an independent branch, integrating the air forces formerly embedded in the Army and the Navy.

The PoAF is an element of the national defense system. It has the mission of cooperating in an integrated way in the military defense of the Republic, through air operations. It is also responsible for Missions derived from international commitments and for Missions of civilian interest.

To better manage the flexible features of the weapons systems, PoAF has a centralized Command and Control and a decentralized execution represented by its Air and Functional Commands. The Air Force structure diagram can be seen at http://www.emfa.pt.

The Air Force structure is defined in the Organic Law for the Air Force (LOFA, 2009), published by the Portuguese Government, and is composed of:

- The Chief of Staff (CEMFA) is the Air Force Commander.
- The Air Force Headquarters (EMFA) is the entity responsible for studying, conceiving and planning the Air Force activities, supporting the CEMFA's decisions.
- The Finance Directorate (DFFA) administers the Air Force finance resources in accordance with the CEMFA's plans and directives.
- The Organs of Cultural Nature (ONC) preserve and display the historical and museum heritage of the Air Force. They are the Air Museum (MUSAR), the Air Force Band and the Air Force Magazine.
- The Counseling Organs (ÓRGÃOS DE CONSELHO) advise the CEMFA on matters related to the administration, discipline and historical. They are the Superior Council, the Discipline Council, the Historical and Cultural Committee and the Council of Health.
- The Inspection (IGFA) supports the CEMFA in the evaluation and control of the Air Force.
- The Logistics Command (CLAFA) manages the material resources and infra-structure of the Air Force in order to accomplish the Chief of Staff's plans and directives while complying with the requirements of airworthiness of military aircraft.
- The Personnel Command (CPESFA) administers the human resources in accordance with the CEMFA's plans and directives.
- The Training and Formation Command (CIFFA) manages training and formation activity on the academic and professional domains, including the draft and preparation of the personnel.
- The Air Command (CA) is responsible for planning, directing and controlling the efficiency of the air power, the air activity and the defense of the national air space.

The annual Flying Regime is the result of an intervention of the General Staff and all the commands, specially the CA and CLAFA and is approved by the CEMFA.

Flying Regime Calculation

As previously stated, the Portuguese Air Force's FR is an essential strategy tool of the organization to achieve its goals since it allows: i) to influence personnel management, anticipating decisions and rationalizing resources, ii) to discipline enforcement agencies, linking them to concrete targets and avoiding the dilution of authority and responsibility; iii) to conduct training, qualification and management of the human resources to maintain the crew qualifications in the air operational and training units.

The Flying Regime Calculation and Monitoring Model includes five phases: Planning, Proposal and Approval, Execution, Monitoring and Analysis.

The calculation of the FR starts with the Planning phase. This phase begins in November of the Year-1 and Ends in January of the Year of its application.

During the Planning phase, the needs identified by the Air and Training and Formation Commands (basic training and qualification, operational and support missions) are considered as the point of departure. They are given in flying hours assigned to each Air Unit. Planning also incorporates the allocated budget and develops a financial analysis to assess the possibility of sustaining the system as requested by the operational component.

In the Proposal and Approval phase, as its name indicates, a FR's draft proposal is prepared; taking into account the needs and available resources and being subject to the approval of the Commanding General.

The Execution phase includes, at first, the monthly planning of the air activity by the Air Command and, then, its publication across the organization.

Figure 2. Ex-Ante and Ex-Post FRCMM applied to the Air Force (Alves et al, 2010)

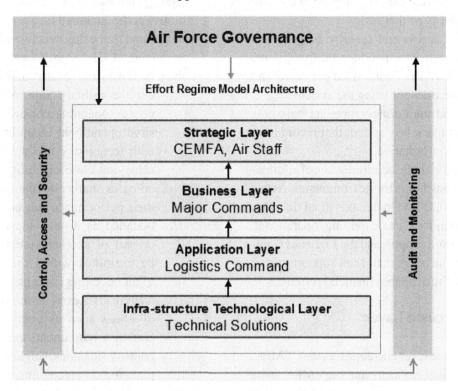

In parallel with the Execution phase, takes place the Control phase, which intends to identify gaps in the planning and to propose corrective actions, if necessary. The FRCMM setting provides a quarterly planning adjustment and a review of the FR itself in the first month of the second semester.

The Analysis phase, as its name indicates, takes the available information of the previous year's FR in the several component areas, analyzes the performance and proposes, if necessary, corrections to the Model.

Although FRCMM already provides insight and guidance for a range of situations, it can be improved with the EX-ANTE and EX-POST Model.

Model Application

Applying the theory of the EX-ANTE and EX-POST, as described above, is part of the creation of an information system associated with the development of the flying hours effort system allowing for the definition of who is authorized to access the information, who adds, changes or deletes and also those who have access to it, adding security and reliability to the system.

Starting with the generic articulated EX-ANTE and EX-POST model presented in Figure 1, the version of the Flying Hours Effort Regime of the Air Force is presented next in Figure 2.

The application of EX-ANTE and EX-POST model, improved FRCMM with the simple application of concepts and systematization. The proposed system is based, doctrinally, in the mechanisms of Air Force governance and consists of:

A central part composed by the Strategic Layer (where the concept of FR proposed and the formulation of the model lies), a Business Layer where the Commands and the activities they develop are, an Application Layer which is responsibility of the IT and a Technological Infrastructure layer which includes the technical solutions and is also the responsibility of that entity.

A control, access and security body, which limits the access to information on the flying hours only to the universe of authorized personnel and which sets the rules for using the system.

An audit and monitoring component that works as an aircraft black box system that records any change in the information.

This would include the introduction of information on the flying hours by the Commands. At this stage, the CA/CIFFA Commands input the planning divided in four areas: training, operational, qualification and support and the Logistics Command inputs the hours that it can support, taking into account the available financial resources.

The Governance Layer

The Governance layer encompasses the CEMFA, which is the final authority and the EMFA, in its role of preparing governance rules and Directives, by coordinating its contents across the Organization, Commands and other major organs. The FRCMM itself is an example of an action of the governance layer.

The Enterprise Architecture Layers

The EX-ANTE and EX-POST Enterprise Architecture, as described previously is formed of four layers that focus on key areas of the Organization. The following description presents the concepts as applied to the Air Force.

- Strategic Layer. The EMFA proposes the Flying Effort, taking in consideration the number of flying hours proposed by the Commands, the financial resources availability and the aircraft maintenance capability and outlines the objectives for the operational dimension of the enterprise assuring its alignement with the Air Force approved Vision and Goals. The EMFA also proposes the Flying Regime

strategy, business goals, business rules, normative codes, standards and regulations that define and frame the objectives designed to be attainned. The plan is analysed by the the CEMFA that gives the final approval.

○ On the military side, Vision focus on key operating constructs and desired operational capabilities dealing with technology investments toward achieving these capabilities. As technologies mature to the point where their performance can be reasonably bounded as a new, separate system or part of another system, they can be examined within the framework of an operating concept that, through analytical means, examine a range of issues such as employment, operating environment, command and control, logistics, organization and planning considerations. Vision statements and vision documents do not address capabilities that are immediately at hand; instead, they leverage the promise of emerging technologies to describe desired operational capabilities. The Vision of the Air Force Chief-of-Staff, however, although written within the business framework, does not forget the military component: *"In the multi-faceted coverage of the mission, I envision an Air Force with a highly deployable nature, while maintaining a high degree of interoperability with other national and multinational forces, supported by the use of equipment that incorporate new technologies, served by a deployable command and control that enables operation in different environments, and a streamlined logistics, based on a modular structure, that eases expedited activation process."* (Araújo, 2008).

○ The Desired Result is expressed by the identification of a set of strategic goals and subsequent strategic objectives that qualify and quantify the Vision published by the Air Force Commander.

○ Goal. Being a statement about a state or condition of the enterprise to be brought about or sustained through appropriate Means, the Portuguese Air Force has established two goals for the strategic level: *"Operate with Efficacy"* and *"Administer with Efficiency"*. These two goals expand the Air Force Commanders Vision and are, in turn expanded by the Strategic Objectives that are described next.

○ Objective. Each objective is statement of an attainable, time-targeted, and measurable target. The Air Force defines its strategic objectives in strict alignment to the presented Goals. Because the objectives have to be time-targeted, they are defined on a yearly basis, and are the basis for the operational (Commands) objectives. The strategic objectives directive is published on the first week of the year. Each objective has an associated metrics, whose fulfillment is accompanied through out the year. For the FR definition, a set of SMART (BRG, 2007) objectives are established, per Flying Unit (FU), in the number of flying hours, the number of aircraft that are needed and the number of qualified crews required to operate the aircraft. For effect of control and the building of the organizational cockpit the objectives are turned into planned values that constitute one of the elements of the

equation that measures operational efficacy.

○ Course of Action. Include Strategies and Tactics and are realized by Business Processes. For the strategy decision several courses of action are taken in consideration. After discussion on the advantages and disadvantages of each in terms of SWOT and risk, one is chosen and the strategy for each goal is then devised.

○ Strategy. The appropriate strategy is designed to attain each goal. At the current moment the Air Force is studying the implementation of a balanced scorecard to monitor the strategy implementation on several levels.

○ Tactic. Tactics are subsets of strategy and a new set of tactics are set to indicate how the desired objectives would be met.

○ Directive. A set of Directives govern the application of the FR. Examples of such Directives are: The "Flying Units Mission Directive" that sets out what are the Mission, and the subsequent elements that each FU can realize; the "Flying Units Personnel Quantities" that sets the number of personnel, divided by operational (crews), maintenance and support for each FC, according to the its Mission and the FR it needs to fly each year, the "Normative for Operational and Maintenance Publications" that sets, what are the publications that each level or the organization must have in order to fly. As an example, a typical FU should have the "Operational Procedures Manual" and the "Qualifications Manual". "The Mission Directive" specifies the "What", the "Personnel Quantities Directive" define the "Who" and the

"Publications Directive" defines the "Why", "When" and "How".

◦ Business Rule. In the military directives can be easily confused with some aspects of doctrine. Military doctrinal maxims are based on experience, hard-won with the blood of people, and tempered by advances in technology allowing, if not ignored, to achieve great success and, if ignored to disaster (USAFDC, 2003). Yet, while forming that baseline for current operations, doctrine also provides a baseline for future thinking. Doctrine deals with the best operating practices for current forces, using currently accepted organizational structures, Command and Control arrangements, functions, and missions. Doctrine is focused on near-term operational issues and talks to the proper employment of current capabilities and current organizations, addressing how best to employ, how to organize, and how to command today's capabilities. A Business Rule, in this article, context, however, has to be seen as an instrument to govern the execution of the operational regime. Therefore, the manuals described before "Operational Procedures Manual"

and "Qualifications Manual", can be considered business rules as they govern operations and qualifications within each FU.

◦ Business Policy. The Air Force Commander issues short statements, usually called orders, indicating his determination on how a particular action (in broad terms) is done. These can be considered a business policy.

• Organization. Focuses on the organizational structure, including the description in terms of positions and functions. Usually the definition of the organizational structure is partially the organization's responsibility (eg definition of specific working groups). It also includes the identification of standards and laws outside the organization. The concepts that define the organization are not static, meaning that all settings and types of relationships may vary over time due to external or internal causes.

• Business Layer. Taking in consideration the business layer contents, as depicted in section "the Enterprise Architecture Layers", in the Portuguese Air Force case, it is decomposed into:

◦ Organization. Focuses on the organizational structure in particular in the organs that contribute for the FR five phases. Table 1 shows the relation

Table 1. Relation between the organs and the FR phases

Phase/Organ	Planning	Proposal & Approval	Execution	Control	Analysis
CEMFA	Orientation	Approval		Approves	Approves
EMFA	Orientation Coordination	Submission	Report	Monthly Analysis	Yearly Analysis
CA & CIFFA	Planning	Monthly Plan	Execute & Report	Report	Feedback
CPESFA	Planning	Monthly Plan	Execute & Report	Report	Feedback
CLAFA	Maintenance Capability	Monthly Plan	Execute & Report	Report	Feedback
DFFA	Financial capability	Monthly Plan	Execute & Report	Report	Feedback

between the phases and the organs in terms of actions performed by each organ.

- Information. It is the structuring of Informational Entities necessary for the pursuit of the business processes of the Organization. It serves to: i) facilitating communication between people and between business and IT people, ii) clarify the fundamental concepts of the business, iii) clarify the life cycle associated with each "information", iv) allow information management; v) planning of Information Systems; vi) manage information regardless of existing Information Systems. The high level Information Entities involved in the Information Architecture are three: Mission, Aircraft and Crew. The following text presents some example of attributes for each one of the high level Information Entities: Mission Entity attributes examples are: type and beneficiary; Aircraft Entity attributes examples are: type, operational status and administrative status; Crew Entity attributes examples are: function on board, qualification status and readiness status.

- Business Processes. The operation business processes described are a subset of the ones needed to fly and maintain the human and material resources. The fundamental business process is the determination of the FR, which determines the operational planning of the activity. For example, it presents also the process of "New Mission" in order to understand how to coordinate the various entities to receive, coordinate, authorize and respond to a request not included in the FR system. The operation process described is an example of how PoAF sets up the alignement between the several organizational sub-systems. The fundamental process is the determination of the FR itself, which is based on a Directive and is part of Governance, which determines the operational planning of the activity. Table 2 to Table 5 shows respectively the process identification, the process objectives, the processo information and the process responsibility.

- Application Layer. The IT dictorate identified the necessary applications and services to support business processes and related

Table 2. Process Identification

Identification		
Process ID	Father Process ID	Process Name
AN--------	AN--	Flying Regime determination

Table 3. Process Objectives

Objectives	
Objective ID	Description
1	In the human resources area, the preparation and achievement of proficiency required for operational and maintenance personnel.
2	In the logistics area, the planning, programming and implementation of timely supply and maintenance support.
3	In the finance área, the planning and management of the financial resources according to the superior decision, that is, the compliance with the FR approved by the CEMFA.

Table 4. Process Information

Necessary Information			
Origin	**Description**	**Input (I)/ Output (O)**	**Artifact**
Governance Directive	Yearly FR Planning Directive	I	Paper or Electronic document
Appropriate Document	Operations and Maintenance Requirements	I	Paper or Electronic document
Governance Directive	Planned Exercises	I	Paper or Electronic document
Governance Directive	Personnel Resources	I	Paper or Electronic document
Governance Directive	FU Missions	I	Paper or Electronic document
Governance Directive	Entity support	I	Paper or Electronic document
FR Directive	FR Directive	O	Paper or Electronic document

Table 5. Process Responsability

Responsability		
Entity	**Responsible**	**Description**
EMFA	Vice Chief-of-Staff	1. Defines: – Financial policy – Operational Level of ambition – Agreements to be established – Priorities and limitations 2. Obtains approval
EMFA	Resources	1. Plans needed human resources
EMFA	Operations	1. Coordinates all activities 2. Plans operational needs 3. Runs coordination meetings
EMFA	Resources	1. Plans needed logistic resources 2. Coordinates with CLAFA 3. Calculates Cost per Flying Hour
CLAFA	Directorates	1. Obtains the logistic resources and executes planned maintenance 2. Proposes the financial support needed for maintenance activities 3. Coordinates with CPESFA the needed human resources
CIFFA	Training Directorate	1. Proposes the Training FR 2. Plans the Training Courses
CA	Staff	1. Proposes the Operational FR 2. Plans the Operational Courses

information in a totally independent view from technology.

- Infra-structural Technological Layer. The IT dictorate described how the applications are physically concretized by specifying the computational infrastructure for processing, for storage and for communications.

Control, Access and Security and Audit and Monitoring Layers

These layers define the mechanisms depicted in section "Control, Access and Security and Audit and Monitoring Layers". The actual requirements are defined in the FRCMM. The periodicity of the audit actions is also defined by the governance board.

CONCLUSION

In the process of making the processes of the Portuguese Air Force more flexible and dynamic, thereby enhancing self-awareness of the organization and its ability to adapt to the changing world, it was proposed to combine an internal definition of essential tools for achieving the Organization's strategy with established models, such as the EX-ANTE and EX-POST, proposed by CODE.

In the architecture model, as shown in Figure 1, various aspects of the organization are included such as elements of management, organizational elements, operational features, applicational elements and infrastructure elements.

The architecture consists of four sections that focus on key areas of the Organization and are crossed by two additional layers, access control and security audit, designed to ensure the security and access control as well as the observability of the Organization, while the architecture is managed by governance mechanisms.

So, the Access Control and Security mechanisms are called EX ANTE and the audit and monitoring mechanisms EX-POST.

The FRCMM, described in section "Flying Regime Calculation", includes five phases: Planning, Proposal and Approval, Implementation, Monitoring and Analysis.

The combination of FRCMM with the concepts of the EX-ANTE and EX-POST model resulted in a system (shown in Figure 3) consisting, among others, of: i) a central part composed by the strategic layer (where lies the concept of existing FRCMM; ii) a business layer where are the Commands and the activities they carried out; iii) an application layer, responsibility of information technology; iv) a layer of technology infrastructure that includes technical solutions and which is also the responsibility of the entity; v) a access and security unit, limiting access to information on FR only to authorized personnel and laying down rules for the system; vi) an audit and monitoring component that works as a black box system and records any and all accesses and / or possible changes in the information.

The definition of application layer provides for the information input related to the FR and command areas. Here, the Air and the Training and Formation Commands input planning divided in four areas: instruction, operational, qualification and outside support, the Logistics Command, taking into account the financial resources, inputs the flying hours that it can support.

The combination of the governance arrangements and definitions advocated by FRCMM with the principles of the EX-ANTE and EX-POST led to the filling of some gaps thus making it more effective and efficient to monitor the stages set and also to monitor and control all interactions between the different actors.

However, the greatest impact lies in the areas of access control and auditing and monitoring and the identification and, also, in the establishment of the various access permissions and the monitoring system.

All in all, the combination of the two resulted in a greater awareness for the Air Force in defining and monitoring all the phases of the FRCMM, thus adding efficiency to its essential tools and mechanisms.

REFERENCES

Alves, A. M. (2010): *Definição de um Modelo de Cálculo e Acompanhamento do Regime de Esforço*, [Defining a Model for Calculating and Monitoring System of Effort] Master Thesis, Academia da Força Aérea, Sintra, Portugal.

Araújo, L. (2008). *Air Force Chief-of-Staff Message to the Air Force, Portuguese Air Force*. Lisboa, Portugal: Alfragide.

Aveiro, D. (2010), *GOD theory for organizational engineering: continuously modeling the (re)Generation, Operationalization and Discontinuation of the Enterprise,* Doctoral dissertation, Department of Computer Science and Engineering, Instituto Superior Técnico, Lisboa.

Bolman, L. G., & Deal, T. E. (2003). *Reframing Organizations* (3rd ed.). San Francisco, USA: Jossey-Bass.

Business Rules Group. (2007): *The Business Motivation Model: Business Governance n a Volatile World,* Revision 1.3, Retrieved (December 2010) from: http://www.businessrulesgroup.org/bmm.shtml.

Chorafas, D. N. (2002). *Enterprise Architecture and New Generation Information Systems.* Florida: St. Lucie Press.

Hoogervorst, J. A. P. (2009). *Enterprise Governance & Enterprise Engineering.* The Netherlands: Springer. doi:10.1007/978-3-540-92671-9

Kaplan, R., & Norton, D. (2000). *The Strategy-Focused Organization: How Balanced Scorecard Companies Thrive in the New Business Environment.* Harvard Business School Press.

Lankhorst, M. (2005). *Enterprise Architecture at Work - Modelling, Communication and Analysis.* Berlin, Heidelberg: Springer-Verlag.

Low, J., & Seisfield, T. (1998). *Measures that Matter.* Boston, USA: Ernst & Young.

Macedo, P.; Zacarias, M.; Tribolet, J. (2005): *Técnicas e Métodos de Investigação em Engenharia Organizacional: Projecto de Investigação em Modelação de Processos de Produção. Bragança* [Techniques and Research Methods in Organizational Engineering: Research Project in Modelling Production Processes. Braganza], 6 ª Conferência da Associação Portuguesa de Sistemas de Informação [6th Conference of the Portuguese Association for Information Systems].

Magalhães, R., Zacarias, M., & Tribolet, J. (2007). Making Sense of Enterprise Architectures as Tools of Organizational Self- Awareness . *Journal of Entreprise Architecture, 3*(4), 64–72.

Magalhães, R., Zacarias, M., & Tribolet, J. (2007a): Making Sense of Enterprise Architectures as Tools of Organizational Self-Awareness (OSA). *Proceedings of the Second Workshop on Trends in Enterprise Architecture Research (TEAR 2007), 6,* 61-70.

Neves, F. M. (2007): *Visualização de Indicadores de Negócio no Contexto de um Sistema de Suporte à Decisão* [View of Business Indicators in the Context of a Decision Support System], Master Thesis, Lisboa: Instituto Superior Técnico.

Páscoa, C., Alves, A., & Tribolet, J. (2010): EX-ANTE and EX-POST Model Development and Monitoring of the Portuguese Air Force Effort Regime, *Minutes of the Conference on ENTERPrise Information Systems held in Viana do Castelo,* Portugal in October 2010, Springer.

Páscoa, C., & Tribolet, J. (2010). Organizational and Design Engineering of the Operational and Support Components of an Organization: the Portuguese Air Force Case Study, Practice-driven Research on Enterprise Transformation (PRET) *Conference on Enterprise Engineering, Springer Lecture Notes in Business Information Processing (LNPIB) Series,* Delft University, The Netherlands.

Poole, M. S., & Van de Ven, A. H. (2004). *Handbook of Organizational Change and Innovation.* New York, NY: Oxford University Press.

Rasmussen, N., Chen, C. Y., & Bansal, M. (2009). *Business Dashboards.* New Jersey: John Wiley & Sons.

Russell-Jones, N. (1998). *The Business Planning Pocketbook* (3rd ed.). Management Pocketbooks Ltd.

Silva, A., Júnior, A., Caetano, A., Pereira, C., Tribolet, J., & Gil, R. (2009). *Arquitectura Empresarial para o SIMP* [Enterprise Architecture for SIMP]. Lisboa, Portugal: INOV.

Tribolet, J. (2005) *"Organizações, Pessoas, Processos e Conhecimento: Da Reificação do Ser Humano como Componente do Conhecimento à "Consciência de Si" Organizacional"* [Organizations, People, Processes and Knowledge: The Reification of Human Knowledge as a Component of the "self-consciousness" Organization], in Amaral, L. (ed) *Sistemas de Informação Organizacionais* [Organizational Information Systems], Nov 2005, Edições Sílabo [Syllabus Revision]

(2003). *United States Air Force Doctrine Center*. Washington, DC: Air Force Basic Doctrine.

Vicente, D. M. (2007): *Towards Organization*, Master Thesis, Instituto Superior Técnico, Lisboa, Portugal.

Weske, M. (2007). *Business Process Management*. Heidelberg, Germany: Springer.

Zacarias, M. (2008) *Business Process Modeling with Objects and Roles*, Doctoral dissertation, Department of Computer Science and Engineering, Instituto Superior Técnico, Lisboa.

Chapter 11
A New Dynamic Framework for Managing ERP Development and Enterprise Strategy

Ben Clegg
Aston University, UK

Yi Wan
Aston University, UK

ABSTRACT

The enterprise management (EM) approach provides a holistic view of organizations and their related information systems. In order to align information technology (IT) innovation with global markets and volatile virtualization, traditional firms are seeking to reconstruct their enterprise structures alongside repositioning strategy and establish new information system (IS) architectures to transform from single autonomous entities into more open enterprises supported by new Enterprise Resource Planning (ERP) systems. This chapter shows how ERP engage-abilities cater to three distinctive EM patterns and resultant strategies. The purpose is to examine the presumptions and importance of combing ERP and inter-firm relations relying on the virtual value chain concept. From a review of the literature on ERP development and enterprise strategy, exploratory inductive research studies in Zoomlion and Lanye have been conducted. In addition, the authors propose a dynamic conceptual framework to demonstrate the adoption and governance of ERP in the three enterprise management forms and points to a new architectural type (ERPIII) for operating in the virtual enterprise paradigm.

INTRODUCTION

Enterprise Systems (ESs) have progressed over the last fifty years as a result of constant interaction between changing business requirements, technological maturity, and organizational structures

DOI: 10.4018/978-1-4666-1764-3.ch011

(Wortmann, 2000). Perceptive people in both enterprise management and information systems suggest that there is soon going to be available a truly integrated technical solution for Enterprise Resource Planning (ERP) systems (Chorafas, 2001), that will make the newly conceived 'virtual value chain' and the e-marketplace concepts a reality (Rayport & Sviokla, 1995; Porter & Millar, 1985). As recent trends in business and technology have focused on inter-organizational collaboration and information system that enhance them (Banker et al., 2010), many companies recognize the critical interdependencies that exist among the firms, suppliers and customers, which cannot be described in terms of simple contractual exchanges, but involve the interactions and network effects with appropriate new enterprise paradigms and information technology. The importance of such inter-firm (i.e. intra-enterprise) relations has been recognized by the structural concepts of vertically integrated enterprises (Lynch, 2003; Joskow, 2003), extended enterprises (Powell, 1990; Davis & Spekman, 2004), virtual enterprises (Byrne & Brandt, 1993; Goranson, 1999), business dynamic networks and strategic alliances (Todeva, 2006; Reuer, 2004) and in the related technical support systems such as web-based Service Oriented Architecture (SOA), Platform as a Service (PaaS), and Software as a Service (SaaS) (Bass & Mabry, 2004; Torbacki, 2008; Candido et al., 2009). Particularly, the *enterprise* here is defined as "...an entity including partnerships or associations that can be made up of parts of different companies". Although some arguments concern the core competences that affect the design and management of the enterprises structures (Binder & Clegg, 2006), the "interconnectedness" of intra-enterprise governance is criticized as there lacks sufficient consideration and contribution to the impact of ERP systems on future enterprise strategies and *vice versa*. In addition, since current prevailing ERP systems are not able to support virtual enterprise structures, we propose a contingency term called "ERPIII" in this chapter to describe such future agile enterprise management systems.

This research study is important because of the increasing competitive and dynamic business circumstance are forcing modern companies to improve their competencies by incessantly learning and re-engineering to adapt to rapid changes around highly complex supply chain in the era of globalization. Along with the emerging multinational virtual networks, more importance has been attached to the inter-organizational network, "agile enterprise" and "agile manufacturing" capabilities (Pal & Pantaleo, 2005; Cummins, 2009; Vazquez-Bustelo & Avella, 2006), in order to continually evolve and optimize the strategic international trade and operations. As consequence, advisable enterprise management strategies and advanced information technologies (e.g. ERP systems) would play as the active tools to enhance intra-enterprise performances, increase the customer-driven markets share and high flexibilities in product/service and business processes, shorter global manufactured product life cycle, narrow niches, handle diverse environmental conditions, and create value within the context of globalized world (Palaniswamy & Frank, 2000). This chapter, therefore, delivers a new dynamic framework for managing ERP systems development and enterprise strategies concurrently.

Extant studies on ERP systems tend to focus on making core system modules better by blending or uniting them with new types of functions or applications to form "extended ERP" (Michel, 2000) as managers have been enticed toward new information technologies for the key to survival and developing a competitive edge (Chen, 2001) rather than investigating how ERP systems can be better designed to support and govern dynamic intra-enterprise management strategies. Also, despite an emerging body of literature about enterprise management strategies has drawn much attention in exploring new enterprise structures and significant organizational forms (Browne & Zhang, 1999; Davis & Spekman, 2004), design and operation to gain core and unique competences (Zhang & Dhaliwal, 2008; Binder & Clegg, 2006), it neglects how enterprise management paradigms can be applied to develop ERP systems from an information systems perspective. Therefore, commencing with: inter-company collaboration as a point of departure from conventional thinking, rather than individual companies, the objectives of this chapter we address are: (1) Reinforce the interdependencies and consistencies between ERP and EM strategy domains; (2) Consider how current and future ERP systems may correspond to different enterprise patterns; (3) Develop a sustainable conceptual dynamic framework to guide enterprise managers for making better decisions about enterprise-wide strategy, structure transformation and technical support.

LITERARY FOUNDATION AND BACKGROUND

Enterprise Resource Planning (Enterprise Systems)

Enterprise systems (ESs) are often explained through the evolution of ERP, which have evolved from highly transaction automation and process management to highly corporate alignment and integration with rapid and dynamic "sense and respond" business model in the context of globalization and growth of virtual organization (Davenport, 2000). At the center of newly virtual value chain notion, we believe that ERP systems can potentially enable the company to integrate the data used throughout its entire organization or intra-enterprise, as well as imposes its logic on the design of enterprise structure and operations in strategic business management.

Enterprise Resource Planning (ERP) systems can be regarded as one of the most innovative developments in information technology (IT) industry, which have become the widespread integrated technical solutions for the enterprise information systems (Al-Mashari, 2003; Chorafas, 2001). The literature on ERP systems was growing steadily in recent years, which has experienced a historical development from MRP to MRPII, and move into the first generation of ERP which was then extended to ERPII. Additionally, a great of issues referring to ERP discipline have been addressed through a taxonomic perspective. These are ERP

systems competitiveness, change and knowledge management accompany by risk migration, business processes management, project-based ERP analysis and design, critical successful factors (CSFs) of ERP adoption, etc. Nevertheless, ERP systems as they exist today represent just a snapshot of one segment of the overall spectrum of information technology since the changes around every field are rapid and constant. Continuing such evolutional insight, we are aware of the urgency of extending ERP modules and functionalities to sustain the next generation of enterprise IS infrastructure and application as well as enterprise strategies during the "post-ERPII" era, in order to face the highly dynamic changes in the turbulent market. Such concept of newly ERP systems is termed as "ERPIII" in this chapter.

ERP vs. ERPII vs. ERPIII

In today's global world, intelligent firms try to provide customers with goods and services faster and less expensively than their rivals. One of the keys to achieve this is to have efficient, integrated information systems (Monk & Wagner, 2009). Over the last twenty years, many firms have made significant investments in ERP suites (Bagchi et al., 2003; Stevens, 2003). The scholarly review depicts that the first generation of ERP systems act as an internal integrated information system which took shape based on manufacturing roots to seek competitive advantage (Blackstone & Cox, 2005, p. 38). These include configurable and off-the-shelf software packages to provide an integrated suite of information systems and resources which coordinate operational and management processes across the internal value chain. The latter ERP systems may also have been accompanied by a broad range of business involving sales and distribution, accounting and finance and human resources, etc. (Davenport, 1998; Al-Mudimigh et al., 2001). Traditionally, ERP systems were highly proprietary (Daniel & White, 2005), incurring a substantial amount of time and considerable financial commitment and effort to integrate or be compatible with other information techniques and systems such as Decision Support System (DSS), Enterprise Application Integration (EAI), and Product Data Management (PDM), whilst requiring additional layers of middleware (Lee et al., 2003; Stevens, 2003). Such challenges and difficulties not only decrease the ability to integrate systems within intra-enterprise boundaries, but also reduce the ability to forge dynamic intra-enterprises linkages (Themistocleous et al., 2001).

Although traditional ERP can often impel business processes re-engineering with high-levels of enterprise-wide inter-functional coordination and integration (Moller, 2005), its capabilities still cannot often fully support the e-business challenge and intensive data requirements (Chen, 2001; Songini, 2002; Moller, 2005). They also often fail to realize the notion of "all things to all people" and future proof users' demands (Bond et al., 2000). By extending more modules and functionalities as 'add-ons', the mantra of "ERP is dead – long live ERPII" often becomes the rule for new enterprise systems development and enabled organizations (Eckartz et al., 2009). This subsequently gives birth to ERPII or 'XRP' (eXtended Resource Planning) systems that are defined as a business strategy to enable inter-organizational collaboration through value chain participation. This requires companies to combine ESs with other new types of intelligent business tools consisted of Advanced Planning and Scheduling (APS), Supply Chain Management (SCM), Customer Relationship Management (CRM), Business Intelligence (BI), and Data Warehouse (DW) to reinforce both upstream and downstream chains. In parallel, by extending traditional ERP capabilities (Moller, 2005) one can put forward the concepts of collaborative-commerce (C-Commerce) and demand chain management (DCM), etc. to optimize the market information management and reinforce business domain re-design. Furthermore, future ERP enabled enterprise

systems development tends to trace transaction automation, process management and knowledge management in order to improve the current ERP gaps and achieve a "co-operation" idea based on the value network concept.

It has been suggested that widespread adoption of standardized ERP within organization may allow improved connectivity between organizations as well as have the potential to enhance the entire supply chain integration (Akkermans et al., 2003). The result of such interconnection were ERPII systems that transcend individual companies and operate at a 'meta level' (Daniel & White, 2005, p. 191), operating at a value chain or even the whole industry level (Davenport & Brooks, 2004). Such systems could also represent known as "Value Chain Resource Planning" (Bendoly et al., 2004), and would not only pass information, data, and knowledge between firms as current linkages can but could integrate processes and relations across all involved participants, in order to add value with extended-ESs beyond the intra-company boundaries.

Even if ERPII seems the current dominant IS infrastructure to support modern enterprise management, and SOA, PaaS, SaaS, and Utility are now emerging as the new IS applications to influence the consistency of multiple ERP systems (Maurizio et al., 2007) as well as offer increased flexibility, agility, efficiency and scalability for ESs with reconfiguration of SCM, EAI, etc. based on service-oriented environment (Torbacki, 2008; Wilkes & Veryard, 2004; Candido et al., 2009). Many firms still endeavor to re-design their enterprise paradigms in order to form highly dynamic and agile units known as virtual enterprises around turbulent markets. Implementing ERP systems in such companies is an entirely different preposition than in a single company scenario. 'Temporary existence' and 'Dynamic agility' requires the corresponding ERP-driven systems to possess a flexible and web-based integrated infrastructure (Candido et al., 2009; Xu et al., 2002). Additionally, since there are some challenges derived from

PaaS, SaaS, and Utility such as interface design, high risk of ROI, time consuming, granularity and culture issues, business secrecy and decomposed objectives (Candido et al., 2009; Wilkes & Veryard, 2004; Torbacki, 2008). "Virtual Enterprise Resource Planning (VERP)" and "Federated ERP" concepts merged with SOA and cloud computing technical solutions also need to be considered to realize the new enterprise structures. As the literature inadequately covers, "ERPIII" – the future of ERP systems – it is contingently defined by the authors as *a flexible, yet powerful information system incorporating web-based SOA and cloud computing version, which enables virtual enterprises to offer increasing degrees of flexibility, agility and dynamic amorphousness.*

The exploration of this chapter begins by considering and discussing the key capabilities of three ERP generations that may consequently affect the design and governance of three dynamic intra-enterprise structures. By reviewing the extant literature with critical assessment, ERP, ERPII, and ERPIII accompanied with related technological tools are all expected to play significant roles in the future of distinct inter-firm relations and management strategies. Moreover, as ERPII and ERPIII are discarding their manufacturing roots and becoming turely enterprise applications or even strategic business tools in the broadest sense, it is imperative to summarize the comparisons between these three systems with respective clear definitions and potential capabilities (as shown by Table 1).

Enterprise Management Strategy

During the recent several decades, many organizational structures are constant transforming for their survival around the fast-changing environment. This has led to the discussions regarding "relation element theory", "chain and network economy" and "virtual inter-organizational alliances". As a result, modern organizational patterns (i.e. enterprises) are becoming a more significant

organizational form (Ketchen & Giunipero, 2004). By reviewing the enterprise management literature, many different enterprise forms have been described such as quasi firm, strategic network, dynamic network, project network, and virtual corporation. By contrasting with above paradigms, we intend to concern more about the three significant newly emerging enterprise management structures involving the vertically integrated enterprise (VIE), extended enterprise (EE), and virtual enterprise (VE) since they can clearly and impressively represent the various contemporary industry-specific firms (e.g. manufacturing, retailing, e-business/SMEs, etc.). Although the characteristics and competitive advantages of these three structures have been remarked by Davis and Spekman (2004) and Goranson (1999), and their similarities and differences have been compared and commented by Browne and Zhang (1999), little has been written about how these three EM structures can transform amongst one another and how they be applied with the respective enterprise information systems implementation and development. Also, we will deeply explore the direct and indirect key factors that influence the design and governance of enterprise management paradigms besides of merely the core competences (Binder & Clegg, 2006).

Three Proposed Enterprise Management Paradigms/ Strategies (VIE, EE, and VE)

Highly competitive and rapidly changing environment, globalized economic conditions, and well-informed and demanding customers urge more and more companies of various sized categories to get involved in activities that are outside the boundaries of the traditional companies (Binder & Clegg, 2006). This is in order to embrace a growing opportunity to see themselves as potential business partners for various business networks, collaborative arrangements (Achrol & Kotler, 1999), and joint ventures. Such relationships are

Table 1. a comparisons between ERP, ERPII, and ERPIII

Element	ERP	ERPII	ERPIII
Role of the ERP systems	Enterprise optimization and integration	Value chain participation /c-commerce enablement	Virtual value chain, value network, and open source
Business **scope/domain**	Manufacturing and distribution, automatic business transactions	Relevant sectors/segments with upstream and downstream	All sectors/segments, strategic alliance, network collaboration
Functions addressed within the domain	Manufacturing, sales and distribution, and finance process	Cross-industry industry sector and specific sector processes	Multinational and global industry sectors and information exchange
Processes required by those functions	Internal, hidden, intra-company boundary	Externally connected, ego-network, inter-company relations	Externally connected, open network to create borderless enterprise
Information system **architecture**	Web-aware, closed, monolithic, PDM, CAD are involved	Web-based, componentized, open, EAI, SCM, CRM, etc. are involved	Web-based communication, service-oriented architecture
The way **data** is handled within those IS architectures	Internally generated and consumed between inter-functional departments	Internally and externally published and subscribed with joint ventures	Externally exchange via open source and cloud computing
	Definitions of three ERP Generations with Typical Capabilities		
Traditional ERP (Capabilities)	*'Traditional ERP is a manufacturing software system for business management, encompassing a variety of modules to support different functional areas. It also facilitate transparent integration of those modules, providing information flow between cross-functions within the company/organization'* • Consist and accurate different systems and data sources • Time saving, company-wide control and decision making • Eliminate bureaucracy		
ERPII (Capabilities)	*'ERPII is a business strategy and a set of industry-domain-specific applications deliver on the integrated value chain, which build supplier, customer, and shareholder value by enabling and optimizing business network, intra-enterprise relations, and collaborative operational processes'* • Reinforce both suppliers and customers sides • Efficiency internal and external operations and collaboration • Bring innovative and effective corporate performance management		
ERPIII (Capabilities)	*'A flexible and powerful information system incorporating web-based SOA, cloud computing version, SaaS, and SLA which enables virtual enterprises paradigm and virtual value network to offer increasing degrees of flexibility, agility and dynamic amorphousness'* • Quick response to the external dynamic markets • Flexibility, efficiency, and agility • Cloud computing accompanied with SLA and other policies/rules around an open environment		

referred to in this chapter as a pattern of intra-enterprise behaviour. Tencati and Zsolnai (2009) state the strength and sustainability of enterprise come from their ability to fit within the environment, social, and culture context in which they function, while Binder and Clegg (2006) claim "the success of collaborative enterprise management depends on the ability of companies to intermediate their internal core competences into other participating companies' value streams and simultaneously outsource their own peripheral activities...". These comments indicate that en-

terprise management strategies now rely much on the performance of its partners in the virtual value chain rather merely look into its internal operations (Choy et al., 2005). Begin with the perspective of IS transformation in different enterprise forms and strategies, we will specifically focus on three proposed inter-company management paradigms known as VIE, EE, and VE, as well as investigate how they can be planned for by three generations of ERP systems.

Vertically integrated enterprises (VIE) that operate close to the traditional large single integrated multi-functional firm (large scale of economy and tall hierarchy) (Lynch, 2003) have been described as "a response to pre-existing market power problems or as a strategic move to create or enhance market power in upstream and downstream markets" (Joskow, 2003). Tall hierarchy, self-control and industrial dominance are major elements existing inside such enterprise management model. VIE normally go through a way of increasing a firm's value-added margins for a particular chain of processing from ultra-raw materials to ultimate consumers (Harrigan, 1985). This is to decide upon the direction (upstream and downstream) and limits of the extensions, which aims at internally balancing potentials and capacities and at externally maximizing the company's manoeuvrability in front of its partners (Vallespir & Kleinhans, 2001). As a result, a set of benefits and competitive advantages such as cost reductions by integrating economies and improved coordinated activities (Harrigan, 1983; 1984), product quality protection by creating product/service-differentiation and building entry barriers (Rothaermel et al., 2006), as well as rapid response with technological adaptations to changing market demands in certain industries (Richardson, 1996) can be gained. Additionally, some scholarly arguments suggest that 'make-or-buy' decision (Vallespir & Kleinhans, 2001), strategic outsourcing and alliances (Rothaermel et al., 2006; Arya et al., 2008), and other alternatives (Harrigan, 1984) could be merged with VIE strategy to synergistically increase and optimize the firm's product portfolio, success, and performance, which can contribute to a competitive advantage in highly dynamic market (Brown & Eisenhardt, 1997).

While the determination of collaborative enterprise boundaries appears to be mediated by industry structure and firm engage-abilities (Argyres, 1996), companies can alter their value chain domain based on IS development and managerial discretion to address more powerful core competences within the intra-enterprise context. Considerable disadvantages and competitive

dangers exist (e.g. increased cost for intra-vertical integration, burden of excess capacity, losing information from suppliers and sellers, etc.) by conducting vertically integrated enterprise management structures. These uncovered newly viewed intra-enterprise structures named 'extended enterprises' (EE). EE is defined by Davis and Spekman (2003; 2004) as "the entire set of collaborating companies…which bring value to the marketplace…". Also, this term is interpreted as "a kind of enterprise which represented by all parts of organizations, customers, suppliers and sub-contractors that engaged collaboratively to the end users" (Browne & Zhang, 1999) or "a business value network where multiple firms own and manage parts of an integrated enterprise" (Lyman et al., 2009). Accordingly, the paradigm of extended enterprise often encompasses just-in-time (JIT) supply chain logistics (Sutton, 2006) and collaborative innovation (Owen et al., 2008), working with data warehouse interoperability (Triantafillakis et al., 2004) and SCM, and focuses on its core business and technical activities, while outsources non-core capabilities from outside suppliers and third parties (Browne & Zhang, 1999; Thun, 2010).

As VIE, or even EE cannot manage to successfully follow the turbulent and unpredictable market behavior of today in all required dimensions, new approach and enterprise paradigms/strategies are requested and recognized as virtual enterprises (VEs) (Martinez et al., 2001). Generally, VE is described as the fluid, flexible combination of components of one or more entities/businesses assigned by decomposed specific objectives to deliver value to a market (Davenport, 2000). Alternatively, VE could be understood as an innovative network from which temporary alignments are formed. Thus, this kind of inter-firm relationship can facilitate agile manufacturing (Cho et al., 1996; Sharp et al., 1999) and manage operation in which ICT plays a major role (Hyvonen et al., 2008), and deal with changing dynamic market needs (Madu & Kuei, 2004).

Browne and Zhang (1999, p. 35) summarize that the extended enterprise and virtual enterprise can be seen as two complementary enterprise strategies as their similarity lies in the fact that they both pursue inter-firm partnerships in order to achieve business success in a very competitive environment. The main difference is represented by the 'temporary' and 'dynamic' nature of one (i.e. VE) versus the relative stability of the other (i.e. EE). Moreover, as management re-engineers the firm for responding well to uncertain business environment, the virtual enterprises (VE) tend to replace the vertically integrated organization (Daniels, 1998) as virtual enterprises are "opportunistic aggregations of smaller units that come together and act as though they were a larger, longer-lived enterprises" (Goranson, 1999) for the purpose of increasing the market share and benefits. In the light of above discussion regarding VIE, EE, and VE, we sum up their comparisons between one another (as shown by Table 2) for enabling the latter hypothesis establishment.

Hypothesize the Relations between ERP and Enterprise Strategies

The above comprehensive insights covering ERP, ERPII, and ERPIII capabilities, as well as

Table 2. a comparisons between VIE, EE, and VE

Key Element	Vertically Integrated Enterprise (VIE)	Extended Enterprise (EE)	Virtual Enterprise (VE)
Core capabilities	Mature and well accepted Well-structured and strong control	Semi-mature with pilot experience Comprehensive for innovators	Quick respond to the changing market and environment
Strategic aims	Stronger-long term objective	Stronger-medium-long term objective	Stronger short-term objective
Partnership purposes	Long-term co-operation for sustain the competitive advantages	Medium-long-term collaboration	Temporary team-working for project or products
Organization stability	Extremely with all hierarchy and inflexible environment	Stable relatively across the product value chain	Dynamic organization with core competences
Duration of partner relationships	Foreseeable as permanent as long as competitive	Medium-long-term depend on mutual trust	Temporary and dynamic
Organization type	Unity of command control Concern more on scales of economies	Product value-chain based	Frequently project or niche market based
Co-ordination of partnership	Always the senior manager supervises the relationship with the partners	Often the manufacturer or prime contractor supervises the partnership	Often the broker supervises the co-operation
Operational challenges	Legacy system transferring approaches (e.g. big bang vs. incremental ways)	The synergistic among the core competencies Compatibility around partners and IS/IT	Dynamic operating and unpredictable environment Psychological issues Low trust leads to high risk
Risk degree	Comparative low	Moderate	Intense high
IS/IT facilitators	In-house development of proprietary systems with traditional ERP system for intra-integration	Advanced IS/IT ERP merged with SCM, CRM, DSS, EAI, BI, etc.	Sophisticated ICT tools SOA, SaaS, SLA, cloud computing Web-based technologies
Main features	External trust is low Inflexible, high overhead Large scale of economy	Hollow the corporation High inter-integration via trust and loyalty	Low overhead Flexibility, agility, temporary and dynamic No hierarchy with rapid changes

VIE, EE, and VE characteristics have revealed the potential correlations for linking these two disciplines. Therefore, this chapter provisionally hypothesize the relationships among three ERP generations and three intra-enterprise strategies (as shown by Figure 1), which tend to be proved and developed by latter two empirical case studies and discussion in order to induce the final sustainable dynamic framework.

Virtual Value Chain and Business Networks

The virtual value chain (VVC) (Rayport & Sviokla, 1995; 1996) is a business model describing the dissemination of value-generating information services throughout extended or virtual enterprises. Alternatively, this novel concept is known as a "Value Net" which re-designs the business using digital supply concepts to achieve both superior customer satisfaction and company profitability.

Figure 1. Hypothetical relationships between ERP and enterprise strategies.

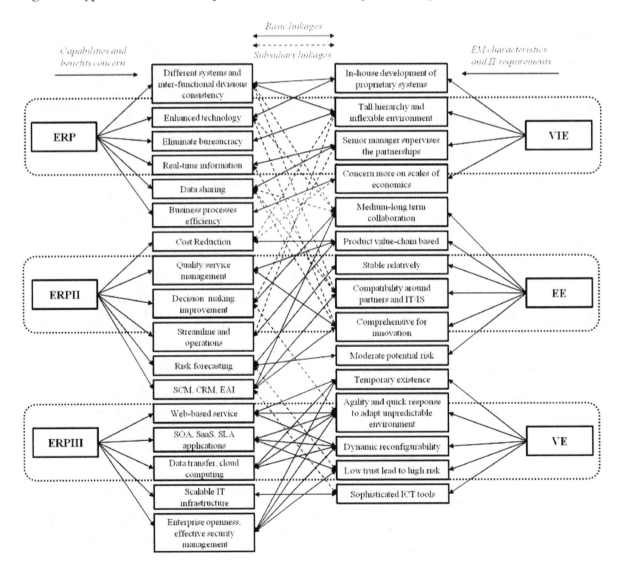

In the virtual value chain (VVC), information has become a dynamic element, rather than a support element in the formation of a businesses' competitive advantage. This transformation produces new benefits and partnerships for suppliers and consumers, which also goes for the manufacturing field. Particularly, "virtual" indicates that information itself can be a source of value and create knowledge (Bhatt & Emdad, 2001).

REFERENCE MODELS

Dynamic Enterprise Reference Grid vs. IS Strategy Formulation Model

The proposed "Dynamic Enterprise Reference Grid" (DERG) model investigates and indicates that the prevailing type of core competence would significantly affect the design and management of the emergent enterprise structure (Figure 2) (Binder & Clegg, 2006). Specifically, the DERG summarizes four different dominant current and future types of enterprise patterns and core competencies and their engage-ability. Each of

Figure 2. Dynamic enterprise reference grid.(Binder & Clegg, 2006)

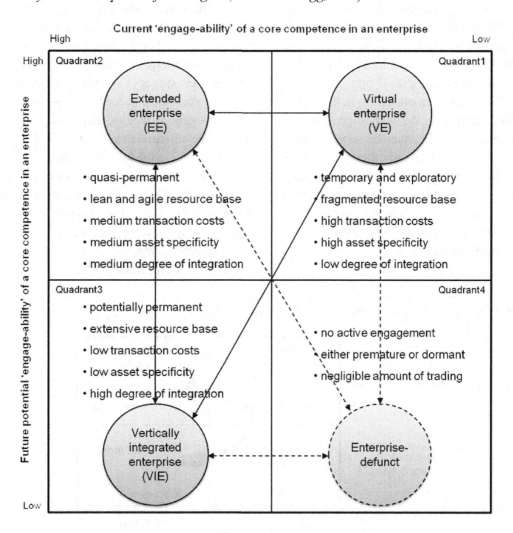

these enterprise structures is considered to be a 'dynamic equilibrium', and one amongst them may change into another as a result of a changed predominance in the type of core competence that it is built upon (Binder & Clegg, 2006). This is a two-way interdependent relationship between each respective pairing.

Limitations of DERG exist as it only focuses on the conspicuous attributes of enterprise structures associated with how their core competencies influence the corresponding enterprise design and management, rather than directly exploring IS strategy. This chapter refers to the "IS formulation strategy transformation" model (Galliers, 1994) simultaneously as Galliers's (1994, p. 60) model (Figure 3) illustrates the changing perceptions of IS strategy shifting from technological efficiency to business competitiveness and collaboration.

Comparatively, Figure 2 demonstrates four distinct structures based on the enterprise management perspective, and Figure 3 presents the associated IS transformation. Even if they look similar and remark on the homologous issues, they are different and cannot be superimposed directly one-on-one. Presently there is a gap in practice and theory referring to how ERP systems satisfy these three enterprise management structures - which is why this research is investigating and addressing it through the following case studies and conceptual induction.

EMPIRICAL CASE STUDIES (RESEARCH METHODOLOGY)

This research methodology was designed to develop a preliminary conceptual framework to explore and understand how governing ERP in inter-company collaboration in dynamic unpredictable circumstances. Case study methods were applied via the narrative research approach to (i) evaluate the companies Zoomlion and Lanye based on the "Collaborative Enterprise Governance" model (Binder & Clegg, 2007), (ii) seek reasons that result in the corporate innovation strategy, and (iii) assesses ERP systems engage-abilities residing in different suggested intra-enterprise structures and rely on the "IS formulation strategy" cycle. These were addressed through the following three major subtopics: mapping and designing the cases at different evolutionary stages, determining the suitable enterprise management structures (i.e. governance strategy) for the engagement with the value members according to both exogenous and endogenous factors, and managing the collaborative enterprise via available ERP systems. Implications derived from Zoomlion and Lanye case studies were then used to refine the "DERG" framework and prove some tentative propositions with respect to the dependencies between the ERP systems development and intra-enterprise management strategies, in order to ultimately achieve agile and flexible ESs.

Figure 3. IS formulation strategy transformation.(Galliers,1994).

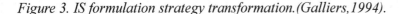

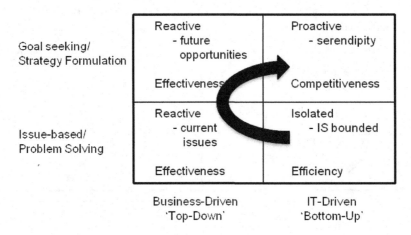

Figure 4. "Collaborative enterprise governance" methodology (Binder & Clegg, 2007)

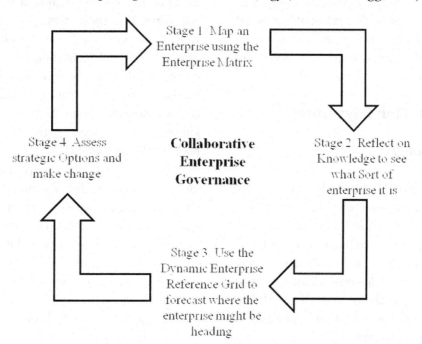

"Collaborative Enterprise Governance" Model

"Collaborative Enterprise Governance" (CEG) model (as shown by Figure 4) provides a methodological approach which considers the "enterprise" to be made up of different modules (parts of companies). Each module is built around highly specific competencies and is integrated with other modules using less specific capabilities and resources (Binder & Clegg, 2007). The tools used in this approach are generally described into four phases. Steps 1 uses the Enterprise Matrix to map enterprise modules, steps 2 uses the theories discussed previously to see which sort of enterprise structure is best suited to, step 3 uses the Dynamic Enterprise Reference Grid (DERG) framework to predict where the enterprise might be heading, and step 4 assesses the options to make available changes. This methodology is cyclical, and therefore, the final stage will start the entire approach again to repeat the above steps.

In the light of foregoing arguments and hypothetical diagram between ERP and intra-enterprise strategies, CEG model was primarily applied to analyze and describe different enterprise structures of Zoomlion and Lanye as well as determining their key value members at different evolutional stages. This model also reinforces the understanding about how ERP systems can mainly influence and satisfy their corresponding enterprise management paradigms and *vice versa* as we would simultaneously explore the ERP systems development within these two cases via a narrative approach.

Empirical Materials of Case Studies

The empirical materials (i.e. primary qualitative data) derived from two cases are gathered from action research at Zoomlion and Lanye. In detail, ease case study involved separate semi-structured interviews of people in three organizational roles: Chief Executive Officer (CEO), the Chief Information Officer (CIO), and the Supply Chain and Sales Manager. Questionnaire survey was only conducted to the staff of relevant functional departments covering market strategy, technical platform and information system divisions, and ERP project teams.

Case A: Zoomlion Case Study

Company Profile

Zoomlion was founded as the Heavy Industry Science & Technology Development Co., Ltd in 1992. Its headquarters is in Changsha and main manufacturing plant in Mainland Chain. Initially, Zoomlion was a hi-tech public company engaging crane and other machines for manufacturing and construction fields, with nearly 20,000 employees. At present, Zoomlion's production line has covered both China and western regions and the company has become a multi-national based manufacturer of consumer products. Also, Zoomlion has its own international management systems for technical development, manufacturing processes and logistics, and a strong sales network and perfect service system covering the whole domestic market, and extending to the oversea market. Zoomlion has continued to achieve rapid development by leaps and bounds with its vision of building up a knowledge-based learning enterprise, and producing top quality and innovative products with enhanced services to the end users on time.

Shifting from Defunct Enterprise into Horizontal Integration and Vertically Integrated Enterprise

The predecessor of Zoomlion was founded on a high-tech academic institution, which could be considered as a "defunct enterprise" without any direct profitable intention. Along with transforming from simple academe into real commercial manufacturing enterprise, the top management realized that 'informationization' would be criti-

cal to replace the physical data flow within the entire operational processes. Thus, IT applications were adopted gradually but with bounded utilization. In parallel, Zoomlion merged other peer companies that supplying logistic and ancillary products/services in order to decrease the sales cost and raise the products' differentiation. Such kind of corporate-level strategy was achieved by horizontal integration (HI).

After combined some competitors in the same business industry, the Zoomlion's enterprise structure and transactions had transformed into a large scope of economies. This type of enterprise management not only decreased the competitive rivalry, but also reinforced Zoomlion's bargaining power to both suppliers and consumers. Following the steps of CEG model, we applied the Enterprise Matrix (which uses 'enterprise modules') to assist mapping out cross-departments within the Zoomlion manufacturing company (as shown by Figure 5). Simultaneously, the 'icons' (i.e. the triangular shapes) were involved to show whereabouts each value member is contributing to the value chain. This tool helped to optimize the whole enterprise operations via the allocation of the most suitable value members (e.g. prime contractor, purchasing, design and manufacturing divisions, after-sale service, etc.) to process stages and tasks (e.g. crane manufacturing and development) of the value stream based on their value proposition to the company.

As cultural diversity, staff turnover (endogenous factors), enormous maintaining expenditure (exogenous factor), etc. occurred unexpectedly, which were induced by a number of piecemeal systems and complex redundant documentations, Zoomlion decided to launch ERP systems to revamp its outdated IT infrastructure for addressing an integration-focused enterprise paradigm. In the same way, the ERP systems facilitated Zoomlion to re-design its business processes dramatically focusing on the high-value departments via the pilot Zoomlion Operations Re-engineering (ZORE) project. The new business model was

Figure 5. The enterprise matrix for Zoomlion (transforming from enterprise-defunct/HI into VIE)

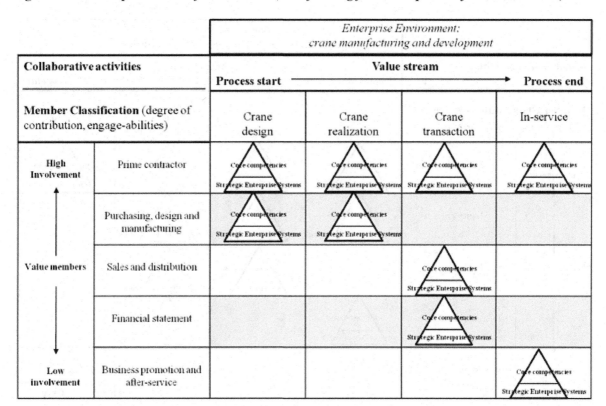

viewed as a tool by which Zoomlion could describe how it wished to conduct its internal operational processes and IT strategy with external customers and suppliers.

Binder and Clegg (2007) state that the number and type of enterprise engagements for any one company is closely aligned with the value proposition of its competencies and the capability of deploying them within collaborative activities of the enterprise, Figure 5 consequently implies and determines that the most appropriate EM paradigm for Zoomlion at this stage is vertically integrated enterprise since the largest contributions are stem from the value members who engaged around the intra-firm. On the other hand, accompany by the substantial impact and strategic changes derived from ERP systems being aware, Zoomlion had been involuntarily realizing the VIE structure which was potentially mature and permanent

with extensive resource and low transaction costs/ specific assets. High degree of intra-integration regarding both cross-functional divisions and diverse resources would lead to high quality of deliverables and investment assets, as well as combine Zoomlion in buyer-seller relationship.

Shifting from Vertically Integrated Enterprise into Extended Enterprise and Virtual Enterprise

Since the industry-specifics of Zoomlion determined that its ERP systems adoption must follow the holistic value chain, new challenges included fast-changing techniques, unpredictable marketing (exogenous factor), and re-intermediation and ownership of assets (endogenous factors) were encountered. Therefore, establishing new corporate-level strategy was imperative. For this

Figure 6. The enterprise matrix for Zoomlion (transforming from VIE into EE/VE)

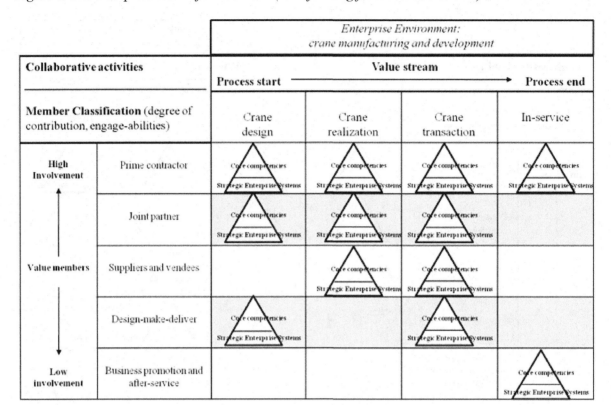

Collaborative activities		Enterprise Environment: crane manufacturing and development			
		Value stream			
		Process start		→	Process end
Member Classification (degree of contribution, engage-abilities)		Crane design	Crane realization	Crane transaction	In-service
High Involvement	Prime contractor	Core competencies / Strategic Enterprise Systems	Core competencies / Strategic Enterprise Systems	Core competencies / Strategic Enterprise Systems	Core competencies / Strategic Enterprise Systems
	Joint partner	Core competencies / Strategic Enterprise Systems	Core competencies / Strategic Enterprise Systems	Core competencies / Strategic Enterprise Systems	
Value members	Suppliers and vendees		Core competencies / Strategic Enterprise Systems	Core competencies / Strategic Enterprise Systems	
	Design-make-deliver	Core competencies / Strategic Enterprise Systems		Core competencies / Strategic Enterprise Systems	
Low involvement	Business promotion and after-service				Core competencies / Strategic Enterprise Systems

purpose, the senior management re-allocated the heterogeneous value members (as shown by Figure 6), which is dependent upon their engage-abilities and contribution to fulfill the final missions via the collaborative value stream. Also, the scope of the member classification tended to go beyond the Zoomlion's organizational boundaries (e.g. joint partner, suppliers and customers, etc.), rather than merely stayed in the interior. These features of the collaborative activities indicate that the most appropriate enterprise management form for Zoomlion at this stage is the extended enterprise due to its value chain (supply network) spanning the whole product life cycle across the inter-company/multi-organizational boundaries.

The asset specificity of Zoomlion's information system was now working against exogenous competitive forces and the company was endeavoring to change its IS strategy with ERP systems

application from merely issue-based problem solving into business tactic seeking. This mission was realized by Toyota's lean management concepts and strategically outsourcing non-core capabilities from other suppliers and third parties in the same heavy industry (e.g. the CIFA manufacturing firm). Moreover, the company ranked the suppliers and consumers in the light of their potential values in order to facilitate its business performances across the entire value chain. In this way, Zoomlion turned to be a quasi-permanent extended enterprise pattern with medium degree of inter-integration, while involved moderate lean and agile resources as well as alliances with other unities within a 'virtual value chain' that accelerated by SCM and CRM.

In spite of setting up collaboration, the senior managers of Zoomlion neglected that great value stemmed from such partnerships, which would

Figure 7. *Corporate innovative roadmap and transformational route in Zoomlion*

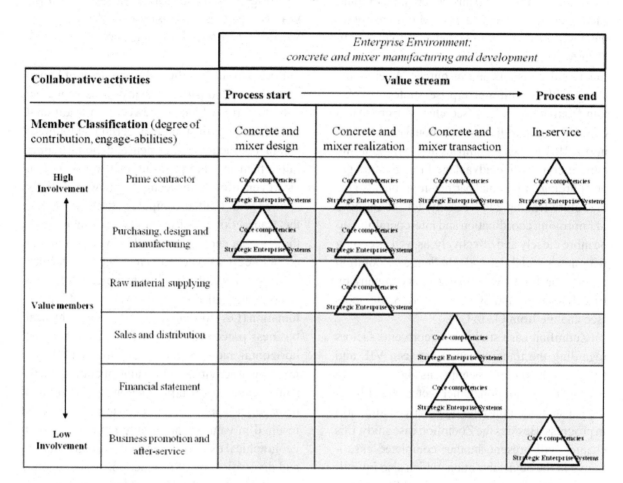

poorly sustain the permanent collaborative venture and long-terms supplier-customer relationships. Hence, we recommends that Zoomlion could test its partial divisions into virtual enterprise structure, which would make the company maximize its flexibility and adaptability for coping with a quick respond environment via cost-effectiveness, product uniqueness, global supply chain optimization, and short-term temporary seamless relations with industrial partners. In this case, ERP systems can be used as another type of weapon with SOA and web-based technologies.

The Transformational Route of Zoomlion's Enterprise Strategies and ERP Development

Figure 7 shows the corporate innovative roadmap and transformational route between different enterprise strategies via ERP systems development at Zoomlion. Particularly, Zoomlion initially shifted from 'enterprise-defunct' form with limited IT usage (see Q4) into horizontal integrated enterprise but still focused on a single company conformation concerning economic investment, in-house data flow and market bargain power. By launching ZORE project and traditional ERP systems through an incremental way, Zoomlion's enterprise structure entered into VIEs (see Q3) which represents the origin of multi-company patterns. Traditional ERP systems work inside this EM form to obtain the high current core-competence with newly IT infrastructure and high intra-integration of functional divisions and resources. Afterwards, along with the intra-enterprise strategy evolution from VIEs to EEs (see change from Q3 to Q2), ERP system has synchronously developed into ERPII to assist company not only gain the current competitive advantage through strategic outsourcing and mutual partnerships, but also for the future leading edge. Finally, for the purpose of improving coordination and interoperability to be more closely and effectively, as well as coping with new crucial network challenges, Zoomlion might morph into VE paradigms accompany by ERPIII systems and SOA, PaaS, SaaS, etc. tools (see change from Q2 to Q1).

Zoomlion case study only represents factors regarding the transformation between VIE and EE, as well as some assumptions about VE with ERP systems adoption. Other factors are still being substantiated through other case studies still in progress. Besides the Zoomlion case study, this chapter will present another completed case – Lanye in the next subsection, which also investigates and proves the possibilities of managing ERP and intra-enterprise strategies within one platform.

Case B: Lanye Case Study

Company Profile

Lanye is a rapidly changing multinational company, which has expanded its supply chain from single company with in-house manufacturing into other organizations all around world along with its IT and ERP systems development.

Shifting from Traditional Manufacturing via Mergers & Acquisitions into a Vertically Integrated Enterprise

Different from Zoomlion, the precursor of Lanye – The Heavy Industry Company – was a concrete manufacturer, which is viewed as a traditional manufacturing firm with a certain amount of commercial active engagement and formal trading rather than an "enterprise-defunct" organization. However, information technologies were initially applied with limited computer efficiency due to the transaction-specific assets of Lanye. With the impetus derived from self-development and economic growth, the senior management decided to bring in a set of advanced technical tools such as computer-aided design (CAD) and office automation (OA) to change the customary physical business processes. Meanwhile, Lanye adopted horizontal mergers and acquisitions (M&As) investment activities for pursuing operating and financial synergies in its production, marketing, and managerial experience. The carrying out of M&As resulted in value creation, internal and external geographical expansion, as well as augmentation and diversification of product portfolios.

After merged three competitors operating in the same industry and on the same industry level through the stock acquisitions strategy, the Lanye's enterprise paradigm had shifted into a larger size of manufacturing firm with more complexity, increased its economies of scale, and boomed the business. Similarly, we used the Enterprise Matrix to map out cross-divisions and value members within the Lanye and its entire value chain (as shown by Figure 8). This approach not only classifies the grade and significance of the most valuable members (e.g. raw material supplying, design and manufacturing department, etc.) involved in contributing to the enterprise transactional operations, but also clarifies each stage and collaborative mission (e.g. concrete and mixer design and realization) to fulfill the ultimate product across the firm's value stream.

As the targeted companies are relatively small compared to Lanye, limited actions and input were laid out to restructure business processes and afterwards led to culture differentiation with desire to preserve own culture, existing routines disruption (endogenous factors), huge amount of M&As expenditure (exogenous factor), etc. Simultaneously, Lanye decided to implement vertical M&As via combing the firms that operate in different stages of the same industry to replace the horizontal strategy, in order to reinforce its competitive advantages and asset investment efficiency. These factors compelled the firm to start-up ERP project to repair the improper information systems and facilitate the real intra-processes integration. According to business strategy, company size, and operational performances on the whole supply chain, Table 5

indicates that the most suitable EM form for Lanye in this phase is vertically integrated enterprise, while ERP systems can subsequently help the firm to achieve the high degree of intra-integration among the cross-functional units and promote the organizational structure re-engineering.

Shifting from Vertically Integrated Enterprise into Virtual Enterprise and Extended Enterprise

During the actual and post vertical integration processes, the top managers spent too long to determine which roles and people should stay, while they had not established available relationships to bring separate entities together. Also, the communication to all constituencies including

Figure 8. The enterprise matrix for Lanye (transforming from Horizontal M&As into VIE)

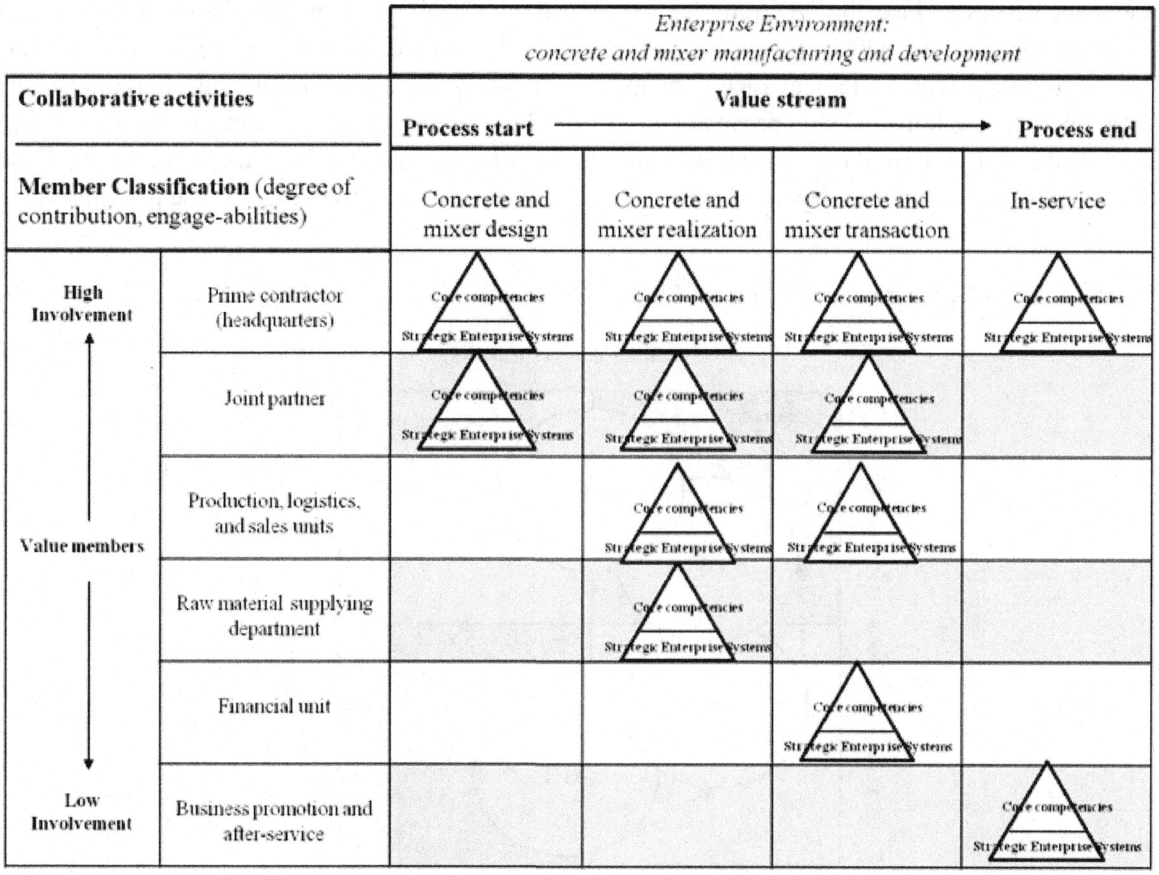

employees, suppliers, customers, and shareholders were not regarded adequately. These endogenous factors forced Lanye to re-conform and streamline its internal diverse resources and assets. On the other hand, the exogenous factors consisted of global economic integration, IT/IS improvement, and transporting costs jack-up occurred unexpectedly. Hence, it was necessary to set up new strategic alignment to combine business, technology, and cross-culture. Aim at this, the senior management re-assigned the value member classification in terms of the degree of their contribution and engage-abilities for completing the respective activities on the collaborative value chain (as shown by Figure 9), in order to achieve an agile or even leagile manufacturing with quick responses to the global marketing demands.

Once the new organizational structure and operational business processes made official, integration and inter-collaboration by gaining the new technologies and capabilities were the true key to the success. Along with changing the previous IS strategy with traditional ERP systems functionalities, the holistic value proposition of Lanye had transferred from issue-based problem solving into goal seeking strategy accelerated by IT tools ('bottom-up') rather than business-driven ('top-down'). Figure 9 determines that the most appropriate EM structure for Lanye in this phase is virtual manufacturing enterprise. Particularly, each functional unit (e.g. joint partner, raw material supplying, logistics division, etc.) extended to the international-bound rather than merely Chinese region. The cooperative tasks were realized by new ERP applications with SCM and CRM systems accompany by Product Data Management (PDM), GPS with Alutec consulting company, and Virtual Private Network (VPN). In this condition, Lanye turned to be a new emerging manufacturing paradigm with operational agility and flexibility for infrastructure commercially, technically, and organizationally via its 'virtual value chain'.

Although VE increased the efficiency of production, logistics, sales, and monitor with lower cost, and improved the management across the inter-departments boundaries, the asset and industry specificity of Lanye constrained the substantial restructuring and reorganization. Meanwhile, the headquarters often used its power to influence and dominant the acquired firms and joint partners, which might cause potential risks

Figure 9. The enterprise matrix for Lanye (transforming from VIE into VE/EE)

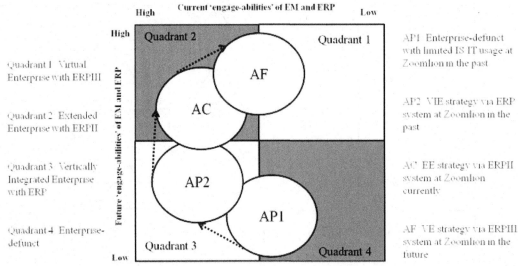

around the dynamic and unpredictable environment. Consequently, we suggest Lanye to apply extended enterprise structure to achieve a more stable organizational structure and long-term relationship with industrial collaborators within the global supply chain network. In this case, ERP systems must be used based on joint venture partnerships instead of web-based technologies.

The Transformational Route of Lanye's Enterprise Strategies and ERP Development

Figure 10 shows the corporate innovative roadmap and transformational route between different enterprise strategies via ERP systems development at Lanye. Comparatively, the evolution path in Lanye case (as shown by Figure 10) indicates that VIEs (see Q3) can not only directly shift to EEs (see Q2) with traditional ERP systems, but also directly morph into VEs with ERPIII or some other IS architecture (e.g. Virtual Private Network) (see change from Q3 to Q1). Once the competencies have matured, Lanye would try to establish a more stable and long-term relations with its critical partners to form EEs with ERPII for chasing

strategic advantages and lower transaction costs (see change from Q1 to Q2).

Lanye case study only represents factors regarding the transformation between VIE and VE, as well as some assumptions about EE with ERP systems adoption. Other factors are still being substantiated through other case studies still in progress. These two cases support the new ideas and dynamic framework that are induced below for managing ERP and inter-firm relationships concurrently.

DISCUSSION OF NOVEL DYNAMIC SUSTAINABLE CONCEPTUAL FRAMEWORK FOR ERP SYSTEMS AND INTRA-ENTERPRISE MANAGEMENT

ERP Systems Engage-abilities in VIE

Since VIEs are highly flexible with self-control, industrial dominance, and proprietary IS (Binder & Clegg, 2006) running applications such as in-house logistic would face uncertain demands and unnecessarily constrained capabilities. Mean-

Figure 10. Corporate innovative roadmap and transformational route in Lanye

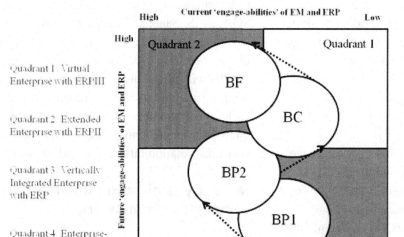

while, the VIE pattern often serves large single organizations or manufacturing firms, which requests ERP systems architecture to be built upon real-time information with a desired level of sales and processes integration. Also, social commitment and risk management for implementing the ERP initiatives need to be practiced carefully in response to the uncertainty and equivocally complex environment.

ERPII Systems Engage-abilities in EE

Shifting from ERP into ERPII, the new systems' capabilities have been extended to undertake the paradigm of EE. First of all, ERPII systems could re-engineer the supply chain and enable a high level of operational process integration. Differing from VIE, this "seamless supply chain" extends towards suppliers and customers rather than being constrained by organizational boundaries. Secondly, as an EE is an entire set of collaborating alliances for sharing common goals and creating superior values, moderate supplier-customer relationships and joint venture partnerships are inevitably and they can be managed efficiently via SCM/CRM that act as integral components of the virtual value chain. With such smart applications, information from both upstream and downstream could be exchanged by ERPII for improving strategic alignment with competencies. However, in view of the EE's essence, this type of cooperation is still pursuing a self-centred approach to IS strategy rather than virtual intercommunication.

ERPIII Systems Engage-abilities in VE

VE key characteristics of 'temporary existence' and 'agility' require corresponding ERPIII systems to contain a flexible, agent-based ICT infrastructure, web-based architecture, and computer integrated manufacturing (CIM) system, and intelligence management based on client/server integrated systems (Xu et al., 2002). As a VE

is an entity with low volume and high diversity inter-collaboration through business process management must be quick and dynamic. This can be achieved by ERPIII systems with supplemental SOA cloud computing versions and internet compliant architecture such as VERP, Dynamic Enterprise Model (DEM) and Business Application Programming Interface (BAPI). Moreover, psychological trust and conflict issues must be taken into account when applying ERPIII systems. EEs and VEs tend to be served by multi-organizational integrated information systems to gain collaborative competitive advantage.

Proposed "ERPIII" System

ERPIII applications integrate enterprise operations within and across enterprise legal entities, or company codes. By extending supply functionality to external enterprises (generally vendor-affiliated companies or enterprises) for reducing cost, improving supply chain efficiency, and performing collaborative innovation based on ERPII applications, ERPIII enterprises will go to the next level of integrating the traditional ERP and ERPII functionalities to include customers and the sales side of the marketplace in general. The end state of the ERPIII enterprise would include a dialog between customers/potential customers, the ERP organization, and the extended supply chain with SOA, PaaS, SaaS, and Service Level Agreement (SLA) tools so that even suppliers would engage in the sales side of the marketplace. Moreover, ERPIII will create the "borderless enterprise" by bringing together a host of technology sources such as collaboration techniques, social media, internet-based technologies, could computing, smart information integration and synthesis, etc.

Novel Dynamic and Sustainable Conceptual Framework

Figure 11 shows how the above ideas can be combined in the context of global value chain and supply chain. These proposed enterprise types do not result from different strategies, but are actually part of the same overall business objective focused on inter-company cooperation. However, at different times and circumstances in its lifecycle the firms may require preferable structures with corresponding ERP systems to satisfy their requirements. At present this is a proposal 'straw man' framework based on the CEG model, literature review on ERP developments and two initial case studies. This is work in progress and further details about the concept testing, theory developing and data can be provided by the authors.

As Figure 11 is a conceptual framework which not only reveals ERP, ERPII, and ERPIII systems engage-abilities within three different intra-en-

terprise strategies and structures respectively, but also demonstrates a cyclical transformation amongst one another. This transformation with empirical examples stem from the above two cases are able to give and explain how and why enterprise strategies changes can be affected and realized by ERP systems development.

FUTURE RESEARCH DIRECTIONS

The thrust of this chapter has been mainly to review the theoretical underpinning and practical approach for research on enterprise information systems integration. It offers adequate theories and concepts that enrich the understanding of

Figure 11. Novel sustainable conceptual framework for managing ERP systems development and dynamic enterprise strategies

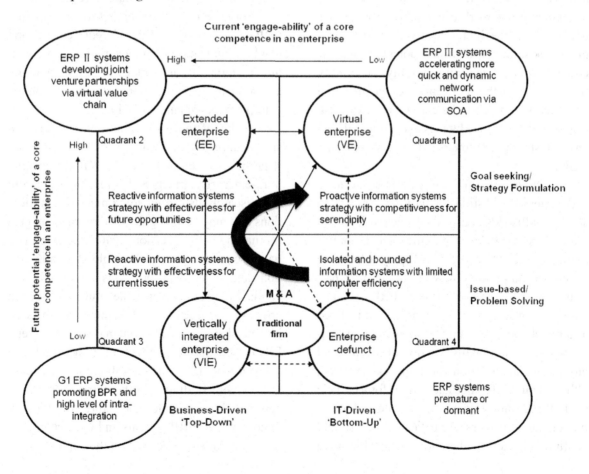

intra-enterprise collaboration with IT governance and contribute towards the combination of ERP systems development and enterprise strategies accompany by appropriate methodology. Overall we hope that the induced dynamic conceptual frameworks will bring more clarity and insight to the analysis of how ERP realize the respective EM paradigms. We also believe that this sustainable approach would be applicable to empirical research.

At present, based on the deep explanation of empirical data and postulated propositions, Figure 11 involving both 'static' and 'dynamic' components has provided a dynamic views of intra-enterprise design and management depending on ERP systems evolution. In other words, the dependencies between ERP development and distinctive inter-company strategies have been uncovered with explicit descriptions. The current achievements, case findings, and new dynamic conceptual framework with a set of propositions are based on the literature review and limited multi-case studies, which might potentially narrow down the generalizability, reliability and validity of results. Thus, the applicability of the proposed approach still needs to be continually explored, tested, and developed by massive empirical data and industrial practitioners in the future research study.

The future direction of enterprise systems and strategies will still keep moving forward the strategic alliances and business network within the context of global economics and virtual e-marketspace. ERP systems can play a key role to realize and promote new intra-enterprise patterns. Nevertheless, how to merge ERP and intra-enterprise management in a whole is considered as a big challenge for both academic and practical worlds. Additionally, we do not recommend any particular direction for empirical research, although our preference naturally is for a holistic study that combines depth with scale and methodological robustness. We believe efforts should continue in multiple directions, to enable us to

address the real-life problems of intra-enterprise information systems management.

CONCLUSION

The scope of this chapter is to propose three generations of ERP systems that focus on corresponding enterprise management patterns and strategies respectively for the purpose of achieving the agility and flexibility. It has not only investigated how ERP works in a VIE, EE, and VE context, but also uncovered developmental issues to present how one enterprise management type morphs into another using the DERG and the "IS strategy formulating" cycle. The findings imply that the design, operations and management of emergent intra-enterprise structures can be affected by preferable information systems (e.g. ERP). Similarly, different intra-enterprise strategies would compel the managers to development ERP systems to satisfy the IT requirements and newly organizational characteristics. Moreover, the theoretical framework can be applied in any area referring to information systems and strategic enterprise management disciplines.

Besides of the above contributions that can significantly fill in the gaps of extant literature regarding the relations between ERP and dynamic intra-enterprise strategies. The results derive from this research also bring some practical implications that may help to guide enterprise managers for making better decisions within the enterprise wide scope. In further, as the exploratory observations and tentative propositions are tended to be validated and developed in the future, the induced novel sustainable dynamic framework can assist both academia and industrial managers to extend ERP modules and capabilities on the new platform

As a conclusion, the Zoomlion and Lanye case studies with findings via the narrative research approach have revealed the future evolutionary trend between ERP systems and intra-enterprise management strategies within the context of the current global business market. These findings are part of an ongoing work, and this chapter demonstrates that the idea has strong potential contribution to make to both theory and practice.

REFERENCES

Achrol, R., & Kotler, P. (1999). Marketing in the network economy. *Journal of Marketing, 63*(Special Issue), 146–163. doi:10.2307/1252108

Akkermans, H., Bogerd, P., Yucesan, E., & Van Wassenhove, L. (2003). The impact of ERP on supply chain management: exploratory findings from a European Delphi Study. *European Journal of Operational Research, 146*(2), 284–294. doi:10.1016/S0377-2217(02)00550-7

Al-Mashari, M. (2003). Enterprise Resource Planning (ERP) systems: A research agenda. *Industrial Management & Data Systems, 103*(1), 22–27. doi:10.1108/02635570310456869

Al-Mudimigh, A., Zairi, M., & Al-Mashari, M. (2001). ERP software implementation: An integrative framework. *European Journal of Information Systems, 10*, 216–226. doi:10.1057/palgrave.ejis.3000406

Argyres, N. S. (1996). Capabilities technological diversification and divisionalization. *Strategic Management Journal, 17*, 395–410. doi:10.1002/(SICI)1097-0266(199605)17:5<395::AID-SMJ826>3.0.CO;2-E

Arya, A., & Mittendorf, B. (2008). Pricing internal trade to get a leg up on external rivals. *Journal of Economics & Management Strategy, 17*(3), 709–731. doi:10.1111/j.1530-9134.2008.00192.x

Bagchi, S., Kanungo, S., & Dasgupta, S. (2003). Modeling use of enterprise resource planning systems: A path analytic study. *European Journal of Information Systems, 12*, 142–158. doi:10.1057/palgrave.ejis.3000453

Banker, R. D., Chang, H., & Kao, Y. (2010). Evaluating cross-organizational impacts of information technology-An empirical analysis. *European Journal of Information Systems, 19*, 153–167. doi:10.1057/ejis.2010.9

Bass, T., & Mabry, R. (2004). Enterprise architecture reference models: A shared vision for Service-Oriented Architectures. *IEEE MILCOM, 1-8.*

Bendoly, E., Soni, A., & Venkataramanan, M. A. (2004). Value Chain Resource Planning (VCRP): Adding Value with Systems beyond the Enterprise. [from http://www.fc.bus.emory.edu/~elliot_bendoly/VCRP_BH.pdf]. *Business Horizons, 1–17.* Retrieved January 17, 2010

Bhatt, D., & Emdad, A. F. (2001). An analysis of the virtual value chain in electronic commerce. *Logistics Information Management, 14*(1-2), 78–84. doi:10.1108/09576050110362465

Binder, M., & Clegg, B. (2007). Designing and managing collaborative enterprises in the automotive industry. *International Journal of Logistics Research and Applications, 10*(2), 135–152. doi:10.1080/13675560701427346

Binder, M., & Clegg, B. T. (2006). A conceptual framework for enterprise management. *International Journal of Production Research, 44*(18-19), 3813–3829. doi:10.1080/00207540600786673

Blackstone, J. H. Jr., & Cox, J.F. (2005). *APICS: The association for operations management.* APICS Dictionary, 11th ed.

Bond, B., Genovese, Y., Miklovic, D., Wood, N., Zrimsek, B., & Rayner, N. (2000). *ERP is dead-long live ERPII.* Retrieved November 8, 2009, from http://www.pentaprise.de/cms_showpdf.php?pdfname=infoc_report

Brown, S. L., & Eisenhardt, K. M. (1997). The art of continuous change: Linking complexity theory and time-paced evolution in relentlessly shifting organizations. *Administrative Science Quarterly, 42*, 1–34. doi:10.2307/2393807

Browne, J., & Zhang, J. (1999). Extended and virtual enterprises-Similarities and differences. *International Journal of Agile Management Systems*, *1*(1), 30–36. doi:10.1108/14654659910266691

Byrne, J. A., & Brandt, R. (1993). The virtual corporation. *Business Week, February 8*, 36-41.

Candido, G., Barata, J., Colombo, A. W., & Jammes, F. (2009). SOA in reconfigurable supply chain: A research roadmap. *Engineering Applications of Artificial Intelligence*, *22*, 939–949. doi:10.1016/j.engappai.2008.10.020

Chen, I. J. (2001). Planning for ERP systems: Analysis and future trend. *Business Process Management Journal*, *7*(5), 374–386. doi:10.1108/14637150110406768

Cho, H., Jung, M., & Kim, M. (1996). Enabling technologies of agile manufacturing and its related activities in Korea. *Computers & Industrial Engineering*, *30*(3), 323–334. doi:10.1016/0360-8352(96)00001-0

Chorafas, D. N. (2001). *Integrating ERP, CRM, supply chain management, and smart materials*. CRC Press LLC, Auerbach Publications. doi:10.1201/9780203997529

Choy, K. L., Lee, H. C. W., & Choy, L. C. (2005). A knowledge-based supplier intelligence retrieval system for outsource manufacturing. *Knowledge-Based Systems*, *18*(1), 1–17. doi:10.1016/j.knosys.2004.05.003

Cummins, F. A. (2009). *Building the agile enterprise with SOA, BPM and MBM*. Burlington, USA: Morgan Kaufmann Publishers, Elsevier Inc.

Daniel, E. M., & White, A. (2005). The future of inter-organizational system linkages: Findings of an international delphi study. *European Journal of Information Systems*, *14*, 188–203. doi:10.1057/palgrave.ejis.3000529

Daniels, S. (1998). The virtual corporation. *Work Study*, *47*(1), 20–22. doi:10.1108/00438029810196685

Davenport, T. H. (1998). Putting the enterprise into the enterprise system. *Harvard Business Review*, 121–131.

Davenport, T. H. (2000). *Mission critical: Realizing the promise of enterprise systems*. Boston: Harvard Business School Press.

Davenport, T. H., & Brooks, J. D. (2004). Enterprise systems and the supply chain. *Journal of Enterprise Information Management*, *17*(1), 8–19. doi:10.1108/09576050410510917

Davis, E. W., & Spekman, R. E. (2003). *The extended enterprise: Gaining competitive advantage through collaborative supply chains*. London: Financial Times Prentice-Hall.

Davis, E. W., & Spekman, R. E. (2004). *Extended enterprise: Gaining Competitive Advantage through Collaborative Supply Chains*. New York, USA: Financial Times Prentice-Hall.

Eckartz, S., Daneva, M., Wieringa, R., & Hillegersberg, J. V. (2009). Cross-organizational ERP management: How to create a successful business case? In *SAC'09 Proceedings of the 2009 ACM Symposium on Applied Computing*. Honolulu, Hawaii, USA.

Galliers, R. D. (1994). Information systems, operational research and business reengineering. *International Transactions in Operational Research*, *1*(2), 159–167. doi:10.1016/0969-6016(94)90017-5

Goranson, H. T. (1999). *The agile virtual enterprise: Cases, metrics, tools. Quorum Books*. USA: Greenwood Publishing Group, Inc.

Harrigan, K. R. (1983a). A framework for looking at vertical integration. *The Journal of Business Strategy*, *3*, 30–37. doi:10.1108/eb038975

Harrigan, K. R. (1983b). *Strategies for vertical integration*. Lexington, MA: Lexington Books.

Harrigan, K. R. (1984). Formulating vertical integration strategies. *Academy of Management Review, 9*, 638–652.

Harrigan, K. R. (1985). Vertical integration and corporate strategy. *Academy of Management Journal, 28*(2), 397–425. doi:10.2307/256208

Hyvonen, E., Viljanen, K., Tuominen, J., & Seppala, K. (2008). Building a national semantic web ontology and ontology service infrastructure-The FinnONTO approach. In *Proceedings of the ESWC 2008*. Tenerife, Span: Springer-Verlag.

Joskow, P. L. (2003). Vertical integration. In *Handbook of New Institutional Economics*. Kluwer.

Lee, B. D., & Schopf, J. M. (2003). Run-time prediction of parallel applications on shared environments. In *Proceedings of the International Conference on Cluster Computing* (pp. 487-491). 1-4 December.

Lyman, K. B., Caswell, N., & Biem, A. (2009) Business value network concepts for the extended enterprise. In *Proceedings of the Network Experience* (PHM Vervest et al., Eds), Springer-Verlag Berlin Heidelberg 2009.

Lynch, R. (2003). *Corporate strategy*. Third ed., Harlow: Prentice Hall Financial Times.

Madu, C. N., & Kuei, C. (2004). *ERP and supply chain management*. Fairfield, CT: Chi Publishers.

Martinez, M. T., Fouletier, P., Park, K. H., & Faurel, J. (2001). Virtual enterprise: Organization, evolution and control. *International Journal of Production Economics, 74*, 225–238. doi:10.1016/S0925-5273(01)00129-3

Maurizio, A., Girolami, L., & Jones, P. (2007). EAI and SOA: Factors and methods influencing the integration of multiple ERP systems (in an SAP environment) to comply with the Sarbanes-Oxley Act. *Journal of Enterprise Information Management, 20*(1), 14–31. doi:10.1108/17410390710717110

Michel, R. (2000). *The road to extended ERP*. Retrieved May 8, 2009, from http://www.manufacturingsystems.com/extendedenterprise

Moller, C. (2005). ERPII: A conceptual framework for next-generation enterprise systems? *Journal of Enterprise Information Management, 18*(4), 483–497. doi:10.1108/17410390510609626

Monk, E. F., & Wagner, B. J. (2009). *Concepts in Enterprise Resource Planning* (3rd ed.). Course Technology, USA: Cengage Learning.

Owen, L., Goldwasser, C., Choate, K., & Blitz, A. (2008). Collaborative innovation throughout the extended enterprise. *Strategy and Leadership, 36*(1), 39–45. doi:10.1108/10878570810840689

Pal, N., & Pantaleo, D. C. (2005). *The agile enterprise: Reinventing your organization for success in an on-demand world*. New York, USA: Springer Science, Business Media, Inc.

Palaniswamy, R., & Frank, T. (2000). Enhancing manufacturing performance with ERP systems. *Information Systems Management, 17*(3), 1–13. doi:10.1201/1078/43192.17.3.20000601/31240.7

Porter, M., & Millar, V. E. (1985). How information gives you competitive advantage. *Harvard Business Review, 63*(4), 149–160.

Powell, W. W. (1990). Neither market nor hierarchy: Network forms of organization. *Research in Organizational Behavior, 12*, 295–336.

Rayport, J. F., & Sviokla, J. J. (1995). 1996). Exploiting the virtual value chain. *The McKinsey Quarterly, 1*, 21–36.

Reuer, J. J. (2004). *Strategic alliances.* New York: Oxford University Press Inc.

Richardson, J. (1996). Vertical integration and rapid response in fashion apparel. *Organization Science, 7*(4), 400–412. doi:10.1287/orsc.7.4.400

Rothaermel, F. T., Hitt, M. A., & Jobe, L. A. (2006). Balancing vertical integration and strategic outsourcing: Effects on product portfolio, product success, and firm performance. *Strategic Management Journal, 27*, 1033–1056. doi:10.1002/smj.559

Sharp, J. M., Bamber, C. J., Desia, S., & Irani, Z. (1999). An empirical analysis of lean & agile manufacturing. In *Proceedings of the IMechE Conference on Lean & Agile for the Next Millennium.* Tuesday 9th March.

Songini, M. L. (2002). J.D. Edwards pushes CRM, ERP integration. *Computerworld, 36*(25), 4.

Stevens, C. P. (2003). Enterprise resource planning: A trio of resources. *Information Systems Management, 20*(3), 61–71. doi:10.1201/1078/43205.20.3.20030601/43074.7

Sutton, S. G. (2006). Extended-enterprise systems' impact on enterprise risk management. *Journal of Enterprise Information Management, 19*(1), 97–114. doi:10.1108/17410390610636904

Tencati, A., & Zsolnai, L. (2009). The collaborative enterprise. *Journal of Business Ethics, 85*(3), 367–376. doi:10.1007/s10551-008-9775-3

Themistocleous, M., Irani, Z., & O'Keefe, R. (2001). ERP and application integration: Exploratory survey. *Business Process Management Journal, 7*(3), 195–204. doi:10.1108/14637150110392656

Thun, J. H. (2010). Angles of Integration: An empirical analysis of the alignment of internet-based information technology and global supply chain integration. *Journal of Supply Chain Management, 46*(2), 30–44. doi:10.1111/j.1745-493X.2010.03188.x

Todeva, E. (2006). *Business networks: Strategy and structure. Milton Park.* Abingdon, UK: Routledge, Taylor & Francis Group.

Torbacki, W. (2008). SaaS – direction of technology development in ERP/MRP systems. *Archives of Materials Science and Engineering, 31*(1), 57–60.

Triantafillakis, A., Kanellis, P., & Martakos, D. (2004). Data warehousing interoperability for the extended enterprise. *Journal of Database Management, 15*(3), 73–82. doi:10.4018/jdm.2004070105

Vallespir, B., & Kleinhans, S. (2001). Positioning a company in enterprise collaborations: Vertical integration and make-or-buy decisions. *Production Planning and Control, 12*, 478–487. doi:10.1080/09537280110042701

Vazquez-Bustelo, D., & Avella, L. (2006). Agile manufacturing: Industrial case studies in Spain. *Technovation, 26*, 1147–1161. doi:10.1016/j.technovation.2005.11.006

Wilkes, L., & Veryard, R. (2004). Service-Oriented Architecture: Considerations for agile systems. *Microsoft Architect Journal, April.* Retrieved May 16, 2010, from http://www.msdn2.microsoft.com

Wortmann, J. C. (2000). Evolution of ERP Systems. In *Proceedings of the International Conference on the Manufacturing Value-Chain.* Klüwer Academic Publishers, Troon, Scotland, UK.

Xu, W., Wei, Y., & Fan, Y. (2002). Virtual enterprise and its intelligence management. *Computers & Industrial Engineering, 42*, 199–205. doi:10.1016/S0360-8352(02)00053-0

Zhang, C., & Dhaliwal, J. (2008). An investigation of resource-based and institutional theoretic factors in technology adoption for operations and supply chain management. *International Journal of Production Economics, 120*(1), 252–269. doi:10.1016/j.ijpe.2008.07.023

ADDITIONAL READINGS

Acemoglu, D., Aghion, P., Griffith, R., & Zilibotti, F. (2010). Vertical integration and technology: Theory and evidence. *Journal of the European Economic Association, 8*(5), 989–1033. doi:10.1162/jeea_a_00013

Beatty, R. C., & Williams, C. D. (2006). ERPII: Best practices for successfully implementing and ERP upgrade. *Communications of the ACM, 49*(3), 105–109. doi:10.1145/1118178.1118184

Bernus, P., Baltrusch, R., Tolle, M., & Vesterager, J. (2002). *Better models for agile virtual enterprises-The enterprise and its constituents as hybrid agents.* Retrieved May 10, 2010, from http://cic.vtt.fi/projects/globemen/book/05_bernus2.pdf

Boden, T. (2004). The grid enterprise-Structuring the agile business of the future. *BT Technology Journal, 22*(1), 107–117. doi:10.1023/B:BTTJ.0000015501.06794.97

Bowersox, D. J., Closs, D. J., & Cooper, M. B. (2002). *Supply chain logistics management* (International eds.). New York: McGraw-Hill.

Brown, A. W., & Johnston, S. (2003). Using Service-Oriented Architecture and component-based development to build web service applications. Retrieved April 29, 2010, from http://citeseerx.ist.psu.edu/viewdoc/download?doi=10.1.1.93.6520&rep=rep1&type=pdf

Caskey, K. R., Hunt, I., & Browne, J. (2001). Enabling SMEs to take full advantage of e-business. *Production Planning and Control, 12*(5), 548–557. doi:10.1080/09537280110042891

Choy, K. L., Lee, W. B., & Lo, V. (2004). An enterprise collaborative management system-A case study of supplier relationship management. *The Journal of Enterprise Information Management, 17*(3), 191–207. doi:10.1108/17410390410531443

Daniel, E. M., White, A., & Ward, J. M. (2004). Exploring the role of third-parties in inter-organizational web service adoption. *The Journal of Enterprise Information Management, 17*(5), 351–360. doi:10.1108/17410390410560982

Goldsby, T. J., Griffis, S. E., & Roath, A. S. (2006). Modeling lean, agile, and leagile supply chain strategies. *Journal of Business Logistics, 27*(1), 57–80. doi:10.1002/j.2158-1592.2006.tb00241.x

Huang, R., & Zmud, R. W. (2010). Lost in translation: Implications of a failed organizing vision for the governance of a multi-organization shared it infrastructure. In *ICIS 2010 Proceedings, AIS Electronic Library: Paper 93* (pp. 1-17).

Hunter, M. G., & Tan, F. B. (2007). *Strategic use of information technology for global organizations.* Hershey, New York: IGI Publishing. doi:10.4018/978-1-59904-292-3

Hyvonen, T., Jarvinen, J., & Pellinen, J. (2008). A virtual integration: The management control system in a multinational enterprise. *Management Accounting Research, 19*, 45–61. doi:10.1016/j.mar.2007.08.001

Jagdev, H. S., & Thoben, K.-D. (2001). Anatomy of enterprise collaborations. *Production Planning and Control, 12*(5), 437–451. doi:10.1080/09537280110042675

Kelechi, N. J. (2007). *The impact of ERP system on the audit process.* Unpublished doctoral dissertation, Swedish School of Economics and Business Administration, Sweden.

Ketchen, D. J. Jr., & Giunipero, L. C. (2004). The intersection of strategic management and supply chain management. *Industrial Marketing Management, 33*, 51–56. doi:10.1016/j.indmarman.2003.08.010

Kleinhans, S., & Poulymenakou, A. (2006). *Managing dynamic networks: Organizational perspectives of technology enabled inter-firm collaboration.* Berlin Heidelberg, Germany: Springer.

Koolwaaij, J., & Van der Stappen, P. (2000). *ERP, XRP & EAI in virtual marketplaces.* Retrieved July 3, 2009, from https://doc.novay.nl/dsweb/Get/Document-15264/Gigats_D228.pdf

Lee, J. H., Shim, H., & Kim, K. K. (2010). Critical success factors in SOA implementation: An exploratory study. *Information Systems Management, 27*(2), 123–145. doi:10.1080/10580531003685188

Liu, J., Zhang, S., & Hu, J. (2005). A case study of an inter-enterprise workflow-supported supply chain management system. *Information & Management, 42,* 441–454. doi:10.1016/j.im.2004.01.010

Malhotra, Y. (2000). *Knowledge management and virtual organization. Covent Garden.* London, UK: Idea Group Publishing. doi:10.4018/978-1-87828-973-5

Markus, M. L., Tanis, C., & Van Fenema, P. C. (2000). Multisite ERP implementations. *Communications of the ACM, 43*(4), 42–46. doi:10.1145/332051.332068

McGinnis, T. C., & Huang, Z. (2007). Rethinking ERP success: A new perspective from knowledge management and continuous improvement. *Information & Management, 44,* 626–634. doi:10.1016/j.im.2007.05.006

Miller, G. (1999). ERP implementation lessons learned. *White Paper*, Proaction Management Consultants.

Moller, C. (2003). ERPII extended enterprise resource planning. In *Proceedings of the 7th World Multi-Conference on Systemics, Cybernetics and Informatics.* Orlando, FL, July/August.

Nezhad, H. R. M., Stephenson, B., Singhal, S., & Castellanos, M. (2009). Virtual business operating environment in the cloud: Conceptual architecture and challenges. In Laender, A. H. F. (Eds.), *ER 2009, LNCS 5829* (pp. 501–514). Berlin, Heidelberg: Springer-Verlag. doi:10.1007/978-3-642-04840-1_37

Norris, G., Hurley, J. R., Hartley, K. M., Dunleavy, J. R., & Balls, J. D. (2000). *E-business and ERP: Transforming the enterprise.* New York, USA: PricewaterhouseCoopers.

O'Reilly, P., & Finnegan, P. (2010). Intermediaries in inter-organizational networks: Building a theory of electronic marketplace performance. *European Journal of Information Systems, 19,* 462–480. doi:10.1057/ejis.2010.12

Palacios, M. C., Alvarez, E., Alvarez, M., & Santamaria, J. M. (2006). Lessons learned for building agile and flexible scheduling tool for turbulent environments in the extended enterprise. *Robotics and Computer-integrated Manufacturing, 22,* 485–492. doi:10.1016/j.rcim.2005.11.004

Papazoglou, M. P., Traverso, P., Dustdar, S., Leymann, F., & Kramer, B. J. (2006). Service-Oriented Computing research roadmap. In *Proceedings of the Dagstuhl Seminar: Paper. 524. Service Oriented Computing (SOC).*

Park, K., & Kusiak, A. (2005). Enterprise Resource Planning (ERP) operations support system for maintaining process integration. *International Journal of Production Research, 43*(19), 3959–3982. doi:10.1080/00207540500140799

Rai, A., & Tang, X. (2010). Leveraging IT capabilities and competitive process capabilities for the management of interorganizational relationship portfolios. *Information Systems Research, 21*(3), 516–542. doi:10.1287/isre.1100.0299

Rotem-Gal-Oz, A., Bruno, E., & Dahan, U. (2007). *SOA patterns.* Manning publications Co., 2007.

Sammon, D., & Adam, F. (2005). Towards a model of organizational prerequisites for enterprise-wide systems integration examining ERP and data warehousing. *The Journal of Enterprise Information Management, 18*(4), 458–470. doi:10.1108/17410390510609608

Segal-Horn, S., & Faulkner, D. (1999). *The dynamics of international strategy.* Hampshire, UK: Thomas Rennie.

Sharif, A. M., & Irani, Z. (2005). Emergence of ERPII characteristics within an ERP integration context. In *Proceedings of the AMCIS 2005: Paper. 235.*

Su, S. Y. W., Meng, J., Krithivasan, R., Degwekar, S., & Helal, S. (2003). Dynamic inter-enterprise workflow management in a constraint-based e-service infrastructure. *Electronic Commerce Research, 3*, 9–24. doi:10.1023/A:1021521209515

Tarafdar, M., & Qrunfleh, S. (2009). IT-business alignment: A two-level analysis. *Information Systems Management, 26*(4), 338–349. doi:10.1080/10580530903245705

Trienekens, J. H., & Beulens, A. J. M. (2001). Views on inter-enterprise relationships. *Production Planning and Control, 12*(5), 466–477. doi:10.1080/09537280110042693

Tugnawat, P. (2008). *Service Oriented approach for ERP integration.* Retrieved June 10, 2010, from http://blogs.oracle.com/pt/2008/03/service_oriented_approach_for.html

Vernadat, F. B. (2010). Technical, semantic and organizational issues of enterprise interoperability and networking. *Annual Reviews in Control, 34*, 139–144. doi:10.1016/j.arcontrol.2010.02.009

Wan, Y., & Clegg, B. (2010). Enterprise management and ERP development: Case study of Zoomlion using the dynamic enterprise reference grid. In Quintela Varajao, J. E. (Eds.), *Proceedings of Springer-Verlag Berlin Heidelberg: CENTERIS 2010, Part I, CCIS 109* (pp. 191–198). doi:10.1007/978-3-642-16402-6_21

Wan, Y., & Clegg, B. (2010, October). *Achieving agility in transforming manufacturing firms through enterprise management and ERP development: Virtual value chain adoption.* Paper presented at the 15th Cambridge International Manufacturing Symposium on the Innovation in Global Manufacturing, Cambridge, UK.

Wang, C., Xu, L., Liu, X., & Qin, X. (2005). ERP research, development and implementation in China: An overview. *International Journal of Production Research, 39*(7-8), 774–782.

Wanger, B., & Paheerathan, S. J. (2000). *Horizontal and vertical integration of organizational IT systems.* Retrieved July 28, 2010, from http://people.dsv.su.se/~perjons/newhv2.pdf

Wood, B. (2010). *ERP vs. ERPII vs. ERPIII future enterprise applications.* Retrieved September 14, 2010, from http://www.r3now.com/erp-vs-erp-ii-vs-erp-iii-future-enterprise-applications

Wylie, L. (1990). A vision of the next-generation MRPII. *Scenario S-300-339* Gartner Group, April 12, 1990.

KEY TERMS AND DEFINITIONS

Case Study: Two critical embedded and cross-sectional cases have been studied within the interpretive case research tradition. This methodology not only helps to prove the transformation between different enterprise structures, but also seeks to build new theories related to information systems discipline.

Dynamic Framework: The dynamic conceptual framework reveals ERP systems engageabilities and development within three enterprise strategies and structures, as well as demonstrating a cyclical change amongst one another.

Enterprise: An enterprise is made up of parts of different companies, including partnerships or associations regularly engaged in economic activities.

Traditional Enterprise Resource Planning (ERP): Traditional ERP is a manufacturing system for business management, encompassing a variety of modules to support different functional areas. It also facilitates transparent integration of those modules, providing information flow between cross-functions within the enterprise.

Enterprise Resource Planning II (ERPII): ERPII is a business strategy and a set of industry-domain-specific applications deliver on the integrated value chain, which build supplier, customer, and shareholder value by enabling and optimizing business network, inter-enterprise relations, and collaborative operational processes.

Enterprise Resource Planning III (ERPIII): ERPIII is a flexible and powerful information system incorporating web-based SOA, cloud computing version, SaaS, and SLA which enables virtual enterprises paradigm and virtual value network to offer increasing degrees of flexibility, agility and dynamic amorphousness.

Extended Enterprise (EE): Extended enterprise is a kind of enterprises which represented by all parts of organizations, customers, suppliers and sub-contractors that engage collaboratively and bring value to the end users and marketplace.

Information Systems (IS) Management: IS management is using information technologies or systems at all levels of business operations, in order to manage people, technology, and organization, and relationships among them.

Information Systems (IS) Strategy: IS strategy is a formation and implementation of strategy with respect to computer-based information systems, which has to be changed continually to adapt to a changing environment and to capitalize on better ideas.

Organization Strategy: Organization strategy is concerned with envisioning a future for business, creating value of the customers, and building and sustaining a strong position in the marketplace with core competitive advantages.

Structural Transformation: Structural transformation refers to widespread change of the fundamental structure. For instance, a manufacturing economy is currently transformed into a servitization economy. This not only imposes the reconfiguration of information systems/technologies (e.g. ERP systems), but also requires the dynamic change of enterprise structures to quickly respond the complex environment.

Service-Oriented Architecture (SOA): SOA enhances and revitalizes technology assets to create an agile, flexible infrastructure that is more responsive to the business with standards-based components that can be developed and deployed rapidly.

Vertically Integrated Enterprise (VIE): Vertically integrated enterprise is an enterprise paradigm which operates close to the traditional large single integrated multi-functional firm (large scale of economy and tall hierarchy), in order to create or enhance market power in upstream and downstream markets.

Virtual Enterprise (VE): Virtual enterprise is a fluid and flexible combination of components of one or more entities/businesses that assigned by decomposed specific objectives, which is understood as an innovative network from which temporary alignments are formed in order to deliver value to a market.

Chapter 12
Electronic Procurement:
The Supplier Perspective

Paulo Andrade
ISCTE – Instituto Universitário de Lisboa, Portugal

Bráulio Alturas
ISCTE – Instituto Universitário de Lisboa, Portugal

Tiago Oliveira
ISEGI, Universidade Nova de Lisboa, Portugal

ABSTRACT

E-procurement systems make purchasing activities more effective in terms of both time and cost. However, over the past years there is evidence that some of the expected benefits have not been achieved. Among several causes, supplier's low adherence to such platforms has been regarded as one. The focus of this work is in supplier adoption of e-Procurement. It will help to better address the issues actually faced by suppliers within e-Procurement. The authors have conducted a questionnaire-based survey to 721 Portuguese companies and performed an empirical analysis of the data. The findings from this work provide evidence that the supplier perceived indirect benefits and business partner pressures are most important to e-Procurement adoption while barriers have a negative impact on their adoption. The main critical success factors on e-Procurement adoption are also presented.

INTRODUCTION

Procurement is a common business activity since companies depend on goods and services provided by other companies. It is estimated that about 75% of sales revenue will be applied to the purchase of goods or services (Cagno, 2004). Suggested by its name, *e-Procurement* is the application of infor-

mation technologies in the procurement process. Gershon (1999) considers e-Procurement as the whole process of acquisition from third parties over the internet; this process spans the whole life cycle from the initial concept and definition of business needs to the end of the useful life of an asset or end of a services contract. E-Procurement allows part or all of purchase activities to be conducted electronically, leading to cost reduction in goods, improved order processing times and

DOI: 10.4018/978-1-4666-1764-3.ch012

gains in transparency (Pereira & Alturas, 2007). E-Procurement has the potential to provide cost and time reductions when ordering from suppliers, and helps to achieve a well-integrated supply chain. A survey conducted in the UK showed that the majority of companies believed that implementation of e-Procurement solutions were critical for the success of their business in the future (Stein & Hawking, 2004). Also an increasing number of public institutions identified electronic purchasing as a priority to e-Government. Many implemented or are in the process of implementing e-Procurement systems. The adoption of e-Procurement in public administration has a huge impact since governments spend large amounts in acquiring materials and services. Some of the benefits are the cost reduction in goods, services and order processing, better transparency to the suppliers and e-commerce development (Pereira & Alturas, 2007).

Companies are approaching e-Procurement implementation with different strategies. Davila *et al.* (2003) identified two main types of companies. The first type is moving aggressively to adopt e-Procurement, frequently experimenting with various solutions. The second type adopts a more conservative strategy by selectively experimenting, typically with one technology. The latter group relies on these limited experiences to provide the capabilities to move quickly into the technology as a dominant design appears.

An e-Procurement system depends on several critical success factors (CSF). Among the different CSF identified in the literature, supplier adoption is one of the most important (Vaidya, Sajeev, & Callender, 2004). A successful e-Procurement system is required to have suppliers willing and able to trade electronically (Benton, 2005). However users of e-Procurement reported that they can acquire goods over the Internet from only 15% of their supply base (Davila, et al., 2003). A report from the European Union (EU) also confirms that only 13% of EU companies are receiving orders online and 27% placing orders online with suppli-

ers (EC, 2005). Engaging suppliers in the process (especially smaller companies) has proven to be difficult given the level of investment required and the different needs of their customer base in terms of technologies and internal procedures. Although suppliers play an important role in the global success of e-Procurement implementations, their adoption factors have been studied very little (Gunasekaran, McGaughey, Ngai, & Rai, 2009).

Users of e-Procurement technologies reported that they can acquire goods over the Internet from only 15% of their supply base (Davila, et al., 2003). A report from EU also confirms that only 13% of EU companies are receiving orders online and 27% placing orders online with suppliers (EC, 2005). Engaging suppliers in the process (especially smaller companies) has proven to be difficult given the level of investment required and the different needs of their customer base in terms of technologies and internal procedures. A successful e-Procurement system is required to have suppliers willing and able to trade electronically. For example, a key learning from a study conducted by the Australian Government (AGIMO, 2005) was that supplier adoption is important to the overall success of an e-Procurement program. They concluded that the more suppliers in the system, the more inclined buyers will be to use it. If suppliers are not correctly involved, then a low adoption rate can constrain users from leveraging the full associated capabilities from e-Procurement solutions. The lack of a critical mass of suppliers accessible through the organization's e-Procurement system might limit the network effects that underlie these technologies, delaying the acceptance and adoption of the solution.

In this study, we will examine the main factors affecting *supplier adoption of e-Procurement*. While the majority of the actual literature focuses only on the buyer side of e-Procurement (Gunasekaran & Ngai, 2008; Soares-Aguiar & Palma-Dos-Reis, 2008), the focus will be on the seller side. Moreover, the identification of the perceived benefits, perceived barriers, CSF and

Figure 1. The purchasing process. Adapted from Caridi et al. (2004).

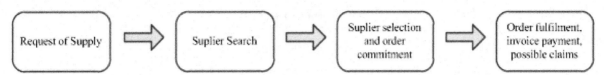

business partner influence will help the research community and the business community to produce a deeper understanding about e-Procurement adoption by suppliers.

BACKGROUND

Procurement Process

In Figure 1, a generic purchasing process is presented. Usually it involves all or part of the activities presented. In the request of supply, technical features, quantity and delivery conditions are specified. Next company looks for the most adequate supplier in the market or in a more restricted list. The selection of the supplier is based on the quality and the pricing of the bids received and finally the selected supplier prepares and delivers goods/services and sends the invoice.

Accordingly to Sparks and Wagner (2003) a purchasing process can range from strategic buying, transactional buying or spot buying. In the first, the main objective is to establish long-term relationship between customers and suppliers and requires a careful vendor selection and a long-term agreement on the supply management. Next, transactional buying implies repetitive purchases with the same vendor, based on yearly blanket orders or outline agreements. Finally, spot buying occurs when urgent requests come out and all the pre-qualified suppliers are not capable of fulfilling them.

Gershon (1999) defines procurement as 'the whole process of acquisition from third parties and covers goods, services and construction projects. This process spans the whole life cycle from the initial concept and definition of business needs through to the end of the useful life of an asset or end of services contract. Thus, Gershon (1999) provides a complete definition of Procurement. However, he doesn't refer anything about the strategic importance of the procurement function.

According to Croom and Giannakis (2002) the purchasing department has been acquiring a more strategic role, coupled with the term Procurement, which continuously strives for new methods of supply, trying to establish collaborative relationships with a selected list of suppliers. Procurement has become a strategic source for firms to compete, since most corporations spend between 50 to 80 percent of sales on goods and services (Cammish & Keough, 1991). Firms need to strategically acquire the materials and services that will enhance their ability to achieve high quality levels, fast delivery and cost savings for exceeding customer requirements (Carr & Pearson, 1999). Thus, the procurement includes all the purchase cycle of a product or service and plays a strategic role, either by its high financial impact or by serving as input to all production of the company.

Definition of E-Procurement

E-Procurement can be seen as part of an automated purchasing system. It is designed to facilitate the acquisition of goods by a commercial or government organization over the Internet. Buyers may log on to the system to view supplier catalogues, and to place orders (Botto, 2003). E-Procurement can be defined as a process which allows any designated user to requisition a product or service through a web interface, which then generates a purchase order to send to a supplier (Falk, 2005).

Figure 2. e-Procurement Lifecycle. Adapted from CIPS (2009).

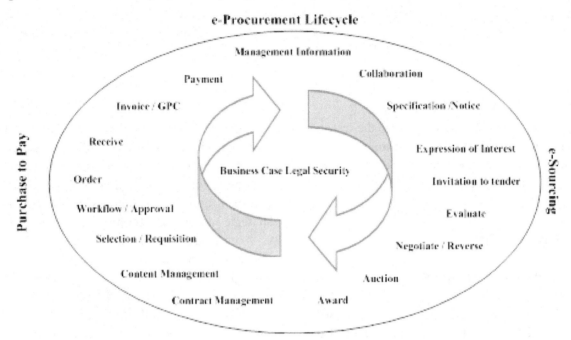

According to the Chartered Institute of Purchasing & Supply e-Procurement is about using the Internet to operate the transactional aspects of requisitioning, authorizing, ordering, receipting and payment processes for the required services or products (CIPS, 2009). This study has determined that this definition is too narrow since they disregard several important activities: the aggregation of orders, monitoring of the supplier's performance, managing and mitigating supplier-connected risks or contract management. Thus, a better definition is that e-Procurement is provided by Gershon (1999). He considers **e-***Procurement* as the whole process of acquisition from third parties over the internet; this process spans the whole life cycle from the initial concept and definition of business needs to the end of the useful life of an asset or end of a services contract.

E-Procurement Tools

E-Procurement is viewed as an end to end solution that integrates and streamlines many procurement processes horizontally trough the organization. In Figure 2 a full e-Procurement lifecycle is presented. The author divides it in the e-Sourcing cycle and Purchase to Pay Cycle (P2P). In the e-Sourcing companies look to what the market has to offer in terms of products or services. Strategic decisions are also performed, like contracts and important sourcing partnerships. In the purchase to pay cycle, the decision of what to buy, when and to whom has already been taken. The focus here is in the execution of the purchase order. Industry and academic analysis indicate that this ideal model is rarely achieved and e-Procurement implementations generally involve a combination of the different tools (Vaidya, Sajeev, & Callender, 2006).

FRAMEWORK FOR THE ADOPTION OF E-PROCUREMENT

Through an extensive literature review some variables were identified as contributing posi-

Figure 3. Framework for e-Procurement adoption by suppliers.

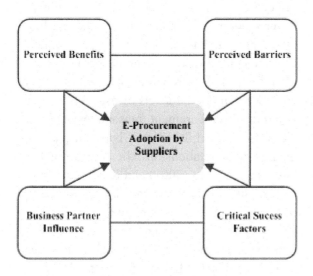

tively or negatively to supplier's adoption of e-Procurement. A framework was developed to structure these variables. Those were divided into perceived benefits, perceived barriers, CSF and business partner influence (Figure 3). This was adapted from the framework developed by Gunasekaran and Ngai (2008) to study e-Procurement adoption.

Perceived Benefits

On this research, we define benefits as the factors having positive impact on the intention to adopt e-Procurement. Gunasekaran and Ngai (2008) describe it as the *perceived benefits of e-Procurement* as seen by companies having tremendous implications whether one goes for the technology or not.

Sales Growth and Reach New Market

For suppliers, the adoption of e-Procurement may be an opportunity to expand sales. According to Sharifi, Kehoe and Hopkins (2006) they will find e-Procurement attractive because they could easily and cost effectively reach new customers. A

greater exposure to larger buying communities, with improved reach, range and efficiency, increases the potential for more transactions. Also, by making the electronic catalogue accessible in a direct way to all employees and buyers, or using e-hubs and e-commerce communities, the seller can widely increase the number of sales orders (Berlak & Weber, 2004). After the implementation, e-Procurement systems can function as a new sales channel improving the chances of sales growth. Suppliers also appreciate the chance to develop new business thought participation on electronic reverse auctions. According to Beall *et al.* (2003) even the most reluctant participants, rarely refuse the chance to participate. This is expected, since electronic reverse auctions (e-RAS) represent a new sales opportunity. For Moser (2002) the fact that supplier´s can change their bids during an online-auction also increases their changes to win the contract. This is because online auctions improve the visibility over the negotiation process. They allow seeing online the competitor price, and while they know how lower they can bid, the chances of winning the action are improved.

Reductions In Order Processing Costs and Better Operational Efficiency

The integration between the buyer and the seller systems allows the exchange of information automatically. Therefore, it is possible for the buyer to make an order more quickly. This will also reduce the chance of occurring errors that are common when an order is dependent on paper (Berlak & Weber, 2004). Linking to a customer directly and collaborating to ensure accurate and on-time delivery provides better service and lower overall procurement costs to the customer. This can result in much more collaborative buyer-seller relationships. As a preferred supplier, or if the buyer begins to provide forecasts of requirements to its vendors, the supplier can begin to predict and prepare for individual buyer requirements well ahead of time, reducing the uncertain on sales (Neef, 2001). Other potential *benefits of e-Procurement* include lower marketing and sales costs (Beall, et al., 2003). The mere conversion of paper documents to electronic can free up employees for higher value tasks such as price negotiation and post bid analysis (Moser, 2002).

Better Negotiable Transparency

E-Procurement tools have been seen as able to provide a better negotiable transparency compared to traditional means. The conclusions of a study conducted by Beall *et. al* (2003) indicated that suppliers considered electronic reverse auctions a fairer process of doing business because they "level the playing field" through increased transparency and much more information. Carayannis and Popescu (2005) analyzed and evaluated the e-Procurement projects carried out by European Commission. They concluded that the transparency of EU public procurement market was improved by a systematic use of electronic tendering. The improvements on the transparency allowed the involved parties to know how the system is intended to work, and all potential suppliers have the same information about procurement opportunities, award criteria, and decision process. Croom and Jones (2007) reinforced the idea that e-Procurement has the potential to improve transparency in supply management, in purchasing companies through greater consolidation of purchases. They also found the majority of respondents had reduced their supply base and had a closer relationship with those remaining. Beall *et. al* (2003) also showed that most of the services associated with goods purchased like design repair, emergency delivers and so forth were now included in the specifications of e-RAS, allowing suppliers to fairly price and bid in the complete package of goods and related services, and allowing the buying firms better know what they were paying for.

Improved Relationship with Clients

In considering how e-Procurement will impact buyer-seller relationships Ellram and Zsidisin (2002) argue that the adoption of e-Procurement contributes to closer buyer–supplier relationships. Therefore, while e-Procurement technology may not deliver improved levels of trust, it has been found that e-Procurement transactions are more likely to be established first between partners in high trust relationships. In addressing this issue, both Croom (2001) and Kumar and Peng (2006) support the view that increased use of e-Procurement and inter-organizational systems enhance opportunities and tend to create more effective customer–supplier relationships over time. According to a EU report "companies maintaining long-term relationships with suppliers and customers are more likely to use technologies supporting inter-company collaboration, in comparison with their peer-group in the same sector" (EC, 2008). However, the number of companies using collaborative tools in Europe is relatively low when compared with non users. The adoption of e-Procurement solutions by supplier´s can improve the relationship with the buyer. But this may depend on the type of tools used by the purchaser. For certain goods the use of tools like electronic reverse auctions may have the opposite effect, by destroying the trust and mutual interdependence between the buying company and a key strategic supplier (Beall, et al., 2003). A good buyer supplier relationship leads to a more robust e-procurement initiative. In Scotland, the government e-Procurement program promoted the collaborative behavior between support staff, buyers and suppliers. Building multi-national and multi-disciplinary networks can also facilitate and foster the exchange of knowledge and develop practical standards (AGIMO, 2005).

Gain of Competitive Advantage

Increased profitability of a supplier will result in an advantage being gained over its competitors. E-Procurement allows procurement activities to be conducted 24 hours a day, 7 days a week, and 365 days a year. It allows going beyond the geographical barriers giving a distinct advantage over other competitors. These improvements in competitiveness are further highlighted by Wong and Sloan (2004). Gains of competitive advantage, reducing order fulfillment costs, and increased profitability are seen as some the most important perceived benefits of e-Procurement for suppliers.

Perceived Barriers

Perceived barriers are considered as factors not contributing to the intention to adopt e-Procurement. Identifying the barriers themselves is part of the major managerial function in developing the right plan for the adoption of e-Procurement among suppliers (Gunasekaran & Ngai, 2008).

Price Reduction Pressures

Buyers are concerned that e-Procurement technologies will push prices down to the point where suppliers cannot invest in new technology, product development, upgrade facilities, or add additional productive capacity. Additional price pressures can even push suppliers down if they have a poor understanding of their cost structure (Davila, et al., 2003). Suppliers need to know how low they can bid, and still observe an acceptable return. They also must consider the buyer's location to calculate shipping costs, and their financial status (Moser, 2002). White and Daniel (2004) concluded that strategic considerations are among the key inhibitors of e-Procurement adoption, as some of the methods deployed in e-Procurement tools such as reverse auctions are perceived to potentially damage long-term supplier relationships, by pushing prices down.

Implementation, Integration, and Maintenance Cost

According to Tanner *et al.* (2008) a main objection of e-Procurement in organizations is the high installation costs of new solutions and it must be taken seriously. The cause, is the high heterogeneity of the supplier and buyer IT environments, organizational structures and business processes. Hawking *et al.* (2004) also identified implementation costs as one of the barriers to e-Procurement adoption in Australia. According to Koorn *et al.* (2001) initial implementation costs may be substantially higher than with those of an EDI system, unless an online intermediary with low enrolment fees is chosen. The potential administrative and implementation costs which will be incurred as companies utilize e-Procurement should also been taken into account. As with all technological adoption, the relatively high cost of maintaining and implementing an e-Procurement system is a major factor when deciding the adoption of e-Procurement (Teo & Ranganathan, 2004).

Lack of Interoperability Between Systems

For e-Procurement technologies to succeed, suppliers should provide e-catalogues in the formats required by customers, reflecting custom pricing or special contractual agreements and send updates on a regular basis (Davila, et al., 2003). However, no common standard has yet emerged for web catalogs. Small suppliers often end up having to provide and regularly update catalogue data in a number of different formats to meet each buyer's specifications. Whereas this approach is satisfactory for small numbers of buyers or suppliers, it is not scalable to many buyers or suppliers. With a large company, there may be hundreds or thousands of suppliers. Each supplier may have thousands of catalogue items (Kim & Shunk, 2004). Hawking *et al.* (2004) support that barriers to e-Procurement also include lack of interoperability and standards with traditional communication systems. Developing standards and systems for facilitating effective interoperability will facilitate the adoption of e-Procurement. However, there is still considerable uncertainty and a lack of clear direction regarding standards for data interchange. Until a clear industry standard is identified and supported, this challenge will continue for all participants (AGIMO, 2005).

Lack of Legal Support

In the EU, Julia-Barcelo (1999) reviewed EU regulation of electronic contracts. Difficulties highlighted by Julia-Barcelo were: lack of specific legal regulation, different national approaches, validity of electronic documents, enforceability or evidentiary problems. Wong and Sloan (2004) also questioned the legal validity of electronic information exchange and considered it as a barrier to e-Procurement. It showed that only 26% of the respondents agreed that electronic documents were admissible as written proof during transactions. The uncertainty surrounding the legal issues of e-Procurement was the top barrier in e-Procurement within Northern Ireland's construction industry. The parallel use of paper copies and electronic documents leaded to difficulties on achieving a fully internet solution using e-Procurement tools (Eadie, Perera, Heaney, & Carlisle, 2007).

Lack of Information Security

According to Neef (2001) some of the reasons for companies not moving into e-Procurement are related to concerns over security and trust. For most companies, some of their most important assets are their buying plans, their pricing models, and their new product designs. Many executives are concerned that once information goes outside the company firewall, these key assets may be exposed to competitors. The lack of security in transactions is an important barrier to e-Procurement (Eadie, et al., 2007). A PriceWaterhouseCoopers

survey with senior business leaders in the U.K., Germany, France, and the Netherlands found that security issues were cited as the most important factor holding back e-procurement progress. This was particularly true in the case of direct procurement (ComputerWeekly, 2000). Concerns about security represent barrier to the systems integration between buyers and suppliers. According to Davila *et al.* (2003) providing other companies with intranet access to company internal data, or integrating applications with company information systems is still unusual. This observation reinforces the prudence that companies demonstrate on integrating e-Procurement technologies into existing systems and relationships.

Lack Skill and Knowledge

Archer *et al.* (2008) conducted a paper with the objective to identify and measure the perceived importance of barriers in the small medium enterprise (SME) community to the adoption of e-Procurement. Few differences were found between adopters and non-adopters. They noticed a lack for education for all SME management on the benefits and drawbacks to using e-business solutions. Some of the informal comments they received indicated that there is a lack of knowledge of e-business and its benefits. The respondents disagreed significantly with the statement "we know what kind of e-business solution is right for us". This shows the need for education about e-Procurement applications.

Critical Success Factors

The factors critical to the use of e-Procurement have been identified based on previous experience and literature available. The critical success factors could be defined as the best practices for the successful use of the e-Procurement system. It encompasses also the successful utilization of the system.

Initial Training

According to Eadie *et al.* (2007) for the successful use of e-Procurement in companies, training is compulsory and should be given, mitigating the effects of the lack of knowledge on this area. Panayiotou *et al.* (2004) also considered training as a critical success factor for e-procurement implementation. The adequate training of the employees will enable them to take advantage of the new system. It should be assured that employees are able to see the benefits derived from e-Procurement technology (Kothari, Hu, & Roehl, 2005). When establishing the electronic reverse auctions implementations framework for the UK public sector the OGC (2005) considered supplier training as part of that framework. Free ongoing training sessions were offered to suppliers. This was responsibility of the change manager, one of the elements recommended by OGC as being critical to help to achieve successful organizational change when implementing e-Procurement.

Integration with Current Systems

A study conducted in the Swiss market revealed that the lack of supplier involvement and infrastructure to optimize B2B processes was an obstacle to integrate B2B scenarios. The integration solutions are not always offered appropriate to suppliers and the majority of companies agree that the position of the suppliers is insufficiently considered (Tanner, et al., 2008). Large companies are increasingly streamlining and integrating their procurement processes, often with advanced e-Procurement schemes based on standardized data exchange. As a result, smaller firms that cannot comply with the technical requirements of their customers, run the risk of elimination from the supply chain (EC, 2008). Large companies must provide several means for suppliers to access their e-Procurement applications. Otherwise smaller suppliers may not be able to meet the requirements.

Top Management Support

If an organization wants to implement e-Procurement successfully top management has to support the e-Procurement implementation into their business. When the top executive level advocates e-commerce, an organization can elevate the importance of e-Procurement for the organization (Pani & Agrahari, 2007). This is even more relevant in SME companies. Due to its reduced hierarchy, the decision to go or not for e-Procurement should be made by top management. Gunasekaran and Ngai (2008) considered top management support as a critical success factor for e-Procurement adoption between Hong Kong industries. Top management involvement and support was viewed by 70% of the respondents as one of the most important of all the factors affecting e-Procurement adoption (Teo & Ranganathan, 2004). Therefore top management support is positively associated with the adoption of e-Procurement.

Business Process Reengineering

The complex relationship between the members of the supply chain leads to different level on accessing and managing information. Gilbert (2000) said that companies were jumping onto e-Procurement without fully understand the inter-organizational collaboration and network effects underlying these technology models, the investment required to move the right information from suppliers to employees, and the complexities of integrating these technologies with existing Enterprise Resource Planning systems. So companies should not model their current paper-based processes into e-Procurement. An implementation of an e-Procurement platform, as any new system, represents an opportunity to reengineering business processes (TIBCO, 2008). The simple introduction of technology into existing processes, may lead to duplication of work, without providing the expected benefits.

Adoption Process Support

Finally, the supplier must be supported throughout the adoption process. This was evident in Scotland and Italy where a supplier engagement process was developed, documented and facilitated to ensure that suppliers business and technical requirements were met. The result was a high incident in supplier activity. In contrast, the buyer centric approach adopted in Western Australia meant that suppliers did not understand the benefits of joining e-Procurement and therefore were reluctant to join (AGIMO, 2005). According to Corini (2000) supplier participation is critical to the successful implementation of any e-procurement solution. He says that without supplier participation the software is useless. Moreover Neef (2001) recommends that key suppliers should be seen as an integral part of the e-Procurement project, provided with clear and attainable milestones and directly included in the change management plan.

Business Partner Influence

Previous research on EDI has found that business partner influence plays an important role in technological adoption. For example, Chwelos *et al.* (2001) concluded that external pressure and readiness is considerably more important than perceived benefits in EDI adoption. Hart and Saunders (1997) concluded that firms with greater power can influence their trading partners to adopt EDI. However, when firms use coercive power to force trading partners to adopt EDI, less powerful partners may be left more vulnerable. And, over time this perceived vulnerability may become a constraint in inter-organizational relationships that prevents improvements in coordination through expanded use of EDI. More recently, Oliveira and Martins (2010) concluded that trading partner collaboration is an important driver for e-business adoption in EU 27 countries context. Similar results were found for e-Procurement. Grandon and Pearson (2004) identified external pressure

as influencing e-commerce adoption. Further Teo *et al.* (2009) examined various factors associated with the adoption of e-Procurement. They found that business partner influence was positively associated with the adoption of e-Procurement.

RESEARCH FOCUS

E-procurement systems can be classified in a number of ways. Kim and Shunky (2004) classify them according to their location. They may be located at the supplier, the buyer or a third party provider. For the buyer side, systems typically owned by large companies, it is their responsibility to ensure that enough suppliers are adopting the system.

The aim of this work is to gain an understanding of the factors affecting e-Procurement adoption by suppliers, with a focus on buyer centric e-Procurement systems, in which typically suppliers have less bargain power (Figure 4). In this context, the buyer plays the role of an initiator, while suppliers act as followers. Consequently, it is fundamental to answer the following question - What are the major factors for the adoption of e-Procurement by suppliers?

EMPIRICAL RESULTS AND ANALYSIS

Characteristics of Data

The industry classification from 721 inquired companies is shown in Table 1. The responses include a broad range of companies based on different types of markets served and products sold. As such, the sample appears to be representing of a wide range of different companies. About 93% of the companies of this sample can be classified as small or medium companies while 7% are considered large companies. About 87% of the respondents were people in relatively high positions at their companies. The high hierarchical

Figure 4. Research Focus.

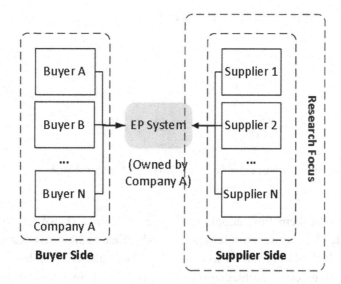

levels of respondents provides some assurance on the validity of responses, since the respondents in higher management levels could generally be expected to be more familiar about their companies' e-Procurement activities than those from lower levels.

Companies were asked to imagine that their company was invited by a client to use an electronic procurement tool, and to classify the intention of their adoption. Figure 5 shows that the majority of the respondents were open to future initiatives of e-Procurement.

The supplier's perception about the benefits of e-Procurement plays a major role in e-Procurement, starting with the decision to go for e-Procurement. Table 2 shows that companies strongly agree that the adoption of e-Procurement will contribute to: achieve a better operational efficiency, reduce order processing costs and provide gains in competitive advantage. However, respondent companies are in average less optimistic about benefits such as improved relationship with clients, negotiable transparency and sales growth.

The concerns of companies regarding the adoption of e-Procurement have a tremendous influence on its success. Companies were asked

Table 1. Industry type, firm size classification and job position.

Industry type	Freq.	%
Financial Services	10	1.4
Retail	188	26.1
Marketing & Advert.	27	3.7
Eng. & Construction	71	9.8
Logistics	13	1.8
Services	247	34.3
Manufacturing	134	18.6
Tourism	31	4.3
Total	721	100.0

Classification	Freq.	%
Small	566	78.5
Medium	101	14.0
Large	54	7.5
Total	721	100.0

Job position	Freq.	%
President/Director	396	54.9
Department Manager	233	32.3
Others	92	12.8
Total	721	100.0

Figure 5. Intention to adopt e-Procurement.

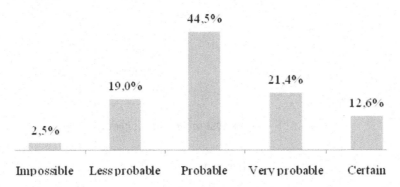

what factors could prevent them from adopting e-Procurement (Table 3). Some companies strongly agree with the lack of information security. However, companies agree that the integration costs and maintenance of a new system are the main impediments against the adoption of e-Procurement. The majority of respondents disagrees or strongly disagrees that price reduction pressures and implementation costs were causes for not implementing e-Procurement.

The respondents were asked what they saw as being critical for their successful adoption and use of e-Procurement (Table 4). The integration with current systems and initial training has been viewed as critical. Top management support and business process reengineering have also been considered as important by the majority of the respondents. However, in comparison to the other factors they were considered the less critical.

The influence of business partners plays a crucial role in e-Procurement adoption. About 74.8% of the respondents admitted to have some kind of influence from business partners to use e-Procurement tools (Table 5).

Validity, Reliability and Correlation

As a first step, we performed a factor analysis (FA) of multi-item indicators (the references of the multi-indicators used are in Appendix) to reduce the number of variables of the survey and to evaluate the validity. We used the principal component technique with varimax rotation (see Table 6) to extract five eigen values, which were all greater than one. The first five factors

Table 2. Perceived benefits.

Perceived benefits	Strongly disagree	Disagree	Uncertain	Agree	Strongly agree
Sales growth	2.6	7.6	32.3	46.0	11.4
Reach new markets	1.5	6.7	25.5	51.7	14.6
Reductions in order processing costs	1.7	5.1	19.3	49.9	24.0
Better operational efficiency	1.4	3.6	11.9	55.5	27.6
Better negotiable transparency	2.5	8.9	34.1	40.5	14.0
Improved rel. with clients	2.5	10.8	27.9	46.0	12.8
Gain of comp. advantage	1.7	4.2	22.2	52.7	19.3

Table 3. Perceived barriers.

Perceived barriers	Strongly disagree	Disagree	Uncertain	Agree	Strongly agree
Price reduction pressures	5.4	27.7	39.0	24.3	3.6
Implementation costs	5.1	30.7	33.6	27.0	3.6
Integration costs and maintenance	1.7	13.3	25.0	51.0	9.0
Lack of interoperability between systems	1.5	17.5	26.9	45.8	8.3
Lack of legal support	1.8	19.1	23.0	49.5	6.5
Lack of information security	3.3	21.1	21.1	41.7	12.8
Lack of skill and knowledge	4.4	25.1	25.1	37.4	7.9

Table 4. Critical Success Factors.

CSF	Unimportant	Less important	Important	Very important	Critical
Initial training	1,0	3,1	31,1	24,3	40,6
Integration with current systems	0,7	3,2	27,3	25,8	43,0
Top management support	1,5	4,6	29,0	30,8	34,1
Business process reengineering	2,4	8,3	36,3	34,0	19,0
Adoption process support	1,4	3,2	28,4	32,0	35,0

explain 64.4% of variance contained in the data. The Kaiser-Meyer-Olkin (KMO) measures the adequacy of sample; general KMO is 0.83 (KMO ≥ 0.80 is good (Sharma, 1996)), which reveals that the matrix of correlation is adequate for FA. The KMO for individual variables is also adequate. All the factors have a loading greater than 0.50. This indicates that our analysis employs a well-explained factor structure. The five factors found are: direct perceived benefits, indirect perceived benefits, perceived barriers of price and costs, perceived barriers and CSF. The factors obtained are in accordance with the literature review. However, there are two variables (perceived benefits and perceived barriers) for which the FA suggests two factors instead one. This reveals that the items of perceived benefits don't have the same factor. These items can be divided into direct and indirect perceived benefits in accordance with other authors (Gunasekaran & Ngai, 2008).

Reliability measures the stability of the scale based on an assessment of the internal consistency of the items measuring the construct. It is assessed by calculating the composite reliability

Table 5. Business partner influence.

Business partner influence	Frequency	Percentage
No influence	182	25.2
Some business partners have recommended us to use e-Procurement.	315	43.7
Some business partners have requested us to use e-Procurement	172	23.9
Majority of business partners have requested us to use e-Procurement	52	7.2

Table 6. Factor Analysis.

	Factors				
	1	2	3	4	5
Direct perceived benefits (Alpha = 0.836)					
Sales growth	0.09	0.24	-0.02	0.86	0.09
Reach new markets	0.11	0.21	0.05	0.85	0.07
Indirect perceived benefits (Alpha = 0.816)					
Reductions in order processing costs	0.15	0.77	0.01	0.06	0.10
Better operational efficiency	0.17	0.83	0.05	0.08	-0.05
Better negotial transparency	0.15	0.73	-0.01	0.17	0.06
Improved relationship with clients	0.17	0.61	0.00	0.33	-0.11
Gain of competitive advantage	0.22	0.55	0.05	0.51	-0.07
Perceived barriers of price and costs (Alpha = 0.482)					
Price reduction pressures	0.04	0.05	0.03	0.16	0.79
Implementation costs	-0.02	-0.08	0.34	-0.06	0.68
Perceived barriers (Alpha = 0.768)					
Integration costs and maintenance	0.12	0.03	0.54	-0.02	0.41
Lack of interoperability between systems	0.06	0.12	0.67	-0.10	0.35
Lack of legal support	0.04	0.07	0.78	-0.10	0.16
Lack of information security	0.04	-0.06	0.76	0.06	-0.07
Lack of skill and knowledge	0.08	-0.03	0.71	0.18	-0.01
CSF (Alpha = 0.875)					
Initial training	0.81	0.04	0.15	0.08	-0.05
Integration with current systems	0.82	0.12	0.12	-0.01	-0.01
Top management support	0.79	0.22	-0.01	0.05	-0.01
Business process reengineering	0.73	0.21	0.02	0.18	0.12
Adoption process	0.83	0.18	0.02	0.08	0.06

for each composite independent variable. Most of the constructs have a composite reliability over the cut off of 0.70, as suggested by Nunnally (1978). All constructs have Cronbach's alpha value higher than 0.70, except perceived barriers of price and cost. For this reasons we excluded this factor from our analysis.

The results of the spearman's rank correlation test are shown below in Table 7. Spearman's rank correlation coefficient is used as a measure of linear relationship between two sets of ranked data (Hill & Hill, 2008). Spearman's rank correlation coefficient (ρ) will take a value between -1 and +1. A positive correlation is one in which the ranks of both variables increase together. A negative correlation is one in which the ranks of one variable increase as the ranks of the other variable decrease (Altman, 1991). Once the value of the difference is significant, that is, its p-value below 0.05, we consider that there is a statistically significant relationship between each of the factors (obtained by factor analysis) and the intention to adopt e-Procurement. The perceived indirect benefits and business partner influence are the most correlated factors.

Table 7. Correlation between perceived factors and business partner influence with the intention to adopt e-Procurement by suppliers.

	Spearman's rank correlation	
	ρ	p-value
Perceived direct benefits (obtained by FA)	0.163	< 0.0001
Perceived indirect benefits (obtained by FA)	0.335	< 0.0001
Perceived barriers (obtained by FA)	-0.108	0.0036
CSF (obtained by FA)	0.119	0.0013
Business partner influence (obtained directly from survey)	0.334	< 0.001

SOLUTIONS AND RECOMMENDATIONS

Among several factors associated with the success of *e-Procurement implementation*, supplier's adherence to such platforms has been regarded as critical. Two main types of supplier perceived benefits were identified with the FA: direct benefits and indirect benefits. Direct benefits are associated with marketing and sales, and represent an opportunity for the company to generate financial gains in the short term. Indirect benefits are related to benefits obtained in the medium and long term that may not directly result in financial gains, but may contribute to improvements on the organizational performance and sustainability of the company. The recommendations are that companies need to explain to their suppliers the real benefits of adopting e-Procurement. Thus it is necessary to develop a communication plan in order to increase the benefits awareness both in the short and mainly in the long term.

As shown, the barriers have a negative impact on the intention to adopt e-Procurement. The main barriers are the costs of integration and maintenance as well as the lack of legal support. Suppliers generally do not consider that e-Procurement leads to a decrease in selling prices. Some informal comments also suggested that the lack of "human interaction" in e-Procurement is not suitable for some types of business, especially in complex products that require significant human interaction. As affirmed by Kothari *et al.* (Kothari, et al., 2005), no advanced technology can replace human interactions in establishing and maintaining business relationships.

All the critical success factors were considered very important in implementing e-Procurement. Less importance was given to business process reengineering. One possible cause is the lack of experience with e-Procurement by business respondents. Compared with benefits and business partner pressure, CSF is less correlated with supplier intention to adopt e-Procurement.

Business partner pressure has a positive and significant influence on the adoption of e-Procurement by suppliers. This is consistent with other studies on technology adoption. For example Chwelos *et al.* (2001) showed that the pressure from business partners in the adoption of EDI contributes more than the perceived benefits of those who will adopt. However, through our analysis we can conclude that the influences of business partners and the indirect benefits have similar importance on e-Procurement adoption.

FUTURE RESEARCH DIRECTIONS

The respondents from our study were from Portuguese companies. Future studies might explore the differences between Portugal and other countries, or between the industries analyzed.

Despite convinced that the proposed objectives for this study were achieved; it is important that future works solve some of the limitations of this study and contribute to the advancement of this area. Some of the factors identified in the literature review were related to the adoption of e-Procurement in a general way and not specifically related to the supplier adoption on buyer centric e-Procurement systems. A deeper analysis on the factors affecting supplier adoption on other models may help to identify additional factors.

Another limitation of the study is that the framework used by Gunasekaran and Ngai (2008) has not yet been widely tested in the literature. Thus, future studies should use this framework in order to test its applicability under other conditions. Future studies may also ponder the analysis of dependency between the factors identified and the intention to adopt e-Procurement. For example the application of logistic regression or structural equations on the present framework may provide more empirical evidence on the impact of each factor on e-Procurement adoption.

REFERENCES

AGIMO. (2005). *Case Studies on E-procurement Implementations: Italy, New South Wales, New Zealand, Scotland, Western Australia*. Canberra: Australian Government Information Management Office.

Altman, D. G. (1991). *Practical Statistics for Medical Research*. London: Chapman & Hall.

Archer, N., Wang, S., & Kang, C. (2008). Barriers to the adoption of online supply chain solutions in small and medium enterprises. *Supply Chain Management: An International Journal*, *13*(1), 73–82. doi:10.1108/13598540810850337

Beall, S., Carter, C., Carter, P. L., Germer, T., Hendrick, T., & Jap, S. (2003). *The role of reverse auctions in strategic sourcing*. CAPS Research.

Benton, P. (2005). E-Procurement's Missing Link. *IT Adviser*(39).

Berlak, J., & Weber, V. (2004). How to make e-Procurement viable for SME suppliers. *Production Planning and Control*, 15–22.

Botto, F. (2003). *Dictionary of e-Business: A De□nitive Guide to Technology and Business Terms*. USA: John Wiley & Sons.

Cagno, E., Giulio, A. D., & Trucco, P. (2004). State-of-art and development prospects of e-procurement in the Italian engineering & contracting sector. *Project Management Journal*, *35*(1), 24–29.

Cammish, R., & Keough, M. (1991). A strategic role for purchasing. *The McKinsey Quarterly*, 22–50.

Carayannis, E. G., & Popescu, D. (2005). Profiling a methodology for economic growth and convergence: learning from the EU e-procurement experience for central and eastern European countries. *Technovation*, *25*(1), 1–14. doi:10.1016/S0166-4972(03)00071-3

Caridi, M., Cavalieri, S., Pirovano, C., & Diazzi, G. (2004). Assessing the impact of e-Procurement strategies through the use of business process modelling and simulation techniques. *Production Planning and Control*, *15*(7), 647–661. doi:10.1080/09537280412331298175

Carr, A. S., & Pearson, J. N. (1999). Strategically managed buyer–supplier relationships and performance outcomes. *Journal of Operations Management*, *17*(5), 497–519. doi:10.1016/S0272-6963(99)00007-8

Chwelos, P., Benbasat, I., & Dexter, A. S. (2001). Research report: Empirical Test of an EDI Adoption Model. *Information Systems Research*, *12*(3), 304–321. doi:10.1287/isre.12.3.304.9708

CIPS. (2009). *The Chartered Institute of Purchasing & Supply*. Retrieved from http://www.cips.org/

ComputerWeekly. (2000). *Bosses voice e-procurement fears.* Retrieved from http://www.computerweekly.com/Articles/2000/07/20/176837/bosses-voice-e-procurement-fears.htm

Corini, J. (2000). Integrating e-procurement and strategic sourcing. *Supply Chain Management Review, 4,* 70–75.

Croom, S. (2001). Restructuring supply chains through information channel innovation. *International Journal of Operations & Production Management, 21*(4), 504–515. doi:10.1108/01443570110381408

Croom, S., & Jones, A. (2007). Impact of e-procurement: Experiences from implementation in the UK public sector. *Journal of Purchasing and Supply Management, 13*(4), 294–303. doi:10.1016/j.pursup.2007.09.015

Croom, S. R., & Giannakis, M. (2002). *Strategic e-Procurement in Global Pharmaceuticals (GP).* Caps Research.

Davila, A., Gupta, M., & Palmer, R. (2003). Moving procurement systems to the internet: the adoption and use of e-procurement technology models. *European Management Journal, 21*(1), 11–23. doi:10.1016/S0263-2373(02)00155-X

Eadie, R., Perera, S., Heaney, G., & Carlisle, J. (2007). Drivers and Barriers to Public Sector e-Procurement within Northern Ireland's Construction Industry. *ITcon, 12,* 103–120.

EC. (2005). *Overview of International e-Business Developments.* Brussels: European Commission.

EC. (2008). *The European e-Business Report 2008 - The impact of ICT and e-business on firms, sectors and the economy.* Brussels: European Commission.

Ellram, L. M., & Zsidisin, G. A. (2002). Factors that drive purchasing and supply management's use of information technology. *IEEE Transactions on Engineering Management, 49*(3), 269–281. doi:10.1109/TEM.2002.803381

Falk, M. (2005). ICT-Linked Firm Reorganisation and Productivity Gains. *Technovation, 25*(11), 1229–1250. doi:10.1016/j.technovation.2004.07.004

Gershon, P. (1999). *Review of civil procurement in central government.* UK: HM Treasury.

Gilbert, A. (2000). E-procurement: problems behind the promise. *InformationWeek,* 48-62.

Grandon, E. E., & Pearson, J. M. (2004). Electronic commerce adoption: an empirical study of small and medium US businesses. *Information & Management, 42*(1), 197–216. doi:10.1016/j.im.2003.12.010

Gunasekaran, A., McGaughey, R. E., Ngai, E. W. T., & Rai, B. K. (2009). E-Procurement adoption in the Southcoast SMEs. *International Journal of Production Economics, 122*(1), 161-175.

Gunasekaran, A., & Ngai, E. W. T. (2008). Adoption of e-procurement in Hong Kong: An empirical research. *International Journal of Production Economics, 113*(1), 159–175. doi:10.1016/j.ijpe.2007.04.012

Hart, P., & Saunders, C. (1997). Power and trust: Critical factors in the adoption and use of electronic data interchange. *Organization Science, 8*(1), 23–42. doi:10.1287/orsc.8.1.23

Hawking, P., Stein, A., Wyld, D. C., & Foster, S. (2004). E-procurement: is the ugly duckling actually a swan down under? *Asia Pacific Journal of Marketing and Logistics, 16*(1), 3–26. doi:10.1108/13555850410765140

Hill, M. M., & Hill, A. (2008). *Investigação por Questionário* [Research by Questionnaire]. 2nd ed.). Edições Silabo. [Syllabus Revision]

Julia-Barcelo, R. (1999). Electronic contracts: a new legal framework for electronic contracts: the EU electronic commerce proposal. *Computer Law & Security Report, 15*(3). doi:10.1016/S0267-3649(99)80032-6

Kim, J.-I., & Shunk, D. L. (2004). Matching indirect procurement process with different B2B e-procurement systems. *Computers in Industry, 53*(2), 153–164. doi:10.1016/j.compind.2003.07.002

Koorn, R., Smith, D., & Müller, C. (2001). *e-Procurement and Online Marketplaces.* The Netherlands: Compact.

Kothari, T., Hu, C., & Roehl, W. S. (2005). e-Procurement: an emerging tool for the hotel supply chain management. *International Journal of Hospitality Management, 24*(3), 369–389. doi:10.1016/j.ijhm.2004.09.004

Kumar, N., & Peng, Q. (2006). Strategic alliances in e-government procurement. *International Journal of Electronic Business, 4*(2), 136–145.

Moser, E. P. (2002). E-Procurement-Reverse Auctions and the Supplier's Perspective. *Pharmaceutical Technology, 26*(5), 82–85.

Neef, D. (2001). *e-Procurement:From Strategy to Implementation.* USA: Prentice Hall.

Nunnally, J., & Bernstein, I. (1978). *Psychometric theory.*

OGC. (2005). *eProcurement in action:A guide to eProcurement for the public sector.* London: Office of Government Commerce.

Oliveira, T., & Martins, M. F. (2010). Understanding e-business adoption across industries in European countries. *Industrial Management & Data Systems, 110*(9), 1337–1354. doi:10.1108/02635571011087428

Panayiotou, N. A., Gayaialis, S. P., & Tatsiopoulos, I. P. (2004). An e-procurement system for governmental purchasing. *International Journal of Production Economics, 90*(1), 79–102. doi:10.1016/S0925-5273(03)00103-8

Pani, A. K., & Agrahari, A. (2007). *E-Procurement in Emerging Economies:Theory and Cases.* India: Idea Group Pub. doi:10.4018/978-1-59904-153-7

Pereira, P., & Alturas, B. (2007, October). *Factores Críticos da Adesão das PME'S Nacionais, Fornecedoras de Materiais de Escritorio ao Procedimento Aquisitivo Público em Portugal: Uma Proposta de Investigação* [Critical Factors of Accession of SMEs National Vendors of office supplies to the Public Purchasing Procedure in Portugal: A Proposal for Research.]. Paper presented at the Conferência IADIS Ibero – Americana.

Sharifi, H., Kehoe, D. F., & Hopkins, J. (2006). A classification and selection model of e-marketplaces for better alignment of supply chains. *Journal of Enterprise Information Management, 19*(5), 483–503. doi:10.1108/17410390610703639

Sharma, S. (1996). *Applied Multivariate Techniques.* USA: John Wiley& Sons.

Soares-Aguiar, A., & Palma-Dos-Reis, A. (2008). Why do firms adopt e-procurement systems? Using logistic regression to empirically test a conceptual model. *IEEE Transactions on Engineering Management, 55*(1), 120–133. doi:10.1109/TEM.2007.912806

Sparks, L., & Wagner, B. A. (2003). Retail exchanges: a research agenda. *Supply Chain Management: An International Journal, 8*(3), 201–208. doi:10.1108/13598540310484609

Stein, A., & Hawking, P. (2004). 2B or not 2B: The real story of B2B e-procurement *Australian CPA 74*(2), 30-33.

Tanner, C., Woumllfle, R., Schubert, P., & Quade, M. (2008). Current Trends and Challenges in Electronic Procurement: An Empirical Study. *Electronic Markets, 18*(1), 6–18. doi:10.1080/10196780701797599

Teo, T. S. H., Lin, S., & Lai, K.-h. (2009). Adopters and non-adopters of e-procurement in Singapore: An empirical study. *Omega*, *37*(5), 972–987. doi:10.1016/j.omega.2008.11.001

Teo, T. S. H., & Ranganathan, C. (2004). Adopters and non-adopters of business-to-business electronic commerce in Singapore. *Information & Management*, *42*(1), 89–102. doi:10.1016/j.im.2003.12.005

TIBCO (2008). *The Case for Business Process Management.*

Vaidya, K., Sajeev, A. S. M., & Callender, G. (2004). *e-Procurement Initiatives in the Public Sector: An Investigation into the Critical Success.* Paper presented at the Annual International Purchasing & Supply Education & Research Association (IPSERA), Catania, Italy.

Vaidya, K., Sajeev, A. S. M., & Callender, G. (2006). Critical Factors That Influence E-Procurement Implementation Success in the Public Sector. *Journal of Public Procurement*, *6*(1/2), 70–99.

White, A., & Daniel, E. M. (2004). The impact of e-marketplaces on dyadic buyer-supplier relationships: evidence from the healthcare sector. *Journal of Enterprise Information Management*, *17*(6), 441–453. doi:10.1108/17410390410566733

Wong, C., & Sloan, B. (2004, September). *Use of ICT for e-procurement in the UK construction industry: a survey of SMES readiness.* Paper presented at the ARCOM Twentieth Annual Conference.

APPENDIX

Table 8. Perceived benefits, perceived and barriers, and critical success factors and literature support for each item.

Items	Authors
Perceived benefits	
Sales Growth	(Beall, et al., 2003; Berlak & Weber, 2004; Moser, 2002; Sharifi, et al., 2006)
Reach New Markets	(Beall, et al., 2003; Sharifi, et al., 2006)
Reductions in order processing costs	(Berlak & Weber, 2004)
Better operational efficiency	(Beall, et al., 2003; Berlak & Weber, 2004; Moser, 2002; Neef, 2001)
Better negotiable transparency	(Beall, et al., 2003; Carayannis & Popescu, 2005; Simon Croom & Jones, 2007)
Improved relationship with clients	(AGIMO, 2005; Beall, et al., 2003; S. Croom, 2001; EC, 2008; Ellram & Zsidisin, 2002; Kumar & Peng, 2006)
Gain of competitive advantage	(Wong & Sloan, 2004)
Perceived barriers	
Price reduction pressures	(Davila, et al., 2003; Moser, 2002)
Implementation costs	(Hawking, et al., 2004; Koorn, et al., 2001; Tanner, et al., 2008)
Integration costs and maintenance	(Teo & Ranganathan, 2004)
Lack of interoperability between systems	(AGIMO, 2005; Davila, et al., 2003; Hawking, et al., 2004; Kim & Shunk, 2004)
Lack of legal support	(Eadie, et al., 2007; Julia-Barcelo, 1999; Wong & Sloan, 2004)
Lack of information security	(Davila, et al., 2003; Eadie, et al., 2007)
Lack of skill and knowledge	(Archer, et al., 2008)
Critical success factors	
Initial training	(Eadie, et al., 2007; Kothari, et al., 2005; OGC, 2005; Panayiotou, et al., 2004)
Integration with current systems	(EC, 2008; Tanner, et al., 2008)
Top management support	(Gunasekaran & Ngai, 2008; Pani & Agrahari, 2007; Teo & Ranganathan, 2004)
Business process reengineering	(Gilbert, 2000; TIBCO, 2008)
Adoption process support	(AGIMO, 2005; Corini, 2000; Neef, 2001)

Chapter 13
End–User Attitude in ERP Post–Implementation:
A Study in a Multinational Enterprise

Tiago Almeida
University of Aveiro, Portugal

Leonor Teixeira
GOVCOPP - University of Aveiro, Portugal, & IEETA, Portugal

Carlos Ferreira
University of Aveiro, Portugal, & CIO - University of Lisbon, Portugal

ABSTRACT

This chapter analyzes the impact of the implementation of SAP R/3 in a Multinational Portuguese Organization (MPO), defining some Critical Success Factors (CSFs). In order to understand the motivations of end-users prior to implementation and to analyze the behavior after a change (post-implementation), a study based on a questionnaire was carried out. The sample included 67 users of SAP R/3 that were present throughout the process. Considering the results, the authors conclude that the implementation of SAP R/3 in MPO was successful, and the respondents consider their work more productive and achieve easier access to information. The existence of a solid team to support the project was established as a major facilitator in the whole process, as opposed to the limited time and lack of training that emerged as barriers to the implementation. It was also found that the learning period assumes a high importance in the success of the implementation, since increasing the training time reduces the need for support to the end-users.

INTRODUCTION

Research literature on Enterprise Resource Planning (ERP) systems has grown significantly in recent years, particularly concerning the identification of Critical Success Factors (CSFs) in

ERP implementation (Ngai, Law, & Wat, 2008; Tchokogué, Bareil, & Duguay, 2005).

Due to the diversity of areas supported by the ERPs, medium and large companies are acquiring this type of application in order to improve their processes through a centralized data management. Most of the ERP systems also allow the redesign

DOI: 10.4018/978-1-4666-1764-3.ch013

of business processes in order to eliminate tasks that have no value, and consequently let the collaborators focus on specific activities that increase productivity. However, implementing such systems requires cultural, organizational and business processes changes that may influence the success of the implementation. Moreover, some projects are too expensive, not only financially, but also in the length of their implementation (from one to three years) involving people, technology and know-how (Abdinnour-Helm, Lengnick-Hall, & Lengnick- Hall, 2003; Ng, Gable, & Chan, 2002; Ngai, *et al.*, 2008; Pinto, 2006).

This chapter examines key aspects in successful implementation of ERP and aims to contribute to the identification of CSFs in the implementation of ERP systems through a study accomplished in a *Multinational Portuguese Organization* (MPO). The system chosen by this MPO was the *SAP R/3* and the present study focus on the perception of the end-users and their behaviors when faced with the changes driven by the ERP system.

THEORETICAL BACKGROUND

Nowadays companies face an increasingly complex and competitive market, which is reflected at the level of needs and requirements of its customers. Consequently, it is necessary to optimize business processes in order to minimize operating costs, and maximize the profit. It is in the perspective of this context that the integrated information systems appeared, now known as ERP systems.

Enterprise Resource Planning

ERP systems are based on integrated modules which aim to collect and process data to provide reliable information to support decision making, increasing the organizational efficiency. Thus, companies can obtain a higher financial return if they adopt and use correctly this kind of system

(Beynon-Davies, 2002; Chou & Chang, 2008; Laudon & Laudon, 2006).

During the last decades ERPs had a rapid growth, becoming one of the most lucrative areas of the software industry during the late '90s (Sprott, 2000). These systems have been extended in order to serve other partners, including suppliers and customers. Thus, other concepts associated to ERPs appeared, such as *Supply Chain Management* (SCM) systems and *Customer Relationship Management* (CRM) systems. Ng *et al.* (2002) consider that ERP systems are today an essential tool for data processing, as well as for the communication of information in enterprises. These systems are currently installed in thousands of organizations around the world, with millions of licenses sold and billions of dollars invested in their implementation. Despite their high cost, many companies seek to adopt these solutions in order to take advantage of the best business practices, as well as achieve competitive advantages.

ERP systems are software packages that need to be integrated, combining operating systems, databases, management systems and telecommunications, through an appropriated logic and fitted to the specific characteristics of the organization. In most cases this involves integration with legacy systems through interfaces among heterogeneous applications (Markus, Tanis, & Fenema, 2000).

Subramanian and Hoffer (2007) refer that ERPs are not intrinsically strategic, but technologies that allow coordination of all intra-organizational operations and transactions flows. As such, and in order to be used by any company, these systems require data, as well as business processes standardization in the organization (Goodhue & Gattiger, 2000, *cit by* (Nah, Faja, & Cata, 2001)).

Moreover, these systems are based on customizable software packages, difficult to adjust to a single organizational process, and therefore, an expensive process. In some cases the business processes of organizations need to be modified in order to adapt to the new system. In this way the re-engineering of business processes turn out

Table 1. Benefit-categories from business perspective (Ng, et al., 2002).

Category	Definition from the literature	Characteristics of ERP
Competitive advantage	Increase and improve the capabilities and power to compete with other competitors	Advanced technologies, best practice, integrated system, worldwide interoperability
Globalization	Enhance information flow to and from customers, suppliers, and other business partners outside the enterprise in a tightly coupled mode, and flexibility to operate in worldwide market	Unified interface, multi-currency and language, integrated system
Integrated system processes	Improve the flow of information through centralized system, better system integration and communication among internal business processes	Cross-functional, single vendor application
Best practice/business processes	Improve business processes and practices, and business performance	Standardized processes, integrated system, off-the-shelf software
Cost reduction	Cost cut in activities related to business administration and processing, and system maintenance, and ensure ongoing system support from the vendor	Real-time, single and centralized database, integrated system, best practice, maintenance support

to be a problem, yet simultaneously becoming a key success factor (Bingi, 1999, *cit by* Nah *et al.*, 2001).

According to Ng *et al.* (2002), there are five major categories that seek benefits in terms of business: (i) competitive advantages; (ii) the possibility of globalization; (iii) adoption of an integrated system; (iv) implementation of best practices/business processes, and finally (v) cost reduction. A brief description of these five dimensions can be found in Table 1, as well as the characteristics of ERP emerging from these categories.

Implementation Process of ERPs

According to Boudreau and Robey (2005), the acceptance and success of ERP systems depend on the implementation process. During this process, users can criticize the project for its costs, effort required, and gaps. Indeed, there are difficult and onerous phases in the implementation process, often with a negative impact on the organizations. Davenport (1998) and Banker *et al.*, 1988 *cit by* (Subramanian & Hoffer, 2007) reveal that more than half of these projects are not successful. Hong and Kim (2002) presented a study with worst results, highlighting the existence of 75% of ERP projects without success. Moreover, Scott

and Vessey (2002) states that 90% of ERP projects are delayed.

The implementation of ERP systems requires organizational changes, cultural and business processes that must be considered and properly analyzed. Thus, it is important to understand the factors that can influence the success or failure of an application, in order to adopt and to maximize the aspects that lead to successful results.

Implementation Risks

Some ERP projects modify the organizational balance of the rights, privileges, obligations, feelings and responsibilities established along the time. Modify these elements may take time, cause disorder and need more resources to support the training (Laudon & Laudon, 2006).

There are risk factors that influence the implementation of ERP, such as the difficulty of acceptance, user's resistance, difficulties transferring the knowledge to computer systems, etc. According to Pinto (2006) and Youngberg, Olsen and Hauser (2009), people not involved and without prior knowledge about the system tend to reject and to create difficulties. Thus, the training process is seen as one of the most important factors in the success of ERP implementation (Barker & Frolick,

2003; Gallivan, Spitler, & Koufaris, 2005; Robey, Ross, & Boudreau, 2002).

Another key-factor in the implementation of ERP is the awareness of end-users for the systems transition (Boudreau & Robey, 2005). In this phase, the organizations should approach the transition process cautiously and with a comprehensive plan (Al-Mashari, Al-Mudimigh, & Zairi, 2003).

Influence of Psychosocial Factors

Nowadays, it is recognized that psychosocial factors are often critical in the implementation of an ERP. Boddy, Boonstra and Kennedy (2002) affirm that organizations sometimes introduce new systems ignoring human factors and using inadequate control methods, causing failures. Abdinnour-Helm *et al.* (2003) state that the user's preparation in the pre-implementation phase is essential to obtain a positive attitude. These attitudes are precursors of a particular behavior pattern, and frequently positive attitudes generate positive behaviors. When an individual does not adopt that attitude, s/he tends to follow practices that will ultimately affect their performance in the medium and long term. People are willing to do their work if they feel they are acting in accordance with their interests and personal goals (Boddy, *et al.*, 2002). Therefore, it is important to measure the motivation levels and user satisfaction, as they are evaluation mechanisms to determine the success of a system (Orlikowski & Barley, 2001).

For Lander, Purvis, McCray and Leigh (2004) the mechanisms of building trust among team members and other stakeholders in the project are also important factors. In turn, Jones, Cline and Ryan (2006) suggest that similar cultures facilitate the exchange of knowledge during the implementation of ERPs.

Whilst end-user training is predominant in early stages of the implementation process, there is an evident need of continuous training (Davenport, 1998; Nah, Faja, & Cata, 2001). Abran and Nguyenkim (1991) show that the maintenance

phase of user support represents 24% of the total time spent by the project team.

IMPLEMENTATION OF AN ERP IN A MULTINATIONAL ENTERPRISE - SAP PROJECT UNIK

Given the fact that it is a distinctive project in Portugal, never before developed in a company with the diversity of business areas that this presents, the project was designate by UNIK. The implementation process had approximately six months becoming due to this reason a demanding project with little margin for error tolerance.

With this project the MPO intended to: (i) increase the mechanisms of business control; (ii) increase the efficiency of operational processes; (iii) standardize processes; (iv) provide scalability beyond borders by creating a shared services centre with international extent; and (v) register the knowledge. This project involved about 550 employees with different responsibilities and levels of affectation, namely, members of the *Department of Information Systems and Business Process* (DIS&BP), key-users and end-users. The DIS&BP members were allocated at 100%, key-users about 40% - 60% and end-users only occasionally (Figure 1). Since the MPO didn't gather the necessary skills and sufficient resources to this implementation, it was necessary to subcontract an outsource consultant.

Implementation Process of the SAP Project UNIK

The implementation process required the engagement and commitment of the entire organization and not only the DIS&BP and consultant. All employees were sensitized with well-defined concepts as well as pragmatism in the evaluation of solutions and decision making. Only then was possible to manage the knowledge intelligently,

Figure 1. Degrees of allocation of actors in the implementation of SAP R/3.

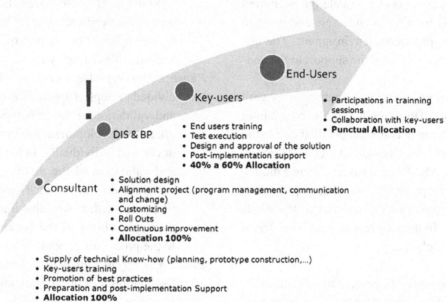

solving problems swiftly and without destabilizing the environment in work teams.

The investment was of great importance to the executive committee, due to the number of people reached and the software cost. Thus, it was necessary to ensure their economic and financial return by taking advantage of best practices provided by *SAP R/3*.

The Integrated Solution – SAP R/3

SAP R/3 is an ERP solution, that integrates different functions of an organization, enabling better planning and control of the business (Davenport, 2002). This system is considered as one of the most complete integrated management software. The *SAP R/3* has become a solution for companies in terms of processes standardization, offering a set of standard integrated modules with different business applications. However, it is seen with some complexity by considering as business process the totality of the functional chain of an organization.

The main features of *SAP R/3* are related to the ability of standardization and customizing, allowing to satisfy the specific needs of a specific business. Although this system is customizable, it is, however, difficult to adjust to a single procedure (Bingi, Sharma, & Godla, 1999; Thomas, 2000; William, 2008).

Implementation Phases of the SAP Project UNIK

The *SAP Company* developed the standard methodology named ASAP (Accelerated *SAP*), recommending it to all those responsible for the implementation of their software (mostly consultants). ASAP consists of five distinct phases. The first phase relates to the preparation of the project, which consists essentially in the planning, identification of main actors and their needs for its implementation. The conceptual design is done in the second phase, responsible by the documentation of the business requirements. In the third phase of the implementation, the customization of the requirements raised in the conceptual design is carried out. The final preparation is the fourth phase, which consists of complete the integrated tests, provide training to end users and migrate all data for a productive environment. The last phase is the "go live" and the support to the end-user starts.

ASAP is a well structured methodology with regard to tasks. However, for small and medium enterprises it can become too detailed due to the large number of tasks included (Esteves & George, 2001). Thus, ASAP is used as a reference model, adjusted to the particularities of each project, in which case appropriately tailored to the needs of the MPO. To develop this project 10 different stages were included.

Phase 1: *Business Blueprint* – In this phase the applications that were running were analyzed, business processes were surveyed and designed according to the customization of *SAP*. As the consultant had no perception of the overall business model, interviews with the responsible of various work areas and observation of the employees in the work field were necessary, to analyze the requirements and procedures to implement. For this, a team of consultants was present for seven months in order to understand the processes of production, maintenance, accounting, logistics, etc. It was also at this stage that the training needs, as well as the definition of inventory were analyzed, in order to plan the implementation of *SAP R/3* (road map). This phase ended after the validation by the administrators and the management, *i.e.*, after the confirmation of the designs of processes and training needs.

Phase 2: *Conceptual Design* – Processes that were previously raised, are at this stage considered in more detail and *SAP* solutions identified to meet the requirements. Thus, the structure of the system was customized in the development environment in order to obtain a global model. The availability of tools necessary

for the functioning of the support team of DIS&BP and key-users was also ensured, as well as the verification of the areas covered by the implementation, its requirements and analysis of existing systems.

Phase 3: *Prototype Development* – This phase is divided in steps of application development and validation of the prototype. In the application development, the processes were developed individually. In the presentation and validation of the prototype what was customized so far and what was still planned was presented. It was also intended to examine the ability of the system to respond to the processes previously drawn.

Phase 4: *Unit and Integrated Testing* – To test the operation of the system unit testing and integrated testing were made. Unit testing were performed by the key-users in the quality environment system. With this procedure, it was intended to verify the performance of individual features of each module. It was necessary to prepare all the files in Excel format provided by the consultant, to serve as support in the integrated testing. This is a slow process, since it is necessary to detail all the steps. The ultimate responsibility of this preparation was from the key-users. Then, it moved to the stage of execution, which aimed at a coherent and effective end, where they performed the tests of integration of different modules. This process involved all key-users divided by their factories.

Phase 5: *End-user Training* – SAP R/3 is not only used by key-users, so it is necessary to provide training for all end users. It is important to correctly identify these people and know that knowledge forward individually, since the training must be objective and licenses are expensive. The training lasted for seven weeks, covering, in stages, people classified as fundamental to operate the *SAP R/3*. Therefore, it was necessary to create manuals and training for different modules.

The preparation of these manuals was done by a support team, checked by the consultant and finally validated by the key users.

Phase 6*: Preparation of the Production Environment*: The preparation phase of the productive environment had four stages of execution.

- *Conversion and Data Migration*: The templates provided to key-users in the development phase of the prototype were, at this stage, collected and verified by DIS&BP and the consultant. Thus, in order to simplify the work the tool *Legacy System Migration Workbench* (LSMW) was used to automatic load the master data.

- *Creating of Profile Authorization*: Given that each employee has specific skills it is necessary to ensure that he/she does not perform tasks that are not his/her responsibility. For this reason, different authorization levels were attributed to the end-users. The first major restriction is made in accordance with the workplace, leading users to view only the data relating to the factory where they belong. Not everyone has access to perform certain transactions, preventing them from creating, modifying, or displaying certain information.

- *Definition of Support Strategy*: problems arose in using the system during the training sessions that were not triggered or nonexistent. Having foreseen this difficulty the DIS opted to create a specific e-mail address for the users support. This application receives requests for help that are rated with a priority level.

- *Sending Login*: Following the requirements of the *SAP Company* it is necessary to allocate a license for each user. These were distributed according to the number of licenses purchased by the MPO and the needs of the system. Each member of the support team was assigned to prepare a "welcome kit" to send to the end-users. This document that served to support the transition to the new system, highlights the following information: i) User ID: user code, password and environment, ii) user support: identification of key-user responsible for aid the resolution of their activities/issues; iii) folder with the first steps towards the use of *SAP*.

Phase 7*: Go Live* – The start of the system was important for all people involved in the project, with special attention for the project managers. This moment marked the end of a run-up and customizing of software and end-user training. In turn, the maintenance and development step begin, such as process redesign and other details that were detected in the early days of use.

Phase 8*: Users Support* – The user support started on system go live and lasted until the time that users were completely independent. A support team was allocated with responsibility for supporting the users in the different factories. The number of requests that followed was high, hampering the role of the support team that tried to lessen the criticality of the situation. Problems such as lack of authorization, errors in the documents of purchases and sales hampered the overall procedures of the organization due in part to the integration of all modules of the *SAP R/3*.

Phase 9*: Acceptance* – The implementation phase of the project was completed. Thus, all results of the development of the *SAP R/3* left by the consultant had to be according to the plan. This process took place with the creation of a final document between the director of DIS and the consultant, later signed by both parties.

Phase 10: *Adjustments, Enhancements and Maintenance System* – This phase appeared mainly when users feel the need to simplify the use of the system. For this reason, evolutionary improvements were needed, through customization and developments. To facilitate the work of the support team members, requirements have been specified and designed. At this stage new employees were still trained, most of them, so as to assume the role of end-users and reduce the workload of their superiors. This process entailed restructuring of the organizational structure.

STUDY OBJECTIVES AND RESEARCH METHODOLOGY

The present study was based on an implementation of the *SAP R/3* system in a MPO, coming to benefit the experience of the researcher who followed all stages of this implementation project.

This research attempts to understand the motivations and behavior of end-users face to the new reality impelled by the new system, and evaluate their satisfaction after a change. To this end, it was used a questionnaire to collect data, having been applied 3 months after the system start-up.

Instrument Validity and Description

The content validity of a questionnaire refers to the representativeness of item content domain. In order to validity the questionnaire used in this study, we followed a validation process in two phases. In the first phase, the questionnaire was validated using judge's method, applied a panel composed by 5 experts, selected according to the following criteria: higher education with knowledge in information systems area and 10 years, at least, of work experience in the same area. Based on results of this phase we developed a second

version of questionnaire (pilot questionnaire). This version was applied to a group of 5 elements, i.e., end-users of *SAP R/3* and employees of the company in the study (MPO). This phase of the validation process also led to small changes in the questionnaire which came to compose the final version.

At the structural level this questionnaire was composed by 27 questions, grouped into 4 areas: characterization socio-professional, training processes in *SAP R/3*, transition process between systems, and changes in job performance.

These areas aim to obtain data to: (i) characterize the sample on demographic and personal data; (ii) assess and characterize training process in *SAP R/3*; (iii) assess the opinions of respondents regarding the duration and relevance of training; (iv) assess the procedures and conditions of respondents regarding the use of the system; (v) assess the opinions of respondents with respect to the transition process between systems and the post-implementation phase; (vi) assess and characterize the job performance of respondents in the face of change; (vii) assess the acceptance degree of the respondents on the system implemented; and, (viii) identify the positive and negative aspects in the implementation, adaptation and utilization of the *SAP R/3* system.

Data Collection

The distribution of the questionnaire was made after the request and authorization of the DIS&BP of the MPO, and applied during April 2009. Ninety (90) questionnaires were delivered and sixty seven (67) were answered correctly. The filling was made individual and manuscripts and the data analysis was performed through software STATISTICA ® (Statsoft-Inc., 2001).

In order to be included in the sample, the participants had to be MPO employees; to use at least one of the modules of the system *SAP R/3* and are present in the transition between systems. The sample consisted by 67 users, of which 32 males and 35 females. Respondents were mostly aged between 20 and 39 years and 66 with Portuguese nationality. The great majority (51) of participants are employed in this company less than 3 years.

RESULTS AND DISCUSSION

In order to carry out this study, we analyzed the three main stages of the implementation processes: i) training process, ii) transition between systems, iii) changes in job performance, covering the pre-implementation, during and post-implementation phases. The main results and discussion of these three stages are the subjects of the next subsections.

Training Process in *SAP R/3*

In the process of training was concluded that the majority of respondents (88.1%) received training on the use of *SAP R/3* in the company studied. However, only 49.2% had training in all the modules that they used. Several authors show that training is a key-factor in the implementation process (Barker & Frolick, 2003; Gallivan, *et al.*, 2005; Peslak, Subramanian, & Clayton, 2006; Robey, *et al.*, 2002). In accordance with the percentage of users that were in the training, it is expected that this factor positively influence the implementation of the system. However, approximately half of the respondents had no training in all the modules that they used, which may arise some difficulties which could threaten the functioning of the ERP in the post-implementation.

Of all the participants, only 30.5% consider that the training time was sufficient. However, and in spite of 50.8% did not have training in all the modules that they use, most of the participants (83.1%) consider that the training received was in accordance with applied modules. This relationship could be identified as a false facilitator in the implementation process, once the behavior may be biased because they have previous knowledge about the functionalities and potentialities of *SAP*

R/3. This way, users can adopt practices that affect their performance in the medium or long term.

Concerning the learning time is noteworthy that 15.3% of respondents have received training lasting less than 1 day, 35.6% between 1 and 3 days, 23.7% at 4 to 5 days and 25.4% more than 5 days. Several authors (Barker & Frolick, 2003; Gallivan, *et al.*, 2005; Robey, *et al.*, 2002) refer that training is one of the most important factors in the success of an ERP implementation, however, those authors don't indicate standardized times. In this sample it was verified that the training time was not uniform, presenting a considerable variability.

Regarding the relevance of training, approximately half of respondents (47.5%) classify the theoretical component with '3' value, in a *Likert* scale from '1' (nothing relevant) to '5' (very important). Of users studied, 33.9% agree with the same level of relevance to the practical component. Most of them consider the theoretical part between '3' and '4', while the practice as a greater dispersion, putting between '3' and '5'. Become evident a greater difference between the components at level '5' (very important), demonstrating that users attach more importance to practice, not forgetting, however, the theoretical component.

Transition Process Between Systems

Respecting the transition process between systems, almost all (95.5%) of people covered in this study understands the reason why the company has implemented the *SAP R/3*. This factor appears as a facilitator in the implementation process, since actors tend to respond positively when objectives are known (Abdinnour-Helm, *et al.*, 2003; Boddy, *et al.*, 2002). It was also observed that the majority (73.1%) of respondents did not feel prepared to use the software. This factor may be incurred as a barrier to the good practices, since the transition between systems is considered by Boudreau and Robey (2005) and Al-Mashari, *et al.* (2003) as a key factor in the implementation of ERP.

During the transition between systems, 94% of users required support, the great majority relied on co-workers (76.2%) and the UNIK team (61.9%) to overcome difficulties. Less frequent was the request for assistance to supervisors and the use of manuals. These results are consistent with the theory of Sarker and Lee (2003) once they defend that the communication between colleagues and a good support team are constituted as essential conditions for successful implementation.

However, despite the difficulties, when utilization problems arise, 92.5% of the respondents know whom to approach, facilitating the transition between systems.

In the perspective of 41.8% respondents, the transition to *SAP R/3* has caused difficulties at work. The lack of time to complete tasks, the lack of training and the inefficient data transfer, emerge as unsatisfactory factors. The lack of computer resources (computer, printer, or other) does not present as a difficulty. Only 7.5% of respondents mentioned that there was another kind of difficulty, such as problems in the transference of the data from legacy systems to *SAP*, producing unreliable and inappropriate information.

The classification of the frequency regarding the difficulties related to the lack of knowledge (theoretical or practical) presents a large-scale, placing it between 'seldom' and 'often'. However, the biggest difficulty presented is the lack of knowledge, marked as 'very often' by 25.4% of respondents.

Changes in the Work Performance

Relatively to the job performance, it was concluded that more than half of the respondents (67.2%) consider their work more productive using the *SAP R/3*, and with this new system the majority (74.6%) have easier access to information they need. According to O'Brien (2001) the facilitated access to information is a fundamental characteristic of the Information Systems (IS), thus will positively influence the work performance. However, 32.8% of respondents do not consider their work more productive, a factor that may be related to the normal organizational restructuring that usually comes from the implementation of a new system (Laudon & Laudon, 2006). After implementation, the great majority (83.6%) of respondents are aware of the specific functions in the *SAP R/3*, appearing as an advantage in efficiency of use (Orlikowski & Barley, 2001). Almost all respondents (98.5%) consider the system as a relevant tool for the company.

Regarding the use of *SAP R/3*, approximately half of respondents consider its use as complex. The fact that users identify the use of *SAP R/3* as complex may be due to their demand of the system and the short contact time (Bueno & Salmeron, 2008). Regarding the information entered into the system, more than half of respondents (61.2%) feel that the information kept is very important. These data provide a better and continuous interaction with the system, which allows the integration and updating of data, improving the performance at work.

Most people consider that in training and usage processes, the system met their expectations. One of the elements favorable to job performance relates to the expectations presented by the actors, which is a critical element of quality management in the project (PMI, 2004). Once the expectations were appropriate, in training and usage, these characteristics emerge as a predictor of quality in the work performed.

Almost all respondents (98.5%) consider the system useful. This factor foresees a systematic and continuous use, contributing once again for the good performance. According to the general opinion of respondents, *SAP R/3* simplified data management (introduction and control), improved access to information and made the work more complete and functional. As disadvantages, were presented difficulties in adapting to the system, an increase of complexity and delays in completion of tasks.

Figure 2. Bar chart of values obtained in questions A and B.

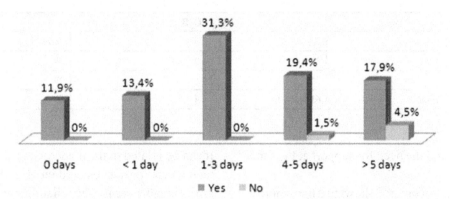

Analyzing the answers to the open question, we can verify that the number of advantages presented is greater than the number of disadvantages, thus is possible to infer that the respondents conceive the system as a positive tool for the implementation of their work. The advantages presented are corroborated by Pinto (2006) and Souza (2000), affirming that the use of a central database originates significant organizational challenges. However, these challenges are offset by the functional scope of the system, simplifying and improving access to all information. Also according to Pinto (2006) and Boudreau and Robey (2005) during the adaptation process can appear criticism and resistance to the project by the effort required and gaps, justifying, this way, the disadvantages presented by those respondents. Bresnahan and Brynjolfsson (2002) affirm that it can take years for people demonstrate a positive feeling in relation to the change, so the presented negative factors will not be reflect of the implementation failure but part of the normal process to the systems implementation.

Association Between Pairs of Variables

After the characterization of individual variables made previously, we present a bivariate analysis that intends to show the existence of a relationship between pairs of variables.

(Q_A) 'Duration of training in SAP R/3 in the MPO' and (Q_B) 'Need for support during the transition to the SAP R/3'.

The data presented in Figure 2 show that all users with training less than or equal to 3 days needed support. This need has decreased slightly with increasing the number of training days. The data indicate that increasing the training time during the implementation of a new system, decrease the need for support. This is essential for the performance of end-users. Burch and Kung (1997) suggest that customer support is more demanding in the first phase, whereat is expected that the need for support decrease until the maturity of the system.

To analyze the relationship between the issues 'A' and 'B', two time periods were considered in training ('<=3 days' and '>3 days'). Using Chi-square test ($\chi 2$) confirms that the hypothesis of independence is rejected for a significance level of 5%, with the value from a *test statistic* (TS) = 5,57>$\chi 2$(1; α=0.05) = 3,84 and *p-value* = 0,02. The data show an association between variables, suggesting that the need for support from users decreases with the increase of the training time. The obtained values are shown in Table 2.

(Q_C) 'Adequacy of preparation for starting to use the SAP R/3' and (Q_D) 'Need for support during the transition to the SAP R/3'.

Questions 'C' and 'D' were analyzed in order to ascertain a possible relationship between feel-

Table 2. Contingency table (Everitt, 1994) resulting from crossing of the answers to questions A and B.

		Q_B		
		Yes	No	Total
Q_A	< 3 days	38	0	38
	> 3 days	25	4	29
	Total	63	4	67

ing prepared and the need for support at the time of transition.

The analysis of Figure 3 shows that the majority of respondents (73%) did not feel prepared to start using the system, felt the need to support during the transition. Moreover, although the majority of respondents (14/18) felt prepared to use the system, the support was required. This may be related to the period of training that possibly did not cover the entire practical component and/or theoretical, failing to foresee all the difficulties.

Figure 3. Bar chart of values obtained in questions C and D.

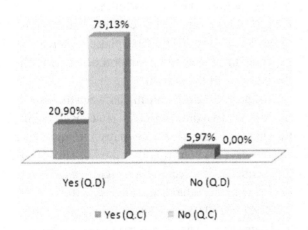

It can be related to the inadequate use of the system, where the data entered incorrectly originate errors in other areas. The reliability and accuracy of these data tend to be a problem in the planning of the operations (Pinto, 2006).

The use of contingency table (Table 3) and Chi-square test ($\chi 2$) confirms that the assumption of independence is rejected for a significance level of 5%, with the value from a test statistic (TS) = 11,58>$\chi 2$ (1; α=0.05) = 3,84 and *p-value* = 0,0007. Thus, there is an association between the variables, suggesting that users who do not feel prepared to use *SAP* needed help at the time of transition.

(Q_E) 'Ease to access information with the SAP R/3' and (Q_F) 'Perception of increased productivity at work after the implementation of SAP R/3'

In order to understand whether the facilitated access to information is related to the perception of work productivity of users, questions 'E' and 'F' were crossed. Figure 4, shows that 76% of users who consider the simplified access to information also agreed that its performance has become more productive with the implementation of the new system. They also show that 24% of respondents think that, although having better ac-

Table 3. Contingency table (Everitt, 1994) resulting from crossing the answers to questions C and D.

		Q_D		
		Yes	No	Total
Q_C	Yes	14	4	18
	No	49	0	49
	Total	63	4	67

Figure 4. Bar chart of values obtained in questions E and F.

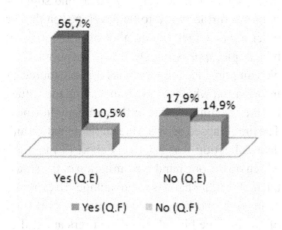

cess to information, the productivity in the tasks will not be increased.

The use of Chi-square test (χ^2) confirms that the assumption of independence is rejected for a significance level of 5%, with the value from a test statistic (TS) = 6,98>$\chi2$(1; α=0.05) = 3,84 and *p-value* = 0,0083.

This result suggests an association between ease access to information with the *SAP R/3* and the perception of work productivity after its implementation, confirming the data previously presented. The obtained values are shown in Table 4.

6. CONCLUSION, LIMITATIONS AND FUTURE RESEARCH DIRECTIONS

Considering our results, we can say that in general the implementation of *SAP R/3* was successful.

However, there are gaps that should be tackled in future implementations to optimize the results.

From the analysis of the training process, we can conclude that more than half of respondents consider their work more productive using the *SAP R/3*, and most access more easily to the information. It was also verified that the majority of those respondents have received training in the company. These factors are positive points, influencing the success of the implementation.

For most individuals the system met the expectations in the training process and usage. In the transition between systems almost all people understood the reason why the administration had to implement the *SAP R/3*. Since these indicators emerge as predictors of quality in the executed work it is important that in future implementations users also have this previous knowledge.

It was also possible to confirm that, when facing difficulties in using the system, the great majority of respondents know where to turn, normally to the support team. This team appears as an essential element in the support of implementations, thus, users should be aware of it to effectively communicate.

It was found that almost half of the participants had no training in all of the modules of *SAP R/3* they use, which may arise some difficulties. Thus, in future implementations the training process should include all areas covered by the end-users.

Most respondents did not consider the training time to be sufficient and did not feel prepared to use the software. However, we can verify that as training time increases, the support need in *SAP R/3* decreases. Therefore, to overcome these

Table 4. Contingency table (Everitt, 1994) resulting from crossing of the answers to questions E and F.

		Q_F		
		Yes	No	Total
Q_E	Yes	38	7	45
	No	12	10	22
	Total	50	17	67

barriers, the increase in training time in future implementations is justified.

The majority of respondents mention that the lack of documentation to help guide the system is an obstacle. However, the DIS&BP created and made available user help guides, so it is necessary to promote the possibility and need for consultation.

Regarding the use of *SAP R/3*, approximately half of respondents consider it complex. In order to blur this negative factor, a solution is to customize the system, which facilitates its use and continuous improvements.

As a member of the implementation process, it was possible to observe that the support team impart positive feelings for key-users is fundamental, which in turn serve as mediators between users and the UNIK team. On the one hand, the more determinate the key-users, the more easily they involve the end-users. On the other hand, the lack of trust by the key-users on the end-users has impact in procedures and underload in the first, since the functions are not decentralized. The fact that all users become independent is crucial for the proper functioning of processes, as well as the support team which can devote to the evolutionary improvements.

With the analysis of the results obtained through questionnaires and attendance the implementation of *SAP R/3*, we can conclude that end-users require ongoing support. Thus, not only the theoretical and practical supports are important in the initial phase, but also the post-implementation practical attendance. In addition, it would be important to determine training time in agreement with the contents to standardize the teaching processes.

According to Cardoso (2003, *cit by* Junior & Ferreira, 2006) the implementation of an integrated management system such as *SAP R/3* consumes on average 2 years. Once the implementation of the project had the duration of 6 months, is possible that more time was needed to customize the whole software, to define procedures, and at the same time to train all users.

As any research, this also presents some limitations, opening, however, new ideas and suggestions for further work to be developed in this or other areas. Given the number of individuals in the sample, approximately 30% of the population, we can consider the results as a good source of information which allows transferring the values for the remaining areas of the company in study. The time elapsed between the implementation and data collection was relatively short (3 months), which on the one hand is a limitation of the study, but on the other hand is an advantage. To evaluate changes in work performance after a short time of use may be biased, since the users are still in an adaption phase to the new system.

In a future research of this nature, it would be pertinent to collect data in a later period (6 months after implementation), to increase the sample number and diversify it in other companies of the Group. It would also be pertinent to accomplish a study on the impact in the organizational structure, analyzing how it suffered modifications. Given that there were changes in procedures, employees may arise with new functions and/or new departments, or even reduce the number of human resources (organizational redesign).

The data obtained in this study appears as prevention indicators and guidelines for the success of future implementations of integrated systems, once for managers it is important to know the impact of the events in all functional areas, as well as its performance, in order to be able to react immediately to market fluctuations.

ACKNOWLEDGMENT

Although maintaining the anonymity, we would like to thank the members of the organization where this whole project took place and particularly those involved in the study.

REFERENCES

Abdinnour-Helm, S., & Lengnick-Hall, M., & Lengnick- Hall, C. (2003). Pre-implementation attitudes and organizational readiness for implementing an enterprise resource planning system. *European Journal of Operational Research*, *146*(2), 258–273. doi:10.1016/S0377-2217(02)00548-9

Abran, A., & Nguyenkim, H. (1991). *Analysis of maintenance work categories through measurement*. Paper presented at the Conference on Software Maintenance, Los Alamitos CA.

Al-Mashari, M., Al-Mudimigh, A., & Zairi, M. (2003). ERP: A taxonomy of critical factors. *European Journal of Operational Research*, *146*, 352–364. doi:10.1016/S0377-2217(02)00554-4

Barker, T., & Frolick, M. N. (2003). ERP implementation failure: A case study. *Information Systems Management*, *20*(4), 43–49. doi:10.1201/1078/43647.20.4.20030901/77292.7

Beynon-Davies, P. (2002). *Information Systems. An Introduction to Informatics in Organisations*. England: Palgrave.

Bingi, P., Sharma, M. K., & Godla, J. K. (1999). Critical issues affecting an ERP implementation. *Information Systems Management*, *16*(3), 7–14. doi:10.1201/1078/43197.16.3.19990601/31310.2

Boddy, D., Boonstra, A., & Kennedy, G. (2002). *Managing Information Systems: An Organizational Perspective* (1st ed.). Edinburgh: Pearson Education.

Boudreau, M., & Robey, D. (2005). Enacting integrated information technology: A human agency perspective. *Organization Science*, *16*(1), 3–18. doi:10.1287/orsc.1040.0103

Bresnahan, T. F., & Brynjolfsson, E. (2002). Information technology, workplace organization, and the demand for skilled labor: Firm-level evidence. *The Quarterly Journal of Economics*, *117*(1), 339–376. doi:10.1162/003355302753399526

Bueno, S., & Salmeron, J. L. (2008). TAM-based success modeling in ERP. *Interacting with Computers*, *20*(6), 515–523. doi:10.1016/j.intcom.2008.08.003

Burch, E., & Kungs, H.-J. (1997). *Modeling software maintenance requests: a case study*. Paper presented at the Proceedings of the International Conference on Software Maintenance.

Chou, S.-W., & Chang, Y.-C. (2008). The implementation factors that influence the ERP (enterprise resource planning) benefits. *Decision Support Systems*, *46*(1), 149–157. doi:10.1016/j.dss.2008.06.003

Davenport, T. H. (1998). Putting the enterprise into the enterprise system. *Harvard Business Review*, *76*(4), 121–131.

Davenport, T. H. (2002). *Missão Critica: obtendo vantagem competitiva com os sistemas de gestão empresarial* [Mission Critical: gaining competitive advantage with enterprise management systems.]. Porto Alegre: Bookman.

Esteves, J., & Jorge, J. (2001). *Análise Comparativa de Metodologias de Implementação de SAP*. [Comparative Analysis of Methodologies for Implementation of SAP.] Associação Portuguesa de Sistemas de Informação (APSI) [Portuguese Association for Information Systems (APSI)]: Évora.

Everitt, B. S. (1994). *The Analysis of Contingency Tables*. New York: Chapman & Hall.

Gallivan, M. J., Spitler, V. K., & Koufaris, M. (2005). Does Information Technology Training Really Matter? A Social Information Processing Analysis of Coworkers' Influence on IT Usage in the Workplace. *Journal of Management Information Systems, 22*(1), 153–192.

Hong, K.-K., & Kim, Y.-G. (2002). The critical success factors for ERP implementation: an organizational fit perspective. *Information & Management, 40*(1), 25–40. doi:10.1016/S0378-7206(01)00134-3

Jones, M. C., Cline, M., & Ryan, S. (2006). Exploring knowledge sharing in ERP implementation: an organizational culture framework. *Decision Support Systems, 41*(2), 411–434. doi:10.1016/j.dss.2004.06.017

Júnior, R., & Ferreira, L. (2006). *Avaliação de um sistema ERP-SAP R/3 como Instrumento para gestão financeira na área de contas a pagar em uma empresa de Telecomunicações.* [Evaluation of an ERP system-SAP R / 3 as a tool for financial management in the area of accounts payable in a company Telecommunications] Brasília.

Lander, M. C., Purvis, R. L., McCray, G. E., & Leigh, W. (2004). Trust-building mechanisms utilized in outsourced IS development projects: a case study. *Information & Management, 41*(4), 509–528. doi:10.1016/j.im.2003.10.001

Laudon, K. C., & Laudon, J. P. (2006). *Management Information Systems: management the digital firm* (9th ed.). New Jersey: Pearson Education.

Markus, M. L., Tanis, C., & Fenema, P. C. v. (2000). Enterprise resource planning: multisite ERP implementations. *Communications of the ACM, 43*(4), 42–46. doi:10.1145/332051.332068

Nah, F. F.-H., Faja, S., & Cata, T. (2001). Characteristics of ERP software maintenance: a multiple case study. *Journal of Software Maintenance and Evolution: Research and Practice, 13*(6), 399–414. doi:10.1002/smr.239

Ng, C. S. P., Gable, G. G., & Chan, T. (2002). An ERP-client benefit-oriented maintenance taxonomy. *Journal of Systems and Software, 64*(2), 87–109. doi:10.1016/S0164-1212(02)00029-8

Ngai, E. W. T., Law, C. C. H., & Wat, F. K. T. (2008). Examining the critical success factors in the adoption of enterprise resource planning. *Computers in Industry, 59*(6), 548–564. doi:10.1016/j.compind.2007.12.001

O'Brien, J. (2001). *Introduction to Information Systems: essentials for the internetworked e-business enterpise* (10th ed.). Irwin/McGraw-Hill.

Orlikowski, W. J., & Barley, S. R. (2001). Technology and institutions: what can research on information technology and research on organizations learn from each other? *Management Information Systems Quarterly, 25*(2), 145–165. doi:10.2307/3250927

Peslak, A., Subramanian, G. H., & Clayton, G. (2006). The phases of ERP software implementation and maintenance: A model for predicting preferred ERP use. *Journal of Computer Information Systems, 48*(2), 25–33.

Pinto, J. P. (2006). *Gestão de Operações na Indústria e nos Serviços* [Operations Management in Manufacturing and Services](2.nd ed.). Lisboa: LIDEL.

PMI. (2004). *A Guide to the Project Management Body of Knowledge* (3rd ed.). Project Management Institute.

Robey, D., Ross, J. W., & Boudreau, M. C. (2002). Learning to implement enterprise systems: An exploratory study of the dialectics of change. *Journal of Management Information Systems, 19*(1), 17–46.

Sarker, S., & Lee, A. S. (2003). Using a case study to test the role of three key social enablers in ERP implementation. *Information & Management, 40*(8), 813–829. doi:10.1016/S0378-7206(02)00103-9

Scott, J. E., & Vessey, I. (2002). Managing risks in enterprise systems implementations. *Communications of the ACM, 45*(4), 74–81. doi:10.1145/505248.505249

Souza, C. A. (2000). *Sistemas Integrados de Gestão Empresarial: estudos de caso de implementação de sistemas ERP* [Integrated Systems Business Management: case studies of implementation of ERP systems]. São Paulo: FEA/USP.

Sprott, D. (2000). Enterprise resource planning: componentizing the enterprise application packages. *Communications of the ACM, 43*(4), 63–69. doi:10.1145/332051.332074

Statsoft-Inc. (2001). *STATISTICA (data analysis software system)*, version 6.

Subramanian, G., & Hoffer, C. (2007). *Implementation of Enterprise Resource Planning (ERP) Systems: Issues and Challenges. Penn State Harrisburg.* Idea Group Inc.

Tchokogué, A., Bareil, C., & Duguay, C. R. (2005). Key lessons from the implementation of an ERP at Pratt & Whitney Canada. *International Journal of Production Economics, 95*(2), 151–163. doi:10.1016/j.ijpe.2003.11.013

Thomas, F. G. (2000). *Understanding the Plant Level Costs and Benefits of ERP: Will the Ugly Duckling Always Turn into a Swan?* Paper presented at the 33rd Hawaii Inter. Conf. on Systems Science., Los Alamitos CA.

William, G. C. (2008). *Implementing SAP ERP Sales & Distribution. Essencial Skills for SAP Professionals.* New York, NY: McGraw-Hill.

Youngberg, E., Olsen, D., & Hauser, K. (2009). Determinants of professionally autonomous end user acceptance in an enterprise resource planning system environment. *International Journal of Information Management, 29*(2), 138–144. doi:10.1016/j.ijinfomgt.2008.06.001

Chapter 14
An Approach for Recovering the Connections between Business Process and Software System

Lerina Aversano
University of Sannio, Italy

Fiammetta Marulli
University of Sannio, Italy

Maria Tortorella
University of Sannio, Italy

ABSTRACT

The relationship existing between a business process and the supporting software system is a critical concern for organizations, as it directly affects their performance. The knowledge regarding this relationship plays an important role in the software evolution process, as it helps to identify the software components involved by a software change request. The research described in this chapter concerns the use of information retrieval techniques in the software maintenance activities. In particular, the chapter addresses the problem of recovering traceability links between the entities of the business process model and components of the supporting software system. Therefore, an information retrieval approach is proposed based on two processing phases including syntactic and semantic analysis. The usefulness of the approach is discussed through a case study.

INTRODUCTION

Fast change in business requirements forces enterprises to a continue evolution of their software systems in order to effectively use them. The change emerging from the business environment

DOI: 10.4018/978-1-4666-1764-3.ch014

immediately affects the business processes that need to be customized to support organizational change (Basili et al., 1994). This scenario offers an important challenge. It regards the software maintenance tasks relatively to the adaptation of software systems to business process changes.

The relationships among organizational and process aspects and software components have already been considered with reference to the development of new software systems (Henderson & Venkatraman, 1993). In particular, a business process consists of the set of activities performed by an enterprise to achieve a goal. Its specification includes the description of the activities and control and data flow among them. The supporting software system is generally an application that provides a support to the user while performing the process activities. Then, it is clear that a change in the process may immediately affects the software components by software change request. However, locating the appropriate components impacted by the change requirements is not always obvious to software maintainers. This is particularly true if the change requirements are expressed in terms of business activities and maintainers have not an evidence of what this means in terms of software components. This immediately suggests the need of adequately managing the links existing between business process activities and software system components. The knowledge regarding these connections is very important for software maintainers while they have to deal with change requirements. Unfortunately, this information is not adequately documented and the impact of a change on the process is often difficult to map to the software components. In the best of the authors' knowledge, there is a lack of studies regarding the definition of methods and tools for recovering and managing the relationships existing between business processes and software systems.

To prove the relevance of the knowledge cited above, an exploratory study was performed with the aim of analyzing the relationship existing between a business process and the supporting software systems and of understanding the contribution of this relation in the software evolution process (Aversano & Tortorella, 2009). The empirical study involved a group of students from the courses of Informative Systems and Project management, in their last year of the master degree in computer science at the University of Sannio, in Italy. They were asked to analyse code and

software documentation of two software systems and identify the software components to be modified on the basis of a set of change requests. In addition, a group of experimental subjects could use the knowledge regarding the business process. The aim of the analysis was evaluating whether the knowledge of the business process using the software systems and the ability of using such a kind of knowledge leads to an improved identification of the impact of a requirement change request on the software system. The results suggested the strong correlation existing between business activities and process components and, according to the initial hypothesis, indicated that the business information effectively provides a significant help to software maintainers.

Learning from this experience, this chapter proposes an approach, based on Information Retrieval, aiming at supporting software maintainers with the business process knowledge that is useful for clarifying change requirements concerning the software systems.

The chapter is organized as follows: Section 2 provides a description of the related work; Section 3 presents the Information Retrieval approach for recovering traceability links between business process activities and software system components; the software tool supporting the approach is presented in Section 4; Section 5 presents the application of the approach in two case studies; finally concluding remarks and future works are discussed in Section 6.

RELATED WORK

The issue of alignment was mentioned for the first time in the late 1970s and since then several studies and researches were conducted highlighting the alignment concerns.

A view of business and technological alignment defines at which degree the information technology mission, objectives, and plans, support and are supported by the business mission, objectives, and plans (Reich & Benbasat, 2000). Moreover, it involves "fit" and "integration" among business strategy, IT strategy, business infrastructure, and IT infrastructure (Henderson & Venkatraman, 1993), (Papp, 2001).

Understanding what business and information systems alignment is, how to obtain it and, therefore, maintain it, is a "problem" (Pereira & Sousa, 2003). Traditional approaches addresses the alignment concern seeking an answer to how can organizations achieve alignment, but with little contribution on how to identify and correct misalignments.

In (Etien & Rolland, 2005), criteria and associated generic metrics are proposed to quantify at which extent there is a fit between the business and the system which supports it. For formulating metrics independent from specific formalisms to express the system and business models, the authors provide a theoretical foundation for their proposal. In addition, for illustrating the use of the proposed generic metrics, they show how to derive a set of specific metrics from the generic ones and discuss the use of the specific metrics in a case study.

In (Wieringa et al., 2003), a framework is presented for analyzing the alignment problem and proposing an approach to application architecture design with reference to a business context. The authors summarize guidelines for application architecture design and illustrate how the approach can be used through an example.

The Business and Information Systems MisAlignment Model (BISMAM), is proposed in (Carvalho & Sousa, 2008), (Thevenet et al., 2006), to understand, classify and manage misalignments. The proposal addresses the alignment problem combining misalignment approach with medical sciences approaches, based on a metaphor between misalignment and disease. The authors believe that the misalignment approach is closer to organizations real life and that medical sciences approaches provide relevant concepts and techniques for misalignment classification and

management. Based on both academic research and years of professional consultancy, the authors propose an initial and possible instantiation to the BISMAM model, establishing a misalignment classification scheme that links enterprise architecture views, misalignment symptoms and causes, and defining techniques for detecting, correcting and preventing misalignments.

Finally, as previously said, the authors of this chapter proposed a coarse grained strategy (Aversano et al., 2005) for detecting misalignment between software systems and supported business processes when a change is executed. The approach considered two attributes: Technological Coverage and Technological Adequacy. A more detailed analysis of these aspects is provided in (Aversano et al., 2010) were a set of metrics are proposed for allowing the evaluation of the two attribute. This chapter considered different and complementary aspects of the alignment relationship, relying on: (i) the use of a modelling notation to represent the software systems and business processes; (ii) the definition of the types of links existing between concepts of these models; (iii) the exploitation of the results of the analysis for identifying evolution changes.

THE TRACEABILITY RECOVERY PROCESS

The method proposed for retrieving the traceability links between the business process activities and supporting software system components relies on the extraction of identifiers from the business process model and discovering of the software components involved in a business activity.

The proposed method is based on a two processing phases, as shown in Figure 1:

- the first phase, named *Semantic Processing*, regards the extraction of semantic information from both business process model, software system model and source code. It

Figure 1. Traceability Recovery Process

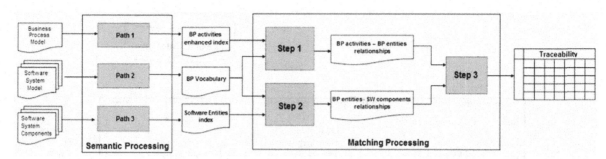

analyses the documentation regarding the business process and software system models, opportunely represented. The output of this phase consists of semantic information regarding both business domain and software components, represented in such a way to permit their automatic processing performed in the next phase.

- the second phase, named *Matching Processing*, aims at discovering the matching existing between the business information found out during the previous phase and software system components. This phase looks for correspondences existing between the business and software information obtained by the previous phase and generates a traceability matrix of relationships.

The two cited phases are composed of a sequence of activities whose detailed description follows in the next two subsections.

SEMANTIC PROCESSING

This phase of the process is made of three independent paths, as shown in Figure 2. Each path is a sequence of steps aiming at extracting identifiers from the software system components and discovering and enhancing information regarding the business process application domain.

Path1 receives as input the business process model containing the list of all relevant activities of the business process, extracts all the identifiers composing the name of each activity and enriches them of semantic information.

During this path, each string composing the name of an activity is subjected to a normalization text step, indicated as *Text Processing*, executing the following tasks:

1. Splitting of each name string, for separating the identifiers composing the activity name;
2. Transformation of capital letters into lower case letters;
3. Removal of stop-words, such as articles, numbers, prepositions, and so on;
4. Morphological analysis for converting plurals into singulars and transforming the flexed verbs into their infinity form.

After the text processing step, the *Semantic Enhancement* step is executed. Its aim is to improve and complete the description of each business process activity, enhancing it with a set of additional information that can be extracted from a lexical ontology. In particular, the lexical ontology is consulted for retrieving a set of semantically related terms of the identifier parts of an activity name. The retrieved terms can be, for instance, synonymous and words contained in the description of the identifiers. If an identifier is a verb, the corresponding nouns are also extracted.

Figure 2. Semantic Processing phase

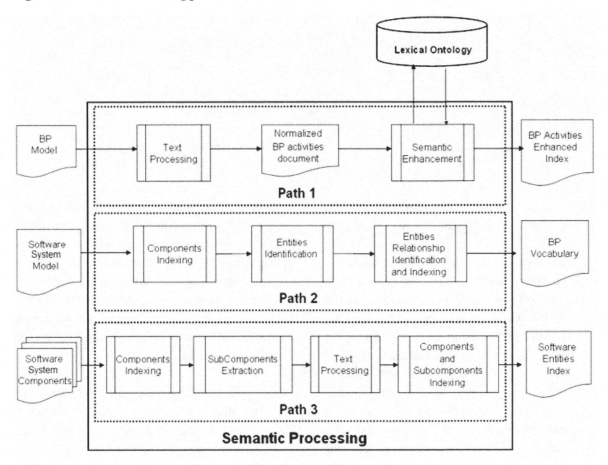

The execution of Path1 generates as output a document containing the enhanced description of each business process activity.

The second path is indicated as Path2 in Figure 2. It receives as input the model of the considered software system and performs an analysis aiming at identifying the entities it uses for modelling the business process domain. Then, the software system components are indexed and explored for finding and extracting the reciprocal dependence and use relationships. The business process entities modelled by the software components and list of the related entities, are stored in a document, that will represent a vocabulary for the business process domain, BP vocabulary.

The Path 3, shown in Figure 2, receives as input the source code of the considered software system and aims at extracting, the list of the subcomponents of each software component (in our case, a list of methods). A Text Processing of all the components and extracted subcomponents name identifiers follows with the aim of removing the useless parts that are next processed in the Components and Subcomponents indexing. The output of this path is represented by a document containing a normalized index, named map, of software components and subcomponents, Software Entities Index.

MATCHING PROCESSING

The *Matching Processing* phase is aimed at verifying the similarity between the syntactical and semantic information extracted by the previous phase, and extracting and classifying links between business process activities and software system components. The result of this phase is a traceability matrix highlighting the software components (i.e., classes and methods) potentially used during the execution of each business process activity.

Figure 1 highlights the three steps composing the *Matching Processing* phase. The first and second steps uses a similarity function that will be later presented. The three steps can be summarized as it follows:

- Computes the similarity level existing between the identifiers included in the BP activities enhanced index and those composing the BP Vocabulary. The first index is composed of the business process activities and all the additional information selected from the lexical ontology. While the BP Vocabulary includes the identifiers representing the entities of the business process domain modelled in the software system.
- Computes the similarity level between the identifiers composing the BP Vocabulary and those of the Software Entities Index, regarding the identifiers extracted from the index document of the software components and subcomponents.
- Analyses the extracted links and related similarity level and merges the intermediate results of the previous two steps for obtaining a complete map of traceability between the business process activities and software system components and subcomponents.

It is worthwhile noticing that the vocabulary is just a mean to discover links between business activities and software system components. This link could not be retrieved if a simple syntactical matching criteria is applied directly to the set of initial identifiers composing the business process and software components description.

Evaluating the similarity between couples of terms related to business process activities names and software components identifiers depends on the adopted Information Retrieval – IR – model. The proposed approach uses a vector space (Harman, 1992) IR model. This model considers the elements of the business process model and software system components organized as vectors in a n-dimensional space, where n is the number of the indexing features. In particular, these features are the identifiers of the entities extracted from the BP Vocabulary.

The similarity criteria are used for linking business process activities with software model entities, and software model entities with software source code components. In particular, it is used:

- Within Step 1 for computing the product of the probabilities that each identifier contained in an entity node of the BP Vocabulary appears in a business activity name;
- and, within Step 2, for evaluating the product of the probabilities that each identifier in an entity node of the BP Vocabulary is also included in the identifier of a source code components.

The cited probabilities will be referenced in the following as weights. They are computed by using the well known IR metric called *term frequency–inverse document frequency (tf–idf)*. According to this metric, the vector of weights of BP Vocabulary terms over BP activities, $wa = [wi,j]$, is made of the weights wi,j, indicating how much important the i-th term of the BP Vocabulary is for the j-th activity. It is derived from the *term frequency* measure, tfi,j , of the i-th term of the BP Vocabulary in the j-th activity, and the *inverse activity frequency, idfiJ*, of the i-th term in the whole set of activities.

In the same way, the weights vector of BP Vocabulary terms over software components, wk = [wi,k], is build by computing the frequency, tfi,k, of the i-th term of the BP Vocabulary in the k-th software component, and the *inverse activity frequency*, $idfiK$, of the i-th term in the entire set of software components. The term frequency tfi,j is the ratio between the number of occurrences of the i-th word over the total number of terms contained in the Aj activity. The inverse activity frequency $idfij$ is defined as follows:

$$idf_{ij} = \frac{\# Activities}{\# ActivitiesContaining_{Term_i}}$$

The vector element wij (respectively wik) is represented as:

wij= $tfi,j*log(idfiJ)$

The term $log(idfiJ)$ represents a weight of the frequency of an entity identifier in an activity (software component): a higher weight means that an entity identifier is more specific to that activity (software component). From experience, we derived that an entity identifier which reach a weight equal or greater than 0.35 against an activity (software component) description can be considered as related to that activity (software component), and, then, the correspondence can be considered.

TOOL SUPPORT

A software system supports the automatic application of the described process. Java and XML technologies were employed for developing the system and representing input and output data. XML technology was also employed for expressing intermediate processing results.

The lexical ontology consulted in the semantic processing phase is Wordnet (www.princeton.edu.net) and the communication with this system was managed by using the JENA API Semantic Framework (http://jena.sourceforge.net/).

This system is characterized by a multi-layer architecture, where each layer directly corresponds to a phase of the process and is made of modules implementing a particular path of activities or a specific processing step. Figure 3 shows the proposed architecture.

The system inputs consist of:

- The business process model described as XML document containing the list of all the business activities;
- The complete set of source code files (classes files) of the software system, including model and functional components;
- A semantic rule file for expressing the criteria adopted for extracting information from the lexical ontology in the semantic enhancement step;
- A splitting rule file, submitted as text file, for introducing the separation characters for the identifiers splitting, according to the system developing conventions;
- A stop-words file, submitted as text file, to introduce the list of useless word.

The system output consist of the complete *traceability matrix* linking business activities and software components in form of XML document.

A short description of the components of the architecture shown in Figure 3 follows.

The first layer represents an *I/O Configuration User Interface layer* built to let system users easily configure the inputs/output information regarding the process. It consists of a friendly tool bar by which users can select the complete path of the input data to be analysed: Business Process Document; Rules file; Stop-words file; Source Code file; destination for the output document. This configuration interface is also used for selecting the two subsets represented by the model and controller components, among the whole set

Figure 3. Architecture of the software system supporting Traceability Recovery Process

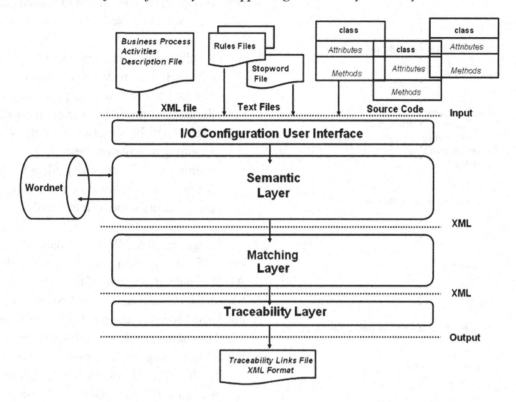

of software system source code components, as used in two different processing paths.

The *Semantic Layer* is made of three modules each one implementing a path of the semantic processing phase.

The first module receives as input an XML file describing the business process, the splitting rules file and the stop-words file. The first performed step regards the splitting of the string composing an activity name as a list of separate identifiers, according to the list of separation characters contained in the rules file. In addition, all identifiers are transformed in lower case letters. The extracted identifiers are saved in a new XML file. Thus, this new file is processed for removing all the useless words listed in the stop-words file. Finally, all the flexed verbs are transformed in their infinite form. At this stage of the elaboration, for each identifier appearing in the normalized list, the Wordnet lexical ontology is consulted for finding

out synonymous and semantically related terms. The default behaviour entails the extraction of five synonymous terms and semantic description. In addition, for each verbal form it was also considered the noun form, if existing. The additional information extracted from Wordnet are stored in a new XML file, with the correspondent root term. The file is organized as shown in Figure 4. Each upper level node represents a business process activity. The description of any activity consists of a set of normalized identifiers, each one represented as a new lower level node. For example, Figure 4 shows that the AA3 activity description, *identification goods donate*, can be decomposed in the following terms: *identification*, *good*, and *donate*. The *good* term has *advantage*, *goodness*, *commodity*, and so on, as the synonyms, and *article of commerce* as sense. The XML file, shown in Figure 4, is elaborated once again for normalizing the text and removing the new stop-

Figure 4. Semantic Enhancement Step

```
- <Activity>
    <id>AA3</id>
    <name>identification good donate</name>
  - <items>
    + <identification>
    - <good>
      - <synonyms>
          <s1>advantage</s1>
          <s2>goodness</s2>
          <s3>commodity</s3>
          <s4>trade good</s4>
          <s5>artifact</s5>
        </synonyms>
      - <sense>
          <ss1>articles of commerce</ss1>
        </sense>
      </good>
    - <donate>
      - <synonyms>
          <s1>give</s1>
          <s2>gift</s2>
          <s3>present</s3>
        </synonyms>
      - <sense>
          <ss1>give to a charity or good cause</ss1>
        </sense>
      - <noun_form>
          <n1>contribution</n1>
          <n2>donation</n2>
        </noun_form>
      </donate>
    </items>
  </Activity>
```

words introduced in the meaning description extracted from the lexical ontology. Finally, it is ready to be processed in the matching module.

The second module receives as input the set of source code components modelling the entities of the business process domain. The first step regards the indexing of all the source code components. The index contains, for each model object, the component identifier and its file name (i.e., in our case study, "Article" and "Article. php") and it is used for exploring in an automated way all the model components and finding out the existing dependence and use relationships between entities. This analysis is implemented by computing an iterative research of each entity identifier in the definition of any other entity. The result of this computation is a new XML document, named BP Vocabulary, listing all the indexed

entities and corresponding list of related entities. As an example, this module:

- Reads out the first entity identifier from the entities index created in the previous step;
- Opens the corresponding file (containing the body definition of the component) and explores it for searching identifiers corresponding to other entities;
- Stores any different entity identifier in the list file, as child node of the currently explored entity node, if it is found.

A fragment of the BP Vocabulary is shown in Figure 5. In particular, Figure 5 shows that the A1class, named *account*, of the software system SantaClaus, discussed in the first case study, is not related to other classes. On the contrary, the A2 class, named *article*, is related to the following classes: *category*, *donation* and *assignation*.

The third module of the Semantic Layer receives as input the set of source code components implementing the entities of the business process domain (controller components). This module creates an XML documents containing an index of all these components and their subcomponents, by applying an iterative procedure. The list of each controller component and its subcomponents is subjected to a text normalization procedure.

The *Matching layer* is made of two modules, each one performing a syntactical comparison between a couple of documents. A comparison procedure computes the identifiers frequency and inverse activity and software component frequencies, as described in the previous section. To this aim, it performs a syntactical comparison among identifiers extracted by the XML documents built in the previous phase. The output of this modules is represented by two new files, containing the list of links identified between the activities of the business process and model entities, and the controller components and model entities, according to the probabilistic matching criteria, discussed in the previous section. In the first module of this

Figure 5. Fragment of a BP Vocabulary

```
<?xml version="1.0" standalone="yes" ?>
- <SANTACLAUS-BP_CLASS>
  - <CLASS>
      <id>A1</id>
      <name>account</name>
      <description />
    </CLASS>
  - <CLASS>
      <id>A2</id>
      <name>article</name>
      <description />
      <CLASS_RELATED>category</CLASS_RELATED>
      <CLASS_RELATED>donation</CLASS_RELATED>
      <CLASS_RELATED>assignation</CLASS_RELATED>
    </CLASS>
  - <CLASS>
      <id>A3</id>
      <name>assignation</name>
      <description />
      <CLASS_RELATED>article</CLASS_RELATED>
      <CLASS_RELATED>user</CLASS_RELATED>
    </CLASS>
  - <CLASS>
      <id>A4</id>
      <name>category</name>
      <description />
    </CLASS>
```

layer, each entity identifier and related entities listed in the BP vocabulary is compared with each activity identifier and searched within its additional information.

A matching is found if the computed weight is equal or greater than the fixed threshold of similarity. The output file will contain the list of model entities matching each BP activity. The second module of this layer is executed in the same way for looking for syntactical matching between model entities and controller components and subcomponents. A new file containing the list of model entities and matched controller components and subcomponents is given as output.

The *Traceability layer*, finally, joins the results obtained by the upper modules using the model entities as primary key for computing the traceability links between activities and software controller components and linking them. The linking criteria is based on common model entities to join activities and components. The output of

this layer is the traceability map, represented as XML document, as shown in Figure 6.

CASE STUDY

To show the applicability of the proposed approach two case study studies, described in the following, have been conducted.

Two widely accepted information retrieval metrics have been used to assess the results, namely *recall* and *precision* (Frakes & Baeza-Yates, 1992). The *Recall* is the ratio of the number of the relevant software components retrieved for a given business process activity over the total number of relevant software components for that activity:

$$\mathrm{Re}\,call = \frac{\sum_i \#(\mathrm{Re}\,levant_i \wedge \mathrm{Re}\,trieved_i)}{\sum_i \mathrm{Re}\,levant_i}\%$$

Figure 6. XML Structure of the Traceability Matrix

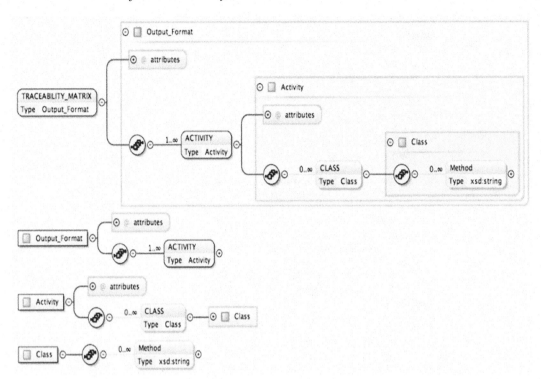

Precision is the ratio of the number of relevant software components retrieved over the total number of software components retrieved:

$$\Pr ecision = \frac{\sum_i \#(\mathrm{Re}\,levant_i \wedge \mathrm{Re}\,trieved_i)}{\sum_i \mathrm{Re}\,trieved_i}\%$$

In this context, a software component is relevant for a business activity if it is executed when the activity is performed. The evaluation have been performed with reference to an oracle that correctly relates software components and business activities.

The main advantage of using an automated traceability recovery process consists of restricting the software components space, while recovering all the software components relevant for each process activity. Indeed, when an activity changes, there is often an impact on the supporting software system. Then, without tool support software maintainers have to analyze all the software components before identifying those impacted by the change, instead with a restricted component space the number of components to be analyzed is generally much lower.

In the first case study the software system, named SantaClaus, is considered, with the business process using it. The relationships of the software system components and supported business process activities are analysed.

Santaclaus is a web application written in PHP and Java. This software system was developed for supporting the business process used by a voluntary association, named Beneslan, to manage object donations for needy children (http://santaclaus.beneslan.it/santaclaus/).

Figure 7 describes the goods *assignation* business process executed by the voluntary association. For sake of space, only the assignation

Figure 7. Model of the business process using SantaClaus

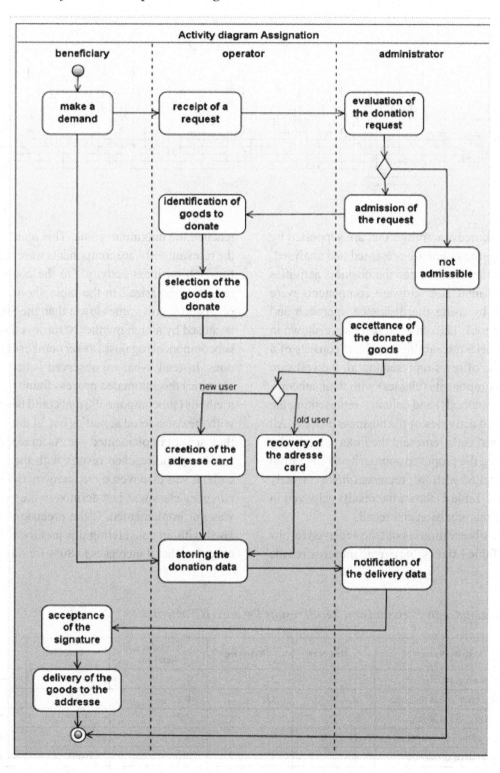

Figure 8. Santaclaus Processing Result: Traceability Links Map

Business Activities	index	indexUser	search	searchUser	post_articoloUser	save_posted	save_Edit	edit	remove	remove_user	assignation	saveAssignation	getProvincesList	getListByProvince	returnListByProvince	getDonationsList	...	index	getUserByAccount	addUser	getAllUserList	getUserById	checkAccount	getRootCategoriesList	getCategoriesListByRoots	getAllCategoriesList	getCategoriesList2	getCategoriesList3	search	index	edit	remove	...
receipt of a request		#		x																													
identification of goods to donate	#	x	#	#			x	#					#									#			x	x	x		x	x	#		#
selection of good to donate						#	#						x	x								#			x	x	x		x	x	#		#
recovery of the addresser card											#	x	x	x	x	x						#	x	#	#								
creation of the addresser card													#	#	#							#											
storing the donation data													x	#																			

x   Not Relevant Retrieved
\#   Relevant Retrieved

business process activities that are supported by the software system are presented and analysed.

The mapping between the business activities and the SantaClaus software components were obtained by using the discussed approach and software tool. The obtained results are shown in Figure 8 as a traceability matrix. It consists of a grid made of rows representing all the software system components (classes) with their subcomponents (methods) and columns representing the considered activities of the business process. All the crossed cells represent the links retrieved by employing the proposed approach and shadowed cells, labelled with '#', represent links correctly retrieved. Table 1 shows the results achieved in terms of the precision and recall.

Some observations about the achieved results follow. Table 1 shows that overall the recall results reached the maximum value. This means that all the relevant software components were identified for each business activity. On the contrary, the results summarized in the table shows that the precision scores values lower than the 50%. This is caused by a high number of retrieved software subcomponents against a lower number of relevant ones. Instead, what we observed is that in these activities the automated process found links with methods (subcomponents) that could be involved with the considered activities but, at the moment, they are not implemented yet. As an example, by analysing the reached results with the software code, it was discovered the many methods of the *category* class was just defined in the model but was not implemented. If the precision is calculated without considering this methods, it can be observed that it increases to 80% for the *identifi-*

Table 1. SantaClaus Precision and Recall results for each BP activity

Activity Name	Relevant	Retrivied	Retrivied and Relevant	Precision	Recall
Receipt of a request	1	2	1	50,00%	100%
Identification of goods to donate	8	15	8	53,33%	100%
Selection of good to donate	5	12	5	41,66%	100%
Recovery of the addresser card	4	9	4	44,44%	100%
Creation of the addresser card	4	4	4	100%	100%
Storing the donation data	1	2	1	50,00%	100%
Total results				**52.27%**	**100%**

cation of goods to donate activity and to 71% for *selection of goods to* donate activity.

In the end, we can affirm that the results obtained by our automated process can be considered as a good suggestion for software engineer, that can use them for cutting the whole set of components to consider as involved with business process activities.

A previous evaluation was performed by executing just a simple syntactical analysis. The obtained results were more poor than those reached by applying the enhanced semantic analysis. In fact, many activities were no traced on any software component. This has demonstrated that the only syntactic analysis is not satisfying for investigating contexts that are human intensive as business processes are.

For sake of completeness another case study was considered for validating the proposed approach. The software system considered, named Jhotel (http://sourceforge.net/projects/jhotel/), is an open source application, written in Java, to manage and support the booking process of small and medium size hotel rooms. Once again, it was considered with the business process using it and the relationships of the software system components and supported business process activities are analysed.

Figure 9 shows the activity diagram of the business process supported by this software application. Results were assessed by the same metrics used in the first case study and a traceability matrix to link software system components and business process activities was obtained as

Figure 9. Model of the business process using JHotel

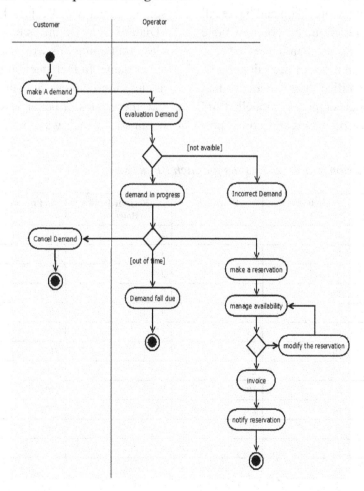

Figure 10.JHotel Processing Result: a fragment of the Traceability Links Map

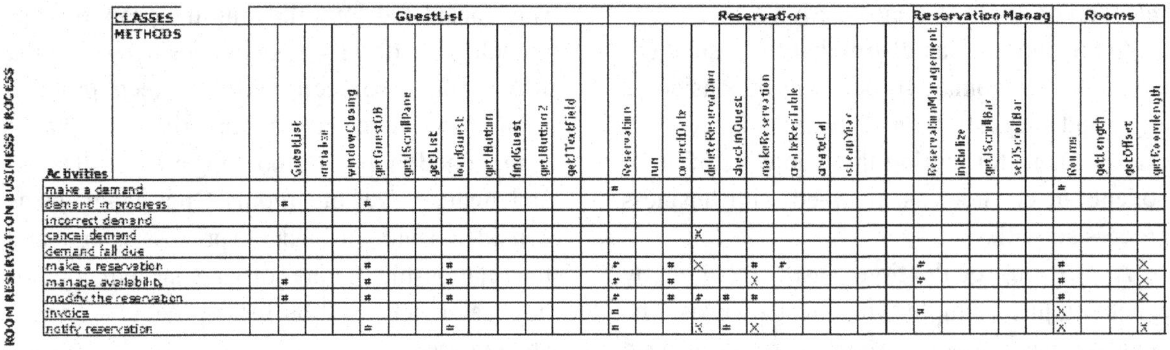

system output. For sake of space, just a portion of the traceability matrix obtained by using the presented approach and tool is shown in Figure 10. Even in this case, the 'X' symbol indicates the links that are not relevant, retrieved by the proposed approach, while the cells labelled with '#' represent the correctly retrieved links.

The evaluation of the precision and the recall with reference to an oracle are proposed in Table 2. In this case, better results than in the first case study were obtained in terms of precision index. This result can be justified by the evidence that the second system was completely modelled and implemented in terms of classes and a more pre-

cise naming convention was adopted by the software programmers. Another important element for the results obtained in the second case study regarded a second list of stop-words, which did not involve the business process identifiers but entailed the indexing process of the software system components. It was simply observed that some typical words, just like "Windows" or "Dialog" suggest the action performed by the class containing this words in

its name. In fact, deciding to discard, as prior assumption, classes whose name contained words like these ones, a better level of precision was obtained. In such way, it was also noticed that,

Table 2. JHotel Precision and Recall results for each BP activity

Activity Name	Relevant	Retrieved	Retrivied and Relevant	Precision	Recall
make a demand	4	6	4	66%	100%
demand in progress	4	6	4	66%	100%
incorrect demand	1	2	2	50%	100%
cancel demand	2	4	2	50%	100%
demand fall due	4	8	4	50%	100%
make a reservation	17	33	17	52%	100%
manage availability	10	14	10	71%	100%
modify the reservation	19	23	19	83%	100%
invoice	7	10	7	70%	100%
notify reservation	16	23	16	69%	100%
Total results				63%	100%

even if the number of the analyzed elements was superior than that one of the first system, the computational times was shorter.

In conclusion, it is reasonably possible to think that the introduction of a business process domain ontology and a software system ontology could significantly improve the obtained results in terms of precision and reduce the computational analysis complexity.

FUTURE RESEARCH DIRECTIONS

The authors will continue to search for additional evidence of the needs of this kind of methods and tools with additional studies also involving subjects working in operative realities.

A further field of investigation in the future is represented by the use of business process domain ontologies and software systems ontologies, as shortly described in the case study section. Business process ontologies represent a strong and efficient way to fully and completely represent business process concepts and their relationships. On the other side, a software system ontology can describe a hierarchical tree of software systems components, their relationship, and point out meaningful paths to be followed for investigating and discard no useful path or elements. In this way, the investigation on the traceability links could be improved as analysing the concepts trees, it is possible to identify dynamical paths and discover links that statically can't be revealed.

The field of Semantic Business Process Management (SBPM) (Filipowska et al., 2008) using ontologies for the representation of the static and dynamic aspects of an enterprise and value chains, is of great interest today in the business process community and many research community are interested to investigate about it (Hepp & Roman., 2007)(Markovic & Kowalkiewicz, 2008).

In the future authors' planned research, there is also a further investigation regarding other text processing tools. In this context, a comparison will be performed between the results obtained by using such processing tools and those obtained by applying the proposed approach and tool. This investigation could also suggest the integration of the described software tool with suitable open source software system. For example, text analysis and semantic annotation could be performed by using the open source software GATE (General Architecture for Text Engineering) (http://gate. ac.uk), that is supported by a large developer community and represents a standard de facto in the text processing problems. It is made of a large family of components, including a complete IDE (Gate Developer) for language processing bundled with widely used and standard Information Extraction system and a rich Java library. The GATE software provides a set of Java API to implement and manage very different types of documents and artefacts and process them. The future use of GATE would provide a greater flexibility degree in analysing different case studies in different domain.

CONCLUSION

Evolving software systems for satisfying requirements change needs requires the analysis and assessment of software documentation. A valid help for understanding software system functionality and requirement change requests can come from the analysis of the business process and its relationships with the used software system. Such a kind of relationships is actually traceability links and can be used for supporting software engineers when dealing with business process and software systems evolution.

The research described in this chapter is concerned with the use of information retrieval techniques to software maintenance and, in particular, to the problem of recovering traceability links between the business process activities and the components of the supporting software system. The introduced approach exploits both syntactic and semantic analysis.

The usefulness of the approach is discussed through two case study. The obtained results in terms of precision and recall encourage to continue investigating in the approach for including more complex analysis and understanding the influence of the practices used by the programmers participating in a project in the quantity and quality of results that can be obtained. For example, the success degree of a matching process strongly depends on the naming (convention) criteria adopted by software systems developers. This issue was experienced in the first case study presented in this chapter, where the software system supporting the business process was developed and implemented in different times and by different developers; the result was a misalignment in the naming convention and a greater difficulty in the text processing step using standard list of separators and stop words.

REFERENCES

Aversano, L., Bodhuin, T., & Tortorella, M. (2005). Assessment and Impact Analysis for Aligning Business Processes and Software Systems. In *ACM Symposium on Applied Computing* (pp. 1338 – 1343). ACM Press.

Aversano, L., Grasso, C., & Tortorella, M. (2010). Measuring the Alignment between Business Processes and Software Systems: a Case Study. In *Symposium on Applied Computing (SAC 2010)* (pp. 2330-2336). ACM Press.

Aversano, L., & Tortorella, M. (2009). Business Process-Aware Maintenance Task: A Preliminary Empirical Study. In *Software Maintenance and Reengineering (CSMR 2009)* (pp. 233-236). IEEE CS Press.

Basili, V. R., Caldiera, G., & Rombach, H. D. (1994). The goal question metric approach. In *Encyclopedia of Software Engineering*. Wiley.

Carvalho, R., & Sousa, P. (2008). (BISMAM): an holistic Model Leveraged on Misalignment and Medical Sciences Approaches. In *BUSiness/IT ALignment and Interoperability (BUSITAL 2008)*. Business and Information Systems Mis-Alignment Model.

Etien, A., & Rolland, C. (2005). Measuring the fitness relationship. *Requirements Engineering Journal, 10*(3), 184–197. doi:10.1007/s00766-005-0003-8

Filipowska, A., Hepp, M., Kaczmarek, M., & Markovic, I. (2008). Organisational Ontology Framework for Semantic Business Process Management. In *Australasian Conference on Information Systems (ACIS 2008)*.

Frakes, W. B., & Baeza-Yates, R. (1992). *Information Retrieval Data Structures and Algorithms*. Englewood Cliffs, NJ: Prentice-Hall.

Harman, D. (1992). Ranking algotithms. In *Information Retrivial: Data Structures and Algorithms* (pp. 363–392). Englewood Cliffs, NJ: Prentice-Hall.

Henderson, J. C., & Venkatraman, N. (1993). Strategic Alignment: Leveraging Information Technology for Transforming Organizations. *IBM Systems Journal, 32*(1), 4–16. doi:10.1147/sj.382.0472

Hepp, M., & Roman, D. (2007). An Ontology Framework for Semantic Business Process Management In *Wirtschaftsinformatik*, 2007.

Korherr, B., & List, B. (2006). A UML 2 Profile for Event Driven Process Chains. In *IFIP International Federation for Information Processing (Vol. 205*, pp. 161–172). Springer Verlag. doi:10.1007/0-387-34456-X_16

Markovic, I., & Kowalkiewicz, M. (2008). Linking Business Goals to Process Models in Semantic Business Process Modeling. In *12th International IEEE Enterprise Distributed Object Computing Conference* (*EDOC 2008*) (pp. 332-338). Washington, DC: IEEE CS press.

Papp, R. (2001). Introduction to Strategic Alignment. In Papp, R. (Ed.), *Strategic Information Technology: Opportunities for Competitive Advantage* (pp. 1–24). Hershey, PA: Idea Group. doi:10.4018/978-1-878289-87-2.ch001

Pereira, C., & Sousa, P. (2003). Getting into the misalignment between Business and Information Systems. In *European Conference On Information Technology Evaluation* (*ECITE 2006*)

Reich, B., & Benbasat, I. (2000). Factors That Influence the Social Dimension of Alignment Between Business and Information Technology Objectives. *Management Information Systems Quarterly*, *24*(1), 81–113. doi:10.2307/3250980

Thevenet, L., Salinesi, C., Etien, A., Gam, I., & Lasoued, M. (2006). Experimenting a Modeling Approach for Designing Organization's Strategies in the Context of Strategic Alignment. In *Australian Workshop on Requirements Engineering* (*AWRE 2006*).

Wieringa, R. J., Blanken, H. M., Fokkinga, M. M., & Grefen, P. W. P. J. (2003). Aligning application architecture to the business context. In *Advanced Information System Engineering* (*CAiSE '03*) (pp. 209–225). Springer Verlag, LNCS 2681.

Chapter 15
Inventory Management, a Decision Support Framework to Improve Operational Performance

Jan van den Berg
Delft University of Technology, The Netherlands

Guido van Heck
Accenture Consulting, The Netherlands

Mohsen Davarynejad
Delft University of Technology, The Netherlands

Ron van Duin
Delft University of Technology, The Netherlands

ABSTRACT

Enterprise Resource Planning systems have been introduced to support the efficient and effective execution of business processes. In practice, this may not fully succeed. This also holds in particular for inventory management (IM), which forms a part of supply chain management. Within this research, by analyzing the IM business process theoretically, eleven potential benefits are indicated. Next, by using a Business Intelligence approach, key performance indicators (KPIs) are selected to measure the performance of IM sub-processes. Integration of these approaches yields an IM performance decision support framework that can be used to obtain a generic, coherent picture of the fundamental IM processes in an organization. In addition, by tracking and analyzing KPI measurements, adequate decisions can be prepared towards the improvement of the operational IM performance. The proposed framework is validated using experts' opinions and a comparative case study. The experts' comments yielded a list of top-10 KPIs,

DOI: 10.4018/978-1-4666-1764-3.ch015

based on the measurements of which a set of quick wins can be determined. The case study results show that some of the identified potential benefits are also observed in practice. Future research may reveal that comparable performance improvements are possible in other IM environments (and even in other supply chain domains) based on similar decision support frameworks.

INTRODUCTION

Over the past decade, the Enterprise Systems (ESs) industry has proven to be an enormous growth market (Gable, 1998; Kumar & Van Hillegersberg, 2000). The broad adoption of ESs by the business world is sometimes considered to be the most important development in the corporate use of information technology during the 1990s (Davenport, 1998; Gable, 1998; Kumar & Van Hillegersberg, 2000). Related to this, the ES market has become a billion dollar market for quite some time already (Klaus et al., 2000; Umble et al., 2003). Annual growth rates up to thirty per cent as observed in the last decade illustrate the rapid growth and significant size of the current ES market. Enterprise Resource Planning (ERP) applications are an example of an ES. ERP packages usually aim to integrate the key business processes, a goal that is typically achieved based on suitable information technologies (Beheshi, 2006; Gupta, 2000; Wier et al., 2007). Consistent, correct and in-time information provision to all members of the organization can be considered as the key enabling characteristic of ERP systems next to the intensive automation of administrative activities. Modern ERP systems tend to include Business Intelligence (BI) functionality as well. To do so, data as available in their databases is usually collected in big data warehouses, then analysed and aggregated, and finally visualized to enable improved business decision-making.

The expectations of ERP are generally quite high: the vendors claim significant improvements in efficiency and effectiveness with their ERP packages (Johnson & Pyke, 2001). For example,

organising the internal logistics using ERP software is supposed to improve related business processes and, due to its integrated nature, to create better performance (Davenport, 1998): production times would be shortened, stock levels lowered, and customers' satisfaction enhanced. Improved performance in its turn is expected to yield higher returns and better competitive advantage. However, to what extent all these claims hold often remains unclear since only a limited number of researchers focused on expressing the benefits gained with ERP in precise quantitative terms (Hunton et al., 2003; Klaus et al., 2000).

Considering the currently available literature on the specific business processes related to inventory management (IM) (Hendricks et al., 2007), (Kleijnen & Smits, 2003), (Gunasekaran et al., 2001), (Fawcett et al., 2007), (Lee & Billington, 1992), we discovered that only a limited number of relevant metrics is mentioned. As an example, the well-known Balanced Score Card (BSC) (Kaplan & Norton, 1992) is sometimes used to create a business intelligence tool for monitoring different aspects of IM. However, a clear prescription or guide describing how to determine what precise metrics should be included in the BSC is not available. Besides the BSC, only limited attempts are made to structure performance measurement of inventories. The Supply Chain Council developed a supply chain performance measurement reference framework named SCOR (SCC, 2006) that provides some ideas about what to measure. Their framework typically takes a strategic supply chain perspective, which is not suitable for the operational measurement of IM. Furthermore some attempts have been made to structure the measurement of performance in terms of different levels (e.g., Gunasekaran et al., 2001). They made an attempt to structure performance metrics into three levels: strategic, tactical and operational. None of these literature references however provides a good overview of the coherence between different performance metrics and it seems that a BI-inspired framework through which this insight can be gained is highly needed.

Based on these considerations, we postulate that there is a need to develop a decision support framework that explains the coherence between the operational activities of a company, hereby focusing on the company activities related to IM (which implies that we do not consider the full supply chain). The framework should also include a set of the (most) relevant metrics to enable measuring of IM operational performance based on which decisions for performance improvement can be made.

The development of such a decision support framework concerns the principal objective of this chapter.

The structure of the rest of this chapter is as follows. The next section provides context information on ERP and IM. The third section presents the results of our theoretical analysis of the IM business process resulting into a basic set of potential ERP-based performance improvements. Section 4 describes the process of selecting Key Performance Indicators (KPIs) as the most promising measurement technique and identifies the KPIs relevant for IM. By integrating the information from the sections 2 till 4, section 5 introduces and illuminates the designed decision support framework in the domain of IM. Based on two cases our designed framework is validated in section 6. Section 7 offers a reflection on future research opportunities including a sketch of the generalization possibilities of the proposed framework, and the last section provides our conclusions.

ENTERPRISE RESOURCE PLANNING AND INVENTORY MANAGEMENT

In this section we elaborate on the above-introduced notions of ERP and IM with the aim of sketching a conceptual background picture. This picture will be used as starting point for our analysis and the following design and testing of the new decision support framework.

Enterprise Resource Planning

ERP packages are complex and comprehensive software solutions, incorporating a wide range of business activities. The concept that distinguishes ERP from other software packages is its aim to totally integrate all different business activities taking place within organisations (Beheshti, 2006). ERP software concerns standardized software, which means that it is generic and customization can be applied for many businesses types across different industries. ERP uses the concept of a totally integrated enterprise solution, across all parts of the enterprise. An integrated solution means that all business activities are integrated in one software solution: information does not have to be inserted and exchanged manually between different departments. A sales order for example almost automatically generates an invoice. When the invoice has been paid by the client the audit reports are immediately updated as well. All the generated information is real-time visible in ERP and transparent for the related departments.

A broadly agreed upon definition of ERP has not been fixed (Klaus et al., 2000). In this research the following definition has been adopted: 'Enterprise resource planning systems are configurable information systems packages that integrate information and information-based processes within and across functional areas in an organization' (Kumar & Van Hillegersberg, 2000). It is often promised that one ERP package can replace dozens of legacy systems. Figure 1 illustrates the

Figure 1. Enterprise software solutions in historical perspective: from non-integrated legacy solutions (left) towards contemporary ERP systems including additional BI software (right).

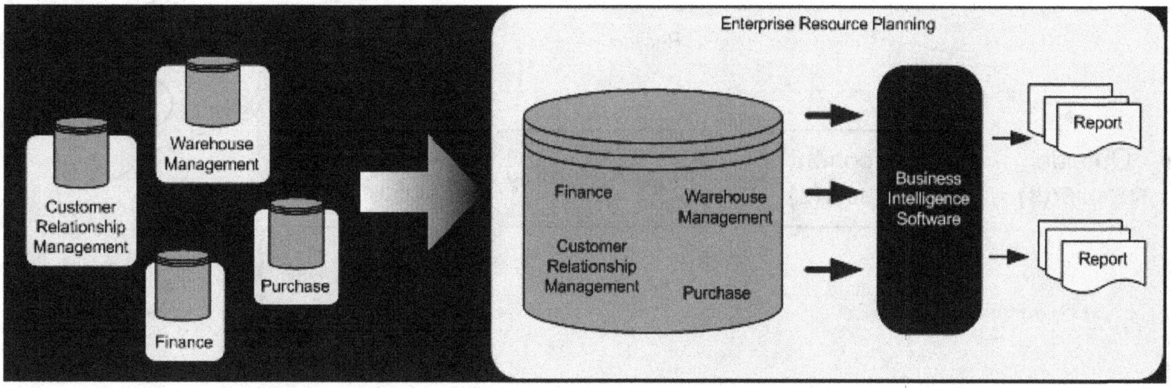

difference between traditional software solutions (where different software packages are not integrated) and the modern ERP solution. Because of its relevance, we explicitly projected the location of BI software tools in the latter.

Looking at the ERP developments in the last decade we observe a rise of extended ERP also referred to as ERP II or e-ERP. ERP traditionally looks into internal processes, whereas ERP II also looks further and uses the Internet. ERP II enables organisations to connect their internal business processes with the (external) systems of their customers and suppliers (Beheshti, 2006). ERP II aims to integrate internet-technology within ERP software in order to enable the exchange of information more easily, for example to coordinate the supply chain between different actors. The future of ERP II clearly includes a perspective in which many companies, customers and vendors are all linked together electronically (Weston Jr., 2003). For example in case of the supply chain management, information sharing plays an important role and therefore ERP II might offer a good tool to support operations across the supply chain. Information sharing could successfully solve all kinds of supply chain inefficiencies including the problems related to the infamous bullwhip effect (Lee et al., 1997).

In practice however, there are still several severe problems that currently block ERP II to becoming a success. Firstly most organisations are still struggling with their internal operations. For organisations to take full advantage of electronic exchange of information across the supply chain, they must ensure that their own ERP systems have already been implemented efficiently. If this is not the case, information sharing will only create up- and downstream problems at 'internet speed' (Búrca et al., 2005). Another huge challenge is the partnership challenge. Because there is usually no control over or access to partners' systems, relationships with business partners are of paramount importance (Búrca et al., 2005). This leads to the second argument why ERP II is not examined: ERP II adoption is currently still very limited. Strategic behaviour plays an important role at this point. Many organisations believe their own information is what gives them a competitive advantage and therefore organisations are hesitative in sharing it (Agrawal & Pak, 2001). Sharing knowledge among all business actors requires a paradigm shift and change of mentality in the economy, which has to take place first (Mohamed & Adam, 2005). These observations motivated us not to focus on ERP II in this research but to limit the focus to operation support based on 'classical ERP'.

Figure 2. Schematic overview of a supply chain.

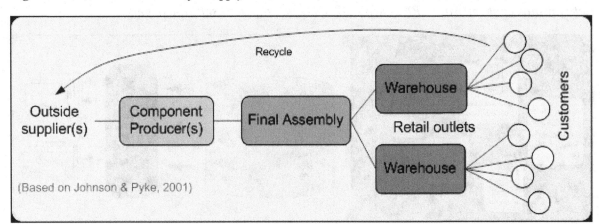

While limiting ourselves to the original ERP, it is remarkable that especially the ERP modules that support the role of organisations as partner in the supply chain have become popular over the past several years due to the fact that the interest and attention paid to supply chain management (SCM) has grown rapidly (Akkermans et al., 2003), (Gunasekaran et al., 2001). Actually, most companies have first reduced their manufacturing costs as much as practically possible, and they are now looking for other means to reduce their costs (Simchi-Levi et al., 2003). One way of doing so is by effectively and efficiently planning and managing their activities in the supply chain. Wal-Mart, Dell, and Cisco are successful example companies showing that good SCM can provide huge benefits. Because of the gains that can be made in SCM, especially when using ERP as the ERP-vendors claim, this has been the scope of this research: to provide more insight onto the gains an organization can achieve by optimising their (internal, company-specific) supply chain activities.

Supply Chain Management

Figure 2 provides a high-level view on an entire supply chain. As can be seen the supply chain reaches very far and therefore SCM incorporates a wide range of companies with different activities which depend on the specific company role in the supply chain. Amongst others, inventory management, manufacturing, operations management and logistic processes and planning all fall within the range of SCM. ERP packages originated from the automation of manufacturing, planning and controlling processes. Manufacturing can therefore often be seen as a core module of ERP packages, around which other activities are concentrated. Actually, most ERP packages that currently available on the market evolved from one core functionality to other business areas as well later on. SAP is a good example hereof, which started off with the finance and control of the production and materials requirements planning (MRP). Later on other activities were incorporated as well, such as human resource management and quality management.

ERP-vendors claim that their ERP-packages are able to support all specific activities of companies along the supply chain. In terms of information management and BI, ERP packages aim to support the information management. By providing intelligent business information, additional efficiency and effectiveness should be reached. ERP vendors also claim that their packages are not only able to support activities, but are also capable of achieving additional benefits

Figure 3. More detailed view on the assembly process.

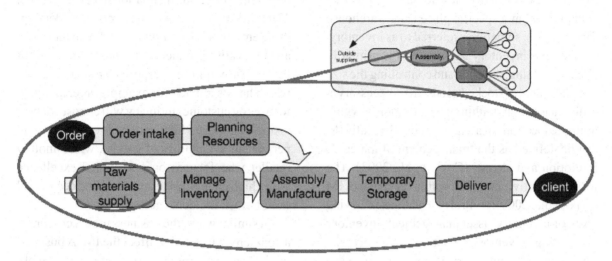

as was already mentioned. However where the exact benefits are and how it is possible to measure those in practice is still vague (Ifinedo, 2008). In other words, a good BI tool is still lacking. This research takes up the challenge to create a tool that can measure performance that, in addition, enables the validation of the claimed benefits provided by ERP packages.

Since SCM stretches out from suppliers to clients with a lot of operations in between, researching the performance of the complete supply chain was too comprehensive for this research project. Therefore the focus has been limited to a small part of SCM: Inventory Management (IM). Figure 3 provides a more detailed view on the typical sub-processes taking place during final assembly in a manufacturing firm. The picture provides a quick overview of the locations where inventories are kept during manufacturing. Typically several different inventories exist, namely, those for raw materials, those for (un)finished products and those for work in process. Like Figure 3 shows, storage of raw materials and finished goods takes place at the beginning and the end of the manufacturing process. During the production, semi-finished products have to be stored occasionally as well; those are called 'work in process inventories'.

This research focuses only on the inbound, the IM of raw materials located at the beginning of the production process. The reasons for this choice are elaborated upon in the next section.

Moreover, the focus of this research took an internal perspective, looking at just the benefits realised in IM due to an ERP implementation. This perspective refers to benefits to be gained in one company while ignoring issues like IM costs and the structure of the costs.

There are many different ERP packages on the market. Assumed benefits of ERP might therefore vary for different packages. Due to time constraints it was not possible to look into all ERP packages. For two reasons, only SAP software is considered in this research. Firstly, SAP claims to be market leader implying that the results of this research apply to the many users of this software (Das, 2006). Secondly, SAP has been chosen due to the comprehensive experience and knowledge at hand about this software.

Inventory Management

'Inventory' and 'stock' are often used to relate to the same thing (Wild, 2002). Yet when the notion of IM is used, there is a slight difference with stock. Stock is usually an amount of goods that is being kept at a specific place (in a warehouse for example), sometimes referred to as inventory. Conversely, inventory *management* is primarily about managing, ordering and controlling the size and placement of stocked goods. IM is necessary at different locations within an organisation or within multiple locations of a supply chain. Basically IM can be defined as the 'management of materials in motion and at rest' (Coyle et al., 2003). The following activities all fall within the range of IM (Wikipedia, 2009): control of lead times, carrying costs of inventory, asset management, inventory forecasting, inventory valuation, inventory visibility, future inventory price forecasting, physical inventory, available physical space for inventory, quality management, replenishment, returns and defective goods and demand forecasting.

IM basically serves two main goals (Reid & Sanders, 2007). First of all good IM is responsible for the availability of goods. It is important for running operations that the required materials are present in the right quantities, quality and at the right time in order to deliver a specific level of service. The second goal is to achieve this service level against optimal costs. Not all items can be held in stock against every cost and therefore choices have to be made. So the main question becomes: *what is the optimal amount of stock to maintain?* Unfortunately, the answer to this question is not unequivocal and always depends on specific business conditions like the chosen corporate strategy, the used business model, and the applied stock prediction method. The most determining factor is the corporate strategy (Dijk et al., 2007) which is fixed by the management. Treacy et al. (1993) and Dijk et al. (2007) define three different key strategies, the first one of which is operational excellence: companies following this strategy aim to offer good quality products against the lowest possible prices. The second strategy concerns customer intimacy: firms operating according to this principle constantly adjust their products to meet the requirements of their clients, in this way

building up an enduring relation with their clients. The third strategy strives for product leadership: these enterprises try to stand out due to their new and innovative products. The choices made in IM have to fit within the corporate strategy chosen, which has its impact: for example, a retailer who focuses on customer intimacy will choose for provision of goods at high service levels (including permanent availability of goods), while another retailer who focuses on operational excellence with a high quality/price ratio may find occasional out-of-stock incidents acceptable.

In similar ways, the business model chosen by a company will usually affect the IM. A business model here concerns the way of operation. (Hoekstra & Romme, 1991), (Dijk et al., 2007, p.38) discriminate four basic types: (*i*) make-to-stock where products are manufactured regardless the orders placed by clients, (*ii*) deliver-from-stock where (usually many different) products are delivered from the stock, (*iii*) assemble-to-order where products are assembled from components based on the desired configuration of the client, and (*iv*) make-to-order where products are only produced on (customers') demand. It is easy to understand that a chosen business model will usually strongly affect the IM approach.

Finally, we would like to mention the impact of the chosen stock level calculation method, which includes the corresponding order-time interval. The literature with respect to these calculation methods is too rich to mention all the references here. Therefore we proceed with the description of the main rationale behind these methods. The point at which new items are ordered is important for good stock control. This point is crucial, because ordering too early could cause overstocking which unnecessarily creates costs, whilst ordering too late may cause a certain item to become out of stock and may cause missed sales. The simplest way to manage a stock would be to use a minimum and maximum stock level. A minimum has to be set in order to create a buffer against the various uncertainties that exist (Coyle et al.,

Figure 4. The five main inventory business process steps.

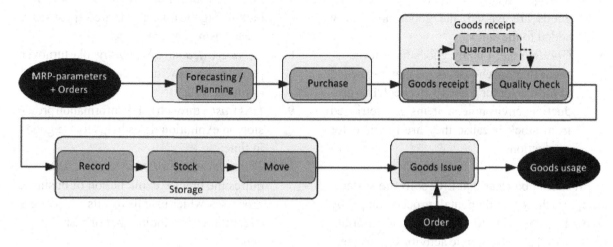

2003). A maximum is set to ensure that not too much stock is kept. Once the minimum level has been reached, items have to be reordered until the maximum is reached again. In practice however it mostly takes a while before ordered goods are actually delivered, therefore a 'review level' is also necessary to ensure that the stock will not fall under the minimum level (Wild, 2002). The review level makes sure that goods are ordered before the minimal level is reached, in such a way that the ordered goods are delivered 'just-in-time' (Van de Klundert, 2003), i.e., when the stock approaches the minimum level. If the review level is reached, items are ordered and, due to the delay, they will be delivered just at the point where the stock level is at its minimum. The minimum stock forms an ultimate buffer to cope with uncertainties.

Having sketched the characteristics of and developments taking place around ERP software, the relationship to SCM, and that to IM more in particular, and having illuminated various dilemmas related to determine the best IM approach for a company, it is now time to analyze in detail the basic inventory business process based on which ERP-supported potential performance improvements can be determined. This very important step will be set in the next section.

POTENTIAL PERFORMANCE IMPROVEMENTS

In order to get a precise picture of what a typical inventory business process entails, literature was reviewed and analysed, and interviews were conducted with experts (Van Heck, 2009). As a result, five main process steps were considered to be key processes in IM: (see also Figure 4)

- *Forecasting*: Forecasting forms the first process step and is necessary to anticipate on future demand in order to maintain a continuous production or service level. Forecasting forms the input to scheduling and planning (Coyle et al., 2003).
- *Purchase*: There are various theories about how purchases should be performed. Here a purchase is viewed as a good being ordered.
- *Goods Receipt*: When new goods arrive at the stock's location, several checks take place. Firstly, the price and quantity are compared to the purchase-order to see whether the delivered quantity and price match. For some materials, the quality is also checked before adding the goods to the stock.

- *Storage*: When all checks for received goods are passed, the goods are finally added to the stock.
- *Goods Issue*: Finally goods have to be issued. In a warehouse, items may be picked to fulfil an order placed by a client. In a production environment, items are retrieved from stock because they are required for production.

It should be clear that ERP software systems support these fundamental process steps by providing facilities to store data and information related to the concrete activities performed. Based on this conceptualisation of the inventory business process, a precise analysis was executed to identify activities that contain possibilities for improving performance:

1. *Improved material resource planning:* the assumption is that ERP software (containing crucial data related to all business processes) can enable better planning of the manufacturing process which includes better forecasts of material resources needed;
2. *Better supplier contracts registration:* effective material purchase from large numbers of vendors requires precise vendor registration (again ERP software can help);
3. *Assign approved suppliers:* suppliers that have shown to meet certain quality standards can be approved as reliable, which can speed up future transaction making with them;
4. *Advanced real-time budget control:* ERP can easily support the application of hard, real-time restrictions on client budgets;
5. *Improved 'three-way-match':* this concerns easy-to-do checks concerning the ordered goods, the receipt goods, and the invoice;
6. *Better supplier reliability monitoring:* this can be applied in order to select new approved suppliers (see above under (3)) and to keep track of their subsequent quality performance;

7. *Improved inventory turnover visibility:* monitoring the time goods are kept at stock is easy using an ERP system;
8. *Enhanced dead stock visibility:* like turnover periods, slow moving stock can be monitored easily as well;
9. *Less waste:* through better information provision on expiration dates helps to use goods in time;
10. *Better handling of rush orders:* ERP requires the precise explicitation of business processes, which usually results into process streamlining, including that of rush orders, and
11. *Less faults through the use of master data:* master data concern data that are centrally stored in an ERP system and can easily be accessed by all kinds of actors in the IM process, if needed.

Figure 5 visualizes the activities by mapping them on the inventory business process steps they relate to. The eleven potential benefits have been validated with the help of some experts working in the field of logistics (Van Heck, 2009).

The eleven points identified actually form *hypotheses* for the potential IM performance improvements due to the use of an ERP system. We consider them as a key result of our research since - due to our fundamental analysis - they seem to hold for any IM process. At the same time, the identified inventory process activities with potential performance improvement are rather concrete. So we expect them to be usable in many practical cases. However, to be able to test their usefulness, a suitable performance measurement technique needs to be selected as well: this selection is executed in the next section.

MEASURING PERFORMANCE

Adequate and reliable measuring of explicitly defined performance is critical for achieving the

Figure 5. The eleven inventory process activities with potential performance improvement.

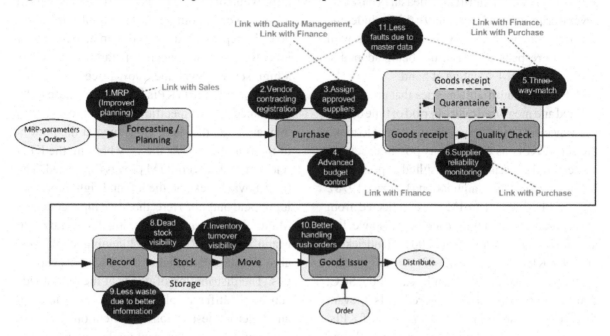

goals set by top-management (Fawcett et al., 2007) and for evaluating changes made to the business. In order to design a measurement tool, a suitable measurement technique has to be selected first. A literature study has been carried out to search for existing methods that might be suitable. In total six important techniques were identified, namely:

1. *Key Performance Indicators* (KPIs) (Rockart, 1979; Bullen & Rockart, 1986);
2. *Balanced Score Card* (BSC) (Kaplan & Norton, 1992);
3. *Return on Investment* (ROI) (Goor & Weijers, 1998; Jones, 2009; Waal, 2002);
4. *Net Present Value* (NPV) (Png & Lehman, 2007);
5. *Critical Success Factors* (CSFs) (Pairat & Jungthirapanich, 2005; Bullen & Rockart, 1986; De Waal, 2002);
6. *Supply Chain Operations Reference-model* (SCOR) (SCC, 2006).

Looking at these techniques, the Balanced Score Card (BSC) of Kaplan is a well-known method. It is occasionally used to create a BI tool for monitoring different aspects of Inventory Management (IM). However, we did not found a clear prescription in literature how to determine the type of metrics to be included since the application of these metrics need to be adjusted to companies specifically.

The disadvantage of ROI and NPV is their purely financial nature, which is too limited to measure performance (Kleijnen & Smits, 2003). Because CSFs are mainly qualitative, they are also considered as less applicable in this case.

The SCOR framework provides some (too) general ideas about what to measure across the complete supply chain, and is for this reason not particularly suitable for IM. Furthermore, some attempts have been made to structure performance measurement in terms of different categories (Neely et al., 1995) or levels (Goor & Weijers, 1998), but again, these approaches are not well applicable in the context of IM (Van Heck, 2009).

Therefore, at the end, Key Performance Indicators (KPIs) have been selected as performance metric to be used, most importantly due to their ability to provide quantifiable measures based on several criteria (Van Heck, 2009): this includes the requirements of being very flexible to work with and, with respect to measuring, being adaptable to the specific IM situation at hand.

KPIs are quantifiable metrics that are usually defined and measured over a period of time or during a specific time interval. In an attempt to make the set of KPIs as complete as possible, several sources and experts were consulted as prescribed by the idea of data triangulation (Denzin, 1978). First, KPIs relevant to IM were collected from various sources of literature including (Fawcett et al., 2007; Gunasekaran et al., 2001; Hendricks et al., 2007; Kleijnen & Smits, 2003; Van de Klundert, 2003; Neely et al., 1995; Krauth et al., 2005; SCC, 2006). In total around one hundred KPIs relevant for IM were listed. From this long-list of KPIs, the most suitable KPIs have next been selected as basis for the creation of the new decision support framework. This selection was done based on a mapping of the KPIs to the different process steps as shown in figure 4, on literature, and on expert-judgments (Van Heck, 2009). The finally selected KPIs are described in the next section, as part of the new IM performance decision support framework.

IM PERFORMANCE DECISION SUPPORT FRAMEWORK

Based on the above-introduced business process steps taking place in IM and the KPIs referred to in the previous section, an overall framework for optimising IM has been designed. It is actually the result of a literature review, scoping of KPIs, and expert judgements, and many more details that can be found in (Van Heck, 2009). The resulting *IM Performance Decision Support Framework* is visualized in Figure 6. The framework provides a structured way of measuring the performance of IM based on which decisions for performance

improvement can be prepared. It can be viewed top-down or bottom up. At the top of it the main goal is represented: optimal management of inventory, which concerns a trade-off between a high service level and a low price. Going one level lower, specific KPIs are shown. These KPIs are linked to the specific business process step they are related to (and are shown at the bottom of the framework). At the very bottom, the KPIs relevant to the overall IM process are listed. The (dark) oval blocks on the left and right represent inputs and outputs. Here, the MRP input concerns Material *Requirements* Planning that, contrary to Manufacturing Resources Planning mentioned above, incorporates human and machinery capacities. The distribution of goods at the output side can be to different places, i.e., to both internal and external destinations. As mentioned before, the blocks on top represent goals that need to be achieved by good IM. The blocks in the middle represent the main processes: within each main process one or more sub-processes take place.

By going from left to right, we can discuss the other dimension of the framework concerning the five IM business process stages (sub-steps) and related KPIs.

1. Problems with forecasting can lead to too much stock (yielding unnecessary higher costs) or to too little stock (negatively affecting the service level). Delivery times should be incorporated in the forecast to cope with latency of delivery. As was described above, both the forecasting interval and the forecasting accuracy are important determinants of the forecasting accuracy, which explains their selection as KPI at this stage.

2. At the purchase step, the order lead times, order cycle times and frequency of delivery are metrics that may cause problems further on in the process if these numbers start to increase. If the order lead times and order cycle times are increasing, it may mean that

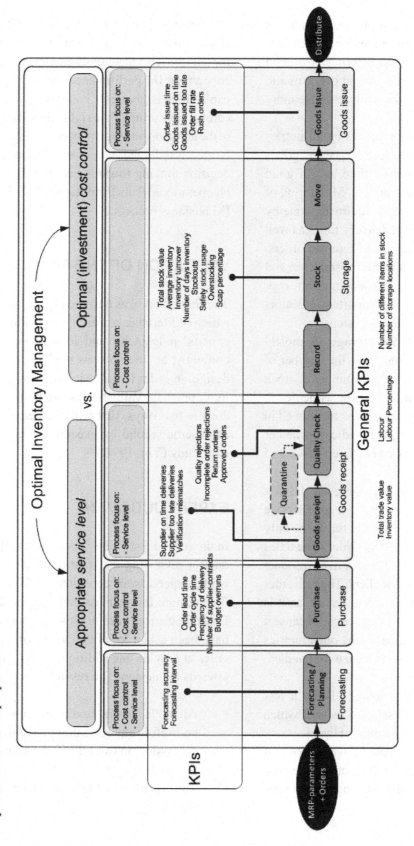

Figure 6. The IM Performance Decision Support Framework showing the dilemma between providing an appropriate high service level versus high cost control. By measuring the KPIs for the five different IM sub-processes and the overall IM process, decisions for IM performance improvement can be prepared.

the goods are delivered later and the stock is already depleted. These metrics are therefore strongly related to the offering of a good service level, whereas budget overruns and the number of vendor-contracts have more to do with costs.

3. At the goods receipt process step, all metrics concern the service level. Whether goods are being delivered on time and in good quality are the main drivers. Monitoring of supplier performance is indirectly done by checking (in)correct delivery times as well as the number of approved/returned orders. In addition, the number of mismatches and rejections (due to either incompleteness or insufficient quality) are important indicators of performance in this sub-step.

4. The metrics related to storage are mostly concerned with costs. Only the number of days of inventory and the number of stock outs are metrics influencing the service level. The metrics at this process as mentioned in figure 6 should together indicate whether the amount of stock kept is effective and efficient.

5. In the final process step, the goods issuing part, the focus is on offering a good service towards the client. Actually this is the only focus of this process step. Order issue times indicate how long it takes to deliver a product that was ordered by the client. The rush order metric has a more external nature, as it is interesting to monitor this metric, because it may negatively influence the other metrics if too much rush orders have to be handled.

Next to the sub-steps' related KPIs, a few general KPIs have been selected as well which relate to the overall performance of the inventory business process. They relate to overall costs of the IM process and include BI metrics like total trade value, inventory value, and number of storage locations.

For many more details we again refer to (Van Heck, 2009), where it is also further explained how the selected KPIs match with the eleven hypotheses concerning IM performance improvement. That explanation is, above all, based on the idea that by careful measuring of the right KPIs, the visibility of the inventory management business process can be greatly enlarged. This enables better, BI-based decision making towards better performance of all operational (sub-)activities taking place in the IM business process.

VALIDATION OF THE FRAMEWORK

The framework was designed based on a combination of literature research, experts' interviews, experts' judgement, and logic reasoning. Accordingly, an attempt was made to validate the design, in order to judge its usability and validity in practise. Validation of the framework was done in two ways, first with the help of a group of experts, second by executing a comparative case study (Yin, 1994).

EXPERT JUDGMENT

In the second test with experts, next to the initial one for reviewing the 'first draft' of the framework, experts were consulted to reflect on the final design: four experts with experience in the field of logistics/inventory management and ERP have been asked to reflect on the framework in order to provide one additional validation check towards the design. The results are as follows:

- All KPIs in the model are considered to be useful (although there have been some discussion on two KPIs that might measure the same thing);
- The list of 33 KPIs was considered to be very long.

Table 1. Potential quick wins: top-10 of most important KPIs

Process Step	KPI number	KPI description
Forecasting	7	Forecasting accuracy
Forecasting	8	Forecasting interval
Purchase	9	Order lead time
Goods receipt	14	Vendor on time deliveries
Goods receipt	15	Vendor too late deliveries
Goods receipt	16	Verification mismatches
Quality check	17	Quality rejections
Quality check	19	Return orders
Goods issue	32	Order fill rate
Goods issue	33	Rush orders

In an ERP environment this may not be a problem (because once an SQL query is available, it can be used again and again), but in a less integrated environment, the calculation of many KPIs may become difficult. For this reason, a TOP-10 was constructed. The TOP-10 list of most important KPIs has been summarized in Table 1, together with the IM sub-process they belong to. These top-ten KPIs combined can be very useful and might serve as a good starting point for IM performance management evaluation, e.g., to detect a set of 'quick-wins'.

Comparative Case Study

In the second, more elaborated test, the framework was applied in two case studies performed in the health care sector. The reasons for choosing this domain are obvious: currently, the Dutch government demands hospitals to work effectively and efficiently, meaning that they have to be competitive against predefined fares and other hospitals. For this reason, budgets are under pressure and hospitals are seeking for means to reduce costs. This also holds for IM in hospitals. The case studies were conducted at two different hospitals. Hospital A does not use ERP, but Vila software for purchase and logistics and SAP FI/CO software at finance. Hospital B uses ERP software (i.e.

SAP SRM, SAP MM and SAP FI/CO) to support purchase, logistics and finance respectively. Both privatised hospitals are medium-sized and classified as non-academic. The operation excellence strategy dominates at both hospitals: their aim is to offer excellent care against the lowest costs. Both a qualitative and a quantitative comparison were performed.

Qualitative comparison: using interviews with purchasers and logistics managers the processes taking place at each hospital were mapped and compared to each other using pattern matching (Yin, 1994). Several differences between the hospitals have been observed. In the ERP case, the *forecasting process* was fully automated via an internal web-application (as a part of SAP SRM), whilst in the non-ERP case, a lot of work had to be done manually, a labour-intensive job requiring more personnel and, as a consequence, more money. To illustrate our way of working, we here show in Figure 7 (as an example) a visualization of the differences at forecasting.

Looking at the *goods receipt sub-process*, the check between the purchase order and the delivered goods takes place automatically in hospital B. Also the invoice is automatically compared to the delivered goods (i.e. numbers/items). No manually checking takes place at this point any-

Figure 7. Comparing sub-steps of the IM business process: differences at forecasting.

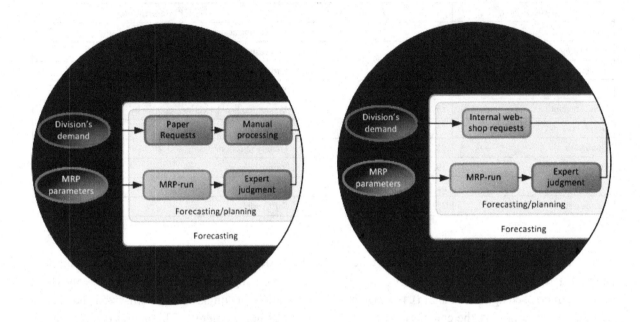

more, whereas in hospital A, faults are occasionally made and have to be repaired (at high costs).

Looking at *goods issue sub-process*, in hospital B not only pick-lists were generated by SAP, but also the routing is taken into account. This saves work for the people working at the warehouse.

Quantitative comparison: to start, relevant data about each KPI have been collected. Unfortunately, not all KPIs could be measured exactly. In those cases, the KPIs were assessed by experts who work in the corresponding inventory department. Data collection was difficult but in the end it was managed for all KPIs, except for the ones from the storage process. Using these metrics, an attempt has been made to *evaluate the eleven potential ERP benefits* identified earlier (see Figure 5). Only slight differences were found. The data pointed out that possibly three of the eleven potential benefits are actually achieved, namely:

1. Improved MRP (improved forecasting/planning);
2. Automatic restricting of approved suppliers;

3. Improved three-way-match (between purchase order, packing note and invoice).

An important remark should be made at this point: due to the limited amount of data this is only an indication and more research is required to further validate the framework and test the potential benefits. In general it was found that in the hospital with ERP, far less people were concerned with inventory management although handling a much bigger volume of goods in relation to the other hospital. For this reason, the ERP-hospital has to operate in any case more efficiently (even if relevant KPIs are not measured at all).

To further illustrate our way of working in the quantitative comparison, we here show *part* of the big table containing metrics data:

In addition, based on the quantitative analysis executed in the two hospitals, many recommendations concerning IM performance improvement could be formulated for the two hospitals. This mainly concerns recommendations with respect to many operational IM activities in both hospitals, some of which can be easily automated using

Table 2. Comparing performance data of the two hospitals (only part of the data is shown).

Metric	Value in hospital A	Measured/ Assessed	Value in hospital B	Measured/ Assessed
Case specific metrics				
Number of beds	386	M	449	M
Number of personnel	1,511	M	2,075	M
Number of personnel (fte)	1,017	M	1,642	M
Number of specialists	117	M	154	M
General metrics				
1. Total trade volume	€ 108,267,000	M	€ 154,720,646	M
2. Inventory Value	0.35%	M	1.07%	M
3. Personnel	Total: 20.4 fte Purchase: 4.6 fte Warehouse: 16 fte	M	Total: 19 fte Purchase: 10 fte Warehouse: 9 fte	M
4. Personnel percentage	53.4%	M	11.4%	M
5. Number of different items in stock	Sterile: 448 Non-sterile: 1490	M	Sterile: 250 Non-sterile: 800	M
6. Number of storage locations	2 (sterile/non-sterile)	M	2 (sterile/non-sterile)	M
Forecasting				
7. Forecasting accuracy	95.0%	A	100.0%	A
8. Forecasting interval	Weekly	M	Daily	M

appropriate ICT tools. Examples of the latter include the adoption of online ordering for all hospital departments, digitally checking of the match between goods ordered and goods received, and optimized routing calculations for goods being delivered. Actually most of the ICT tools needed to implement these recommendations are available in current ERP systems (Van Heck, 2009). In any case, all recommendations should be evaluated taking into account the existing dilemmas between optimal service levels and optimal cost control.

FUTURE RESEARCH DIRECTIONS

The research executed may be considered as a first since our scope limitation towards IM has been quite strict. Below, we therefore sketch some potentially interesting future research directions.

Generalization Opportunities

The framework has been used to analyze ERP-based IM performance within the healthcare domain based on which certain suggestions for improvement could be formulated. It seems quite interesting to know whether the framework can also be applied in other domains. Using the framework to evaluate IM is presumably no problem, because in other organizations like a production company or grocery store, the same five main basic inventory sub-processes take place. Actually most of the literature we have seen focuses on a production environment and thus a lot of the collected KPIs are supposed to be valid for production companies as well. Of course, the precise outcomes (benefits) in those environments might be different, for example, due to other business strategies or other business models that are being applied.

Another interesting topic for further research would be to broaden the scope towards other parties in the supply chain. As the introduction argument, the focus of this research is on IM at a single organisation only: it might be very interesting to research the applicability of this model in a full supply chain. It would be a challenge to get a performance decision support framework in place for most actors in the supply chain at stake, and to analyse what can be achieved by letting the different actors align their activities. Of course, this challenge is no sinecure and, in order to be successful, requires agreement on an underlying supply chain-wide business model in which all the related actors would have to participate.

A third opportunity for extending the use of the framework lies in its possibility to test other technologies as well. In this research the framework was used to validate hypotheses concerning the IM improvements using ERP technology. Yet it is quite well possible to use the framework for studying the effects on IM (or other supply chain activities) as enabled by other technologies. The steps that were taken in this study to evaluate the impact of ERP can be formulated in the following, more general terms:

- Formulate hypotheses about the impact of a certain technology on the performance of a certain business process;
- Describe what KPI(s) should be selected to measure potential performance improvements;
- Measure all KPIs;
- Reflect on the outcomes, test each hypothesis, and come up with suggestions for activity changes that improve operational performance.

Following these steps it is supposed to be possible to investigate the effects of other technologies. As an example, the effect of the use of the Radio Frequency Identification (RFID) (IEEE, 2007) on the supply chain performance can be considered.

The framework currently focuses on measuring and analyzing operational performance. Further research might be aimed at finding a detailed method to aggregate the results and, therewith, to create a dashboard to support performance improvement decision-making at tactic and strategic level.

The current version of the decision support framework makes explicit the fundamental dilemma between optimal service levels and optimal cost controls. This basic dilemma should be elaborated in more detail in order to give more reliable suggestions for performance improvement measures. Especially the notion of return-on-investment (ROI) is key here and it seems natural to extend the current set of IM KPIs with metrics that enable the calculation of ROI for different IM scenarios, i.e., for different sets of possible IM measures. This would also include an additional dimension to the framework: measurement over time.

A final extension to mention here concerns investigating external factors, especially the human factor in more detail. This was left outside the scope of this research, but human experience can certainly influence the measures of the model in a drastic way. Finding a way to standardize this influence would make comparisons between organisations more reliable and, in general, would provide more insight.

Practical Business Cases

The above-given generalization opportunities are quite generic and still somewhat theoretical. It is also interesting to describe what the practical use of the current decision support framework might be. First of all, one of the things a consultant can achieve is giving a client more insight into his/

her business, for example, by extracting relevant IM performance data from the clients' ERP (or similar) system and to aggregate these data into information that is published in (control) reports. In a more advanced approach, the framework might be used to analyse the available data and to put relevant information aggregated from it into a dashboard for real-time, operational monitoring of the IM process of a client.

Additionally the framework might be used during the commercial activities of a consultancy firm. The TOP-10 of most important KPIs for instance might form an interesting trigger for a client to allow the implementation of the full framework or the execution of a performance scan which incorporates all KPIs from the framework.

Finally, the framework might very well be applicable at all types of clients with IM performance problems. Actually, the possible range of clients that can profit from a type of decision support framework like this, is supposed to be quite large. On the other hand, for the organisations that have already reached a certain maturity level towards the use and implementation of their ERP-software, the proposed framework is probably less interesting, because they might already have some kind of performance measurement dashboard in place. The framework will especially help organisations that have a lower maturity level with respect to ERP use and performance measurement.

CONCLUSION

The aim of this research has been to develop a decision support framework for improving IM performance. As a concrete result, such a framework has become available. The framework incorporates a set of metrics to evaluate performance based on which a coherent view on and performance of IM processes in all kinds of organizations can be induced. In more detail, we conclude that the

new decision support framework has the following advantages:

- Based on the business process approach applied, a coherent set of metrics has been designed and structured into one overall framework.
- The framework clearly describes the stages of the inventory business process, which PKIs should be measured at each stage to enable both evaluation of its performance and doing suggestions for performance improvement measures while having in mind the fundamental dilemmas between optimal service level and optimal cost control.
- A top-10 of most relevant metrics has been defined based on which companies interested in finding quick wins can easily start using a simpler performance management approach.
- Due to the span of the framework, different actors involved are represented. This characteristic makes sure that the focus is not just on a single sub-process, input, or output, but that, instead, the interests of all IM stakeholders are taken into account.

From the case studies performed, it may be concluded that the framework provides a practical tool for making standardised comparisons between IM situations. The designed framework matches with practice and it turned out that all metrics proposed are valuable and relevant. Despite of the limited testing of the framework, the obtained measurements suggest that certain performance benefits can be expected in case (integrated) ERP software is in use.

More research is needed to fully validate the framework and to discover under which conditions and to what extent performance benefits are consistently present, by just applying the proposed decision support framework in other IM cases. Other suggestions focus on ideas about widening the scope, for example, towards other operational activities in the supply chain, towards other business levels (tactic and strategic level), or towards adoption of an extra dimension in the framework (by introducing additional metrics for calculating of ROI of performance improvement measures). The latter suggestions, of course, require some adaptations of the decision support framework that we have pioneered with in this work. The currently very popular research domain of 'global supply chains' might provide an interesting challenge for extending the framework: the goal to be achieved would be to realize, in a way analogous to our analysis and design, global supply chain performance improvements for (all) partners linked in such a supply chain, most probably based on new upcoming data sharing technologies like RFID, e-ERP, XML and Web Services (Tan et al., 2011).

REFERENCES

Agrawal, M. K., & Pak, M. H. (2001). Getting smart about supply chain management. *The McKinsey Quarterly*, *2*, 22–25.

Akkermans, A. H., Bogerd, P., Yücesan, E., & Wassenhove, L. N. v. (2003). The impact of ERP on supply chain management: exploratory findings from a European Delphi study. *European Journal of Operational Research*, *146*, 284–301. doi:10.1016/S0377-2217(02)00550-7

Beheshti, H. M. (2006). What managers should know about ERP/ERP II. *Management Research News*, *29*(4), 184–193. doi:10.1108/01409170610665040

Bullen, V., & Rockart, J. F. (1986). A Primer on Critical Success Factors. In Bullen, C. V., & Rockart, J. F. (Eds.), *The Rise of Managerial Computing: The Best of the Center for Information Systems Research* (pp. 383–423). Homewood, IL: Dow Jones-Irwin.

Búrca, S. d., Fynes, B., & Marshall, D. (2005). Strategic technology adoption: extending ERP across the supply chain. *Journal of Enterprise Information Management*, *18*(4), 427–440. doi:10.1108/17410390510609581

Coyle, J. J., Bardi, E. J., & Langley, C. J. Jr. (2003). *The Management of Business Logistics: A Supply Chain Perspective* (7th ed.). Cincinnati, Ohio: South-Western/Thomson Learning.

Das, S. (2006). *SAP Holds Top Rankings in Worldwide Market Share for SAP(R) Business Suite Applications*. Retrieved June 22, 2009, from http://www.reuters.com/article/pressRelease/idUS87519+30-Jul-2008+PRN20080730

Davenport, T. H. (1998). Putting the enterprise into the enterprise system. *Harvard Business Review*, *76*(4), 121–131.

de Waal, A. A. (2002). *Quest for Balance, The human element in performance management systems*. Chichester: John Wiley & Sons Ltd.

Denzin, N. K. (1978). *Sociological Methods: A Sourcebook*. New York: McGraw Hill.

Dijk, E. v., Leeuw, S. d., & Durlinger, P. (2007). *Voorraadbeheer in perspectief: Zeven invalshoeken van het vak*. Deventer, The Netherlands: Slimstock B.V.

Fawcett, S.E., Ellram, L.M. & Ogden, J.A. (2007). *Supply Chain Management: From Vision to Implemention*. New Jersey: Pearson Education, Inc.

Gable, G. G. (1998). Panel Discussion. In B. Edmundson and D. Wilson (Eds.), *9th Australasian Conference on Information Systems*. Sydney: NSW.

Goor, A. R. v., & Weijers, S. J. (1998). *Poly Logistiek Zakboekje*. Arnhem, The Netherlands: PBNA.

Gunasekaran, A., Patel, C., & Tirtiroglu, E. (2001). Performance measures and metrics in a supply chain environment. *International Journal of Operations & Production Management, 21*(1/2), 71–87. doi:10.1108/01443570110358468

Gupta, A. (2000). Enterprise resource planning: the emerging organizational value systems. *Industrial Management & Data Systems, 100*(3), 114–118. doi:10.1108/02635570010286131

Hendricks, K. B., Singhal, V. R., & Stratman, J. K. (2007). The impact of enterprise systems on corporate performance: A study of ERP, SCM and CRM system implementations. *Journal of Operations Management, 25*, 65–82. doi:10.1016/j.jom.2006.02.002

Hoekstra, S., & Romme, J. H. (1991). *Integral logistic structures: developing customer-oriented good flow*. London: McGraw-Hill.

Hunton, J. E., Lippincott, B., & Reck, J. L. (2003). Enterprise resource planning systems: comparing firm performance of adopters and nonadopters. *International Journal of Accounting Information Systems, 4*(3), 165–184. doi:10.1016/S1467-0895(03)00008-3

IEEE. (2007). About IEEE, Technologies, Emerging Technology Portal - RFID. Retrieved on October 22, 2009, from http://www.ieee.org/portal/site/emergingtech/index.jsp?techId=864.

Ifinedo, P. (2008). Measuring Enterprise Resource Planning (ERP) Systems Success: A Structural Equation Modeling Approach. In J. Cordeiro, Y. Manolopoulos, J. Filipe, P. Constantopoulos (Eds.), *Enterprise Information Systems: 8th International Conference* (pp. 86-97), Springer-Verlag, Berlin Heidelberg.

Johnson, M. E., & Pyke, D. F. (2001). Supply Chain Management. In Harris, C., & Gass, S. (Eds.), *Encyclopedia of Operations Research and Management Science*. Boston, Massachusetts: Kluwer Academic Publishers. doi:10.1007/1-4020-0611-X_1022

Jones, B. (2009). *Balanced Scorecard Tower: a framework for comparing IT investment against business benefits*. Unpublished Master's thesis, Delft University of Technology, The Netherlands.

Kaplan, R. S., & Norton, D. P. (1992). *The Balanced Scorecard, Measures that Drive Performance. Harvard Business Review, 71*. Boston, MA: Harvard Business Publishing.

Klaus, H., Rosemann, M., & Gable, G. G. (2000). What is ERP? *Information Systems Frontiers, 2*(2), 141–162. doi:10.1023/A:1026543906354

Kleijnen, J. P. C., & Smits, M. T. (2003). Performance metrics in supply chain management. *The Journal of the Operational Research Society, 54*(5), 507–551. doi:10.1057/palgrave.jors.2601539

Krauth, E., Moonen, H., Popova, V., & Schut, M. C. (2005). Performance Measurement in Control and Logistics Service Providing. In C.-S. Chen, J. Filipe, I. Seruca, J. Cordeiro (Eds.), *Proceedings of the Seventh International Conference on Enterprise Information Systems (ICEIS2005)* (pp. 25-28), Miami, USA.

Kumar, K., & Van Hillegersberg, J. (2000). ERP Experiences and Evolution. *Communications of the ACM, 43*(4), 22–26. doi:10.1145/332051.332063

Lee, H. L., & Billington, C. (1992). Managing Supply Chain Inventory: Pitfalls and Opportunities. *Sloan Management Review, 33*, 65–73.

Mohamed, M., & Adam, F. (2005). ERP II: Harnessing ERP Systems with Knowledge Management Capabilities. *Journal of Knowledge Management Practice, 1* (2). Retrieved january 19, 2011, from http://www.tlainc.com/articl91.htm.

Neely, A., Gregory, M., & Platts, K. (1995). Performance measurement system design. *International Journal of Operations & Production Management, 15*(4), 80–116. doi:10.1108/01443579510083622

Pairat, R., & Jungthirapanich, C. 2005. A chronological review of ERP research: an analysis of ERP inception, evolution, and direction. In *Proceedings of 2005 IEEE International Engineering Management Conference* (pp. 288-292), St John's, Newfoundland & Labrador, Canada.

Png, I., & Lehman, D. (2007). *Managerial economics*. Malden, MA, USA: Blackwell Publising.

Reid, R., & Sanders, N. R. (2007). *Operations Management: an integrated approach* (3rd ed.). New York: John Wiley & Sons.

Rockart, J. F. (1979). Chief executives define their own data needs. *Harvard Business Review*, *57*(2), 81–93.

SCC (2006), *Supply-Chain Operations Reference-Model, Plan, Source, Make, Deliver*, SCOR Model Handbook v. 8.0, Cypress: Supply-Chain Council.

Simchi-Levi, D., Kaminsky, P., & Simchi-Levi, E. (2003). *Managing the Supply Chain: The Definitive Guide for the Business Professional*. New York: McGraw-Hill.

Tan, Y.-H., Bjørn-Anderson, N., Klein, S., & Rukanova, B. (Eds.). (2011). *Accelerating Global Supply Chains with IT-Innovation, ITAIDE Tools and Methods*. Berlin, Heidelberg: Springer-Verlag. doi:10.1007/978-3-642-15669-4

Treacy, M., & Wiersema, F. (1993). Customer intimacy and other value disciplines. *Harvard Business Review*, *71*(1), 84–93.

Umble, E. J., Haft, R. R., & Umble, M. M. (2003). Enterprise resource planning: implementation procedures and critical success factors. *European Journal of Operational Research*, *146*(2), 241–257. doi:10.1016/S0377-2217(02)00547-7

Van de Klundert, J. J. (2003). *Supply Chain Management en Technologie*. Unpublished Technical Report. Venlo, The Netherlands: Mateum/Universtiteit Maastricht.

Van Heck, G. F. N. (2009). *Inventory Management: Performance Measurement, Designing a Framework to Assess Inventory Management's Performance*. Unpublished Master's thesis. Delft University of Technology, The Netherlands. Retrieved 18 January 2011 from http://www.tbm.tudelft.nl/live/pagina.jsp?id=70163a1a-37c1-4f78-8cb0-50653874a96b&lang=en, #104.

Weston, F. D. T. Jr. (2003). ERP II: The extended enterprise system. *Business Horizons*, *46*(6), 49–55. doi:10.1016/S0007-6813(03)00088-0

Wier, B., & Hunton, J.E. & HassabElnaby, H.R. (2007). Enterprise Resource Planning & Non-Financial Performance Incentives: The Joint Impact on Corporate Performance. *International Journal of Accounting Information Systems*, *8*(3), 165–190. doi:10.1016/j.accinf.2007.05.001

Wikipedia. (2009). *Inventory*. Retrieved January 21, 2011, from http://en.wikipedia.org/wiki/Inventory

Wild, T. (2002). *Best Practice in Inventory Management* (2nd ed.). Oxford: Butterworth-Heinemann (imprint of Elsevier).

Yin, R. K. (1994). *Case Study Research: Design and Methods* (2nd ed.). Beverly Hills, CA: Sage Publishing.

Chapter 16
Automation of the Approval and Control Process of Documents

Rui Pedro Figueiredo Marques
ALGORITMI, Universidade do Minho, Portugal

Henrique Manuel Dinis dos Santos
Universidade do Minho, Portugal

Carlos Alberto Lourenço dos Santos
Universidade de Aveiro, Portugal

ABSTRACT

Traceability systems, including the approval and control of documents, are increasingly assuming a pivotal role in the workflow of information across an organization and they can be classified as an element of any internal control system at the organizational context which contributes for a continuous auditing and helps to manage and minimize organizational risk. RFID (Radio Frequency Identification) is a technology that can enable the development of architectures which provide an adequate response to this requirement of internal control. Thus, this chapter, as main objective, raises awareness of the importance of these systems in an organizational environment. Moreover this chapter's objective is to propose a modular and flexible solution which simultaneously traces, monitors, and searches the flow and location of documents in an organization, using RFID technology.

INTRODUCTION

Traceability systems of documents have been increasingly critical to ensure an efficient document management in an organizational environment and consequently an essential internal control system. Thus these systems are contributing for a continuous auditing as a tool to help manage

and minimize organizational risk. This type of systems is an important asset for organizations where the documents have a high value and where the temporary or permanent loss of documents has negative impacts on the organization (Marques, Santos, & Santos, 2010).

A business process can involve different actors and can be seen as a set of activities formalized by a set of actions and procedures. In general, there is a sequential order between the activities and,

DOI: 10.4018/978-1-4666-1764-3.ch016

for example, an activity can start only when other activities have been concluded. In these activities some paper documents can be produced from some offices and/or signed from the person in charge. For example, legal, administrative, financial and government business processes are characterized by paper documents, and it is difficult to follow and locate all these documents during their management. In addition, they and their correlations with other documents can be lost (Bodhuin, Preziosi, & Tortorella, 2006). Thus, Bodhuin et al. (2006) consider that a control of the causal relations of paper documents and their flow could represent a way for improving the organizational business.

In addition, Marques et al. (2010) affirm that in the definition of documental control function and in the identification of the respective responsible it is common to meet the required document cycles and their verification. Thus, associated with the business processes of any organization there is a set of documents that requires monitoring so that you can have access to all orders and information about them formally drawn up and so that you can clearly identify employees who carried out operations as well as their efficiency on that (Marques et al., 2010).

Moreover, the approval and control of documents can be identified as an essential component of an internal control system even because this definition is supported by some legislation, regulation and other standards, such as ISO/IEC 27001:2005, ISO 9001:2000 and some official charts and plans of accounting refer the necessity for control of documents.

Any type of organization (public or private) can benefit from the adoption and use of traceability systems for documents, for example hospitals or other health institutions, government offices, bookshops, libraries, law or accountancy firms, and other organizations with large volume and flow of documents (Marques et al., 2010). Easily we can find very common everyday scenarios in organizations which clearly demonstrate the necessity

of an efficient document management. Just as an example (Bodhuin, Preziosi, & Tortorella, 2007):

- An accounting office is obliged to keep payment receipts, faxes, invoices and other paper documents for a given number of years, in accordance with the current body of legislation;
- Staff's private information (e.g., curricula, contracts) are stored and their access must be mandatorily secure;
- Some administrative procedures have to follow a given bureaucratic course to be concluded. A sequence of operations or given orders often have to cross a certain number of places and people, and some users could need to know the state of these procedures before taking their decisions.

With reference to the traceability, management and control of state and location of paper documents several rewards emerge, such as: reduction in the number of errors and fraudulent and irregular operations with consequent economic advantages, additional meticulous ability for scheduling, planning and making decisions, reduction of time for performing a business process and more control on a business process. These organizational advantages are possible because the documental management allows to check whether certain documents were properly and timely made, verify who took which document, detect whether a document is outside of the defined and/ or authorized circuit within organization and whether a given document suffers an interruption or delay (Bodhuin et al., 2006, 2007; Marques et al., 2010).

Besides satisfying the requirements of the internal control system, an organization which adopts a system of traceability and management of paper documents saves time and money by reducing the document search time and diminishing the financial and legal impacts associated to the loss of documents or the omission/ delay of necessary and required operations in the usual circuit of such documents in an organization. Thus the system enables you to hold those who cause any delays or failures in documents in crucial procedures responsible. Moreover, it allows you to monitor and subsequently obtain statistical data to enable the optimization of the document flow in an organization. In addition, the adoption of a document traceability solution increases the transparency of bureaucratic procedures of the organization (Marques et al., 2010; Puliafito, 2006).

In this chapter we are focusing on the use of RFID (Radio Frequency Identification) systems for traceability of documents, assigning a specific identifier to physical documents (Lopresti & Nagy, 2005). This new identifier will distinguish a document from all the remaining and will monitor the location and its circuit across an organization. The integration of RFID technology into an organizational information system combined with a whole set of procedures (consistent with the requirements of usability predetermined when designing the information system) can underpin a system of traceability, monitoring and search for documents since it allows you to assign an identification and a memory unique to each document, and thus control its circuit within an organization (Marques et al., 2010).

The main objective of this chapter is to present the architecture of a functional and viable solution applicable to the traceability, monitoring and search for paper documents at any organization using RFD technology suggested by Marques et al. (2010). So that the implementation of the proposed architecture becomes a reality, we need to convince organizations about the importance of such solutions and additional work of applied research in a specific organizational context. Therefore, this chapter intends essentially to raise awareness of the importance of the traceability systems, including control and approval of documents, in an organization.

This chapter is structured as follows: in the next section a brief discussion traceability and monitoring of documents including some definitions and

brief reviews are given in order to demonstrate the importance of this topic in organizational environments; after that, a modular solution is presented, one that allows you to trace, validate, monitor and search for documents at an organization, constituting thus the proposed functional architecture also addressing some security details. Then, a methodology for implementation and evaluation of the proposed solution and the future research directions in this subject are given. Finally, the last section presents the authors' conclusions about this theme.

BACKGROUND

The previous section of this chapter shows how important it is for an organization to implement a system which is able to trace, control and manage paper documents, since they still represent the core of some organizational processes for their legal value and the need to manage and keep them. Hence, some researches and studies have been made in order to meet this need.

The technology of radio frequency identification, commonly known as RFID, can have an important and crucial role in the development of systems for management, approval and monitoring of documents, and thus control its circuit within an organization (Marques et al., 2010). Bodhuin et al. (2006) affirm that RFID is a capable technology for addressing the questions related with traceability and monitoring of documents and bringing new benefits to the organizations having business processes where the circulation of documents is very important. In addition, the same authors added saying that, however, there are not as many applications based on this technology for document management which can prove this opinion.

Radio Frequency Identification (RFID) is a non-contact, proximity based, automatic identification and information technology that indentifies and locates objects attached with RFID tags which are devices that contain a unique identifier and information. In the scenario of management of paper documents, the identification and memory allocated to the documents correspond to the identifier and the ability of non-volatile memory of the RFID tags, which are attached to the document.

An RFID system includes three components: a tag or transponder located on the object to be identified; an interrogator (reader), which may be a read or write device; and an antenna which emits radio signals to activate the tag and read/write data to it. The use of RFID technology for documents traceability is justified as it presents a set of very favorable advantages compared to other identification technologies (e.g. bar code). The main advantages of using this technology are (Sybase, 2006): no need line of sight for communication between tag and reader; and depending on the RFID tag type used, it is possible to benefit from the tag memory capacity to provide the document with very useful information, for example data of its creation, approval, notes about their circuits across the organization and data about the users responsible for the operations made in the document. In addition to these advantages, which distinguish the RFID technology, there are various types, shapes and sizes of pluggable tags on documents which allow different functional options. The identifier of the tag (and therefore the document which carries it) can be a vehicle to obtain more information about the documents in other sources (e.g. database).

However, the RFID technology has emerged in various organizational applications to meet the various needs and its potential applications are vast. It is already widely deployed in such diverse application areas such as: transportation, railway transport monitoring, livestock identification, highway fees and charges, anti-counterfeiting, tracing and monitoring of different types of goods and services, optimization of logistics processes, supply chain automation and optimization, security systems and protection counterfeiting, control of temperature and pressure, among others (Fer-

nando & Abawajy, 2009; Gupta & Joseph, 2006; Li & Chen, 2009; Marques, 2008; Sybase, 2006).

As example of a system which allows to monitor, control and manage paper documents we can present the proposal of Bodhuin et al. (2007). This research study discusses how the RFID can create value in an organization and describes the RFID service defined for supporting document management. They state that this service aims at monitoring paper documents, with special attention to their circulation in addition to the activity flows in order to capture further information about them and improve the knowledge of who manages, carries out and uses the organizational business processes and, consequently, offers an advantage to its business. This proposal consists in the verification of the location, the flow and the state of documents using RFID antennas attached to the desks and in other some strategic points of the offices.

Marques et al. (2010) states that traceability systems of documents may use passive tags like RFID smart labels operating at high frequency - 13.56 MHz - and mobile or fixed readers according to its application. This type of technology already supports standard protocols on the market (such as ISO/IEC 15693:2000), has a lifespan of more than 10 years, a low cost, and can be rewritten about 100,000 times (DAILY RFID CO., 2009). Bodhuin et al. (2006) as ubiquitous computing experts also confirm that RFID passive tags are the ones more compliant to the intended goal and they decided to use passive tags to monitor paper documents.

As already mentioned, there are not many applications based on RFID technology for document management to evaluate and conclude whether this type of proposals is sustainable and effective. Notwithstanding, Marques (2008) did a research study in which he designed a solution to identify, manage the use and control the flow of tools and equipment used in a metal factory for plastic items manufacturing in order to improve and optimize the traceability of this equipment and tools, using

RFID technology. The architected solution presumes the placement of RFID tags in equipments and tools which are intended to monitor and trace. It uses a mobile terminal that has attached a RFID reader and antenna to communicate with RFID tags. In turn, the mobile terminal incorporates the necessary features to synchronize in real-time the current data to a central database. This solution can also be classified as an internal control system since it is endowed with mechanisms that can manage locations and states of equipment and trace its flows. This solution is similar with the one presented in the next section of this chapter because every change of location and/ or state of given equipment is registered in database and in tag memory. Thus, it is possible to know in real-time the location and the state of every equipment within the factory. A prototype system was developed in a real manufacturing environment, and the results were quite satisfactory because it has shown that RFID technology enables the improvement of traceability and monitoring of equipment and can be used as an internal control system.

FUNCTIONAL ARCHITECTURE FOR A SOLUTION OF TRACEABILITY, MONITORING AND SEARCH FOR DOCUMENTS

This section intends to present a modular and flexible solution which was suggested by Marques et al. (2010) as one which allows you to trace, validate, monitor and search for documents in an organization.

Therefore, the solution presented in this chapter can be classified as a traceability system which allows control and approval of documents and consequently as an internal control system that can support organizational continuous auditing.

The architecture proposed for this solution (Figure 1) distinguishes itself by actuating in two areas: monitoring and validation, and search for documents. Since both areas have a common a database, it is possible to trace the flow and the entire life cycle of documents circulating in an organization with main focus on the stages and operations of each of the areas mentioned, since the entry/ creation of the document in the organization until its archive in storage space (Marques et al., 2010).

Figure 1. Architecture of a control solution, validation and search for documents

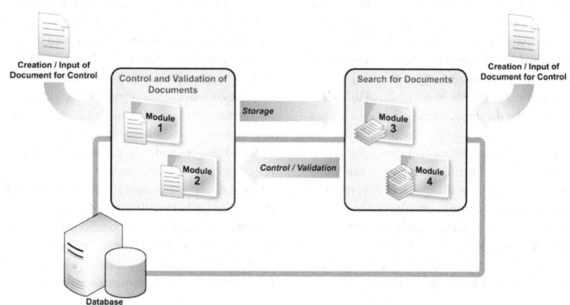

Furthermore, this solution presents for each of its main areas modules that execute the operations and the stages of the corresponding areas. Modules 1 and 2 described below are designed to monitor and validate documents which are generated or input into an organization and have a circuit with assessments and/ or validations to be performed. Modules 3 and 4, also presented below, are intended to search for documents in a storage space.

In Figure 1 we can see the circuit of a document that is received or created in an organization and initially goes through a process and a set of validation and control operations, being subjected to the procedures of modules 1 or 2. After control and validation, the document may be archived, and in this situation, when you need to search for the location of the document, modules 3 or 4 can be used, depending on the amount of storage space and the amount of stored documents. In the module of monitoring and validation, the choice of the module to be used (module 1or module 2) depends on the type of document, the type and quantity of validations, approvals and assessments which is submitted. The choice of the module 3 or 4 in the area of searching for documents depends solely in the dimensions of the storage space. With the descriptions of these modules below it is easier to differentiate them and to infer which one is the best choice for each possible situation.

The first operations executed when documents are created or input into the organization are the actions related to the placing of the RFID tag in the document and to the registration of this association in the database. These operations are the responsible to give a unique identification within the organization to each document. This identification will provide the control and a validation of the document in its life cycle. In the proposed solution, these operations are planned as ones of the procedures of validation and control modules - module 1 or 2 (Marques et al., 2010).

Alternatively to the circuit described above, after the document has been created in or input into

the organization, its life cycle can be initiated by a temporary archive and then submitted to validation and control. In this situation the search modules (modules 3 or 4) are the first to be used and then the control and validation modules (modules 1 or 2). After monitoring and validation, the document can be re-stored. In this situation, the placing of the RFID tag in the document and the registration of this association in the database must be made when creating the document or when inputting it into the organization. This demonstrates the feasibility and modularity of the solution presented regardless of the type of circuit made by documents in the organization.

The proposed solution (architecture shown in Figure 1), allows a modular and flexible usability. Hence, it can be necessary to use only some of the modules depending on the specificity and the type of document in question. Namely the adoption of the modules depends solely on the circuit of this document within the organization and the operations that documents will be subjected to (control and/or search). Moreover, each module can exist isolated; however, there may be combinations of modules or even all modules, which together represent a complete solution that simultaneously traces, monitors and searches for documents in a particular organization (Marques et al., 2010).

In addition to several individual modules described below, Marques et al. (2010) propose that some mechanisms must be implemented in order to automate the monitoring of the physical flow of documents within an organization in order to increase control over the document location, minimizing the risks caused by loss of documents due to user error. Thus, it is suggested the placement of RFID readers and antennas in some strategic doors/ gateways within an organization. Then, when a document goes through these strategic points, the database will be updated automatically with the current document location. That is, it is possible to get an idea of the macroscopic physical location of the documents in the organization and their flows based on information received on the

RFID readers and antennas placed on the defined strategic points. The objective of this mechanism is not to create redundant information about the location of the documents but to make it possible to compare this data with that derived from the various modules described below, and find operational unconformities and, in certain way, audit the modules of control, validation and search.

Description of Module 1

Module 1 belongs to the area of monitoring and validation of documents and Marques et al. (2010) designed it to be used to control the documents that have a life cycle with multiple staging points, and in each of them there are operations which are performed possibly by different people.

The architecture of this module (see Figure 2) requires that when a document is created or input into an organization, it will be attached to one RFID tag that will follow it through its life cycle. The user who creates or receives this document will have access to a computer with an RFID reader connected to it. At this stage with

the support of an application developed for this purpose, the user will read the tag and associate its identifier with the identification number of the document they want to trace. This association will be registered in a database, and from that moment on, the document has a unique identifier and a memory which can be used to store information about operations drawn up on it.

Each bit of memory will be associated with a staging point belonging to the document circuit. When the document is in one of these staging points, the bit that corresponds to it will be activated and the database will be automatically updated accordingly. This operation is left to the users of the system who are in each of the staging points of the document circuit (Marques et al., 2010).

The monitoring of the document flow is done by evaluating the bits of the tag memory reserved for this purpose. This operation can be done at anytime and any place or situation. Simultaneously, at each point of the circuit, you can also give an indication to the database if the document was or was not validated at this point, and more

Figure 2. Architecture of module 1

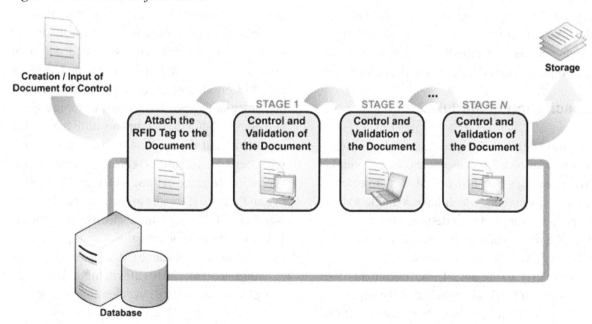

information may be added if necessary (e.g. user, date, time, type of validation in the case of more than one type of validation at the same point, etc). Simply map the tag memory to make possible specific bytes of memory to be allocated to certain staging points. Hence, only a simple query to the database may have information about the present state of a certain document (Marques et al., 2010).

When an operation at some staging point is only possible to be carried out after the completion of operations of previous staging points, the system application with the RFID reader should examine the bits of the memory tag to allow or not this operation in accordance with the document history. It demonstrates the importance of having two sources for data storage (the database and the tag memory), which enables you to verify the state of a document not only by queries to the database but also by analyzing the tag memory which is attached to the document.

If the application to this solution possesses the appropriate validation rules, it will be possible to prevent an operation from being carried out before the preceding and mandatory ones have been duly performed (Marques et al., 2010).

Figure 2 shows module 1 in the solution depicted in Figure 1 in a specific situation. This representation refers to the situation where the document is validated and controlled in multiple staging points soon after its creation or input into the organization and only then will it be archived.

Description of Module 2

This module also belongs to the area of monitoring and validation of documents and is very similar to the previous one; however, this is projected to control documents which have a single validation whereas module 1 is designed to control and validate documents with a circuit with multiple points of validation and control.

Similarly to module 1, the documents will also have an RFID tag attached at the beginning of their life cycle. Likewise, the identifier of this tag will be responsible for establishing the relationship between the document and its record in the database.

When the document gets the expected validation, the user will order the writing on the tag, where the user who validated the operation and eventually the date and time of validation will be registered. At the same time in the database it will be registered that this document was controlled and validated. It is also possible to register this information (user, date and time of validation) in the database. This repetition is not at all redundant since deterioration in the tag attached to the document can occur, being the historical data of document in this way safeguarded in the database (Marques et al., 2010).

Description of Module 3

Module 3 belongs to the area of search and Marques et al. (2010) designed it to allow the search for documents in a small or medium sized archive.

As in previous modules, tags are attached to documents and this association is registered in the database, in case these operations have not been implemented.

In this module, a search for a document begins with a query to the database, searching for the requested document in order to obtain the identifier of the RFID tag associated with that document. With the tag identifier and using a portable terminal which contains an RFID reader and antenna the user moves to the storage space and goes through the documents until having the indication that the document which has the tag with the desired identifier is in the read range. This is possible because in these situations the mobile or handheld RFID reader allows the user to know whether a RFID tag with a specific identifier is in its communication range. Thus it is possible to diminish the area of search (Marques et al., 2010).

Marques et al. (2010) affirm that this module can also be optimized, accelerating the search process. Thus, to achieve this optimization, it is proposed that it is necessary to divide the storage space in matrix form. When you search for a document in the database, you will be informed of what cell in the matrix, which represents the storage area, contains the document. After this, we use the mobile RFID terminal to search for the document within the limits of the cell matrix (this matrix had its origins in the division of storage space) indicated by the database.

Note that this module is not resilient to premeditated or accidental change, deposit or withdrawal of documents of their initial location without registration in the database. Hence, the automation of the traceability of the physical flow of documents becomes very important. Its implementation happens by placing RFID readers in some strategic doors/ gateways within the organization, as explained above.

In an attempt to reduce the number of abnormal situations, the access to storage areas can be controlled by biometric mechanisms (e.g. fingerprint) to control deposits, withdrawals and changes of document locations within those areas, increasing the security and integrity of data (Marques et al., 2010).

Description of Module 4

This module also belongs to the area of search and Marques et al. (2010) designed it to allow the search for documents in large dimension storage spaces.

In the proposed architecture for this module the storage space is divided in matrix form, and each of its cells contains an RFID antenna, which covers the entire cell area. The multiple antennas are connected to a reader (note that one reader may have associated multiple antennas to it, depending on the number of connectors it has). As for the reader, it is connected to the server which contains the database via a CAN (Controller Area Network) bus (Marques et al., 2010). The architecture of this module is depicted in Figure 3.

The search for documents is done using an application connected to the database. The user gives an indication of the desired document and then a signal will be sent to the readers to search for the document. As for the readers, they verify if the document was detected by any antenna connected to it. The user will be informed of which antenna (which represents the location) detected the document. When we take it after having the antenna area, the process is similar to module 3 within that storage area (area covered by the antenna which detected the desired document) (Marques et al., 2010).

As implicitly stated in the description of the modules, the presented solution needs an application connected to the database to make the management of traceability of documents. Besides the main functionalities for the deployment of the solution, the front-office of this application may also offer a set of queries and reports. These queries and reports turn the proposed solution into

Figure 3. Architecture of module 4

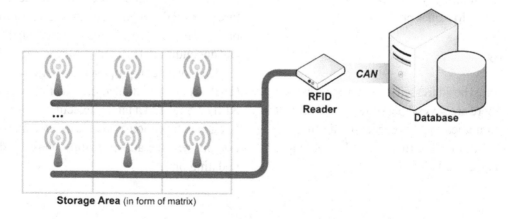

Storage Area (in form of matrix)

a document management system. Marques et al. (2010) gave examples of some of these queries and reports:

- Document location;
- Current and historical data about the document state and location;
- Inventory report and location;
- Real-time stock;
- Documents inserted in the system during a certain period of time;
- Documents out of the storage area;
- List of items removed in a specific period of time;
- List of items which were created but were never at the storage area and/or validated;
- Report of the missing documents (not removed from the system, but that do not appear anywhere in the storage area);
- List of all documents in a specific location;
- List of operations/ validations and flow of documents and the related responsible user;
- Activity report for a certain document or set of documents in a specific period.

However, the availability of each of these functionalities depends only on the modules adopted by the organization, because some of these functionalities need data provided by a specific module or by multiple modules. Thus, adopting all modules or, at least, one of each area, it is possible to have all presented functionalities becoming their utilization a very potential tool for organizational continuous auditing, in this case, in documental management (Marques et al., 2010).

Security

Security must be addressed in this solution as well because there are several possible attacks against RFID communication that can jeopardize its reliability (Gandino, Montrucchio, & Rebaudengo, 2010; Langheinrich, 2009).

Song and Mitchell (2009) stated the following attacks against RFID communications which have compromised the tag information privacy as well as the tag location privacy:

- Tag impersonation: an attacker can impersonate a tag to a server without knowing the internal data of tag.
- Server impersonation: an attacker can impersonate an authentic server to a tag using knowledge of the tag internal state. For example, the attacker can request the tag to update its internal state so that no other server can communicate successfully with the tag, except the attacker.
- Replay Attack: messages sent between server and tag can be replayed without being detected.
- Man-in-the-Middle (MitM) attack: messages sent between a server and a tag can be changed by the attacker, for example inserting, modifying or deleting data.
- Denial-of-Service (DoS) attack: messages transmitted between a server and a tag can be blocked.
- Backward and forward traceability: an attacker might be able to trace past transactions and future transactions respectively between a server and a compromised tag using knowledge of the tag internal state.

Thus, we suggest the use of the protocol presented in (Alomair, Lazos, & Poovendran, 2010) which provides a successful communication between RFID reader and tag and mitigates security threats to RFID communication. The proposed protocol is shown to achieve unconditional secrecy and unconditional integrity (Alomair et al., 2010).

This protocol proposed by Alomair et al. (2010) enables mutual authentication between an RFID reader and a tag by executing four phases: a tag identification phase, a reader authentication phase, a tag authentication phase, and a key updating phase.

At first, each tag is loaded with an identifier A and a secret key composed of five subkeys, i.e. K = (ka; kb; kc; kd; ku). The security is ensured by the ability of the reader to convey a random nonce to the tag in an authenticated and secret way.

When an RFID reader interrogates a tag, it responds to the reader with its identifier A. The reader looks up the database for the key K corresponding to the current identifier A. Then, the reader generates a random nonce n. With kb, kc, and n, the reader broadcasts messages to the tag while the tag verifies the integrity of the reader.

In the following phase, the tag is authenticated by its ability to extract the nonce n from the reader messages. After the authentication of the reader, a bitwise XOR operation is applied to n and kd and the tag broadcasts a message with the result of this operation. After receiving this message, the reader is able to check the message and to validate the tag. Otherwise, the communication is aborted.

Finally, after a mutual authentication between the RFID reader and the tag, the parameters are updated for the next communication. In this phase, the reader and the tag update the key K and the tag identifier A. The parameters for the next authentication run are updated at the reader, at the tag and at the database according to a set of rules and operations defined in the protocol implementation using the parameters of the current authentication run. With the update procedures and the randomness nature of the generated nonces, we have different parameters in each mutual authentication run. Therefore, the adversary will have difficulties to obtain meaningful information to attack.

FUTURE RESEARCH DIRECTIONS

This chapter presents a conceptual architecture for a feasible solution but there has not been the opportunity and the ability yet to develop and implement the proposed architecture in its entirety and in the context of approval and control of documents; however, the practical results expected prove to play a crucial role in the organizational internal control and consequently an efficient tool for continuous auditing. Moreover, there are already reports of other studies with developed prototypes and tested in a real environment which were explained above and which prove the viability of RFID in the traceability of items and search for location, similar to the modules in this work.

Therefore, we present in this section methodology of deployment and evaluation for the proposed system, because we know that the deployment of proposed solution should be one of the first steps in future research directions.

A user-centered design and research typically follows an iterative cycle which comprises some fundamental processes, in which we understand, study, design, build and evaluate the solution (Harper, Rodden, Rogers, & Sellen, 2008). The previous sections of this chapter have contents that fit in the first three stages of the iterative cycle – understanding, study and design stages. In fact, this chapter contributes to the recognition of the documents control/ validation problem and to the formulation of objectives for this type of solutions.

The methodology intended for the fourth stage (building stage) of this solution consists in the construction of prototypes. Bonner and Schaik (2004) use the terms low- and high-level and define a high-fidelity prototype as one where all or most of the functionality and often the form of the interface is fully represented. We think that the best type to prototype the system at the organizational context is a high-fidelity prototype. At first the development of this prototype will go through the deploying of each module separately during a certain period of time. Then, after evaluating each module separately, we should gradually implement different combinations of modules until we have all modules implemented. To validate the effectiveness of the proposed solution, we suggest using different types of documents with different cycles within the organization and in different types of organizations.

The evaluation (fifth stage of the user-centered, five-stage design/research model) should be made in the prototype deployments since it is easier to understand the impact of the solution in a real context rather than in labs. Nonetheless, before the first deployment, in the early stages, some lab studies should be carried out to evaluate the technological feasibility and to solve the technological issues. Evaluation is needed and very important to determine if the solution objectives are accomplished. We suggest evaluating the system, getting user opinions by interview or observation since they reflect the system usefulness and the level of user's satisfaction. A heuristic evaluation is also relevant. For that Jakob Nielsen's ten heuristics can be used (Nielsen, 2005).

It is also significant to have some quantitative data for evaluation when using the system as the example of error rate. These data mechanisms, which count the successful and unsuccessful situations during the period of test, must be created in the prototype systems. Another important aspect in the system evaluation is to compare results from the various experiences in order to assess what improvements are needed in each module and to evaluate which modules work better or worse in each situation.

The emergence of digital document technology offers a different perspective to the organizational business processes and in their management. Therefore, it would be interesting to think of solutions with functionalities and features similar to the ones which were considered in the solution presented in previous section of this chapter to enable to control, validate and monitor digital documents. However, it would be still more interesting to think of an architecture to control, validate and monitor documents in both digital and paper supports. But this challenge represents different approaches of those we intend to focus on this chapter because digital documents are immaterial and their information is represented by logical bits that can be stored on, and copied to, any suitable electronic medium and only become meaningful to users when represented through a physical medium such as a computer screen. But if we analyze with attention the current technological scenario, we have at our disposal some technologies that can eventually meet the requirements of a solution identical to that presented in this chapter, such as digital signatures and digital watermarks (Miyazaki, Hanaoka, & Imai, 2006; Yamada, Fujii, Echizen, Tanimoto, & Tezuka, 2004). So, we think there are all technological conditions to project in the future a solution that validates and manages digital documents over the business processes in an organization.

In addition, and to strengthen the importance of this subject under the control of digital documents, new regulations have been formulated and implemented. These new regulations will lead to the implementation of solutions which must guarantee that digital documents will be maintained and supported by controls to ensure data authenticity and integrity, and other requirements of control and monitoring equivalent to the control requirements under paper documents. See, for example, the rules of the recent code of federal regulations title 21, part 11 of U.S. Department of Health and Human Services.

The solution presented in this chapter may deserve special attention in future researches in another area: management and control of locations and flows of medical equipment in healthcare institutions. The solution presented here is designed for document management, but it can easily be extended to other types of items. In fact, the presented solution has modules of search which can be adapted to search for location of medical equipment and has modules of control and monitoring which can be modified to manage the states of this medical equipment (e.g. whether it is in use or it is operational to be used). This idea is very similar to that presented by

Marques (2008) which manages locations, flows and states of equipment and tools in industrial environments. Moreover, this idea can be also adapted to different areas where there are assets in which it is necessary to have internal controls to manage, trace and monitor them.

CONCLUSION

Traceability systems of documents are a vehicle for an optimized and controlled information workflow within an organization, from the input/creation of documents to the end of their life cycle. The solution depicted in Figure 1 is flexible and modular and can meet the needs of document monitoring before its archive or it just meets the needs of search for documents in storage spaces. The adoption of the complete solution represents the acquisition of a system capable of controlling the document flow and of managing its location.

The adoption of the proposed architecture will provide organizations with the ability to meet the basic requirements of an internal control, particularly the approval and control of documents as referred in several standards and legislation. The solution allows to control procedures and data related to internal documents, increasing their reliability and the review of operations as well as to hold the participants responsible.

The competent use of the presented solution will allow a reduction in the number of fraudulent and irregular operations, check whether related documents were properly and timely made (for example, whether all the necessary permits were given and whether certain operations were settled, ordered, paid or registered). However, it is important to note that the feasibility and success of such solutions is strongly dependent of the introduction of adjusted procedures and in their compliance in all situations.

A system of approval and control of documents enables the operations to be transparent and verifiable as well as to have a reliable and trustworthy character. Simultaneously, it ensures in real time the compliance with the requirements of the internal control system provided in legislation.

REFERENCES

Alomair, B., Lazos, L., & Poovendran, R. (2010, June). *Securing Low-Cost RFID Systems: an Unconditionally Secure Approach*. Paper presented at the Sixth Workshop on RFID Security, Singapore.

Bodhuin, T., Preziosi, R., & Tortorella, M. (2006, November). *Building an RFID Document Management Service*. Paper presented at the Innovations in Information Technology, Dubai.

Bodhuin, T., Preziosi, R., & Tortorella, M. (2007). Integrating RFID Services and Ubiquitous Smart Systems for Enabling Organizations to Automatically Monitor, Decide, and Take Actions. In J. Indulska, et al. (Eds.), *Ubiquitous Intelligence and Computing, 4th International Conference: Vol. 4611. Lecture Notes in Computer Science* (pp. 225-234). Heidelberg: Springer-Verlag Berlin Heidelberg.

Bonner, J., & Schaik, P. V. (1998). The use of high and low level prototyping methods for product user interfaces. In Hanson, M. (Ed.), *Contemporary Ergonomics 1998* (pp. 253–257). London: CRC Press.

DAILY RFID CO. (2009). RFID File Tracking System optimizes file inventory management. *DAILY RFID CO., LIMITED Web Site*. Retrieved May 12, 2010, from http://www.rfid-in-china.com/2009-03-23/info_3199.html

Fernando, H., & Abawajy, J. (2009, December). *A RFID architecture framework for global supply chain applications*. Paper presented at the 11th International Conference on Information Integration and Web-based Applications & Services, Kuala Lumpur, Malaysia.

Gandino, F., Montrucchio, B., & Rebaudengo, M. (2010). Tampering in RFID: A Survey on Risks and Defenses. *Mobile Networks and Applications, 15*(4), 502–516. doi:10.1007/s11036-009-0209-y

Gupta, P., & Joseph, A. (2006). Using Radio Frequency Identification in Cash Management. *HSBC's Guide to Cash and Treasury Management in Asia Pacific*, 191-194.

Harper, R., Rodden, T., Rogers, Y., & Sellen, A. (2008). *Being Human: Human-Computer Interaction in the Year 2020*. Cambridge, England: Microsoft Research Ltd.

Langheinrich, M. (2009). A survey of RFID privacy approaches. *Personal and Ubiquitous Computing, 13*(6), 413–421. doi:10.1007/s00779-008-0213-4

Li, M., & Chen, C. (2009, December). *RFID Complex Event Processing Mechanism for Logistics Tracking and Tracing*. Paper presented at the International Forum on Computer Science - Technology and Applications, Chongqing, China.

Lopresti, D., & Nagy, G. (2005, January). *Chipless ID for Paper Documents*. Paper presented at the International Symposium on Electronic Imaging - Document Recognition and Retrieval XII, San Jose, CA.

Marques, R. P. (2008*). Ferramentas de Apoio ao Ciclo de Fabricação de Produto: um caso de estudo na indústria dos moldes*. [Tools to Support Cycle Product Manufacturing: a case study in the mold industry] Unpublished master's dissertation, University of Aveiro, Portugal.

Marques, R. P., Santos, C., & Santos, H. (2010) Automation of the Approval and Control Process of Documents. In J. E. Quintela Varajão, et al. (Eds.), *Enterprise Information Systems: Vol. 109. Communications in Computer and Information Science* (pp. 328-337). Heidelberg: Springer-Verlag Berlin Heidelberg.

Miyazaki, K., Hanaoka, G., & Imai, H. (2006, March). *Digitally signed document sanitizing scheme based on bilinear maps*. Paper presented at the 2006 ACM Symposium on Information, computer and communications security, Taipei, Taiwan.

Nielsen, J. (2005). Heuristic Evaluation. *useit. com: Jakob Nielsen's Website*. Retrieved January 8, 2010, from http://www.useit.com/papers/heuristic/

Puliafito, A. (2006, May). *An Example of Applied Research: RFID and Administrative Processes*. Paper presented at the Workshop RFID Application Domains and Emerging Trends, Brussels, Belgium.

Song, B., & Mitchell, C. J. (2009, October). Scalable *RFID Pseudonym Protocol*. Paper presented at the Third International Conference on Network and System Security, Gold Coast, Australia.

Sybase. (2006). *Estado da Arte em RFID*. Unpublished Technical Report, Sybase Portugal - RFID Solutions Center, Portugal.

Yamada, T., Fujii, Y., Echizen, I., Tanimoto, K., & Tezuka, S. (2004, October). *Print Traceability Systems Framework using Digital Watermarks for Binary Images*. Paper presented at the IEEE International Conference on Systems, Man and Cybemetics, Hague, Netherlands.

Chapter 17
Vector Consensus Model

José M. Monguet
Universitat Politécnica de Catalunya, Spain

Carlos Córdoba
Universitat Politécnica de Catalunya, Spain

Alfredo Gutiérrez
Universitat Politécnica de Catalunya, Spain

Joaquín Fernández
Universitat Politécnica de Catalunya, Spain

Marco Ferruzca
Autonomous Metropolitan University, Spain

Teresa Sanguino
Universitat Politécnica de Catalunya, Spain

Yadira Alatriste
Universitat Politécnica de Catalunya, Spain

José Aguilá
Universitat Politécnica de Catalunya, Spain

Claudia Martínez
Universitat Politécnica de Catalunya, Spain

Miguel Ramírez
Universitat Politécnica de Catalunya, Spain

ABSTRACT

Collaborative workgroups have to make decisions, so it is necessary to have a good mechanism in order to make better decisions. Consensus decision-making helps organizations to process that, based on a diagnosis- and discussion-based approach to current and idealized future scenarios regarding a set of topics of interest. The model incorporates a mechanism that allows the comparison of personal opinion with the average group's opinion. Besides, it allows users to prioritize the topics evaluated, or agree about the potential risks in a specific field, with the aim of facilitate to take decisions about how and where to start actions. The model is presented within the dynamic context of an innovation community. A prototype of such consensus support system in which members provide their opinion in relation to some drivers that support and encourage their organization has been implemented. In such a way, the chapter provides a new consensus framework which can be applied to support web-based consensus and decision processes in different environments.

Two case studies are presented; the first one is focused on the prioritization of the drivers that motivate a researcher in an innovative group, and the second is dedicated to the assessment of the drivers for the future internet.

DOI: 10.4018/978-1-4666-1764-3.ch017

INTRODUCTION

To examine the context for taking better decisions is an important task for any kind of organization (Choo, 1996). Overall today when it is more difficult to keep a competitive advantage on the basis of common knowledge and new business models. The aim of a decision process is to reach an agreement by sharing ideas with the intention to take the best decision, and thus to achieve some advantage for an organization.

The decision-making process should include a representative number of members in the organization and its stakeholders, generally if an environmental change is being planned (Lozada & Calantone, 1996).

The aim of this chapter is to present a model of consensus decision making, denominated Vector Consensus[1], for helping organizations to manage a consensus decision-making process based on a diagnosis and discussion approach of current, and idealized future scenario of a specific topic of interest. The model incorporates a mechanism that allows comparing the personal opinion to the average group's opinion.

The Consensus Process may focus on different aspects of the topic of study. Once identified the drivers or aspects that are going to be evaluated, the attention may be put in many different matters, from how well the things go today, to which is the risks in the future for a particular item, of not to be considered properly.

In the first case the focus is dedicated to prioritize the topics evaluated with the aim of taking decisions about where to start actions. The model is presented within the dynamic context of an innovation community, so group of participants are the researchers of that community. A prototype of such consensus support system in which members provide their opinion in relation to some drivers that support and encourage their organization has been implemented. In such a way, we provide a new consensus framework which can be applied to support web-based consensus and decision processes in different drivers: motivation, cooperation, collaboration, etc.

The second case study is applied to the evaluation of future internet by a representative group of experts of the internet community. The drivers that influence the evolution of internet in the future are put under the assessment of the experts, with the intention of determining a shared scenario for the internet of the future. The goal is to get an agreement about the relevance of a selected group of "drivers" and to agree about the existing risk that these drivers are not correctly managed by the internet community.

Sometimes there are decisions situations in which the members' ideas cannot be put in common and thus the uses of a consensus decision-making approach is necessary (Pérez, Cabrerizo, & Herrera-Viedma, 2011). But, even when the consensus idea is popular as a way to take decisions, sometimes it is hard for organizations to build a consistent and efficient consensus model (Butler & Rothstein, 2001).

A good consensus process can support the elements that drive effective decisions (Yeager & Sommer, 2010). For example:

- By helping members to clarify themselves about their position in the organization they belong to.
- To clarify the role that each member must play in his or her job.
- To build a common language.
- To build a shared decision-making process.

On the other hand, we believe that in many domains the activities of an organization are already open and distributed and those who can stimulate and support this kind of collaboration to leverage their local and dispersed resources will have more chances to succeed (Hansen & Nohria 2004). This is the case of collaborative innovation communities like: research groups, living labs or multinational organizations.

Even when strategies and tools exist to support collaboration practices, there is a need to help organizations to keep competitive and to build a consensus about developing their core capabilities. Web-based consensus systems can be useful to achieve these goals, considering also that they haven't been sufficiently explored (Cihnho Lin & Hsu, 2007; Chinho Lin, Liu, Hsu, & Wu, 2008). The incorporation of new ICT in the consensus decision making process, besides solving the geographical dispersion of members participating in an open organization, expand the opportunities to take better decisions for successfully transforming the organizational mindset (Pourdehnad & Bharathy, 2004).

Something similar may be considered in relation to the process of establishing scenarios about the future of complex systems like dynamic sectors of activity, and this is the case for Internet.

With the aim to make it operational, a first prototype system was developed. It was implemented within an innovation community where it was important to achieve an agreement about some drivers affecting collaboration and then take decisions for future actions. The system can be configured to discuss about any kind of topic. It allows gathering information from participants, comparing a personal opinion with the collective opinion, and it promotes sharing knowledge.

From this point a second prototype was developed to share opinions about the evolution of a field of study, and a representative group of experts, with political, economic, social and technical dominant profiles where invited to try to converge their opinions about the drivers that will manage the future of internet. That's the case for the internet community.

The present research has followed a constructive and explorative methodology based on building and test prototypes. The web-based system developed are described we are particularly interested in intensive knowledge domains, like

research groups where distributed individuals in several countries interact with each other in order to achieve personal and collective goals. However, this experience should be also useful for other kind of innovative communities.

The effects on users' perception have been assessed through a survey. The results can be of interest for those organizations trying to implement mechanisms for consensus decision-making process.

BACKGROUND

To scan the context in order to take better decisions is an important task for any kind of organization (Choo, 1996). It is a "must-do". Decisions are normally about trying to achieve some advantage for an organization or community. Including all the members in the organization and all the stakeholders is imperative in achieving environmental change (Lozada & Calantone, 1996). The decision-making process can improve and obtain a realistic perspective if the following aspects are considered (Frishammar, 2003): First, include soft and hard information. While soft information is tied to an individual person and can be subjective (tacit knowledge), hard information is explicit and can be easily quantified and processed. The first one is important because individuals can provide guidance, advice and encouragement. Second, decision-makers should rely on information received on a solicited and unsolicited basis. Third, it is recommended to utilize the organization's internal and external resources to obtain information.

Consensus is an idea associated with the decision-making process and the common-agreement building among most of the participants of an organization or a community. In simple words, this concept is thus concerned with decision-making procedures.

In Collaborative Innovation Communities (CIC) as research groups, Living Labs Spaces or multinational organizations, it is ever more difficult to maintain competitive advantage on the basis of the traditional knowledge and economic models. Those who can stimulate and support open collaboration to leverage their local and dispersed resources should have more chances to succeed (Hansen & Nohria, 2004).

Nowadays, there are many current studies that highlight various factors affecting collaboration effectiveness and efficiency (AMI@Work, 2009; Riege, 2005; Fawcett, Magnan, & McCarter, 2008; Cramton, 2001). Some of the main collaboration barriers have to do with: a lack of clear leadership, a lack of mutual trust, a lack of motivation, unbalanced intellectual property rights and a lack of common knowledge and meaning. These factors create different types of barriers among collaborating people working in CIC's.

Some of the principles enounced for CIC's may be extended to Virtual CIC's, a groups of experts, which although they don't work together, belong to the same environment or region and share the fact that work in the same area from different positions. In this case, it may be said that the group of experts through their behavior, participate or influence with decisions and actions on the scenario that finally will result.

Although, there are a lot of strategies and tools oriented to solve collaboration practices, more efforts are needed to help CIC's ability to sustain competitive and to build cognition and consensus in developing their core capabilities (Cihnho Lin & Hsu, 2007). These problems can be solved by implementing web-decision-making systems which are rarely explored (Chinho Lin, Liu, Hsu, & Wu, 2008).

MODEL FOR CONSENSUS DECISION-MAKING: VECTOR CONSENSUS

Vector Consensus is a model of consensus decision-making process that depends on the collective participation of users. Individuals have different personal opinions in relation to the main drivers that support and encourage organizations (Aguilá & Monguet, 2010). If we take a group of experts in a particular field we will discover that they have different sensibilities and interests that biased their visions about future scenarios of that field.

Vector Consensus is a tool that aims to allow experts to share views and approach opinions about the drivers that will determine the development and/or the priorities of the object of study.

Vector Consensus is a model based on series of surveys, where the user progresses through them, and have the particularity to be kept open to allow the experts to approximate their positions on the various aspects that make the object of study, and that should be discussed. Experts may be changing the meaning of their vote based on the assessment made of point of view of other participants, and based also on the moderated discussions by the presenters or conductors of the process.

The kind of debate that takes place is characterized by the fact that is structured, progressive and asynchronous:

- Structured as it follows a very specific sequence of steps that previously has been studied in detail.
- Asynchronous because the participants have some time intervals to change the sense of their votes, to the various surveys in order to promote consensus.
- Progressive to reach the final result, the vision on the future of the object of study, going through intermediate results.

The proposed framework evolves in three steps. In the first prototype the process was managed in two steps but in the second prototype, the first step was divided in two phases, so the final model of Vector Consensus is presented to the participants in three steps called: 1. Model, 2. Today, and 3. Future.

Table 1. Consensus Decision-Making Process

1. Drivers. Model	2. Today Current Scenario		3. Future Desirable Scenario	
Preparation	Evaluation	Consensus/ Discussion	Consensus/ Discussion	Decision Making
Presentation of the proposal and the drivers to be discussed. The list of participants is open.	It implies an individual diagnosis about each driver to be evaluated.	A test for consensus is applied. Individual should define the current level of a specific driver..	A test for consensus is applied. Individual should define the desirable future level of a specific driver.	On the basis of consensus, participants should prioritize drivers requiring more attention or where to start solving problems.
The participants understand the goal of the project and engage with it.	The idea is to gather information about how the groups of participants share the topic to be discussed.	A discussion process is started with the aim to build a common agreement and converge as much as possible.	Again a discussion strategy is required for individuals to try to converge as much as possible.	Again a discussion strategy is required for individuals to try to converge as much as possible.
The participant is able to propose changes in the model	The participant can compare his or her result to the average answer of the organization.	All different opinions by individuals are shared.	All different opinions by individuals are shared.	As a result of the whole process an action plan can be designed by the organization.

In the first step, the discussion is focused on the proposed model, which is based in a number of drivers. The participants familiarize with the drivers proposed as a model of the object of study, and the meaning of drivers may be clarified if necessary. Finally the participant may eventually propose the exclusion of drivers and the inclusion of new ones.

In the second step, each participant evaluates the current state of each specific driver in the organization or in the community. The participant can view his or her personal result and compare it with the average of the other answers. Then, a first consensus process about the current level of drivers is sustained in order to achieve a common agreement about the drivers being evaluated. A discussion process is started with the aim to expose and defend the personal point of view and convince others. Participants can change their point of view at anytime he or she desires it.

In the third step participants start one more consensus process in order to define the desirable future level of performance for each of the drivers evaluated in the organization or in the community. After a common agreement has been achieved, participants should decide the priority to solve the issues found at each driver. They also share a discussion process to establish a priority order or the risk or any other relevant aspect. It is important also to establish at which term the future is considered.

With all the information gathered, an action plan can be designed. Table 1 summarizes Vector Consensus.

In conclusion, the aim is to reduce the dispersion level between the personal opinion manifested in the evaluation step at the beginning of the consensus decision making process and the collective opinion built during the whole process. The group's consensus around the actual and desirable scenario in the organization or in the community is promoted by using a discussion strategy about each driver and comparing personal opinions every time. Figure 1 represents the conceptual model of Vector Consensus.

RESEARCHER'S PRIORITIES AND CONCERNS

Taking the model into account, it was developed a web-based system – the Vector Consensus system – aimed at improving consensus in a research community involved with the develop-

Figure 1. Framework for consensus decision-making model.

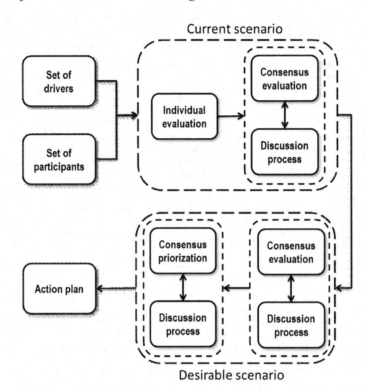

ment of Internet-based innovative projects. Vector Consensus addresses simultaneously: gathering information about a collective thought, promoting sharing knowledge and diminishing collaborative barriers (Figure 2).

Figure 2. System flow scheme

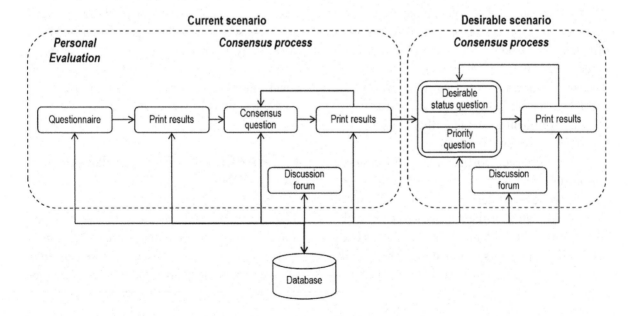

Questionnaires and forums were implemented as tools to gather information from the users. See Figure 3. The questionnaires are based in a Semantic Differential Scale (SDS). Their results are analyzed and published graphically in real time. Figure 4 represents the main interface of Vector Consensus.

In order to visualize the results, it is necessary to calculate for each driver during the whole consensus process the following values:

a. Mean value from personal user answers.
b. Mean value from the group answers.
c. Dispersion.

Results are then presented to users with a graphic code using a simplified color code: red for the mean value which represents the personal opinion, green for the mean value representing the group's opinion, and gray to standard deviation (± 1) from the group's mean value to represent the statistical dispersion (Figure 5).

Figure 3. An example of the interface for the semantic differential scale questionnaire and forum

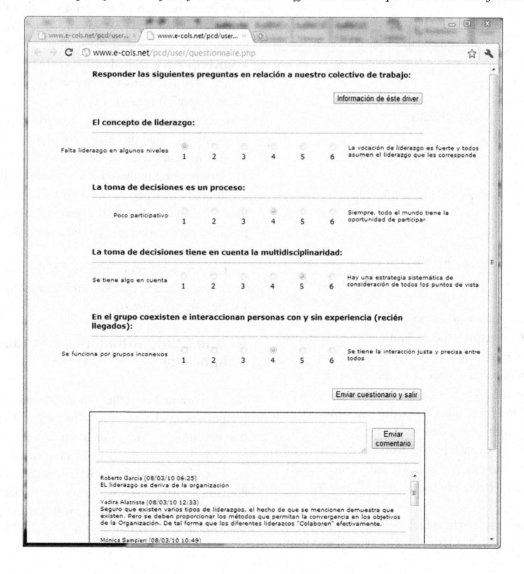

Figure 4. Vector Consensus main graphical interface.

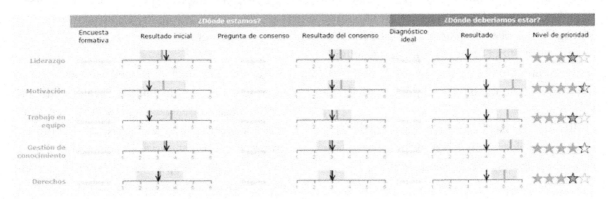

Figure 5. Vector Consensus statistical data representation.

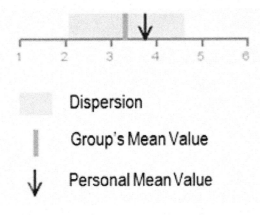

In synthesis, the first prototype of Vector Consensus was based on five user-interfaces:

- Personal evaluation
- Consensus process in the current scenario component
- Consensus process in the future scenario component
- One to be queried by the user when more information is needed and
- User's central panel working as start point to the others interfaces and as a feedback center, already presented in Figure 4.

The first interface includes a set of questions to be answered (Figure 3). The second and third interfaces with consensus process include a single question to be answered and a discussion forum where users can also post any message. This can be displayed in real-time to other users obtaining a between users knowledge flow and a better basis to get a well set of answers that will represent the group's opinion (Figure 4).

Every user's activity is logged, including every initial value or change to an answer, and publishing comments in the discussion forums. The information gathered is a support for future depth analysis work in order to understand the user's behavior during the group's consensus process, and to explore the consensus mechanisms in organizations.

The second prototype changed the interface and evolved to a more clear and easy interaction for the users (Figure 6).

A Case Study within an Innovation Community

A first exploration of the Vector Consensus prototype was in charge of a collaborative innovation community. The innovation process of this group is based in the lead of multidisciplinary teams which bring experts in several knowledge domains, mostly business, design, and technology. Members of this group are distributed in Spain, Venezuela, Mexico, Portugal, and USA. The main

Figure 6. Interface of the second prototype.

activity of this group is focused in creating new internet-based business models.

In order to support their innovation activities, the group has created its own web platform to coordinate their collaborative work.

Because of the complexity to stimulate and support the collaboration practices to leverage their local and distributed resources, the organization has adopted the Vector Consensus Model as a strategy to discuss about some drivers affecting it. Specifically, they were interested in building a common agreement about how the organization understands the following drivers before taking decisions and implementing an action plan in the near future: leadership, motivation, collaborative work, intellectual propriety rights, and knowledge management.

The consensus decision-making process was explained to users. They also received complementary information about each driver with the aim to have a reference framework. They interacted with the system during nine days. The first three days were designated to present a personal evaluation of the drivers and to discuss with others the personal opinion. The following two consensus processes had the same duration each one. In each of these three moments, users had to answer a SDS questionnaire and interchange opinions through a forum. The evaluation test included 20 items (4 per driver). The consensus process for discussing current driver's status in the organization included five items (1 per driver), while the consensus for defining the desirable future level of the studied drivers included 8 items (2 per driver). Every item

Table 2. Drivers and adjective used in the semantic differential scale questionnaire

Driver	1=Negative status	6=Positive status
Leadership	Lack	Have
Motivation	Lack	Motivating environment
Collaborative work	Lack	Integrative environment
Knowledge environment	Inappropriate	Appropriate
Intellectual Propriety Rights	Non respected	Respected

was represented as a 6-point SDS (See Table 2). Participants were asked to rate each item.

After the consensus process, and to explore the group´s awareness about the effects of the strategy and the system usability they was asked to answer an on-line survey with six questions.

Results

In each of the two possible scenarios, the current and the desirable, the mean value for the personal answers was compared with the mean value representing the collective opinion about the drivers studied. The standard deviation was also calculated to represent the dispersion (See Table 3).

If the two level of dispersion obtained in the "Current scenario" are compared, we can conclude that there is a trend to consensus. The dispersion related to the collective opinion is lower than the average personal opinion for each driver. This

suggests that users achieved a common agreement of the drivers' current status within the organization. Diminutions on dispersion levels during consensus have a stronger meaning since there were also changes in the mean collective opinion for each driver going up to 16.2% from initial position, obtaining mostly lower levels. Based on this evidence, we can conclude there was a change in most of the personal opinions due to the consensus and discussion process in the model (See Figure 7, and Figure 8).

The levels of dispersion in the "Desirable scenario", as well as in "Consensus" as in "Priority" sections follow the same consensus trend as in the "Current scenario" which can be interpreted as a collective ability to get into get an easier consensus opinion.

In relation to the survey applied to users, these were the answers:

Table 3. Trend to consensus

Driver	Current				Desirable			
	Personal Opinion		Consensus		Consensus		Priority	
	Mean	Dispersion	Mean	Dispersion	Mean	Dispersion	Mean	Dispersion
Leadership	3.42	0.87	3.38	0.60	4.80	0.93	4.20	0.75
Motivation	3.34	0.87	3.56	0.79	5.50	0.74	4.50	0.59
Collaborative work	3.80	1.06	3.19	0.73	5.20	0.60	4.15	0.73
Knowledge Management	3.39	0.86	2.88	0.78	5.37	0.67	4.32	0.65
Intellectual Propriety Rights	3.09	0.95	2.94	0.75	5.00	0.71	3.90	0.77

Figure 7. Mean value for each driver across different scenarios.

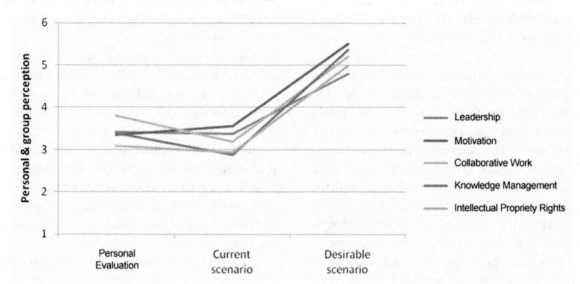

Figure 8. Statistical dispersion related to each driver across different scenarios.

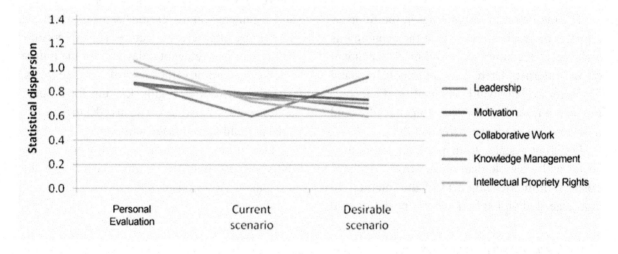

- All of them suggest that the proposed strategy affords to increase the knowledge about the organization.
- Most of them (85.7%) consider this consensus decision-making model a good strategy to achieve common goals.
- Most of them (85.7%) affirm it is a useful channel to share personal contributions to the group.
- It fosters personal commitment because it brings awareness about the personal role in the organization (57.1% of the users affirm this idea).
- And finally, some of them (50%) think the system is a good tool to share knowledge between members of the organization.

A CASE STUDY WITH A GROUP OF EXPERTS FROM THE INTERNET COMMUNITY

The second prototype is the result of the application of the former model to different researching groups. The aim with this second group was to help the researchers to get a shared view of the internet of the future. This research team was devoted to the development of an internet architecture for the future based in a service composition through the aggregation of a variety of atomic services. The model is designed to allow both sensors for things, as well as services requiring large bandwidth.

Whatever the architecture that eventually evolve into, the Internet, there will be necessary to support the development of new cost models in order to face a complex socio-economic environment.

The evolution of the Internet in the future is a matter of great interest, since the economy as a whole, is becoming more and more dependent on the Internet. There is a continuous demand for increased bandwidth and quality of telecommunications services, competition intensifies and new opportunities arise permanently.

Different agents, from political, economic, social and technological areas have a decisive position in the development of the Internet. To converge and/or explicit views, positions and interests of different stakeholders can contribute to facilitate optimal and healthy growth of the network and its applications.

The aim of the research project was to define a realistic scenario for the future of the Internet, taking into account and combine the views of the Internet with technical, social, economic and political bias.

To share which is the importance and priorities is essential, to design and develop an architecture of the Internet where all drivers are taken into account and the balance is found to optimize growth and profitability of the network and maximize its use and benefits for all stakeholders.

From the literature review and discussion with experts, have been identified a set of 24 drivers that together constitute a framework to explain and predict the development of Internet in the future and consequently be better able design and arguments on the various aspects that could set a future Internet architecture. The drivers may be more or less relevant today and for the Future Internet, according to the views of various experts. The consensus was finally looking for a better understanding between views in order to facilitate a deeper and conscious discussion.

The following table is a framework for the 24 promoters identified, sorted according to the 4 points of view considered.

Table 4. Future Internet Drivers

Politic	Economic	Social	Technical
Promote the use of internet	Jobs based on knowledge	Promote the knowledge of internet	Give control to the user
Incentivize innovation and entrepreneurship	Productivity	User as inspiration of innovation	Efficiency and liability
Intensive use of the e-administration	Sectorial prioritizing	Ensure participation and inclusion	Edge technology public purchase
Ensure law accomplishment	Protect and incentive market	Protect privacy	Consensus in technology regulation
Surveillance of services and products	Fair concurrency and open market	Balance between prices and products	Ensure quality and sustainability of services
Promote neutrality	Opportunities to invest	Allow the user to select services	Open and transparent architecture.

Finally Vector Consensus in its current version has become an active tool, since once the experts have had a convergence, the system may be open to other individuals and / or groups to compare their particular point of view with the opinion established and shared by first level experts who have agreed their vision.

FUTURE RESEARCH DIRECTIONS

Although this consensus process itself can show what the collectiveness opines, and contributes to generate a collective knowledge, it is possible and maybe necessary to find a way to give a specific weight to every opinion commented during the discussion process in order to reinforce the pure statistical results.

So the next step is to generate a Semantic Analysis Model to be suitable to the Vector Consensus Model. That Semantic Analysis Model should be capable to read the comments and, as result, to give some statistical value which could be used as well as to modify the current statistics that system deliveries as to generate new possible drivers to be taken into account by the collectiveness.

Since many specific drivers affects collectiveness, and it is not convenient to take all of them but delimitate a good sample of topics according to the group's necessities, it will be generated a model to find the best set of drivers to be taken into account in a consensus process. The model will take as much as possible of drivers that matter to the collective and then, following the model's process, every driver will be ranked, according to the ranking it will be possible obtain the set of drivers to be used at consensus process.

As Vector Consensus has been created as a decision-making support tool, a future research direction consists in evaluate the taken decisions. After a while from the consensus process some surveys or maybe another adapted consensus process could be applied in order to evaluate the new collective's environment on the same drivers.

CONCLUSION

We have presented a consensus decision-making model based on a mixed strategy of diagnosis and discussion. We have also implemented a system prototype of this model. It is designed to deal with consensus and decision-making issues in organizations. The system is based in web, so organizations interested in involving its members distributed in local and remote places doesn't represent a problem. This consensus decision-making strategy can be a useful to diagnostic and discuss about the current, idealized and future scenario of a specific topic of interest in the organization.

The first version of the system has been tested in a collaborative innovation community where thirty experts have participated building a consensus about some drivers affecting their collaborative efficiency and efficacy during collaboration practices. Experts could share their personal opinion about the current status of the topic analyzed and compare it to the average group's opinion. Also, they could assess the future desirable scenario of the same topic. At the end of the consensus process, they had to prioritize the drivers in order to determine which aspect was more important to attend.

Results suggest that this consensus framework allows users to augment their context knowledge awareness about the organization and their role in it.

Another conclusion is that tools like the Vector Consensus model can be considered a good approach to achieve consensus and support decision-making, helping align the different individuals' opinion in an organization. Moreover, a better knowing on others' opinions has beneficial effects in the social capital of the organization.

In the future, we are interested in applying this model in several organizations. We consider that this studio can be useful for those organizations which need tools to support their decision processes.

The web-based system innovates by implementing a conceptual model for consensus, originally thought for enterprises, allowing distributed individuals discuss and subjectively measure some barriers affecting collaboration in the community. Furthermore, it innovates because it offers to each individual the possibility to compare his personal opinion with respect to rest of the community, given as a real-time feedback.

REFERENCES

Aguilá, J., & Monguet, J. M. (2010) *¿Por qué algunas empresas tienen éxito y otras no?* [Why do some companies succeed and others do not?] (1st ed.) Barcelona, Spain: Planeta.

AMI@Work. (2009) "ECOSPACE Newsletter No 11." *ECOSPACE Consortium.* Retrieved February 10, 2010 from: http://www.ami-communities.eu/wiki/ECOSPACE_Newsletter_No_11

Butler, C.T.L., & Rothstein, A. (2001). *On conflict and consensus: a handbook on formal consensus decisionmaking.* Takoma Park, MD: Food Not Bombs Publishing. Retrieved January 19, 2011 from: http://wandreilagh.org/consensus.pdf

Choo, C. W. (1996). The knowing organization: How organizations use information to construct meaning, create knowledge and make decisions. *International Journal of Information Management, 16*(5), 329–340. Available at http://dx.doi.org/10.1016/0268-4012(96)00020-5 doi:10.1016/0268-4012(96)00020-5

Cramton, C. D. (2001). The Mutual Knowledge Problem and Its Consequences for Dispersed Collaboration. *Organization Science, 12*(3), 346–371. doi:10.1287/orsc.12.3.346.10098

Fawcett, S. E., Magnan, G. M., & McCarter, M. W. (2008). Benefits, barriers, and bridges to effective supply chain management. *Supply Chain Management: An International Journal 13*(1): 35-48. Available at: http://www.nasstrac.org/membersonly/ArticlesOnline/PDFs/2008/NASSTRAC_Benefits_Barriers_Bridges_To_Effective_SCM.pdf.

Frishammar, J. (2003). Information use in strategic decision making. *Management Decision, 41*(4), 318–326. Available at http://www.emeraldinsight.com/Insight/ViewContentServlet?Filename=Published/Emerald-FullTextArticle/Articles/0010410401.html doi:10.1108/00251740310468090

Hansen, M. T., & Nohria, N. (2004.) How To Build Collaborative Advantage. *MIT Sloan Management Review 46*(1): 22-30. Available at: http://sloanreview.mit.edu/the-magazine/articles/2004/fall/46105/how-to-build-collaborative-advantage/.

Lin, C. (2008). Pursuing excellence in firm core knowledge through intelligent group decision support system. *Industrial Management & Data Systems, 108*(3), 277–296. doi:10.1108/02635570810858723

Lin, C., & Hsu, M. (2007). A GDSS for ranking a firm's core capability strategies. *Journal of Computer Information Systems, 47*(4), 111–130.

Lozada, H. R., & Calantone, R. J. (1996). Scanning behavior and environmental variation in the formulation of strategic responses to change. *Journal of Business and Industrial Marketing, 11*(1), 17–41. Available at http://www.emeraldinsight.com/Insight/ViewContentServlet?Filename=Published/EmeraldFullTextArticle/Articles/0800110102.html doi:10.1108/08858629610112274

Pérez, I. J., Cabrerizo, F. J., & Herrera-Viedma, E. (2011). Group decision making problems in a linguistic and dynamic context. *Expert Systems with Applications, 38*(3), 1675–1688. Available at http://dx.doi.org/10.1016/j.eswa.2010.07.092 doi:10.1016/j.eswa.2010.07.092

Pourdehnad, J., & Bharathy, G. K. (2004). Systems Thinking and Its Implications in Organizational Transformation. In *Conference on Systems Thinking in Management*, Philadelphia, PA.

Riege, A. (2005). Three-dozen knowledge-sharing barriers managers must consider. *Journal of Knowledge Management, 9*(3), 18–35. Available at http://lpis.csd.auth.gr/mtpx/km/material/JKM-9-3b.pdf doi:10.1108/13673270510602746

Yeager, J., & Sommer, L. (2010). The Four Key Factors That Drive Successful Decisions. *Qualitative Report, 15*(5), 1114–1123. Available at http://www.nova.edu/ssss/QR/QR15-5/yeager.pdf

ADITIONAL READING

Dennis, A. R., George, J. F., Jessup, L. M., Jay, F., Nunamaker, J., & Vogel, D. R. (1988). Information technology to support electronic meetings. *Management Information Systems Quarterly, 12*(4), 591–624. doi:10.2307/249135

Gould, S. J., & Kramer, T. (2009). "What's it Worth to Me?" Three interpretive studies of the relative roles of task-oriented and reflexive processes in separate versus joint value construction. *Journal of Economic Psychology, 30*(6), 840–858. doi:10.1016/j.joep.2009.08.003

Grudin, J. (1994). Computer-supported cooperative work: History and focus. *Computer, 27*(5), 19–26. doi:10.1109/2.291294

Karlsson, G. (1989). Rules and strategies in decision making: A critical analysis from a phenomenological perspective. In Montgomery, H., & Svenson, O. (Eds.), *Process and structure in human decision making* (pp. 51–64). Chichester, UK: H. Montgomery and O. Svenson.

ENDNOTE

[1] The name "Vector Consensus" was selected as an analogy to Euclidian vector in physics, and more specifically in a vector space, where each single member in an organization would be represented by a single vector, and a vector space would be the collectiveness. So as a vector space has a vector addition, an organization will have results based on the addition of multiple personal efforts. If individual vectors align then vector addition increases.

Chapter 18
Efficient Alternatives in the Adoption of Software for Public Companies

Carmen de Pablos Heredero
Universidad Rey Juan Carlos, Spain

David López Berzosa
Instituto de Empresa Business School, Spain

ABSTRACT

Public Administrations are seeking more efficient alternatives for the use of information and communication technologies in terms of a cost-benefit analysis. Open source standards can offer them rational alternatives. Up to this moment one can find some good experiences in the implementation of open source software in Public Administrations worldwide. This study offers the results of research where a group of eighteen Public Administration experiences of integral systems migration to open software standards have been analyzed. Public Administrations perceive improvements in the way they offer services, a reduction of the costs, and better secured information systems. The authors think this analysis can be of value for IT decision makers at Public Administrations.

INTRODUCTION

In the last two decades a great number of structuralism models have appeared in the applied technology areas. They all have generated a great debate around the role that information and communication technologies play in the organizations

DOI: 10.4018/978-1-4666-1764-3.ch018

(Poole & de Sanctis, 1990; Walsham 1993; de Sanctis & Poole, 1994). These models consider information and communication technologies as tools that allow more efficient alternatives in the management of the information system. The human action occupies a central place in these models, in particular, the actions that have to do with the use given to these technologies. New approaches that give a special importance, not only to the information and communication technologies in the firm, but the use that firms make of these technologies and derived consequences (Weick, 1990; Roberts & Gravowski, 1995) have also been analysed. In this orientation Orliwoski (2000) from a structuralism orientation on the information technologies' field proposes a practical understanding of the relationship amongst people, technology and social action.

The development of Public Administration IT policies can have positive impacts in the creation of more efficient relationships with citizens. People constitute the main asset in the information society, so the emphasis must be put on them. Policies trying to build the information society worldwide must promote social integration and make people be active and critic users of information and communication technologies. We must build a culture centered in the relationships between users. In our information society users must be the builders apart from consumers (Casacuberta, 2003). Open source software can mean an opportunity to this fact and an alternative in a cost-benefit analysis for Public Administrations.

In this study we present real experiences of open source migration in Public Administrations worldwide. And from them we try to identify behavioral models in the way they adopt this kind of software.

We really think that the results that we offer can help policy makers to define public policies to promote the adoption of free software tools. We have obtained the data thanks to the 2009 project "Migrafloss, migration to open source software" financed by CENATIC, A Spanish National Centre of Reference for Information and Communication Technologies".

OPEN SOURCE SOFTWARE: AN OPORTUNITY FOR ORGANIZATIONS

Open source migration (F/OSS) was first applied in the sixties. In the nineties it becomes a quite consolidated business alternative. Since then, the free software implementation has been studied from both, the technical point of view (Raymond, 1999; Hunter, 2006; Rossi, 2006; Berry, 2008) as an economic emergent possibility in the market (Lerner & Tirole, 2002; Lerner & Tirole, 2005; Riehle, 2007).

Free software migration means an efficient solution in terms of costs, specially for the public industry and in contexts demanding great technological resources as it is the case of education (Lerner and Tirole, 2002; Riehle, 2007; Lakhan & Jhunjhunwala, 2008). The implementation of free software tools promotes the innovation and the development in enterprise information systems worldwide (David & Steinmueller, 1994; Shiff, 2002; Hippern & Krogh, 2003; Bitzer, 2005; Osterloh & Rota, 2007). Most experiences have just been started in the twenties and they are still in progress (Ahmed, 2005; UOC Report, 2009).

This kind of technological option can favorite the creation of a more interactive civil society. Paradoxically, as Tascón indicates (2006) *"Despite the access to the information is today more universal thanks to Internet, we can find more sophisticated systems to have some access prohibited"*. In some countries there are still today barriers for the access to Internet mainly due to the technological infrastructure or the lack of Internet segmentation, amongst others. Despite the benefits provided by free software to organizations, there are still some barriers for its use. In a Report published in April 2009 (EOI Report) some positive effects of the use of open source software tools are stressed. We cite amongst others that it means an opportunity for firms and Public Administrations, since it implies a global technological option, it promotes the public participation, a decrease in the computing costs is produced, it can increase the choices to optimize hardware and software devices, and it can have a direct effect in the increase of the information society rates.

Venkatesh et al. (2003) and Sameh e Izak (2009) that have studied the processes for technology adoption have stressed the importance for modeling the user's behavior. The implementation of open source software in different firm's processes can produce impacts in wide business areas. Final customers can also perceive benefits of it. For this reason, we require for this analysis an organizational approach. For applying this approach we demand quantitative approaches as it has been previously suggested in the literature review (Gonzalez-Barahona, 1991; 2004; Wheeler, 2007) and also positivistic ones. These last ones can help us to build hypothesis around free software implementations. We lack of the description of cases up to now. As a different perspective to other approaches, theory must be built as data are being processed. From our own perspective, both, the firm's level and the macro analysis are complemented when trying to find a global perspective that explains the progressive adoption of free software at firms.

Then for this analysis we need a wider perspective since we lack of the description on the experience of real cases. This is the reason why we have decided to apply the grounded theory (Myers, 2009). It is a qualitative method of research that tries to build theories from data collected in real scenarios. Grounded theory is then an inductive method that allows the production of emergent theories where some knowledge gaps are identified.

This methodology specially applies for descriptions centered in a context where organizational phenomena appear (Myers, 2007). The grounded theory has first been applied to psychology (Glaser & Strauss, 1967; Strauss & Corbin, 1990) and later in the information systems area (Orliwoski, 1991; 1993) including our area of interest, the research in open source software (Dedrick & West, 2005).

THE EMPIRICAL STUDY

In this research we have analyzed eighteen Public Administrations. In the following Table 1 we show

Table 1. The cases analyzed

Organization	Country
Munich Town Hall	Germany
National Policy	France
Postal Service	United States
Birmingham Town Hall	Great Britain
Zaragoza Town Hall	Spain
Valencia Education Counsel	Spain
Bucarest Meteorology Service	Rumania
Finnish Justice Ministry	Finland
Castilla La Mancha Health Service	Spain
Amorebieta-Extano Town Hall	Spain
Toledo Counsel, Spain	
Valencia Transport and Infrastructure Council	Spain
Murcia University	Spain
Saint Bartolomeu del Grau Town Hall	Spain
Brasil Education Ministry	Brasil
Sao Paulo Metro	Brasil
Brasil Public Administration	Brasil
Arles Town Hall	France

the analyzed organizations and the countries where they are based. The projects have been selected according to criteria of maximum variability in terms of context, size, main objective and degree of use of ICT amongst others, by making use of the technique suggested by Glaser and Strauss (1967). Strauss and Corbin (1990) consider that whenever there are many factors that can intervene at different levels, it is important to define concepts, categories and relationships that allow us design an emergent theory as it is our case.

The theoretical sampling is cumulative due to the fact that future experiences in migration add value to the existent knowledge suggesting new concepts that can be relevant for open source migration initiatives. We posit that adopting an evolutionary approach for theory building moderates the obsolescence that technical migration guides can present when disruptive technologies or new standards emerge.

So we have studied experiences coming from Public Administrations of six different countries (Brasil, France, Germany, Great Britain, Spain, Finland). Besides, for each of them we have considered the following aspects: main objectives for the migration, time estimated for the migration, kind of software and migrated service, cost for the migration, critical success factors in the migration, critical failure factors in the migration, the obtained results, the perceived benefits.

The collection of data based in the grounded theory has been developed in an iterative way (Glaser & Strauss, 1967) starting by an exploratory perspective and searching afterwards for approaches more centered in the relevant aspects and structured interviews.

The case studies analyzed can be seen at: http://cenatic.interoperabilidad.org:8080/web/guest/administraciones-publicas and in, http://cenatic.interoperabilidad.org:8080/web/guest/grandes-empresas

For the analysis of the collected data we have followed an inductive analysis. It searches for relevant concepts and relations amongst them.

By making use of the Strauss and Corbin's methodology (1990), initially the existent data are analyzed. We have grouped them in open coding categories. After this, and in a second phase, we have performed an axial coding. The initial categories are grouped into sub-categories that answer to questions of the kind: when, how, why, where and what for. In our concrete case:

1. When did the open source software implementation take place?
2. How did the open source software implementation happen?
3. Why did they perform it?
4. Where did they promote it?
5. For what did they migrate into open source software?

Software migration experiences mean internal processes for change, from an intra-firm point of view. We believe that this approach centered on processes offers a view of real organizational structures therefore fostering its adoption by different business units.

As it is shown in Figure 1, the projects for open source migration present three stages: the process of adoption, the migration process and the evaluation of obtained results. Each stage, or main category according to the grounded theory, entails a series of secondary categories that intervene in the migration process.

The secondary categories take their own meaning in a progressive way according to the exam of the case studies considered. As it is shown in the previous figure, the following factors condition the way in which the migration takes place.

In the process of open source software adoption,

*   The existence of external collaborators
*   The size of the organization
*   Where the decision making process comes from
*   The IT strategy of the firm

Figure 1. The life cycle for the migration to free software

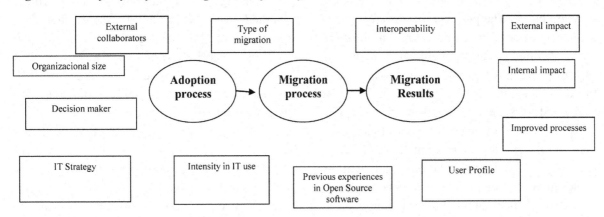

In the process of migration to open source software

- The type of migration
- The intensity of IT use
- The degree of interoperability
- The existence of previous experiences in open source software
- The user profile

In the results of open source software migration

- The external impact
- The internal impact
- The improvement of firm's processes

So we have to take into main how concepts as the interoperability (defined as the compatibility with the software running in the organization), previous experiences or internal ICT competencies moderate the following main categories: migration process and results.

THE RESULTS: MODELS FOR OPEN SOURCE MIGRATION

In our analysis we can distinguish three different ways for the implementation of free software in Public Administrations:

- Public Administrations that consider that free software is a strategic asset.
- Public Administrations that consider that open source software means a better option than proprietary software in terms of results and new options.
- Public Administrations that count on with budgetary restrictions and see free software as an attractive option.

Group One: Strategic Movers

We find in this group, organizations have been forced to migrate for different reasons, as for example the end of service maintenance of previous software or the need to decrease the costs of information and communication technologies. For this group, removing the barriers imposed by the provider of proprietary software is a clear priority, even in the definition of the firm's strategic plans.

These organizations count on with qualified human resources and a generous ICT budget. Besides they also assign specific personal to the development and support of ICT services.

Although they are intensive in ICT use, they face some interoperability problems amongst existing services and the natural resistance of users to change from the established routines and procedures to new ones. These companies perform a gradual approach in the migration of software that often demands timetables that can support years in finishing the migration. Besides, schedules are adapted according to the some contextual factors, as for example, resistance to change, interoperability problems, development of additional functionalities, etc.

The migration processes in this case require of external collaborators with the technical expertise and further experience in similar developments, especially in the case that the organization lacks of previous experiences or faces challenging scenarios involving non-interoperable ICT services.

The result of the migration initiatives in these cases is positive in general in terms of improvement in the internal processes. Besides, normally positive externalities are created in other business units. The nature at a great extent of this initiatives are often reflected in the general society providing new services or improved software that is available in a public way. Clear examples in this group are the French Policy, the Munich Town Hall and the USA Postal Service. Next figure shows the typical characteristics of this group.

Group Two. Feature Seekers

We often find in this group medium to big size organizations that use in an intensive way ICT in their business processes. These organizations are also searching for new opportunities to improve

Table 2. Strategic movers

Group one. Strategic movers	
Process of adoption	
Organisation size	Normally big
Decisión makers	Top management
ICT strategy	Independence from provider, flexibility to specific requirements
The personal experience	High, normally there are specific units in ICT
The intensity in ICT	Great intensity, good equipment in hardware and software
External collaborators. Degree of autonomy	Often they count on them depending on their experiences and internal capabilities
Previous analysis	yes, cost and technical analysis
Process of migration	
Kind of migration	Structural or key services
Previous experiences in OSS	No normally
External collaborators. Implementation	The vast majority of cases
Barriers to inter-operability	Normally high barriers due to the existent applications
The management of change	Emphasis in educational programs, gradual approaches
Business process reengineering	High, especially when there are pre-established procedures
Users base	Big
Time horizon	Years
Results of the migration	
Re-trials for migration	They often do not stop the started tendency
Impact in other units	Practically always
Impact in external organisations	Quite often
Objectives reached	Often reached, sometimes a re-planning of the Project is required
Improved processes	Almost always

the availability of ICT capabilities, as for example, embedded systems, supercomputing, etc. In this group we find the University of Murcia or Amorebieta-Extano Town Hall.

The projects of migration are started by internal experts. They take into account the advantages that the new developments in software and hardware can offer. As a proof of this statement we can describe an IT expert working in a financial Institution stating *"There are no fans of open source software; we search for the best solution in a context plenty of different possibilities"*.

To get the specific experience, normally they collaborate with external agents, instead of having the technical expertise.

The interoperability does not play an essential role, due to the lack of strategic nature of the affected services. At the same time, if we consider that the final users are experts already, there is not great resistance to change. Contrary to the previous category, migration deadlines are maintained with processes clearly defined beforehand. The success criteria are clearly determined.

The results in this initiative do not normally show big transformations in the sense of producing impacts exclusively in internal services and not in other units. The following figure shows the most frequent characteristics for this group.

Table 3. Seekers for functional opportunities

Group two. Seekers for functional opportunities	
Process of adoption	
Firm size	Medium of big
Decision makers	Normally internal staff or technical units
The ICT strategy	Oriented to business support or new opportunities
Employee experiencies	High, normally there are specific ICT units
ICT intensity of use	Great intensity, good equipment in hardware and software
External collaborators. Degree of autonomy	Sometimes
Previous analysis	Sometimes
Process of migration	
Kind of migration	In no key services
Previous experience in OSS	Not necessarily
External collaborators. Implementation	Almost always
Barriers to interoperability	Normally it is not relevant except in applications that requires it from the legal point of view
The management of change	Procedures to make sure the lowest impact in the operations
Business process reengineering	Mínimum
Users base	Minimum
Time horizon for the migration	Months
Results of the migration	
Re-trials for migration	Yes, always that it is needed
Impact in other units	Minimum
Impact in external organisations	Often
Objectives reached	Yes
Improved processes	Yes, additional services

Group Three. Budget Optimizers

In this last group we find small and medium size Public Administrations that often adopt open source software as the best option in terms of cost-benefit analysis. They usually implement not critical new services by using open source software. They consider it as a less cost alternative.

The typical profile is a local ICT administrator that operates in a small and medium size organization in a market that it is not intensive in the use of ICT. Examples of this group can be the Toledo Council or the Arles Town Hall. The following figure shows the most important characteristics for this group.

CONSEQUENCES FROM OPEN SOURCE SOFTWARE MIGRATION

The implementation of open source software in firm's processes helps to search for interoperable technologies. These technologies can promote the independence of the software provider from the firm and the flexibility to be adapted to new possible scenarios.

The Spanish Acts RD 3/2010, for interoperability and RD 4/2010, for security, mean an evolution for the IT industry and an opportunity for consumers of IT devices. Both Acts define a group of appropriate practices that can help to remove potential situations for technological

Table 4. Budget optimizers

Group three. Budget optimizers	
Process of adoption	
Firm size	Usually small or medium size firm
Decision makers	Internal staff normally
The ICT strategy	Oriented to main business support and cost minimization
Employee experiences	Medium or low
ICT intensity of use	Medium or low
External collaborators. Degree of autonomy	Sometimes
Previous analysis	Minimum
Process of migration	
Kind of migration	In no key services
Previous experience in OSS	Medium or mínimum
External collaborators. Implementation	Sometimes
Barriers to interoperability	They do not exist normally
The management of change	It is not required normally
Business process reengineering	It is not required normally
Users base	Frequent
Time horizon for the migration	Months
Results of the migration	
Re-trials for migration	Yes, always a cost decrease is justified
Impact in other units	Few times
Impact in external organisations	Few times
Objectives reached	Yes
Improved processes	Yes, new proceses

lock in facing software providers. These Acts will probably allow, as it is mentioned in the disposition 11/2007, the required adaptation of Public Administrations to the global access to the information society and derived services. The disposition 11/2007 is known as the Act for the citizen's electronic access to public services.

Previous experiences in migration can help companies to decide and proof new prototypes that can be better adapted to their own circumstances according to the feedback that they have received. We consider this a very good approach since it assures the continuity of the business and it makes users to be participants at the same time. It reinforces the idea that software migration initiatives require of business process reengineering efforts from the technical and organizational perspectives.

According to the results obtained in this research, frequently big size Administrations hires the services of external organizations that offer them the technical knowledge or their own migration experience. No matter the way of adoption: strategic, functional or optimizer, initially the open source software is considered as an alternative in specific areas and it is later extended in a gradual way to other business areas. This behavior based in the previous experience trust agrees with other models for technology acceptance at different organizational levels (Venkatesh et al., 2003).

Implications for the Organizations that Decide to Implement Open Source Software

For open source projects we must take into consideration four different enabling aspects: managerial support, clear routines that promote the change efforts, an effective management of the project and the implication of the agents and end users that take part in the project.

Support of managers: Finney and Corbett (2007) develop a whole analysis of the literature review where they stress the importance of the

support of managers in ICT projects. Additionally and in view of our recent interviews with people responsible of open source migration processes in the Spanish market, the managerial support is mentioned as one of the most important aspects for the final success of the projects. Kotter (1995) and the UOC Report (2009) affirms how the

Managerial support offers leadership and trust in the long term. The leadership styles that we have observed in the Public Administrations match with relevant changes in the organization promoted by ICT implementations.

The redesign of processes: Al-Mashari et al. (2003), Fui-Hoon et al. (2003) and Finney and Corbett (2007) relate the existence of clear procedures when facing business process redesigns in the organizations with the search of positive results in ICT implementations and with the management of the needed cultural change in the organization.

The migration to new systems requires of the redesign of previous processes in the organization. Often new implementations fail because firms underestimate the reach of the processes of change. Motwani et al. (2002) affirm that firms must be prepared for radical changes.

The observation in software migration processes in large Organizations takes time and gradual executions. As Garvin recognizes (1998), this last statement fits with the need of inducing incremental change processes.

An efficient processes management. Implementing a a new system implies working in a variety of activities. All these activities can be immersed in different functionalities and can demand a global vision in the long term (Falwoski et al., 1998, Holland & Light, 1999, Rosario, 2000, Mabert, 2003). The plans for the management of processes coordinate and control the complex activities of the industrial and commercial projects.

Whenever the migration to open source software attempts to integrate information at different organizational levels, to get the required support in the functional areas of the organization is of crucial importance. Everyone must be responsible of the whole system and the key users in different areas must have clear their needs for the implementation of the new projects.

For achieving success in the final results of the implementation, it is useful to follow a methodology. It can help to establish in a clear way the steps of the project and the involvement of each key user and the consultancy team that might take part in the project.

Sommers and Nelson (2003) and Al Mashari et al. (2003) show how the selection of tools must be related to a reliable external support and the relationship between the firm and the external services.

To align the implementation of the services with the objectives established for the project is of great importance for both the Organization that decides to migrate to a new system and the providers. The design document elaborated once that the collect of information and analysis of requirements have finished, must include the objectives for the system. This document must include the situation of the processes before the implementation and the expectations on the future desired situation.

FUTURE RESEARCH DIRECTIONS

This research confirms a group of hypotheses that can be of interest for firms thinking about changing their integrated systems into open source software possibilities. We show that the open source software is a real alternative to the private one; it offers a solution for unsatisfied segments, it also reduces the dependence in the software provider, and optimizes hardware at a certain time.

We have shown how implementing open source software offers good opportunities so that firms can reach efficiency, flexibility and security in the organizational processes. However open source software also offers some challenges. The technology acceptance models (Olson & Davis, 1989) offer some answers to users about the changes in

technologies. They consider software as a social actor in the organization. Samez et Izak (2009) affirm how information technologies are capable of making users interact at different levels in the organization. We think that future research areas can deliver interesting results since they can complement these models with other constructs at firms.

The open source software is also having political support. This circumstance provides of some help to organizations. The two mentioned Acts RD 3/2010 y RD 4/2010, on interoperability and security make it possible a proper context to enable interactions with this kind of software. There is always an internal sponsor or a group of persons leading the initiative as an essential part of each migration project. Forthcoming research in the leadership styles can help to identify better scenarios to influence the success in the adoption of this kind of software.

Public Administrations are intensive consumers of ICT and they also interact daily with many different agents. These circumstances joint to their political positions towards the use of open source applications can male of them great promoters of innovation by being early adopters of this kind of technology.

The open source software does not necessarily imply budget savings, as we have observed for all the analyzed cases. As our analysis shows it seems more dependent in other dimensions such as own user experiences, the removal of the provider dependence, security issues, the reuse of hardware elements, etc.

Today there is a positive consensus on the importance of information and communication technologies in the educational systems over the development of the economies in general. The Berkman Report (2009) shows that a 10% of the increase in the penetration of bandwidth increases a 1.2 per cent the NGP in the developed economies. As far as open source software is able to offer technological resources at better costs, political incentives could be established for the promotion of public administration information systems based in the paradigm of open source. In this paper we have found of interest to document some of the successful initiatives that have been already performed in different countries.

REFERENCES

Ahmed, O. (2005). *Migrating from proprietary to Open Source: Learning Content Management Systems,* Unpublished doctoral dissertation, Department of Systems and Computer Engineering, Carleton University, Ottawa, Ontario, Canada.

Al-Mashari, M., Al-Mudimigh, A., & Zairi, M. (2003). Enterprise Resource Planning: a taxonomy of critical factors. *European Journal of Operational Research, 146,* 352–364. doi:10.1016/S0377-2217(02)00554-4

Berkman Center (2009). *Berkman Center for Internet and Society Broadband Study for FCC,* Report.

Berry, D. M. (2008). *Copy, rip, Burn: the Politics of Copyleft and Open Source.* London: Pluto Press.

Bitzer, J. (2005). The impact of entry and competition by Open Source Software on Innovation Activity, *Industrial Organization 051201,* EconWPA.

Casacubierta, D. (2003). *Collective creation.* Barcelona: Gedisa.

David, P., & Steinmueller, E. (1994). Information Economics and Policy. *Special Issue on The Economics of Standards, 6*(3-4), 134–148.

Davis, F. (1989). Perceived uselfulness, perceived ease of use and end user acceptance of information technology. *Management Information Systems Quarterly,* (September): 219–339.

Dedrick, J. & West, J. (2005). Why firms adopt Open Source Platforms: A grounded Theory of Innovation and Standards Adoption. *MIS Quarterly. Special Issue on Standard Making,* Seatle.

DeSanctis, G. M., & Poole, M. S. (1994). Capturing the complexity in advanced technology use: adaptive structuration theory. *Organization Science, 5*(2), 121–147. doi:10.1287/orsc.5.2.121

EOI. (2009). *The opportunities of free software: capacities, rights and innovation, Report.* Madrid: EOI.

Falkowski, G., Pedigo, P., Smith, B., & Swamson, D. (1998). A recipe for ERP success. Beyond Computing. *International Journal of Human-Computer Interaction, 16*(1), 5–22.

Finney, S., & Corbett, M. (2007). ERP implementation: a compilation and analysis of critical success factors. *Business Process Management Journal, 13*(3), 329–347. doi:10.1108/14637150710752272

Fui-Hoon, F., Zuckweiler, K. M., & Lee-Shang, J. (2003). ERP implementation: Chief Information Officers' Perceptions on Critical Success Factors. *International Journal of Human-Computer Interaction, 16*(1), 5–22. doi:10.1207/S15327590IJHC1601_2

Garvin, D. A. (1998). The processes of Organization and Management. *Sloan Management Review, 39*(4), 33–50.

Glaser, G., & Strauss, A. (1967). *The discovery of Grounded Theory: Strategies for qualitative research.* New York: Aldine Publishing Company.

Gonzalez-Barahona, J. (2001). Counting Potatoes: the Size of Debian 2.2. *The European Online Magazine for the IT Professional, 2*(6), December.

Gonzalez-Barahona, J. (2004). *About free software.* Madrid: Rey Juan Carlos University- Dykinson.

Hammer, M. (2000). Reengineering Work: Do not Automate, Obliterate. *Harvard Business Review,* 37–46.

Hippern, L., & Krogh, S. (2003). Open source software and the private-collective innovation model: Issues for organization science. *Organization Science, 14*(2), 241–248.

Holland, C. P., & Light, B. (1999). A critical success factors model for ERP implementation. *IEEE Software*, (May/June): 30–36. doi:10.1109/52.765784

Hunter, H. (2006). *Open Source Data Base Driven Web Development*. Oxford: Chandos.

Kotter, J. P. (1995). Leading change: Why transformation effort fail. *Harvard Business Review*, (September): 42–56.

Lakhan, R., & Jhunjhunwala, V. (2008). Open Source in Education. *EDUCAUSE Quarterly*, *31*(2), 32–40.

Lerner, J., & Tirole, J. (2002). The simple economics of Open Source. *The Journal of Industrial Economics*, *50*(2), 197–234. doi:10.1111/1467-6451.00174

Lerner, J., & Tirole, J. (2005). The Economics of Technology Sharing: Open Source and Beyond. *The Journal of Economic Perspectives*, *19*(2), 99–120. doi:10.1257/0895330054048678

Mabert, V., Soni, A., & Venkatamara, M. (2003). Enterprise Resource Planning: managing implementation process. *European Journal of Operational Research*, *146*(2), 302–314. doi:10.1016/S0377-2217(02)00551-9

Motwani, J., Mirchandani, M., & Gunasekaran, A. (2002). Successful implementation of ERP Projects: evidence from two case studies. *International Journal of Production Economics*, *75*, 83–96. doi:10.1016/S0925-5273(01)00183-9

Myers, M. D. (1997). Qualitative Research in information systems. *Management Information Systems Quarterly*, 209–223.

Myers, M. D. (2009). *Qualitative Research in Business and Management*. London: Sage.

Orlikowski, W. (1991). Information Technology and the Structuring of Organizations. *Information Systems Research*, winter, 27-38.

Orlikowski, W. (1993). CASE Tools as Organizational Change: investigating Incremental and Radical Changes in Systems Development. *MIS Quarterly,* Septermber, 209-223.

Orliwoski, W. (2000). Using technology and constituing structures: a practice lens for studying technology in organizations. *Organization Science*, *11*(4), 404–428. doi:10.1287/orsc.11.4.404.14600

Osterloh, R., & Rota, M. (2007). Open source software development, just another case of collective invention. *Research Policy*, *36*(2), 157–171. doi:10.1016/j.respol.2006.10.004

Poole, M. S., & DeSanctis, G. (1990). Understanding the use of group decisions support systems: the theory of adaptive structuration. In Fulk, J., & Steinfield, C. W. (Eds.), *Organizations and communication technology* (pp. 173–193). California: Sage.

Raymond, E. (1999). The Cathedral and the bazaar. *Knowledge, Technology & Policy*, *12*(3), 23–49. doi:10.1007/s12130-999-1026-0

Riehle, D. (2007). The Economic Motivation of Open Source: Stakeholder Perspectives. *IEEE Computer*, *40*(4), 25–32. doi:10.1109/MC.2007.147

Roberts, K. H., & Grabowski, M. (1995). *Organizations, technology and structuring*. In S.R: Clegg, C. Hardy, W.R. Nord, (Eds). *Handbook of Organization Studies*, 409-423. California: Sage.

Rosario, J.G. (2000). On the leading edge: critical success factors in ERP implementation projects, *Business World*, May, 21-27.

Rossi, D. (2006). Decoding the green open source software puzzle: A survey of theoretical and empirical contributions. *The Economics of Open Source Software Development, 22nd IEEE International Parallel and Distributed Processing Symposium*, New York.

Sameh, B., & Izak, J. (2009). The Adoption and Use of IT Artifacts: A New Interaction Centric Model for the Study of User-Artifact Relationships. *Journal of the Association for Information Systems, 10*(9), 661–685.

Shiff, T. (2002). The Economics of Open Source Software: a survey of the early literature. *Review of Network Economics, 1*(1), 66–74. doi:10.2202/1446-9022.1004

Sommers, G., & Nelson, C. (2003). A taxonomy of players and activities across the ERP project life cycle . *Information & Management, 41*(3), 257–278. doi:10.1016/S0378-7206(03)00023-5

Strauss, A., & Corbin, J. (1990). *Basics of Qualitative Research: Grounded theory, procedures and techniques.* London: Sage.

Tascón, M. (2006). Development of a place fotr the information society. In R. Casado (coord.). *Keys for digital literacy.* Seminar on Digital Literacy. Madrid: Telefónica Foundation, 187-194 Retrieved from: http://sociedaddelainformación. telefónica.es/documentos/articulos/clavesdelaalfabetizacióndigital.pdf

UOC. (2009). *The use of open source in Public Administrations in Spain. Report.* Barcelona: Universitat Oberta de Calalunya.

Venkatesh, V., & Brown, S. A. (2003). User acceptance of information technology: Toward a unified view. *Management Information Systems Quarterly, 27*(3), 425–478.

Walsham, G. (1993). *Interpreting information systems in organizations. Nueva York.* Wiley.

Weick, K. (1990). *Technology as equivoque.* In P.S. Goodman, L.S. Sproull and Associates, (eds.), *Technology and organizations,* 1-44, San Francisco: Jossey-Bass.

Wheeler, D. (2007). *Why Open Source Software. Look at the Numbers.* Retrieved 30th January 2010 from: dwheeler.com/oss_ls_why_html.

ADDITIONAL READING SECTION

Akkermans, H., & Van Helden, K. (2002). Vicious and virtuous cycles in ERP implementation: a case study of interrelations between critical success factors. *European Journal of Information Systems, 11*(1), 35–46. doi:10.1057/palgrave/ejis/3000418

Ang, J. S. K., Sum, C. C., & Yeo, L. N. (2002). A multiple-case design methodology for studying MRP success and CSFs. *Information & Management, 39*(4), 271–281. doi:10.1016/S0378-7206(01)00096-9

Esteves, J., & Pastor, J. (2001). Analysis of critical success factors relevance along SAP implementation phases. *Proceedings of the Seventh Americas Conference on Information Systems,* 1019-1025.

Moor, J. H. (1985). What is computer ethics? *Metaphilosophy, 16*(4), 266–275. doi:10.1111/j.1467-9973.1985.tb00173.x

Nah, F., Lau, J., & Kuang, J. (2001). Critical factors for successful implementation of enterprise systems. *Business Process Management, 7*(3), 285–296. doi:10.1108/14637150110392782

Parker, D. (1988). Ethics for Information Systems Personnel. *Journal of Information Systems Management, 5,* 44–48. doi:10.1080/07399018808962925

Smith, A. (2009). New framework for enterprise information systems. *International Journal of CENTERIS, 1*(1), 30–36.

Summer, M. (1999). *Critical success factors in enterprise wide information management systems projects.* Proceedings of 5th Americas Conference on Information Systems, 232-234.

Tiwari, R., et al. (2007) *Mobile Banking as Business Strategy: Impact of Mobile Technologies on Customer Behaviour and its Implications for Banks.* Working Paper, Germany. Retrieved Feb. 2007

Umble, E. J., Haft, R. R., & Umble, M. M. (2003). Enterprise Resource Planning: implementation procedures and critical success factors. *European Journal of Operational Research, 146*, 241–257. doi:10.1016/S0377-2217(02)00547-7

Wang, E., Sheng-Pao, S., Jianj, J. J., & Klein, G. (2008). The consistency among facilitating factors and ERP implementation success: A holistic view of kit. *Journal of Systems and Software, 81*, 1601–1621. doi:10.1016/j.jss.2007.11.722

Chapter 19
IT Governance State of Art in the Colombian Health Sector Enterprises

Andrea Herrera
University of Los Andes, Colombia

Olga Lucía Giraldo
University of Los Andes, Colombia

ABSTRACT

The Colombian healthcare industry has been growing since the late 90's and the amount of spending allocated to this sector is the highest proportion of GDP in Latin American countries. Those facts have increased the importance of this sector for the economy and national development. Furthermore, enterprises with IT governance that focus on organizational objectives have yielded superior results than their competitors. The authors performed a research project to find out if there are similarities amongst Colombian Health Sector Enterprises that have obtained positive results. In this project, the authors studied IT governance, operational model, engagement model, and portfolio management of twelve companies, all of them large to medium-sized. The results show that the IT governance behavior of the Colombian healthcare industry is not homogeneous. Different subsectors have different behavior; some perform as large superior global enterprises and others are beginning their journey.

INTRODUCTION

Researches of the Center for Information Systems Research (CISR), of MIT, show that enterprises that carefully govern their IT assets usually have superior results than other enterprises in their industrial sector. Frequently their ROI and ROA is about 20% greater than that of competitors (Weill

& Ross, 2004), (Weill, 2004). More often than not superior enterprises have set up IT governance schemes with common constituents such as: IT governance scheme, intentional operation model, coordination mechanisms between corporative and local objectives, engagement mechanisms linking IT projects goals with business goals, IT portfolio management aligning IT investment with business objectives.

DOI: 10.4018/978-1-4666-1764-3.ch019

Our research objective is to find out how superior health enterprises with operations in Colombia govern their IT to compare results among them and with those of CISR. The sample we observed was composed of twelve companies, both large multinationals and large and medium-sized Colombian companies, all of them with nonstop growth during last five years. Our research framework is CISR IT governance. The main concepts we used were IT Governance arrangements matrix, operational model, IT portfolio, and Engagement model.

The contribution of our work is that we show a trend of IT governance in Colombia, and that we provide Colombian enterprises with a framework to think about their actual and future IT governance and to decide consciously its composition looking for coherence between its elements and for better results. We begin this chapter with a background, then, we show the IT governance components for each company studied and partial findings. Finally, we present our main conclusions and future directions of our research.

BACKGROUND

This section is divided in three parts, in the first one, we state the importance of the IT governance and we provide the main IT governance concepts. Then, we discuss the key characteristics of the Colombian health sector and finally, we offer a general description of the methodology used in this work.

IT Governance Background

Today companies manage many assets: human, financial, physical, intellectual, and relationships; but information and the technologies that they use to manage it, have an increasing importance. This importance is not just because of the key role IT plays inside an organization but also because companies need to get more value from their IT investments. Therefore, as a key asset IT must be

governed to create value. This require different people to be involved in IT decisions, new ways of making those IT-related decisions, and new techniques for implementing and monitoring those decisions. As a result of this, it has been a proliferation of academic theories and practical solutions, some of the most known are:

- ISO/IEC 38500:2008: "provides guiding principles for directors of organizations (including owners, board members, directors, partners, senior executives, or similar) on the effective, efficient, and acceptable use of Information Technology (IT) within their organizations" ("ISO organization", 2008).
- COBIT: "is an IT governance framework and supporting toolset that allows managers to bridge the gap between control requirements, technical issues and business risks" ("ISACA organization", 2006)
- CISR IT governance model: "an approach to systematically planning IT input and decision rights in key IT decisions". It is designed mainly for "executives to will make a difference in the performance of their enterprises" and for IT managers to have a "framework, best practices, and clear examples of how to work with their business collages to improve IT governances" (Weill & Ross, 2004).

Those models and standards have allowed many organizations to study how a well-designed IT governance can positively impact enterprises' performance. Particularly, a series of research project conducted by CISR explored IT governance in more than three hundred enterprises spanning Americas, Europe, and Asia Pacific. They studied who had input to and who held decision rights for key IT decisions and also they "measured governance and financial performance and the effectiveness of the mechanisms used to implement governance" (Weill & Ross, 2004).

These researches analyzed different governance patterns and identified what governance arrangements work best and also they correlated those arrangements with financial performance. From this information, the researchers identified lessons learned from leading companies that can help other enterprises to design consciously their IT governance. Based on those results, our work is to study companies with operations in Colombia, in order to achieve the main objective we mentioned before.

Now, we will delve into the CISR's framework. Weill define IT governance as "Specifying the decision rights and accountability framework to encourage desirable behavior in the use of IT", and also complemented this definition by emphasizing that "IT governance is not about what specific decisions are made. That is management. Rather, governance is about systematically determining who makes each type of decision (a decision right), who has input to a decision (an input right), and how these people (or groups) are held accountable for their role." (Weill, 2004). Therefore, an effective IT governance scheme addresses both a behavioral and normative side.

By focusing in decision rights, the authors group IT decisions in *five domains: IT principles*, clarifies the business role of IT; *IT architecture*, defines integration and standardization requirements; *IT infrastructure*, determines shared and enabled services; *Business application needs*, specifies the business need for purchase, or internally developed IT applications; and, *IT investment and prioritization*, chooses which initiatives to fund and how much to spend. These decisions cannot be isolated. Consequently, IT governance must ensure that these reinforce each other to successfully achieve organization's objectives.

The authors also classified the way of specifying decision rights or input to IT decisions in *six archetypes: Business monarchy*, Top managers; *IT monarchy*, IT specialists; *Feudal*, each business unit makes independent decisions; *Federal*, combines the corporate center and the business units

with or without IT people involved; *IT duopoly*, IT group and other groups; and *Anarchy*, where an isolated individual or a small group makes decisions. Crossing domain against archetypes forms the IT governance arrangements matrix, where the governance scheme of a particular company can be depicted. This matrix also helps identify the level of centralization of each decision according to each archetype; being monarchy, the level most centralized and anarchy, the most decentralized.

IT governance intentions must be supported by the company's *operating model*, which is defined as "the necessary level of business process integration and standardization for delivering goods and services to customers". Standardization of a business process defines "how a process will be executed regardless of who is performing the process of where it is completed" and Integration "links the efforts of organizational units through shared data" (Ross et al, 2006). Using this two-dimensional model, CISR scientists generate four types of operating models:

- *Diversification:* low standardization and integration. This model applies to companies whose business units have the following characteristics: few shared customers or suppliers, independent transactions, different ways doing business, few data standards, among others. These companies may look for economies of scale in a model of independence with shared services.

- *Coordination:* low standardization, high integration. Business units for which this model applies share some of the following: customers, products, or suppliers. Also, transactions can impact different units; however, they have unique functions. This model promotes process expertise strengthening, so that companies can attract new customers and sell more products to existing customers through seamless access to shared data.

- *Replication:* high standardization, low integration. This model allows business units to maintain autonomy while managing operations in a well-regulated way. Consequently, the success of the company is dependent of a set of efficient standardized business processes rather than on shared customers. Franchises are clear examples of this model; those have standardized independent transactions that are added up at corporate level.
- *Unification:* high standardization and integration. The last model applies to organizations that typically have integrated supply chains around global customers or suppliers and they can take advantage of economies of scale. The unification model could benefit companies whose products or services are commodities rather than those whose are focused on innovation.

Additionally, IT portfolios are an approach to "enable a manager team to match IT investments with corporate strategic objectives" (Weill et al, 2008). IT portfolios divide IT asset in four classes: *Strategic,* gains competitive advantage or position in the market place; *Informational,* provides information for any purpose; *Transactional,* cuts costs or increase throughput; and *Infrastructure,* supplies a foundation for shared IT services.

Finally, the IT engagement model (Fonstad, 2006), aims to realize and maintain the IT business value by linking *six internal stakeholder groups*: IT and non-IT managers at the corporate, business unit and project level. Using this model we can align IT and non-IT stakeholders and coordinate organizational levels. Said model has three types of components: at a corporate level, the *Company-wide IT governance*, when IT outsources include shared IT Business Governance; at an operational level, *project management* to bind IT and non-IT stakeholders; and *linkage mechanisms* between IT and non-IT stakeholders. There are three types of linking mechanisms: Business linkages, link projects with business unit strategies and with corporate strategies; Alignment linkages, link IT project objectives with those of business units; and Architecture linkages, link IT projects architecture to the corporative IT architecture, adjusting the former to the second or allowing exception if necessary.

Health Sector in Colombia

Now we address some key features of the health sector in Colombia, its main actors and its basic regulation. Currently, in Colombia inequality between the riches and the poor continues to be very strong, although, it is noteworthy that the amount of spending allocated to health is the highest proportion of GDP in Latin American countries. This has led to a general improvement in Colombia's health indicators (Santa-María et al, 2007). But this was not always so, before 1993 the social security health system in Colombia had three main problems: inefficiency in spending, low coverage rates and low quality of services.

Given these problems in 1993, the law 100 approved the creation of the Colombian General Social Security Health System or SGSSS because of its name in Spanish. The SGSSS introduced three basic principles in the provision of health services: efficiency, universality, and solidarity. To support these principles, the SGSSS is founded on two pillars: the universal coverage, and regulated competition (Santa-María et al, 2007). The SGSSS establishes a mandatory health plan (POS) with some specific benefits and also it divides Colombian population according to their ability to pay in two different schemes: the contributory (RC) and the subsidized (RS). Also, it defines three kinds of entities to manage and deliver health services:

- *Health Promoting Enterprises (EPS):* Insurance companies that are responsible for providing directly or indirectly the POS to the members of the RC,

- *Subsidized Scheme Administrators (EPS-S):* These entities are also insurance companies and they are responsible directly or indirectly the POS to the members of the RS, and
- *Medical Care Institutions (IPS):* Public, private, mixed or community hospitals or health centers to which the EPSs and EPS-Ss will engage the services defined in the POS. The IPS can be of different levels (from I to III), depending on the complexity of the services they offer.

Additionally, the reform of 1993 delegated the regulation and surveillance of the SGSSS to three bodies: the National Council of Social Security in Health (CNSSS)[1], supreme authority responsible for updating and designing the content of the POS; the Ministry of Social Protection (MPS), responsible for the formulation of the sector policies towards quality and efficient management of the system; and the National Health Authority,

responsible for monitoring, inspecting and controlling the actors in the system.

According to the structure of the SGSSS explained above, we can divide the health sector in Colombia in three main subsectors and two special groups, see Figure 1:

- Providing subsector: is responsible for providing the main external sourced materials to deliver health services to the final users, for example, in this subsector we find pharmaceutical laboratories, and medical instrument companies, among others.
- Commercial subsector: is responsible for promoting uncovered groups' membership and collecting the quota from members of both RC and RS systems. Therefore, both the EPSs and EPS-Ss belong to this subsector.
- Operation subsector: is responsible for delivering health services to final users,

Figure 1. Colombia's Health Sector: Main subsectors and actors

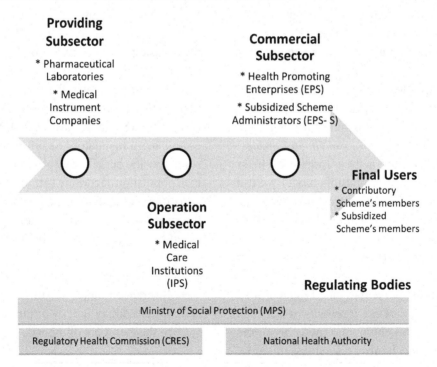

therefore, all medical care institutions belong to this one.

- Final users: is the first special group and it is composed by all members assigned to one of the two schemes defined by the SGSSS.
- Regulating bodies: as we explained before this special group is responsible for designing, implementing and controlling policies for the health sector in Colombia.

For this research we studied some companies belonging to each of the three subsectors identified and next subsection presents the methodology we followed in our research.

Methodology

This subsection shows how we use the previous elements to analyze the IT governance in Colombian health sector enterprises. We begin by defining the instruments we used to analyze IT governance practices in leading enterprises of Colombia. These included interviews and inquiries applied to IT and non-IT managers and employees.

Then, we selected twelve companies with operations in Colombia that belong to the three different subsectors in the Colombian health sector: providers, commercial, and operations. After selecting the companies, we contacted CxO level to obtain approval and cooperation. Then, we studied the history, products, processes, and organizational structure of each company. Afterwards, we gathered information and analyzed it; and we presented and discussed the results with IT and non-IT CxO level. Then, we interviewed selected managers and employees from IT and business units, project managers and stakeholders, and the CxO level. Next, we showed and discussed the results with the CxO participating in the study and adjusted it when necessary. Finally, we consolidated the results, drafted conclusions looking for trends, and compared with those of CISR.

IT GOVERNANCE AT THE HEALTH SECTOR IN COLOMBIA

We focused on large and medium-sized enterprises. We studied twelve enterprises belonging to the health sector, five pharmaceutical laboratories from the providing subsector, three EPSs from the commercial subsector and four level III IPSs from the operation subsector.

IT Governance at Five Pharmaceutical Laboratories

The pharmaceutical laboratory industry is the tenth most notable economical sector in Colombia. Its assets had a real increase of 69% between 2002 and 2006; in the same period sales rose by 78%. In 2006 ROA was 7.72% and ROE 12.27%, both doubled those of 2002. The market share of the top five laboratories is more than 28% of the sector, and assets are about 30%. SMEs in the industry increased from 23 (36%) in 2002, to 105 (62%) in 2006 ("Portafolio", 2007). Now, we present the laboratories and their IT governance (Lavilla & Moreno, 2008), (Kuperman, 2009). We do not give their names for reasons of confidentiality; we refer to them as Lab1 to Lab5.

First Pharmaceutical Laboratory: Lab1

Lab1, established at the end of the 19th century, is a multinational that researches, develops, manufactures, and merchandizes pharmaceutical and biopharmaceutical products. It has more than 130 subsidiaries in 47 countries, and more than 40,000 employees around the world. Lab1 belongs to the 20 largest pharmaceuticals in the world and in Colombia it is in the top 10. In Colombia, Lab1 manufactures and supplies liquid and semisolid products to Latin American markets; its sales increase from 2006 to 2007 was 7.4% ("Cambio", 2008).

Our analysis showed that both IT and non-IT staff have a clear vision about IT governance style and its benefits. The decision making process is centralized, such as in Business monarchy, coming from headquarters. In Lab1 information input is also centralized, IT monarchy, for all domains except Business application needs; this last one uses IT duopoly to address local needs and compliance.

Process standardization level at Lab1 is very high, which helps them have global contracts with IT providers. Although, geographic units share information at the local level, they do not share among them or with the corporate level. As a result, global integration level is low, but locally it is high. These facts allow us to classify Lab1 as using two operating models: Unification at local level, and Replication at regional and global level.

IT investment in 2008 was 3.5% of annual sales. Its IT Portfolio distribution is: Strategic, 13%, focused on improving customer relationships; Informational, 13%, concentrated on customers and order control and business intelligence. The focal point of Transactional, 27% was cost control and process integration using an ERP system, antivirus software, and recovery plans and tools; and the focal point of Infrastructure, 53% was sharing local, regional and corporative services.

In Lab1 the IT engagement model elements are:

- IT companywide governance: Executive committee including CIO, Architecture committee, and Capital approval committee; and Project prioritization process. Shared IT governance uses regular meetings and Service Level Agreements-SLA.
- Project management: Early business project objectives definition; Good practices and standards; and Project sponsor and accountable person.
- Linking mechanisms:
  ○ Business: Project prioritization, Sponsoring, Post-implementation re-
  views; and Aligning project with corporate objectives.
  ○ Alignment: Level, Area, and Project committees; and Business/IT relation manager.
  ○ Architecture: Infrastructure standardization, and Architecture Exception management.

Second Pharmaceutical Laboratory: Lab2

Lab2 is a Colombian medium-sized enterprise established in the mid 90's. It has two business units, the first manufactures and merchandizes pharmaceutical, cosmetic and nutritional products for human consumption; the second business unit makes-up other laboratory products. Lab2 exports products in association with other Colombian medium-sized pharmaceutical laboratories.

Even though archetypes of IT governance exist and are known by non-IT managers and employees, their benefits are not clear. IT investment domain archetype is Business monarchy. Other archetypes used for input of information are Federal and IT duopoly, and the decision right predominant archetype is IT duopoly.

Lab2 was reengineered to focus on processes using an ERP system with high integration and standardization of processes, generating a unique operational model, Unification. As a collateral result, IT changed its role and then began to be strategic.

IT portfolio is aligned with the priorities of reengineering. So, the objective of Strategic investment, 30%, is to gain market share by managing customer relationships; Informational focuses on process control by means of a balanced scorecard referring to fulfillment of corporate objectives; Transactional looks to control costs; and the aim of Infrastructure investment, 50% is to share IT services.

In Lab2 the IT engagement model elements are:

- IT companywide governance: similar to Lab1 but Shared IT governance without a SLA.
- Project management: similar to Lab1.
- Linking mechanisms:
  - Business: Project prioritization; Sponsoring, Regular and post-implementation reviews and Aligning project with corporate objectives.
  - Alignment: Area committees, and Business/IT relation manager.
  - Architecture: Infrastructure standardization.

Third Pharmaceutical Laboratory: Lab3

Lab3, a multinational enterprise with geographical business unit in more than 100 countries, around 70.000 employees, has been in Colombia more than 30 years, and researches and supplies pharmaceutical products for catastrophic diseases. Lab3 is in the 2008 Fortune Magazine top 500 and top 10 pharmaceutical laboratories. In Colombia there are two business units, Pharmaceutical and Diagnosis.

IT and non-IT staffs have a clear vision about IT governance style and its benefits, particularly, the CEO is the direct sponsor for IT projects when is necessary. IT area has a very important role in IT governance: input of IT principles and Business need applications archetype is IT duopoly and IT infrastructure decision right archetype it is also.

All around the world processes are standardized, but integrated only at local level, neither regionally nor globally, then local operating model is Unification, regional and global operation models are Replication.

Its global IT investment is around 7% of global annual sales; last five years local IT investment has been 1% of annual incomes due to the former investment, IT service centralization and global and regional shared IT services. IT portfolio distribution shows low Transactional, 20%, due to

regional and global shared services, and high Infrastructure, 50%, to gain access to those services. Strategic, 25%, looks for competitiveness, innovation and new business particularly at the Diagnosis business unit, giving an idea about enterprise trust in IT. Informational had been 5%.

In Lab3 the IT engagement model elements are:

- IT companywide governance: similar to Lab1 plus Purchase and Accountable committee, and Infrastructure renewal process. No outsourcing then no Shared IT governance.
- Project management: similar to Lab1 plus PMO and Project monitoring.
- Linking mechanisms:
  - Business: in addition to those of Lab1 we found Regular reviews and Early stakeholder involvement.
  - Alignment: Business/IT relation manager and Project advances approval.
  - Architecture: Project early ensure conform to Architecture standard and Project carry-over according to former results.

Fourth Pharmaceutical Laboratory: Lab4

Lab4 is multinational with geographical business units in more than 130 countries, around 50.000 employees, and more than 70 years in Colombia. As Lab3, Lab4 is in the 2008 Fortune Magazine top 500 and top 10 pharmaceutical laboratories; Lab4 researches and supplies pharmaceutical products. Locally it has three business units. CIO is responsible for Colombian and Ecuadorian IT services and operation.

IT and non-IT staffs have a clear vision about IT governance style and its benefits. IT governance archetypes are the same than those of Lab3 except for Infrastructure decisions right and Business applications needs; for the first one the archetype is IT monarchy, and for the second one are Federal for input and IT duopoly for decision right. Critical factors for IT governance success are the same than Lab3.

Processes are standardized all around the world and integrated at local and regional level, not globally, then local and regional operating model are Unification, and global operation models is Replication.

Its global IT investment is around 5% of global annual sales; meanwhile local IT investment is around 2.3% of annual incomes for similar reason of Lab3. Infrastructure, 50%, and Transaction, 25%, are similar to Lab3, but Strategic, 5%, and Informational, 20%, are exactly opposed. Reasons of high Infrastructure, Transaction and Informational investment is supporting the local Unification operating model.

Lab4 and Lab3 IT engagement models are similar. Lab4 specific mechanisms are:

- IT companywide governance: equal to Lab3. Shared governance uses regular meetings and SLA.
- Project management: same of Lab3.
- Linking mechanisms:
  ◦ Business: are alike Lab3 although Periodical project review is not always done.
  ◦ Alignment and Architecture: are the same as Lab3.

Fifth Pharmaceutical Laboratory: Lab5

Lab5 is a multinational located in more than 130 countries, and around 100.000 employees. As Lab3 and Lab4, Lab5 is in the 2008 Fortune Magazine top 500 and top 10 pharmaceutical laboratories. Lab5 imports, markets and supplies medicines, vaccines and holistic health solutions; locally it has three business units.

Contrary to other pharmaceutical laboratories in this study, there is no clear vision of IT gover-

nance. CxO level sees IT as a support tool; IT is under CFO so it has no visibility neither empower. Archetypes for input are IT duopoly, but Business application needs Federal; decisions making of IT principles and IT investment archetypes are IT monarchy, remaining are IT duopoly.

Like previous multinational laboratories, processes standardization -globally, regionally and locally- and locally integration are high. And like almost every pharmaceutical multinational company, process integration at global and regional level is low. Then operational models are Unification at local level and Replication at regional and global levels. At global and regional levels IT focuses on providing standardized infrastructure and developing centralized applications; at local level IT is looking for greater integration to achieve advantages of Unification model.

As in previous two multinational laboratories, global IT portfolio is high, 5% of annual incomes, but unlike them, local IT portfolio is also high, 8% of annual local incomes. IT portfolio distribution is correlated with IT current state; IT is developing a project to export regionally and its main issues are synergies, and value generation, so strategic. Then, Infrastructure, 35%, and Transactional, 30%, are higher than Informational, 10%, and Strategic, 25%.

Its IT engagement model is similar to earlier laboratories; specific mechanisms are:

- IT companywide governance: the same than Lab3, but no Purchase committee.
- Project management: same of Lab3.
- Linking mechanisms:
  ◦ Business: the same than Lab4 but no Periodical project revisions.
  ◦ Alignment: the sole is Business/IT relation manager.
  ◦ Architecture: the single is Architecture Exception management.

Findings for Pharmaceutical Laboratories

We present our findings for this first group of enterprises (Giraldo et al, 2010) divided in four parts: IT governance arrangements matrix, operating model, IT portfolio, and IT engagement model.

Regarding to the IT governance arrangements matrix, we noticed that IT governance trend absolutely differs from CISR. Table 1 presents the main IT governance trend in Colombian pharmaceutical laboratories.

IT Monarchy and IT duopoly are the most frequently archetypes for information input, meanwhile for CISR research it is Federal. It looks like if subsidiaries input information through IT; IT monarchy and IT duopoly gather local information and input it to headquarter. Partial exception is Business application needs that use Federal archetype like CISR; normally business units know local needs and regulations and input it to corporate center to obtain approval for adapting global applications. For decision making there is also a mismatch. We do not find a clear explanation, but it looks like that IT monarchy and IT duopoly roles were reversed.

About operating models, those were predictable at all levels: local, regional and global. This industry use best practices, and then processes are standardized from corporate to local level. Furthermore, process integration level is high in the local level and low in regional and global level. Local high integration tries to find transparency behind client and supplier, efficiency and control cost. Regional and global low integration pursue flexibility. Financial indicators reveal that operating models results to be positive.

Observing global IT investment for Lab3, Lab4 and Lab5 – 8%, 5% and 5% of annual incomes respectively- is amazingly superior to the average IT investment of enterprises researched in CISR, 4.2%, (Weill & Ross, 2004). High IT investment seems to be standard in this industry; more research must be done to confirm this hypothesis. Additionally, according to CISR research, enterprise average investments are: Infrastructure 54%, Transactional 13%, Informational 20%, and Strategic 13% (Weill et al, 2008). Our result for Infrastructure is similar 48%, except Lab5. But in the other types of investment - Transactional 22%, Informational 11%, and Strategic 20% respectively - there is a big difference and a large variance in our sample. Although, we do not have enough evidence to formulate a hypothesis about this difference, we believe that it has to do with local strategy and being a subsidiary.

Table 1. IT Governance Arrangements Matrix: 5 Pharmaceutical Laboratories.

	IT principles		IT architecture		IT infrastructure		Business appl. needs		IT investment	
	I	D	I	D	I	D	I	D	I	D
Business Monarchy		L1		L1		L1		L1	L2	L1 L2
IT Monarchy	L1	L3 L4 L5	L1 L3 L4	L3 L4	L1 L3 L4	L4		L3	L1 L3 L4	L3 L4 L5
Federal	L2						L2 L4 L5			
IT Duopoly	L3 L4 L5	L2	L2 L5	L2 L5	L2 L3 L5		L1 L3	L2 L4 L5	L5	

I Information input   D Decision Making Right   ▮ Most common pattern in CISR research
L1: Lab1; L2: Lab2; L3: Lab3; L4: Lab4; L5: Lab5

Finally, concerning the IT engagement model in all pharmaceutical laboratories the strongest component is IT companywide governance. All have Executive committee frequently including CIO, Architecture committee, and Capital approval committee often with Project prioritization process. Project management is also mature. All laboratories have Early business project objectives definition, Project management good practices and standards; and Project sponsor and accountable person. Alignment linkage sole common mechanism is Business/IT relation manager. Other frequently mechanism is Project advances approval. Architecture linkages are Infrastructure standardization, and Architecture exception management. Business linkage mechanisms are well developed. All laboratories use Project prioritization, and sponsoring. Frequently mechanisms are Regular project and post-implementation reviews, Incentives, and Aligning project with corporate objectives. Shared IT governance frequently used mechanisms are regular meeting and SLA. The most outsourced processes are help desk, document management, and hardware and communication support.

IT Governance at three Health Promoting Enterprises: EPSs

All the EPSs in Colombia are large-sized enterprises because they need a critical mass to be profitable. Given this situation many small or medium-sized enterprises after the reform of the health system in 1993, had to merge to meet this need.

Next, we present the EPSs and their IT governance (Díaz, 2010). Again, we do not give their names for reasons of confidentiality. The first one, EPS1 is a business unit of a family compensation company, and then it focuses in having a big amount of affiliates of mass sector. EPS2 was established when the health sector was open in 1993, as looking to catch the opportunity. EPS3

is a business unit of a prepaid health company, with focus on high incomes population.

First EPS- EPS1

EPS1 is among the top 10 of its subsector. Its strategy is being a leader in the social protection business so quality is a key factor to promote its services. EPS1 is a business unit of a family compensation company; let's call it "Caja".

Family compensation companies are a very particular business established in some countries such as Colombia and Chile. Even though they are a private business, they are delivering a public service in order to achieve a more equitable and fair society by helping the working-class to have better living condition. Their incomes are from a percentage of Colombian enterprises payroll. Actually, they have many different business units like health, education, housing, financial services, retail, and recreation and tourism.

Caja is one of the top 100 biggest Colombian enterprises. Organizational culture of Caja is customer focused, so it uses IT to improve its services' quality while having competitive costs. Just before our study, the company reengineered itself to achieve a process-centered structure. The reengineering process gives IT a central role for the organization's operations and strategies. IT helps both, Caja and EPS1, to establish its IT governance, so currently IT and non-IT staff is aware about it and its benefits. The resulting IT governance archetypes for information input are IT duopoly for business related domains, and IT monarchy for IT related domains; the same is for decisions making but IT investment archetype is business monarchy.

The operational model of Caja, thus of EPS1, is Coordination. Business units generate synergies using common data, so integration is high. They also share information about products and services with its suppliers and customers.

IT investment is about 3% of annual sales. Infrastructure, 54%, focal point is technology standardization to share data between business processes and with suppliers and customers. Transactional, 16% objective is cut costs. Informational, 17%, looks for better data integration. Strategic, 13%, is focus on client relationship management.

The IT engagement model mechanisms of EPS1 are:

- IT companywide governance: Executive, Technical and Architectural committees, and Project prioritization; technical committee includes non-IT senior leaders and it is in-charged of approving, controlling, and reviewing IT projects. Shared IT governance uses regular meetings and SLA.
- Project management: PMO office for all IT and non-IT projects at corporate level, Caja, thus for EPS1.
- Linking mechanisms:
  ◦ Business: Project prioritization, Sponsoring, Approval; Aligning IT project with corporate objectives; and IT project improvement process.
  ◦ Alignment: Project and Areas committees.
  ◦ Architecture: Infrastructure standardization, and Architecture Exception management.

Second EPS: EPS2

At its very beginning EPS2 was a prepaid health company. In 1993, when public health care law allows private companies to be EPSs, the company established two new business line EPS and EPS-S. Nowadays, the prepaid business line disappeared, and the company covers almost all the country and its strategy is cost control because the company only offers services defined by law and they quality is controlled by law.

Currently, IT and non-IT staff are aware about IT governance and its benefits, which are communication, fair and transparent negotiations between IT and business, and IT projects focus on

corporative objectives. EPS2 encourages business participation on IT decision using IT duopoly and Federal archetypes for information input. The resulting IT governance archetypes for information input are IT monarchy for principles, IT duopoly for IT related domains, Federal for Business application needs, and IT monarchy for Investments; decisions making is completely different, principles and IT related domains archetypes are IT monarchy, while Business application needs archetype is IT duopoly and Investment decisions are reserved for business monarchy.

The operational model of EPS2 is Unification to generate one company image to customers, suppliers, and regulators. Business processes standardized are those related with medical care services authorization, marketing, quality control and business planning and control. Shared information is: members', medical care institutions, and services' general data.

IT investment is about 1.5% of annual sales. Infrastructure, 34%, focal point is communication channel and hardware improvement. Transactional, 21% objective is processes automation. Informational, 13%, looks for data integration. Strategic, 32%, is focus on services enhancement so EPS2 achieves competitive advantage.

Its IT engagement model elements are:

- IT companywide governance: Executive committee including CIO, Capital approval committee, Renewal process, Project prioritization process, and Application acquisition accountable. Shared IT governance uses SLA, regular meetings and Shared IT architecture definition.
- Project management: Early business project objectives definition; Good practices and standards; and Project sponsor and accountable person.
  • Linking mechanisms:
    ▪ Business: Project prioritization, Early stakeholders involvement, Sponsoring, Post-

implementation reviews, and Aligning project with corporate objectives.

- Alignment: Requirements definition and Project committees.

o Architecture: Infrastructure standardization, and Architecture Exception management.

Third EPS: EPS 3

As EPS2, EPS3 initially was a prepaid health care company that started an EPS business line after regulation opens the business to private companies, but unlike EPS2, currently the main business line continues to be the prepaid health care services. EPS3 strategy was to maintain its early costumers and complementing its services with the POS in order to give a better service. Consequently, EPS3 strategy is services' quality.

The IT governance main benefit for this company is the aligning business needs with the IT resources; therefore, decisions about IT services and its sourcing are made according with the importance of those services for the business. Consequently, all decision making domains archetype is IT monarchy, except for IT investments which archetype is Business monarchy.

EPS3 and the prepaid business line share the IT area and its operational model which is Unification. Shared information is: members', medical care institutions, and services' general data. Standardized processes are affiliation, services authorization, services quality control, and financial and operational management.

IT investment is about 1.1% of annual sales. Infrastructure, 34%, focal point is infrastructure and communication enhancement. Transactional, 15%, objective is integrating internal and external sourced applications. Informational, 28%, pursues business intelligent development. Strategic, 23%, is focus on customer relationship management by offering best services and new channels to achieve competitive advantage.

Its IT engagement model elements are:

- IT companywide governance: Executive committee including CIO, Capital approval committee, and Corporative architectural committee. Shared IT mechanisms are the same as to EPS2.
- Project management: Project objectives definition; Good practices and standards; and Project sponsor and accountable person.
  - Linking mechanisms:
    - Business: Project prioritization, Early stakeholders involvement, Sponsoring, Regular reviews, and Aligning project with corporate objectives.
    - Alignment: Level, Area and Project committees.
    - Architecture: Infrastructure standardization, and Architectural projects align.

Findings for Health Promoting Enterprises: EPSs

We present our findings for this second group of enterprises with the same structure we used before. Regarding to the IT governance arrangements matrix, we noticed that inputs to IT decisions trend absolutely differs from CISR while decision rights trend is quite similar to CISR, Table 2 presents the main IT governance trend in Colombian EPSs.

As for the pharmaceutical laboratories, IT Monarchy and IT duopoly are the most frequent archetypes for information input, meanwhile for CISR research it is Federal. However, in this case this behavior could be a little bit strange because they do not have a regional or corporate level that will define specific needs and policies on the use of IT in the organization. The EPSs do not seem to be looking directly to the business areas to identify IT needs in their companies. This suggests that the EPSs are using other mechanisms as a

Table 2. Governance Arrangements Matrix: 3 EPSs.

	IT principles		IT architecture		IT infrastructure		Business appl. needs		IT investment	
	I	D	I	D	I	D	I	D	I	D
Business Monarchy	E2, E3									E1, E2, E3
IT Monarchy		E2, E3	E1, E3	E1, E2, E3	E1	E1, E2, E3		E3	E2, E3	
Federal							E2			
IT Duopoly	E1	E1	E2		E2, E3		E1, E3	E1, E2	E1	

I Input of Information   D Decision Making Right   ▓   Most common pattern in CISR research
E1:EPS1; E2: EPS; E3: EPS3

source of information to make its major decisions. For decision making, in contrast, we found a clear match between CISR and our findings. We do not have a clear explanation, but it looks like companies in this case are not subsidiaries, they are independent companies.

About operating models, we have identified a clear trend towards Unification in our sample. Although, one of them uses Coordination model we concluded that it is because it belong to a very special business where its units are quite different so it does not need to standardized its process. However, if we analyze in an isolate way the EPS line, we could ensure that standardized processes operate along this line.

Observing global IT investment of annual incomes, 1.87, is much lower compare to the average IT investment of enterprises researched in CISR, 4.2%, (Weill & Ross, 2004). More research must be done to confirm if low IT investment is the standard in this subsector and why. Additionally, there is a big difference and a large variance in our sample. Therefore, we do not have enough evidence to formulate a hypothesis about IT investment in this subsector. However, it is important to note that Strategic investments show a percentage far outweighs with nearly 23% versus 13% of the CISR research and we believe it is due to the importance for these companies to establish innovative projects that allow them to offer new services and new communication channels with their customers.

Finally, concerning the IT engagement model we found linking mechanisms of the three types in all EPSs: alignment, architecture, and business. Those mechanisms enable them to align IT projects with business strategies at all organizational level. Similarly, we found a clear trend towards the outsourcing of IT services and therefore, we found that the three studied companies have Shared IT governance, whose main objective is to establish a well-defined liaison. This relationship allows them to control the processes that have been outsourced. However, not all the companies studied have established architectural policies with their IT services providers. They just monitor compliance with SLAs.

IT Governance at Four Medical Care Institutions: IPSs

IPSs are the companies to which the EPSs and EPS-Ss will engage the services defined in the POS. We studied four III level IPSs (Figueredo, 2009). As we explained before, IPSs are all the public, private, mixed or community hospitals or health centers so there are too many of them, and we do not have a clear composition of this subsector in terms of how many companies belong to it. Whereas, our sample is composed of four

III level IPSs, in other words, IPSs that offer the most complex services in the sector.

First IPS: IPS1

IPS1, a public institution, was established 60 years ago to offer pediatric care. The organization is process oriented; main processes are admissions, external consult, hospitalization, surgery, and pharmacy. Even though its nature, it serves RC and RS members.

It is clear for both, IT and non-IT staff, how and who takes IT decisions and who is accountable of its results. It is important to notice that there is no CIO; instead the IT staff takes care of IT services and when necessary they are part of project teams. The IPS1 IT governance arrangement matrix is really atypical: first it uses the Feudal archetype to input information about business applications needs; and second, uses Federal archetype to input and take decisions about IT principles, and input information for IT infrastructure. As a common pattern, IT investment decision archetype is Business monarchy.

Its process orientation has driven IPS1 to the Unification model that is supported by an ERP system that has just been implemented. This system manages the processes mentioned above. Other processes, such as diagnosis and laboratory, have their own proprietary IT, that, in some cases have to be manually processed to provide financial information to some of the firm's processes.

IT investment during 2009 was 2.9% of its annual sales, about 12.6% of total investments of IPS1. Infrastructure, 37%, focal point is IT infrastructure strengthens. Transactional, 22%, objective is IT support for call center and human resources. Informational, 7%, supposes to develop business intelligent but currently information is not available. Strategic, 34%, is focused on customer relationship management by offering best services and new channels to achieve competitive advantage.

IT engagement model elements are:

- IT companywide governance: Executive committee, IT committee. No outsourcing thus no Shared IT governance.
- Project management: Sponsoring and accountable person.
  - Linking mechanisms:
    - Business: Project prioritization, and Early stakeholders involvement.
    - Alignment: Business needs identification process.
    - Architecture: Help desk and Technological committee.

Second IPS: IPS2

IPS2 is a private institution leader on family and prepaid medical care. The organization business processes are admissions, urgencies, hospitalization, surgery, intensive care (UCI), pharmacy, diagnosis, and vaccination. It focuses on high incomes CR members with health prepaid plans.

As for IPS1, IPS2 has clear for both, IT and non-IT staff, how and who takes IT decisions and who is accountable of its results. Also, IPS2 does not have a CIO, so IPS2 IT governance arrangements matrix never uses IT monarchy archetype for decision making; on the contrary all information input on IT-related domains use this archetype. As a common place IT investment decision use Business monarchy.

It operational model is Unification. Just as IPS1, the same business processes are supported by an ERP system, and diagnosis and vaccination have their own proprietary support systems that are integrated to previous processes.

IPS2 IT portfolio is bizarre: Strategy, 53%, is out of the ordinary, very high. Last year IPS2 has been changing its IT strategy looking for better client services, so they have invested a lot on strategic assets. Consequently, Transactional has been very low, 5%, and Informational disappear. Infrastructure is pretty similar to the other studied enterprises.

IT engagement model elements are:

- IT companywide governance: Executive committee, IT committee, Project tracking committee. No outsourcing thus no shared Governance.
- Project management: Regular and post-implementation reviews.
  - Linking mechanisms:
    - Business: Project prioritization, and Early stakeholders involvement.
    - Alignment: Business needs identification process and Project committees.
    - Architecture: Help desk, Technological committee, and Architecture approval committee.

Third IPS: IPS3

IPS3 is a university hospital thus it has a wide number of specialized cares, educational and researched units. Main processes are admissions, external consult, hospitalization, surgery, and patient monitoring. IPS3 has efficiently grown during 2009 after business processes were standardized and an ERP system was implanted strengthening its IT infrastructure. Although, these results, non-IT staff is aware of the IT importance.

IT and non-IT staffs know who take IT decisions and who is accountable of its results. Just like the previous IPSs, IPS3 does not have a CIO, but different from the previous ones, IPS3 is establishing the role. IT governance arrangements matrix has some common characteristics to the IPS1, it uses the Feudal archetype to input information for Business applications needs. Federal archetype is used to input information of IT-related domains. IT investment decisions archetype is Business monarchy as the previous ones.

Support processes share information among them but no with medical care processes, then IPS3 operational model is Replication. IPS3's IT portfolio figures were not available during our

research, and it was not possible to calculate the figures because they were part of the corporate investments.

IT engagement model is completely different from the other IPSs, its elements are:

- IT companywide governance: Executive corporative committee including the corporative CIO, and the IT committee. No outsourced activities thus no Shared IT governance.
- Project management: Project prioritization.
  - Linking mechanisms:
    - Business: Early stakeholders' involvement.
    - Alignment: Business needs identification process and IT committee.
    - Architecture: Help desk, and Architecture approval committee.

Forth IPS: IPS4

IPS4 is a public institution willing to give health complex services with high standing staff. It is focused on the care of EPS-S members.

IPS4 just, as the other IPSs, does not have a CIO. IT governance arrangements matrix has some peculiar characteristics as: they are using Business monarchy to input information and take decision in IT principles domain, and IT duopoly to take IT infrastructure decision. And like previous IPSs IT investment decisions use Business monarchy archetype.

IPS4 operational model is Replication. Although the institution uses an ERP system to support its financial and administrative processes, only financial information of patients is in this system; patient's illness and medical care data is in hard copy only.

IPS4 total IT investment as percentage of annual sales was not available, but clearly its focus is supporting financial and administrative processes. Consequently, main investments are in Infrastructure, 56%, and Transactional, 24%, issues; Informational, 15%, and Strategic, 5%, investments are less important.

IT engagement model elements are:

- IT companywide governance: Executive committee, and Steering committee. No outsourcing thus no Shared IT governance.
- Project management: Early business project objectives definition, Early stakeholders involvement and Post-implementation reviews.
  - Linking mechanisms:
    - Business: Project prioritization and Aligning project with corporate objectives.
    - Alignment: Business/IT relation manager and Project accountability identification.
    - Architecture: IT project coordination, Early stakeholders involvement, and Business standardization processes.

Findings for Medical Care Institutions: IPSs

To present our findings for this third group of enterprises we use the same structure we used before. Even though studied IPSs are large-sized enterprises according to the Colombian laws, their behavior about the topics covered makes it seem as if they were not. For none of them, IT is strategic. Its role mainly is supportive for both nonprofit and for-profit ones. Therefore, business core units – medical units - and support units share only information for financial purposes.

As a result, IT role is unplanned and the IT director role is not on the C level. Currently, two IPSs are pursuing better performance and want IT to be strategic, so they are rethinking IT role. Certainly, they hope to improve not only their

financial performance but also their medical services.

Looking at the IT governance arrangement matrix we noticed that IT governance trend of Colombian Medical Care Institutions have unusual characteristics, Table 3.

First, we noticed that there is no clear trend for the three first domains. It seems that having IT as a non-strategic asset gives no importance to decisions on these domains, so any archetype is used. This behavior is particularly well-founded for IT related domains: architecture and infrastructure. Second, we found the Feudal archetype in half of the IPSs studied for Business applications needs' input; the explanation for this behavior is based on the relationship between medical units and IT: IT knows nothing about IPSs' business while medical units know better than anyone else their needs, so they make independent decisions. Finally, we found a common pattern for decision rights between CISR research and our sample in this group of enterprises. For Business applications needs and IT investment the rule is it does not matter if IT is strategic or not, the board of director wants to decide where the organization is putting their monetary resources.

Operational model also diverge, IPS1 and IPS2 have Unification model, and IPS3 and IPS4 have Replication model. On the one hand, the use of ERP systems to support financial and administrative processes has allowed standardizing them; on the other hand, medical units' current practices look as a barrier for sharing information in these IPSs.

IT portfolio management surprises us. The first finding is that IT investment as a percentage of annual incomes, except for IPS2 2.9%, was not available during our study. Sometimes because it is part of the technological investment that includes medical equipment, and in other cases because it is done with corporate resources. IPS3 gets out for our analyses about this topic because there were no figures.

IPSs average investment are Infrastructure, 45%, Transactional 17%, Informational 7%, and

Table 3. Governance Arrangements Matrix: 4 IPSs.

	IT principles		IT architecture		IT infrastructure		Business appl. needs		IT investment	
	I	D	I	D	I	D	I	D	I	D
Business Monarchy	I4	I2, I4		I1						I1, I2, I3, I4
IT Monarchy			I2, I4	I3, I4	I2	I1,I3	I2	I3	I3	
Federal	I1, I3	I1	I3		I1, I3, I4	I2	I4			
IT Duopoly	I2	I3	I1	I2		I4		I1, I2, I4	I1, I2, I4	
Feudal								I1, I3		

I Input of Information   D Decision Making Right   ▓   Most common pattern in CISR research

I1: IPS1; I2: IPS2; I3: IPS3; I4: IPS4

Strategic 30% and standard deviations are: 21%, 61%, 102%, and 79%. Differences are amazing but even more surprising are the deviations. Notwithstanding we have little evidence about IT portfolio management, we can conclude that IT its behavior is non-standard and non-mature for Colombian IPSs.

IPSs IT engagement model is really fragile. Its weaker component is Project management: none of the IPSs do use project management best practices or standards. IT companywide governance is also fragile: Executive committee and IT committee are the sole elements; a common feature is no Shared IT governance. Linking mechanisms do not perform better: Business linkage most general elements are Early stakeholder's involvement and Project prioritization; Alignment linkage regular element is Business needs identification process; and Architecture linkage frequently element is Help desk and is followed by Technological committee and Architecture approval committee. The frequent mechanisms used by CISR enterprises, were not found at IPSs. We conclude that IT engagement model is immature at this subsector.

Solutions and Recommendations

We present the main similarities and differences between CISR research and Colombian health sector enterprises, and among the subsectors.

IT Governance Arrangements Matrix

Regarding to the IT governance arrangements matrix, we noticed that IT governance trend absolutely differs from CISR. Table 4 presents the main IT governance trend in the Colombian health sector.

There is a mismatch for information input between Colombian health sector enterprises and CISR enterprises. In Colombian health sector enterprises the most frequent archetypes are: IT monarchy and IT duopoly, meanwhile for CISR research it is Federal; the sole exception is Business application needs that uses Federal archetype like CISR. For decision making there are two similarities on IT architecture and IT infrastructure. Its looks like that IT technical domains were reserved for IT monarchy. However, Investment decisions in our research are totally reserved for Business monarchy (75%); it looks like IT governance is not mature enough, so C business level let financial decisions on them. Particularly, we truly believe that IT areas in IPSs and EPSs have a long way to go to achieve an IT governance arrangement matrix that first, help the enterprises get their corporative objectives; and second, realize the true impact IT can have on business, not only on cost reduction, but in strategy as well.

In contrast, we found that pharmaceutical laboratory industry enterprises are quite mature in this

Table 4. IT Governance Arrangements Matrix: 12 Colombian Health Sector Enterprises

	IT principles		IT architecture		IT infrastructure		Business appl. needs		IT investment	
	I	D	I	D	I	D	I	D	I	D
Business Monarchy										
IT Monarchy					☐					
Federal	▨		▨		▨			▨	▨	▨
IT Duopoly		▨	▨							▨
Feudal										

I Input of Information   D Decision Making Right   ▨ Most common pattern in CISR research
☐ Most common pattern in Colombian Health sector   ☐ Most common pattern in both researches

aspect. Multinational pharmaceutical laboratories have well-established practices for their processes that have influenced positively their IT governance and their local business lines have adopted them.

Operating model

Beginning with the local level the model pattern that we found is Unification, 75%, next Replication, 16.6%, and finally Coordination at one EPS. Unification model increases efficient and cost control, are very universal objectives for any organization, particularly, when companies have integrated supply chains around global customers or suppliers and they can take advantage of economies of scale as multinational pharmaceutical laboratories local business unit, EPSs and IPSs.

IPS3 and IPS4 use Replication model because they do not share information between support business processes and medical care processes. These IPSs must analyze if this is the model they need or sharing data will really contribute with their strategic objectives. Coordination model fits for businesses having quite different business units so they cannot standardize its process, as EPS1 for instance.

Operational model, at regional and global level, for pharmaceutical laboratories is a tool to reinforce corporative strategies, 75% Replication,

25% Unification. This reflects they have mature best practices for core processes, so they have high standardization, but they need global flexibility, and so they have low integration.

IT Portfolio

One alarming fact we found was that we could not have data about IT investment as a percentage of annual incomes for three companies, 25%. These companies do not handle IT investments as a portfolio, as a logical result of IT non-strategic role. Pharmaceutical laboratories' IT investment is higher than CISR average, 4.2%, in contrast EPSs' average IT investment is 1.87% of annual incomes.

In addition, the distribution among the different kind of assets have a very strong relationship with the current IT and business situation. Let us explain why. First, the difference among the pharmaceutical laboratories studied could be explained because sometimes regional or corporative levels invest on a particular asset for all the company, then the local level concentrates in other types of investments. Second, the current EPSs' investments on Transactional and Strategic assets are higher than CISR average, showing that their present need is to have more reliable information for operational and strategic decisions. Finally, the few data available for this topic in IPSs shows us the undeveloped role of IT in this kind of companies.

Those facts show us a diverse behavior that leads us to conclude that IT investment is managed as a portfolio, just when the company has achieved a minimum level of maturity in their IT use and its governance.

IT Engagement Mechanisms

IT engagement model has a pretty similar behavior just as other IT governance components. Pharmaceutical laboratory industry enterprises have strong IT engagement models, EPSs have medium developed IT engagement models, and IPSs have a weak IT engagement models. Other interesting point is that IPSs do not have Shared IT governance because they do not outsource IT services.

Another remarkable characteristic in enterprises with mature IT governance is the importance of controlling the IT architecture and the IT project management. Pharmaceutical laboratory industry enterprises have a wide variety of mechanisms and artifacts to control their IT architecture, EPSs have less but some, while IPSs have none at all. The same happens with Project management; IPSs have none or eventually general mechanisms to manage it, but specific good practices are absent; meanwhile pharmaceutical laboratories have solid practices.

FUTURE RESEARCH DIRECTIONS

Our future research direction must focus in the generation of tools to support IT governance implementing, measuring, strengthen and controlling. The first topic we propose is creating an IT governance maturity model. The model must provide: a diagnostic tool for evaluating IT governance effectiveness, a tool for producing consistent data from which benchmark analyses could be done, and a tool for formulating objectives to move IT

governance forward in order that companies can achieve their suitable maturity level.

Another research direction is developing tools to measure coherence and harmony among IT governances' components: IT governance arrangements matrix, operating model, IT portfolio management, and IT engagement model, in order to achieve stronger synergies that lever up the organizational efforts and reinforces business competiveness. A complementary research is defining a set of tools to measure coherence and harmony among IT governance levels: local, regional, and global.

CONCLUSION

Companies must measure their IT governance arrangements matrix effectiveness; not having a better tool a benchmark in their subsector may help to rank themselves. Companies whose IT governance arrangements matrix effectiveness is under its subsector average, surely, have to develop an IT road map to reach and strength the IT role that companies need nowadays. This road map must include a radical cultural change not only in IT areas but in organization's C level. Those over the average should continue working on strengthening its mechanisms to monitor the coherence and harmony of their IT governance arrangement's elements.

In addition, enterprises have to measure the impact of their operating models. After they decide which model works better for their businesses and before they implement it, IT areas should measure their current performance by business indicators; and, when they have the operation model implanted, IT areas should measure again to show the impact, so IT areas take or reinforce their strategic role.

Organizations must manage IT investment as a portfolio. To achieve the competences they need to do it, IT and non-IT staff should develop competences on project management, as a first step. We can identified during our research that when companies have good project management practices, they begin to manage IT investment as a portfolio; on the contrary, companies without those practices manage IT investments as costs.

IT engagement model is a fundamental part of IT governance. It reinforces, monitors and controls the other IT governance elements, in order to realize and maintain the IT business value. IT engagement model is not the end, not the beginning of IT governance. It goes with the other elements, growing and complementing each other. But its foundation and appropriate design highlight IT governance, so company's competitiveness increases.

REFERENCES

Díaz, L. (2010). *Gobierno de TI en Sector Salud - Subsector EPS*. [IT Governance in the Health Sector - Subsector EPS] Unpublished Master dissertation, University of Los Andes, Colombia

Figueredo, M. (2009). *Gobierno de TI en el Sector Salud de Colombia: IPS Nivel III*. [IT Governance in Colombia's Health Sector: IPS Nivel III] Unpublished Master dissertation, University of Los Andes, Colombia

Fonstad, N.O. (2006). Engagement Matters: Enhancing Alignment with Governance Mechanisms. *CISR Research Briefing4*(3e)

Giraldo, O. L., Herrera, A., & Gómez, J. E. (2010). IT Governance State of Art at Enterprises in the Colombian Pharmaceutical Industry. *Communications in Computer and Information Science109*(5), 431-440. Springer Link Press Information Systems Audit and Control Association. (2006). *COBIT Framework for IT Governance and Control*. Retrieved January 13, 2011, from http://www.isaca.org/Knowledge-Center/COBIT/Pages/Overview.aspx

International Organization for Standardization. (2008). *ISO/IEC 38500:2008*. Retrieved January 13, 2011, from http://www.iso.org/iso/iso_catalogue/catalogue_tc/catalogue_detail.htm?csnumber=51639

Kuperman, D. (2009). *Gobernabilidad de TI en el Sector Farmacéutico Colombiano: Investigación de Buenas Prácticas en Empresas Modelo*. [IT Governance in the Columbian Pharmaceutical Sector: Researching Good Practices in Model Businesses] Unpublished Master dissertation, University of Los Andes, Colombia

Lavilla, A., & Moreno, J. J. (2008). *Gobierno de Tecnologías de Información en el Sector Farmacéutico Colombiano*. [Information Technololgy Governance in the Columbian Pharmaceutical Sector] Unpublished Bachelor dissertation, University of Los Andes, Colombia

Portafolio Nestlé. (2007) *Afine: Empresas Líderes de Colombia Información Financiera 2002-2006*. [Tune: Business Leaders of Columbia Financial Information 2002-2006] Bogotá, Colombia: Casa Editorial El Tiempo.

Revista Cambio de Mayo 15-21/ 2008 (2008): *Las 1.001 Compañías* [1001 Companies].(776) Casa Editorial El Tiempo.

Ross, J., Weill, P. & Robertson, D. (2006). *Enterprise Architectures as Strategy*. Boston, MA: Harvard Business School Press.

Santa María, M., García, F., Rozo, S., & Uribe, M. (2007). *Un diagnóstico general del sector salud en Colombia: evolución, contexto y principales retos de un sistema en transformación*. [A General Assessment of the Health Sector in Columbia: Evolution, Context and Main Challenges for a Changing System] Retrieved March 2, 2009 http://www.med-informatica.net/FMC_CMCB/VeeduriaCiudadana/CIDMEDvcacelapss/SaludRetosRegulacion_MauricioSantamaria_cap1_final.pdf.

Weill, P. (2004). Don't Just Lead, Govern: How Top performing Firms Govern IT. *MIS Quarterly Executive, 3*(1)

Weill, P., Aral, S., & Johnson, A. (2007). Compilation of MIT CISR Research on IT Portfolio, IT Savvy and Firm Performance (2000-2006). *CISR Working Paper* (368).

Weill, P., & Ross, J. (2004). *IT Governance: How Top Performers Manage IT Decision Rights for Superior Results*. Boston, MA: Harvard Business School Press.

Weill, P., Woerner, S. & Rubin, H. (2008) Managing the IT Portfolio: It´s all about what´s new. *CISR Research Briefing, 8*(2b).

ENDNOTE

[1] Replaced by the Regulatory Health Commission (CRES) in 2007

Chapter 20

Enterprise Tomography Driven Root–Cause–Analysis and Integration Lifecycle Management of Federated ERP in Green Clouds

Jan Aalmink
Carl von Ossietzky Universität Oldenburg, Germany

Jorge Marx Gómez
Carl von Ossietzky Universität Oldenburg, Germany

ABSTRACT

Cloud Computing is finding its way into the architecture of current IT landscapes. The present chapter depicts the challenges of the required changes and transitions of Enterprise Data Centers from non-integrated on-premise solutions towards fully integrated on-demand systems in silo-free clouds. Cloud standardization in the context of the Open Cloud Manifesto is discussed as well as a reference model based upon semantic composition and federation (Federated ERP Systems and Corporate Environmental Information Management Systems CEMIS 2.0). How Enterprise Tomography can support the governance process is described as the Root-Cause-Analysis procedure and Integration Lifecycle Management of an Enterprise Cloud and by comparing different system states. On the basis of an operator-based approach, Root-Cause-Analysis and data integrity can be ensured. Finally, an outlook on an approach involving environmental aspects (Green Clouds) is given.

INTRODUCTION

Enterprise Cloud Computing becomes more and more prevalent in the IT and Business Application Industry. The quality of integration, i.e. the extent of vertical and horizontal Business Process

Integration and its efficient management is to be seen as a key IT asset in Enterprise Data Centers. The scientific approach now is to overcome most of the disadvantages of legacy on-premise solutions. Therefore, existing different research streams, requirements and semantic perspectives need to be converted into one central ubiquitous,

DOI: 10.4018/978-1-4666-1764-3.ch020

optimized and standardized architectural approach. The goal is to perform on-demand and cross-enterprise business processes in the context of Very Large Business Applications (VLBAs). Also in this context cloud standardization is one of the biggest challenges of the Open Cloud Manifesto. This chapter discusses and outlines, how a semantic composition and federation based reference model (Federated ERP-System) can be established for Enterprise Cloud Computing and set up for business operation. Furthermore, it is debated, how enterprises can develop and maintain enterprise software solutions in the Cloud Community in an evolutionary, self-organized way complying Cloud Standards. In this context a metric driven Semantic Service Discovery and the Enterprise Tomograph can be seen as an entry-point to an organic, gradable marketplace of processes exposed by cloud based Service Grids and Data Grids in graded levels of granularity and semantic abstractions.

Regarding Enterprise Cloud Computing, conflictual requirements and design principles need to be resolved. A convergence of the polymorphic streams towards a shared, cloud-based platform can be observed. The main motivation in utilizing Enterprise Cloud Computing for a customer is the reduction of TCO in different aspects: Pooling of resources and services regarding consumption peaks or simplification of legacy infrastructure from on-premise solutions towards an on-demand solution. From the perspective of an Enterprise Cloud Provider virtualization with multi-tenancy functionality proves as suboptimal. There is a higher degree of sharing and reuse possible. This leads to federated service-based cloud software which can grow organically. The scientific challenge is to provide a controllable reference model which serves as a common standard, where standards overcome the typical vendor-lock-in phenomenon and are prerequisite for acceptance.

In general, Federated ERP Systems (FERP Systems) based on web-services are heterogeneous software systems processing business data complying integration rules, so different customers have different views, i.e. access points to the FERP. Since the typical software ownership (provider-consumer) is transformed from 1:n to m:n (Brehm, Marx Gómez & Rautenstrauch, 2006, pp. 99-111; Brehm, Luebke, Marx-Gómez, 2007, pp. 290-305) and the complexity of such information eco-systems is increasing in the course of the life cycle, the superordinate target in the context of Enterprise Cloud Computing is to provide methodologies and mechanisms for streamlining and controlling the integration in federated ERP systems. The organic growth of interlinked Enterprise Services Networks needs to follow compliance rules. Therefore, semantic deviation-analysis of enterprise service consumption, Monitoring and Tracking becomes essential in distributed consumer-provider networks along the life cycle.

The Enterprise Tomography approach enables monitoring of the complete life cycle of federated Enterprise Software or Corporate Environmental Management Information Systems CEMIS 2.0 described in (Marx Gómez, 2009): With Enterprise Tomography it is possible to make consumption patterns comparable. This comparison is based on a common interlingua represented as lightweight hierarchical ontologies and is achieved by applying the Delta Operator which determines the differences between system-status A and system-status B in a cloud. To be more precise, the comparison and evolution-tracking of integrated business process scenarios in a cloud represented as interlinked enterprise services ensembles is possible. The Enterprise Tomography approach provides the possibility to visualize differences with help of tomograms which aggregate indicators, metrics and serve as a decision basis in the governance process and Integration Lifecycle Management of an Enterprise Cloud (Aalmink & Marx Gómez, 2009).

Figure 1 illustrates an overview of the topology of a Cloud Farm. Different aspects and fundamental pillars of the FERP reference model are shown. The procedure, how Enterprise Cloud Evolution can be controlled is outlined in Figure 2.

Figure 1. Topology of an Enterprise Cloud Computing Farm based on FERP and Enterprise Tomography

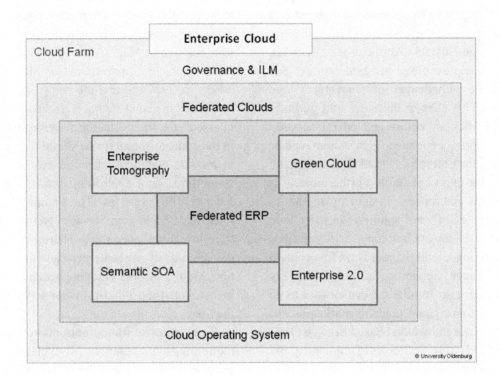

Figure 2. Enterprise Tomography driven Governance of FERP in a Cloud Farm

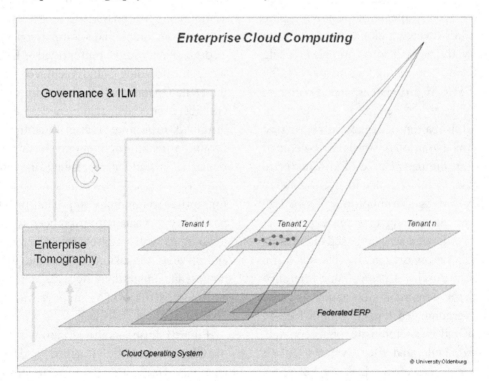

FEDERATED ERP IN A CLOUD

In reality, on-premise Standard Enterprise Software is widely used within the enterprise community. Standard means, there are common business process patterns which are highly configurable and extensible according to the business requirements. Typically, this methodology results in similar composed, configured and enhanced CEMIS-Systems deployed to many Enterprise Data Centers. Similarity means redundancy, which can be eliminated with the FERP approach.

According to Figure 2, in the cloud-based Federated ERP approach we have one single software instance active for all participating enterprises. Each enterprise is encapsulated in a Cloud Tenant according to the Separation of Concerns Paradigm. Each Tenant is provided a view on the single software and data instance. Basically, the software and data instance is a network of shared Business Objects that are projected on columnar In-Memory databases (Plattner, 2009). The In-Memory Databases can be regarded as intelligent Caches (Heuser, Alsdorf & Woods, 2008). In-Memory Columnar Databases significantly reduce the redundancy in the data volume and provides instantaneous access to non-materialized aggregates and business object collections. Aggregates are being calculated on the fly and are exposed as services via endpoints of Data Grids. It is possible to keep the Business Object Network consistent according to the ACID transactional OLTP methodology. Columnar In-Memory Database Models provide extensibility by nature.

Non-frequent used Business Objects are physically stored in a distributed fashion. A read access of a Business Object means data retrieval of distinct fragments for reconstruction of the original Business Object. A Business Object is regarded as a tree serialized to a document. This document is fragmented. The fragments are coded and distributed within the Data Grids. A document can be seen as a sequence of numbers which defines

a mathematical polynomial. According to the fundamental theorem of algebra, this document can be uniquely reconstructed, if there are only n distinct fragments (out of a redundant coded set) available. While retrieving, inconsistent fragments can be ignored and substituted by distinct consistent fragment retrieved from remote Data Grids (Heuser, Alsdorf & Woods, 2007).

In the FERP approach technical references to Business Objects are the payload of messages. E.g. if company A wants to send company B an invoice (Business Object) only the reference of the Invoice is sent as a payload. The invoice is in this case a shared and ubiquitous accessible Business Object. Company A has an individual view-based access to the Invoice via the reference only. The same applies to company B. Receiving the message, company B will change the status of the invoice to the value 'paid' as soon as the real payment is executed.

Columnar Databases are based on Inverted Indexing known in classical Information Retrieval. In (Plattner, 2009) it is shown that this algorithmic approach is well-suited for parallel multi-core hardware. Systolic Arrays are in the position to accelerate string position/value matching even further with the rate of clock frequency speed (Epstein, 2004).

View-based access via references to Business Objects has the big advantage, that no mapping and technical transformation of the Business Objects is required. Business Objects needs not to be moved within the memory. There is no need for asynchronous processing and updating anymore. This leads to tremendous scalability which is a prerequisite for cloud computing. Having instantaneous services in places, completely new quasi real-time applications will be possible in future.

In addition, the FERP reference model leads to a more data-consistent behavior. The cloud software can become much leaner in comparison to classical stacked on-premise enterprise software solutions and are therefore less error-prone. A closed-loop feedback development process ensures a promptly iterative correction cycle. This leads to quality insurance.

GOVERNANCE OF INTEGRATION LIFECYCLE MANAGEMENT IN GREEN CLOUDS

The Federated ERP model can be regarded as a central shared and ubiquitous accessible network based approach. An error in the enterprise cloud software can lead to dramatic consequences and might have serious business impact.

An enterprise client can extend its own business processes or even create and compose its individual business process schemas. The individual part of functionality can be shared with related tenants. So FERP leaves the classical software vendor / software client ownership model. In FERP approach each individual tenant can be simultaneously in the role of a service consumer as well as a logical service provider. The services are exposed via a Semantic Service Discovery (Heuser, Alsdorf, & Woods, 2008). The essential point here is, that each service, composite service or business process is potentially provided with a set of alternatives distinguished by Quality of Service (QoS) and metrics.

To be more general, the FERP approach can be seen as a definition of a governed service marketplace. Each individual participant can contribute materialized cloud content as shared services and shared (sub)-processes. Each participant can virtually compose his own ERP. In fact he gets a view on a service of an one software and data instance.

With Enterprise Tomography it is possible to make similar data contexts comparable. The comparison is based on a common Interlingua represented as lightweight ontologies. With a Delta Operator it is realizable to determine dynamically the differences between service offering A and service offering B. The Enterprise Tomograph provides the possibility to visualize semantic differences with help of tomograms. A comparison between two service offerings is possible as well as a comparison of a service offerings between two points in time. E.g. in a project a consulting team implements business processes and therefore changes customizing or alters the composition of an Enterprise Service Ensemble. This delta is of common interest, e.g. as an indicator for the quality of security evolvement in the last period of time. Another use-case is to determine the delta after a functional upgrade in the cloud. The delta is calculated between the previous reference version and the active version of Enterprise Service Ensemble. The delta in this case is the equivalent of new or changed functionality. This delta, represented as a hierarchical ontology tree, is a good basis for evaluation of new functionality. Test and training teams therefore can focus on new/changed functionality only. This results automatically in cost containment.

One more interesting use case for Enterprise Tomography is to calculate the data footprint of a selected business transaction or a business process in a cloud. Between two points in time the update on database is calculated with help of the Delta Operator. Based on the business data delta, the IT experts are in the position to assess the correctness of the behavior of the executed business transactions more efficiently. This is a highly efficient diagnostics approach for root cause analysis for given error symptoms. Based on the delta, the Undo Operator resets the business transaction. This business transaction can be executed again with same preconditions and data contexts. In this way repetitive testing of business processes is enabled.

The Enterprise Tomography approach allows the construction of an early warning system based on semantic metrics and indicators. If the distance - computed by the Delta Operator - exceeds a threshold, actions (= cloud based services) can be executed to control the usage of dedicated Enterprise Services. For example, the Enterprise Tomograph can execute process mining. When the quota exceeds a threshold, the Enterprise Tenant needs to be invoiced for funding the cloud infrastructure he has used. This is a simple example to implement self-organized feedback control system based on the generic Enterprise Tomography approach.

Each participant can contribute service based software as materialized cloud content. This naturally leads to high redundancy in offerings of business processes. The Enterprise Tomograph can evaluate the services and business processes according real consumption patterns. Business processes with low traffic on the cloud infrastructure are regarded as non-value added processes and will be disabled. The decision of disablement is based on dynamic calculated results of the

Enterprise Tomograph. The most useful services - or more general - the services with the highest Quality of Services will survive the market competition. This example illustrates how Enterprise Tomography approach can control the Integration Lifecycle Management of Enterprise Clouds and increase the overall quality in an Enterprise Cloud according to free definable metrics while fulfilling requirements in a prioritized manner.

In Figure 3 an advanced VLBA (FERP) across Data Centers of distinct owner (Enterprises) is displayed. The Enterprise Cloud encompasses federated clouds which exposes services and infrastructures. The lifecycle of the cross-federated VLBA is managed by the Enterprise Tomograph. Crawling of cloud entities, i.e. of business data,

Figure 3. Controlled Cross-Datacenter VLBA residing in an Enterprise Cloud

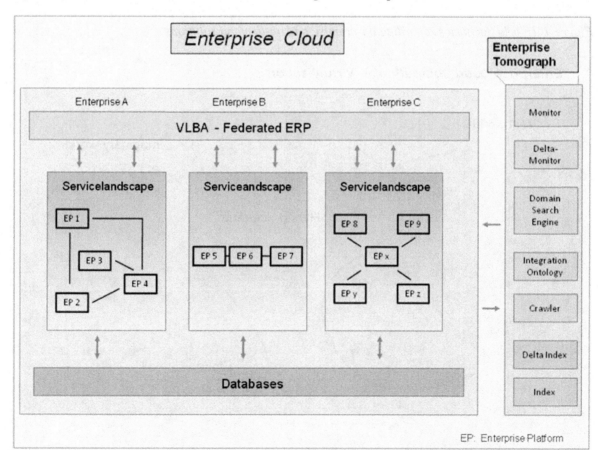

log files, data, metadata, operational data, master data, configuration data, service repositories and infrastructure content is executed on a permanent basis. Changes in ontologies can be calculated via delta determination of the Enterprise Tomograph. Deviation analysis and metric based rule infringement detection leads to immediate adaptive actions and events.

A more business relevant use-case is a partial architectural transformation from real world data centers to virtual data centers as shown in Figure 4. A subset of static infrastructures can be converted in virtual infrastructures. This allows a better sharing and assignment of resources. This enables an adaptive pooling of virtual resources. From user perspective, the transformation is non-transparent. Keeping Hybrid Scenarios in sync according to Business Process Integration requires

definition of dedicated compliance rules which can be enforced with the Enterprise Tomography approach.

Scientific purpose of the research field Green Clouds is analyzing enterprise software within cloud environments for the reduction of company-made environmental pollution. Solutions are worked out, to harmonize legal compliance, environmental compliance, cost indicators, complexity, and the degree of integrating environmental information systems. Centralized cloud solutions are used to avoid isolated views on enterprises. This can result in a federated ERP system enhanced by environmental aspects. The approach is showing similarities to an enhanced Balanced Scorecard model.

Enterprise Tomography approach can be advantageous to identify environmental indica-

Figure 4. Hybrid Scenarios regarding on-premise and on-demand solutions

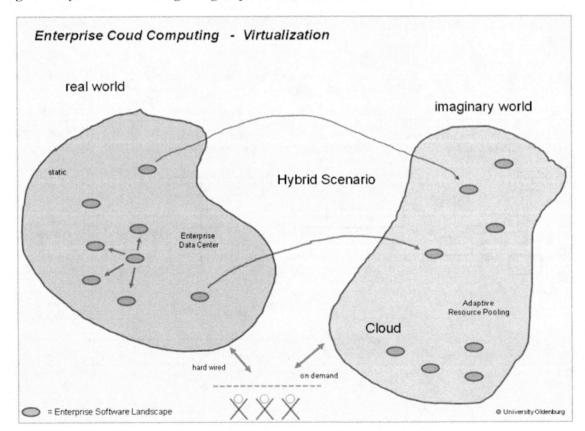

tors from ontology based network structures or reference models. A further domain of enterprise tomography is the integration management of environmental information systems (Integration Lifecycle Management). Integration of isolated and siloed solutions in virtual cloud environments is in the center of interest.

Operator Based Approach for Root-Cause-Analysis in Cloud Environments

Environmental Information Systems do have inherent complex integration concepts. Because of cascading effects, internal errors can accumulate, propagate and have massive negative impacts regarding data integrity. Finding the root-cause of error symptoms is time-critical, generally very time consuming and requires high skilled software engineers. The following sections outlines a generic methodology supporting the Root-Cause-Analysis phase using scientific algorithms defined in discrete mathematics, spectral graph-theory and bio-informatics. An operator-based approach alleviates the error finding procedure in a systematic and efficient way. Semantic Debugging Patterns can be defined upon generic operators provided by an Enterprise Tomography diagnosis system.

In Enterprise Software Engineering industrialization made significant progress over the last years. However, regarding automatization, the progress in Root-Cause-Analysis of Environmental Information Systems Maintenance is far behind. Especially the diagnostics in maintenance is not standardized and provides high potential regarding efficiency. Operative Enterprise Software System Landscapes in their entirety are heterogenic and complex. Defect analysis and corrections in integrated software conglomerates is often extremely difficult and risky, is time consuming and needs to be performed by highly specialized software engineers on a case-by-case basis. In this section the procedure of Enterprise Software Maintenance is standardized according to the

metaphor Computer Tomography established in medical diagnostics. In medical root-cause and comparative diagnostics Computer Tomography is a de-facto standard, is a generic concept for defect location along with minimized preconditions and non-surgical intervention for diagnosing scenarios. Both characteristics are essential and advantageous in the context of Root-Cause-Analysis of Enterprise Software Systems as well. Dedicated approaches and concepts of Semantic Web, Social Networking, Spectral Graph-Theory and Bio-Informatics are transferred to Enterprise Software Diagnostics. The resulting approach is called Enterprise Tomography (Aalmink & Marx Gómez, 2011). To increase efficiency in maintenance of Environmental Information Systems, the concepts are adapted individually and combined to a holistic error-approximation concept.

In the present chapter generic operators are constructed with interdisciplinary algorithms and methods. These operators are in the position to categorize polymorphic integration concepts by semantic views in Enterprise Platforms both, in dimension space and time (Aalmink & Marx Gómez, 2009). The generic operators facilitate repetitive maintenance tasks and point the maintenance engineer in the periphery of the root-cause. In accordance to apparatus supported medical diagnostics, the proposed Enterprise Tomography approach enables localization of semantic integration concepts, enables visualization and makes the tracking of the semantic integration concepts in dimension time and space possible. A domain-specific delta analysis between Enterprise Platforms is possible as well. The concept Enterprise Tomography contains algorithm-based Semantic Debugging Patterns and enables system-based guidance for defect approximation and defect detection. In this chapter the scientific contribution is primarily seen in a novel methodology for automatization and streamlining of continuous Enterprise Software Maintenance. The presented Enterprise Tomography approach supports the Root-Cause-Analysis and is therefore to be positioned in the context of Application Lifecycle Management for Environmental Information Systems.

Typically, in the context of enterprise software maintenance, externally reported defect issues are to be corrected in Enterprise Software Systems in a very short period of time with no side-effects. The defect issues contains the whole description, how to reproduce the error symptom in the productive enterprise software system or in a reference system hosted at the enterprise software manufacturer site. Reproducing the error symptom means executing business transactions, individual business process steps or performing operations or fine granular enterprise services according to the defect description. All those steps leave a footprint in the system. Assuming, a system at point-in-time t_0 before reproducing the error symptom and at point-in-time t_1 after reproducing the error symptom is introspected. This results in two system states S_0 and S_1 respectively. Abstract speaking, the difference of the system states $D = S_1 - S_0$ is a good approximation for the root-cause of the error symptom. This assumption can be made in most cases, because executing a business transaction touches in an enterprise software system a small amount of data in comparison to the whole system. Therefore, it is assumed, that the delta of the system state contains a small amount of data, i.e. in terms of formula $|D| << |S|$ where S denotes the volume of the whole Enterprise Software System data with its associated set of S_0 and S_1 of artifacts. The delta D, i.e. the Delta-Centrality represents the entry-point for the Root-Cause-Analysis with the advantage, being in the environment of the origin error. It is a close periphery of the root-cause for the error symptom. The touched data is a small sub-space D of the full space S with S containing D. Intuitively speaking, there are integration paths from the delta D to the origin defect in the space S beyond delta space D. In the context of this chapter the space is modeled as a multirelational property graph. This graph spans a decision space for the Root-Cause-Analysis. Delta-determination reduces the decision space

drastically and therefore this approach of defect location procedure will become more efficient. Technically, the delta can be calculated using algorithms of the virtualization context. With help of virtualization it is technically an easy task to determine a delta between two different system states in linear time complexity $O(|S|)$. The enterprise software system needs in this case to be virtualized, i.e. needs to be operative in a virtual environment. The big disadvantage here is, that the delta contains neither semantic nor structured data that can be evaluated in the course of the Root-Cause-Analysis scenario. The delta in this case is merely a bit-level sequence and therefore not useful for Root-Cause-Analysis purposes. Therefore, an alternative modeling approach is to be established.

Semantic Representation

The challenge is to model the Environmental Information System integration complexity in an appropriate way. Conclusively, an alternative representation of the physical Environmental Information System covering all relevant aspects for the Root-Cause-Analysis is needed. This model will be a projection, i.e. logical representation of the physical Environmental Information System. The model can be compared as a generalized Semantic Web - a Web of Data enriched by semantics.

Ontologies are good concept to represent the semantic reality of the interior of an Environmental Information System. Ontologies correlate to the Semantic Web in the same way as schemas do for databases. All the logical artifacts are represented with ontology concepts and ontology instances. The elements of the ontologies are in possibly different semantic relationships. Applying these semantic principles on a graph will result in a multirelational property graph. The nodes contain the artifacts, i.e. the ontology instances and the edges represent the semantic relationship between the nodes. It is worth noting, that there are also multiple edges between two nodes possible. Those edges contain different semantics. Let V denote a finite set of nodes and let $E\sigma$ be a subset of $(V x V)$ and $\sigma \in M$, and M a finite set of semantic views. In addition to that, let f_V be a function, that maps every node $v \varepsilon V$ to a set of 2-tuples of string. f_V assigns each node v a set of key-value pairs to. An individual character of the key-value-pairs is an element of a finite alphabet Σ. Similarly, let f_σ with σ in the set of M according to $f_\sigma: E_\sigma \rightarrow D_\sigma$. that assigns in the semantic view σ each edge in E_σ a subset of key-value pairs in D_σ.

Furthermore, let $\hat{E} = < E_0, E_1, ..., E_{|M-1|} >$ be a family of semantic relationships. Then the graph $G = (V, \hat{E}, f_V, f_0, f_1, ..., f_{|M-1|})$ is called a multirelational property graph. The property graph is a simplistic representation of the Semantic Web of data. The interior of the Enterprise Software System can be mapped to the multirelational property graph defined before. This is a projection of the real world Environmental Information System status S_t onto a knowledge representation system G. For example business objects like production orders, business partner, customer order, service order or financial accounts can be mapped to a specific semantic view in terms of key-value assignment in the property graph G. Business objects are special kinds of ontology instances. Other meaningful semantic views include coding, i.e. the coding artifacts and its relationships to each other. Further examples for semantic views include: metadata view based on business objects and its dependencies. The database view with all native data entries of the database tables and their relationships to each other can be a semantic view. Documentation of development artifacts and their relationships is another semantic view to be mapped onto the multirelational property graph G. It is worth noting, that the multirelational property graph is a systematic textual representation of the integration ontology of an operative Environmental Information System at point-in-time t_0. The Root-Cause-Analysis is now reduced to the problem of finding the relevant smallest subgraph in the multirelational property Graph G causing the error symptom. The aspects of integration of an Environmental Information System are represented as integration paths within the graph: nodes with integrative dependencies are linked via edges to overlapping paths. Dependency trees as spanning subgraph reflect the aspects of integration. Here, the integration can cover different semantic views. This provides huge flexibility in appropriate modeling of integration concepts.

Traversal in Decision Space

The property graph spans a decision space for the enterprise software maintenance engineer. Contextual traversal along the edges can easily be performed within a semantic view (intra-traversal) as well as between the different semantic views (inter-traversal). It needs to be mentioned, that the decision space is quite big. Therefore, several decision space reduction algorithms are outlined in the course of this chapter. The reduction can either be a subgraph as a result of delta-determination of a multirelational property graph G at point-in-time t_0 and t_1. In terms of discrete mathematics this means determination of the delta between two similar graphs representing the states of an Environmental Information System at point-in-time t_1 and t_0. Another decision space reduction is the prioritization of the decision space. This means e.g. that some nodes are more important, if they are connected to important nodes. This definition is recursive and leads to recursive or iterative determination of the relevancy regarding the integration aspects. In the Social Networking research area a bunch of graph centrality algorithms is defined. Google PageRank is one prominent example. The PageRank can be calculated iteratively based on linear equation system. Other graph centralities are the Eigenvector Centrality defined by Bonacich, the Betweeness Centrality or the Bridging Centrality (Bader et. al., 2007, Bunke et. al, 2007).

Let $G_\sigma = (V, E_\sigma, f_V, f_\sigma)$ be a subgraph of the multirelational property graph G containing the semantic view σ. Then an adjacency matrix A can be derived. Linearcombinations of term A^k, with k a positive natural number, can build a polynom of matrices according to:

$$p(A)x = (\delta_k A^k + \delta_{k-1} A^{k-1} + ... + \delta_1 A^1 + \delta_0 A^0)x \tag{1.1}$$

with

$$\sum_{i \leq k} \delta_i = 1, \delta_i \geq 0, i = 0, ..., k \tag{1.2}$$

The adjacency matrix is a square matrix with dimensions $(|V|, |V|)$. The k-times multiplication of the matrix A according to A^k contains in each component (u, v) the number of distinct paths from node $u \in V$ to node $v \in V$ in the subgraph G_σ with path length k. The δ_i can carry the semantic of weights or damping factors for path traversals. So, the resulting polynom $p(A)$ is a matrix which can be regarded as weighted composition of integration paths of different length. Above mentionend centrality algorithms like PageRank or Bridging Centrality can be calculated on basis of the constructed matrix as denoted in Equation 1.1. This definition takes the importance of the path length into consideration. In the context of Root-Cause-Analysis paths with short length should be higher weigthed than paths with greater length. Centrality algorithms, mentioned above, can now prioritize the set of nodes V in the semantic view σ respecting path length.

Another, a rather lightweight approach of reduction of decision spaces is the separation of the components of the graph G_σ. If the software engineer starts Root-Cause-Analysis in node v containing in subgraph P as subset of G_σ and the defect is located in the same component, other non-connected components can be ignored. The spectrum of the Laplace Matrix - a matrix derived from the degrees of the nodes $v \in V$ - represents the number of components: The amount of Eigenvalues $= 0$ is the number of disconnected components. So if there are more than one Eigenvalue with value equal to 0 then there is potential for graph

reduction, which makes the Root-Cause-Analysis more efficient. The reduction can be done with dedicated standard algorithms from graph theory.

Up to here, only one semantic view $\sigma \in M$ of the multirelational property graph G is taken into consideration for decision space reduction. Taking the different semantics views into consideration, linear combinations of the adjacency matrixes of each individual semantic view can be established. The topology of the multirelational property graph G can be represented not as matrices but as tensors known in discrete mathematics. In our case 3-way tensors with dimensions $(|V|, |V|, |M|)$, a kind of cuboid of numbers with cells denoting the adjacency between node $u \in V$ and $v \in V$ in semantic view σ in M are constructed. Building the linear combinations over the layers of the tensors (weightening of the semantic views) can be done easily. As a result, in Root-Cause-Analysis individual layers, e.g. the coding layer and the database layer can be prioritized and the proportion of e.g. the metadata layer can be decreased. Centrality algorithms now can be applied on basis of weighted matrices.

The tensors and its calculus mentioned above play a significant role in the context of path algebra (Rodriguez & Shinavier, 2009). Searching and finding of relevant integration paths in the multirelational property graph can be performed with the expressiveness of the path algebra. E.g. find all function modules a, that are indirectly called by class method b that contain a remote function call c in system Y that inserts database entries d_i into database table T. This example outlines a typical integration path in Root-Cause-Analysis to be identified by a path algebra query.

A path algebra is a mathematical formalized description for retrieval of subgraphs of the multirelational property graph G. The procedure of determining the subgraph based on a path algebra query is therefore a decision space reduction algorithm. The path algebra cannot only determine a subgraph in read-mode. The path algebra can enrich or modify the graph in change mode as well. With help of tensor multiplication, addition, subtraction, weightening et. al. it is possible to identify the relevant integration paths in the decision space of the multirelational property graph G. So the path algebra is a very generic mechanism for reducing the decision space.

One disadvantage needs to be mentioned here: The path algebra is based on matrices, more generally on tensors, which can contain billions of components, i.e. cells. Having operative Environmental Information Systems in mind, a graph derivation leads to multirelational graphs with billions of nodes and billions of edges in the individual semantic views. The density is not necessarily high, but the resulting tensors are too big for efficient calculation. Recent research is heading in the direction of ring algebra instead of tensor calculation. Regarding performance and efficiency this seems to become an interesting alternative approach (Rodriguez & Shinavier, 2009).

Up to here, the reduction of the decision space with help of methods of spectral graph theory was discussed. Another algorithmic approach is the evaluation of the structure of the multirelational property graph G. For example dense subgraphs (highly and complex integrated software components) is typically more error-prone than regions with low density subgraphs. Therefore, to increase efficiency in, Semantic Debugging, the detection of such subgraphs with high density is always a good approach. The identified regions are prioritized regions and therefore the decision space is reduced. Algorithms for community detection in the context of Social Networking Research can be applied. A community in a social network is the pendant of an complex integrated subsystem represented as a high density subgraph within a multirelational property graph. Also k-means clustering algorithms can be very useful to exclude subspaces in the decision space. All algorithms need to cope with mass-data, which can be a knock-out criterion in the context of Semantic Debugging or Root-Cause-Analysis. Interactivity given in classical technical debuggers is

also expected in semantic debuggers. Therefore, algorithms need to be constructed, that work in a relaxative mode without loosing the correctness regarding defect location.

The methodology of prioritizing a whole decision space is called ranking. All nodes and edges of a multirelational property graph is taken into consideration. Another approach is the scoring of a path query. This means subgraphs, resulting from a concrete path algebra query, are ranked e.g. with centrality algorithms. So the ranking happens in combination with the path algebra query. The ranking takes place only on a subgraph. Depending on the query, the result is ranked. This scoring is very useful in diagnosis scenarios.

The concept of recommendation is also a practice proven approach in Root-Cause-Analysis. When the software maintenance engineer is at a specific stage in the semantic debugging scenario, he has many degrees of freedom to follow paths. This can result in false-positive, true-negative, positive or negative hits regarding approaching the defect location. A recommendation engine provides hints in terms of nodes to follow with higher rated root-cause hit rate. This is a probabilistic approach. Recommendations can be calculated on basis of tensors mentioned above. Therefore recommendations take different semantic views into considerations. This leads to a more efficient routing to the root-cause location. All in all the concept of recommendations leads to decision space reduction. Finally, in category of decision space reduction algorithms, the semantic inference based on multirelational property graphs needs to be mentioned. Semantic interference in our context means making the implicit knowledge of a specific integrationgraph G explicit. This can be done with help of interference algorithm used in artificial intelligence. Typically, the interference algorithms do not modify the multirelational property graph G. The graph G is rather extended to G', i.e. in terms of formula G is a subset of G'. This set-theoretical inclusion is to be interpreted in the following sense: All information retrievable from the multirelational property graph G can also be retrieved from the multirelational property graph G'. The graph G' contains more information. In other words, G' can have additional nodes, additional edges, additional semantic views or additional key-values on existing nodes and edges. The time consumption for provisioning of the additional knowledge in the graph G' can be reused in multiple follow-up queries and therefore amortized over the amount of path algebra queries.

Delta-Operator

In the previous section a flexible schema-free model for adequate knowledge representation covering integration aspects in an Environmental Information System at point-in-time t_0 is discussed. The model is schema-free, because if the integration aspects are extended, or the system states change, the multirelational property graph is in the position to absorb those cross-cutting concerns and represent the data in an appropriate way without the need of static extension of the data model. This section is concerned with the comparison of two similar systems. Basically, two multirelational property graphs need to be compared. If the comparison is based on graphs with large node sets and edge sets in the range of beyond billions of entities, the comparison cannot be executed in reasonable time. Although mathematically correct and exact, the results are not provided in a reasonable time-frame and therefore this option is not applicable. Nevertheless, the procedure shall be outlined for having a better understanding of the algorithms involved. It is worth noting, that the comparison exceeds the entity-by-entity comparison. The comparison of two similar multirelational property graphs is rather a structural comparison. So it needs to be figured out, what is the algorithm for detecting the structural difference of two similar graphs. The involved indices can based upon a graph G_1 at t_0 and its modified version G_2 at t_1, i.e. comparison of one Environmental Information System, which

changes over a short period of time. The other use case is the comparison of two different Environmental Information Systems. The comparison of a productive system with the test system is based on data close to production system. Test cases can be verified based on this comparison of physical similar systems. The comparison is based on two physical software instances at different locations. The delta is the footprint of the test scenarios executed based on copied productive data.

Especially in the case of physical distributed comparison the entity-by-entity comparison is not sufficient. Here, the structural comparison is the path forward to go. Alternatively speaking, nodes in different systems with the same semantics can be labeled with different IDs. E.g. the labeling is based on number ranges or based on GUIDs which is a rather randomized labeling procedure. The probabilistic distribution or the policy-based labeling is different; the semantic relationships are rather invariant. This case of relationship association with different labeling needs to be taken into consideration. Consequently, nodes with the same semantics are belonging cross-system together and therefore need to be structural compared. The structure of two similar systems is nearly invariant, not necessarily the individual labeling of the nodes.

Basically, the comparison reflects the changes of the multilayered represented semantic. If e.g. a business transaction in an Environmental Information System is executed, the semantic in the multirelational property graph will get modified at point in time t_0 which results in a changed graph G_2. The delta is the footprint of the business transaction executed. More generally, the delta is the footprint of any tool, process step, user interaction, service execution, maintenance task. The delta is represented in different layers of the multirelational property graph, which reflects not only the data, i.e. the labeling, but the semantic topology as well. This generic delta-approach embeds inter alia the mathematics of several domain specific topics of applied computer science like

Business Process Mining, SAP Standard Proximity (Sekatzek & Krcmar, 2009), Architecture Deviation Analysis or Software-Tracking and Tracing in the context of Software Evolution. The delta in this context is a subset, i.e. a multirelational subgraph of a multirelational property graph. It is a holistic semantic representation useful for a family of algorithms in the area of in-depth structural analysis. The Delta-Operator in this context can be seen as a reusable component for those algorithms. This enables significant complexity reduction while simultaneously the quality of the resulting compositions increases. The delta is to be seen as a means for defining a graph centrality in the context of Root-Cause-Analysis. This is comparable to the approaches of Eigenvector Centrality, Closeness Centrality, Bridging Centrality, Google Page-Rank Centrality or Vitality Centrality inter alia as defined and used in Social Network Analysis or Spectral Graph Theory, respectively. The new Delta Centrality points the software maintenance engineer close to the regions of relevancy in the decision space that is spanned by the multirelational property graph. To put it in other words, there is an analogon of approaches and the fuzzy Root-Cause-Analysis procedure can be formulized and captured more precisely. This leads to concrete derivation of approximative algorithms.

It is worth noting, that the theory of Software Metrics can build on the abstraction of Delta Centrality as presented in this chapter. In this chapter the Delta Centrality is primarily used for the Root-Cause-Analysis, i.e. for approximation of the defect location. The approximation happens in the decision space spanned by the multirelational property graph. The Root-Cause-Analysis is therefore based on the indirection of the delta graph centrality.

In the following section the precise mathematical calculus of the Delta-Operator is developed. For the sake of simplicity, the focus is based on one single semantic view $\sigma \in M$. This reduction can be made without loss of generality. Levenshtein

has developed the Levenshtein-Distance for two single finite sequences $\tau_1, \tau_2 \in \sum^n$. By the way - a sequence can be seen as a very simplistic chained labeled graph. The positions are the node IDs and the elements of the sequences are the labels. In the Levenshtein theory, the concept of Edit Script, denoted as Π, is developed. The length of the minimal Edit Script is defined as the Levenshtein Distance $\pounds(\tau_1, \tau_2) = |\Pi|$. The Edit Script represents a sequence of elementary operation *insert, delete, update* needed to be performed on τ_1 to morph τ_1 sequentially into τ_2. Calculation of the Edit Script and consequently for the Edit Distance can be done with help of the generic Simplex Method known in in the theory of Linear Programming for integer based programs. The concept of Levenshtein Distance can be formulated more generically and transferred to Tree Distance. With help of Tree Distance Algorithms a minimum Edit Script, representing the shortest sequence of elementary operations on the tree for transforming tree F into tree H, can be calculated. Elementary operations may be performed on nodes, edges and the associated labels. Deleting of a node implies deleting of the incident edge. Inserting a node implies inserting of the related edge at the specific parent node. The Tree Edit Script and Tree Edit Distance can be calculated with Simplex Method as well, but the asymptotic time complexity is exponentially in the number of nodes of the tree.

In the context of Root-Cause-Analysis, the Tree-Edit-Distance is generalized to the Graph-Edit-Distance. Referring to the complexity of the Tree-Edit-Distance, the complexity of the Graph-Edit-Distance is much higher, but still remains exponential. Also the Graph-Edit-Distance can be calculated with help of Simplex Method, well known, that this approach is not necessarily the optimal one regarding time and space complexity.

Let $G_1 = (V_1, E_1, f_1, g_1)$ and $G_2 = (V_2, E_2, f_2, g_2)$ be two labeled graphs and S the set of possible Edit Scripts transforming graph G_1 morphologically into graph G_2. f_1 is a label function that maps the nodeset V_1 onto a finite discrete set of labels

L. The label function g_1 maps the set of edges E_1 to the set of labels *L.* Likewise, f_2 and g_2 maps the set of nodes V_2 and the set of edges E_2 into *L.* Furthermore, let c be a cost function for the set of individual elementary graph operation sequences based on *insert, update, delete*, which maps those sequence sets into the field of positive rational numbers. Then the Graph-Edit-Distance is calculated according to (Neuhaus & Bunke, 2006):

$$d(G_1, G_2) = min_{<s1,...sk> \, = \, s \, \epsilon \, S} \sum_{i \, \epsilon \, [1:k]} c_i \qquad (1.3)$$

As mentioned before, this definition of distance according to the optimization schema can be generalized to multirelational graphs. The Graph-Edit-Distance $d(G_1, G_2)$ and the Edit Script is leading to the Graph-Edit-Distance, that is the center of interest. Having the minimal Graph Edit Script in place, the delta subgraph can easily be derived from the source graph G_1. This delta subgraph is referred to as Delta or Delta Centrality throughout the chapter. The Delta encompasses the nodes and edges, that are close to the defect location, i.e. most relevant for continuing Root-Cause-Analysis in direction to the error. The Delta-Centrality in generalization can encompass different semantic views in *M.*

Consequently, the error i.e. the root-cause of the error symptom can be approached from different angles. The defect itself can also affect different semantic views. Delta determination according to Equation 1.3 is very time consuming, in theory as well as in practice for operational data. Therefore, determination of the Delta, utilizing optimization techniques is not applicable in the context of Root-Cause-Analysis, where in general the graphs have a large extent. Asymptotically with the extent of graphs, the time for semantic debugging would exceed the time for manual Root-Cause-Analysis. To enable drastic acceleration, relaxation techniques to Equation 1.3 are to be applied.

The basic idea of the Delta-Operator is that calculation does not take place on the level of the graphs, but rather on the level of indices.

Speaking more precisely, the involved graphs are to be indexed. The index construction algorithms need to fulfill the characteristic of redundancy elimination of the multirelational property graph to a large extent while preserving the topology structure of the graph. It can be shown, that multirelational property graphs can be mapped to tensors which, technically speaking, are a homogeneous set of matrices. Those matrices, derived from operational Corporate Environmental Management Information Systems with help of crawlers, are in fact sparse, i.e. have low density in values not equal to 0. Beyond that, it can empirically be shown, that there are patterns in such matrices, e.g. many adjacent equal values. This leads to high redundancy in the set of matrices. This redundancy can easily be removed with help of a multilevel inverted indexing technique. In addition to that, different further redundancy elimination techniques can be applied. Amongst others, interval determination for neighboring positions or codes of label values according to the probabilistic distribution in that way, that the labels with higher frequency will be assigned the codes with smaller length to. This is a very easy but efficient redundancy eliminating technique in combination with inverted indexing. A good, with linear time complexity indexing algorithm for matching subsequences or patterns is the $DC\mu$ Difference Cover Modulo μ algorithm, a generalized indexing algorithm of $DC3$ used in bio-informatics (Kärkkäinen, Sanders & Burkhardt 2006, Nulens, 2006). The resulting index is a PAT-Array, which is a compact representation of the logically involved PAT-tree. PAT-Arrays allow logarithmic access to the indexed sequence, which is very advantageous for primary access to the inverted index via the lexicon. This sequence indexing algorithm can be combined with the inverted indexing for defining an index-path to the lexicon of the distinct values of the multirelational property graph.

Basically, the Delta-Operator compares rather the redundancy eliminated indices instead of the involved redundant graphs. This leads to performance gains. It constructs the indices of the involved multirelational property graphs in a first step. A Delta-Index is constructed based on the previously constructed indices. The indices are systematically organized and allow easy light-weight comparison. In the case of high redundancy, as given in Enterprise Software Systems (Plattner, 2009), the Delta-Index is quasi-isomorphic to the Delta of the involved multirelational property graphs. A small Delta-Index indicates that the involved multirelational property graphs are similar. The Delta-Operator is an efficient algorithm for handling of similar Enterprise Software Systems or for tracing the changes of an Enterprise Software System over a short period of time.

The efficiency of the Delta-Operator is given only in the case of highly redundant and sparse graphs. The approach of the Delta-Operator is in general not loss-free, i.e. it may result in an incorrect delta-subgraph. Nevertheless, if the characteristics of high redundancy and low density of the involved graphs are given, the resulting Delta is quasi-correct and therefore suitable in most practicable use cases. At the same time, the time and space complexity is reasonable in this situation in the context of Semantic Debugging. In addition to that, the parameter μ can rebalance time complexity against space complexity to a certain extent.

If the involved graphs are orthogonal to each other, i.e. with high entropy in the set of nodes, edges and labels, then the approach of the Delta-Operator has no value-added advantage in comparison to the optimization approach outlined in Equation 1.3. A comparison of two complete structural different integrated Enterprise Software Systems is suboptimal in conjunction with the Delta-Operator. The decision space will not be reduced significantly. In this situation, the indices degrade and the Delta-Centrality provides non-relevant hints regarding defect location in the context of Semantic Debugging. The Delta-Operator is applicable for similar and redundant Enterprise Software Systems only. Nevertheless,

this restriction leaves many options for practicable use-cases in the context of Root-Cause-Analysis.

Join-Operator

In Root-Cause-Analysis it is essential to have effective means in place for reducing the decision space in order to approach or at least approximate the defect location. Using multirelational property graphs in Semantic Debugging implies the need for grouping the nodes and edges according to specific semantic criteria. The nodes may be topologically adjacent via direct or indirect edges or the nodes are distributed, but connected semantically across different semantic views $\sigma \in M$. Those nodes have a semantic link rather than an edge relationship. The nodes are grouped in a semantic bundle. This semantic bundle can be refined iteratively with help of the Join-Operator. As a result, a subgraph of the multirelational property graph encompasses the defect location or the graph periphery is in the proximity of the defect location. This iteratively approximation is very effective in Semantic Debugging, because there is no need to define a complex path algebra query at the very beginning. The decision space reduction can be done iteratively with help of a sequence of elementary queries. Each intermediate step, i.e. each query depends on the result of the previous semantic grouping. The iteratively constructed subgraphs of the multirelational property graph can be prioritized. In each individual step all nodes and edges can be prioritized with help of centrality rankings, e.g. the Delta Centrality, Google PageRank Centrality, Bridging Centrality, Betweeness Centrality to name but a few. This is called multirelational property graph scoring, because the ranking, i.e. prioritizing is depending on the previous query, more precisely on the previous materialized queries executed in a sequence. With help of centralities the most relevant nodes can be emphasized in the decision space. E.g. Degree Centrality, Bridging Centrality or the Betweeness Centrality are good means to identify intensive integrated software regions with high correction risks. Defect locations are primarily to be found in areas with high grade of integration. Basically, from the perspective mathematics the algorithms of the Join-Operator are included in the Delta-Operator. In essence, the Join-Operator is executed in the first step for each operand of the Delta-Operator.

The Join-Operator constructs a multilayered inverted index for two multirelational property graphs. Also here the $DC\mu$ Difference Cover Modulo μ indexing algorithm is involved. As a result, the Join-Operator performs the union of the multirelational property graphs and constructs a reusable inverted index for efficient query access.

As mentioned before, the Join-Operator enables identification and grouping of distributed elements of the multirelational property graph. Those elements are bundled. The semantic bundle is a not necessesarily connected subspace in the decision space in the context of semantic debugging. There is an analogon to Cross-Cutting Concerns as known from Aspect-Oriented-Programming AOP. More precisely, the Join-Operator is an algorithm for identification of aspects in an Enterprise Software System. The aspects may include Security, Logging, Numerical Precision, Connectivity, Software Enhancements and Modifications to name but a few. Those aspects are cross-cutting and therefore are distributed in the multirelational property graph. Not to be mentioned, that the aspects can freely be defined by a sequence of elementary queries.

The Join-Operator has two operands and enables iterative refinements of the Cross-Cutting-Concerns in the decision space spanned by the multirelational property graph. The index is redundancy eliminated, structured and allows an efficient materialization of the queries, i.e. the reconstruction of the subgraphs implied by the queries.

In summary, the Join-Operator as well as the Delta-Operator spans a subspace in the decision space. This subspace can be prioritized to segregate

defect location relevant from the non-relevant subspaces. The queries take place not on the graph level but rather on the level of the inverted index of the involved graph. This indexing procedure is redundancy eliminating to a large extent and enables the reconstruction of the subgraphs. If redundancy of Enterprise Software System can be assumed (Plattner, 2009) and in the case of system similarity, the algorithms work efficient and correct also for multirelational graphs of a larger extent. This relaxation approach can ensure the quasi-correctness in most practical use-cases. It circumvents the extreme time consumption needed for the exact calculation in the optimization approach mentioned in equation 1.3.

SEMANTIC DEBUGGING PATTERNS

In the previous sections basically two generic operators for reducing the decision space have been constructed. This paragraph covers the topic of Semantic Debugging Patterns based upon the operators defined before. In this context, Semantic Debugging Patterns are best practice blueprints for defect location approximation. Assuming, an erroneous business process needs to be diagnosed in an Corporate Environmental Management Information System. The business process can be seen as a sequence of individual business process operations leaving a footprint in the Enterprise Software System each. The sequence of business process steps changes the Enterprise Software System from the initial system status S_{t0} to S_{t1} until the final business process step, which transforms the system into the target state S_{tn}. In terms of mathematics, this means a trajectory in the decision space. The sequence of system states $< S_{t0}, S_{t1, ...,} S_{tn} >$ represents the set of consecutive intermediate states in the decision space. The Delta of the system states $\Delta_k = S_{tk} - S_{tk-1}$, $k \, \varepsilon \, [1, n]$ represents the footprint of an individual business process step k. The system deltas Δ_k can easily be calculated utilizing the Delta-Operator. All in all, the Delta is the incremental composition of the trajectory of the business process in the decision space. The Delta-Centrality points to the periphery of the defect location. Traversal from the individual delta is possible. Elements in the delta-subgraph can be ranked or scored according to the centralities mentioned in the previous sections. With the Join-Operator it is possible to traverse from an individual delta subgraph Δ_k to the periphery of the defect location. This can be done in different semantic views $\sigma \in M$ of the multirelational property graph G. Up to here, a fundamental Semantic Debugging Pattern has been discussed. Another Semantic Debugging Pattern is related to the Join-Operator only. With the aid of Join-Operator it is possible to refine the decision space of the multirelational property graph iteratively. This leads, in comparison to a trajectory, to a monotone decreasing sequence of multirelational subgraphs according to $G = G_{t0} \geq G_{t1} \geq ... \geq G_{tn}$. The relation $\geq$ denotes the inclusion of graphs. A query q_k is based on G_k and results in an indexed multirelational subgraph G_{k+1}. In terms of mathematics, this iteration is the analogy to fixed point determination or invariant point determination of a graph operator. This allows a very flexible decision space reduction in an easy way. The Join-Operator, the Delta-Operator and the Inference-Operator of the next section are multivariate operators, respectively. The algorithms can be parameterized and be reused and composed for individual Semantic Debugging Patterns. This enables a specific target-oriented defect location approximation strategy. Enterprise Tomography encompasses the set of Semantic Debugging Patterns based on generic graph operators utilizing redundancy eliminating indexing techniques.

FUTURE RESEARCH DIRECTIONS: INFERENCE-OPERATOR

A strong limitation of the Delta-Operator and of the Join-Operator is the fact, that approximation for the defect location and for the root cause can be performed iteratively only. For reconstruction and traversal of the integration graph, each individual step requires human interaction and decision. Therefore, this diagnosis apppoach is semiautomatic.

For Semantic Debugging it would be advantageous to have an operator in place that is in the position to evaluate deep queries based on multirelational property graphs. The depth, the attributes and the topology of the graph should be taken into consideration. The Inference-Operator, based on path-algebra, should be aligned to techniques mentioned in (Rodriguez & Shinavier, 2009). Basically, it is an open research question, how to build graph based queries based on path algebra and simultaneously employ the indexing techniques as used for the Delta-Operator and for the Join-Operator. On the one hand side, the Inference-Operator shall provide more flexibility and genericity in the queries and on the other hand side, there is a big potentiality for runtime-efficient algorithms based on graph redundancy eliminating indexing techniques. The research for the Inference-Operator should address the fact, that the graph based queries not to be executed on the extrinsic level of the Multirelational Property Graph, but rather on the intrinsic level of the graph representation, i.e. on basis of the index representation. In summary, graph theoretic algorithms and the path algebra based queries need to be performed on indices directly. The query results can be materialized to the extrinsic graph representation.

To make the Inference-Operator useful for reducing decision spaces in Semantic Debugging, different Centrality Algorithms shall be applied. The open research question results in finding a good balanced and practice relevant combination of graph traversal and evaluation algorithms, indexing techniques and decision space reduction algorithms with help of centrality prioritization. The compatibility of the operators regarding the operands as indices enables a harmonized approach for Semantic Debugging Patterns. This provides potentiality for standardization in software maintenance as part of Application Lifecycle Management and leads to efficiency in the Root-Cause-Analysis phase.

RELATED WORKS

The approach Enterprise Tomography driven Governance of Federated ERP in a Cloud is complementary to the research areas Application Lifecycle Management of VLBAs and governance of Semantic SOA respectively. In Semantic SOA there are dedicated procedures in alignment of semantic entities and semantic services (Panchenko, 2007). The Enterprise Tomography approach generically unifies a set of ontology matching approaches and is primarily based on algorithms for genetic engineering known in Bio-Informatics (Tiun, Abdullah & Kong, 2001; Haak & Brehm, 2008; Aalmink & Marx Gómez, 2009; Abels, Haak & Hahn, 2005). The mathematical model of a family of matching algorithms for large data sets in genetic engineering is transformed to semantic matching and delta determination. The delta indicators can be interpreted as generic software metrics in a specific domain called semantic view. The software metrics are the decision basis in the governance procedure. Regarding metrics, service provisioning and consumption (dependency graph), business data as well as meta-data is taken into consideration.

CONCLUSION

In previous sections we have outlined the Federated EPR approach in the context of Green Computing. It was discussed how FERP can increase scalability in a Green Cloud. In addition we adumbrated the Integration Lifecycle Management of a Federated ERP network in a Cloud. With help of closed-loops the evolution of a shared Feder-

ated ERP system can be controlled according to cloud metrics, which are indicators calculated by the Enterprise Tomograph. The Enterprise Tomograph acts as a generic Delta-calculating search engine, which permanently crawls and observes the materialized cloud content. The search engine of the Enterprise Tomograph can be executed in delta mode as well as in full mode. With help of extractors for the Enterprise Tomograph we can have polymorphic search operator or delta operator which delivers the indicators as decision basis in the governance procedure.

This chapter proposes a set of Semantic Debugging Patterns based on generic graph operators as blueprints for efficient Root-Cause-Analysis regarding defect location in Enterprise Software Systems. With help of Enterprise Tomography it is possible to perform efficient systematic structural system analysis regarding approximation towards defect locations. The decision space can effectively be reduced while simultaneously minimizing the algorithmic time consumption during the diagnosis iteration. The chapter outlines the generic Join-Operator and the Delta-Operator. The Delta-Operator determines and prioritizes the decision space according to the Delta Centrality. The Delta-Centrality is a metric on multirelational property graphs for defining the periphery and proximity of the defect location. The operator-based approach is applicable for Environmental Information Systems with high redundancy in software and data artifacts. With help of relaxation techniques the performance of graph algorithms can be increased drastically while preserving the correctness to a large extent. In particular, the Delta-Operator is applicable and efficient only for similar systems. However, these restrictions leave many, in practice useful semantic debugging patterns for large and complex integrated Corporate Environmental Management Information Systems.

REFERENCES

Aalmink, J., & Marx Gómez, J. (2009). Enterprise Tomography - an efficient approach for semi-automatic localization of integration concepts in VLBAs. In (Ed) Cruz-Cunha, M. M., *Social, Managerial and Organizational Dimensions of Enterprise Information Systems*, Hershey, PA: IGI Global ISBN: 978-1-60566-856-7.

Aalmink, J., & Marx Gómez, J. (2011). Enterprise Tomography - an efficient Application Lifecycle Management approach supporting semiautomatic localization, delta-tracking and visualization of Integration Ontologies in VLBAs. In (Ed.) Kumar, S., Bendoly, E., Esteves, J., *Frontiers of Research in Enterprise Systems*. SAGE.

Abels, S., Haak, L., & Hahn, A. (2005). Identification of common methods used for ontology integration tasks. Interoperability Of Heterogeneous Information Systems. In *Proceedings of the first international workshop on Interoperability of heterogeneous information systems*, (pp. 75-78) Bremen, Germany. ACM.

Bader, D. A., Kintali, S., Madduri, K., & Mihail, M. (2007). Approximating Betweeness Centrality. In (Eds) Bonato A, Chung F R K.: *Algorithms and Models for the Web Graph, 5.th International Workshop WAW 2007, San Diego, CA, USA, December 2007, Proceedings*, (pp. 124-134) LNCS 4863.

Brehm, N., Lübke, D., & Marx Gómez, J. (2007). Federated Enterprise Resource Planning (FERP) Systems. In Saha, P. (Ed.), *Handbook of Enterprise Systems Ar-chitecture in Practice* (pp. 290–305). Hershey, PA, USA: IGI Global. doi:10.4018/978-1-59904-189-6.ch017

Brehm, N., Marx Gómez, J., & Rautenstrauch, C. (2006). An ERP solution based on web services and peer-to-peer networks for small and medium enterprises. [IJISCM]. *International Journal of Information Systems and Change Management*, *1*(1), 99–111. doi:10.1504/IJISCM.2006.008288

Bunke, H., Dickinsion, P. J., Kraetzl, M., & Wallis, W. D. (2007). *A Graph-Theoretic Approach to Enterprise Networks Dynamics* (pp. 71–117). Birkhäuser Verlag.

Epstein, A. (2004). *Parallel hardware architectures for the life science*. Doctoral thesis, Delft University Press.

Grünwald, C., & Marx Gómez, J. (2007). Conception of System Supported Generation of Sustainability Reports in a Large Scale Enterprise. In (Eds) Marx Gomez, J., Sonnenschein, M., Müller M., Welsch H. Rautenstrauch C.: *Information Technologies in Environmental Engineering. ITEE 2007 - Third International ICSC Symposium*, (pp. 60-68) Berlin, Heidelberg, New York: Springer Verlag.

Haak, L., & Brehm, N. (2008). Ontologies supporting VLBAs Semantic integration in the context of FERP. In *3rd International Conference on Information and Communication Technologies: From Theory To Applications, ICTTA 2008*. (pp.1-5.)

Heuser, L., Alsdorf, C., & Woods, D. (2007). *Enterprise 2.0 - The Service Grid –User-Driven Innovation - Business Model Transformation*. International Research Forum 2007, Potsdam, SAP Research, Evolved Technologist Press.

Heuser, L., Alsdorf, C., & Woods, D. (2008). *The Web-Based Service Industry – Infrastructure for Enterprise SOA 2.0, Potential Killer Applications - Semantic Service Discovery*. International Research Forum 2008, Potsdam, SAP Research, Evolved Technologist Press.

Kärkkäinen, J., Sanders, P., & Burkhardt, S. (2006). *Linear Work Suffix Array Construction.* In: Journal *of the ACM (JACM). 53*(6) 918-936.

Marx Gómez, J. (2009). Corporate Environmental Management Information Systems - CEMIS 2.0. In (Eds) Davcev D, Marx Gómez J.: *Proceedings of the ICT Innovations Conference 2009,* (pp. 1-4) Ohrid, Macedonia, Springer Heidelberg.

Neuhaus, M., & Bunke, H. (2006). A Random Walk Kernel Derived from Graph Edit Distance. In (Eds) Yeung D- Y, Kwok J T, Fred A, Roli F, de Ridder D.: *Structural, Syntactic and Statistical Pattern Recognition. Joint IAPR International Workshops, SSPR 2006 and SPR 2006,* (pp. 191-199.) Hong Kong, China, August 2006, Proeedings LNCS 4109, Berlin Heidelberg: Springer-Verlag.

Nulens, R. (2006). *Sequentie Analyse.* Doctoral Thesis, transnationale Universiteit Limburg, School voor Informatietechnologie. pp 67-77.

Panchenko, O. (2007). Concept Location and Program Comprehension in Service-Oriented Software. In *Proceedings of the IEEE 23rd International Conference on Software Maintenance: Doctoral Symposium,* (pp. 513 – 514), Paris, France: ICSM.

Plattner, H. (2009). A Common Database Approach for OLTP and OLAP using an In-Memory Column Database. International Conference on Management of Data. *Proceedings of the 35th SIGMOD international conference on Management of data. Providence.* (pp 1-2) Rhode Island. USA. ISBN: 978-1-60558-55.

Rodriguez, M. A., & Shinavier, J. (2009). Exposing Multi-Relational Networks to Single-Relational Network Analysis Algorithms. DOI: 10.1016/j.joi.2009.06.004. *Journal of Informetrics, 4*(1), 29-41 ISSN:1751-1577.

Sekatzek, P. E., & Krcmar, H. (2009). *Measurement of the Standard Proximity of Adapted Standard Business Software.* In: DOI 10.1007/s12599-009-0045-4. BISE Research Paper. (pp. 1-11.)

Tiun, S., Abdullah, R., & Kong, T. E. (2001). Automatic Topic Identification Using Ontology Hierarchy. In *Proceedings, Computational Linguistic and Intelligent Text Processing, Second International Conference CICLing,* (pp 444-453) Mexico City, Mexico: Springer

Chapter 21
Corporate Governance of IT in Spanish Family Owned Enterprises

Alberto J. Arroyo
ALAMCIA S. L, Spain.

ABSTRACT

IT Corporate governance is the information technology-governing discipline of corporate governance.. Governing IT is not a simple discipline: researchers and practitioners have developed frameworks, best practices, etc. The standard ISO/IEC 38.500 sets the principles and activities to be carried in the organization to implement corporate governance of IT. Family-owned enterprises introduce a specific particularity regarding governance: the family. This paper presents an analysis of corporate governance of IT in family owned enterprises, considering this singularity, from the Spanish perspective. Also, it introduces two examples of implementation in family owned enterprises.

INTRODUCTION

Corporate governance is the system in which organizations are directed and controlled (ISO, 2008). Corporate governance is not new, and the effects of bad governance are suffered every day by the organizations. In fact, reports are pointing to bad governance as the key factor for the recent credit crunch (Moxey, 2008). The importance of corporate governance began with the publication of COSO (COSO, 1992) and the Cadbury Report (Cadbury, 1992). Codes of conduct were published on the different countries (ASX, 2007; Vienot, 1995), and then the release of the OECD Principles of Corporate Governance (OECD, 2004) was a milestone in order to standardize the contents and extent of corporate governance code of conducts and practices around the world.

According with the standard ISO/IEC 38.500 (ISO, 2008), corporate governance of IT is the system by which the current and future use of IT is directed and controlled. It is recognized as a part of corporate governance nowadays even in codes of conduct (IDSA, 2009), defining rules and recommendations.

DOI: 10.4018/978-1-4666-1764-3.ch021

Family owned enterprises differs from traditional companies or organizations. The difference is based on the family. Family is a key element not only from the ownership perspective, but also from the management perspective: family members are usually involved in top and medium-level management, and tend to make decisions just because of their condition of family members. The importance of family owned enterprises in the world economy is huge. Statistics (IEF, 2009) show that family owned enterprises represents about 80% of the companies in the United States, 60% of the companies in the European Union. In Spain, where the current analysis is done, statistics shows that 85% of the companies are family owned enterprises, and that represents about 70% of the national GDP. In Spain, family owned enterprises have tools to govern and direct the company and separate family issues from company issues. This paper describes this tools, its impact in corporate and IT governance, and also illustrates this with the experience of two family owned enterprises.

CORPORATE GOVERNANCE AND FAMILY OWNED ENTERPRISES

Corporate governance has its origins on the Agenda problems (AECAE, 2007), that is, the separation between ownership and management, and the need that the ownership has to control the management. Mechanisms such as internal controlling and auditing, the different committees and the existence of independent directors are to be implemented on the companies to try to cover the gap of the Agenda problems.

In family owned enterprises, as said before, a third factor comes to reality: the family. Family does not only own the company, but also is involved in the management, and separating management from the family is a thought task. Real situations, in which family members (siblings, in-laws and other relatives) are located at different positions in organizations, are normal in this type of companies. And this is a simple situation, in which first and second generation (founders and his/her sons/daughters) is only considered.

But there are family owned enterprises in which not only first and second generations are involved on the company, but also the third generation, spouses and also other family members (cousins, uncles, etc.) The more complex is the family, the more issues can be found on that type of companies. Other factors needed to be considered. For instance, the condition of being a family member is sometimes assumed by some people to take decisions affecting the operating and the strategy of the company. And these decisions are taken isolated, and with the only justification of being family members. Moreover, the conflicts between family members can take to the situations in which decisions taken by the top management are not only questioned but also prevented from being implemented by other family members.

Thus, it is not a problem of management or ownership; it is also a problem of governance. Ownership, management and family are intertwined and it is important to define mechanisms to separate clearly the three dimensions.

In Spain, this problem tends to be solved with some tools, especially two: a family protocol, and the Family Council. According with the Instituto de la Empresa Familiar (IEF, 2005), the family protocol is a written and approved document, with

Figure 1. The three dimensions of family owned enterprises

Figure 2. The governing structure in family owned enterprises

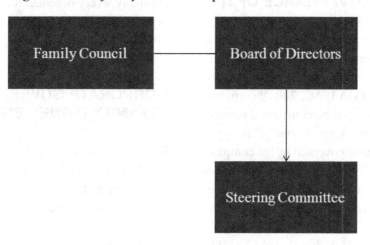

legal bases, by the family members that "contents explicitly the manner in which the family wishes to give answers to corporate objectives". The protocol set rules related to: ownership of the company, transmission of shares, degree of involvement of the family members in the company, transition and retiring rules, establishment of family strategy and corporate directions, approving of big issues and investments, use of the company resources by family members, and so on.

Family protocol set the rules, but there is but there is another tool to be considered: the constitution and implementation of the Family Council. The Family Council is like the Board of Direc-

tors of the family. It is composed by key family members (not spouses), and is the forum in which big issues are handled. The Family Council sets the family objectives, strategy, and rules regarding with the company, and also sets directions for the strategy of the company. Moreover, it is responsible to approve big investments, especially those that can affect the family wealth. The Family Council has a great impact in the company and in the family, because also handles conflicts between family members related to the company and the transition from one to next generation.

Roles with this new governance structure differ from traditional structure. Functions are described on the next table:

Table 1. Roles and responsibilities of the governing components

Structure	Roles and responsibilities
Family Council	Defines the vision and values of both the family and the company Approves high level strategy/directions for the company Approves major investments and also major financing and legal agreements Handles family issues and company family related issues Informs about the performance of the family Is the forum of debate about family objectives and goals Debates and approves changes on the family protocol
Board of Directors	Sets direction for establishing and implementing the company strategy, according with the Family Council Approves major investments according to rules defined by the family council, or leaves them to the Family Council when necessary Those roles that are usually attributed to the Board of Directors
Management	Those who are usually attributed to the Management

CORPORATE GOVERNANCE OF IT

Corporate governance of IT is the discipline that deals with the corporate management of IT (ISO, 2008). CIMA considers two dimensions of corporate governance (CIMA IFAC, 2003); corporate governance of IT should be considered more in the performance dimension, as one of the types of assets that should be governed by the company (Weill & Ross, 2003). From this start, practitioners and professionals have defined different frameworks for implementing IT governance in the organizations. The IT Governance Institute has developed COBIT (ITGI, 2007), Val IT (ITGI, 2008) and Risk IT (ITGI, 2009) frameworks. CISR from MIT has analyzed corporate governance of IT in different publications, identifying best practices from the best players (CIMA IFAC, 2003) (Weill & Broadbent, 1998), and also defining a framework for governing and managing the risk of IT (Westerman & Hunter, 2007). Other institutions and authors (Calder, 2007; Symons, Oliver Young, & Lambert, 2005; Van Grembergen, 2004), etc.) have also developed their own framework or recommendations for implementing corporate governance of IT.

Publications points out to different elements to be covered by Corporate Governance of IT: strategic alignment between IT and the business, value delivery of IT to the company, performance management, IT risk management, organizational structures and processes, etc. As can be perceived, Corporate governance of IT was a set of different rules, methodologies, frameworks, best practices, etc. The conception and publication of the standard ISO/IEC 38.500 was a key element to set the common basis to implement it in the organizations. ISO/IEC 38.500 conceives Corporate governance of IT based in three tasks (direct, monitor and evaluate), and 6 principles: responsibility, strategy, acquisition, performance, conformance and human behaviour.

There is no general solution; Corporate governance of IT implementation depends on every

company, every organization, just because every organization has its own particularities (Toomey, 2009).

CORPORATE GOVERNANCE OF IT IN FAMILY OWNED ENTERPRISES

In family owned enterprises, the existence of the family protocol and the Family Council affects to corporate and IT governance systems. The Family Council and its attributions, as well as the attributes of the Board of Directors, makes that the three tasks defined in the standard ISO/IEC 38.500, as well as the principles, are to be considered in a different way that in other type of organization. Differences in the managing and governing structure have impacts in all the principles, as described next.

Responsibility

Responsibility is perhaps the principle that is impacted the most. Assigning responsibility is not only to be done by the Board of Directors, but also by the Family Council. In fact, since the family protocol is the document that establishes the role of the Family Council, the Board of Directors, and (more important) the way in which the family is involved in the decision making process, assigning responsibility is primarily a role of the Family Council. Not only for what is established in the Family Protocol, but also because of the Family Council can re-interpret and modify this document. According with this, Family Council sets the framework and directions for assigning responsibility with regard of IT. Is the role of the Board of Directors to interpret this framework and direction, and to set the schema and directions for assigning responsibility in the company. Then, the role of the CEO and top management to implement and accept responsibility adequately, according with the Family Council and the Board of Directors.

Strategy

Strategy in also a Corporate governance of IT principle that is importantly impacted in family owned enterprises. Strategy definition and implementation of the entire company, but also regarding IT, must be directed, evaluated, and monitored by the Board of Directors, but it is the Family Council who must first set the rules and principles for defining it, and then approving the strategic direction set on the IT strategy according with the rules defined in the Family Protocol. Not only this: Family Council must validate business strategy, and any modification that this strategy can have. Just because of this, the Family Council has to define specific strategic elements such as the appetite for risk, the availability of resources (family and other resources), etc. Also, the Family Council must propose and validate strategic indicators and the mechanisms for measuring and evaluating it. Thus, implementation of the IT strategy should also be validated and modified by the Family Council not only due to its attributions, but also when unexpected facts happen; anticipation of the transition between generations, family issues, etc. In these situations, the Family Council needs to begin the wheel, that is, recommence the process of strategy definition.

Acquisition

Acquisition, as said in the ISO/IEC 38.500 standard, "are made for valid reasons", and an appropriate analysis should be done to support the decision making process. Business case for family owned enterprises should consider the stakeholders appetite for risk, and be tailored for the family appetite for risk: the main stakeholder is the family and thus the business case must be done according with the family's direction, and also with family owned tendencies and rules for major investing.

According with Family Council attributions, major investments should be approved by this institution. That implies that Family Council (interpreting the family protocol or by its own rules) must set thresholds for investment approval and also the approval process.

Performance

Performance is the principle that does not suffer too much impact in family owner enterprises. Since the Family Council is worried about the performance of the company and its IT, top management and the Board of Directors should inform the Family Council adequately.

Nevertheless, performance should evaluate also specific issues regarding the family, such us the CEO attributes regarding investments.

Also, most of the families establish, as said before, a formal process that evaluates the behaviour and performance of family members, that should consider the IT dimension of the company.

Conformance

Conformance is not only about regulations and compliance; is also about the rules defined in the family protocol, or established by the Family Council. The family protocol is a legal document, and the governing mechanisms should consider this. The Family Council is a legal forum defined, established and supported by the family protocol.

IT must support conformance accordingly, assuring the right level of integrity, confidentiality, availability, etc., at both levels: Family Council and the Board of Directors. Especially important is the confidentiality of the information with regard to the family (salaries, compensations, but other type of information such as financial information), and IT must grant the information has the right degree of integrity, confidentiality, that is sought by the Family Council.

Figure 3. Organizational structures of company – Case Study 1

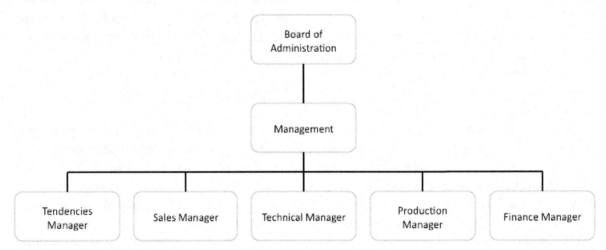

Human Behaviour

In family owned enterprises, family members can be located in any position of the company. Family members can have access to (and make decisions about) IT. And these decisions are not only affecting to the low operational level. Family members tend to re-interpret strategy or family directions.

The family protocol is the document in which rules are defined and mechanisms to interpret them are put in place. The Family Council is the forum in which issues about the family are discussed, interpretation of the rules is made and consensus is taken, when the management and the Board of Directors cannot re-direct doubtful family members behaviours and decisions. Processes such as communication, handling with the unconformists or the resistance, must be made at the Family Council when family is involved (Weill & Ross, 2003), and this also applies to IT.

CASE STUDIES

Taking all al this into account, we present two case studies of implementation of IT governance in family owned enterprises. The first is an SME (small and medium enterprise); the second company is in fact a holding of various SMEs.

Case Study 1

Case Study 1 is a furniture manufacturer small company based in the Southeast of Spain. Company has around 70 employees, with the organizational structure as depicted next:

The founder (manager) is working in the company, as well as the older son (Sales Manager). The younger son had just had his university degree, and joined the company as Technical Manager. When that happened, he began to make technical and financial decisions by himself. Relationship between brothers was not very good, with huge impacts on the management of the company. Importance is the figure of the Finance and Production Manager (a unique person), a reference in the company and acting as a referee when disputes arise between brothers.

The company had an ERP installed (Microsoft's Navision), only covering the admin and finance department, sales and purchasing. There is a need to implement numerical controls in production, and in finished and raw materials inventory. The version installed was outdated, and the system most likely needed to be updated to the new version to introduce new requirements. The IT infrastructure was outsourced, and the contract was to be negotiated shortly. Also, there was a tendency in the clients to require 3D visualization of the products in order to allow designers to show the ambient to its clients. This can have impacts in terms of requiring a technical system to produce 3D designs. Moreover, PCs/laptops needed to be renewed, and back-up systems were not performing well, so there was a need to change it to a more updated technology.

Initially, IT decisions were taken by the Sales Manager (the older son), and approved by the Manager. In case of big investments, the approval is done in the Board of Directors, composed by the founder, the two sons, and the Finance Manager. The youngest son arrival implied that he took ownership of IT on both Technical and Production Departments, and began to take decisions about it by himself, as said.

The definition and implementation of a family protocol, and the Family Council served to put things in order. The Family Council is composed by the founder, his spouse, and the two sons. The Board of Directors is composed by the two sons and the Finance and Production manager. All of this had a great impact on the business but also on IT. Disputes arose between the two brothers, not only regarding the management of the company, but also about IT. The younger brother big investments proposals (updating the ERP to the newest version and also implement production and inventory requirements, but also all with regard the technical department) could have a great impact in the company, and should be approved appropriately.

Investments were prioritized according not only to strategy, but also with family evaluation (considering the family patrimony). Decisions in IT regarding inventory were prioritized, according with the new rules. The family protocol implied that family accounting was performed in the company, and the privacy of the information needed to be assured. Rules were implemented regarding access to the information that was restricted to specific workers of the company. Lastly, emphasis in observing the right behaviour was not only putted into the company's personnel, but also into family members, and adherence to a specific set of value was observed.

Case Study 2

The second company is a holding of three companies: two competing companies manufacturing agricultural machinery, and a third company that manufactures components for the two companies. The structure of the group is depicted in the figure, which also includes the structure of each company.

In terms of IT, all companies had legacy information systems. Regarding IT infrastructure, maintenance was outsourced only in Company 2.

The founder (81 years old) was in an assessing position. His son is the manager of companies 1 and 3, and supervises de facto the management of company 2. Company 2 is being managed by his brother-in-law (his spouse is a secretary). The other daughter has a business outside the family business, acting only as a shareholder in all the companies. Two figures needed to be considered: Administration Manager in Company 1 that is being carried on by a very valuable non-family member, and Sales Manager in Company 2 that is being held by the nephew of the manager of companies 1 and 3, and thus the grandson of the founder.

The implementation of a family protocol was the result of a process of reflection of the founder and his son. There was a need for a family-based holding structure, with the vision of having the best people, but promoting the family among the workers, and centralizing the decision making structures from the family and strategic point of view. This reflection was accompanied with a business reflection that pursued the specialization of the companies (less competition). This implied the centralization of finance and administration services, and the creation of an R&D department

Figure 4. Organizational structures of company – Case Study 2

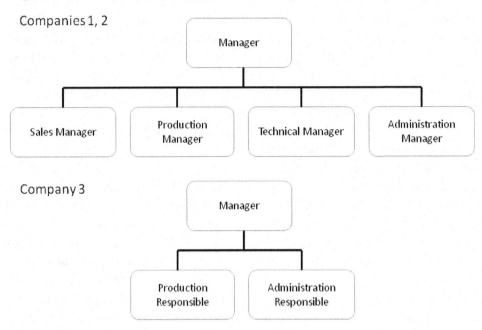

for the three companies. The Board of Administration was established for all four companies. Composition of Boards of Administration was different, with a common element: the nephew of the manager, the Administration Manager in Company 1 and also the son of the founder were on all the Boards. This allowed implementing a common view in all the companies. Family Council was implemented, and it was composed by the first and second generation of the family.

In terms of IT, the implementation of the family protocol had big consequences. The first is the implementation of the same information system for the three companies, in order to allow common accounting and finance services, and consolidation in a holding company. Moreover, the information system covered inventory and production, which allowed to Company 3 to be integrated on the supply chain of Company 1 and Company 2. IT infrastructure was standardized, and was outsourced for all three companies by the same provider. Secondly, there was a rationalization of the approval process for investments, that was now centralized and any major investment decision need to go through the Board of Administration

first, and approved by the Family Council. This happened with the investment in the information system implemented.

And third, there were an effort to take advantage of synergies and best practices, implementing them in all the companies. For instance, allowing sales person to remotely connect to the information system. This was firstly implemented in Company 1 for its sales team, allowing introducing product requests on the systems on a daily basis (instead of weekly), which allowed the company to tune the production, and improve economics. This practice was then implemented in the other companies.

CONCLUSION

Family owned enterprises have special particularities in implementing not only corporate governance but also IT governance. The existence of a family protocol and a Family Council implies that the governing body is divided into two, and the family reserves the right to define direction in setting strategies, objectives, investment prioritization, etc.

Implementing IT governance has to consider the above specificities, assuring also the right level to access, accuracy and security of the information. Behaviour is also important, and adherence to family's values is a must in family owned enterprises. And values depend on the family, not on the company.

REFERENCES

AECAE. (2007). *Gobierno y Responsabilidad Social de la Empresa* [Government and Corporate Social Responsibility]. Asociación Española de Contabilidad y Administración de Empresas. [Spanish Association of Accounting and Business Administration]

ASX. (2007). *Corporate Governance Principles and Recommendations* (2nd ed.). Australian Stock Exchange.

Cadbury, A. (1992). *Report of the Committee on the Financial Aspects of Corporate Governance*. G. P. Publishing.

Calder, A. (2007). *IT Governance Pocket Guide*. IT Governance Publishing.

CIMA IFAC. (2003). *Enterprise Governance. Getting the balance right*. CIMA.

COSO. (1992). *Internal Control - Integrated Framework*. COSO.

IDSA. (2009). *Code of Governance Principles for South Africa (King Code)*. Institute of Directors of Southern Africa.

IEF. (2005). *Guía de Buen Gobierno en la Empresa Familiar* [The Guide to Good Governance in Family Business]. Instituto de la Empresa Familiar. [Institute of Family Business]

IEF. (2009). *Folleto Corporativo* [/Corporate Brochure]]. Instituto de Empresa Familiar.

ISO. (2008). *ISO/IEC 38500*. Corporate Governance of Information Technology.

ITGI. (2007). *Control Objectives for Information and Related Technology, version 4.1*. IT Governance Institute.

ITGI. (2008). *Enterprise Value: Governance of IT Investments. The Val IT Framework 2.0*. IT Governance Institute.

ITGI. (2009). *Enterprise Risk: Identify, govern and manage risk. The Risk IT Framework*. IT Governance Institute.

Moxey, P., Berendt. (2008). *A Corporate Governance and the Credit Crunch*. ACCA.

OECD. (2004). *OECD Principles of Corporate Governance*. OECD.

Symons, C., M., Oliver Young, G., & Lambert, N. (2005). *IT Governance Framework*. Forrester.

Toomey, M. (2009). *Waltzing with the Elephant*. Infonomics.

Van Grembergen, W. (2004). *Strategies for Information Technology Governance*. Idea Group Publishing.

Vienot, T. (1995). *Le Conseil d'Administration des Societés Cotées*. [The Board of Directors of listed companies] Conseil National du Patronal Français and L'Association Française des Enterprises Privées [National Council of French Employers and The French Association of Private Enterprises]

Weill, P., & Broadbent, M. (1998). *Leveraging the new Infrastructure*. Harvard Business School Press.

Weill, P., & Ross, J. W. (2003). *IT Governance. How top performers manage IT decision for superior results*. Harvard Business School Press.

Westerman, G., & Hunter, R. (2007). *IT Risk: Turning Threats into Competitive Advantage*. Harvard Business School Press.

Chapter 22
Towards Effective Tourism and People Alignment

Luís Ferreira
Polytechnic Institute of Cávado and Ave, Portugal

Goran Putnik
University of Minho, Portugal

Maria Manuela Cruz-Cunha
Polytechnic Institute of Cávado and Ave, Portugal

Hélio Castro
University of Minho, Portugal

ABSTRACT

The new (e)commerce/(e)business paradigms forced enterprises to undertake important transformations and reorganizations. It happened with the web and will be repeated in the Cloud and social networks, following Eric Schmidt's (Google CEO) thoughts, "better thinking now on WWC – World Wide Computer, that is, what is behind u-commerce, ubiquity". The tourism is no more only a traditional commercial activity but ever more social- and information-oriented. The tourism services need to be effective to be aligned with tourist requirements. The globalization and easy access allows tourists to change their plans constantly. Dynamic services reconfiguration and resulting impact on their information systems need to be supported. The theme here presented explores new tourism services requirements as the ubiquity and dynamic reconfiguration, new brokering mechanisms, and reliable integration processes, and human-to-human synchronous collaboration allow the natural involvement of the tourist on the co-creation of his activity plan with other agents (humans).

INTRODUCTION

The web is surely the main event after the appearance of the personal computer and quickly became the main mediator for information sharing, communication and presence on a worldwide scale.

However, we assist to a complete and definitely "disintegrated" amount of data, business and processes. We are facing now the opposite situation of the initial isolated processing power, having disperse units (now services) struggling to get in touch. Transform data into useful information and

DOI: 10.4018/978-1-4666-1764-3.ch022

opportunity into business is a high challenge of nowadays. Client's fidelity and trust were relegated to opened concurrency, QoS (Quality of Services) and effectiveness.

The new (e)commerce/(e)business paradigms forced enterprises to undertake important transformations and reorganizations (intra- and inter-organization). It happened with the web and will be repeated in the Cloud and social networks, following Eric Schmidt (Google CEO) thoughts "better thinking now on WWC – World Wide Computer, that is, what is behind u-commerce, ubiquity".

The tourism activities and enterprises are particular cases which show clearly this continuous transformation and impacts of internet acceptance. There are a lot of web places which offer multiple tourism services, from simple information to complete activity planning, including accommodation reservation and travel. However, not everything looks easy indeed. The general web tourism service focuses essentially the business activity and not the tourists. By one side it is complex to get several (unknown, distinct or distrustful) entities working together according to a specific dynamic changing plan; on the other, the personal perspective and participation of tourist are not fully considered on delivery of the results.

The tourism is no more a traditional commercial activity but more social and information-oriented. The tourism services need to be effective to be aligned with tourist requirements. The globalization and easy access (to information and proposals), allows tourists to change constantly their plans. Future challenge requires dynamic tourism services reconfiguration and consequent impact on related information systems, for one hand, and collaboration mechanisms to allow tourist participate on the decision, to the other.

Being cloud computing the most recent emerging paradigm (Coppinger, 2007), it comes nothing more than another "advanced" tentative to get the same, unless tourism services becomes ubiquitous "processing units" which are easily discovery,

composed and coordinated. The same happened with traditional tourism activities: those who remained unknown did not survive!

Since future context demands new tourism services, sustained by new ubiquity and dynamic reconfiguration requirements, an effective brokering mechanism and innovative reliable integration processes based on human-to-human synchronous collaboration which allows the natural involvement of the tourist on the co-creation/co-design (co-management) of his activity plan with other agents (humans).

BACKGROUND

Tourism Business

Tourism is one of the main global industries. Worldwide tourism receipts reached US$ 852 billion in 2009, and accounted for a contribution of some 5% to global economic activity, becoming fourth in main ranking export category, after fuels, chemicals and automotive products (UN-WTO, 2010). Moreover, tourism contributes to one of the highest offer of employment (direct and indirect), which tends to be slightly higher relatively to 2010 and is estimated in the order of 6-7% of the overall number of jobs worldwide.

Many developing countries strive for sustainable tourism, as it represents an opportunity of economic growth, high unemployment, and environmental protection (Watson, Akselsen, Monod, & Pitt, 2004).

Information is the essence for tourism sustainability as a dynamic business activity. Until recently, information technology was not more than a tool for managing purposes; with the advent of the Web, ICT (Information and Communication Technology) progress and tourism (as almost all business activities) have been going "hand in hand"; Nowadays, the Web is no more just a marketing place or a showcase. It became a potential tool to support most of the necessary processes (search, selection, reservation, monitoring, simulation, etc.) to prepare a tourism activity, for supplier (which needs to promote) and for tourist (which needs to discover) as well.

But it still exist an important gap. The tourist (as human) easily changes his plans, and needs immediately to know the impact of that occurrence. The tourist needs to analyse new context and to decide according to new circumstances. The requirement of having anytime, anywhere, any details about anything means ubiquity and emergent technological platforms already announce its support.

Since the ubiquity of the Web is evident, to get that advantage it is necessary to quickly adapt actual processes that take lot of time to be implemented and assimilated. The emerging need (and ability) to systematically integrate technologies and processes, towards efficient and effective alignment of information variants and its useful utilization, represents the major challenge for computing sciences. In actual economic activities, client-supplier frontiers were vanished. E-Business, e-Commerce, u-Commerce, transformed radically business and commerce processes, making them less self and unique, less "ours" and more global (Berners-Lee, 2008; Zabel, Bönke, & Constanta, 2000).

Buhalis (1998) was one of the first authors to propose an efficient utilization of technology in tourism by adopting a strategic perspective. Later, (Buhalis & Law, 2008) presents a very comprehensive review of the R&D in e-Tourism, a kind of mix of ICT and tourism domain, occurred during the last 20 years, highlighting the main efforts in the field and the challenges that tourism researchers are and will be facing. Although, traditional tourist life cycle is well identified, it is no more an advantage to mobile tourist guide design since mobile devices and their applications changed tourist profile ((Eriksson, 2007)). The future of the travel agencies is to become virtual tourism enterprises, based on the existence of a flexible virtual travel agent (VTA) information system (Assimakopoulos, Dimitriou, & Sotiriou-Xanthopoulos, 2011).

Since the web becomes gradually the main commercial support for tourism activities, it is natural that promoting companies by one hand, and the customers, on the other, change their way to participate in this process. The distance between the tourist and the service providing company is growing to the point that effectiveness becomes the critical success factor, independently of how and who executes it.

Besides the announced ubiquity of services, the main present concern focuses customers' expectations. Since a tourism activity involves a wide and heterogeneous set of variables (values and resources), such as time, schedules, travelling, accommodation, food, etc., it will easily appear factors that constrain and change an initial plan or specification. Ideally, these changes should not be related to the set of events that constitute the activity itself (avoid disturbing the customer), but be restricted to the way the events will be performed, and keep the tourist away from the implications of these changes. In short, these changes should not affect the tourist activity, only the service providers.

Considering the actual typical tourism business activities, it is unanimous that they are composed by several integrated services (transportation, accommodation, etc.) and usually are not accomplished by a single company. Several entities work together, each one specialist in a particular service, and the combination of their capabilities result in the final activity offer. To archive this cooperation, the service providers must be able to be integrated as members of a more complex "company" of other providers that, as a whole, assure the activity execution. As the tourist request changes or some other factor conditions, the service could also need to change and consequently this new "company" can be different in their members, his capability, etc. The current tourism companies do not cope well with unpredictable factors as usually happens, for instance, when there are strikes (transports, public services, etc.) or environmental disasters that prevent flights between travel points.

In almost all tourism solutions there is a considerable discrepancy between the announced service and the real support of it, especially from the customer point of view. Web sites advertisements and current publicity, even well explored, are made without tourist participation and focused on estimated tourist interest or motivation. Sometimes publicity is erroneous. Once disappointed, the tourist needs ever more to have an activity according to his interest and capacities.

It is also clear that there are a lot of factors which influences new tourism frontiers, and not only ICT (Swarbrooke, Beard, Leckie, & Pomfret, 2003). But focusing on technological trends, it will have impact on particular and critical areas, such as planning, booking, business management, marketing and communications which tends to be individualized and no more massive.

Looking at the present and imagining the future tourism activity, it is a fact that the web, and now, the cloud services, encouraged and enabled a new way to reach and construct tourism activities, where participants are each day geographically more distant, could be in everywhere and any region. Therefore, could this social activity be completely transformed into a cyber activity? How could it be possible if the tourists still prefer to decide for themselves, according to their preferences or possibilities of tourism complex scenarios?

Tourism Technological Support

To better address the idea of this topic, it is necessary to clarify some particular terms: integration and interoperability, efficiency and effectiveness. They are not necessarily the same but sometimes are used as so.

IEEE (1990) presents a reductive definition of integration (we interpret that it considers both concepts: integration and interoperability): "*... the ability of two or more systems or components to exchange information and to use the information that has been exchanged...*". Li et al. (2006) used interoperability and integration with no clear difference: "*system interoperability is a growing interest area, because of the continuously growing need of integration of new, legacy and evolving systems, in particular in the context of networked businesses and eGovernment*"; on the other hand (Tripathi, Gupta, & Bhattacharya, 2006) stress that interoperability is a necessary dimension for the effectiveness on corporate portals; Chen et al. (2008) evidences that, presenting interoperability as the capability to "talk" and integration as "to be part of". Agreeing with Chen, any system to result integrated, all their "parts" need to be interoperable. In short, *interoperability* demands coexistence, autonomy and federated environment and *integration* requires coordination, coherence and uniformization.

Talking about efficiency and effectiveness, the evident difference is even more tenuous. *Efficiency* means "doing the thing right", producing results with little wasted effort; *Effectiveness* means "doing the right thing", producing powerful effects and the desired results, comes from taking the time to stop and evaluate, rather than running faster and faster. Sometimes the price of greater efficiency is less effectiveness.

The increasing socialization of the web and its cloudscale to services architectures, supported by emergent collaboration tools (social network engines as Facebook, Twitter, etc.), promotes the active participation of people in almost all kind of decision process. Since the access to and the rights of web use is almost completely democratized, the social values are increasingly exposed to be scrutinized or explored.

In future scenarios, the tourist may want to clarify or define his motivation or interest regardless of the information system. The tourist constructs or defines his activity through conversation and or through interpretation of available information. If the tourist needs, he can use an information system or other auxiliary "systems" to help him in get the weather forecast, know transit conditions, planning map course, or else. So, the tourist and the "systems" work together to co-construct a tourism activity and to reconfigure its services composition, towards the alignment with tourist's interests. This construction and reconfiguration imply a dynamics which can change initial requirements. In spite the dynamics of the interests inherent to everyone, and even though they are distant from technical specifications, it is essential that they are considered in the definition, composition or selection of the best activity or even on its change (reconfiguration).

This dynamics requires all available tourism service providers properly integrated in a single solution. For that, the interoperability of their information systems is crucial. Considering this, the future tourism information system must be supported by a platform of interoperability which allows dynamic reconfigurations of tourism packages, considering: a) the integration and management of offers multiple tourism services providers; b) the subjective tourist evaluation support and his way of see and understand "things"; c) answer to the necessary changes (reconfigurations) both by the willingness of the tourist or by implications related to the support to the activities and d) support tourist interactions (communication) and their dynamics behavior, allowing co-construction of the tourism activities.

Considering that the actual information systems are not sufficiently prepared for the above requirements, the Virtual and Agile Enterprise model (Putnik & Cunha, 2007) and its inherent capacity to reconfigure, together with integrated real-time collaboration mechanisms is seen as the more adequate model to support these requirements, make them effective in sense to keep them permanent alignment with customers (tourists).

So, it seems clear that next generation of e-Tourism infrastructure will have to support flexible automation, integration, computation,

storage, and collaboration (Jaatun, Zhao, Rong, & Zhang, 2009).

In following we present the more relevant research contributions on technologies and processes, initiatives or developments related with tourism and information technology.

The Open Tourism Consortium

With the emergence of u-commerce, the integration technologies and interoperability becomes the backdrop to identifying a series of information products that will improve searching, management, delivery, and sharing of tourism data. Watson et al. (2004) proposed the creation of The Open Tourism Consortium (OTC) to support the development of several integrated and complementary products, using a XML based open source model (Figure 1).

However, after some research we conclude that OTC is a standby consortium of companies, government agencies, individuals, and universities participating in the open development of publicly available standards and software applications to support tourism activities. Their major goals were to develop u-Tour, a XML based data exchange objects and events of interest to tourists (TourML) and an open source parser for this language, able to insert the data into a relational database based on the standard data model. It focuses the capability to describe touristic information since it could be available in multiple devices.

Besides, by one hand, this initiative promotes u-Commerce and is supported by a XML Schema, on the other, due to its tightly components dependency, it disables or makes difficult the necessary agile reconfiguration of a tourism service (Monod, 2004).

Dynamic Tourist Packages

Although emergent, the concept of Dynamic Packaging is not specific of tourism activities.

Figure 1. Open Tourism Consortium Concept: (a) model; (b) Information Architecture

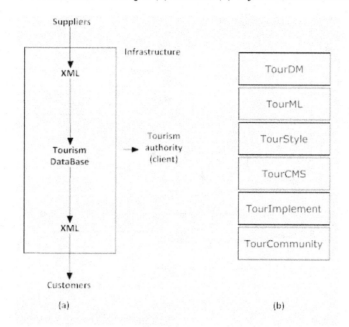

Moreover, the concept is not new, having been mainly explored in computer network area, where the Dynamic Packet Transport (DPT) protocol proposed an optimized transport protocol suitable to deliver fundamental cost and functionality advantages over existing IP network solutions (CISCO, 2000). Efficient use of bandwidth, multiple-service support, optimization of packets transmission, failure self-healing capabilities, etc. may have been some of the features which inspired software developers and systems architects to adapt the concept to business software applications area.

Considering the current tourism and its computational support, web sites, even being the most common applications currently, are nothing but searching tools that offer to the tourist some autonomy and new possibilities in defining his vacation schedule.

Cardoso & Lange (2007) provide a study of the strategic opportunities enabled by dynamic packaging (Figure 2), highlighting the key success factors, stating that an appropriate level of integration of tourism information systems is a key factor for further realizing the strategic opportunities of dynamic packaging. This is consistent with the

proposal for tourism supply chain management by Zhang et al. (2009), as well as data tourism aggregation using metadata and syndication of (Murua, Lladó, & Llodrá, 2005).

The Collaborative Travel Agent System (CTAS) based on a scalable, flexible, and intelligent Multi-Agent Information System (MAIS) architecture, is a proposal of Chiu et al. (2009) to respond to the increasing demands for ubiquitous access to tourist information systems for service coordination and process integration.

Denicolai et al. (2010) explore the relationship between the networking approach of tourism firms and the development of tourism core-competencies, reinforcing the need of solutions networking based.

The dependence on the context where the activity will take place and the tourist's interest and preference (Abbaspour & Samadzadegan, 2008), as well as the application of case-based reasoning and multi criteria decision making on tourism activity planning (Alptekin & Büyüközkan, 2011) are other relevant scientific contributions which refer the main subjects of our research.

Figure 2. Dynamic Packages supporting architecture (Cardoso & Lange, 2007)

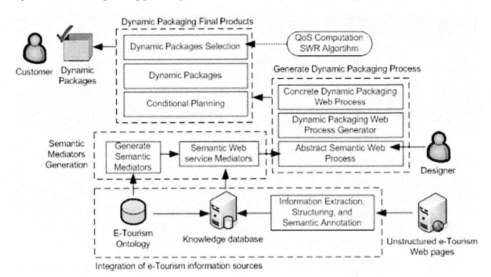

Ontologies and Service Oriented Architecture

The increasing "webization" of applications and platforms implied important changes in the development processes and business paradigms. The service is the main processing units of practically all recent web applications, similar to the class importance in the object oriented paradigm.

The main current difficulty is the orchestration and ascertaining the quality of those (web) services (which one is the best?), even known that their technological support assures their discovery and interoperability.

To compare and evaluate (QoS) services, ontologies are needed. Through ontologies it is possible to enhance those services with semantic (meta) information, as done with Web Services Modeling Ontologies (Bruijn, Fensel, & Keller, 2005) and Semantic Annotation for WSDL and XML Schema (Kopecký, 2007).

Considering the interoperability among services providers (enterprises) it is necessary now to "deal with" their own architectures or information systems, some of them legacy. Due to the existence of different internal architectures models (several

of them following service oriented architectures), it is necessary to interoperate among those architectures too (Sprott & Wilkes, 2004).

So, the advantage to explore now is SOA (Services Oriented Architecture) integration and web services enhancement (Erl, 2007). The existence of SOA ontologies (Workgroup, 2010) becomes useful to promote and facilitate that process. The integration (or composition) of processes or solutions, represented by solutions-agnostics services (eventually coming from several SOA) (Figure 3), is placed to multiple and continuous contextual changes in a tentative to react to them and maintains the initial objectives. It should behave like an event driven architecture, or, as suggested for ontologies (Kopecký, 2007) a context-aware architecture. We should not ignore that events are not all predictable (Hoof, 2006).

Considering tourism context, the scenario can be staged by multiple tourism services (providers), multiple tourists (clients) and multiple distinct tourism activities (architectures) already implemented and experimented, some recent and some old. To satisfy tourist expectations, these activities need to be flexible, extensible, dynamic and composable. A new activity can result for the

Figure 3. SOA integration using services interoperability (Erl, 2005)

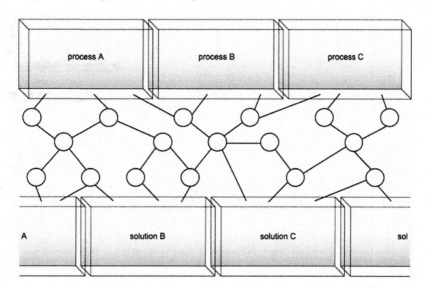

reorientation and composition of existent ones, for instance (Ferreira, Putnik, Cruz-Cunha, & Putnik, 2011; Najdawi, 2009). However, to allow distinct activities to "understand" each other they must have a *lingua franca* between them. Here ontologies can do their job, as (Escórcio & Cardoso, 2007; Gouveia & Cardoso, 2007; Murua et al., 2005) well describe.

Web "Tourism" Services

After relevant literature review we are convinced that the tourist profile has been changing, as well as, his interests or preferences. The emergence of the winning "team" composed by the amazing handheld devices (mobile smart devices) and the ubiquity of the information that anyone can looks for (GS1, 2008) is a fact! Despite of the potentiality of these devices, it is not easy for the tourist to plan its tourist activity. But this is the common scenario of tourism in the web, indeed!

Talking about web tourism services leave us to the features (or services) and interaction modes of current and future web applications: engines, layouts, contents, styles, templates, accessibility and portability.

Due to the generalist behavior of existent web search engines, it is not easy enough for the tourist to find the expected information. However, important scientific contributions are still emerging. (Murua et al., 2005) present the ANOTA web pilot on Balearic Islands, exploring metadata and syndication (Figure 4) on data tourism aggregation. The Travelocity (an e-marketplace) service demonstrated the new potentialities of human-computer interaction (Hudge, 2009), Schiaffino in (2009a) explored intelligent agent technology to support travel planning, Huang in (Huang & Bian, 2009) reinforced the personalized recommendations systems of tourist attractions, integrating heterogeneous online travel information and advanced selection and matching algorithms (Bayesian Networks and Analytic Hierarchy Processes); (Alptekin & Büyüközkan, 2011) integrated case-based reasoning processes and multi criteria decision making (another Analytic Hierarchy Process) system to enhance efficiency in tourism destination planning. Context-based adaptation (Höpken, Scheuringer, Linke, & Fuchs, 2008) and context-aware services (Abbaspour & Samadzadegan, 2008), are others contributions

Figure 4. ANOTA: (a) System model (b) Pilot portal (Murua et al., 2005)

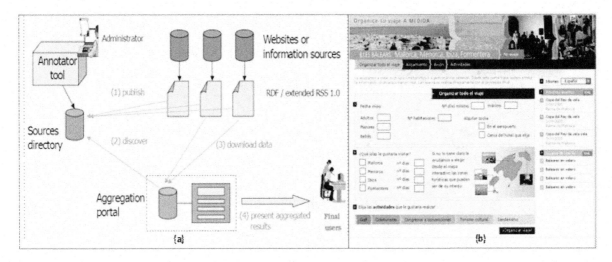

which evidence the emergent aware with the context of the activity.

Considering emergent technological potentialities and tourist requirements, we can conclude that tourism is clearly an activity which claims for services virtualization. A common travel agent (system, not person) will be efficient if it is able to offer services packages geographically distributed. It should have predictable and guaranteed quality of the service. For that, it must to be able to analyze the historical quality of the services.

Assuming this, it is no longer necessary to sub-contract many enterprises or to physically visit several places to make sure that everything is properly planned. As conclusion, everything must be integrated.

Information Retrieval, Searching and Selection Strategies

Several proposals for frameworks and technological support focus in the knowledge discovery and its interpretation to better respond to tourist.

Agents and web services (to enhance the discovery process), advanced matching algorithms (to enhance the accuracy and efficiency), case-based and context-related inference mechanisms, ontologies and Web Semantic, summarize the

technical topics of relevant scientific contributions. A hybrid combination of several of these technologies is the basis for most architectures and frameworks analyzed.

Since the mobile commerce (m-commerce) is prevailed, the tourism activities must to adapt to this new channel of information, requiring new tourism marketing strategies (S. Liu, 2005). Paraphrasing (Ferreira & Putnik, 2008), the *"possibility to get useful information depends on the capacity to retrieve, search and interpret it. Considering this and accepting tourist information ubiquity, the actual mobile tourist profile looks real and mobile devices should be the key tool for information retrieval"*.

In sense to reinforce the previous context importance reference, many others variants must be considered, namely, temporality, user preference, geographical information and pragmatics. Kenteris et al. (2007) present personalized online tourism services; (Hill & Wesson, 2008) explores preference-based searching capacities to align searching results with tourist interests; and Lorenzi (2007) explores multiagent knowledge-based recommender system to deal better with disperse information and improve the consistency of recommended results; (Barta, Feilmayr, & Grun, 2009), modularized ontologies shows their capacities to model contextual information, towards semantic alignment between tourism service and user context.

A service-oriented travel portal is being proposed to provide tourists with composite travel packages through dynamic composition among travel-related services from distributed providers and across business domains (Y. Li et al., 2011). The developments of Dinh & Thi (2010) are conducting to the development of a conceptual framework for service modeling in a network of service systems, based on network configuration and shared information.

(Alptekin & Büyüközkan, 2011) propose a framework integrating case-based reasoning system with the Analytic Hierarchy Process multi criteria decision making technique to enhance the accuracy and speed in search and selection of suppliers in tourism destination planning.

Selecting and ranking several results using collaborative filtering or recommendations over previous similar experiences and making intuition on user's past behavior and user's stereotype similarities (Blanco-Fernández, Pazos-Arias, Gil-Solla, Ramos-Cabrer, & López-Nores, 2009; Schiaffino & Amandi, 2009b); doing knowledge-based inference on user needs and preferences (Middleton, Shadbolt, & Roure, 2003); applying case-based reasoning and multi-criteria decision making of (Alptekin & Büyüközkan, 2011); delivering relevant content to tourist under location-based systems (Schwinger, Grün, Pröll, Retschitzegger, & Werthner, 2006); data-mining over relational databases with online analysis processes (Chaudhuri & Dayal, 1997) ; integrating data using patterns and markup languages (Hohpe & Woolf, 2004); adapting context-based multimodal adaptive systems (Höpken et al., 2008); etc. are all well referred technical initiatives, essentially based on events and transactions and applied to concretes and objective scenarios.

However, all these technical initiatives only can "infer" new information from existing and registered information or facts. The information which belongs to tourist perspective is impossible to get before his manifestation (spoken, written, other) or could not be interpreted unless by another human. It still exists an important gap between the man and the machine communication.

Collaborative Behaviors and Supporting Technologies

Although it may looks different, the communication model persists today as the three entities Shannon and Weaver model (1949) and follows its inherent transmission pattern. As in the beginning, it is need a transmitter, a receiver and a channel, as the medium used to transmit the content of the message to receiver (Figure 5). With obvious different technical support, the systems continue to be classified as discrete, continuous or mixed and suffer with "noise" problems too. The actual agent (foregoing transmitter or receiver) of the communication use the team (mixed), virtual (continuous) or face-to-face (discrete) models to collaborate (foregoing communicate) and the "noise" resides in things like confidence ("men in the middle" pattern), trustiness, etc. So, if in that time these were technical particularities, now we assume the analogy more to the way how and for what they are used for.

As Weaver defended, the accuracy (technical), the precision (semantic) and the effectiveness

Figure 5. Shannon and Weaver model

continue to be the critical levels of actual communication goals. The syntax (form), the semantics (meaning) and the pragmatics (use) of the language, are the essence of these levels, respectively. The terms syntax, semantics and pragmatics were introduced in linguistic and semiotic theory of Ferdinand de Saussure (1916).

This dynamic collaborative behavior might be further enhanced with the emergent technological opportunities. In nowadays, information society the persons are focused on common electronic social media as form of collaborative systems. The people are adopting a new social cyber-behavior, motivating them to adopt new habits in working as well as in thinking (Mickel, Agosto, Vignollet, & Marty, 2006).

We are now better related persons and we can easily share our point of view or send intended information. However, there is an insufficient utilization of this new capacity in actual information systems. The majority of systems were made to minimize the human dependency in the decision making and reduce the complexity (the human being is naturally complex). In consequence to this, the actual systems are "distant" from human being and can hardly be fully functional to him. Although the user can more easily interact it is difficult (almost impossible) to "pass" his interpretation of the context to the system. The system does not need that information to work too, is just a mechanical behavior.

Paraphrasing Giuseppe Begnis "the behavior of the collaborators and the collaborative artifacts are affected by the ability of the infrastructure to facilitate desired and appropriate behaviors".

The increase of technological capacities (considering devices and applications) for real-time social interaction, using online meetings, distributed multimedia brainstorms, synchronous and virtual interactions, etc., as evident on social software as Facebook, Twitter, Skype, Twiddla, Thinkature, etc., can be models to follow or to integrate on future applications. Pragmatics is possible when human beings can share and react directly among themselves, if the information systems support it, the information systems will be (more) aligned with user's interests and improve the result of the collaborative effort.

Pragmatics as Necessary Technology Complement

Pragmatics is one of the semiotic fields and concerns the relation between 'signs' and their interpreters (Morris, 1938). The 'sign' is the foundation of semiotic theory, formulated by Saussure (1916) as a 'dyadic' model: significant (the form which the sign takes) and *signifié* (the concept it represents) and by Peirce (1958) as a triadic model: *representamen* (the form which the sign takes), *interpretant* (the sense made by the sign) and object (to which the sign refers). Both authors formulated a theory for the relationship between the elements of their models: signification (Saussure) and *semiosis* (Peirce) which results in a different argumentation for the same proof: all elements must behave as a whole. Paraphrasing Saussure *"you cannot have a totally meaningless signifier or a completely formless signified"* and Peirce *"nothing is a sign unless it is interpreted as a sign"*.

For example, in linguistic terms, the word 'full' (used, for instance, when a recipient cannot have more contents) is a 'sign' with: signifier (the word 'full') and signified (the recipient cannot have more), according to Saussure. But the same signifier ('full') could means different signified and thus be a different 'sign' ('full' as 'have no patience', for instance). Another example, the semaphore's red light as a 'sign' have: red light (the *representemen*), cars stop (the object) the idea that the red light indicates that cars must stop (the *interpretant*), according to Peirce. But how it is perceived the same element of those who know nothing about traffic?

Each one of these examples exposes well the meaning of pragmatics because, and paraphrasing Charles Moris (1995), *"deals with the origin, uses and effects of signs within the behavior in which they occur*". The fundamental, qualitative, differences between the pragmatics, semantics and syntactic, are virtually the best described by Carnap (1942), based on their degree of abstractness in relation to complete signs and semiosis: "*If in an investigation explicit reference is made to the speaker, or, to put it in more general terms, to the user of language, then we assign it to the field of pragmatics. . . . If we abstract from the user of the language and analyze only the expressions and their designate, we are in the field of semantics. And if, finally, we abstract from the designate also and analyze only the relations between the expressions, we are in (logical) syntax*" (Carnap, 1942, p. 9) (cited in (Recanati, 2004)).

The implication is that any (information) system that aims at considering true needs of a customer, i.e. needs closest to the real customer's needs, with as less as possible abstractions, should consider pragmatic aspects of communication with him.

Sign interpretations are, thus, context dependent, meaning that actually is hardly possible to exist an 'absolute', common and universal, interpretation of reality (in our case the reality of the customer needs), but, rather, there are multiple interpretations by multiple communities (i.e. specific for each one customer and by multiple scenarios for satisfying customer's needs) and in different times (i.e. in continuous change).

Considering several distinct scenarios, we identified three main dimensions of their complex and unpredictable behavior:

1. The linguistic competence on communication
2. The behavior of the tourist during context evolution
3. The technological conditions

Although most of people think that technological problems (legacy systems, not integrated systems, insufficient support, methodologies, etc.), it represents the main argument for the deficient

alignment among tourism business and IT. We are convinced that personal (tourist) factors represents the strongest (or valuable) argument, most of them related with the ability to well communicate (in sense of to be able to transmit und understand a message) or with the behavior dynamics of the tourist. Let us explore these dimensions better with some possible real practical scenarios.

Considering the language meaning, a subset of linguistic knowledge (Fromkin, 2000), present in the intra-tourist (or agents) communication, several factors (educational, cultural, social, religious, intends, etc.) can easily respond for the high probability of incapacity, error or failure in the meaning transmission process. This means that any two persons in the context of tourism (tourist agent and customer, for instance), might have difficulties in communicating. Paraphrasing Mey, the ability to understand another speaker's intended meaning is called pragmatic competence (Mey, 1993). So, to have the capacity to communicate cannot be enough.

In a completely different aspect (dimension) of the scenario, the tourist, as human, could easily change his interest or motivation regarding a given objective, depending on the context where the activity is to take place as well as his new interest or preference. The tourist may have had presented their initial requirements; they were well understood for the tourism Agent (so the first scenario was surpassed), and the activity was prepared according to those requirements. But the tourist can easily change them or have new ones, later on. This is a typical situation where the tourist, independently of any information systems or language problems, changes his behavior or interest. Since the human behavior is not constant (most of the times, the behavior is irregular or ambiguous), the patterns of behavior are not more than empirical or just a representation of part of the real information.

In the technological dimension of the problem (and not only informatics) and according to the tourist's requirements, the system will suggest a set of possible activities. In case of doubts or indecisions about what activity to choose, what to do when the activity changes or when his interest diverges, the tourist will need to have more (new or different) information or even to interact with someone (tourist agent, another tourist, etc.) in order to refine some requirements or to clarify eventual (new) questions. A great effort of interoperability among all tourism services providers are the essence for effective tourist support. If those particular systems are not interoperable and somehow integrated, the "global" system hardly satisfies the tourist expectation.

The emergence of pragmatic web was a tentative to support pragmatics aspects and complement the syntactic web (common web) and the semantic web. This initiative tried to get relevant information applying human interaction, i.e., concerning not only with the form but also with the meaning of the information. Since pragmatics is a field, rather than a discipline (however, there should not be confused with a discipline of pragmatics when applied within the human communication), and, additionally, belonging to the human communication, the tentative to implement the pragmatics in an information system as its part is a paradox.

Other technological initiatives explored several collaborative mechanisms with semiotic frameworks but were no more than technical experimentations to give some intelligence capacity to existing technologies, as happened with agents or web services (Booy, Liu, Qiao, & Guy, 2008; K. Liu, 2008). Once again, these attempts tried to "transform" human particularities following to technical requirements towards their integration (utilization) in the information systems.

The satisfaction of customer's expectation must not be seen as an easy and completely defined process. The tourist participates as a customer in a set of complex and unpredictable scenarios where the conditions might be completely unpredictable.

The regularity with which these scenarios can happen requires agility on the management of tourism service composition, of tourist request as well as the capacity to allow tourists to communicate each other and generate their own activities outside the idiosyncrasy of the information systems.

In conclusion, a new P (from Personalized and Pragmatic) should be put on the previous marketing tourism strategies bet on 8P's Morrison's elements (price, product, place, promotion, people, partnership, package and programming) (Ma & Crestan, 2009), since the tourist perception and interpretation of the context will be an important criteria on the final decision.

Effective Open Tourism Initiative

"...we will live in a transparent 3D mobile media cloud that surrounds us everywhere. In this cloud, we will use intelligent machines, to whom we delegate both simple and complex tasks. Therefore, we will loose the skills we needed in the old days (e.g., reading paper maps while driving a car). But we will gain the skill to make better choices (e.g., knowing to choose the mortgage that is best for you instead of best for the bank)..." Marcel Bullinga in (Anderson & Rainie, 2010).

From (Anderson & Rainie, 2010) and several other trends analysis, it is clear that the future of internet (Internet 3.0 (Paul, Pan, & Jain, 2010)) and applications goes to align technology with human being requirements, where the collaboration between persons will be the key point. If someone needs to interact with other to decide, it must be allowed to do that.

Agreeing with this perspective, our proposal, Effective Open Tourism Initiative (EOTI) is based on the transition from a traditional transactional to a communicational architecture. This means, an integration between three main "components": a) existent development patterns; b) emergent cloud services architecture and c) Semiotc bases framework. A step further of OTI - Open Tourism Initiative (Ferreira et al., 2011), making it effective.

In short, Open Tourism Initiative promoted the evolution of several others related initiatives, integrating two innovative components (Figure 6): a) a Brokering mechanism over Tourism Market of Resources (Putnik & Cunha, 2007) and b) a Pragmatic renderer, which is responsible for human-to-human collaboration services.

Being already projected as a services oriented architecture (SOA), this decision sustains the transition from the transactional multilayer architecture (Figure 7), where layers services are semantically interoperable (thanks to API syntactical and semantic signatures), to an innovative architecture (communicational) where, apart from being transactional, is allowed a human-to-human real and synchronous collaboration towards the co-creation of the final decision. So, apart from actual aesthetically rich user interfaces, future applications need to be aligned with human direct interaction, having real and easy conversation tools as essential requirements.

Moreover EOTI, as required for nowadays tourism business, needs to grant sufficient flexibility, reliability and ubiquity of services. Considering actual impacts of social software,

and the potential of cloud services architecture, EOTI represents the cloudscale progress of OTI to a Solution as a Service (SaaS).

Indeed, the EOTI (Figure 8), having the Agile Virtual Enterprise (AVE) as the underlying organizational model, could be seen as a set of semiotic-based models in continuous change, i.e. a set of communication models, or a set of pragmatics based collaboration decisions (following the semiotic-based systems integration (Putnik & Putnik, 2010).

EOTI will be supported by a Ubiquity Tourism System (UTS) which allows ubiquitous tourism service management and direct human communication for decision taken by humans.

Considering open-source technologies, the presentation layer will be accomplish by: a) use of emergent Internet 3.0/Web 2.0 agnostic devices technologies, as HTML5, CSS3, JQuery and AJAX framework for asynchronous support of rich interfaces design:, b) integration of VOIP components developed using specific SDK API of existent social tools (as Skype, XMMP, Facebook, Google, etc.).

Figure 6. Previous OTI UML components model (Adapted from (Ferreira et al., 2011))

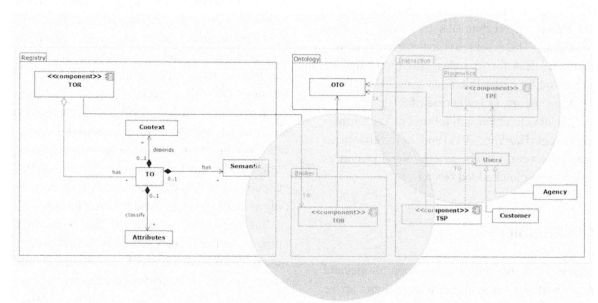

Figure 7. OTI transactional architecture

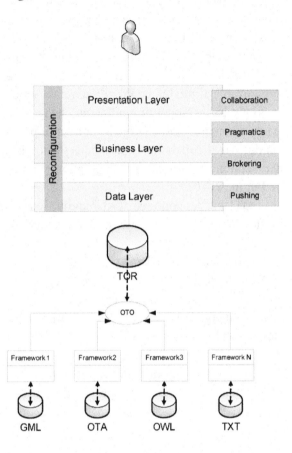

Business Layer will be (mainly) support by cloud (SOA) services developed with SDK API of existent social computing, which will support the brokering mechanisms on Cloud Tourism Resources. This resources repositorium provides cloud services for its management and will be supported by extensible open source social networking engine, as is the case of Elgg.

The development will follows cloud computing model (Harding, 2011) and, at the end, there may be several clouds, several cloud providers and several cloud added services.

CONCLUSION

New technologies promote new opportunities and new challenges. Usually new paradigms arrive from (considered) deprecated ones since there supporting sciences can take advantage no more on new technology potentialities. New patterns (for analysis, development, etc.) are accepted when previous experiences grant no more efficiency and appropriateness. New features appear when new applications and technical devices prove user's acceptability. All these facts sustain a skewed and restricted purely technical perspective, where tangible measures are easily managed.

But in nowadays social concerns are present in almost all kind of activities, demanding human behavior support over the traditional technical-centric submission. The people need and demand to be themselves and not represented by a machine. This fact sustains the complementary perspective where tangible measures are replaced for intangible and not-supported measures by technical solutions (Goldstein, Lazaris, & Weyl, 2011) (Moffitt, 2010).

As answer to this and cause to its relevance, new technologies offer new mechanisms or process to allow human approach and consequent more natural interaction and cooperation. An alignment between people and technology is needed.

With the advent of the "clouds" the "weather" comes again unpredictable and the forecast evidences that there are not only good conditions for technological (and commercial) growth. Coming as consequence of the increased capacity of connectivity, availability of data and "services", and their emergent potentiality, the essence of this new "style" is essentially based on technical infra-structures (Reese, 2009). The announced commercial success mainly comes from its capability to support any infra-structure requirements. Paraphrasing the Expert Group (Group, 2010), "Clouds are of particular commercial interest not only with the growing tendency to outsource IT, ..., but even more importantly, they reduce the entrance barrier for new service providers to offer their respective capabilities to a wide market with a minimum of entry costs and infrastructure requirements..". Clearly, it is a technical perspective!

Figure 8. EOTI communicational architecture

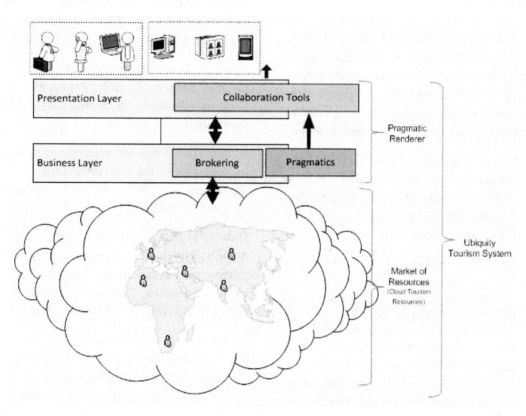

But this new "paradigm" will quickly represent no more than a new technical change if the participants (users, applications and processes) don't change themselves according to it, mainly in order how they explore their potentiality. For instance the Facebook, an evidence of cloud importance, appeared as a social network platform with a lot of new interaction ways (likes, wall, etc.) and tools (chat, video, avatars, etc.) between participants. According to several literatures, its exponential grown is sustainable by a new set of ways and tools which allows their participants to interact, being the communication and availability the main arguments for this tremendous phenomenon. Until now, only internet (nowadays called internet of things) can be proud for similar happening. In that case, however, due to the excessive "distance" between participants (surfers, managers, producers, promoters, etc.) and consequent lack of confidence between them,

has made it nothing more than a data repository. That's one of the reasons why several internet activities (eCommerce, eBusiness, etc.) took too much time to grow, below expectations!

It is clear the technical capability and potentiality of the cloud concerning scalability, robustness, security, interoperability, flexibility and many others attributes (Betts et al., 2010). However the emergent cloud services make us feel some obdurate about its effectiveness and knowledge constructiveness capability.

Considering this we proposed an integrated solution for tourism support where integration parts are represented by technology and human. Summarizing, cloud technology will support integration technologies and semiotic tools will support human-to-human interaction. The system will be a way to allow humans to (inter) communicate and relate.

REFERENCES

Abbaspour, A., & Samadzadegan, F. (2008). Building a context-aware mobile tourist guide system base on a Service oriented architecture. In *Proceedings of The International Archives of the Photogrammetry, Remote Sensing and Spatial Information Sciences. Vol. XXXVII. Part B4.* Beijing.

Alptekin, G. I., & Büyüközkan, G. (2011). An integrated case-based reasoning and MCDM system for Web based tourism destination planning. *Expert Systems with Applications, 38,* 2125–2132. doi:10.1016/j.eswa.2010.07.153

Anderson, J. Q., & Rainie, L. (2010). *The Future of the Internet.* Pew Research Center.

Assimakopoulos, N. A., Dimitriou, N. K., & Sotiriou-Xanthopoulos, E. (2011). VITRO: a flexible and innovative architecture for virtual travel agent information systems. *International Journal of Services Technology and Management, 15*(1-2), 4–26. doi:10.1504/IJSTM.2011.038659

Barta, R., Feilmayr, C., & Grun, C. (2009). *Covering the Semantic Space of Tourism - An Approach based on Modularized Ontologies.* Paper presented at the 1st Workshop on Context, Information and Ontologies, Heraklion, Greece.

Berners-Lee. (2008). *The Web Of Things*: ECRIM New 72.

Betts, D., Densmore, S., Dunn, R., Narumoto, M., Pace, E., & Woloski, M. (2010). *Developing Applications for the Cloud on the Microsoft® Windows AzureTM Platform.* Microsoft.

Blanco-Fernández, Y., Pazos-Arias, J., Gil-Solla, A., Ramos-Cabrer, M., & López-Nores, M. (2009). Semantic Web Technologies in the Service of Personalization Tools. In Cunha, M., Oliveira, E., Tavares, A., & Ferreira, L. (Eds.), *Social Dimensions of Semantic Technologies and Web Services* (*Vol. I*). doi:10.4018/978-1-60566-650-1.ch004

Booy, D., Liu, K., Qiao, B., & Guy, C. (2008). *A Semiotic Multi-Agent System for Intelligent Building Control.* Paper presented at the Ambi-Sys '08

Bruijn, J., Fensel, D., & Keller, U. (2005). *Using the Web Service Modelling Ontology to enable Semantic eBusiness.* Paper presented at the Communications of the ACM.

Buhalis, D. (1998). Strategic use of information technologies in the tourism industry. *Tourism Management, 19*(5), 409–421. doi:10.1016/S0261-5177(98)00038-7

Buhalis, D., & Law, R. (2008). Progress in information technology and tourism management: 20 years on and 10 years after the Internet--The state of eTourism research. *Tourism Management, 29*(4), 609–623. doi:10.1016/j.tourman.2008.01.005

Cardoso, J., & Lange, C. (2007). A Framework for Assessing Strategies and Technologies for Dynamic Packaging Applications in E-Tourism. *Information Technology &#38. Tourism, 9*(1), 27–44.

Carnap, R. (1942). *Introduction to semantics.* Cambridge, MA: Harvard University Press.

Chaudhuri, S., & Dayal, U. (1997). An overview of data warehousing and OLAP technology. *SIGMOD Record, 26*(1), 65–74. doi:10.1145/248603.248616

Chen, D., Doumeingts, G., & Vernadat, F. (2008). Architectures for enterprise integration and interoperability: Past, present and future. *Computers in Industry, 59*(7), 647–659. doi:10.1016/j.compind.2007.12.016

Chiu, D., Yueh, Y., Leung, H.-f., & Hung, P. (2009). Towards ubiquitous tourist service coordination and process integration: A collaborative travel agent system architecture with semantic web services. *Information Systems Frontiers, 11*(3), 241–256. doi:10.1007/s10796-008-9087-2

CISCO. (2000). *Dynamic Packet Transport Solution*. CISCO Systems.

Coppinger, R. (2007). *Cloud computing to enable virtual development*. Retrieved 5th June, 2011, from http://www.flightglobal.com/articles/2010/04/27/340790/cloud-computing-to-enable-virtual-development.html

Denicolai, S., Cioccarelli, G., & Zucchella, A. (2010). Resource-based local development and networked core-competencies for tourism excellence. *Tourism Management, 31*(2), 260–266. doi:10.1016/j.tourman.2009.03.002

Dinh, T. L., & Thi, T. T. P. (2010). A Conceptual Framework for Service Modelling in a Network of Service Systems. In Aalst, W., Mylopoulos, J., Sadeh, N. M., Shaw, M. J., & Szyperski, C. (Eds.), *Exploring Services Science* (*Vol. 53*, pp. 192–206). Berlin: Springer Berlin Heidelberg. doi:10.1007/978-3-642-14319-9_15

Eriksson, C. I. (2007). *Multi-users and multi-contextuality: a mobile tourism setting*. Paper presented at the 12th international conference on Human-computer interaction: applications and services.

Erl, T. (2005). *Service-Oriented Architecture: Concepts, Technology, and Design*. Pearson Education.

Escórcio, A. L. N., & Cardoso, J. (2007). *Developing an ontology for e-tourism using the Zachman framework*. Unpublished Master's Thesis, Universidade da Madeira

Ferreira, L., Putnik, G., Cruz-Cunha, M. M., & Putnik, Z. (2011). Towards effective Tourism Dynamic Packages: *Information Resources Management Journal (IRMJ)*.

Ferreira, L., & Putnik, G. D. (2008). Open Tourism Initiative. In *Tékhne Vol. VI*,(pp. 91-110): IPCA.

Fromkin, V. B. H. S. C. Anna Szabolcsi, Tim Stowell, Donca Steriade. (2000). *Linguistics: An Introduction to Linguistic Theory*: Oxford: Blackwell.

GS1. (2008). Mobile Commerce: opportunities and challenges, *A GS1 Mobile Com White Paper*: GS1.

Goldstein, A., Lazaris, L., & Weyl, E. (2011). *HTML5 & CSS3 for the Real World*. SitePoint Pty.

Gouveia, M. B. L. d., & Cardoso, J. (2007). *Arquitectura semântica para a integração de sistemas no domínio do turismo*.[Semantic architecture for systems integration in the field of tourism] Unpublished Master's Thesis, Universidade da Madeira.

Group, E. (2010). *The Future of Cloud Computing: Opportunities for European Cloud Computing behond 2010*. Europe Comission.

Harding, C. (2011). *Cloud Computing for business*. The Open Group Guide.

Hill, R., & Wesson, J. (2008). *Using Mobile Preference-Based Seraching to Improve Tourist decision Support, SAICSIT 2008*. ACM.

Hohpe, G., & Woolf, B. (2004). *Enterprise Integration Patterns: Designing, Building, and Deploying Messaging Solutions*. Boston, MA: Addison-Wesley.

Höpken, W., Scheuringer, M., Linke, D., & Fuchs, M. (2008). Context-based Adaptation of Ubiquitous Web Applications in Tourism. In O'Connor, P., Höpken, W., & Gretzel, U. (Eds.), *Information and Communication Technologies in Tourism 2008* (pp. 533–544). New York: Springer. doi:10.1007/978-3-211-77280-5_47

Huang, Y., & Bian, L. (2009). *A Bayesian network and analytic hierarchy process based personalized recommendations for tourist attractions over the Internet: Expert Systems with Applications*.

Hudge (2009). The City of New York Teams Up with HUGE to Launch NYCGo.com. *Journal*. Retrieved from http://www.hugeinc.com/news/the-city-of-new-york-teams-up-with-huge-and-google-to-launch-nycgo

IEEE. (1990). *IEEE Standard Computer Dictionary: A Compilation of IEEE Standard Computer Glossaries*. Institute of Electrical and Electronics Engineers.

Jaatun, M., Zhao, G., Rong, C., & Zhang, X. (2009). A Semantic Grid Oriented to E-Tourism. In *Cloud Computing* (*Vol. 5931*, pp. 485–496). Berlin, Heidelberg: Springer.

Kenteris, M., Gavalas, D., & Economou, D. (2007). *An innovative mobile electronic touris guide application*. London: Springer-Verlag.

Kopecký, J. (2007). *SAWSDL - Status and relation to WSMO, WSMO teleconference*. Universität Innsbruck.

Li, M.-S., Cabral, R., Doumeingts, G., & Popplewell, K. (2006). *Enterprise Interoperability Research Roadmap*. CORDIS.

Li, Y., Chen, H., Zheng, X., Tsai, C.-F., Chen, J.-H., & Shah, N. (2011). A service-oriented travel portal and engineering platform. *Expert Systems with Applications, 38*(2), 1213–1222. doi:10.1016/j.eswa.2010.05.014

Liu, K. (2008). *Pragmatic Computing - A Semiotic Perspective to Web Services*. Paper presented at the ICETE2007, E-Business and Telecommunications

Liu, S. (2005). *A Theoretic Discussion of Tourism E-commerce*. Chongqing Technology and Business University.

Lorenzi, F. (2007). *A Multiagent Knowledge-Based Recommender Approach with Truth Maintenance, RecSys'07*. ACM.

Ma, Y.-T., & Crestan, A. (2009). *Taiwan's challenges for Significant International Tourism Market Growth*. Paper presented at the The Proceedings of the 10th International Digital Government Research Conference.

Mey, J. L. (1993). *Pragmatics: An Introduction*. Oxford: Blackwell.

Mickel, P., Agosto, L., Vignollet, L., & Marty, J.-C. (2006). A Contact Recommender System for a Mediated Social Media. In J. C. Isabel Seruca, Slimane Hammoudi, Joaquim Filipe (Ed.), *Enterprise Information Systems VI*: Springer

Middleton, S. E., Shadbolt, N. R., & Roure, D. C. D. (2003). *Capturing interest through inference and visualization: ontological user profiling in recommender systems*. Paper presented at the Proceedings of the 2nd international conference on Knowledge capture.

Moffitt, J. (2010). *Professional XMPP Programming with JavaScript and jQuery*. Wiley Publishing.

Monod, E. (2004). *Open Tourism: Cultural heritage tourism enhanced by open technologies and u-commerce*.: European Comission - FP6 The Sixth Framework Programme RTD.

Morris, C. (1938). Foundations of the theory of signs. In Neurath, O., Carnap, R., & Morris, C. (Eds.), *International Encyclopaedia of Unified Science I* (pp. 77–138). Chicago: University of Chicago Press.

Morris, C. (1995). *Signs, Language and Behavior*. George Braziller.

Murua, I., Lladó, E., & Llodrá, B. (2005). *The Semantic Web for Improving Dynamic Tourist Packages Commercialisation*. Madrid: Fundación IBIT, ROBOTIKER.

Najdawi, A. (2009). *SOA and Web Services for Leveraging Inter-organizational Integration in Travel and Tourism* Paper presented at the Services - I, 2009 World Conference.

Paul, S., Pan, J., & Jain, R. (2010). Architectures for the future networks and the next generation Internet: A survey. *Computer Communications*, *34*, 2–42. doi:10.1016/j.comcom.2010.08.001

Peirce, C. S. (1958). *Collected Papers of Charles Sanders Peirce* (Vol. 1-6).

Putnik, G. D., & Cunha, M. M. (2007). *Knowledge and Technology Management in Virtual Organizations*. Hershey, PA: IDEA Group Publishing.

Putnik, G. D., & Putnik, Z. (2010). A semiotic framework for manufacturing systems integration -Part I: Generative integration model. *International Journal of Computer Integrated Manufacturing*, *23*(8), 691–709. doi:10.1080/095119 2X.2010.510292

Recanati, F. (2004). Pragmatics and semantics. In Ward, L. R. H. G. (Ed.), *The Handbook of Pragmatics*. Oxford, UK: Blackwell Publishing.

Reese, G. (2009). *Cloud Applications Architectures*. O'reilly.

Saussure, F. d. (1916). *Course in general linguistics* (W. Baskin, Trans.): McGraw-Hill Book Company.

Schiaffino, S., & Amandi, A. (2009a). Building an expert travel agent as a software agent. *Expert Systems with Applications*, *36*(2), 1291–1299. doi:10.1016/j.eswa.2007.11.032

Schiaffino, S., & Amandi, A. (2009b). Intelligent User Profiling. *Artificial Intelligence: An International Perspective*, *5640*, 193–216. doi:10.1007/978-3-642-03226-4_11

Schwinger, W., Grün, C., Pröll, B., Retschitzegger, W., & Werthner, H. (2006). Pinpointing Tourism Information onto Mobile Maps —A Light-Weight Approach. In M. Hitz, M. Sigala & J. Murphy (Eds.), *Information and Communication Technologies in Tourism 2006* (pp. 29-43). Viena: Springer Computer Science.

Shannon, C. E., & Weaver, W. (1949). *A Mathematical Model of Communication*. Urbana, IL: University of Illinois Press.

Sprott, D., & Wilkes, L. (2004). *Understanding Service-Oriented Architecture, The Arquitecture Journal*. Microsoft.

Swarbrooke, J., Beard, C., Leckie, S., & Pomfret, G. (2003). *Adventure Tourism - The new Frontier*. Butterwortk Heinemann.

Tripathi, R., Gupta, M. P., & Bhattacharya, J. (2006). *Dimensions of Interoperability for an Effective Portal*. Indian Institute of Technology.

UNWTO. (2010). *UNWTO Tourism Highlights*: World Tourism Organization (UNWTO), United Nations. avaliable online at http://www.unwto. org/facts/menu.html.

Watson, R., Akselsen, S., Monod, E., & Pitt, L. (2004). The Open Tourism Consortium: Laying The Foundations for the Future of Tourism. *European Management Journal*, *22*(3), 315–326. doi:10.1016/j.emj.2004.04.014

Workgroup, S. (2010). *Service-Oriented Architecture Ontology*. The Open Group.

Zabel, J., Bönke, D., & Constanta, P. (2000). *Open Network for Tourism (OnTour): A Concept for Electronic Commerce in the Business Processes of the Tourism Industry*. Paper presented at the Information and Communication Technologies in Tourism 2000, Proceedings of the International Conference in Barcelona, Barcelona, Spain.

Zhang, X., Song, H., & Huang, G. Q. (2009). Tourism supply chain management: A new research agenda. *Tourism Management*, *30*(3), 345–358. doi:10.1016/j.tourman.2008.12.010

Compilation of References

(2003). *United States Air Force Doctrine Center*. Washington, DC: Air Force Basic Doctrine.

Aalmink, J., & Marx Gómez, J. (2009). Enterprise Tomography - an efficient approach for semi-automatic localization of integration concepts in VLBAs. In (Ed) Cruz-Cunha, M. M., *Social, Managerial and Organizational Dimensions of Enterprise Information Systems*, Hershey, PA: IGI Global ISBN: 978-1-60566-856-7.

Aalmink, J., & Marx Gómez, J. (2011). Enterprise Tomography - an efficient Application Lifecycle Management approach supporting semiautomatic localization, delta-tracking and visualization of Integration Ontologies in VLBAs. In (Ed.) Kumar, S., Bendoly, E., Esteves, J., *Frontiers of Research in Enterprise Systems*. SAGE.

Abbaspour, A., & Samadzadegan, F. (2008). Building a context-aware mobile tourist guide system base on a Service oriented architecture. In *Proceedings of The International Archives of the Photogrammetry, Remote Sensing and Spatial Information Sciences. Vol. XXXVII. Part B4*. Beijing.

Abdinnour-Helm, S., & Lengnick-Hall, M., & Lengnick- Hall, C. (2003). Pre-implementation attitudes and organizational readiness for implementing an enterprise resource planning system. *European Journal of Operational Research*, *146*(2), 258–273. doi:10.1016/S0377-2217(02)00548-9

Abels, S., Haak, L., & Hahn, A. (2005). Identification of common methods used for ontology integration tasks. Interoperability Of Heterogeneous Information Systems. In *Proceedings of the first international workshop on Interoperability of heterogeneous information systems*, (pp. 75-78) Bremen, Germany. ACM.

Abran, A., & Nguyenkim, H. (1991). *Analysis of maintenance work categories through measurement*. Paper presented at the Conference on Software Maintenance, Los Alamitos CA.

Abreu, M., & Tribolet, J. (2008). *Considerações Sobre a Medição de Factores Soft nas Organizações* [Considerations on the Measurement of Soft Factors in Organizations]. Portugal: Center for Organizational and Design Engineering, INESC-INOV.

Achrol, R., & Kotler, P. (1999). Marketing in the network economy. *Journal of Marketing*, *63*(Special Issue), 146–163. doi:10.2307/1252108

Ackoff, R. L. (1974). *Redesigning the Future: A Systems Approach to Societal Problems*. New York: Wiley.

Ackoff, R. L. (1999). Transformational leadership. *Strategy and Leadership*, *2*(1), 20–25. doi:10.1108/eb054626

AECAE. (2007). *Gobierno y Responsabilidad Social de la Empresa* [Government and Corporate Social Responsibility]. Asociación Española de Contabilidad y Administración de Empresas. [Spanish Association of Accounting and Business Administration]

AGIMO. (2005). *Case Studies on E-procurement Implementations: Italy, New South Wales, New Zealand, Scotland, Western Australia*. Canberra: Australian Government Information Management Office.

Agrawal, M. K., & Pak, M. H. (2001). Getting smart about supply chain management. *The McKinsey Quarterly*, *2*, 22–25.

Aguilá, J., & Monguet, J. M. (2010) *¿Por qué algunas empresas tienen éxito y otras no?* [Why do some companies succeed and others do not?] (1st ed.) Barcelona, Spain: Planeta.

Aguinis, H. (2004). *Regression Analysis for Categorical Moderators. New York, NY.* New York: Guilford Press.

Ahmed, O. (2005). *Migrating from proprietary to Open Source: Learning Content Management Systems,* Unpublished doctoral dissertation, Department of Systems and Computer Engineering, Carleton University, Ottawa, Ontario, Canada.

Aidemark, J. (2007), *IS planning and socio-technical theory perspectives - Växjö University. Retrieved* from: http://www.iseing.org/emcis/EMCIS2007/emcis07cd/EMCIS07-PDFs/571.pdf

AIMMP. (2008). *A fileira da madeira em Portugal - 2008. Caracterização estatística do sector da madeira e mobiliário* [The row of wood in Portugal - 2008. Statistical characterization of the wood and furniture sector]. Retrieved January 02, 2011, from www.aimmp.pt

Akbari, H., & Land, F. (2010) *Socio-technical theory,* Retrieved from http://www.fsc.yorku.ca/york/istheory/wiki/index.php/Socio-technical_theory.

Akkermans, A. H., Bogerd, P., Yücesan, E., & Wassenhove, L. N. v. (2003). The impact of ERP on supply chain management: exploratory findings from a European Delphi study. *European Journal of Operational Research, 146,* 284–301. doi:10.1016/S0377-2217(02)00550-7

Akkermans, H., Bogerd, P., Yucesan, E., & Van Wassenhove, L. (2003). The impact of ERP on supply chain management: exploratory findings from a European Delphi Study. *European Journal of Operational Research, 146*(2), 284–294. doi:10.1016/S0377-2217(02)00550-7

Akkermans, H., & van Helden, K. (2002). Vicious and virtuous cycles in ERP implementation: a case study of interrelations between critical success factors. *European Journal of Information Systems, 11,* 35–46. doi:10.1057/palgrave/ejis/3000418

Aladwani, A. M. (2001). Change management strategies for successful ERP implementation. *Emerald -. Business Process Management Journal, 7*(3), 266–275. doi:10.1108/14637150110392764

Albritton, M., Oswald, S., & Anderson, J. (2008). Leadership quality and follower affect: A study of U.S. presidential candidates. *The Journal of Leadership Studies, 1*(4), 6–22. doi:10.1002/jls.20035

Al-Fawaz, K. (2009) *An Investigation of The Factors That Impact Users Satisfaction In ERP Implementations* Paper presented at Ph.D. Symposium, Brunel University, UK.

Al-Mashari, M. (2002). Enterprise resource planning (ERP) systems: a research agenda. *Industrial Management & Data Systems, 102*(3), 165–170. doi:10.1108/02635570210421354

Al-Mashari, M. (2003). Enterprise Resource Planning (ERP) systems: A research agenda. *Industrial Management & Data Systems, 103*(1), 22–27. doi:10.1108/02635570310456869

Al-Mashari, M., Al-Mudimigh, A., & Zairi, M. (2003). Enterprise resource planning: A taxonomy of critical factors. *Elsevier -. European Journal of Operational Research,* (146): 352–364. doi:10.1016/S0377-2217(02)00554-4

Al-Mashari, M., Al-Mudimigh, A., & Zairi, M. (2003). ERP: A taxonomy of critical factors. *European Journal of Operational Research, 146,* 352–364. doi:10.1016/S0377-2217(02)00554-4

Almeida, R., & Azevedo, A. (2011) Collaborative business networks - Evaluation of technological tools for decision support making. *e-LP Engineering and Technology Journal.*

Almeida, R., & Azevedo, A. (2009). The needed adaptability for ERP systems. In Cruz-Cunha, M. M. (Ed.), *Enterprise Information Systems Design, Implementation and Management: Organizational Applications.* Hershey, PA: IGI Global.

Al-Mudimigh, A., Zairi, M., & Al-Mashari, M. (2001). ERP software implementation: An integrative framework. *European Journal of Information Systems, 10,* 216–226. doi:10.1057/palgrave.ejis.3000406

Alomair, B., Lazos, L., & Poovendran, R. (2010, June). *Securing Low-Cost RFID Systems: an Unconditionally Secure Approach.* Paper presented at the Sixth Workshop on RFID Security, Singapore.

Alptekin, G. I., & Büyüközkan, G. (2011). An integrated case-based reasoning and MCDM system for Web based tourism destination planning. *Expert Systems with Applications, 38,* 2125–2132. doi:10.1016/j.eswa.2010.07.153

Altman, D. G. (1991). *Practical Statistics for Medical Research.* London: Chapman & Hall.

Alves, A. M. (2010): *Definição de um Modelo de Cálculo e Acompanhamento do Regime de Esforço*, [Defining a Model for Calculating and Monitoring System of Effort] Master Thesis, Academia da Força Aérea, Sintra, Portugal.

AMI@Work. (2009) "ECOSPACE Newsletter No 11." *ECOSPACE Consortium*. Retrieved February 10, 2010 from: http://www.ami-communities.eu/wiki/ECO-SPACE_Newsletter_No_11

Anderson, C., Spataro, S., & Flynn, F. (2008). Personality and organizational culture as determinants of influence. *The Journal of Applied Psychology*, *93*(3), 702–710. doi:10.1037/0021-9010.93.3.702

Anderson, J. Q., & Rainie, L. (2010). *The Future of the Internet*. Pew Research Center.

Angeles, R. (2008). Anticipated IT Infrastructure and Supply chain Process Integration Capabilities for RFID and Their Associated Deployment Outcomes. In *Proceedings of the ACM iiWAS Workshops: ERPAS 2008: Business and Service Model* (pp. 634-646).Springer.

Angeles, R. (2009). Anticipated IT Infrastructure and Supply Chain Integration Capabilities for RFID and Their Associated Deployment Outcomes. *International Journal of Information Management*, *29*(3), 219–231. doi:10.1016/j.ijinfomgt.2008.09.001

Angeles, R. (2010). Moderated Multiple Regression of Absorptive Capacity Attributes and Deployment Outcomes: The Importance of RFID IT Infrastructure Integration and Supply Chain Process Integration. *International Journal of Information Systems and Supply Chain Management*, *3*(2), 25–51. doi:10.4018/jisscm.2010040102

Anonson, J. M., Ferguson, F., MacDonal, M. B., Murray, B. L., Fowler-Kerry, S., & Bally, J. M. (2009). The anatomy of interprofessional leadership: An investigation of leadership behaviors in team-based health care. *The Journal of Leadership Studies*, *3*(3), 17–35. doi:10.1002/jls.20120

Ansell, C., & Gash, A. (2007). Collaborative Governance in Theory and Practice. *Journal of Public Administration and Theory Advance Access*, *18*(4), 543–571.

Araújo, L. (2008). *Air Force Chief-of-Staff Message to the Air Force, Portuguese Air Force*. Lisboa, Portugal: Alfragide.

Araújo, L. (2008). *Portuguese Air Force Chief-of-Staff Speech*. Portugal: Portuguese Air Force.

Archer, N., Wang, S., & Kang, C. (2008). Barriers to the adoption of online supply chain solutions in small and medium enterprises. *Supply Chain Management: An International Journal*, *13*(1), 73–82. doi:10.1108/13598540810850337

Argyres, N. S. (1996). Capabilities technological diversification and divisionalization. *Strategic Management Journal*, *17*, 395–410. doi:10.1002/(SICI)1097-0266(199605)17:5<395::AID-SMJ826>3.0.CO;2-E

Ariely, D. (2008). *Predictably irrational: The hidden forces that shape our decisions*. New York: HaperCollins.

Arya, A., & Mittendorf, B. (2008). Pricing internal trade to get a leg up on external rivals. *Journal of Economics & Management Strategy*, *17*(3), 709–731. doi:10.1111/j.1530-9134.2008.00192.x

Ask, U., Juell-Skielse, G., Magnusson, J., Olsen Dag, H., & Päivärinta, T. (2008). Enterprise Systems as Vehicles of Pedagogic Innovation - Enterprise System Inclusion in Higher Education. *Proceedings of the 5th International Conference on Enterprise Systems, Accounting and Logistics (5th ICESAL '08)*, 7-8 July 2008, Crete Island, Greece.

Assimakopoulos, N. A., Dimitriou, N. K., & Sotiriou-Xanthopoulos, E. (2011). VITRO: a flexible and innovative architecture for virtual travel agent information systems. *International Journal of Services Technology and Management*, *15*(1-2), 4–26. doi:10.1504/IJSTM.2011.038659

ASX. (2007). *Corporate Governance Principles and Recommendations* (2nd ed.). Australian Stock Exchange.

Aveiro, D. (2010), *GOD theory for organizational engineering: continuously modeling the (re)Generation, Operationalization and Discontinuation of the Enterprise*, Doctoral dissertation, Department of Computer Science and Engineering, Instituto Superior Técnico, Lisboa.

Aversano, L., & Tortorella, M. (2009). Business Process-Aware Maintenance Task: A Preliminary Empirical Study. In *Software Maintenance and Reengineering* (*CSMR 2009*) (pp. 233-236). IEEE CS Press.

Aversano, L., Bodhuin, T., & Tortorella, M. (2005). Assessment and Impact Analysis for Aligning Business Processes and Software Systems. In *ACM Symposium on Applied Computing* (pp. 1338 – 1343). ACM Press.

Aversano, L., Grasso, C., & Tortorella, M. (2010). Measuring the Alignment between Business Processes and Software Systems: a Case Study. In *Symposium on Applied Computing* (*SAC 2010*) (pp. 2330-2336). ACM Press.

Bader, D. A., Kintali, S., Madduri, K., & Mihail, M. (2007). Approximating Betweeness Centrality. In (Eds) Bonato A, Chung F R K.: *Algorithms and Models for the Web Graph, 5.th International Workshop WAW 2007, San Diego, CA, USA, December 2007, Proceedings*, (pp. 124-134) LNCS 4863.

Bagchi, S., Kanungo, S., & Dasgupta, S. (2003). Modeling use of enterprise resource planning systems: A path analytic study. *European Journal of Information Systems, 12*, 142–158. doi:10.1057/palgrave.ejis.3000453

Baker, R. S. J. d., Barnes, T., & Beck, J. E. (Eds.). (2008). Educational Data Mining 2008: 1st International Conference on Educational Data Mining. *Proceedings*, Montreal, Quebec, Canada.

Balloni, A. J. (2004) *Why GESITI?: Why Management of System and Information Technology? Book Series IFIP International Federation for Information Processing*, Boston, Book Virtual Enterprises and Collaborative Networks: Springer

Balloni, A. J. (2010) Challenges and Reflections on Knowledge Society & Sociotechnical Systems. JMIT/2010 – International Journal of Managing Information Technology – Book /V.2, Nr.1, 06-26 Digital/IJMI: http://airccse.org/journal/ijmit/papers/0210ijmit3.pdf

Balloni, A. J., & Bermejo, P. H. S. (2010) Governance, Sociotechnical Systems and Knowledge Society: Challenges and Reflections. ENTERprise Information Systems *-Springer- International Conference, CENTERIS 2010, Part I*,(pp. 42-51.) Springer.

Balloni, A. J., (2006) *Por que GESITI?: Por que Gestão em Sistemas e Tecnologia da Informação?* Editora. Komedi, Livro I, 06-25. Retrieved April 21, 2012, from http://repositorio.cti.gov.br/repositorio/bitstream/10691/152/2/AJBLivro%20POR%20QUE%20GESITI.pdf

Banker, R. D., Chang, H., & Kao, Y. (2010). Evaluating cross-organizational impacts of information technology-An empirical analysis. *European Journal of Information Systems, 19*, 153–167. doi:10.1057/ejis.2010.9

Barker, T., & Frolick, M. N. (2003). ERP implementation failure: A case study. *Information Systems Management, 20*(4), 43–49. doi:10.1201/1078/43647.20.4.20030901/77292.7

Barling, J., Christie, A., & Turner, N. (2008). Pseudo-transformational leadership: towards the development and test of a model. *Journal of Business Ethics, 81*(4), 851–861. doi:10.1007/s10551-007-9552-8

Barney, J. B., & Clark, D. N. (2007). *Resource-based theory: Creating and sustaining competitive advantage.* Oxford: Oxford University Press.

Barta, R., Feilmayr, C., & Grun, C. (2009). *Covering the Semantic Space of Tourism - An Approach based on Modularized Ontologies.* Paper presented at the 1st Workshop on Context, Information and Ontologies, Heraklion, Greece.

Basili, V. R., Caldiera, G., & Rombach, H. D. (1994). The goal question metric approach. In *Encyclopedia of Software Engineering.* Wiley.

Bass, T., & Mabry, R. (2004). Enterprise architecture reference models: A shared vision for Service-Oriented Architectures. *IEEE MILCOM*, 1-8.

Baudrillard, J. (1994). *Simulacra and simulation* (Glaser, S. F., Trans.). Ann Arbor: The University of Michigan Press.

Beall, S., Carter, C., Carter, P. L., Germer, T., Hendrick, T., & Jap, S. (2003). *The role of reverse auctions in strategic sourcing.* CAPS Research.

Becerra-Fernandez, I., Murphy, K., & Simon, S. (2000). Integrating ERP in the business school curriculum. Association for Computing Machinery. *Communications of the ACM, 43*(4), 39–41. doi:10.1145/332051.332066

Becker, G. F. (2007). Organizational climate and culture: Competing dynamics for transformational leadership. *Review of Business Research, 7*(6), 116–123.

Beheshti, H. M. (2006). What managers should know about ERP/ERP II. *Management Research News*, *29*(4), 184–193. doi:10.1108/01409170610665040

Belew, R., & Mitchell, M. (1996), "Introduction", in R. Belew and M. Mitchell (editors), *Adaptive Individuals in Evolving Populations: models and algorithms, Chapter 1, Proceedings volume XXVI*, Santa Fe, CA: Addison Wesley

Bendoly, E., Soni, A., & Venkataramanan, M. A. (2004). Value Chain Resource Planning (VCRP): Adding Value with Systems beyond the Enterprise. [from http://www.fc.bus.emory.edu/~elliot_bendoly/VCRP_BH.pdf]. *Business Horizons*, 1–17. Retrieved January 17, 2010

Benton, P. (2005). E-Procurement's Missing Link. *IT Adviser*(39).

Berkman Center (2009). *Berkman Center for Internet and Society Broadband Study for FCC*, Report.

Berlak, J., & Weber, V. (2004). How to make e-Procurement viable for SME suppliers. *Production Planning and Control*, 15–22.

Bermejo. P. H. S., & Tonelli, A. O., (2011) Planning and Implementing IT Governance in Brazilian Public Organizations. *44th Hawaii International Conference on System Sciences*

Berners-Lee. (2008). *The Web Of Things*: ECRIM New 72.

Bernroider, E., & Koch, S. (2001) ERP selection Process in Mid-size and Large Organizations. *Business Process Management Journal 7* (3) 251, 257.

Berry, D. M. (2008). *Copy, rip, Burn: the Politics of Copyleft and Open Source*. London: Pluto Press.

Betts, D., Densmore, S., Dunn, R., Narumoto, M., Pace, E., & Woloski, M. (2010). *Developing Applications for the Cloud on the Microsoft® Windows Azure TM Platform*. Microsoft.

Beynon-Davies, P. (2002). *Information Systems. An Introduction to Informatics in Organisations*. England: Palgrave.

Bhatt, D., & Emdad, A. F. (2001). An analysis of the virtual value chain in electronic commerce. *Logistics Information Management*, *14*(1-2), 78–84. doi:10.1108/09576050110362465

Binder, M., & Clegg, B. (2007). Designing and managing collaborative enterprises in the automotive industry. *International Journal of Logistics Research and Applications*, *10*(2), 135–152. doi:10.1080/13675560701427346

Binder, M., & Clegg, B. T. (2006). A conceptual framework for enterprise management. *International Journal of Production Research*, *44*(18-19), 3813–3829. doi:10.1080/00207540600786673

Bingi, P., Sharma, M., & Godla, J. (1999). Critical Issues Affecting an ERP Implementation. *Information Systems Management*, *16*(3), 7–14. doi:10.1201/1078/43197.16.3.19990601/31310.2

Bitzer, J. (2005). The impact of entry and competition by Open Source Software on Innovation Activity, *Industrial Organization 051201*, EconWPA.

Blackstone, J. H. Jr., & Cox, J.F. (2005). *APICS: The association for operations management*. APICS Dictionary, 11th ed.

Blanco-Fernández, Y., Pazos-Arias, J., Gil-Solla, A., Ramos-Cabrer, M., & López-Nores, M. (2009). Semantic Web Technologies in the Service of Personalization Tools. In Cunha, M., Oliveira, E., Tavares, A., & Ferreira, L. (Eds.), *Social Dimensions of Semantic Technologies and Web Services* (*Vol. I*). doi:10.4018/978-1-60566-650-1.ch004

Boddy, D., Boonstra, A., & Kennedy, G. (2002). *Managing Information Systems: An Organizational Perspective* (1st ed.). Edinburgh: Pearson Education.

Bodhuin, T., Preziosi, R., & Tortorella, M. (2006, November). *Building an RFID Document Management Service*. Paper presented at the Innovations in Information Technology, Dubai.

Bodhuin, T., Preziosi, R., & Tortorella, M. (2007). Integrating RFID Services and Ubiquitous Smart Systems for Enabling Organizations to Automatically Monitor, Decide, and Take Actions. In J. Indulska, et al. (Eds.), *Ubiquitous Intelligence and Computing, 4th International Conference: Vol. 4611. Lecture Notes in Computer Science* (pp. 225-234). Heidelberg: Springer-Verlag Berlin Heidelberg.

Bolman, L. G., & Deal, T. E. (2003). *Reframing Organizations* (3rd ed.). San Francisco, USA: Jossey-Bass.

Bolman, L. G., & Deal, T. E. (2008). *Reframing organizations: Artistry, choice, and leadership*. San Francisco: Jossey-Bass.

Bond, B., Genovese, Y., Miklovic, D., Wood, N., Zrimsek, B., & Rayner, N. (2000). *ERP is dead-long live ERPII*. Retrieved November 8, 2009, from http://www.pentaprise.de/cms_showpdf.php?pdfname=infoc_report

Bonner, J., & Schaik, P. V. (1998). The use of high and low level prototyping methods for product user interfaces. In Hanson, M. (Ed.), *Contemporary Ergonomics 1998* (pp. 253–257). London: CRC Press.

Booher, D. E. (2005). Collaborative Governance Practices and Democracy. *National Civic Review, 93*(4), 32–46. doi:10.1002/ncr.69

Booy, D., Liu, K., Qiao, B., & Guy, C. (2008). *A Semiotic Multi-Agent System for Intelligent Building Control*. Paper presented at the Ambi-Sys '08

Borges, J. G., & Falcão, A. Miragaia, C., Marques, P. &Marques, M. (2003). A decision support system for forest resources management in Portugal. In T. M. Barrett and G. J. Arthaud (Eds.) *System Analisys in Forest Resources: Managing Forest Ecosystems* (pp.155-164). Dordrecht, Netherlands, Kluwer Academic Publishers.

Bostrom, R., P, & Heinen, J. S. (1977). MIS Problems and Failures: A Socio-Technical Perspective, Part II: The Application of Socio-Technical Theory. *Management Information Systems Quarterly, 1*, 345–349. doi:10.2307/249019

Botto, F. (2003). *Dictionary of e-Business: A Deꞏnitive Guide to Technology and Business Terms*. USA: John Wiley & Sons.

Boudreau, M., & Robey, D. (2005). Enacting integrated information technology: A human agency perspective. *Organization Science, 16*(1), 3–18. doi:10.1287/orsc.1040.0103

Boyle, T. A., & Strong, S. E. (2006). Key Skills Organizations Expect from ERP Graduates. Proceedings of the 2006 Conference, Production and Operations Management Division. *Administrative Sciences Association of Canada, 27*(7), 109-124.

Boyle, T. A. (2007). Technical-Oriented Enterprise Resource Planning (ERP): Body of Knowledge for Information Systems Programs: Content and Implementation. *Journal of Education for Business*, (May/June): 267–274. doi:10.3200/JOEB.82.5.267-275

Brancheau, J. C., & Wetherbe, J. C. (1987). Key Issues in Information Systems Management. *Management Information Systems Quarterly, 11*(1), 23–45. doi:10.2307/248822

Branden, N. (1969). *The psychology of self-esteem*. San Francisco: Jossey-Bass.

Brehm, N., Lübke, D., & Marx Gómez, J. (2007). Federated Enterprise Resource Planning (FERP) Systems. In Saha, P. (Ed.), *Handbook of Enterprise Systems Ar-chitecture in Practice* (pp. 290–305). Hershey, PA, USA: IGI Global. doi:10.4018/978-1-59904-189-6.ch017

Brehm, N., Marx Gómez, J., & Rautenstrauch, C. (2006). An ERP solution based on web services and peer-to-peer networks for small and medium enterprises. [IJISCM]. *International Journal of Information Systems and Change Management, 1*(1), 99–111. doi:10.1504/IJISCM.2006.008288

Bresnahan, T. F., & Brynjolfsson, E. (2002). Information technology, workplace organization, and the demand for skilled labor: Firm-level evidence. *The Quarterly Journal of Economics, 117*(1), 339–376. doi:10.1162/003355302753399526

Bromiley, P. (2005). *The behavioral foundations of strategic management*. Malden, MA: Blackwell Publishing.

Brown, A. E., & Grant, G. G. (2005). Framing the frameworks: A review of IT Governance research. *Communications of the Association for Information Systems, 15*, 696–712.

Browne, J., & Zhang, J. (1999). Extended and virtual enterprises-Similarities and differences. *International Journal of Agile Management Systems, 1*(1), 30–36. doi:10.1108/14654659910266691

Brown, S. L., & Eisenhardt, K. M. (1997). The art of continuous change: Linking complexity theory and time-paced evolution in relentlessly shifting organizations. *Administrative Science Quarterly, 42*, 1–34. doi:10.2307/2393807

Bruijn, J., Fensel, D., & Keller, U. (2005). *Using the Web Service Modelling Ontology to enable Semantic eBusiness.* Paper presented at the Communications of the ACM.

Brusilovsky, P. (1996). Methods and Techniques of Adaptive Hypermedia. *User Modeling and User-Adapted Interaction, 6*(2-3), 87–129. doi:10.1007/BF00143964

Buckhout, S., Frey, E., & Nemec, J., Jr. (1999) *Making ERP Succeed: Turning Fear into Promise.* Retrieved from: http://www.strategy-business.com/article/16678?gko=49d43

Bueno, S., & Salmeron, J. L. (2008). TAM-based success modeling in ERP. *Interacting with Computers, 20*(6), 515–523. doi:10.1016/j.intcom.2008.08.003

Buhalis, D. (1998). Strategic use of information technologies in the tourism industry. *Tourism Management, 19*(5), 409–421. doi:10.1016/S0261-5177(98)00038-7

Buhalis, D., & Law, R. (2008). Progress in information technology and tourism management: 20 years on and 10 years after the Internet--The state of eTourism research. *Tourism Management, 29*(4), 609–623. doi:10.1016/j.tourman.2008.01.005

Bulkeley, H. (2005). Recon□guring environmental governance: towards a politics of scales and networks. *Political Geography, 24*(8), 875–902. doi:10.1016/j.polgeo.2005.07.002

Bullen, V., & Rockart, J. F. (1986). A Primer on Critical Success Factors. In Bullen, C. V., & Rockart, J. F. (Eds.), *The Rise of Managerial Computing: The Best of the Center for Information Systems Research* (pp. 383–423). Homewood, IL: Dow Jones-Irwin.

Bunke, H., Dickinsion, P. J., Kraetzl, M., & Wallis, W. D. (2007). *A Graph-Theoretic Approach to Enterprise Networks Dynamics* (pp. 71–117). Birkhäuser Verlag.

Búrca, S. d., Fynes, B., & Marshall, D. (2005). Strategic technology adoption: extending ERP across the supply chain. *Journal of Enterprise Information Management, 18*(4), 427–440. doi:10.1108/17410390510609581

Burch, E., & Kungs, H.-J. (1997). *Modeling software maintenance requests: a case study.* Paper presented at the Proceedings of the International Conference on Software Maintenance.

Büsch, S., Nissen, V., & Schmidt, L. (2010). Praxisnahe und effiziente ERP-Ausbildung am Beispiel der TU Ilmenau. In M. Schumann, L. M. Kolb, M. H. Breitner, & A. Frerichs (Eds.), *Multikonferenz Wirtschaftsinformatik 2010 [Multi-Industry Computer Science Conference, 2010]* (pp. 1697-1708). Göttingen: Universitätsverlag.

Business Rules Group. (2007): *The Business Motivation Model: Business Governance n a Volatile World*, Revision 1.3, Retrieved (December 2010) from: http://www.businessrulesgroup.org/bmm.shtml.

Business.com (2009): *Business Social Media Benchmarking Study.*

Butler, C.T.L., & Rothstein, A. (2001). *On conflict and consensus: a handbook on formal consensus decisionmaking.* Takoma Park, MD: Food Not Bombs Publishing. Retrieved January 19, 2011 from: http://wandreilagh.org/consensus.pdf

Byrne, J. A., & Brandt, R. (1993). The virtual corporation. *Business Week, February 8*, 36-41.

Cadbury, A. (1992). *Report of the Committee on the Financial Aspects of Corporate Governance.* G. P. Publishing.

Cadbury, A. (2002). *Corporate Governance and Chairmanship.* Oxford: Oxford University Press. doi:10.1093/acprof:oso/9780199252008.001.0001

Cagno, E., Giulio, A. D., & Trucco, P. (2004). State-of-art and development prospects of e-procurement in the Italian engineering & contracting sector. *Project Management Journal, 35*(1), 24–29.

Calder, A. (2007). *IT Governance Pocket Guide.* IT Governance Publishing.

Callan, S. (2003). Charismatic Leadership in Contemporary Management Debates. *Journal of General Management, 29*(1), 1–14.

Callon, M. (2002). Writing and re(writing) devices as tools for managing complexity. In Law, J., & Mol, A. (Eds.), *Complexities: Social studies of knowledge practices* (pp. 191–217). Durham: Duke University Press.

Cama, Z. J. (2011)- *Brazil unbound - How investors see Brazil and Brazil sees the world. An HSBC report produced in co-operation with the Economist Intelligence Unit*. Retrieved from: http://www.hsbcculturalexchange. com/uploaded_files/HSBC_EIU_%20report_Brazil_Unbound.pdf or, http://www.globalautoindustry. com/images/HSBC_EIU_%20report_Brazil_Unbound. pdf or, http://www.100thoughts.hsbc.co.uk/downloads/ Festival_Brazil_Report.pdf or, Brazil unbound: How investors see Brazil and Brazil sees the world download the report and watch the webcast or http://viewswire.eiu. com/report_dl.asp?mode=fi&fi=1857301570.PDF -Last access 01/08/2011.

Camarinha-Matos, L., & Afsarmanesh, H. (2004). *Collaborative Networked Organizations - A research Agenda for emerging Business Models*. Springer. doi:10.1007/ b116613

Cammish, R., & Keough, M. (1991). A strategic role for purchasing. *The McKinsey Quarterly*, 22–50.

Campos, P., Brazdil, P., & Brito, P. (2006). Organizational survival in cooperation networks: the case of automobile manufacturing. In Camarinha-Matos, L., Afsarmanesh, H., & Ol-lus, M. (Eds.), *Network-Centric Collaboration and Supporting Frameworks* (pp. 77–84). Heidelberg: Springer. doi:10.1007/978-0-387-38269-2_8

Candeloro, R. (2009). *Modelo de Negócio e Estratégia. Você tem?* [Business Model and Strategy. Do you?] Retrieved October 2009 from: http://www.gestaoetc.com. br/213/modelo-de-negocio-e-estrategia-voce-tem/

Candido, G., Barata, J., Colombo, A. W., & Jammes, F. (2009). SOA in reconfigurable supply chain: A research roadmap. *Engineering Applications of Artificial Intelligence*, *22*, 939–949. doi:10.1016/j.engappai.2008.10.020

Cantor, P. A. (2001). *Gilligan unbound: Pop culture in the age of globalization*. London: Rowman & Littlefield Publishers, Inc.

CAP. (2004). *Código de Boas Práticas para a Gestão Florestal Sustentável.*[Code of Practice for Sustainable Forest Management.] Retrieved January 02, 2011, from www.pefc-portugal.cffp.pt/pdfs/Boas_Prt_final.pdf

Capra, F. (1996). *The web of life. A new scientific understanding of living systems*. New York: Anchor Books.

Carayannis, E. G., & Popescu, D. (2005). Profiling a methodology for economic growth and convergence: learning from the EU e-procurement experience for central and eastern European countries. *Technovation*, *25*(1), 1–14. doi:10.1016/S0166-4972(03)00071-3

Cardoso, J., & Lange, C. (2007). A Framework for Assessing Strategies and Technologies for Dynamic Packaging Applications in E-Tourism. *Information Technology & #38. Tourism*, *9*(1), 27–44.

Caridi, M., Cavalieri, S., Pirovano, C., & Diazzi, G. (2004). Assessing the impact of e-Procurement strategies through the use of business process modelling and simulation techniques. *Production Planning and Control*, *15*(7), 647–661. doi:10.1080/09537280412331298175

Carnap, R. (1942). *Introduction to semantics*. Cambridge, MA: Harvard University Press.

Carr, A. S., & Pearson, J. N. (1999). Strategically managed buyer–supplier relationships and performance outcomes. *Journal of Operations Management*, *17*(5), 497–519. doi:10.1016/S0272-6963(99)00007-8

Carvalho, R., & Sousa, P. (2008). (BISMAM): an holistic Model Leveraged on Misalignment and Medical Sciences Approaches. In *BUSiness/IT ALignment and Interoperability (BUSITAL 2008)*. Business and Information Systems MisAlignment Model.

Casacubierta, D. (2003). *Collective creation*. Barcelona: Gedisa.

Cavaye, A. L. M. (1996). Case study research: a multifaceted research approach for IS. *Information Systems Journal*, *6*(3), 227–242. doi:10.1111/j.1365-2575.1996. tb00015.x

CELPA. (2008). *Boletim estatístico da Industria Papeleira Portuguesa*. [Statistical Bulletin of Portuguese Paper Industry.] Retrieved January 02, 2011, from www.celpa.pt

Chadwick, S. (2006): Client-driven change: The impact of Changes in Client Needs on the Research Industry. *International Journal of Market research 48*, 391–414.

Chang, E. (2010) *Magnetic Data Storage and Nanoparticles*. Retrieved from http://www.eng.uc.edu/~gbeaucag/ Classes/Nanopowders/ Applications/ErnieChang_Na-MagneticMemory.pdf. Last access 01/08/2011.

Charron, C., Favier, J., & Li, C. (2006). *Social Computing*. Forrester Research.

Chaudhuri, S., & Dayal, U. (1997). An overview of data warehousing and OLAP technology. *SIGMOD Record*, *26*(1), 65–74. doi:10.1145/248603.248616

Chen, D., Doumeingts, G., & Vernadat, F. (2008). Architectures for enterprise integration and interoperability: Past, present and future. *Computers in Industry*, *59*(7), 647–659. doi:10.1016/j.compind.2007.12.016

Chen, I. J. (2001). Planning for ERP systems: Analysis and future trend. *Business Process Management Journal*, *7*(5), 374–386. doi:10.1108/14637150110406768

Chia, R. (1996). The problem of reflexivity in organizational research: Towards a postmodern science of organization. *Organization*, *3*(1), 31–59. doi:10.1177/135050849631003

Chisnall, P. S. (2001). Virtual ethnography [Review of the book Virtual ethnography]. *International Journal of Market Research*, *43*(3), 354–356.

Chiu, D., Yueh, Y., Leung, H.-f., & Hung, P. (2009). Towards ubiquitous tourist service coordination and process integration: A collaborative travel agent system architecture with semantic web services. *Information Systems Frontiers*, *11*(3), 241–256. doi:10.1007/s10796-008-9087-2

Cho, H., Jung, M., & Kim, M. (1996). Enabling technologies of agile manufacturing and its related activities in Korea. *Computers & Industrial Engineering*, *30*(3), 323–334. doi:10.1016/0360-8352(96)00001-0

Choi, J. (2006). A motivational theory of charismatic leadership: envisioning, empathy, and empowerment. *Journal of Leadership & Organizational Studies*, *13*(1), 24–43. doi:10.1177/10717919070130010501

Choo, C. W. (1996). The knowing organization: How organizations use information to construct meaning, create knowledge and make decisions. *International Journal of Information Management*, *16*(5), 329–340. Available at http://dx.doi.org/10.1016/0268-4012(96)00020-5doi:10.1016/0268-4012(96)00020-5

Chorafas, D. N. (2001). *Integrating ERP, CRM, supply chain management, and smart materials*. CRC Press LLC, Auerbach Publications. doi:10.1201/9780203997529

Chorafas, D. N. (2002). *Enterprise Architecture and New Generation Information Systems*. Florida: St. Lucie Press.

Chou, S.-W., & Chang, Y.-C. (2008). The implementation factors that influence the ERP (enterprise resource planning) benefits. *Decision Support Systems*, *46*(1), 149–157. doi:10.1016/j.dss.2008.06.003

Choy, K. L., Lee, H. C. W., & Choy, L. C. (2005). A knowledge-based supplier intelligence retrieval system for outsource manufacturing. *Knowledge-Based Systems*, *18*(1), 1–17. doi:10.1016/j.knosys.2004.05.003

Chwelos, P., Benbasat, I., & Dexter, A. S. (2001). Research report: Empirical Test of an EDI Adoption Model. *Information Systems Research*, *12*(3), 304–321. doi:10.1287/isre.12.3.304.9708

CIMA IFAC. (2003). *Enterprise Governance. Getting the balance right*. CIMA.

CIPS. (2009). *The Chartered Institute of Purchasing & Supply*. Retrieved from http://www.cips.org/

CISCO. (2000). *Dynamic Packet Transport Solution*. CISCO Systems.

Clarke, T. (2007). *International Corporate Governance: A comparative approach*. New York: Routledge.

Cochran, W. G. (1977). *Sampling Techniques* (3rd ed.). Chichester: Wiley.

Colley, J., Wallace, S., Doyle, J., & Logan, G. (2005). *What is Corporate Governance?* New York: McGraw-Hill.

Collins, J. (2001). *Good to great: Why some companies make the leap and others don't*. New York: HarperCollins Publishers, Inc.

ComputerWeekly. (2000). *Bosses voice e-procurement fears*. Retrieved from http://www.computerweekly.com/Articles/2000/07/20/176837/bosses-voice-e-procurement-fears.htm

Cooke, M., & Buckley, N. (2008): Web 2.0, Social Networks and the Future of Market research. *International Journal of Market research 50*(2).

Coppinger, R. (2007). *Cloud computing to enable virtual development*. Retrieved 5th June, 2011, from http://www.flightglobal.com/articles/2010/04/27/340790/cloud-computing-to-enable-virtual-development.html

Corini, J. (2000). Integrating e-procurement and strategic sourcing. *Supply Chain Management Review*, *4*, 70–75.

COSO. (1992). *Internal Control - Integrated Framework*. COSO.

Covey, S. M. R. (2006). *The speed of trust: The one thing that changes everything*. New York: Free Press.

Coyle, J. J., Bardi, E. J., & Langley, C. J. Jr. (2003). *The Management of Business Logistics: A Supply Chain Perspective* (7th ed.). Cincinnati, Ohio: South-Western/ Thomson Learning.

Cramton, C. D. (2001). The Mutual Knowledge Problem and Its Consequences for Dispersed Collaboration. *Organization Science*, *12*(3), 346–371. doi:10.1287/orsc.12.3.346.10098

Cranti, J., & Bateman, T. (2000). Charismatic leadership viewed from above: The impact of proactive personality. *Journal of Organizational Behavior*, *21*(1), 63–75. doi:10.1002/(SICI)1099-1379(200002)21:1<63::AID-JOB8>3.0.CO;2-J

Crewe, F. (2009). *Shock of the Old*. Evaluation Centre.

Croom, S. (2001). Restructuring supply chains through information channel innovation. *International Journal of Operations & Production Management*, *21*(4), 504–515. doi:10.1108/01443570110381408

Croom, S. R., & Giannakis, M. (2002). *Strategic e-Procurement in Global Pharmaceuticals (GP)*. Caps Research.

Croom, S., & Jones, A. (2007). Impact of e-procurement: Experiences from implementation in the UK public sector. *Journal of Purchasing and Supply Management*, *13*(4), 294–303. doi:10.1016/j.pursup.2007.09.015

Cummins, F. A. (2009). *Building the agile enterprise with SOA, BPM and MBM*. Burlington, USA: Morgan Kaufmann Publishers, Elsevier Inc.

Dagger, D. (2007). Service oriented e-Learning platforms: From monolithic systems to flexible services. *IEEE Internet Computing*, *11*(3), 28–35. doi:10.1109/MIC.2007.70

DAILY RFID CO. (2009). RFID File Tracking System optimizes file inventory management. *DAILY RFID CO., LIMITED Web Site*. Retrieved May 12, 2010, from http://www.rfid-in-china.com/2009-03-23/info_3199.html

D'Amours, S., Ronnqvist, E. M., & Weintraub, A. (2008). Using Operational Research for Supply Chain Planning in the Forest Products Industry. *INFOR*, *46*(4), 265–281.

Daneva, M. (2007). *Approaching the ERP Project Cost Estimation Problem: an Experiment*. Paper presented at the Proceedings of the First International Symposium on Empirical Software Engineering and Measurement.

Daneva, M. (2004). ERP Requirements Engineering Practice: Lessons Learnt. *IEEE Software*, *21*(2), 26–33. doi:10.1109/MS.2004.1270758

Daniel, E. M., & White, A. (2005). The future of inter-organizational system linkages: Findings of an international delphi study. *European Journal of Information Systems*, *14*, 188–203. doi:10.1057/palgrave.ejis.3000529

Daniels, S. (1998). The virtual corporation. *Work Study*, *47*(1), 20–22. doi:10.1108/00438029810196685

Das, S. (2006). *SAP Holds Top Rankings in Worldwide Market Share for SAP(R) Business Suite Applications*. Retrieved June 22, 2009, from http://www.reuters.com/article/pressRelease/idUS87519+30-Jul-2008+PRN20080730

Davenport, T. H. (1998). Putting the enterprise into the enterprise system. *Harvard Business Review*, 121–131.

Davenport, T. H. (2000). *Mission critical: Realizing the promise of enterprise systems*. Boston: Harvard Business School Press.

Davenport, T. H. (2002). *Missão Critica: obtendo vantagem competitiva com os sistemas de gestão empresarial* [Mission Critical: gaining competitive advantage with enterprise management systems.]. Porto Alegre: Bookman.

Davenport, T. H., & Brooks, J. D. (2004). Enterprise systems and the supply chain. *Journal of Enterprise Information Management*, *17*(1), 8–19. doi:10.1108/09576050410510917

Davenport, T. H., & Harris, J. G. (2007). *Competing on analytics: The new science of winning*. Boston: The Harvard Business School Press.

David, P., & Steinmueller, E. (1994). Information Economics and Policy. *Special Issue on The Economics of Standards*, *6*(3-4), 134–148.

Davila, A., Gupta, M., & Palmer, R. (2003). Moving procurement systems to the internet: the adoption and use of e-procurement technology models. *European Management Journal, 21*(1), 11–23. doi:10.1016/S0263-2373(02)00155-X

Davis, E. W., & Spekman, R. E. (2003). *The extended enterprise: Gaining competitive advantage through collaborative supply chains.* London: Financial Times Prentice-Hall.

Davis, E. W., & Spekman, R. E. (2004). *Extended enterprise: Gaining Competitive Advantage through Collaborative Supply Chains.* New York, USA:Financial Times Prentice-Hall.

Davis, F. (1989). Perceived uselfulness, perceived ease of use and end user acceptance of information technology. *Management Information Systems Quarterly*, (September): 219–339.

Davis, F. D. (1989). Perceived Usefulness, Perceived Ease of Use, and User Acceptance of Information Technology. *Management Information Systems Quarterly, 13*(3), 319–339. doi:10.2307/249008

Davis, F. D., Bagozzi, R. P., & Warshaw, P. R. (1989). User Acceptance of Computer Technology: A Comparison of Two Theoretical Models. *Management Science, 35*, 982–1003. doi:10.1287/mnsc.35.8.982

Day, G. S., & Schoemaker, P. J. H. (2006). *Peripheral Vision: Detecting the Weak Signals that will Break or Make your Company.* Cambridge: Harvard Business School Press.

de Waal, A. A. (2002). *Quest for Balance, The human element in performance management systems.* Chichester: John Wiley & Sons Ltd.

Dedrick, J.& West, J. (2005). Why firms adopt Open Source Platforms: A grounded Theory of Innovation and Standards Adoption. *MIS Quarterly. Special Issue on Standard Making*, Seatle.

Deithering, F. G. (1995). *Selbstgesteuertes Lernen* [Self-directed learning.]. Göttingen: Verlag für Angewandte Psychologie.

DeLanda, M. (2006). *A new philosophy of society: Assemblage theory and social complexity.* London: Continuum.

Delbecq, A., Van de Ven, A., & Gustafson, D. (1975). *Group techniques for programme planning: a guide to nominal group and Delphi processes.* Glenview, Illinois: Scott, Foresman & Company.

Den Hartog, D., De Hoogh, A., & Keegan, A. (2007). The interactive effects of belongingness and charisma on helping and compliance. *The Journal of Applied Psychology, 92*(4), 1131–1139. doi:10.1037/0021-9010.92.4.1131

Denicolai, S., Cioccarelli, G., & Zucchella, A. (2010). Resource-based local development and networked core-competencies for tourism excellence. *Tourism Management, 31*(2), 260–266. doi:10.1016/j.tourman.2009.03.002

Denning, S. (1999), Enlisting Management Support for Knowledge Management, *Knowledge Management Symposium: Applications for Government and Non-Profit Organizations, World Bank Headquarters, Washington DC, October 2, 2000. Committee on Science, Engineering, and Public Policy, Evaluating Federal Research Programs,* Washington DC: National Academy of Sciences, National Academy Press

Denning, S. (2005). Transformational innovation: a journey by narrative. *Strategy and Leadership, 33*(3), 11–16. doi:10.1108/10878570510700119

Denzin, N. K. (1978). *Sociological Methods: A Sourcebook.* New York: McGraw Hill.

Derrida, J. (1976). *Of grammatology* (Spivak, G. C., Trans.). Baltimore: The Johns Hopkins University Press.

DeSanctis, G. M., & Poole, M. S. (1994). Capturing the complexity in advanced technology use: adaptive structuration theory. *Organization Science, 5*(2), 121–147. doi:10.1287/orsc.5.2.121

Díaz, L. (2010). *Gobierno de TI en Sector Salud - Subsector EPS.* [IT Governance in the Health Sector - Subsector EPS] Unpublished Master dissertation, University of Los Andes, Colombia

Dick, B. (2000). *Delphi face to face* Retrieved December 4, 2009, from http://www.scu.edu.au/schools/gcm/ar/arp/delphi.html

Dietz, J. (2006). *Enterprise Ontology: Theory and Methodology.* Delft: Springer. doi:10.1007/3-540-33149-2

Dijk, E. v., Leeuw, S. d., & Durlinger, P. (2007). *Voorraadbeheer in perspectief: Zeven invalshoeken van het vak*. Deventer, The Netherlands: Slimstock B.V.

Dinh, T. L., & Thi, T. T. P. (2010). A Conceptual Framework for Service Modelling in a Network of Service Systems. In Aalst, W., Mylopoulos, J., Sadeh, N. M., Shaw, M. J., & Szyperski, C. (Eds.), *Exploring Services Science* (*Vol. 53*, pp. 192–206). Berlin: Springer Berlin Heidelberg. doi:10.1007/978-3-642-14319-9_15

Doolin, B. (2003). Narratives of change: Discourse, technology and organization. *Organization, 10*(4), 751–770. doi:10.1177/13505084030104002

Drucker, P. F. (1997). Toward the new organization. In Hesselbein, F., Goldsmith, M., & Beckhard, R. (Eds.), *The organization of the future* (pp. 1–5). New York: The Peter F. Drucker Foundation for Nonprofit Management.

Eadie, R., Perera, S., Heaney, G., & Carlisle, J. (2007). Drivers and Barriers to Public Sector e-Procurement within Northern Ireland's Construction Industry. *ITcon, 12*, 103–120.

Ebers, M. (1997). Explaining Inter-Organizational Network Formation. In Ebers, M. (Ed.), *The Formation of Inter-Organizational Networks* (pp. 3–40). New York: Oxford University Press.

EC. (2005). *Overview of International e-Business Developments*. Brussels: European Commission.

EC. (2008). *The European e-Business Report 2008 - The impact of ICT and e-business on firms, sectors and the economy*. Brussels: European Commission.

Eckartz, S., Daneva, M., Wieringa, R., & Hillegersberg, J. V. (2009). Cross-organizational ERP management: How to create a successful business case? In *SAC'09 Proceedings of the 2009 ACM Symposium on Applied Computing*. Honolulu, Hawaii, USA.

Eden, C., & Ackermann, F. (2004). Cognitive mapping expert views for policy analysis in the public sector. *European Journal of Operational Research, 152*(3), 615–630. doi:10.1016/S0377-2217(03)00061-4

Edwards, J. (2009, July 27). An RFID Fashion Statement. *RFID Journal*. Retrieved November 1, 2010, from http://www.rfidjournal.com/article/view/5081

Ehin, C. (2008). Un-managing knowledge workers. *Journal of Intellectual Capital, 9*(3), 337–350. doi:10.1108/14691930810891965

Eicker, S., Kress, S., & Mense, L. (2007). ERP-ELearn – e-Learning für ERP-Systeme im Hochschulbetrieb am Beispiel von SAP R/3. In Breitner, M., Bruns, B., & Lehner, F. (Eds.), *Neue Trends im E-Learning* [New Trends in E-Learning]. (pp. 59–74). Physica. doi:10.1007/978-3-7908-1922-9_5

Eikebrokk, T. R., Iden, J., Olsen, D. H., & Opdahl, A. L. (2008). Validating the Process-Modelling Practice Model. *EMISA, 3*(2), 3–17.

Eisenhardt, K. M. (1989). Building theories from case study research. [AMR]. *Academy of Management Review, 14*(4), 532–550.

Ellram, L. M., & Zsidisin, G. A. (2002). Factors that drive purchasing and supply management's use of information technology. *IEEE Transactions on Engineering Management, 49*(3), 269–281. doi:10.1109/TEM.2002.803381

Emery, F. E., & Trist, E. (1981). Introduction to Volume 1, First Edition. Systems Thinking (Volume 1), selected readings. F. E. Emery. Harmondsworth, Penguin.

Engen, M. L., Leeden, R., & Willemsen, T. M. (2001). Gender, context and leadership styles: A field study. *Journal of Occupational and Organizational Psychology, 5*(74), 581–598. doi:10.1348/096317901167532

EOI. (2009). *The opportunities of free software: capacities, rights and innovation, Report*. Madrid: EOI.

Epstein, A. (2004). *Parallel hardware architectures for the life science*. Doctoral thesis, Delft University Press.

Erez, A., Misangyi, V., Johnson, D., LePine, M., & Halverson, K. (2008). Stirring the hearts of followers: Charismatic leadership as the transferal of affect. *The Journal of Applied Psychology, 93*(3), 602–616. doi:10.1037/0021-9010.93.3.602

Erickson, A., Shaw, J., & Agabe, Z. (2007). An empirical investigation of the antecedents, behaviors, and outcomes of bad leadership. *The Journal of Leadership Studies, 1*(3), 26–43. doi:10.1002/jls.20023

Eriksson, C. I. (2007). *Multi-users and multi-contextuality: a mobile tourism setting.* Paper presented at the 12th international conference on Human-computer interaction: applications and services.

Erl, T. (2005). *Service-Oriented Architecture: Concepts, Technology, and Design.* Pearson Education.

Ernst & Young. (1998). *Measures that Matter.* Boston, USA.

Escórcio, A. L. N., & Cardoso, J. (2007). *Developing an ontology for e-tourism using the Zachman framework.* Unpublished Master's Thesis, Universidade da Madeira

Esteves, J., & Jorge, J. (2001). *Análise Comparativa de Metodologias de Implementação de SAP.* [Comparative Analysis of Methodologies for Implementation of SAP.] Associação Portuguesa de Sistemas de Informação (APSI) [Portuguese Association for Information Systems (APSI)]: Évora.

Etien, A., & Rolland, C. (2005). Measuring the fitness relationship. [REJ]. *Requirements Engineering Journal, 10*(3), 184–197. doi:10.1007/s00766-005-0003-8

European Commission. (2010) *Étymologie du terme "gouvernance"* [The origin of the term "governance"], Retrieved 08/01/2011 from: http://ec.europa.eu/governance/docs/doc5_fr.pdf.

Evans, M. G. (1985). A Monte Carlo Study of the Effects of Correlated Method Variance in Moderated Multiple Regression Analysis. *Organizational Behavior and Human Decision Processes, 36,* 302–323. doi:10.1016/0749-5978(85)90002-0

Everitt, B. S. (1994). *The Analysis of Contingency Tables.* New York: Chapman & Hall.

Falcão, A., Borges, J. G., & Tomé, M. (1999). SagFlor – an automated forest management prescription writer. *Faculty of Forestry Research Notes 97.* (pp. 211-218.) University of. Joensuu

Falcão, A., M. Próspero M. S. & Borges, J. G. (2006). A real-time visualization tool for forest ecosystem management decision support. *Computers and Electronics in Agriculture, 53,* 3–12. doi:10.1016/j.compag.2006.03.003

Falcão, A., & Borges, J. G. (2005). Designing decision support tools for Mediterranean forest ecosystems management: a case study in Portugal. *Annals of Forest Science, 62,* 751–760. doi:10.1051/forest:2005061

Falk, M. (2005). ICT-Linked Firm Reorganisation and Productivity Gains. *Technovation, 25*(11), 1229–1250. doi:10.1016/j.technovation.2004.07.004

Falkowski, G., Pedigo, P., Smith, B., & Swamson, D. (1998). A recipe for ERP success. Beyond Computing. *International Journal of Human-Computer Interaction, 16*(1), 5–22.

Fawcett, S. E., Magnan, G. M., & McCarter, M. W. (2008). Benefits, barriers, and bridges to effective supply chain management. *Supply Chain Management: An International Journal 13*(1): 35-48. Available at: http://www.nasstrac.org/membersonly/ArticlesOnline/PDFs/2008/NASSTRAC_Benefits_Barriers_Bridges_To_Effective_SCM.pdf.

Fawcett, S.E., Ellram, L.M. & Ogden, J.A. (2007). *Supply Chain Management: From Vision to Implemention.* New Jersey: Pearson Education, Inc.

Felfe, J., & Schyns, B. (2004). Is similarity in leadership related to organizational outcomes? The case of transformational leadership. *Journal of Leadership & Organizational Studies, 10*(4), 92–102. doi:10.1177/107179190401000407

Fernando, H., & Abawajy, J. (2009, December). *A RFID architecture framework for global supply chain applications.* Paper presented at the 11th International Conference on Information Integration and Web-based Applications & Services, Kuala Lumpur, Malaysia.

Ferreira, L., & Putnik, G. D. (2008). Open Tourism Initiative. In *Tékhne Vol. VI,* (pp. 91-110): IPCA.

Ferreira, L., Putnik, G., Cruz-Cunha, M. M., & Putnik, Z. (2011). Towards effective Tourism Dynamic Packages: *Information Resources Management Journal (IRMJ).*

Fichman, R. G. (1992). Information Technology Diffusion: A Review of Empirical Research. In *Proceedings 13th International Conference on Information Systems* (pp. 195-206). Dallas, TX: ICIS.

Fiedeldey-Van Dijk, C., & Freedman, J. (2007). Differentiating emotional intelligence in leadership. *The Journal of Leadership Studies, 1*(2), 8–20. doi:10.1002/jls.20012

Figueredo, M. (2009). *Gobierno de TI en el Sector Salud de Colombia: IPS Nivel III*. [IT Governance in Colombia's Health Sector: IPS Nivel III] Unpublished Master dissertation, University of Los Andes, Colombia

Filipowska, A., Hepp, M., Kaczmarek, M., & Markovic, I. (2008). Organisational Ontology Framework for Semantic Business Process Management. In *Australasian Conference on Information Systems (ACIS 2008)*.

Finney, S., & Corbett, M. (2007). ERP implementation: a compilation and analysis of critical success factors. *Business Process Management Journal, 13*(3), 329–347. doi:10.1108/14637150710752272

Fonstad, N.O. (2006). Engagement Matters: Enhancing Alignment with Governance Mechanisms. *CISR Research Briefing4*(3e)

Fosnot, C. T. (1996). Constructivism: A Psychological Theory of Learning. In Fosnot, C. T. (Ed.), *Constructivism: Theory, Perspectives and Practice* (pp. 8–33). New York: Teachers College Press.

Frakes, W. B., & Baeza-Yates, R. (1992). *Information Retrieval Data Structures and Algorithms*. Englewood Cliffs, NJ: Prentice-Hall.

Frankfort-Nachmais, C., & Nachmais, D. (2008). *Research methods in the Social Science* (7th ed.). New York, NY: Worth Publishers.

Freeman, J. (1982). Organizational life cycles and natural selection processes. In Staw, B., & Cummings, L. (Eds.), *Research in Organizational Behavior* (pp. 1–32). JAI Press Inc.

Frishammar, J. (2003). Information use in strategic decision making. *Management Decision, 41*(4), 318–326. Available at http://www.emeraldinsight.com/Insight/ViewContentServlet?Filename=Published/EmeraldFullTextArticle/Articles/0010410401.html-doi:10.1108/00251740310468090

Frith, C. (2007). *Making up the mind: How the brain creates our mental world*. Malden: Blackwell Publishing.

Fromkin, V. B. H. S. C. Anna Szabolcsi, Tim Stowell, Donca Steriade. (2000). *Linguistics: An Introduction to Linguistic Theory*: Oxford: Blackwell.

Fui-Hoon, F., Zuckweiler, K. M., & Lee-Shang, J. (2003). ERP implementation: Chief Information Officers' Perceptions on Critical Success Factors. *International Journal of Human-Computer Interaction, 16*(1), 5–22. doi:10.1207/S15327590IJHC1601_2

Gable, G. G. (1998). Panel Discussion. In B. Edmundson and D. Wilson (Eds.), *9th Australasian Conference on Information Systems*. Sydney: NSW.

Gabriel, R., Gersch, M., Weber, P., & Venghaus, C. (2006). Blended Learning Engineering: Der Einfluss von Lernort und Lernmedium auf Lernerfolg und Lernzufriedenheit - Eine evaluationsgestützte Untersuchung. [The influence of place of learning and learning medium of learning success and learning satisfaction - An evaluation based study] In Breitner, M. (Ed.), *Technologiebasiertes Lehren und Lernen* [[Technology-based teaching and learning]]. Passau.

Galliers, R. D. (1994). Information systems, operational research and business reengineering. *International Transactions in Operational Research, 1*(2), 159–167. doi:10.1016/0969-6016(94)90017-5

Gallivan, M. J., Spitler, V. K., & Koufaris, M. (2005). Does Information Technology Training Really Matter? A Social Information Processing Analysis of Coworkers' Influence on IT Usage in the Workplace. *Journal of Management Information Systems, 22*(1), 153–192.

Gambon, J. (2009, June 1). Benefits Up and Down the Ski Slope. *RFID Journal*. Retrieved November 10, 2010, from http://www.rfidjournal.com/article/view/5120

Gandino, F., Montrucchio, B., & Rebaudengo, M. (2010). Tampering in RFID: A Survey on Risks and Defenses. *Mobile Networks and Applications, 15*(4), 502–516. doi:10.1007/s11036-009-0209-y

Gardner, H. (1983). *Frames of mind: The theory of multiple intelligences*. New York: Basic Books.

Gardner, H. (2006). *Multiple intelligences: New horizons*. New York: Basic Books.

Gardner, H. (2007). *Five minds for the future*. Boston: Harvard Business School Press.

Garvin, D. A. (1998). The processes of Organization and Management. *Sloan Management Review, 39*(4), 33–50.

Gehrke, S. J. (2008). Leadership through meaning-making: An empirical exploration of spirituality and leadership in college students. *Journal of College Student Development, 49*(4), 351–359. doi:10.1353/csd.0.0014

German Science Council. 2006 (Wissenschaftsrat (2006)) Empfehlungen zum arbeitsmarkt- und demographiegerechten Ausbau des Hochschulsystems. [Recommendations to the labor market and demographic requirements of the expanding higher education system], Berlin: Wissenschaftsrat.

Gershon, P. (1999). *Review of civil procurement in central government*. UK: HM Treasury.

Gherardi, S. (2000). Practice-based theorizing on learning and knowing in organizations. *Organization, 7*(2), 211–223. doi:10.1177/135050840072001

Gibbs, A. (1997). Focus groups. *Social Research Update, Department of Sociology, 19*. Retrieved from www.soc.surrey.ac.uk/sru/sru19.html

Gilbert, A. (2000). E-procurement: problems behind the promise. *InformationWeek*, 48-62.

Giles, J. (2005): Internet Encyclopedias Go Head to Head. *Nature* (December).

Gilheany, S. (2004) *Moore's Law and Knowledge Management*, Retrieved 01/08/2011 from: http://www.ee.ic.ac.uk/pcheung/teaching/ee4_asic/notes/ Lec%201%20Moore%20Law%20and%20Knowledge%20Management.pdf.

Gilovich, T., & Griffin, D. (2002). Introduction – Heuristics and biases: Then and now. In Gilovich, T., Griffin, D., & Kahneman, D. (Eds.), *Heuristics and biases: The psychology of intuitive judgment* (pp. 1–18). Cambridge: Cambridge University Press.

Giraldo, O. L., Herrera, A., & Gómez, J. E. (2010). IT Governance State of Art at Enterprises in the Colombian Pharmaceutical Industry. *Communications in Computer and Information Science 109*(5), 431-440. Springer Link Press Information Systems Audit and Control Association. (2006). *COBIT Framework for IT Governance and Control*. Retrieved January 13, 2011, from http://www.isaca.org/Knowledge-Center/COBIT/Pages/Overview.aspx

Glaser, B. G., & Strauss, A. L. (1967). *The discovery of grounded theory: Strategies for qualitative work*. New Brunswick: Aldine Transaction.

Glaser, G., & Strauss, A. (1967). *The discovery of Grounded Theory: Strategies for qualitative research*. New York: Aldine Publishing Company.

Goffman, E. (1959). *The presentation of self in everyday life*. New York: Anchor Books.

Goffman, E. (1974). *Frame analysis: An essay on the organization of experience*. Boston: Northeastern University Press.

Goldman, A. I. (1999). *Knowledge in a social world*. Oxford: Oxford University Press. doi:10.1093/0198238207.001.0001

Goldratt, A. Y. (2009) *The Theory of Constraints and its Thinking Processes*, http://www.goldratt.com/toctpwhitepaper.pdf. Last access 01/08/2011

Goldratt, M. V. (1999) *"Theory of Constraints" Thinking Processes: A Systems*

Goldstein, A., Lazaris, L., & Weyl, E. (2011). *HTML5 & CSS3 for the Real World*. SitePoint Pty.

Goleman, D., & Boyatzis, R. (2008). Social intelligence and the biology of leadership. *Harvard Business Review*, (September): 1–8.

Gonzalez-Barahona, J. (2001). Counting Potatoes: the Size of Debian 2.2. *The European Online Magazine for the IT Professional, 2*(6), December.

Gonzalez-Barahona, J. (2004). *About free software*. Madrid: Rey Juan Carlos University- Dykinson.

Goor, A. R. v., & Weijers, S. J. (1998). *Poly Logistiek Zakboekje*. Arnhem, The Netherlands: PBNA.

Goranson, H. T. (1999). *The agile virtual enterprise: Cases, metrics, tools. Quorum Books*. USA: Greenwood Publishing Group, Inc.

Gordon, R. (1991). Innovation, Industrial Networks and High-technology Regions. In Camagni, R. (Ed.), *Innovation Networks: Spatial Perspectives* (pp. 174–195). London: Belhaven Press.

Gouveia, M. B. L. d., & Cardoso, J. (2007). *Arquitectura semântica para a integração de sistemas no domínio do turismo.*[Semantic architecture for systems integration in the field of tourism] Unpublished Master's Thesis, Universidade da Madeira.

Grandon, E. E., & Pearson, J. M. (2004). Electronic commerce adoption: an empirical study of small and medium US businesses. *Information & Management*, *42*(1), 197–216. doi:10.1016/j.im.2003.12.010

Green, D. D. (2007). Leading a postmodern workforce. *Academy of Strategic Management Journal, 6*, 15–26.

Grohmann, G., Kraemer, W., Milius, F., & Zimmermann, V. (2007). Modellbasiertes Curriculum-Design für Learning Management Systeme: Ein Integrationsansatz auf Basis von ARIS und IMS Learning Design. [Model-Based Curriculum Design for Learning Management Systems: An approach to integration based on ARIS and IMS Learning Design] In A. Oberweis, C. Weinhardt, H. Gimpel, A. Koschmieder, V. Pankratius, & B. Schnitzler (Eds.), *Tagungsband 8. Internationale Konferenz Wirtschaftsinformatik [*Proceedings of 8th International Conference economy computer science,], Karlsruhe.

Gross, N. (2009). A pragmatist theory of social mechanism. *American Sociological Review, 74*(3), 358–379. doi:10.1177/000312240907400302

Group, E. (2010). *The Future of Cloud Computing: Opportunities for European Cloud Computing behond 2010.* Europe Comission.

Grover, K. S. (2005). Linking leader skills, follower attitudes, and contextual variables via an integrated model of charismatic leadership. *Journal of Management, 31*(2), 255–277. doi:10.1177/0149206304271765

Grünwald, C., & Marx Gómez, J. (2007). Conception of System Supported Generation of Sustainability Reports in a Large Scale Enterprise. In (Eds) Marx Gomez, J., Sonnenschein, M., Müller M.,Welsch H. Rautenstrauch C.: *Information Technologies in Environmental Engineering. ITEE 2007 - Third International ICSC Symposium*, (pp. 60-68) Berlin, Heidelberg, New York: Springer Verlag.

GS1. (2008). Mobile Commerce: opportunities and challenges, *A GS1 Mobile Com White Paper*: GS1.

Guang-hui, C., Li, C., & Sai, Y. (2006)... *Critical Success Factors for ERP Life Cycle Implementation International Federation for Information Processing Digital Library, 205*, 553–562.

Guevara, A., & Catgarina Dib, V. (2000) *The Age of Knowledge and the growing relevance of human and social capital*, Retrieved 01/08/2011 from: http://in3. dem.ist.utl.pt/downloads/cur2000/papers/S26P05.pdf

Gunasekaran, A., McGaughey, R. E., Ngai, E. W. T., & Rai, B. K. (2009). E-Procurement adoption in the Southcoast SMEs. [doi: DOI: 10.1016/j.ijpe.2009.05.013]. *International Journal of Production Economics, 122*(1), 161-175.

Gunasekaran, A., & Ngai, E. W. T. (2008). Adoption of e-procurement in Hong Kong: An empirical research. *International Journal of Production Economics, 113*(1), 159–175. doi:10.1016/j.ijpe.2007.04.012

Gunasekaran, A., Patel, C., & Tirtiroglu, E. (2001). Performance measures and metrics in a supply chain environment. *International Journal of Operations & Production Management, 21*(1/2), 71–87. doi:10.1108/01443570110358468

Gupta, P., & Joseph, A. (2006). Using Radio Frequency Identification in Cash Management. *HSBC's Guide to Cash and Treasury Management in Asia Pacific*, 191-194.

Gupta, A. (2000). Enterprise resource planning: the emerging organizational value systems. *Industrial Management & Data Systems, 100*(3), 114–118. doi:10.1108/02635570010286131

Guzman, P. M. (2007). *Strategic leadership: Qualitative study of contextual factors and transformational leadership behaviors of chief executive officers.* Unpublished doctoral dissertation, University of Phoenix, Phoenix, Arizona.

Haak, L., & Brehm, N. (2008). Ontologies supporting VLBAs Semantic integration in the context of FERP. In *3rd International Conference on Information and Communication Technologies: From Theory To Applications, ICTTA 2008.* (pp.1-5.)

Haddara, M., & Päivärinta, T. (2011). *Why Benefits Realization from ERP in SMEs Doesn't Seem to Matter?* Paper presented at the HICSS 44, Kauai, Hawaii.

Haddara, M., & Zach, O. (2011). *ERP Systems in SMEs: A Literature Review.* Paper presented at the HICSS 44, Kauai, Hawaii.

Hakansson, H. (1987). *Industrial Technological Development: a Network Approach.* London: Croom Helm.

Hakansson, H., Havila, V., & Pedersen, A.-C. (1999). Learning in Networks. *Industrial Marketing Management, 28,* 443–452. doi:10.1016/S0019-8501(99)00080-2

Hakansson, H., & Snehota, I. (1995). *Business Networks.* London: Routledge.

Hamaker, S. (2003). Spotlight on Governance. *Information Systems Control Journal., 1,* 15.

Hamel, G. (2009). Moon shots for management. *Harvard Business Review, 2008*(February), 91–08.

Hammer, M. (2000). Reengineering Work: Do not Automate, Obliterate. *Harvard Business Review,* 37–46.

Hancock, P., & Tyler, M. (2001). *Work, postmodernism and organization: A critical introduction.* Thousand Oaks: Sage Publications.

Handy, C. (1991). *Gods of management: The changing work of organizations.* Oxford: Oxford University Press.

Hansen, M. T., & Nohria, N. (2004.) How To Build Collaborative Advantage. *MIT Sloan Management Review 46*(1): 22-30. Available at: http://sloanreview.mit.edu/the-magazine/articles/2004/fall/46105/how-to-build-collaborative-advantage/.

Hardgrave, B. C. (2009, July). Charles Vogele: Reaping the Benefits of Source-to-Store RFID. *Apparel Magazine, 50*(11), 17–20.

Hardgrave, B., Langford, S., Waller, M., & Miller, R. (2008). Measuring the impact of RFID on out of stocks at Wal-Mart. *MIS Quarterly Executive, 7*(4), 181–192.

Harding, C. (2011). *Cloud Computing for business.* The Open Group Guide.

Harman, D. (1992). Ranking algotithms. In *Information Retrivial: Data Structures and Algorithms* (pp. 363–392). Englewood Cliffs, NJ: Prentice-Hall.

Harper, R., Rodden, T., Rogers, Y., & Sellen, A. (2008). *Being Human: Human-Computer Interaction in the Year 2020.* Cambridge, England: Microsoft Research Ltd.

Harrigan, K. R. (1983a). A framework for looking at vertical integration. *The Journal of Business Strategy, 3,* 30–37. doi:10.1108/eb038975

Harrigan, K. R. (1983b). *Strategies for vertical integration.* Lexington, MA: Lexington Books.

Harrigan, K. R. (1984). Formulating vertical integration strategies. *Academy of Management Review, 9,* 638–652.

Harrigan, K. R. (1985). Vertical integration and corporate strategy. *Academy of Management Journal, 28*(2), 397–425. doi:10.2307/256208

Hart, P., & Saunders, C. (1997). Power and trust: Critical factors in the adoption and use of electronic data interchange. *Organization Science, 8*(1), 23–42. doi:10.1287/orsc.8.1.23

Hautala, T. (2005). The effects of subordinates' personality on appraisals of transformational leadership. *Journal of Leadership & Organizational Studies, 11*(4), 84–92. doi:10.1177/107179190501100407

Hawking, P., & McCarthy, B. (2000). Industry Collaboration: A Practical Approach for ERP Education. *Australasian Conference on Computer science education. 8,* 129-133.

Hawking, P., Stein, A., Wyld, D. C., & Foster, S. (2004). E-procurement: is the ugly duckling actually a swan down under? *Asia Pacific Journal of Marketing and Logistics, 16*(1), 3–26. doi:10.1108/13555850410765140

Helic, D. (2006). *A Didactics-Aware Approach to Management of Learning Scenarios in E-Learning Systems.* Graz University of Technology.

Hempel, L. C. (1996). *Environmental Governance: The Global Challenge.* Washington, DC: Island.

Henderson, J. C., & Venkatraman, N. (1993). Strategic Alignment: Leveraging Information Technology for Transforming Organizations. *IBM Systems Journal, 32*(1), 4–16. doi:10.1147/sj.382.0472

Hendricks, K. B., Singhal, V. R., & Stratman, J. K. (2007). The impact of enterprise systems on corporate performance: A study of ERP, SCM and CRM system implementations. *Journal of Operations Management*, *25*, 65–82. doi:10.1016/j.jom.2006.02.002

Hepp, M., & Roman, D. (2007). An Ontology Framework for Semantic Business Process Management In. *Wirtschaftsinformatik*, 2007.

Herold, D., Fedor, D., Caldwell, S., & Liu, Y. (2008). The effects of transformational and change leadership on employees' commitment to a change: A multilevel study. *The Journal of Applied Psychology*, *93*(2), 346–357. doi:10.1037/0021-9010.93.2.346

Hesselbein, F., & Goldsmith, M. (2009). *The organization of the future 2*. San Francisco: Jossey-Bass.

Hetemaki, L., & Nilsson, S. (2005). *Information Technology and the Forest Sector (Vol. 18)*. Vienna: IUFRO World Series.

Heuser, L., Alsdorf, C., & Woods, D. (2007). *Enterprise 2.0 - The Service Grid –User-Driven Innovation - Business Model Transformation*. International Research Forum 2007, Potsdam, SAP Research, Evolved Technologist Press.

Heuser, L., Alsdorf, C., & Woods, D. (2008). *The Web-Based Service Industry – Infrastructure for Enterprise SOA 2.0, Potential Killer Applications - Semantic Service Discovery*. International Research Forum 2008, Potsdam, SAP Research, Evolved Technologist Press.

Hill, M. M., & Hill, A. (2008). *Investigação por Questionário* [Research by Questionnaire]. 2nd ed.). Edições Sílabo. [Syllabus Revision]

Hill, R., & Wesson, J. (2008). *Using Mobile Preference-Based Seraching to Improve Tourist decision Support, SAICSIT 2008*. ACM.

Hine, C. (2000). *Virtual ethnography*. London: Sage Publications.

Hines, T. (2000). A Evaluation of Two Qualitative Methods (Focus Group Interviews and Cognitive Maps) for Conducting Research into Entrepreneurial Decision Making. *International Journal of Qualitative Market Research*, *3*(1), 7–16. doi:10.1108/13522750010310406

Hinkin, T., & Tracey, J. B. (1999). The relevance of charisma for transformational leadership in stable organizations. *Journal of Organizational Change Management*, *12*(2), 105–119. doi:10.1108/09534819910263659

Hinttu, S., Fosman, S., & Kock, S. (2004). A network perspective of international entrepreneurship. In Dana, L.-P. (Ed.), *Handbook of research on International Entrepreneurship*. USA: Edward Elgar Publishing Limited.

Hippern, L., & Krogh, S. (2003). Open source software and the private-collective innovation model: Issues for organization science. *Organization Science*, *14*(2), 241–248.

Hoekstra, S., & Romme, J. H. (1991). *Integral logistic structures: developing customer-oriented good flow*. London: McGraw-Hill.

Hohpe, G., & Woolf, B. (2004). *Enterprise Integration Patterns: Designing, Building, and Deploying Messaging Solutions*. Boston, MA: Addison-Wesley.

Holland, C. P., & Light, B. (1999). A critical success factors model for erp implementation. In *IEEE Software*. Washington, DC: IEEE Press. doi:10.1109/52.765784

Holland, J. (2001). *Adaptation in Natural and Artificial Systems - an Introductory Analysis with Applications to Biology, Control and Artificial Intelligence, 6th printing*. The MIT Press. (Original work published 1975)

Holland, J. H., & Miller, J. (1991). Artificial Adaptive Agents in Economic Theory [AEA papers and proceedings]. *The American Economic Review*, *81*, 365–370.

Hong, K.-K., & Kim, Y.-G. (2002). The critical success factors for ERP implementation: an organizational fit perspective. *Information & Management*, *40*(1), 25–40. doi:10.1016/S0378-7206(01)00134-3

Hoogervorst, J. (2009). *Enterprise Governance & Enterprise Engineering*. The Netherlands: Springer. doi:10.1007/978-3-540-92671-9

Hoogervorst, J. A. P. (2009). *Enterprise Governance & Enterprise Engineering*. The Netherlands: Springer. doi:10.1007/978-3-540-92671-9

Hoopes, J. (2003). *False prophets: The gurus who created modern management and why their ideas are bad for business today*. New York: Basic Books.

Höpken, W., Scheuringer, M., Linke, D., & Fuchs, M. (2008). Context-based Adaptation of Ubiquitous Web Applications in Tourism. In O'Connor, P., Höpken, W., & Gretzel, U. (Eds.), *Information and Communication Technologies in Tourism 2008* (pp. 533–544). New York: Springer. doi:10.1007/978-3-211-77280-5_47

Hoyt, C. L., & Blascovich, J. (2003). Transformational and transactional leadership in virtual and physical environments. *Small Group Research, 34*(6), 678–715. doi:10.1177/1046496403257527

Huang, Y., & Bian, L. (2009). *A Bayesian network and analytic hierarchy process based personalized recommendations for tourist attractions over the Internet: Expert Systems with Applications.*

Huang, M., Cheng, B., & Chou, L. (2005). Fitting in organizational values: The mediating role of person-organization fit between CEO charismatic leadership and employee outcomes. *International Journal of Manpower, 26*(1), 35–49. doi:10.1108/01437720510587262

Huber, G. (1990). A Theory of the effects of advanced information technologies on organizational design, intelligence, and decision making. *Academy of Management Review, 15*(1), 47–71.

Hudge (2009). The City of New York Teams Up with HUGE to Launch NYCGo.com. *Journal.* Retrieved from http://www.hugeinc.com/news/the-city-of-new-york-teams-up-with-huge-and-google-to-launch-nycgo

Hunter, H. (2006). *Open Source Data Base Driven Web Development.* Oxford: Chandos.

Hunton, J. E., Lippincott, B., & Reck, J. L. (2003). Enterprise resource planning systems: comparing firm performance of adopters and nonadopters. *International Journal of Accounting Information Systems, 4*(3), 165–184. doi:10.1016/S1467-0895(03)00008-3

Hurt, H., & Hubbard, R. (1987, May). The Systematic Measurement of the Perceived Characteristics Of Information Technologies: Microcomputers as Innovations. In *Proceedings of The ICA Annual Conference.* Montreal, Quebec.

Hyvonen, E., Viljanen, K., Tuominen, J., & Seppala, K. (2008). Building a national semantic web ontology and ontology service infrastructure-The FinnONTO approach. In *Proceedings of the ESWC 2008.* Tenerife, Span: Springer-Verlag.

IDSA. (2009). *Code of Governance Principles for South Africa (King Code).* Institute of Directors of Southern Africa.

IEEE. (1990). *IEEE Standard Computer Dictionary: A Compilation of IEEE Standard Computer Glossaries.* Institute of Electrical and Electronics Engineers.

IEEE. (2007). About IEEE, Technologies, Emerging Technology Portal - RFID. Retrieved on October 22, 2009, from http://www.ieee.org/portal/site/emergingtech/index.jsp?techId=864.

IEF. (2005). *Guía de Buen Gobierno en la Empresa Familiar* [The Guide to Good Governance in Family Business]. Instituto de la Empresa Familiar. [Institute of Family Business]

IEF. (2009). *Folleto Corporativo* [[Corporate Brochure]]. Instituto de Empresa Familiar.

Ifinedo, P. (2008). Measuring Enterprise Resource Planning (ERP) Systems Success: A Structural Equation Modeling Approach. In J. Cordeiro, Y. Manolopoulos, J. Filipe, P. Constantopoulos (Eds.), *Enterprise Information Systems: 8th International Conference* (pp.86-97), Springer-Verlag, Berlin Heidelberg.

IIBA. (2009). *A Guide to the Business Analysis Body of Knowledge (Babok Guide). Version 2.0.* Toronto, Canada: IIBA.

Indvik, L. (2010). *Nike+ Meets Gowalla in Vail Resorts App for Skiers and Snowboarders.* Retrieved November 12, 2010, from http://mashable.com/2010/08/30/epicmix-app/

INE. (2007). *Estatísticas agrícolas 2007.* [Agricultural statistics 2007] Retrieved January 02, 2011, from www.ine.pt

Instituto Português da Qualidade [Portuguese Institute for Quality](2000). ISO 9000:2000, *Quality Management Systems – Fundamentals and Vocabulary,* Lisboa.

International Organization for Standardization. (2008). *ISO/IEC 38500:2008*. Retrieved January 13, 2011, from http://www.iso.org/iso/iso_catalogue/catalogue_tc/catalogue_detail.htm?csnumber=51639

ISACA. (2009) Information Systems Audit and Control Association. In Summary: Taking Governance Forward Mapping Initiative. *ISACA Journal, 1*: 1-10

ISO, International Organization for Standardization. (2008). *ISO/IEC 38500 Corporate Governance for Information Technology.* Switzerland.

ISO. (2008). *ISO/IEC 38500.* Corporate Governance of Information Technology.

ISO/IEC 2382-1:1993. *Information technology - Vocabulary - Part 1: Fundamental terms.* Retrieved January 02, 2011, from http://www.iso.org/iso

ITGI. (2007). *Control Objectives for Information and Related Technology, version 4.1.* IT Governance Institute.

ITGI. (2008). *Enterprise Value: Governance of IT Investments. The Val IT Framework 2.0.* IT Governance Institute.

ITGI. (2009). *Enterprise Risk: Identify, govern and manage risk. The Risk IT Framework.* IT Governance Institute.

ITGI. Information Technology Governance Institute. (2007) *COBIT 4.1: Control objectives, Management guidelines, Maturity models.* Rolling Meadows: ITGI.

Jaatun, M., Zhao, G., Rong, C., & Zhang, X. (2009). A Semantic Grid Oriented to E-Tourism. In *Cloud Computing* (*Vol. 5931*, pp. 485–496). Berlin, Heidelberg: Springer.

Jacoby, R. (2008). The CIO's Role in Enabling Innovation. *Thoughtleaders, 2007*(4), Retrieved April 22, 2008, from http://www.bmighty.com/printableArticle.jhtml;jsessionid=VNC2O21E3AHJCQSNDLOSKH0CJUNN2JVN?articleID=205208507

Jäger, P. (2001). Der Erwerb von Kompetenzen als Konkretisierung der Schlüsselqualifikationen, [*The acquisition of skills as a specification of the key skills*] Universität Passau.Retrieved from: http://www.opus-bayern.de/uni-passau/volltexte/2003/17/pdf/jaeger.pdf [24.02.2010]

Jägers, H., Jansen, W., & Steenbakkers, W. (2007). *New Business Models for the Knowledge Economy.* Hampshire: Gower Publishing Limited.

Jamrog, J., & Overholt, M. (2005). The future of HR metrics. *Strategic HR Review, 5*(1), 3–3. doi:10.1108/14754390580000837

Johnson, M. E., & Pyke, D. F. (2001). Supply Chain Management. In Harris, C., & Gass, S. (Eds.), *Encyclopedia of Operations Research and Management Science.* Boston, Massachusetts: Kluwer Academic Publishers. doi:10.1007/1-4020-0611-X_1022

Johnson, T., Lorents, A. C., Morgan, J., & Ozmun, J. (2004). A Customized ERP/SAP Model for Business Curriculum Integration. *Journal of Information Systems Education, 15*(3), 245–253.

Jones, B. (2009). *Balanced Scorecard Tower: a framework for comparing IT investment against business benefits.* Unpublished Master's thesis, Delft University of Technology, The Netherlands.

Jones, C. (2007). *Estimating software costs Bringing realism to estimating* (2nd ed.). New York: McGraw-Hill Companies.

Jones, M. C., Cline, M., & Ryan, S. (2006). Exploring knowledge sharing in ERP implementation: an organizational culture framework. *Decision Support Systems, 41*(2), 411–434. doi:10.1016/j.dss.2004.06.017

Joskow, P. L. (2003). Vertical integration. In *Handbook of New Institutional Economics.* Kluwer.

Journal, R. F. I. D. (2009). RFID Journal's Best RFID Implementation of 2009: Source-to-Store Visibility at Charles Vögele (Part 1). *RFID Journal.* Retrieved November 3, 2010, from http://www.rfidjournal.com/videos/view/120

Julia-Barcelo, R. (1999). Electronic contracts: a new legal framework for electronic contracts: the EU electronic commerce proposal. *Computer Law & Security Report, 15*(3). doi:10.1016/S0267-3649(99)80032-6

Jung, D., & Sosik, J. (2006). Who are the spellbinders? Identifying personal attributes of charismatic leaders. *Journal of Leadership & Organizational Studies, 12*(4), 12–26. doi:10.1177/107179190601200402

Júnior, R., & Ferreira, L. (2006). *Avaliação de um sistema ERP-SAP R/3 como Instrumento para gestão financeira na área de contas a pagar em uma empresa de Telecomunicações.* [Evaluation of an ERP system-SAP R / 3 as a tool for financial management in the area of accounts payable in a company Telecommunications] Brasília.

Kahiigi, E., Ekenberg, L., & Hansson, M. (2007). Exploring the e-Learning State of art. *Proceedings of the Conference on E-Learning.*

Kahneman, D., & Frederick, S. (2002). Representativeness revisited: Attribute substitution in intuitive judgement. In T. Gilovich, D, Griffin, & D. Kahneman (Eds.) *Heuristics and biases: The psychology of intuitive judgment* (pp. 49-81). Cambridge: Cambridge University Press.

Kahneman, D., Slovic, P., & Tversky, A. (Eds.). (1982). *Judgment under uncertainty: Heuristics and biases.* Cambridge: Cambridge University Press.

Kahneman, D., & Tversky, A. (1982). Causal schemas in judgments under uncertainty. In Kahneman, D., Slovic, P., & Tversky, A. (Eds.), *Judgment under uncertainty: Heuristics and biases* (pp. 117–128). Cambridge: Cambridge University Press.

Kahneman, D., & Tversky, A. (Eds.). (2000). *Choices, values, and frames.* Cambridge: Cambridge University Press.

Kallinikos, J. (2009). On the computational rendition of reality: Artifacts and human agency. *Organization, 16*(2), 183–202. doi:10.1177/1350508408100474

Kamann, D. J. F., & Strijker, D. (1991). The Network Approach: concepts and Applications. In Camagni, R. (Ed.), *Innovation Networks: Spatial Perspectives* (pp. 145–172). London: Belhaven Press.

Kang, S., Park, J. H., & Yang, H. D. (2008). ERP alignment for positive business performance: Evidence from Korea's ERP market. *Journal of Computer Information Systems, 48*(4), 25–39.

Kaplan, R. S., & Norton, D. P. (1992). *The Balanced Scorecard, Measures that Drive Performance. Harvard Business Review, 71.* Boston, MA: Harvard Business Publishing.

Kaplan, R. S., & Norton, D. P. (1997). *A Estratégia em Ação: Balanced Scorecard* [The Strategy in Action: Balanced Scorecard]. Rio de Janeiro, Brazil: Elsevier.

Kaplan, R., & Norton, D. (2000). *The Strategy-Focused Organization: How Balanced Scorecard Companies Thrive in the New Business Environment.* Harvard Business School Press.

Kärkkäinen, J., Sanders, P., & Burkhardt, S. (2006). *Linear Work Suffix Array Construction.* In: Journal *of the ACM (JACM). 53*(6) 918-936.

Karlsson, J., Ronnqvist, M., & Frisk, M. (2006). RoadOpt: A decision support system for road upgrading in forestry. *Scandinavian Journal of Forest Research, 21,* 5–15. doi:10.1080/14004080500487102

Kassem, G. (2007). *Application Usage Mining.* Aachen: Grundlagen und Verfahren. Shaker Verlag.

Kastrup, J., & Tenfelde, W. (2008). *Werkstattbericht Lern- und Testaufgaben für die Konstruktion von Lehr-Lernarrangements und die Diagnose von Kompetenzentwicklung im Modellversuch HaBiNa* [Workshop report, learning and assessment tasks for the design of teaching-learning arrangements and the diagnosis of skills development in the pilot HaBiNa], Universität Hamburg, URL: http://www.habina.de/files/downloads/Werkstattbericht%201_Endversion.pdf [14.02.2010]

Katz, D., & Kahn, R. L. (1978). *The social psychology of organizations.* Hoboken: John Wiley & Sons, Inc.

Kauffeld, S. (2003). Weiterbildung: eine lohnende Investition in die berufliche Zukunft? [Training: a worthwhile investment in their future careers?] In A. Frey, R. S. Jäger, & U. Renold (Eds.), *Kompetenzmessung – Sichtweisen und Methoden zur Erfassung und Bewertung von beruflichen Kompetenzen* [Measuring competence - perspectives and methods for evaluation and assessment of professional competence], (pp. 176–195) Landau: Empirische Pädagogik Verlag.

Kearney, E. (2008). Age differences between leader and followers as a moderator of the relationship between transformational leadership and team performance. *Journal of Occupational and Organizational Psychology, 81*(4), 803–811. doi:10.1348/096317907X256717

Kehl, V., Kunzendorf, M., & Wolf, M. (2006). Die berufliche Handlungskompetenz im Zeichen visualisierter Arbeitskontexte. [The professional competence in work contexts visualized characters] In Ott, B. (Ed.), *Eigene Kompetenzen erkennen und fördern* [/Own skills to recognize and promote]]. (pp. 47–70). ChangeX-Edition, Erding.

Kenteris, M., Gavalas, D., & Economou, D. (2007). *An innovative mobile electronic touris guide application.* London: Springer-Verlag.

Kerres, M., & Jechle, T. (2002). Didaktische Konzeption des Telelernens. [Instructional design of telelearning] In Issing, L. J., & Klimsa, P. (Eds.), *Information und Lernen mit Multimedia und Internet* [/Information and learning with multimedia and Internet]]. (pp. 267–281). Weinheim: BeltzPVU.

Kilduff, M., & Krackhardt, D. (2008). *Interpersonal networks in organizations: Cognition, personality, dynamics, and culture.* New York: Cambridge University Press. doi:10.1017/CBO9780511753749

Kimberling, E. (2010) *What Was the Cause of the SAP Failure at Lumber Liquidators?* 360° ERP Blog. Retrieved from: http://panorama-consulting.com/erp-blog/

Kim, J.-I., & Shunk, D. L. (2004). Matching indirect procurement process with different B2B e-procurement systems. *Computers in Industry, 53*(2), 153–164. doi:10.1016/j.compind.2003.07.002

Kitzinger, J. (1995). Qualitative Research: Introducing focus groups. *BMJ (Clinical Research Ed.), 311*(7000), 299–302. doi:10.1136/bmj.311.7000.299

Klaus, H., Rosemann, M., & Gable, G. G. (2000). What is ERP? *Information Systems Frontiers, 2*(2), 141–162. doi:10.1023/A:1026543906354

Kleijnen, J. P. C., & Smits, M. T. (2003). Performance metrics in supply chain management. *The Journal of the Operational Research Society, 54*(5), 507–551. doi:10.1057/palgrave.jors.2601539

Komninos, N. (2009). Intelligent Cities: towards interactive and Global Innovation Environments. *International Journal of Innovation and Regional Development, 1*(4), 337–355. doi:10.1504/IJIRD.2009.022726

Konorti, E. (2008). The 3D transformational leadership model. *Journal of American Academy of Business, Cambridge, 14*(1), 10–20.

Konrad, K., & Traub, S. (1999). *Selbstgesteuertes Lernen in Theorie und Praxis* [/Self-directed learning in theory and practice]]. München: Oldenbourg Verlag.

Konstantinidis, C., Kienegger, H., Wittges, H., & Krcmar, H. (2010). Planspiele in der ERP-Lehre: Eine empirische Untersuchung deutscher Bildungseinrichtungen. [Simulation games in ERP Education: An Empirical Investigation of German educational institutions.] In M. Schumann, L. M. Kolb, M. H. Breitner, & A. Frerichs (Eds.), *Multikonferenz Wirtschaftsinformatik 2010 [Multi-Industry Computer Science Conference, 2010]* (pp. 1709-1721). Göttingen: Universitätsverlag.

Koorn, R., Smith, D., & Müller, C. (2001). *e-Procurement and Online Marketplaces.* The Netherlands: Compact.

Kopecký, J. (2007). *SAWSDL - Status and relation to WSMO, WSMO teleconference.* Universität Innsbruck.

Korherr, B., & List, B. (2006). A UML 2 Profile for Event Driven Process Chains. In *IFIP International Federation for Information Processing (Vol. 205*, pp. 161–172). Springer Verlag. doi:10.1007/0-387-34456-X_16

Kothari, T., Hu, C., & Roehl, W. S. (2005). e-Procurement: an emerging tool for the hotel supply chain management. *International Journal of Hospitality Management, 24*(3), 369–389. doi:10.1016/j.ijhm.2004.09.004

Kotlyar, I., & Karakowsky, L. (2007). Falling over ourselves to follow the leader: conceptualizing connections between transformational leader behaviors and dysfunctional team conflict. *Journal of Leadership & Organizational Studies, 14*(1), 38. doi:10.1177/1071791907304285

Kotter, J. P. (1995). Leading change: Why transformation effort fail. *Harvard Business Review*, (September): 42–56.

Kouzes, J. M., & Posner, B. Z. (2009). To lead, create a shared vision. *Harvard Business Review, 2009*(January), 20–21.

Krauth, E., Moonen, H., Popova, V., & Schut, M. C. (2005). Performance Measurement in Control and Logistics Service Providing. In C.-S. Chen, J. Filipe, I. Seruca, J. Cordeiro (Eds.), *Proceedings of the Seventh International Conference on Enterprise Information Systems (ICEIS2005)* (pp. 25-28), Miami, USA.

Kreuger, R. (1988). *Focus groups: a practical guide for applied research*. London: Sage.

Krüssel, H. (1993). *Konstruktivistische Unterrichtsforschung* [[*Constructivist teaching research*]]. Frankfurt am Main: Lang.

Krüssel, H. (1996). Unterricht als Konstruktion. [Lessons as a design] In Voß, R. (Ed.), *Die Schule neu erfinden* [Reinventing the School]. (pp. 92–104). Luchterhand, Neuwied.

Kuechler, T., Thissen, D., & Zimmermann, V. (2009). Into the great wide open: Responsive Learning Environments for Personalised Learning. In O'Donoghue, J. (Ed.), *Technology Supported Environment for Personalised Learning: Methods and Case Studies*. London: IGI Global.

Kumar, K., & Van Hillegersberg, J. (2000). ERP Experiences and Evolution. *Communications of the ACM, 43*(4), 22–26. doi:10.1145/332051.332063

Kumar, N., & Peng, Q. (2006). Strategic alliances in e-government procurement. *International Journal of Electronic Business, 4*(2), 136–145.

Kundra, V. (2010). *25 Point Implementation Plan to Reform Federal Information Technology Management*. White House Document.

Kuperman, D. (2009). *Gobernabilidad de TI en el Sector Farmacéutico Colombiano: Investigación de Buenas Prácticas en Empresas Modelo.* [IT Governance in the Columbian Pharmaceutical Sector: Researching Good Practices in Model Businesses]Unpublished Master dissertation, University of Los Andes, Colombia

Kurbel, K. (2009). Das Studium der Wirtschaftsinformatik. [The study of the computer science industry] In Kurbel, K., Brenner, W., Chamoni, P., Frank, U., Mertens, P., & Roithmayer, F. (Eds.), *Studienführer Wirtschaftsinformatik 2009/ 2010* [/Business computer science study guide 2009/2010]]. (pp. 17–23). Wiesbaden: Gabler. doi:10.1007/978-3-8349-8057-1_3

Lakhan, R., & Jhunjhunwala, V. (2008). Open Source in Education. *EDUCAUSE Quarterly, 31*(2), 32–40.

Lamb, R., & Kling, R. (2003). Reconceptualizing Users as Social Actors in Information Systems *Research. Management Information Systems Quarterly, 27*(2), 197–235.

Lander, G. (2003). *What Is Sarbanes-Oxley?*Blacklick, OH, USA: McGraw-Hill Trade.

Lander, M. C., Purvis, R. L., McCray, G. E., & Leigh, W. (2004). Trust-building mechanisms utilized in outsourced IS development projects: a case study. *Information & Management, 41*(4), 509–528. doi:10.1016/j.im.2003.10.001

Langheinrich, M. (2009). A survey of RFID privacy approaches. *Personal and Ubiquitous Computing, 13*(6), 413–421. doi:10.1007/s00779-008-0213-4

Lankhorst, M. (2005). *Enterprise Architecture at Work - Modelling, Communication and Analysis*. Springer-Verlag Berlin Heidelberg.

LaRue, B., Childs, P., & Larson, K. (2006). *Leading organizations from the inside out: Unleashing the collaborative genius of action-learning teams*. New York: Wiley.

Latour, B. (2005). *Reassembling the social: An introduction to actor-network-theory*. Oxford: Oxford University Press.

Laudon, K. C., & Laudon, J. P. (2007) *Sistemas de informação gerenciais. (7th.ed)*. [Management information systems.] São Paulo: Pearson Prentice Hall.

Laudon, C. K., & Laudon, J. P. (2004). *MIS (Activebook)*. Prentice Pearson.

Laudon, K. C., & Laudon, J. P. (2006). *Management Information Systems: management the digital firm* (9th ed.). New Jersey: Pearson Education.

Lavilla, A., & Moreno, J. J. (2008). *Gobierno de Tecnologías de Información en el Sector Farmacéutico Colombiano.* [Information Technololgy Governance in the Columbian Pharmaceutical Sector] Unpublished Bachelor dissertation, University of Los Andes, Colombia

Law, J. (1994). *Organizing modernity*. Oxford: Blackwell Publishers.

Law, J. (2004). *After method: Mess in social science research*. New York: Routledge.

Law, J., & Mol, A. (2002). Complexities: An introduction. In Law, J., & Mol, A. (Eds.), *Complexities: Social studies of knowledge practice* (pp. 1–22). Durham: Duke University Press.

Lazarica, M. *The Virtual Enterprise – Opportunity for SMES in the Digital Economy.*

Leal, P. (2010). *Definição do Modelo de Negócio da Força Aérea.* [Definition of Business Model of the Air Force] Master Thesis, Portuguese Air Force Academy, Department of University Education, Sintra

Leal, P., Páscoa, C., & Tribolet, J. (2010), *A Business Model for the Portuguese Air Force*, Springer CCIS Series on Minutes of the CENTERIS 2010 Conference on ENTERprise and Information Systems, Viana do Castelo, Portugal.

Lee, B. D., & Schopf, J. M. (2003). Run-time prediction of parallel applications on shared environments. In *Proceedings of the International Conference on Cluster Computing* (pp. 487-491). 1-4 December.

Lee, D., Trauth, E., & Farwell, D. (1995). Critical skills and knowledge requirements of IS professionals: A Joint Academic/Industry Investigation. *Management Information Systems Quarterly, 19*(3), 313–340. doi:10.2307/249598

Lee, H. L., & Billington, C. (1992). Managing Supply Chain Inventory: Pitfalls and Opportunities. *Sloan Management Review, 33*, 65–73.

Lee, H. L., Padmanabhan, V., & Whang, S. (1997). The Bullwhip Effect in Supply Chains. *Sloan Management Review, 38*(3), 93–102.

Léger, P.-M. (2006). Using a Simulation Game Approach to Teach ERP Concepts. *Journal of Information Systems Education, 17*(4), 441–447.

Lempert, W. (2002). Prinzipien der Auswahl, Entwicklung und Verwendung moralischer Dilemmata als Materialien für die berufliche und berufspädagogische Aus- und Weiterbildung, [Principles of selection, development and use of moral dilemmas as materials for the professional and vocational education and training] *Zeitschrift für Berufs- und Wirtschaftspädagogik, 98* [Journal of Vocational and Business Education], 330-353.

Leoni, W. Leoni, &Hart, D. (1996), *The Impact of Organizational Politics on Information Systems Project Failure - A Case Study*, Retrieved: 01/08/2011. from http://www.computer.org/plugins/dl/pdf/proceedings/hicss/1996/7333/00/73330191.pdf?template=1&loginState=1&userData=anonymous-IP%253A%253A201.82.72.62

Lepelley, D. M. (2001). *Exploring the adaptability of leadership styles in senior business executives: Life narratives and self discovery of factors contributing to adaptability.* Unpublished doctoral dissertation, Fielding Graduate Institute, California). Retrieved January 28, 2009, from ABI/INFORM Global database. (Publication No. AAT 3037966).

Lerner, J., & Tirole, J. (2002). The simple economics of Open Source. *The Journal of Industrial Economics, 50*(2), 197–234. doi:10.1111/1467-6451.00174

Lerner, J., & Tirole, J. (2005). The Economics of Technology Sharing: Open Source and Beyond. *The Journal of Economic Perspectives, 19*(2), 99–120. doi:10.1257/0895330054048678

Leyking, K., Angeli, R., Faltin, N., Giorgina, F., Martin, G., Siberski, W., & Zimmermann, V. (2010). Towards an Open SOA for Learning Management. In Schumann, M., Kolbe, L. M., Breitner, M. H., & Frerichs, A. (Eds.), *Multikonferenz Wirtschaftsinformatik 2010* [Multi-industry computer science conference]. (pp. 355–368). Universitätsverlag Göttingen.

Li, M., & Chen, C. (2009, December). *RFID Complex Event Processing Mechanism for Logistics Tracking and Tracing.* Paper presented at the International Forum on Computer Science - Technology and Applications, Chongqing, China.

Li, M.-S., Cabral, R., Doumeingts, G., & Popplewell, K. (2006). *Enterprise Interoperability Research Roadmap.* CORDIS.

Lin, C. (2008). Pursuing excellence in firm core knowledge through intelligent group decision support system. *Industrial Management & Data Systems, 108*(3), 277–296. doi:10.1108/02635570810858723

Lin, C., & Hsu, M. (2007). A GDSS for ranking a firm's core capability strategies. *Journal of Computer Information Systems, 47*(4), 111–130.

Linstone, H., & Turoff, M. (1975). *The Delphi Method: Techniques and Applications*. London: Addison-Wesley.

Liu, K. (2008). *Pragmatic Computing - A Semiotic Perspective to Web Services.* Paper presented at the ICETE2007, E-Business and Telecommunications

Liu, S. (2005). *A Theoretic Discussion of Tourism E-commerce*. Chongqing Technology and Business University.

Li, Y., Chen, H., Zheng, X., Tsai, C.-F., Chen, J.-H., & Shah, N. (2011). A service-oriented travel portal and engineering platform. *Expert Systems with Applications, 38*(2), 1213–1222. doi:10.1016/j.eswa.2010.05.014

Lopresti, D., & Nagy, G. (2005, January). *Chipless ID for Paper Documents*. Paper presented at the International Symposium on Electronic Imaging - Document Recognition and Retrieval XII, San Jose, CA.

Lorenzi, F. (2007). *A Multiagent Knowledge-Based Recommender Approach with Truth Maintenance, RecSys '07*. ACM.

Low, J., & Seisfield, T. (1998). *Measures that Matter*. Boston, USA: Ernst & Young.

Lozada, H. R., & Calantone, R. J. (1996). Scanning behavior and environmental variation in the formulation of strategic responses to change. *Journal of Business and Industrial Marketing, 11*(1), 17–41. Available at http://www.emeraldinsight.com/Insight/ViewContentSe rvlet?Filename=Published/EmeraldFullTextArticle/Articles/0800110102.htmldoi:10.1108/08858629610112274

Lucas, H. C. Jr, & Baroudi, J. (1994). The role of information technology in organization design. *Journal of Management Information Systems, 10*(4), 9–23.

Lunardi, G. L., Becker, J. L., & Maçada, A. C. G. (2009) The financial impact of IT governance mechanisms' adoption: an empirical analysis with Brazilian firms. *42nd Hawaii International Conference on System Sciences*, (pp. 1-10).

Lundberg, C. (1988). Working with culture. *Journal of Organizational Change, 1*(2), 38–47. doi:10.1108/eb025598

Lyman, K. B., Caswell, N., & Biem, A. (2009) Business value network concepts for the extended enterprise. In *Proceedings of the Network Experience* (PHM Vervest et al., Eds), Springer-Verlag Berlin Heidelberg 2009.

Lynch, R. (2003). *Corporate strategy.* Third ed., Harlow: Prentice Hall Financial Times.

Ma, Y.-T., & Crestan, A. (2009). *Taiwan's challenges for Significant International Tourism Market Growth.* Paper presented at the The Proceedings of the10th International Digital Government Research Conference.

Mabert, V. A., & Venkatraman, M. A. (1998). Special Research Focus on Supply Chain Linkages: Challenges for Design and Management in the 21st Century. *Decision Sciences, 29*(3), 537–550. doi:10.1111/j.1540-5915.1998.tb01353.x

Mabert, V., Soni, A., & Venkatamara, M. (2003). Enterprise Resource Planning: managing implementation process. *European Journal of Operational Research, 146*(2), 302–314. doi:10.1016/S0377-2217(02)00551-9

Mabin, V. J., & Balderstone, S. J. (2000). *The world of the theory of constraints: a review of the international literature*. The St. Lucie Press.

Macedo, P.; Zacarias, M.; Tribolet, J. (2005): *Técnicas e Métodos de Investigação em Engenharia Organizacional: Projecto de Investigação em Modelação de Processos de Produção. Bragança* [Techniques and Research Methods in Organizational Engineering: Research Project in Modelling Production Processes. Braganza], 6ª Conferência da Associação Portuguesa de Sistemas de Informação [6th Conference of the Portuguese Association for Information Systems].

Machado, R. J. M., Costa, L. A. A. F., & Gomes, J. L. F. (2008). *Processo de implementaçao de ERPs: um método para o ajuste de requisitos e optimizaçao de funcionalidades* [Process of implementing ERP: a method for setting requirements and sparing use of features]. Portugal: Universidade do Minho.

Madu, C. N., & Kuei, C. (2004). *ERP and supply chain management*. Fairfield, CT: Chi Publishers.

Magalhães, R., & Silva, A. (2009). A White paper on Organizational and Design Enginering, Center for Organizational and Design Engineering, *INESC INOV*, Portugal.

Magalhães, R., Zacarias, M., & Tribolet, J. (2007a): Making Sense of Enterprise Architectures as Tools of Organizational Self-Awareness (OSA). *Proceedings of the Second Workshop on Trends in Enterprise Architecture Research (TEAR 2007), 6*, 61-70.

Magalhães, R., Zacarias, M., & Tribolet, J. (2007). Making Sense of Enterprise Architectures as Tools of Organizational Self- Awareness. *Journal of Entreprise Architecture, 3*(4), 64–72.

Malhotra, A., Gosain, S., & El Sawy, O. A. (2005). Absorptive Capacity Configurations in Supply Chains: Gearing for Partner-Enabled Market Knowledge Creation. *Management Information Systems Quarterly, 29*(1), 145–187.

Mandl, H., Gruber, H., & Renkl, A. (2002). Situiertes Lernen in multimedialen Lernumgebungen. [Situated learning in multimedia learning environments] In Issing, L. J., & Klimsa, P. (Eds.), *Information und Lernen mit Multimedia und Internet* [Information and Learning with Multiedia and the Internet]. (pp. 139–148).

Mangan, J., Lalwani, C., & Butcher, T. (2008). *Global Logistics and Supply Chain Management*. Hoboken, NJ: John Wiley & Sons.

Manning, T. T. (2003). Leadership across cultures: Attachment style influences. *Journal of Leadership & Organizational Studies, 9*(3), 20–30. doi:10.1177/107179190300900304

Marcuse, H. (1964). *One-dimensional man*. Boston: Beacon Press.

Markovic, I., & Kowalkiewicz, M. (2008). Linking Business Goals to Process Models in Semantic Business Process Modeling. In *12th International IEEE Enterprise Distributed Object Computing Conference (EDOC 2008)* (pp. 332-338). Washington, DC: IEEE CS press.

Markus, M. L., Tanis, C., & Fenema, P. C. v. (2000). Enterprise resource planning: multisite ERP implementations. *Communications of the ACM, 43*(4), 42–46. doi:10.1145/332051.332068

Marques, R. P. (2008*). Ferramentas de Apoio ao Ciclo de Fabricação de Produto: um caso de estudo na indústria dos moldes*. [Tools to Support Cycle Product Manufacturing: a case study in the mold industry] Unpublished master's dissertation, University of Aveiro, Portugal.

Marques, R. P., Santos, C., & Santos, H. (2010) Automation of the Approval and Control Process of Documents. In J. E. Quintela Varajão, et al. (Eds.), *Enterprise Information Systems: Vol. 109. Communications in Computer and Information Science* (pp. 328-337). Heidelberg: Springer-Verlag Berlin Heidelberg.

Marques, A. F., Borges, J. G., Sousa, P., Diaz, E., Moura, P., & Ferrinho, M. (in press). A hybrid approach for integrating harvest scheduling and product assortment and assignment to transformation centers. *Forest Science*.

Marques, A. F., Borges, J. G., Sousa, P., & Pinho, A. M. (2010). An enterprise architecture approach to forest management support systems design. An application to pulpwood supply management in Portugal. *European Journal of Forest Research*. doi:doi:10.1007/s10342-011-0482-8

Marques, A., Borges, J. G., Pina, J. P., Lucas, B., & Garcia, J. (in press). A participatory approach to design a regional forest management planning decision support toolbox. *Annals of Forest Science*.

Marr, B. (2006) *Strategic Performance Management. 1.ᵃ ed*. Oxford: Elsevier Ltd.

Martinez, M. T., Fouletier, P., Park, K. H., & Faurel, J. (2001). Virtual enterprise: Organization, evolution and control. *International Journal of Production Economics, 74*, 225–238. doi:10.1016/S0925-5273(01)00129-3

Martin, M. H. (1998, Feb. 2). An ERP Strategy. *Fortune*, 95–97.

Marx Gómez, J. (2009). Corporate Environmental Management Information Systems - CEMIS 2.0. In (Eds) Davcev D, Marx Gómez J.: *Proceedings of the ICT Innovations Conference 2009*, (pp. 1-4) Ohrid, Macedonia, Springer Heidelberg.

Matos, M. G. (2007), *Organizational Engineering: An Overview of Current Perspectives*, Master Thesis in Computer Science, IST/UTL, Lisboa.

Maurizio, A., Girolami, L., & Jones, P. (2007). EAI and SOA: Factors and methods influencing the integration of multiple ERP systems (in an SAP environment) to comply with the Sarbanes-Oxley Act. *Journal of Enterprise Information Management, 20*(1), 14–31. doi:10.1108/17410390710717110

McAfee, A. (2006). Enterprise 2.0: The Dawn of Emergent Collaboration, *MIT. Sloan Management Review, 47*(3).

McLaurin, J. R., & Al Amri, M. B. (2008). Developing an understanding of charismatic and transformational leadership. *Allied Academies International Conference. Academy of Organizational Culture, Communications and Conflict. Proceedings, 13*(2), 15–19.

McMullen, T. B. Jr. (1998). *Introduction to the theory of constraints (TOC) management system.* The St. Lucie Press.

Methodology linking Soft with Hard, Retrieved from: http://www.systemdynamics.org/conferences/1999/PA-PERS/PARA104.pdf. Last access: 01/08/2011.

Mey, J. L. (1993). *Pragmatics: An Introduction.* Oxford: Blackwell.

Michel, R. (2000). *The road to extended ERP.* Retrieved May 8, 2009, from http://www.manufacturingsystems.com/extendedenterprise

Mickel, P., Agosto, L., Vignollet, L., & Marty, J.-C. (2006). A Contact Recommender System for a Mediated Social Media. In J. C. Isabel Seruca, Slimane Hammoudi, Joaquim Filipe (Ed.), *Enterprise Information Systems VI*: Springer

Microsoft Corporation. (2009, June). Resort *Streamlines Skier Check-In, Improves Data Collection with RF Technology.* Retrieved November 10, 2010, from http://www.microsoft.com/casestudies/Case_Study_Detail.aspx?CaseStudyID=4000004666

Middlebrooks, A. E., & Haberkorn, J. T. (2009). Implicit leader development: The mentor role as prefatory leadership context. *The Journal of Leadership Studies, 2*(4), 7–22. doi:10.1002/jls.20077

Middleton, S. E., Shadbolt, N. R., & Roure, D. C. D. (2003). *Capturing interest through inference and visualization: ontological user profiling in recommender systems.* Paper presented at the Proceedings of the 2nd international conference on Knowledge capture.

Miller, M. (2007, July). Transformational leadership and mutuality. *Transformation, 24*(3/4), 180–192.

Mintzberg, H., Lampel, J., Quinn, J.B., & Ghoshal, S. (2003). *The strategy process: Concepts, contexts, cases.* Edinburgh Gate: Pearson Education Limited.

Miyazaki, K., Hanaoka, G., & Imai, H. (2006, March). *Digitally signed document sanitizing scheme based on bilinear maps.* Paper presented at the 2006 ACM Symposium on Information, computer and communications security, Taipei, Taiwan.

Moffitt, J. (2010). *Professional XMPP Programming with JavaScript and jQuery.* Wiley Publishing.

Mohamed, M., & Adam, F. (2005). ERP II: Harnessing ERP Systems with Knowledge Management Capabilities. *Journal of Knowledge Management Practice, 1* (2). Retrieved january 19, 2011, from http://www.tlainc.com/articl91.htm.

Moller, C. (2005). ERPII: A conceptual framework for next-generation enterprise systems? *Journal of Enterprise Information Management, 18*(4), 483–497. doi:10.1108/17410390510609626

Monk, E. F., & Wagner, B. J. (2009). *Concepts in Enterprise Resource Planning* (3rd ed.). Course Technology, USA: Cengage Learning.

Monod, E. (2004). *Open Tourism: Cultural heritage tourism enhanced by open technologies and u-commerce.*: European Comission - FP6 The Sixth Framework Programme RTD.

Moon, Y. (2007). Enterprise Resource Planning (ERP): A review of the literature. *International Journal of Management and Enterprise Development, 4*(3), 200. doi:10.1504/IJMED.2007.012679

Moore, G. C., & Benbasat, I. (1991). Development of an Instrument to Measure the Perceptions of Adopting an Information Technology Innovation. *Information Systems Research, 2*(3), 192–222. doi:10.1287/isre.2.3.192

Morris, L. (2006). *Top-down innovation: leaders define innovation culture.* Retrieved April 26, 2008 from http://www.realinnovation.com/content/c070528a.asp

Morris, C. (1938). Foundations of the theory of signs. In Neurath, O., Carnap, R., & Morris, C. (Eds.), *International Encyclopaedia of Unified Science I* (pp. 77–138). Chicago: University of Chicago Press.

Morris, C. (1995). *Signs, Language and Behavior.* George Braziller.

Moser, E. P. (2002). E-Procurement-Reverse Auctions and the Supplier's Perspective. *Pharmaceutical Technology, 26*(5), 82–85.

Motwani, J., Mirchandani, M., & Gunasekaran, A. (2002). Successful implementation of ERP Projects: evidence from two case studies. *International Journal of Production Economics, 75,* 83–96. doi:10.1016/S0925-5273(01)00183-9

Moxey, P., Berendt. (2008). *A Corporate Governance and the Credit Crunch.* ACCA.

Mueller, R. K. (1981). Changes in the wind of corporate governance. *The Journal of Business Strategy, 1*(4), 8–14. doi:10.1108/eb038907

Müller, K. R. (2006). Berufliches Lernen und Lerntheorie. [Vocational learning and learning theory] In Kaiser, F.-J., & Pätzold, G. (Eds.), *Wörterbuch Berufs- und Wirtschaftspädagogik* [Dictionary of Professional and Business Education]. 2nd ed., pp. 86–89). Klinkhardt, Bad Heilbrunn.

Murua, I., Lladó, E., & Llodrá, B. (2005). *The Semantic Web for Improving Dynamic Tourist Packages Commercialisation.* Madrid: Fundación IBIT, ROBOTIKER.

Mutka, K. A., Broster, D., Cachia, R., Centeno, C., Feijóo, C., & Haché, A. (2009). *The Impact of Social Computing on the EU Information Society and Economy - European Commission.* Joint Research Centre Institute for Prospective Technological Studies.

Myers, M. D. (1997). Qualitative Research in information systems. *Management Information Systems Quarterly,* 209–223.

Myers, M. D. (2009). *Qualitative Research in Business and Management.* London: Sage.

Myers, M. D., & Newman, M. (2007). The qualitative interview in IS research: Examining the craft. *Information and Organization, 17*(1), 2–26. doi:10.1016/j.infoandorg.2006.11.001

Nah, F. F.-H., Faja, S., & Cata, T. (2001). Characteristics of ERP software maintenance: a multiple case study. *Journal of Software Maintenance and Evolution: Research and Practice, 13*(6), 399–414. doi:10.1002/smr.239

Nah, F. F., Lau, J. L., & Kuang, J. (2001). *Critical factors for successful implementation of enterprise systems.* Emerald - Business Process Management Journal.

Najdawi, A. (2009). *SOA and Web Services for Leveraging Inter-organizational Integration in Travel and Tourism* Paper presented at the Services - I, 2009 World Conference.

Neef, D. (2001). *e-Procurement: From Strategy to Implementation.* USA: Prentice Hall.

Neely, A., Gregory, M., & Platts, K. (1995). Performance measurement system design. *International Journal of Operations & Production Management, 15*(4), 80–116. doi:10.1108/01443579510083622

Neuhaus, M., & Bunke, H. (2006). A Random Walk Kernel Derived from Graph Edit Distance. In (Eds) Yeung D- Y, Kwok J T, Fred A, Roli F, de Ridder D.: *Structural, Syntactic and Statistical Pattern Recognition. Joint IAPR International Workshops, SSPR 2006 and SPR 2006,* (pp. 191-199.) Hong Kong, China, August 2006, Proeedings LNCS 4109, Berlin Heidelberg: Springer-Verlag.

Neuhauser, C. (2007). Project manager leadership behaviors and frequency of use by female project managers. *Project Management Journal, 38*(1), 21–31.

Neves, F. M. (2007): *Visualização de Indicadores de Negócio no Contexto de um Sistema de Suporte à Decisão* [View of Business Indicators in the Context of a Decision Support System], Master Thesis, Lisboa: Instituto Superior Técnico.

Nevo, D., & Chan, Y. E. (2007). A Delphi study of knowledge management systems: Scope and requirements. *Information & Management, 44*(6), 583–597. doi:10.1016/j.im.2007.06.001

Newman, M., & Zhao, Y. (2008). The process of enterprise resource planning implementation and business process re-engineering: tales from two chinese small and medium-sized enterprises. *Information Systems Journal, 18*(4), 405–426. doi:10.1111/j.1365-2575.2008.00305.x

Ngai, E. W. T., Law, C. C. H., & Wat, F. K. T. (2008). Examining the critical success factors in the adoption of enterprise resource planning. *Computers in Industry, 59*(6), 548–564. doi:10.1016/j.compind.2007.12.001

Ng, C. S. P., Gable, G. G., & Chan, T. (2002). An ERP-client benefit-oriented maintenance taxonomy. *Journal of Systems and Software, 64*(2), 87–109. doi:10.1016/S0164-1212(02)00029-8

Nielsen, J. (2005). Heuristic Evaluation. *useit.com: Jakob Nielsen's Website*. Retrieved January 8, 2010, from http://www.useit.com/papers/heuristic/

Nisbett, R. E., Borgida, E., Crandall, R., & Reed, H. (1982). Popular induction: Information is not necessarily informative. In Kahneman, D., Slovic, P., & Tversky, A. (Eds.), *Judgment under uncertainty: Heuristics and biases* (pp. 101–116). Cambridge: Cambridge University Press.

Nulens, R. (2006). *Sequentie Analyse*. Doctoral Thesis, transnationale Universiteit Limburg, School voor Informatietechnologie. pp 67-77.

Nunnally, J., & Bernstein, I. (1978). *Psychometric theory*.

O'Brien, J. (2001). *Introduction to Information Systems: essentials for the internetworked e-business enterpise* (10th ed.). Irwin/McGraw-Hill.

O'Connor, M. C. (2010, September 2). Vail Resorts Links RFID with Social Media. *RFID Journal*. Retrieved November 10, 2010, from http://www.rfidjournal.com/article/view/7845

O'Brien, J. A., & Marakas, G. (2009). *Introduction to Information Systems*. McGraw-Hill.

OECD. (2004). *OECD Principles of Corporate Governance*. OECD.

OGC, Office of Government Commerce. (2007). *The Official Introduction to the ITIL Service Lifecycle*. London: The Stationery Office.

OGC. (2005). *eProcurement in action: A guide to eProcurement for the public sector*. London: Office of Government Commerce.

Oliveira, T., & Martins, M. F. (2010). Understanding e-business adoption across industries in European countries. *Industrial Management & Data Systems, 110*(9), 1337–1354. doi:10.1108/02635571011087428

Op 't Land, M, Proper, E., Maarten, W., Cloo, J., & Steghuis, C. (2009): Enterprise Architecture – Creating Value by Informed Governance, Springer – Verlag Berlin Heidelberg.

Orlikowski, W. (1991). Information Technology and the Structuring of Organizations. *Information Systems Research*, winter, 27-38.

Orlikowski, W. (1993). CASE Tools as Organizational Change: investigating Incremental and Radical Changes in Systems Development. *MIS Quarterly*, Septermber, 209-223.

Orlikowski, W. J., & Barley, S. R. (2001). Technology and institutions: what can research on information technology and research on organizations learn from each other? *Management Information Systems Quarterly, 25*(2), 145–165. doi:10.2307/3250927

Orliwoski, W. (2000). Using technology and constituing structures: a practice lens for studying technology in organizations. *Organization Science, 11*(4), 404–428. doi:10.1287/orsc.11.4.404.14600

Osborn, A. F. (1957). *Applied Imagination* (revised ed.). New York: Scribners.

Osterle, H., Fleisch, H., & Alt, R. (2001). *Business Networking - shaping Collaboration between enterprises* (2nd ed.). Berlin, Germany: Springer.

Osterloh, R., & Rota, M. (2007). Open source software development, just another case of collective invention. *Research Policy, 36*(2), 157–171. doi:10.1016/j.respol.2006.10.004

Osterwalder, A., & Pigneur, Y. (2010). *Business Model Generation – A Handbook for Visionaries, Game Changers, and Challengers*. Hoboken, NJ: John Wiley and Sons, Inc.

Owen, L., Goldwasser, C., Choate, K., & Blitz, A. (2008). Collaborative innovation throughout the extended enterprise. *Strategy and Leadership, 36*(1), 39–45. doi:10.1108/10878570810840689

Pairat, R., & Jungthirapanich, C. 2005. A chronological review of ERP research: an analysis of ERP inception, evolution, and direction. In *Proceedings of 2005 IEEE International Engineering Management Conference* (pp. 288-292), St John's, Newfoundland & Labrador, Canada.

Palaniswamy, R., & Frank, T. (2000). Enhancing manufacturing performance with ERP systems. *Information Systems Management, 17*(3), 1–13. doi:10.1201/1078/43192.17.3.20000601/31240.7

Pal, N., & Pantaleo, D. C. (2005). *The agile enterprise: Reinventing your organization for success in an on-demand world.* New York, USA: Springer Science, Business Media, Inc.

Panayiotou, N. A., Gayaialis, S. P., & Tatsiopoulos, I. P. (2004). An e-procurement system for governmental purchasing. *International Journal of Production Economics, 90*(1), 79–102. doi:10.1016/S0925-5273(03)00103-8

Panchenko, O. (2007). Concept Location and Program Comprehension in Service-Oriented Software. In *Proceedings of the IEEE 23rd International Conference on Software Maintenance: Doctoral Symposium,* (pp. 513 – 514), Paris, France: ICSM.

Pani, A. K., & Agrahari, A. (2007). *E-Procurement in Emerging Economies:Theory and Cases.* India: Idea Group Pub.doi:10.4018/978-1-59904-153-7

Papp, R. (2001). Introduction to Strategic Alignment. In Papp, R. (Ed.), *Strategic Information Technology: Opportunities for Competitive Advantage* (pp. 1–24). Hershey, PA: Idea Group. doi:10.4018/978-1-878289-87-2.ch001

Parnes, J., & Meadow, A. (1959). Effects of Brain-Storming Instruction on Creative Problem-Solving by Trained and Untrained Subjects. *Journal of Educational Psychology, 50.*

Parr, A., & Shanks, G. (2000). A model of ERP project implementation. *Emerald-.Journal of Information Technology, 15*(4), 289–303. doi:10.1080/02683960010009051

Páscoa, C., & Tribolet, J. (2010). Organizational and Design Engineering of the Operational and Support Components of an Organization: the Portuguese Air Force Case Study, Practice-driven Research on Enterprise Transformation (PRET) *Conference on Enterprise Engineering, Springer Lecture Notes in Business Information Processing (LNPIB) Series*, Delft University, The Netherlands.

Páscoa, C., Alves, A., & Tribolet, J. (2010): EX-ANTE and EX-POST Model Development and Monitoring of the Portuguese Air Force Effort Regime, *Minutes of the Conference on ENTERPrise Information Systems held in Viana do Castelo*, Portugal in October 2010, Springer.

Pastor, J., Mayo, M., & Shamir, B. (2007). Adding fuel to fire: the impact of followers' arousal on ratings of charisma. *The Journal of Applied Psychology, 92*(6), 1584–1596. doi:10.1037/0021-9010.92.6.1584

Patnayakuni, R., Rai, A., & Seth, N. (2006). Relational Antecedents of Information Flow Integration for Supply Chain Coordination. *Management Information Systems Quarterly, 23*(1), 13–49. doi:10.2753/MIS0742-1222230101

Paul, S., Pan, J., & Jain, R. (2010). Architectures for the future networks and the next generation Internet: A survey. *Computer Communications, 34*, 2–42. doi:10.1016/j.comcom.2010.08.001

Pawar, B. (2003). Central conceptual issues in transformational leadership research. *Leadership and Organization Development Journal, 24*(7), 397–406. doi:10.1108/01437730310498596

Pearce, C. L., Sims, H. P. Jr, Cox, J. F., Ball, G., Schness, E., Smith, K., & Trevino, L. (2003). Transactors, transformers and beyond: A multi-method development of a theoretical typology of leadership. *Journal of Management Development, 22*(4), 273–307. doi:10.1108/02621710310467587

Peirce, C. S. (1958). *Collected Papers of Charles Sanders Peirce* (Vol. 1-6).

Pereira, C., & Sousa, P. (2003). Getting into the misalignment between Business and Information Systems. In *European Conference On Information Technology Evaluation (ECITE 2006)*

Pereira, P., & Alturas, B. (2007, October). *Factores Críticos da Adesão das PME'S Nacionais, Fornecedoras de Materiais de Escritório ao Procedimento Aquisitivo Público em Portugal: Uma Proposta de Investigação* [Critical Factors of Accession of SMEs National Vendors of office supplies to the Public Purchasing Procedure in Portugal: A Proposal for Research.]. Paper presented at the Conferência IADIS Ibero – Americana.

Pérez, I. J., Cabrerizo, F. J., & Herrera-Viedma, E. (2011). Group decision making problems in a linguistic and dynamic context. [Accessed January 19, 2011]. *Expert Systems with Applications, 38*(3), 1675–1688. Available at http://dx.doi.org/10.1016/j.eswa.2010.07.092doi:10.1016/j.eswa.2010.07.092

Person, R. (2009). *Balanced Scorecards and Operational Dashboards with Microsoft Excel.* Indianapolis, IN: Wiley Publishing, Inc.

Peslak, A. (2005). A twelve-step, multiple course approach to teaching enterprise resource planning. *Journal of Information Systems Education, 16*(2), 147–155.

Peslak, A., Subramanian, G. H., & Clayton, G. (2006). The phases of ERP software implementation and maintenance: A model for predicting preferred ERP use. *Journal of Computer Information Systems, 48*(2), 25–33.

Peters, D., Haak, L., & Marx Gómez, J. (2010). Learner-oriented Approach for Enterprise Systems in Higher Education using TEL-based Concepts. In J. Cordeiro (Ed.), *Proceedings of the 2nd International Conference on Computer Supported Education* (pp. 521-526), INSTICC Press, Setúbal, Portugal.

Peterson, H. (2005). *Data Mining. Verfahren, Prozesse, Anwendungsarchitektur.* Oldenbourg. doi:10.1524/9783486593334

Pillai, R., Schriesheim, C. A., & Williams, E. S. (1999). Fairness perceptions and trust as mediators for transformational and transactional leadership: A two-sample study. *Journal of Management, 25*(6), 897–933. doi:10.1177/014920639902500606

Pinto, J. P. (2006). *Gestão de Operações na Indústria e nos Serviços* [Operations Management in Manufacturing and Services] (2.nd ed.). Lisboa: LIDEL.

Plattner, H. (2009). A Common Database Approach for OLTP and OLAP using an In-Memory Column Database. International Conference on Management of Data. *Proceedings of the 35th SIGMOD international conference on Management of data. Providence.* (pp 1-2) Rhode Island. USA. ISBN: 978-1-60558-55.

PMI. (2004). *A Guide to the Project Management Body of Knowledge* (3rd ed.). Project Management Institute.

Png, I., & Lehman, D. (2007). *Managerial economics.* Malden, MA, USA: Blackwell Publising.

Poole, M. S., & DeSanctis, G. (1990). Understanding the use of group decisions support systems: the theory of adaptive structuration. In Fulk, J., & Steinfield, C. W. (Eds.), *Organizations and communication technology* (pp. 173–193). California: Sage.

Poole, M. S., & Van de Ven, A. H. (2004). *Handbook of Organizational Change and Innovation.* New York, NY: Oxford University Press.

Popper, K. (1959). *The logic of scientific discovery.* London: Hutchinson and Company.

Portafolio Nestlé. (2007) *Afine: Empresas Líderes de Colombia Información Financiera 2002-2006.* [Tune: Business Leaders of Columbia Financial Information 2002-2006] Bogotá, Colombia: Casa Editorial El Tiempo Revista Cambio de Mayo 15-21/ 2008 (2008): *Las 1.001 Compañías* [1001 Companies].(776) Casa Editorial El Tiempo, Ross, J., Weill, P. & Robertson, D. (2006). *Enterprise Architectures as Strategy.* Boston, MA: Harvard Business School Press

Porter, M. (1996) *What is strategy?* Harvard Business Review

Porter, M., & Millar, V. E. (1985). How information gives you competitive advantage. *Harvard Business Review, 63*(4), 149–160.

Pourdehnad, J., & Bharathy, G. K. (2004). Systems Thinking and Its Implications in Organizational Transformation. In *Conference on Systems Thinking in Management,* Philadelphia, PA.

Powell, R., & Single, H. (1996). Focus groups. *International Journal for Quality in Health Care, 8*(5), 499–504. doi:10.1093/intqhc/8.5.499

Powell, W. W. (1990). Neither market nor hierarchy: Network forms of organization. *Research in Organizational Behavior, 12,* 295–336.

Puliafito, A. (2006, May). *An Example of Applied Research: RFID and Administrative Processes.* Paper presented at the Workshop RFID Application Domains and Emerging Trends, Brussels, Belgium.

Putnik, G. D., & Cunha, M. M. (2007). *Knowledge and Technology Management in Virtual Organizations.* Hershey, PA: IDEA Group Publishing.

Putnik, G. D., & Putnik, Z. (2010). A semiotic framework for manufacturing systems integration -Part I: Generative integration model. *International Journal of Computer Integrated Manufacturing, 23*(8), 691–709. doi:10.108 0/0951192X.2010.510292

Rahim, M. A., & Psenicka, C. (2002). A model of emotional intelligence and conflict management strategies: A study in seven countries. *The International Journal of Organizational Analysis, 10*(4), 302–326. doi:10.1108/ eb028955

Ramesh, B., & Tiwana, A. (1999). Supporting Collaborative Process Knowledge Management in New Product Development Teams. *Decision Support Systems, 27,* 213–235. doi:10.1016/S0167-9236(99)00045-7

Rang, M., Hohn, B., & Rühl, O. (2008). *Wirtschaftswissenschaftler: Neue Chancen auf dem Europäischen Arbeitsmarkt?* [Economists: New Opportunities in the European labor market?]. (pp. 283–287). Wirtschaftsstudium. [Business studies]

Rasmussen, N., Chen, C. Y., & Bansal, M. (2009). *Business Dashboards.* New Jersey: John Wiley & Sons.

Ratti, R. (1991). Small and Medium-Size Enterprises, Local. Synergies, and Spatial Cycles of Innovation. In Camagni, R. (Ed.), *Innovation Networks: Spatial Perspectives* (pp. 71–88). London: Belhaven Press.

Raymond, E. (1999). The Cathedral and the bazaar. *Knowledge, Technology & Policy, 12*(3), 23–49. doi:10.1007/ s12130-999-1026-0

Rayport, J. F., & Sviokla, J. J. (1995). 1996). Exploiting the virtual value chain. *The McKinsey Quarterly, 1,* 21–36.

Rebmann, K. (2001). *Planspiel und Planspieleinsatz* [*Simulation and simulation applications*]. Hamburg: Kovac.

Rebmann, K., & Tenfelde, W. (2008). *Betriebliches Lernen* [Workplace learning]. München: Hampp.

Rebmann, K., Tenfelde, W., & Uhe, E. (2005). *Berufs- und Wirtschaftspädagogik* [Vocational and Business Education]. Wiesbaden: Gabler.

Recanati, F. (2004). Pragmatics and semantics. In Ward, L. R. H. G. (Ed.), *The Handbook of Pragmatics.* Oxford, UK: Blackwell Publishing.

Reese, G. (2009). *Cloud Applications Architectures.* O'reilly.

Reetz, L. (1999). Zum Zusammenhang von Schlüsselqualifikationen – Kompetenzen – Bildung. [On the relationship of key skills - skills – Education] In Tramm, T., Sembill, D., Klauser, F., & John, E. G. (Eds.), *Professionalisierung kaufmännischer Berufsausbildung* [Professional commercial training]. (pp. 32–51). Frankfurt am Main: Lang.

Reich, B., & Benbasat, I. (2000). Factors That Influence the Social Dimension of Alignment Between Business and Information Technology Objectives. *Management Information Systems Quarterly, 24*(1), 81–113. doi:10.2307/3250980

Reid, R., & Sanders, N. R. (2007). *Operations Management: an integrated approach* (3rd ed.). New York: John Wiley & Sons.

Reinmann, G., & Mandl, H. (2006). Unterrichten und Lernumgebungen gestalten. [Teaching and learning environments.] In Krapp, A., & Weidenmann, B. (Eds.), *Pädagogische Psychologie* [educational Psychology]. 5th ed., pp. 613–658). Weinheim: Beltz.

Reinmann-Rothmeier, G., & Mandl, H. (1997). Lehren im Erwachsenenalter. [Lessons in adulthood.] In F.E. Weinert, & H. Mandl (Eds.), *Psychologie der Erwachsenenbildung* [Psychology of Adult Education] *4* (pp.355-403). Hogrefe, Göttingen.

Remberg, J. (2009). *Grundlagen des Process* [Fundamentals of Process]. Mining. GRIN Verlag.

Reuer, J. J. (2004). *Strategic alliances.* New York: Oxford University Press Inc.

Reynolds, K. M., Twery, M., Lexer, M. J., Vacik, H., Ray, D., Shao, G., & Borges, J. G. (2007). Decision support systems in natural resource management. In Burstein, F., & Holsapple, C. (Eds.), *Handbook on decision support systems.* Springer Verlag International.

Ribeiro, R. P., Borges, J. G., Pereira, C., Sousa, P., & Lé, J. (2005). Designing an Integrated Forest Planning System for the forest industry: an application in Portugal. In: *Proceedings of the 2003 Symposium on Systems Analysis in Forest Resources.* Stevenson, WA, USA.

Richardson, J. (1996). Vertical integration and rapid response in fashion apparel. *Organization Science, 7*(4), 400–412. doi:10.1287/orsc.7.4.400

Riege, A. (2005). Three-dozen knowledge-sharing barriers managers must consider. *Journal of Knowledge Management, 9*(3), 18–35. Available at http://lpis.csd.auth.gr/mtpx/km/material/JKM-9-3b.pdf-doi:10.1108/13673270510602746

Riehle, D. (2007). The Economic Motivation of Open Source: Stakeholder Perspectives. *IEEE Computer, 40*(4), 25–32. doi:10.1109/MC.2007.147

Rizzolatti, G., & Sinigaglia, C. (2006). *Mirrors in the brain: How our minds share actions and emotions* (Anderson, F., Trans.). Oxford: Oxford University Press.

Robert, M. (2010, March 22). The Age of RFID Pilots is Over --- Deployments Crank Up. *RFID Journal.* Retrieved November 13, 2010, from http://www.rfidjournal.com/article/view/7471

Roberti, M. (2009, May 11). RFID Moves Beyond Tracking. *RFID Journal.* Retrieved November 10, 2010, from http://www.rfidjournal.com/article/view/4860

Roberti, M. (2010, August 2). Putting Wal-Mart's Apparel Tagging in Context. *RFID Journal.* Retrieved November 13, 2010, from http://www.rfidjournal.com/article/view/7769

Roberti, M. (2010, January 11). The Decade Ahead. *RFID Journal.* Retrieved November 13, 2010, from http://www.rfidjournal.com/article/view/7308

Roberti, M. (2010, July 26). Wal-Mart Takes a New Approach to RFID. *RFID Journal.* Retrieved November 13, 2010, from http://www.rfidjournal.com/article/view/7756

Roberts, K. H., & Grabowski, M. (1995). *Organizations, technology and structuring.* In S.R: Clegg, C. Hardy, W.R. Nord, (Eds). *Handbook of Organization Studies,* 409-423. California: Sage.

Robey, D., Ross, J. W., & Boudreau, M. C. (2002). Learning to implement enterprise systems: An exploratory study of the dialectics of change. *Journal of Management Information Systems, 19*(1), 17–46.

Rockart, J. F. (1979). Chief executives define their own data needs. *Harvard Business Review, 57*(2), 81–93.

Rodriguez, M. A., & Shinavier, J. (2009). Exposing Multi-Relational Networks to Single-Relational Network Analysis Algorithms. DOI: 10.1016/j.joi.2009.06.004. *Journal of Informetrics, 4*(1), 29-41 ISSN:1751-1577.

Rogers, E. M. (1983). *Diffusion of Innovations.* New York, NY: Free Press.

Ronnqvist, E. M. (2003). Optimization in Forestry. *Mathematical Programming, 97*(1-2), 267–284.

Rosario, J.G. (2000). On the leading edge: critical success factors in ERP implementation projects, *Business World*, May, 21-27.

Rossi, D. (2006). Decoding the green open source software puzzle: A survey of theoretical and empirical contributions. *The Economics of Open Source Software Development, 22nd IEEE International Parallel and Distributed Processing Symposium*, New York.

Roth, R. M., & William, C. Wood, I. (1990). *A Delphi approach to acquiring knowledge from single and multiple experts.* Paper presented at the Proceedings of the 1990 ACM SIGBDP conference on Trends and directions in expert systems.

Rothaermel, F. T., Hitt, M. A., & Jobe, L. A. (2006). Balancing vertical integration and strategic outsourcing: Effects on product portfolio, product success, and firm performance. *Strategic Management Journal, 27*, 1033–1056. doi:10.1002/smj.559

Rubin, H. J., & Rubin, I. S. (2005). *Qualitative interviewing: The art of hearing data* (2nd ed.). Thousand Oaks, CA: Sage.

Russell-Jones, N. (1998). *The Business Planning Pocketbook* (3rd ed.). Management Pocketbooks Ltd.

Sambamurthy, V., & Zmud, R. W. (1999). Arrangements for Information Technology governance: A Theory of Multiple Contingencies. *Management Information Systems Quarterly, 23*(2), 261–291. doi:10.2307/249754

Sameh, B., & Izak, J. (2009). The Adoption and Use of IT Artifacts: A New Interaction Centric Model for the Study of User-Artifact Relationships. *Journal of the Association for Information Systems, 10*(9), 661–685.

Sandel, M. J. (2009). *Justice: What's the right thing to do?* New York: Farrar, Straus, and Giroux.

Santa María, M., García, F., Rozo, S., & Uribe, M. (2007). *Un diagnóstico general del sector salud en Colombia: evolución, contexto y principales retos de un sistema en transformación.* [A General Assessment of the Health Sector in Columbia: Evolution, Context and Main Challenges for a Changing System] Retrieved March 2, 2009 http://www.med-informatica.net/FMC_CMCB/VeeduriaCiudadana/CIDMEDvcacelapss/SaludRetos-Regulacion_MauricioSantamaria_cap1_final.pdf.

Sarker, S., & Lee, A. S. (2003). Using a case study to test the role of three key social enablers in ERP implementation. *Information & Management, 40*(8), 813–829. doi:10.1016/S0378-7206(02)00103-9

Saussure, F. d. (1916). *Course in general linguistics* (W. Baskin, Trans.): McGraw-Hill Book Company.

SCC (2006), *Supply-Chain Operations Reference-Model, Plan, Source, Make, Deliver,* SCOR Model Handbook v. 8.0, Cypress: Supply-Chain Council.

Scheider, F. W., Gruman, J. A., & Coutts, L. M. (Eds.). (2005). *Applied Social Psychology: Understanding and addressing social and practical problems.* Thousand Oaks: Sage Publications.

Schekkerman, J. (2009). *Enterprise Architecture Good Practices Guide: How to Manage the Enterprise Architecture Practice.* IFEAD / TOGAF Open Standards.

Schelling, T. (1978). *Micromotives and Macrobehaviour.* New York: Norton.

Schiaffino, S., & Amandi, A. (2009a). Building an expert travel agent as a software agent. *Expert Systems with Applications, 36*(2), 1291–1299. doi:10.1016/j.eswa.2007.11.032

Schiaffino, S., & Amandi, A. (2009b). Intelligent User Profiling. *Artificial Intelligence: An International Perspective, 5640,* 193–216. doi:10.1007/978-3-642-03226-4_11

Schimm, G. (2003). Mining most specific Workflow Models from Event-based Data. In W. van der Aalst, A. ter Hofstede, & M. Weske (Eds.), *Proceedings of the International Conference BPM* (pp. 25-40), Springer-Verlag, Berlin.

Schlömer, T. (2008). Die Sustainability Balanced Scorecard als Lerngegenstand in der Berufsbildung für eine nachhaltige Entwicklung. [The Sustainability Balanced Scorecard as a learning object in professional education for sustainable development.] In Duensing, M., Schwithal, T., & Tredop, D. (Eds.), *Kapital, Kompetenz, Konflikte* [Capital, expertise, conflicts]. (pp. 175–193). Oldenburg: BIS.

Schmidt, R. C. (1997). Managing Delphi Surveys Using Nonparametric Statistical Techniques. *Decision Sciences, 28*(3), 763–774. doi:10.1111/j.1540-5915.1997.tb01330.x

Schmidt, S. J. (1992). *Der Kopf, die Welt, die Kunst. Konstruktivismus als Theorie und Praxis* [The head, the world of art. Constructivism as a theory and practice]. Wien: Böhlau.

Schwinger, W., Grün, C., Pröll, B., Retschitzegger, W., & Werthner, H. (2006). Pinpointing Tourism Information onto Mobile Maps — A Light-Weight Approach. In M. Hitz, M. Sigala & J. Murphy (Eds.), *Information and Communication Technologies in Tourism 2006* (pp. 29-43). Viena: Springer Computer Science.

Scott, J. E. (1999) The FoxMeyer Drugs' bankruptcy: Was it a failure of ERP. In *Americas Conference on Information Systems, August,* 13–15.

Scott, B., Colquitt, J., & Zapata-Phelan, C. (2007). Justice as a dependent variable: Subordinate charisma as a predictor of interpersonal and informational justice perceptions. *The Journal of Applied Psychology, 92*(6), 1597–1609. doi:10.1037/0021-9010.92.6.1597

Scott, J. E., & Vessey, I. (2002). Managing risks in enterprise systems implementations. *Communications of the ACM, 45*(4), 74–81. doi:10.1145/505248.505249

Seddon, P. (2003). *Second-Wave Enterprise Resource Planning Systems.* New York, NY: Cambridge University Press.

Sekatzek, P. E., & Krcmar, H. (2009). *Measurement of the Standard Proximity of Adapted Standard Business Software*. In: DOI 10.1007/s12599-009-0045-4. BISE Research Paper. (pp. 1-11.)

Shannon, C. E., & Weaver, W. (1949). *A Mathematical Model of Communication*. Urbana, IL: University of Illinois Press.

Sharifi, H., Kehoe, D. F., & Hopkins, J. (2006). A classification and selection model of e-marketplaces for better alignment of supply chains. *Journal of Enterprise Information Management*, *19*(5), 483–503. doi:10.1108/17410390610703639

Sharma, S. (1996). *Applied Multivariate Techniques*. USA: John Wiley& Sons.

Sharp, J. M., Bamber, C. J., Desia, S., & Irani, Z. (1999). An empirical analysis of lean & agile manufacturing. In *Proceedings of the IMechE Conference on Lean & Agile for the Next Millennium*. Tuesday 9th March.

Shiff, T. (2002). The Economics of Open Source Software: a survey of the early literature. *Review of Network Economics*, *1*(1), 66–74. doi:10.2202/1446-9022.1004

Sillince, J. A. (2007). Organizational context and the discursive construction of organizing. *Management Communication Quarterly*, *20*(4), 363–394. doi:10.1177/0893318906298477

Silva, A., Júnior, A., Caetano, A., Pereira, C., Tribolet, J., & Gil, R. (2009). *Arquitectura Empresarial para o SIMP* [Enterprise Architecture for SIMP]. Lisboa, Portugal: INOV.

Simchi-Levi, D., Kaminsky, P., & Simchi-Levi, E. (2003). *Managing the Supply Chain: The Definitive Guide for the Business Professional*. New York: McGraw-Hill.

Sloman, S. A. (2002). Two systems of reasoning. In Gilovich, T., Griffin, D., & Kahneman, D. (Eds.), *Heuristics and biases: The psychology of intuitive judgement* (pp. 379–396). Cambridge: Cambridge University Press.

Smith, A., & Stirling, A. (2006). *Moving Inside or Outside? Positioning the Governance of Sociotechnical Systems. Science and Technology Policy Research*. *Falmer*. UK: University of Sussex.

Soares-Aguiar, A., & Palma-Dos-Reis, A. (2008). Why do firms adopt e-procurement systems? Using logistic regression to empirically test a conceptual model. [Article]. *IEEE Transactions on Engineering Management*, *55*(1), 120–133. doi:10.1109/TEM.2007.912806

Soh, C., Kien, S. S., & Tay-Yap, J. (2000). Enterprise resource planning: cultural fits and misfits: is ERP a universal solution? *Communications of the ACM*, *43*(4), 47–51. doi:10.1145/332051.332070

Solé, F., & Valls, J. (1991), "Networks of Technological Cooperation between SMEs: Strategic and Spatial Aspects", in Camagni (ed.) *Innovation Networks: Spatial Perspectives*, (pp. 174-195) London: Belhaven Press

Sommers, G., & Nelson, C. (2003). A taxonomy of players and activities across the ERP project life cycle. *Information & Management*, *41*(3), 257–278. doi:10.1016/S0378-7206(03)00023-5

Song, B., & Mitchell, C. J. (2009, October). Scalable *RFID Pseudonym Protocol*. Paper presented at the Third International Conference on Network and System Security, Gold Coast, Australia.

Songini, M. L. (2002). J.D. Edwards pushes CRM, ERP integration. *Computerworld*, *36*(25), 4.

Sorlin, S., & Hebe, V. (2007). *Knowledge Society vs. Knowledge Economy: Knowledge, Power, and Politic*. New York, NY: Palgrave Macmillan. doi:10.1057/9780230603516

Soulsby, A., & Clark, E. (2007). Organization theory and the post-socialist transformation: Contributions to organizational knowledge. *Human Relations*, *60*(10), 1419–1442. doi:10.1177/0018726707083470

Sousa, P., & Pereira, C. (2005). Enterprise Architecture: Business and IT Alignment. In ACM. *Symposium on Applied Computing*. (pp. 1344-1345). New York, NY: ACM Press.

Souza, C. A. (2000). *Sistemas Integrados de Gestão Empresarial: estudos de caso de implementação de sistemas ERP* [Integrated Systems Business Management: case studies of implementation of ERP systems]. São Paulo: FEA/USP.

Sparks, L., & Wagner, B. A. (2003). Retail exchanges: a research agenda. *Supply Chain Management: An International Journal, 8*(3), 201–208. doi:10.1108/13598540310484609

Spewak, S., & Hill, S. (1992). *Enterprise Architecture Planning: Developing a Blueprint for Data, Applications and Technology.* Wiley-QED Publication.

Spivack, N. (2009)- *Web Evolution Nova Spivack Twine,* Retrieved from: http://www.novaspivack.com/uncategorized/the-evolution-of-the-web-past-present-future or http://www.novaspivack.com/technology/powerpoint-deck-making-sense-of-the-semantic-web-and-twine or http://novaspivack.typepad.com/nova_spivacks_weblog/files/nova_spivack_semantic_web_talk.ppt

Sprott, D. (2000). Enterprise resource planning: componentizing the enterprise application packages. *Communications of the ACM, 43*(4), 63–69. doi:10.1145/332051.332074

Sprott, D., & Wilkes, L. (2004). *Understanding Service-Oriented Architecture, The Arquitecture Journal.* Microsoft.

SPSS for Windows. (2007). *Rel. 15.0.* Chicago: SPSS Inc.

Statsoft-Inc. (2001). *STATISTICA (data analysis software system),* version 6.

Stein, A., & Hawking, P. (2004). 2B or not 2B: The real story of B2B e-procurement *Australian CPA 74*(2), 30-33.

Stelzner, M. (2010): *2010 Social Media Marketing Industry Report: how marketers are using social media to grow their businesses.*

Stensrud, E. (2001). Alternative Approaches to Effort Prediction of ERP Projects. *Information and Software Technology, 43*(7), 413–423. doi:10.1016/S0950-5849(01)00147-1

Stevens, C. P. (2003). Enterprise resource planning: A trio of resources. *Information Systems Management, 20*(3), 61–71. doi:10.1201/1078/43205.20.3.20030601/43074.7

Stevens, G. C. (1990). Successful Supply Chain Management. *Management Decision, 28*(8), 25–30. doi:10.1108/00251749010140790

Stone, G. A., Russell, R. F., & Patterson, K. (2004). Transformational versus servant leadership: A difference in leader focus. *Leadership and Organization Development Journal, 25*(4), 349–361. doi:10.1108/01437730410538671

Strauss, A., & Corbin, J. (1990). *Basics of Qualitative Research: Grounded theory, procedures and techniques.* London: Sage.

Streibel, M. J. (1993). Queries About Computer Education and Situated Critical Pedagogy. *Educational Technology, 33*(3), 22–26.

Strong D. M., Fedorowicz J., Sager J., Stewart G., & Watson E. (2006). Teaching with Enterprise Systems. *Communications of AIS,* (17), article 33.

Subramanian, G., & Hoffer, C. (2007). *Implementation of Enterprise Resource Planning (ERP) Systems: Issues and Challenges. Penn State Harrisburg.* Idea Group Inc.

Supply Chain Council. (2008). *SCOR: The Supply Chain Reference Model.* Retrieved January 02, 2011, from www.supply-chain.org

Sutton, S. G. (2006). Extended-enterprise systems' impact on enterprise risk management. *Journal of Enterprise Information Management, 19*(1), 97–114. doi:10.1108/17410390610636904

Swarbrooke, J., Beard, C., Leckie, S., & Pomfret, G. (2003). *Adventure Tourism - The new Frontier.* Butterwortk Heinemann.

Swedberg, C. (2009, April 29). Charles Voegele Group Finds RFID Helps It Stay Competitive. *RFID Journal.* Retrieved November 2, 2010, from http://www.rfidjournal.com/article/view/4836

Sybase. (2006). *Estado da Arte em RFID.* Unpublished Technical Report, Sybase Portugal - RFID Solutions Center, Portugal.

Symons, C., M., Oliver Young, G., & Lambert, N. (2005). *IT Governance Framework.* Forrester.

Tanner, C., Woumllfle, R., Schubert, P., & Quade, M. (2008). Current Trends and Challenges in Electronic Procurement: An Empirical Study. *Electronic Markets, 18*(1), 6–18. doi:10.1080/10196780701797599

Tan, Y.-H., Bjørn-Anderson, N., Klein, S., & Rukanova, B. (Eds.). (2011). *Accelerating Global Supply Chains with IT-Innovation, ITAIDE Tools and Methods*. Berlin, Heidelberg: Springer-Verlag. doi:10.1007/978-3-642-15669-4

Tarde, G. (1899). *Social laws: An outline of sociology* (Warren, H. C., Trans.). New York: The Macmillan Company.

Tascón, M. (2006). Development of a place fotr the information society. In R. Casado (coord.). *Keys for digital literacy*. Seminar on Digital Literacy. Madrid: Telefónica Foundation, 187-194 Retrieved from: http://sociedad-delainformación.telefónica.es/documentos/articulos/clavesdelaalfabetizacióndigital.pdf

Taylor, F. (1911). *The principles of scientific management*. New York: Harper & Brothers Publishers.

Taylor, V. (2007). Leadership for service improvement: part 3. *Nursing Management, 14*(1), 28–32.

Tchokogué, A., Bareil, C., & Duguay, C. R. (2005). Key lessons from the implementation of an ERP at Pratt & Whitney Canada. *International Journal of Production Economics, 95*(2), 151–163. doi:10.1016/j.ijpe.2003.11.013

Tekleab, A. G., Sims, H. P., Yun, S., Tesluk, P. E., & Cox, J. (2008). Are we on the same page? Effects of self-awareness of empowering and transformational leadership. *Journal of Leadership & Organizational Studies, 14*(3), 185–201. doi:10.1177/1071791907311069

Tencati, A., & Zsolnai, L. (2009). The collaborative enterprise. *Journal of Business Ethics, 85*(3), 367–376. doi:10.1007/s10551-008-9775-3

Teo, T. S. H., Lin, S., & Lai, K.-h. (2009). Adopters and non-adopters of e-procurement in Singapore: An empirical study. *Omega, 37*(5), 972–987. doi:10.1016/j.omega.2008.11.001

Teo, T. S. H., & Ranganathan, C. (2004). Adopters and non-adopters of business-to-business electronic commerce in Singapore. *Information & Management, 42*(1), 89–102. doi:10.1016/j.im.2003.12.005

Thaler, R. H. (2000). Mental accounting matters. In Kahneman, D., & Tversky, A. (Eds.), *Choices, values, and frames* (pp. 241–268). Cambridge: Cambridge University Press.

The Business Rules Group. (2007). *The Business Motivation Model: Business Governance in a Volatile World. Version 1.3* Retrieved October 2009 from: http://www.businessrulesgroup.org/bmm.shtml.

The Open Group. (2007). *The Open Group: A Pocket Guide to TOGAF Version 8.1.1 Enterprise Edition*. Retrieved from: http://www.opengroup.org/togaf.

Themistocleous, M., Irani, Z., & O'Keefe, R. (2001). ERP and application integration: Exploratory survey. *Business Process Management Journal, 7*(3), 195–204. doi:10.1108/14637150110392656

Thevenet, L., Salinesi, C., Etien, A., Gam, I., & Lasoued, M. (2006). Experimenting a Modeling Approach for Designing Organization's Strategies in the Context of Strategic Alignment. In *Australian Workshop on Requirements Engineering (AWRE 2006)*.

Thomas, F. G. (2000). *Understanding the Plant Level Costs and Benefits of ERP: Will the Ugly Duckling Always Turn into a Swan?* Paper presented at the 33rd Hawaii Inter. Conf. on Systems Science., Los Alamitos CA.

Thompson, C. (2010). Group think: When it comes to what we say we like, often we're just following the herd. *Wired, 18.01*.

Thompson, C. J. (1995). A contextualist proposal for the conceptualization and study of marketing ethics. *Journal of Public Policy & Marketing, 14*(2), 177.

Thun, J. H. (2010). Angles of Integration: An empirical analysis of the alignment of internet-based information technology and global supply chain integration. *Journal of Supply Chain Management, 46*(2), 30–44. doi:10.1111/j.1745-493X.2010.03188.x

TIBCO (2008). *The Case for Business Process Management.*

Tichy, N. M., & Devanna, M. A. (1986). *The transformational leader*. New York: John Wiley & Sons, Inc.

Tiun, S., Abdullah, R., & Kong, T. E. (2001). Automatic Topic Identification Using Ontology Hierarchy. In *Proceedings, Computational Linguistic and Intelligent Text Processing, Second International Conference CICLing*, (pp 444-453) Mexico City, Mexico: Springer

Todeva, E. (2006). *Business networks: Strategy and structure. Milton Park.* Abingdon, UK: Routledge, Taylor & Francis Group.

Todorovic, W., & Schlosser, F. (2007). An entrepreneur and a leader! A framework conceptualizing the influence of leadership style on a firm's entrepreneurial orientation-performance relationship. *Journal of Small Business & Entrepreneurship, 20*(3), 289–307.

Toomey, M. (2009). *Waltzing with the Elephant.* Infonomics.

Torbacki, W. (2008). SaaS – direction of technology development in ERP/MRP systems. *Archives of Materials Science and Engineering, 31*(1), 57–60.

Travica, B. (1999). *New organizational designs: Information aspects.* Stamford: Ablex Publishing Corporation.

Treacy, M., & Wiersema, F. (1993). Customer intimacy and other value disciplines. *Harvard Business Review, 71*(1), 84–93.

Triantafillakis, A., Kanellis, P., & Martakos, D. (2004). Data warehousing interoperability for the extended enterprise. *Journal of Database Management, 15*(3), 73–82. doi:10.4018/jdm.2004070105

Tribolet, J. (2005) *"Organizações, Pessoas, Processos e Conhecimento: Da Reificação do Ser Humano como Componente do Conhecimento à "Consciência de Si" Organizacional"* [Organizations, People, Processes and Knowledge: The Reification of Human Knowledge as a Component of the "self-consciousness" Organization], in Amaral, L. (ed) *Sistemas de Informação Organizacionais* [Organizational Information Systems], Nov 2005, Edições Sílabo [Syllabus Revision]

Tribolet, J., & Páscoa, C. (2008). *Apontamentos das aulas de Engenharia Organizacional I.* Academia da Força Aérea. [Lecture notes and Organizational Engineering, Air Force Academy.]

Tripathi, R., Gupta, M. P., & Bhattacharya, J. (2006). *Dimensions of Interoperability for an Effective Portal.* Indian Institute of Technology.

Tsai, C. (2010, November 4). Ski resorts storm the slopes with new apps. *Taiwan News Online.* Retrieved November 11, 2010, from http://today.msnbc.msn.com/id/39892850/ns/today-todaytravel

Tuomo, T. (2006). How to be an effective charismatic leader: lessons for leadership development. *Development and Learning in Organizations, 20*(4), 19–21. doi:10.1108/14777280610676963

Ulwick, A. (1999). *Business Strategy Formulation: Theory, Process, and the Intellectual Revolution.* Westport: Quorum Books.

Umble, E. J., Haft, R. R., & Umble, M. M. (2002). *Enterprise resource planning: Implementation procedures and critical success factors* (pp. 241–257). Elsevier.

Umble, E. J., Haft, R. R., & Umble, M. M. (2003). Enterprise resource planning: implementation procedures and critical success factors. *European Journal of Operational Research, 146*(2), 241–257. doi:10.1016/S0377-2217(02)00547-7

Unterrichts. [Self-directed learning as a prerequisite, method and aim of teaching] *Unterrichtswissenschaft,* [Teaching Science] *10*(2), 99-110.

UNWTO. (2010). *UNWTO Tourism Highlights*: World Tourism Organization (UNWTO), United Nations. avaliable online at http://www.unwto.org/facts/menu.html.

UOC. (2009). *The use of open source in Public Administrations in Spain. Report.* Barcelona: Universitat Oberta de Calalunya.

Vaidya, K., Sajeev, A. S. M., & Callender, G. (2004). *e-Procurement Initiatives in the Public Sector: An Investigation into the Critical Success.* Paper presented at the Annual International Purchasing & Supply Education & Research Association (IPSERA), Catania, Italy.

Vaidya, K., Sajeev, A. S. M., & Callender, G. (2006). Critical Factors That Influence E-Procurement Implementation Success in the Public Sector. *Journal of Public Procurement, 6*(1/2), 70–99.

Vallespir, B., & Kleinhans, S. (2001). Positioning a company in enterprise collaborations: Vertical integration and make-or-buy decisions. *Production Planning and Control, 12*, 478–487. doi:10.1080/09537280110042701

Van de Klundert, J. J. (2003). *Supply Chain Management en Technologie.* Unpublished Technical Report. Venlo, The Netherlands: Mateum/Universtiteit Maastricht.

Van de Ven, A., & Delbeco, A. (1971). Nominal versus Interacting Group Processes for Committee Decision-Making Effectiveness. *Academy of Management Journal, 14*(2), 203–212. doi:10.2307/255307

Van de Ven, A., & Delbecq, A. (1974). The Effectiveness of Nominal, Delphi, and Interacting Group Decision Making Processes. *Academy of Management Journal, 17*(4), 605–621. doi:10.2307/255641

Van Everdingen, Y., Van Hillegersberg, J., & Waarts, E. (2000). Enterprise resource planning: ERP adoption by European midsize companies. *Communications of the ACM, 43*(4), 27–31. doi:10.1145/332051.332064

Van Grembergen, W. (2004). *Strategies for Information Technology Governance*. Idea Group Publishing.

Van Grembergen, W., & De Haes, S. (2007). *Implementing Information Technology Governance: Models, Practices, and Cases.* Hershey, PA: IGI Publishing. doi:10.4018/978-1-59904-924-3

Van Grembergen, W., & De Haes, S. (2009). *Enterprise Govrernance of Information Technology: Achieving Strategic Alignment and Value.* New York: Springer.

Van Heck, G. F. N. (2009). *Inventory Management: Performance Measurement, Designing a Framework to Assess Inventory Management's Performance.* Unpublished Master's thesis. Delft University of Technology, The Netherlands. Retrieved 18 January 2011 from http://www.tbm.tudelft.nl/live/pagina.jsp?id=70163a1a-37c1-4f78-8cb0-50653874a96b&lang=en, #104.

Varner, I., & Beamer, L. (2005). *Intercultural communications in the global workplace.* New York: McGraw-Hill/Irwin.

Vazquez-Bustelo, D., & Avella, L. (2006). Agile manufacturing: Industrial case studies in Spain. *Technovation, 26*, 1147–1161. doi:10.1016/j.technovation.2005.11.006

Venkatesh, V., & Brown, S. A. (2003). User acceptance of information technology: Toward a unified view. *Management Information Systems Quarterly, 27*(3), 425–478.

Verville, J. C. (2000) *An empirical study of organizational buying behavior: a Critical investigation of the acquisition of ERP software,*.

Verville, J.C. & Halingten, A. (2002) A Qualitative study of the influencing factors on the decision process for acquiring ERP software. *Qualitative Market Reasearch: An International Journal 5*(3) 188, 198.

Vicente, D. M. (2007): *Towards Organization*, Master Thesis, Instituto Superior Técnico, Lisboa, Portugal.

Vienot, T. (1995). *Le Conseil d'Administration des Sociétés Cotées.* [The Board of Directors of listed companies] Conseil National du Patronal Français and L'Association Française des Enterprises Privées [National Council of French Employers and The French Association of Private Enterprises]

Visich, J. K., Li, S., Khumawala, B. M., & Reyes, P. M. (2009). Empirical evidence of RFID impacts on supply chain performance. *International Journal of Operations & Production Management, 29*(12), 1290–1315. doi:10.1108/01443570911006009

Von Foerster, H. (1985). *Sicht und Einsicht* [Perspective and insight]. Braunschweig: Vieweg.

Vossen, G., & Westerkamp, P. (2003). E-learning as a web service. In *7th International Database Engineering and Applications Symposium (IDEAS 2003)* (pp. 242-249). IEEE Computer Society.

Walsham, G. (1993). *Interpreting information systems in organizations. Nueva York.* Wiley.

Walumbwa, F. O., Avolio, B. J., & Zhu, W. (2008). How transformational leadership weaves its influence on individual job performance: the role of identification and efficacy beliefs. *Personnel Psychology, 61*(4), 793–825. doi:10.1111/j.1744-6570.2008.00131.x

Wang, R. Y., Pierce E. M., Stuart, E. M., & Fisher C. W. (2005). A*dvances in Management Information Systems.*

Watson, R., Akselsen, S., Monod, E., & Pitt, L. (2004). The Open Tourism Consortium: Laying The Foundations for the Future of Tourism. *European Management Journal, 22*(3), 315–326. doi:10.1016/j.emj.2004.04.014

Watts, M., & Ebbutt, D. (1987). More than the sum of the parts: research methods in group interviewing. *British Educational Research Journal, 13*, 25–34. doi:10.1080/0141192870130103

Wee, S. (2000) Juggling toward Erp Sucess: Keep key success factors high. *ERP News*, (February).

Weick, K. (1990). *Technology as equivoque*. In P.S. Goodman, L.S. Sproull and Associates, (eds.), *Technology and organizations*, 1-44, San Francisco: Jossey-Bass.

Weill, P. (2004). Don't Just Lead, Govern: How Top performing Firms Govern IT. *MIS Quarterly Executive, 3*(1)

Weill, P., Aral, S., & Johnson, A. (2007). Compilation of MIT CISR Research on IT Portfolio, IT Savvy and Firm Performance (2000-2006). *CISR Working Paper* (368).

Weill, P., Woerner, S. & Rubin, H. (2008) Managing the IT Portfolio: It´s all about what´s new. *CISR Research Briefing, 8*(2b).

Weill, P., & Broadbent, M. (1998). *Leveraging the new Infrastructure*. Harvard Business School Press.

Weill, P., & Ross, J. (2004). *IT Governance: How Top Performers Manage IT Decision Rights for Superior Results*. Boston, MA: Harvard Business School Press.

Weill, P., & Ross, J. W. (2003). *IT Governance. How top performers manage IT decision for superior results*. Harvard Business School Press.

Weill, P., & Ross, J. W. (2004). *Governança de tecnologia da informação: Como as empresas com melhor desempenho administram os direitos decisórios de TI na busca por resultados superiores. { Governance of information technology: As the best performers manage IT decision-making rights in the quest for superior results]*. São Paulo: M. Books do Brasil.

Weinert, F. E. (1982). *Selbstgesteuertes Lernen als Voraussetzung*. Methode und Ziel des.

Weinert, F. E. (1996). Lerntheorien und Instruktionsmodelle. [Learning theories and instructional models] In Weinert, F. E. (Ed.), *Psychologie des Lernens und der Instruktion* [Psychology of learning and instruction]. (pp. 1–48). Göttingen: Hogrefe.

Weintraub, A., Epstein, R., Morales, R., Seron, J., & Traverso, P. (1996). A truck scheduling system improves efficiency in the forest industries. *Interfaces, 26*(4), 1–11. doi:10.1287/inte.26.4.1

Wersching, K. (2005), "Agglomeration in an Innovative and Differentiated Industry with Heterogeneous Knowledge Spillovers", Workshop Regional Agglomeration, growth and multilevel governance: the EU in a comparative perspective", Ghent (Belgium), 24-25 Nov.

Weske, M. (2007). *Business Process Management*. Heidelberg, Germany: Springer.

Westerman, G., & Hunter, R. (2007). *IT Risk: Turning Threats into Competitive Advantage*. Harvard Business School Press.

Weston, F. D. T. Jr. (2003). ERP II: The extended enterprise system. *Business Horizons, 46*(6), 49–55. doi:10.1016/S0007-6813(03)00088-0

What is Actor-Network Theory? (2010), Retrieved 08/01/2011 from: http://carbon.ucdenver.edu/~mryder/itc_data/ant_dff.html

Wheeler, D. (2007). *Why Open Source Software. Look at the Numbers*. Retrieved 30th January 2010 from: dwheeler.com/oss_ls_why_html.

White, A., & Daniel, E. M. (2004). The impact of e-marketplaces on dyadic buyer-supplier relationships: evidence from the healthcare sector. *Journal of Enterprise Information Management, 17*(6), 441–453. doi:10.1108/17410390410566733

Wier, B., & Hunton, J.E. & HassabElnaby, H.R. (2007). Enterprise Resource Planning & Non-Financial Performance Incentives: The Joint Impact on Corporate Performance. *International Journal of Accounting Information Systems, 8*(3), 165–190. doi:10.1016/j.accinf.2007.05.001

Wieringa, R. J., Blanken, H. M., Fokkinga, M. M., & Grefen, P. W. P. J. (2003). Aligning application architecture to the business context. In *Advanced Information System Engineering (CAiSE '03)* (pp. 209–225). Springer Verlag, LNCS 2681.

Wikipedia. (2009). *Inventory*. Retrieved January 21, 2011, from http://en.wikipedia.org/wiki/Inventory

Wild, T. (2002). *Best Practice in Inventory Management* (2nd ed.). Oxford: Butterworth-Heinemann (imprint of Elsevier).

Wilkes, L., & Veryard, R. (2004). Service-Oriented Architecture: Considerations for agile systems. *Microsoft Architect Journal, April*. Retrieved May 16, 2010, from http://www.msdn2.microsoft.com

William, G. C. (2008). *Implementing SAP ERP Sales & Distribution. Essencial Skills for SAP Professionals*. New York, NY: McGraw-Hill.

Willinger, W. &,Doyle J., (2002) *Robustness and the Internet: Design and evolution*. Retrieved from

Willis, C. L., & Miertschin, S. L. (2006). Mind maps as active learning tools. *J. Comput. Small Coll., 21*(4), 266–272.

Winkelmann, A., Leyh, C., & Frick, N. (2010). ERP-Systeme in der Lehre - ein vergleichendes hochschulübergreifendes Seminar mit mittelgroßen ERP-Systemen. [ERP systems in education - a comparative inter-university seminar with medium-sized ERP systems.] In Schumann, M., Kolb, L. M., Breitner, M. H., & Frerichs, A. (Eds.), *Multikonferenz Wirtschaftsinformatik 2010* [Multi-industry computer science conference]. (pp. 1625–1636). Göttingen: Universitätsverlag.

Wong, C., & Sloan, B. (2004, September). *Use of ICT for e-procurement in the UK construction industry: a survey of SMES readiness*. Paper presented at the ARCOM Twentieth Annual Conference.

Workgroup, S. (2010). *Service-Oriented Architecture Ontology*. The Open Group.

Wortmann, J. C. (2000). Evolution of ERP Systems. In *Proceedings of the International Conference on the Manufacturing Value-Chain*. Klüwer Academic Publishers, Troon, Scotland, UK.

Wren, D. A. (2005). *The history of management thought*. New Jersey: John Wiley & Sons.

Wu, C., Neubert, M., & Xiang, Y. (2007). Transformational leadership, cohesion perceptions, and employee cynicism about organizational change: The mediating role of justice perceptions. *The Journal of Applied Behavioral Science, 43*(2), 327–351. doi:10.1177/0021886307302097

Wylie, S. (2009), *Enterprise 2.0: What, Why and How, White paper for the Enterprise 2.0 Conference, Boston, 2009*, Retrieved from: http://www.e2conf.com/whitepaper

Xu, W., Wei, Y., & Fan, Y. (2002). Virtual enterprise and its intelligence management. *Computers & Industrial Engineering, 42*, 199–205. doi:10.1016/S0360-8352(02)00053-0

Yamada, T., Fujii, Y., Echizen, I., Tanimoto, K., & Tezuka, S. (2004, October). *Print Traceability Systems Framework using Digital Watermarks for Binary Images*. Paper presented at the IEEE International Conference on Systems, Man and Cybemetics, Hague, Netherlands.

Yanhong, Z. (2009) ERP Implementation Process Analysis Based on the Key Success Factors. *Information Technology and Applications, IFITA '09*.

Yeager, J., & Sommer, L. (2010). The Four Key Factors That Drive Successful Decisions. [Accessed January 19, 2011]. *Qualitative Report, 15*(5), 1114–1123. Available at http://www.nova.edu/ssss/QR/QR15-5/yeager.pdf

Yin, R. K. (1994). *Case Study Research: Design and Methods* (2nd ed.). Beverly Hills, CA: Sage Publishing.

Yin, R. K. (2003). *Case study research: Design and methods* (3rd ed., *Vol. 5*). Thousand Oaks, CA: Sage.

Youngberg, E., Olsen, D., & Hauser, K. (2009). Determinants of professionally autonomous end user acceptance in an enterprise resource planning system environment. *International Journal of Information Management, 29*(2), 138–144. doi:10.1016/j.ijinfomgt.2008.06.001

Youngjin, Y., Boland, R., & Lyytinen, K. (2006). From Organization Design to Organization Designing. *Organization Science, 17*(2), 215–229. doi:10.1287/orsc.1050.0168

Yu, B., Venkatamaran, M., & Singh, M., P. (2003). An adaptive social network for information access: theoretical and experimental issues. *Applied Artificial Intelligence, 17*, 21–38. doi:10.1080/713827056

Zabel, J., Bönke, D., & Constanta, P. (2000). *Open Network for Tourism (OnTour): A Concept for Electronic Commerce in the Business Processes of the Tourism Industry.* Paper presented at the Information and Communication Technologies in Tourism 2000, Proceedings of the International Conference in Barcelona, Barcelona, Spain.

Zacarias, M. (2008) *Business Process Modeling with Objects and Roles,* Doctoral dissertation, Department of Computer Science and Engineering, Instituto Superior Técnico, Lisboa.

Zebra Technologies. (2009). *Vail Resorts: Zebra Technologies Case Studies.* Retrieved November 10, 2010, from www.zebra.com/.../zebra/.../vail_resorts.../ CS_P1011336_VailResorts2010.pdf

Zhang, C., & Dhaliwal, J. (2008). An investigation of resource-based and institutional theoretic factors in technology adoption for operations and supply chain management. *International Journal of Production Economics, 120*(1), 252–269. doi:10.1016/j.ijpe.2008.07.023

Zhang, D., Zhao, J. L., Zhou, L., Jay, F., & Nunamaker, J. (2004). Can e-learning replace classroom learning? *Communications of the ACM, 47*(5), 75–79. doi:10.1145/986213.986216

Zhang, X., Song, H., & Huang, G. Q. (2009). Tourism supply chain management: A new research agenda. *Tourism Management, 30*(3), 345–358. doi:10.1016/j. tourman.2008.12.010

About the Contributors

João Eduardo Varajão is professor of information systems management, project management and software engineering at the University of Trás-os-Montes e Alto Douro. He graduated in 1995, received his master degree in Computer Science in 1997 and, in 2003, received his PhD in Technologies and Information Systems, from University of Minho (Portugal). He supervises several Msc and PhD thesis in the information systems field. His current research includes information systems management, project management and enterprise information systems. He has over 200 publications, including books, book chapters, refereed publications, and communications at international conferences. He serves as associate editor and member of editorial board for international journals and has served in several committees of international conferences. He is co-founder of CENTERIS – Conference on ENTERprise Information Systems and HCist - Conference on Health and Social Care Information Systems and Technologies. He is also a member of AIS, IEICE and APSI.

Maria Manuela Cruz-Cunha is currently an Associate Professor in the School of Technology at the Polytechnic Institute of Cavado and Ave, Portugal. She holds a Dipl. Eng. in the field of Systems and Informatics Engineering, an M.Sci. in the field of Information Society and a Dr.Sci in the field of Virtual Enterprises, all from the University of Minho (Portugal). She teaches subjects related with Information Systems, Information Technologies and Organizational Models to undergraduated and post-graduate studies. She supervises several PhD projects in the domain of Virtual Enterprises and Information Systems and Technologies. She regularly publishes in international peer-reviewed journals and participates on international scientific conferences. She serves as a member of Editorial Board and Associate Editor for several International Journals and for several Scientific Committees of International Conferences. She has authored and edited several books and her work appears in more than 100 papers published in journals, book chapters and conference proceedings. She is the co-founder and co-chair of several international conferences: CENTERIS – Conference on ENTERprise Information Systems, ViNOrg - International Conference on Virtual and Networked Organizations: Emergent Technologies and Tools and SeGAH – IEEE International Conference on Serious Games and Applications for Health.

António Trigo is an Assistant Professor of Computer Science at Institute of Accounting and Administration of Coimbra, which is part of the Polytechnic Institute of Coimbra, Portugal, where he teaches business intelligence, management information systems, software engineering and computer programming, supervising several MSc students. He received his PhD in informatics from the University of Trás-os-Montes e Alto Douro. His research interests include information systems management and enterprise information systems. He worked as software engineer, project manager and software engineering consultant in several companies including Portugal Telecom, Cabo Verde Telecom, Meditel, Telesp Celular and Portuguese National Institute of Statistics. He has publications in international journals, book chapters and international conferences. He serves as editorial board member for international journals and has served in several organization and scientific committees of international conferences.

* * *

Jan Aalmink was born in 1967, Nordhorn, Northern Germany. His interest in computer science began in the early 80th. He received the university-entrance diploma in 1987 from Fachgymnasium Technik in Nordhorn. He studied both, informatics and mathematics at Technical University of Clausthal. After receiving degrees Dipl.-Inf. and Dipl.-Math from Technical University of Clausthal in 1991, he entered the business IT world. After 3 years in IT Consulting Industry as a freelancer he joined SAP AG in 1994. Prior to his recent appointment to Senior Software Architect he was responsible for Enterprise Systems Engineering in the areas of Logistics-Controlling, Cost Containment, Financial Services, Foundation, Manufacturing Industries and Supply Chain Management. In addition to SAP he joined the research department VLBA - Very Large Business Applications at University of Oldenburg as an external PhD student in 2008. His research interests include Enterprise Systems Engineering and Diagnostics, Enterprise Tomography, Cloud Computing, In-Memory Computing, Search Engine Technology, Algorithm Engineering, Graph-Theory and Development Efficiency.

José Aguilá. Business consultant. Graduated in business Intenational Direction by Harvard, old student in IMD of Lausanne. Graduated by IESE Business School, and inengineering degree from the Polytechnic Catalunya Universirtat (UPC). Founding partner of IOR Consulting and member of Advisory Council of the Faculty of Economics (Universitat Pompeu Fabra). He was president of Tecniberia-Management (Madrid) and the Federación Europea de Asociaciones de Consultores en Management FEACO (Brussels), and Member of Governance and Social Council of the UPC. Columnist inthe newspaper Expansión, is author of the books *Personas, Gestión y Logros, y Hojas de Ruta para directivos*, both with Management 2000.

Yadira Alatriste. Master in Design. Professor of the Faculty of Design and Arts, Metropolitan Autonomus University [2006-2009]. Currently doing doctoral studies at the Polytechnic University of Catalonia, Spain in multimedia engineering about living lab and user experience.

Ricardo João Costa Almeida. Born in 1974 and graduated in 1997 on Management Software Engineering at Universidade Portucalense Infante D. Henrique, has an MsC at Universidade de Aveirto in the area of order decision making considering production capacity. Currently he is a PhD student from MIT Portugal EDAM Program and Researcher at Inesc Porto (one of the main research and technology transfer institutes in Portugal). He also is the Director of Computer Engineering's course and Professor at Universidade Lusófona do Porto. Before heading for the PhD study, he had 2 major professional experiences on Portuguese software market, acting as a software developer (Microsoft technologies) and project manager. One of his major challenges was as a software development director for almost 9 years, applying their software to almost 130 industrial companies.

Tiago Almeida graduated in Management and Industrial Engineering, received a MSc in the same subject and he is currently attending the PhD in Information Systems area. At this moment he is a logistics and maintenance consultant at Novabase. He has worked in different companies to implement and maintain SAP ERP system. During his studies, he has published in some conferences.

Bráulio Alturas is an Assistant Professor at ISCTE – Lisbon University Institute (ISCTE-IUL) at the ISCTE-IUL School of Technology and Architecture (ISTA), where he is responsible for courses in degree programs and master's programs. He is also partner and researcher of ADETTI-IUL (Advanced IS/IT Research Center). He received is PhD in Management with a specialization in Marketing from ISCTE-IUL in 2005. He also received his Master of Sciences in Management Information Systems from ISCTE-IUL in 1995 and a five-year degree in Business Organization and Management from the same University in 1989. Before joining academia he worked in the private sector as a financial manager and consultant. His current research interests include Digital Marketing, E-Commerce, E-Procurement, Databases and Information Systems Analysis. He has several articles in the fields of Marketing and Management Information Systems.

António Manuel Alves joined the Air Force Academy in September 2005 for the Master's Degree in Military Aviation, specializing in Aviator Pilot. Having completed it at 25 February 2010, with the master degree dissertation in the area of Organizational Engineering. Then starting the apprenticeship in April 12th 2010, in the TB 30 Epsilon aircraft, at the Air Base No. 1, in Sintra. At March 31 2011 as Second Lieutenant, he finished the apprenticeship, then joining in the Permanent Board of the Air Force. After completing the instruction phase he was placed at 13 June 2011 in 103 Squadron, at Air Base No. 11, Beja.

Paulo Andrade works as a consultant for a global consulting firm based in Switzerland. He received his Master degree in Information Systems Management from ISCTE-Instituto Universitário de Lisboa, Portugal in 2009. He also received a Bachelor degree in Management and Industrial Engineering from the same University in 2007. During his professional career he worked as Information Systems Consultant for several companies in Europe including BMW AG, GDD and Portugal Telecom. His research interests include Information systems adoption and electronic Procurement systems having several articles published in international conferences.

Rebecca Angeles is Full Professor, Management Information Systems Area, Faculty of Business Administration, University of New Brunswick Fredericton, Canada. She has published in Information & Management, Decision Support Systems, Supply Chain Management: An International Journal, Industrial Management & Data Systems, International Journal of Integrated Supply Management, International Journal of Management and Enterprise Development, International Journal of Value Chain Management, International Journal of Physical Distribution & Logistics Management, Logistics Information Management, Journal of Business Logistics, among others. Her current research interests are in radio frequency identification, supply chain management issues, outsourcing and its consequences on supply chains, electronic trading partnership management issues, business-to-business exchanges, electronic trading partnerships, electronic data interchange (EDI), and innovative approaches to teaching Management Information Systems.

Lerina Aversano is a Researcher at the Department of Engineering, University of Sannio. She received the laurea degree in computer engineering in 2000 and the PhD degree in computer engineering in 2003 at the University of Sannio in Benevento, Italy. Her research interests include process and information system modelling, evaluation and alignment; workflow management and document management; software reengineering and migration, and service-centric software engineering. She has served program and organizing committees of conferences and workshops such as, CSMR, CSSE, SAC, ICPC.

Antonio José Balloni is currently a researcher at the Center for Information Technology Renato Archer, working with MIS (Management of Information Systems) in the GESITI Project, Ph.D. in Experimental Plasma Physics/1988, by the Institute of Physics Gleb Wataghin – University of Campinas and Pos Doctor researcher/1992 at Interuniversity Microelectronics Centrum/Belgium. Since January 2003 has been Manager of the GESITI Project. Author of the books: *Why GESITI? (Why management of system and information technology towards organizations?*, and *"Why GESITI? Security, Innovation and Society"*. Creator and Organizer of the Workshop GESITI, an workshop about MIS towards organizations, editions I to VIII. He is a Visiting Professor at the Institute of Economy, at UNICAMP, lecturing about MIS. He has about 30 articles in international and national magazines. Since February 2008 is Coordinator of the GESITI Network, with about 2300 collaborators.

Jan van den Berg studied mathematics and physics at Delft University of Technology in the '70-ies. He worked at several institutes of higher indication in the Netherlands while lecturing mathematics, physics, information & communication technology, and economics. When working at the Econometric Institute at Erasmus University Rotterdam, he finalized his PhD research in 1996: this concerned a mathematical-physical analysis of recurrent neural networks. His current research interests focus on computational intelligence techniques and its applications as well as on information security. Since 2007 he works as an associate professor at Delft University of Technology within the section of ICT of the Faculty of Technology, Policy and Management.

Paulo Henrique de Souza Bermejo received his post-doctorate in Information Systems Management and Innovation at Bentley University (U.S.A.) in 2012 and his PhD in Knowledge Engineering and Management at Federal University of Santa Catarina (Brazil) in 2009. Currently, he is Associate Professor in the Department of Computer Science at Federal University of Lavras (Brazil), and researches about information technology governance, knowledge management, software innovation and software engineering. Author of the book *"Gerência de riscos em projetos de software"*, he is ISACA advocate member and Cobit certified. Over his 15-years career, Bermejo has published 35 refereed papers on knowledge management, IT governance and software engineering, and has developed over 24 software products in partnership with public and private institutions. In the period of 2009 to 2011, he worked as Associate Dean for Graduate Studies at Federal University of Lavras.

José G. Borges holds a PhD from the College of Natural Resources, University of Minnesota, USA and is Associate Professor at the School of Agriculture of the Technical University of Lisbon, Portugal as well as member of its Forest Research Centre. He was member of the European Forest Institute Mediterranean Regional Office (EFIMED) Advisory Group and of the IUFRO Task Force on Information Technology and the Forest Sector. He has participated in research and teaching in several universities in Europe and in North and South America. Teaching and research interests are on the development of stand, forest and landscape-level management models, on environmental resources management modeling and on the development of forest resources decision support systems. He has wide experience of participation and coordination of national and international research projects. He is co-author of 43 international refereed publications and of over 100 other publications.

Billy Brocato is a graduate research & teaching assistant in the Graduate Department of Sociology at Sam Houston State University in Huntsville, Texas. Billy also serves as the Managing Editor of the Journal of Rural Sociology. Billy holds an MBA from the University of Phoenix, and a Bachelor of Science from Eastern New Mexico University. Billy has worked 20 years as an international, national, and local business journalist with major news wire services and as a managing editor in Tokyo with the McGraw Hill Companies. Billy is a member of the Alpha Kappa Delta International Sociology Honor Society, American Sociological Association, Southwestern Social Science Association, and Society of Judgment and Decision Making.

Pedro Campos is an Assistant Professor at the Faculty of Economics of the University of Porto (UP), with a PhD in Management Sciences by U. Porto, Bsc in Applied Maythematics (U. Portucalense). He is a member of LIAAD (Laboratory of Artificial Intelligence and Decision Support), which is a research group belonging to INESC Porto, LA. He coordinates the Post-Graduate Programme in of Information Management and Marketing Intelligence at the University of Porto Business School. Pedro is actually Deputy Director of the international Statistical Literacy Project (ISLP). His main research interests are Statistics (Data Analysis, Sampling Techniques, Statistical Education) and Artificial Intelligence (Multi-Agent Systems). The main areas of applications are Demography and Organizational Networks. He is also member of the Portuguese AI Association (APPIA), of the Portuguese Statistical Society (SPE), and of the Portuguese Association for Classification and Data Analysis (CLAD).

Hélio Castro is a Researcher at the Department of Production and Systems Engineering in University of Minho. He is currently working in European R&D and transnational cooperation projects for manufacturing. His research interests are agile manufacturing and entrepreneurship, virtual and ubiquitous enterprises, meta-organizations and advanced business models, concurrent and collaborative engineering. He is also a member of research group "Distributed and Virtual Manufacturing Systems and Enterprises," within the CITEPE – Interdisciplinary Centre for Production and Energy Technologies, at the University of Minho.

Ben Clegg is an academic at Aston Business School. He has worked for GEC, De Monfort, Portsmouth, Birmingham City and Stanford (USA) Universities before joining Aston. His research, training and consulting activities focus on strategic and operational transformation. He has published over 100 articles and secured over £1.5m of research funding.

Carlos Córdoba. Associate Professor in the Design Department at the University of Nariño (Colombia) since 2004. Currently doing doctoral studies at the Polytechnic University of Catalonia (Spain) in multimedia engineering about user experience and learning systems.

Mohsen Davarynejad is a PhD researcher at Delft University of Technology, Faculty of Technology, Policy and Management, Department of Multi-actor Systems, Section of Systems Engineering. He has previously held research position at the Section of Information and Communication Technology at the same university. His current research focuses on the development and analysis of nature-inspired optimization algorithms, especially for transportation systems.

Ron van Duin studied econometrics at the Erasmus University Rotterdam. He worked for 5 years on logistic business/military problems at the applied science organization TNO. Afterwards he started as an entrepreneur implementing logistic IT-projects (SAP/R3), developing and teaching educational courses, and building advanced simulations models. Now Ron is working as an assistant professor logistics within Delft University of Technology, Faculty of Technology, Policy and Management. Main research interest is focused on policymaking for (urban) freight transport. The challenge to work on policy making in a multi-actor-environment with a lot of conflicting goals makes an interesting research area for developing tools and methods which really can help to support the decision-making process.

Ahmed Elragal is an Associate Professor of Information Systems at the German University in Cairo (GUC). He has got his PhD in Decision Support Systems (DSS) from the University of Plymouth in the UK, 2001. He has over twenty publications in both enterprise systems and business intelligence. He is deeply involved in industry projects mainly with SAP and Teradata. In 2010 he has won Teradata International BI case study competition. He is a member of the AIS and ACM. He is a member of the Information & Management Editorial Board.

Joaquín Fernandez. Doctor in Computer Science, Polytechnic University of Catalonia, 2005. Bachelor of Fine Arts, University of Barcelona, 1983. director of the Master DAM, UPC, 1992-2009 Director of the Degree in Design, UPC, 2002-2007 Director of the Master in Business Telecom, Telefonica, 2006-2009 Director of Multimedia Applications Laboratory, UPC, 2000-2009. Professor of Multimedia Studies. UPC-UOC. 2000-2002. Professor Degree in Design, UPC. 2002-2008. Professor ETSEIB. 1990 - 1993.

Carlos Ferreira graduated in Electrical Engineering, received a MSc degree in Statistics and Operational Research and a PhD in Mathematics. He is currently an Associate Professor with the Department of Economics, Management and Industrial Engineering at the University of Aveiro. He has published in several journals as European Journal of Operational Research, Decision Support Systems, Multimedia Tools and Applications, Haemophilia, Computer Methods and Programs in Biomedicine. His teaching interests are in Operations Research, Data Analysis, Information Management and Research Methodology.

Ferreira Luís, is currently an Invited Assistant Professor in the School of Technology at the Polytechnic Institute of Cavado and Ave, Portugal. He teaches subjects related with Computer Sciences, Information Systems Integration and Software Engineering to undergraduate and pos-graduate studies.

Marco Ferruzca. He has been a researcher and professor at Department of Research and Knowledge of the Faculty of Sciences and Arts for Design at Universidad AutónomaMetropolitana – Azcapotzalco since 1997. He is currently Liaison Coordinator in the same faculty. He has more than 15 years of experience in design, development and exploitation of multimedia spaces. He has participated in different events about design and multimedia. His research focuses on design and innovation of products and services supported on the Internet. His researching works have been presented in different national and international publications. Is member of National Council of Science and Technology of Mexico.

Manuel Fonseca is an expert in IT and Services, currently working for Link Consulting as a Senior Consultant. He has been coordinating several IT projects, including three IST 7th Framework Program in the e-Health area. Was also responsible for the development of an locally funded project in the forest industry sector. He has also been an evaluator and expert reviewer for the IST on the 6th Program. His expertise also includes a degree in Computer Sciences from Universidade Autonoma de Lisboa (1990-1994).

Olga Lucía Giraldo. She has been Associate Professor of the Systems and Computing Engineering Department at the University of Los Andes, Colombia, since 1994. She is the leader and cofounder of the TION- Technology, Information, Organization, and Business- line of the TICSw research group. She has been working as teacher in the Systems and Computing Engineering Department at the University of Los Andes since 1982 where she had participated in the creation and redefinition of the master level program. She has lead the introduction of IT business line in the current undergraduate program curricula. Her main research interests are related to ICT, Information and Communication Technologies, appropriation in small and medium-size enterprises and IT governance state of the art in Colombian enterprises. She received her bachelor in Systems and Computing Engineering at the University of Los Andes, and her D.E.A (Diplôme de Etude Approfondie) en Informatique at the Université Scientifique et Médicale de Grenoble, France.

Stuart Gold is an experienced professional and teacher. As an Adjunct Professor, he has taught management and information systems management courses in the United States and the Caribbean during the past several years. During a 30-year career in industry, he held a number of senior-level corporate positions, including chief information officer and vice president of systems and planning. Dr. Gold has a broad background in a number of industries, including health care, personal products, and industrial products.

Jorge Marx Gómez studied Computer Engineering and Industrial Engineering at the University of Applied Science of Berlin (Technische Fachhochschule). He was a lecturer and researcher at the Otto-von-Guericke-Universität Magdeburg (Germany) where he also obtained a PhD degree in Business Information Systems with the study Computer-based Approaches to Forecast Returns of Scrapped Products to Recycling. In 2004, he received his post-doctorate for the study into Automated Environmental Reporting through Material Flow Networks at the Otto-von-Guericke-Universität Magdeburg. From 2002 until 2003, he was a visiting professor for Business Informatics at the Technical University of Clausthal (Germany). In 2004, he became a full Professor and Chair of Business Information Systems at the Carl von Ossietzky University of Oldenburg (Germany). His research interests include Business Information Systems, E-Business, Enterprise Systems in Higher Education, Material Flow Management Systems, Federated ERP-Systems, Data Warehousing, Recycling Program Planning, Disassembly Planning and Control, Simulation and Neuro-Fuzzy-Systems.

João Gonçalves is carrying out since 2006 Forest Direction at Europac – Papeles e Cartones de Europa; 2005 – 2006 Responsible for Logistics and Wood Procurement Development StoraEnso-Celbi; 1999 - 2005 Responsible for Forest Operations Development StoraEnso – Celbi; 1997 – 1999 Technical Director at H.P. Madeiras, Alcácer do Sal. This company's work is dedicated to full planning and services, from infrastructures to transport operations, including road construction, harvesting and forwarding; 1997 Land Evaluations and Indemnity Department at EN (Northern Power Network Company); 1994 – February 1997 Technical Director at H.P. Madeiras. EDUCATION: Portuguese Catholic University Advanced Executive Management Program Post – graduate degree 1999 Politechnical Institute of Coimbra Degree in Management and Agrarian Extension Politechnical Institute of Coimbra degree in Forest Operations Engineering.

Alfredo Gutiérrez Is the Professor of Normal Education at Jalisco's Education Secretariat in México since 1994, where he has leaded the Virtual Education official project. He is Professor at Computer Sciences Department in Universitary Centre of Exact Sciences and Engineering of Universidad de Guadalajara in México since 2001 teaching to Computer Science students. From 2009 to 2011 member at TARIFA researching group in I2CAT in Barcelona, Spain. From 2009 student in Phd in Engineering of Processes and Systems at Universitat Politécnica de Catalunya in Barcelona, Spain. His researching line goes on online evaluation and assessment, Consensus opinion in collective workgroups, and Future Internet Socioeconomics. Granted by EMCW18 from European Community, and CONACYT from México he develops his PhD thesis on GDSS and consensus web-based model and tools.

Liane Haak studied Business Economics with major in Computer Science and worked many years in the Department of Computing Science at the Carl von Ossietzky University of Oldenburg (Germany) in teaching and research. She operated industrial technology transfer projects in cooperation with OFFIS research institute in the area of Enterprise Systems (ES). 2007 she received her PhD (Dr. rer. nat.) and get assistant professor in the working group of Business Information Systems. Besides her teaching in Oldenburg, she taught at Wadi International University (Syria) and was project leader of the bi-national PhD-net DEEBIS-Net with Cuba from 2008 to 2010. Her PhD was in the research field of Semantic Integration of Data Warehousing and Knowledge Management and her actual research focuses on teaching methods for ES. Therefore she published several publications in international conferences and was chair of three ESHE-Workshops (2009, 2010 and 2011).

Moutaz Haddara is a Research Fellow in Enterprise Systems at the Centre of Enterprise Systems, at the department of Information Systems, University of Agder (UiA), Norway. He has several publications in the areas of enterprise systems, research methods, open source software, and query optimization techniques. Haddara serves as a reviewer for several top information systems conferences and publishers. Haddara has worked closely to the industry and government and has been a consultant for several ERP and web related projects, including European Union funded projects. He is a member of the AIS and served as a bulletin director for the Egyptian AIS chapter.

Guido van Heck studied Systems Engineering, Policy Analysis and Management (SEPAM) at Delft University of Technology, Faculty of Technology, Policy and Management from 2002 until 2009. This period was interrupted for one year due to Guido's full time role in the study association's board. Within

SEPAM, Guido focused on the Information Technology domain; however not only on the technique itself, but also on the managerial aspects that are also involved and play an important role.

Carmen de Pablos Heredero is a Professor in the Business Administration Area at the Rey Juan Carlos University in Madrid, Spain from 1994. She is the main researcher for the Openinnova group centered on the research of Open innovation and is responsible for the Master's degree and Doctoral program on Business Administration and Organization Theory. She is specialized in the impact of information technologies over organizational systems and entrepreneurship where she develops main research. She has presented communications in different international venues and has published in specialized journals. She has also worked as a consultant in the area of IS management at Primma Consulting.

Andrea Herrera. Currently, she is a Lecturer at the department of Systems and Computing Engineering, School of Engineering at the University of Los Andes. She worked as a system and computer engineer in the Central Bank of Colombia (Banco de la República), in the information technology VP as business continuity specialized engineer. She had participated in the redefinition of the undergraduate Systems and Computing Engineering program. Particularly, she designed and developed one professional course for the current curricula "Enterprise Systems" and one professional elective course "Continuity Management in IT Services". Her main research interests are focused on issues related to the management and use of information technology in organizations, especially risk management, IT strategies for disaster recovery, enterprise systems, and IT Governance. She is also member and cofounder of the TION- Technology, Information, Organization, and Business- line of the TICSw research group.

Jeanne Holm is the Evangelist for Data.Gov (an open government flagship project for the Obama Administration managed by GSA) leading collaboration with educators, developers, and governments in the use of open government data. As the Chief Knowledge Architect at NASA's Jet Propulsion Laboratory, her team helps to transform NASA into a learning organization through innovative techniques in developing communities of practice, harnessing the power of social media, and ensuring lessons are shared and embedded across the organization. She was the architect behind the award-winning NASA public (www.nasa.gov) and internal (InsideNASA/Spacebook) portals. Her work for DoD focuses on multi-generational learning, social media, collaborative structures, and driving innovation. For the UN, she leads teams that set standards for how space missions should manage knowledge and share data in the future. And, as an instructor at UCLA, her courses focus on knowledge management, social network analysis, and collaborative systems. She has been awarded numerous honors, including the NASA Exceptional Service Medal for leadership (twice), three Webby's, the 2011 UCLA Professional Achievement Award, and led NASA to three global Most Admired Knowledge Enterprise (MAKE) awards.

Alberto Javier Arroyo Jávega holds a Degree on Computer Science. He also holds an Executive MBA for the IEDE. Currently, he is doing his Ph. D. in IT Governance. With more than 20 years of experience in the consulting arena, Alberto has a deep knowledge of family business. He is responsible for the module Transitioning a Family Business in the MBA of the IIB, and also is a professor for IT, strategy, and family business in the Escuela de Organización Industrial. Member of ISACA (responsible for the subcommittee responsible for analyzing the status of the IT Governance in the Spanish organizations), and member of the GT25 commission of AENOR (Spanish body for ISO), responsible for ISO 38500 among others.

Jonatan Jelen is a business owner, manager, as well as Assistant Professor of Business at Parsons The New School for Design, where he is also the director of the graduate program 'MS in Design Business Management'; he is involved in several social ventures as investor, advisor, and founder, and one of his main research interests and publication efforts is leadership. He earned a Doctorate from University of Pau, France; he is currently finishing his PhD in Computer Information Systems at Baruch College/ Graduate School and University Center of CUNY and is pursuing a Doctorate a DBA with Edinburgh Business School of Heriot Watt-University.

Pedro Miguel Barardo Leal was born in Caldas da Rainha, at 30 December 1987. He joined the Air Force Academy in September 2005 for the Master's Degree in Military Aviation, specializing in Aviator Pilot. Having completed it at 25 February 2010, with the master degree dissertation in the area of Organizational Engineering. Then starting the apprenticeship in April 12th 2010, in the TB 30 Epsilon aircraft, at the Air Base No. 1, in Sintra. At March 31 2011 as Second Lieutenant, he finished the apprenticeship, then joining in the Permanent Board of the Air Force. After completing the instruction phase he was placed at 13 June 2011 in 502 Squadron, Elephants, at Air Base No. 6, Montijo.

David López is with Department of Operations and Technology at I.E Business School. He has more than 10 years of professional and academic experience in telecommunications and healthcare. He has consulted for firms such as IBM, Ericsson, Telefónica, O2 and several public agencies. His research interests are related to knowledge-intensive servicings, open innovation and complex system.

Alexandra Marques is an expert in forest economics and decision support, currently carrying out research in the framework of her PhD in Forest Operational Planning in the Technical University of Lisbon (TUL). Her expertise combines a forestry background - forest engineering 5 year undergraduate degree (TUL,1996-2002) - with the operations research background - Master degree in Operations Research (Lisbon University, 2003-2005). She acquired consultancy working experience in two private IT companies. There, she applied Enterprise Architecture methodologies in the course of several research and consultancy projects with the major Portuguese forest-based companies, as well as public transportation companies, telecom and logistics operators. Additionally, she is an IPMA certified project manager (since 2006), with specific training and auditing skills. She co-supervised 3 Master theses and is the author of more than 20 publications, including scientific articles, book chapters and outreach articles.

Rui Pedro Figueiredo Marques is a student of the joint doctoral program in Computer Science offered by the University of Minho, the University of Aveiro and by the University of Porto, three of the top universities in the north of Portugal. In 2008 he concluded his Masters degree in Electronics and Telecommunications Engineering, at the University of Aveiro, and in 2005 he graduated in the same area, also from the University of Aveiro. His main research interests are on organizational information systems. He has been lecturing Informatics classes since 2007 at the University of Aveiro, at the Higher Institute of Accounting and Administration.

Claudia Martínez. She has worked in design and developing web environments (2005-present). Works in managing and personalizing content of the web environments. She was also professor in the area of Information Technologies and Communication in Universidad Tecnológica del Sureste de Veracruz (2006-2007). Currently she is doing a PhD in Multimedia Engineering at Universidad Politécnica de Catalunya, Spain. Her researching area is knowledge management, personalization and user model.

Fiammetta Marulli received the Laurea Degree in Computer Engineering in 2007 at the University of Sannio in Italy. She worked as research assistant at the Department of Engineering at the University of Sannio, from October 2007 to October 2011. She currently works as software consultant at HP Enterprise Services. Her research interests and skills regard: Software Design and Development by using JavaSE and JavaEE platforms; software maintenance and evolution; distributed programming and computing; wireless and wired networking.

Josep Monguet. PhD in Industrial Engineering and professor at Superior Technical Engineering School in Polytechnic University of Barcelona. Founding partner of the company SICTA (Sistemas de Información Comunicación y Tele Asistencia), specialized in e-health. Coordinator of Industry Cluster at I2Cat Foundation. Hisrprofessional activity and research labor are focused on innovation in business models based on the application of Information and Communication Technologies. He has been Vice Chancellor for Permanent Learning Group and UPC (Universitat Politècnica de Catalunya), Director of the Superior Grade in Design at UPC, Director of the Grade in Multimedia at UPC, and UOC, Director of Multimedia Applications Laboratory, among other positions.

João Oliveira is an expert in forest economics and management support, currently is a Fund Manager in a Forestry Real Estate Investment Funds Management Company in Portugal. Ger expertise combines a forestry background - forest engineering 5 year undergraduate degree (Technical University of Lisbon, 1996-2002) with the Master in Business Management (ISCTE-IUL, 2008-2010). He was a controller for European Aids for agriculture and forest were he acquired experience in European legislation, Geographical Information System and GPS technologies (GIS) and field work. Afterwards he gained experience in financial managing, accounting and compliance in a Forestry Real Estate Investment Fund.

Tiago Oliveira is an invited Assistant Professor at Instituto Superior de Estatística e Gestão de Informação da Universidade Nova de Lisboa (ISEGI-UNL). He received his PhD degree in Information Management from Universidade Nova de Lisboa (UNL), Portugal in 2011. He also received Master degree in Statistics and Information Management from ISEGI-UNL, Portugal, in 2006 and a degree in Industrial Engineering and Management from Instituto Superior Técnico (IST), Universidade Técnica de Lisboa (UTL), Portugal, in 2001. Before joining academia he worked in the Private Sector as a Product Management and Account Management in the largest Portuguese Information Technology Company, Portugal Telecom. His current research interests include Technology Adoption, Technology Diffusion and the Economic Impact of Technology. His publications have appeared in Industrial Management and Data Systems, Electronic Journal of Information Systems Evaluation, Applied economics Letters, and American Journal of Mathematical and Management Sciences among others.

Carlos Páscoa is a PhD Student supervised by Dr. José Tribolet at IST/UTL - Instituto Superior Técnico, Technical University of Lisbon, in the area of Information Systems and Organizational and Design Engineering. He works for the Portuguese Air Force, at the Headquarters in the Operations Division and teaches Organizational and Design Engineering at the Air Force Academy. He has taught Operational

Force Employment and Staff Studies at the Air Force Staff College and he is a frequent speaker at the Joint Staff College. He has, since 2009, more than 15 publications on Enterprise Architecture, Enterprise Engineering, Enterprise Governance, Organizational Change and Organizational Competencies. He has co-oriented 12 master thesis in the area of Organizational and Design Engineering at the Air Force Academy.

Dirk Peters studied Computer Science with major in Business Information Systems. In his diploma thesis he developed a case study design for teaching the Business Intelligence-compontents of SAP NetWeaver 7.0. These case studies can be used as practical exercises in higher education institutes like universities. Since October 2008 he is a research assistant in the Department of Computing Science at the Carl von Ossietzky University of Oldenburg (Germany) and continues his research in the field of Enterprise Systems in Higher Education (ESHE). He is involved in teaching and administrative tasks at the VLBA department. In his doctoral thesis, he is creating a concept for an "Adaptive Enterprise Systems Learning Environment in the field of Higher Education" based on transaction data. The aim is to generate and analyze behaviour patterns to offer the learner a technology-enhanced, dynamic and adaptive learning environment. He was chair of three ESHE-Workshops (2009, 2010 and 2011).

Goran D. Putnik, Dr. Habil., DrSc., Full Professor, Department of Production and Systems Engineering. His scientific and engineering interests are distributed, agile and virtual production systems and enterprises design and management theory, and complexity management in organizations. His publishing record comprises more than 200 publications in international and national journals and conferences, including 9 books, of which the 'Encyclopedia of Networked and Virtual Organizations' is distinguished. He serves as a member of Editorial Board for several International Journals. He is an associate member of the International Academy for Production Engineering CIRP.

Miguel Ramírez. Was born at Barcelona in 1953. He received a Master in Telecommunications Engineering for the Universitat Politécnica de Catalunya in 1976. He has been working from 1976 to 2005 in Telefonica designing corporative networks and network planning. From 2005 he works has independent consultant in communications and also as business angel in the BCNBA network. From 2006 he is dean of the College of telecomm engineers in Catalonia, a public corporation with more the 1500 affiliates. From 1977 he teaches engineering at La Salle University. The fields of interest are teletraffic applications and wideband networks.

Teresa Sanguino. Law degree from the University of Barcelona, 1989. Graduate studies in Political Science and Sociology at the Autonomous University of Barcelona, 1988. Currently working in PhD in the UPC. Project Manager in several companies in the sector e-learning and eHealth. Tutor of International Public Law at UNED.

Henrique M. Dinis Santos received his first degree in Electric and Electronic Engineering, by the University of Coimbra, Portugal, in 1984. In 1996 he got his PhD in Computer Engineering, at the University of the Minho, Portugal. Currently he is an Associate Professor at the Information Systems Department, University of Minho, being responsible for several graduate and postgraduate courses, as well as the supervision of several dissertations, mainly in the Information Security and Computer

Architecture areas. He is also the president of a national Technical Committee (CT 136) related with the information system security standards. During the second semester of 1990, under an ERASMUS program, he was teaching at the University of Bristol, United Kingdom, where he was recognized as University Academic staff.

Carlos Santos has a PhD degree in Information Systems from Instituto Superior Técnico (Technical Institute of Lisbon), a Masters degree in Sciences of Technology and graduated from Coimbra University (Portugal). Currently he teaches in the Higher Institute of Accounting and Administration of Aveiro University (Portugal) and he is interested in researching information systems auditing, accounting information systems, and XBRL. He has presented and published about 25 papers in national and international conferences and in technical Journals.

Thomas M. Schmidt is currently the Campus College Chairman for Information Systems and Technology at the Jersey City Campus of the University of Phoenix. He holds a Doctor of Science degree from Tulane University in Computer Science, with a concentration in databases, and is the author of several published articles and book chapters. His research interests include databases and information theory, and social networking and management issues.

Pedro Sousa is an Associate Professor at Technical University of Lisbon, responsible for the courses in Information and Enterprise Architecture. He is also a researcher at Organizational Engineering Group (CEO), where he has more than 70 articles and presentations on subject of Enterprise Architectures and IT Alignment. He also works as senior consultant of link consulting (www.link.pt), an Aitec company. During the past seven years he has been involved in more than 20 professional projects on Enterprise Architectures both in public and private sector, mostly in finance and telecommunication industries in Portugal, Luxemburg and Brazil.

Miguel Nuno de Oliveira Teixeira. Born in 1976, Graduated in Management at Universidade de Trás-os-Montes e Alto Douro in 2004, with optional specialization in Marketing Management & Research. Is currently working on the final stages of an MsC thesis at Universidade de Trás-os-Montes e Alto Douro, on the subject of Consumer Satisfaction and Aquisition process on ERPs. As professional experience, he has worked in marketing developer in Food & Beverage industry, for a bottled water company, as a Marketing & Product Developer for the medical devices industry and has been for the last 6 years marketing and sales Manager for a top Portuguese player on the ERP market.

Leonor Teixeira graduated in Management and Industrial Engineering, received a MSc degree in Information Management and a PhD in Health Information Systems area. He is currently an Assistant Professor with the Department of Economics, Management and Industrial Engineering at the University of Aveiro and teaching in Technology and Information Systems areas. He has published in several conferences and journals, and currently she is researcher at the Governance, Competitiveness and Public Politics (GOVCOPP) and of the Institute of Electronics and Telematics Engineering (IEETA) of Aveiro research units.

Adriano Olímpio Tonelli is currently a Researcher at Department of Computer Science/Federal University of Lavras and MSc candidate in Management at Department of Management end Economics/ Federal University of Lavras. BSc in Computer Science and MBA in IT Governance by Federal University of Lavras, Tonelli is currently working with IT Governance, IT Service Management and Software Innovation. Teacher of the MBA Executive in IT Governance at Federal University of Lavras, Tonelli has published 6 refereed papers and worked on consulting projects involving strategic planning, information security management, software development and IT governance in public and private organizations.

Maria Tortorella is an associate professor at the Faculty of Engineering of the University of Sannio since 2007. She was assistant professor in the same University since 2001. She received the Ph.D. in Electronic Engineering and Computer Science from the University of Naples "Federico II", Italy, and M.Sc. degree in Computer Science from the University of Durham, UK, where she was visiting student. Her research interests include software maintenance, program comprehension, reverse engineering, reengineering, migration, business process modelling, business process evolution, software system evolution, software quality.

José Manuel Tribolet is Full Professor of Information Systems at IST/UTL - Instituto Superior Técnico, Technical University of Lisbon, responsible for the courses in Enterprise Information Systems and Organizational Engineering, and President of INESC, the largest Portuguese private research institute. He is senior researcher at the Center for Organizational Design and Engineering (CODE) of INOV - INESC INOVAÇÃO, where he has, since 2000, more than 100 publications on Enterprise Architecture, Enterprise Engineering and Governance. Under his supervision, 5 Ph.D. theses have been successfully defended in 2007, 2008, and 2010, with 3 more coming up for defence in the next 3 years. He also works as private executive counsellor for top executives in business and public administration. Among is present commitments is counselling the Attorney General on the architecture and deployment of the next generation information systems of the Portuguese Justice System.

Vasco Vasconcelos. After several years as Chief Marketing Officer in a multinational industrial company, he is currently Chief Marketing Officer and Chief Blogging Officer at a private Healthcare group in Portugal. He is also an external consultant/trainer at Competinov, working closely with IAPMEI and Small and Medium Businesses, sharing his expertise in the fields of Internationalization Processes, Social Media and Competitive Intelligence. With a college degree in Public Relations, he later graduated on a Post-Graduation Program on Information Management and Marketing Intelligence at EGP – University of Porto Business School, where he developed his passion for Social Media and Competitive Intelligence.

Yi Wan is a doctoral researcher in Operations and Information Management at Aston Business School. He has a Bachelor in Computer Networks for Business from Birmingham City University and Master's in Information Systems Management from Warwick Business School. His research, investigating enterprise information systems with operation management for business, which focuses on IS strategy and enterprise integration perspective. He specializes in the areas of information systems management, inter-firm collaboration governance, and strategic change. He has published three articles at '15th Cambridge International Manufacturing Symposium' in UK, 'CENTERIS'2010 – Conference on Enterprise Information Systems' in Portugal (Springer-Verlag), and 'POMS 22nd Annual Conference' in USA.

Index